THE

ARCANA

OF

ASTROLOGY

BY

W. J. SIMMONITE

NEWCASTLE PUBLISHING COMPANY, INC.
1521 NO. VINE ST.   HOLLYWOOD, CALIF. 90028

1974

Library of Congress Cataloging in Publication Data

Simmonite, William Joseph.
    W. J. Simmonite's The complete arcana of astral
philosophy; or, The celestial philosopher.

    (Newcastle occult book T-26)
    Reprint of the 1890 ed. published by W. Foulsham,
London.
    Cover title: The arcana of astrology.
    1. Astrology. I. Title: The complete arcana of
astral philosophy. II. Title: The arcana of astrology.
BF1701.S55 1974   133.5   74-6220
ISBN 0-87877-026-7

W. J. SIMMONITE'S

COMPLETE ARCANA

OF

ASTRAL PHILOSOPHY

OR THE

CELESTIAL PHILOSOPHER

BEING

GENETHLIOLOGY SIMPLIFIED, OR THE DOCTRINE OF NATIVITIES,

TO WHICH IS ADDED THE

RULING OF THE MICROCOSM.

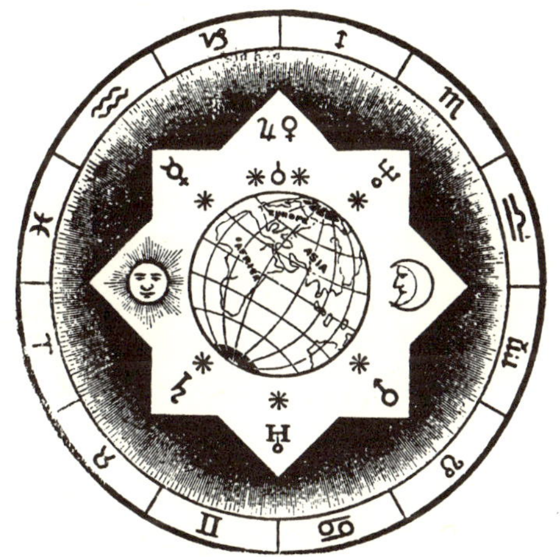

ASTRO DIAGRAM (COPYRIGHT).

*"Nature, which is the Timevesture of God, and reveals
Him to the wise, hides Him from the foolish."*
—CARLYLE.

LONDON :

W. FOULSHAM & CO., LTD., 10/11, RED LION COURT, FLEET STREET, E.C. 4.

INDEX.

The Ruling of the Microcosm, by John Story.
Letter to the Editor on Neptune.

Preface to the New Edition.

I make no apology for republishing Dr. Simmonite's " Arcana of Astrology." Dr. Simmonite was the master of this science in his day ; his work has ever been eagerly sought after, and fabulous prices have been asked and obtained for it. Its republication was an imperative necessity that truth might the more fully abound.

I commenced the republication of this great work at such a time as the superior powers appointed for me to do so, for the good of mankind and the benefit of all students in the grand, noble, and sublime study of astrology, and when the influences indicated a permanent and ever-growing fame. This book will ever stand in the first rank with all students of astrological lore. Generations shall pass away, and the centuries roll on, but this work shall endure and remain ; remain as a preacher of laws, as a teacher of truth, and as an evidence of the power of times and of seasons. It is already making its way over the Continents of Europe, America, and Australia, and will eventually be found in the uttermost parts of the earth.

The old edition contained a great number of printer's errors, and I have given great attention to this reprint to make it as correct and free from error as possible ; and that it might be clear to the sight, I have had it printed with new type bought expressly for the purpose.

I have added short notes on the planet Neptune (page 84, 98, 134, 146, and other parts) as I am of opinion that it is time the nature and influence of this planet was brought before the notice of students. Although discovered September 23rd, 1846, the professors of astrology have not generally made up their minds as to what they can, or will, say for it. Writing this as I am, 44 years after its discovery, I find them still saying, " Let us watch it," " We must compare notes for sometime to come yet," etc. This is very good and very proper, but it seems to me they are unwilling to let go their old notions. It is with planets as with men, " By their works ye shall know them." Then let us look at Neptune's works and know it. It has just left the sign Taurus, ruling Ireland, and such history has been made for that country that future generations will read with amazement and awe. Remember Dublin, May 6th, 1882. At the present time the planet is slowly wending its way through Gemini, the ruling sign of our Capital City London, and it has already begun to show its disposition. It has just been passing over the Sun, Moon, and Ascendant of our Sovereign Lady, Queen Victoria, and the result is shown in the discontent and trouble in the army, police, postal service, etc., and when it reaches the ruling degree of the city it will, according to the aspects thrown to it, cause such events as will long be remembered. It will put to nought the wisdom of our legislators, and show, " 'tis not in mortals to command success." At the same time I do not wish you to understand by this that his influence will be, and produce, all evil. His positions at birth, his aspects, transits over him, and he over others, will show the thoughtful student his power and influence, and I expect he will produce some very novel and striking features in the near future. Most of the readers of this work began their lives in the most important, intellectual, and progressive period of human history : the period of such marvels as the telegraph, telephone, phonograph, electric lighting, anæsthetics, new and powerful explosives, the spectroscope, etc., but I look for great wonders to be unfolded during the next decade. The preacher, the laywer, and the medical man, will have to take long strides to keep pace with the times ; and who shall say that the undying vigil of the astronomer shall not be rewarded by discovering other intelligent dwellers in other planets, and even discover means of intercourse with them.

I have added at the end of this work an article on Neptune, forwarded me by a very thoughtful and erudite professor of astrology, in which I trust you will find matter for thought and consideration.

I see it is becoming the fashion amongst a certain class of writers to entirely repudiate any power or influence to the ☊, ☋, and ⊕ I advise you to take no man's word upon them, but look to the ⊕ in your money affairs, and note the passage of the ☉ over the radix ☋, and then judge for yourselves. There are too many superficial professors of this art. It requires as much study as medicine or law, and years of experience before any man should consider himself sufficiently proficient to follow it as a profession.

And now, in conclusion let me say,—do not simply read this book, but be a student of it, study to understand the mysteries therein set forth, divest your mind of all prejudices, notions, and educational acquirements which are in opposition to this science, and come to it, even as a little child, knowing nothing, but desiring to know all the truth.. Herein is stored the wisdom of the ages of the past ; here is the lore of the shepherds of old, the Egyptians, Hindoos, Greeks, Arabians, and a long line of philosophers have added to the store of this knowledge, and you, standing in their lot, can take hold of the threads where they have left them, and follow knowledge and truth for its own sake and for the uprooting of prevailing superstition and error. The mind of mankind is bounding onward. The spirit of the age is one of enquiry. Reason, not faith, is the prevailing tendency. Sacerdotal ascendency is on the wane, and proof for every assertion is demanded. Old beliefs are shaking, their errors are being detected, and the cry upon every side is for Light and Truth. 'Tis now the mental crisis of the race, and the mysteries of nature are now the subjects of thought and of study. Then, if you would know the secrets of Humanity, survey the universe around you, mark its wonderful laws and workings, then turn to the pages of this work and study the application of the wonderful laws and works there seen, and you will find mankind and his works no longer a mystery to you, but that he is acting in perfect subserviency to laws which have been set in operation by the Maker and Creator of the universe.

I have added a very choice little work which will be found at the end of this book, entitled, " The Ruling of the Microcosm," being an astrological and physical discourse on the human virtures in the body of man, both principal and administrating, which students will find of inestimable value, and which may probably throw light upon some points which have seriously puzzled them.

I also desire to add that I have some very valuable manuscripts and tables of houses for different latitudes, which I may probably at some future date put into print and introduce to your notice.

Now, if each reader will introduce the " Arcana of Astrology " to some other seeker after truth he will be hastening the time for the public recognition of the grand old science, and the universal acceptation of its grand, noble, and elevating truths.

Wishing and hoping for each reader a long, bright, and prosperous future, each in his own sphere, and that each may do his utmost to advance the work,

I am, yours very truly,

JOHN STORY.

THE

ARCANA

OF

PRACTICAL ASTRAL PHILOSOPHY.

BOOK THE FIRST.

CHAPTER I.

THE TWELVE SIGNS OF THE ZODIAC, AND THEIR DIVISIONS.

1. The Zodiac being the great circle of the sphere, is divided into 360 degrees; every degree into 60 minutes; every minute into 60 seconds, thirds, fourths, and farther, if necessary.

2. Every sign contains 30 of these degrees, and thus 12 signs comprise the Zodiac.

NORTHERN SIGNS.			SOUTHERN SIGNS.	
♈	Aries	opposite to ...	♎	Libra.
♉	Taurus ...	ditto	♏	Scorpio.
♊	Gemini ...	ditto	♐	Sagittarius.
♋	Cancer ...	ditto	♑	Capricorn.
♌	Leo	ditto	♒	Aquarius.
♍	Virgo ...	ditto	♓	Pisces.

3. The first six signs are called *Northern*, because the Sun is longer above the earth than below, and because they decline from the equator towards the North Pole.

The latter six are called *Southern*, because they decline towards the South Pole, or our opposite hemisphere; and the Sun remains longer below the Earth than above.

4. There are also *nine* other bodies, called Planets, and their

Symbols are as follows:

♆	Neptune	♃	Jupiter	♀	Venus
♅	Herschel	♂	Mars	☿	Mercury
♄	Saturn	☉	Sol, or Sun	☽	Luna, or Moon

5. The Asteroids are found to have some influence: they are Vesta, Juno, Pallas, Ceres, but at the present day their influence is very little known.

6. There are also three Points in the Heavens which must be considered, viz.,

☊ The Dragon's Head, or Moon's N. Node.
☋ The Dragon's Tail, or Moon's S. Node.
⊕ The Part of Fortune, and the Earth.

7. The *fourth class* of Symbols used in Astronomy is called Aspects, viz.,

☌ *Conjunction*, or same degree of longitude.

S ✱ *Semisextile*, or 30 degrees apart, a geometrical figure called a dodecagon.

Dc. *Decile*, or 36 degrees apart, divides a circle into ten sides, which forms ten angles, called a decagon.

Nonagon, or 40 degrees, divides the Heavens into nine equal sides, a polygon of some importance.

S □ *Semisquare*, or 45 degrees, forms a regular octagon, a figure of eight sides and angles, or half a semiarc.

✱ *Sextile*, or 60 degrees apart, which is the angle of a regular spherical triangle, or figure of three angles, or two-thirds of a semiarc.

Qu. *Quintile*, or 72 degrees apart, which is the supplemental angle of a regular pentagon, or figure of five sides and angles, or one-fifth of the Zodiac.

□ *Square*, or 90 degrees apart, or one quarter of the entire heavens, or a semiarc and a half, a figure of four sides, called a quadrangle.

Y *Sesquiquintile*, 108 degrees, a quintile and half, or a whole semiarc and one fifth.

△ *Trine*, 120 degrees in the Zodiac, and forms the angle of a regular hexagon, or figure of six angles and six sides; it is the whole of a semiarc and one third of another in the world.

SSQ. *Sesquisquare*, 135 degrees, and is the angle of a regular octagon, or figure of eight sides, the whole semiarc and one-half.

BQ. *Biquintile*, or 144 degrees, a double quintile, the angle of a regular decagon, or ten sides and ten angles, or four-fifths of a diurnal arc.

QX. *Quincunx*, or 150 degrees, and consists of five signs.

  Opposition, or 180 degrees, the sum of two right angles.

P. *Parallel*, the same distance from the equator, North or South.

8. We divide these angular positions, or aspects, into four classes, according to their species, and into fifteen divisions, in reference to angular directions, according to their strength or influence, namely,

CLASS

1. *Solar Aspects*, or those formed between the Sun and Planets.
2. *Mutual Aspects*, or those found among the Planets.
3. *Lunar Aspects*, or those formed between the Moon and the Planets.

4. *Astronomical Positions,* are those peculiar positions of the Planets which are said to be Stationary, Retrograde, or when they are said to be in their Exaltation, Fall, House, Detriment, Combustion, Cadent, or any other accidental position.

LESSON FIRST.

Questions to be answered before the Student proceeds to the next Chapter.

How many degrees in the zodiac ?
How many degrees in the sphere ?
How many minutes in a degree ?
How many degrees in a sign ?
Tell the names of the Northern signs.
Tell the names of the Southern signs.
How many Planets ? Name them.
How many asteroids ? Name them.
What other influential points in the heavens ?
What are Lunar aspects.
What is the Globe sometimes called ?
How many signs are there ?
Why are some called Northern signs ?
Why are others called Southern signs ?
Mark the Symbols on paper or slate.
Mark out the Asteroids and the influential points.

Mention the signs which are opposite each other.
What are Mutual aspects ?
How many aspects are there ? Name them.
What are Solar aspects ?
What are Astronomical positions?
What is a parallel ?
What is a conjunction ?
What is a trine ?
What is a square ?
What is a sextile ?
What is a semisquare ?
What is a semisextile ?
What is a quintile ?
What is a decile ?
What is a nonagon ?
What is a sesquiquintile ?
What is a sesquisquare ?
What is a biquintile ?
What is a quincunx ?
What is an opposition ?
Into how many classes are these divided ? Name them.

CHAPTER II.

DEFINITIONS OF ASTRO-PHILOSOPHICAL TERMS, ETC.

ASTROLOGY is compounded of two Greek words—(Aster) a Star and (Logos) discourse, science, word, or reason ; and literally implies the doctrine and law of the Stars—hence the noble Art or Science of foretelling events. It is based on Astronomy, and the motions, influences, aspects, qualities, and positions of the heavenly bodies. It comprehends the most excellent part of the noble science of Physiology, or Natural Philosophy, which is the doctrine of natural bodies in the construction of the work of nature.

Astrology consists of three parts or branches, namely : 1. Genethliology, which teaches us by certain mathematical rules to judge from the figure, or chart, of the heavens, at the moment of birth; the form, temperament, and character of the individual; the blemishes, hurts, mental and bodily diseases; the quality of the intellectual faculties and mental propensities, the probability of friends and enemies, their nature and description; of marriage, of offspring; of success in business; strength of constitution, natural disposition, and many of the most remarkable periods of life, either advantageous or otherwise.

2. Astrology, Mundane, or State, or the Art of Foreseeing, from the position of the heavenly bodies, at the time of eclipses, great conjunctions, and other periods, the changes and circumstances of nations as to war, pestilence, famine, earthquakes, and other physical phenomena.

3. Astrology, Horary, or the Art of Foreseeing Events from the positions of the heavens at the moment a question is propounded, or when an individual may be anxious about any matter, the result of any business, or circumstance whatever. This part of the science is the easiest understood and the most advantageous to mankind. It furnishes the Astral Student with the actual means of satisfying those doubts to which the minds of all men are subject, by an apparently simple means, which presumes that the same sympathetic power which causes the iron and magnet to attract and approach each other exists throughout nature.

Abcission of light, is when a light planet goes to a ☌ of a ponderous planet, but before his ☌ the ponderous planet goes to a more ponderous, whereby the light of the inferior is cut off. See Frustration.

Affliction, a planet, or the cusp of a house, being in evil aspect to any planet, or in ☌ to a malefic.

Airy signs, ♊, ♎, and ♒.

Accochoden, is the planet giving years or term of life in a nativity; an Arabic name for the Hyleg.

Almuten, is the principal lord of any house or sign, or of the whole figure.

Ambient, the heavens when spoken of in a general way.

Anabibayon, the dragon's head.

Angle, is the opening between two straight lines, which meet, but are not in the same straight line. The opening between the lines A B and C B is an angle, termed the angle B, or the angle A B C; the letter at the point where the lines meet is placed in the middle.

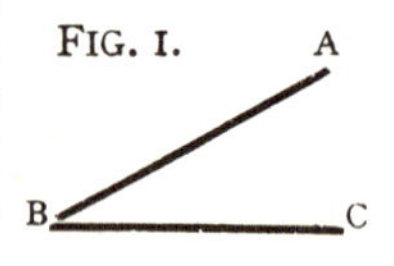

Angle, right, is the angle formed when one straight line stands upon another in such a direction that the angles on each side are equal to one another. A B is a perpendicular line.

Angle, obtuse, is one which is greater, or has a wider opening than a right angle. In FIG. 3, D E F is an obtuse angle.

Angle, acute, is one which is less, or has a narrower opening than a right angle. In FIG. 1, A B C is an acute angle.

Anareta, is the planet destroying life, or the killing planet in a nativity, which are ♅, ♄, and ♂; but, in some particular cases, the ☉, ☽, and ☿, will kill. The ☉ in particular will kill, when the ascendant, the ☽, is hyleg.

Apheta, from the Greek; "the Hyleg," from the Hebrew; and "the Prorogator," from the Latin: they all signify one thing, i.e., the "Giver of Life."

Apogee, a planet at its greatest distance from the earth.

Arc of Direction, See Direction.

Angles, the 1st, 4th, 7th, and 10th houses. When planets are therein they are more powerful than in any other situation.

Application, to apply. These terms mean the approach of any planet to the body or aspect of another, or to the cusp of any house.

Aldebaran, a fixed star of the first magnitude, situated in the 2nd face of ♊, the nature of ♂, produces eminence in martial affairs.

Algeneb, a fixed star of the 2nd magnitude, in the right side of Perseus, in the 2nd face ♈, of the nature of ♂ and ☿. A violent, unfortunate star.

Algol, or Medusa's Head, a fixed star of the 3rd magnitude, in the constellation Perseus, in the 5th face of Taurus, of the nature of ♄ and ♃.

Altair, or Ara, a southern constellation, consisting of nine stars, in the last face of ♑, of the nature of ♅.

Andromeda Caput, a northern constellation, consisting of sixty stars, of the 1st magnitude, in the 3rd face of ♈, of the nature of ♃ and ♀. Zona Andromeda, in the last face of ♈, of the 2nd magnitude, the nature of ♀.

Antares, a fixed star of the 1st magnitude, in the 2nd face of ♐, the nature of ☿ and ♂.

Antecedentia, a motion of any of the heavenly bodies which is contrary to the order of the signs; as from ♈ towards ♓, etc. See Retrograde.

Acquarius, a zodiacal constellation, consisting of 108 stars. It is sanguine, aërial, hot, moist, masculine, humane, rational, southern, obeying sign; the house of Herschel.

Acquirius, a fixed star of the 3rd magnitude, in the face of ♒, nature of ♅: denoting erudition.

Arcturus, a fixed star of the 1st magnitude, situated in the skirt of the constellation Bootes, in the 5th face of ♎, of the nature of ♃ and ♂, giving riches and honour.

Aries, the Ram, the first zodiacal constellation, consisting of 66 stars ; it is vernal, dry, fiery, masculine, cardinal, equinoxinal, diurnal, moveable, commanding, eastern, choleric, violent, and a quadrupedian sign.

Ascendant, the 1st house, or that space between the eastern horizon and one-third of the distance towards the meridian under the Earth ; also the cusp of that house which represents the party ; as the cusp of the 5th is the ascendant for a child of the querent, the 10th for business, etc.

Ascending, a term denoting any planet which is between the 4th and 10th houses, more especially when rising above the eastern horizon.

Ascension, Right, the distance any body or point in the heavens is from the beginning of the ecliptic, or 1st point of ♈ in a right sphere.   It is measured upon the equator in degrees and minutes, or hours, minutes, and seconds.   It is thus abbreviated, A.R.

Ascension, Oblique, if a star be not on the equator, it will, when it rises, form an angle with that part of the equator which is rising at the same time, and this is called its

Ascensional Difference (A.D.): this, added to its right ascension (A.R.) if it have south declination, but subtracted therefrom if it have north declination, gives its oblique ascension.

Aspect, from aspicio, to behold, the being placed at certain distances from a planet, or the cusp of a house, as, if ♃ be 60 degrees from ☽, then they are both said to be in sextile aspect to each other.   They are zodiacal and mundane.

Barren Signs, ♊, ♌, ♍.

Benefics, the two planets ♃ and ♀, and sometimes ♅.

Bellatrix a star of the 2nd magnitude, in the 4th face of ♊, the nature of ☿ and ♂, giving military or civic honours, and wealth.

Betelguese, a star of the 2nd magnitude, in the east shoulder of Orion, in 6th face of ♊, the nature of ♂ and ☿, giving martial honours, preferment and wealth.

Bull's South Eye (Occulus Taurus), a star of the 3rd magnitude, in the 2nd face of ♊, the nature of ♀, fortunate.

Bull's North Horn, a star of the 2nd magnitude, in the 5th face of ♊, the nature of ♂, fortunate and eminent.

Bull's South Horn, a star of the 3rd magnitude, in the 5th face of ♊, the nature of ♂, a mischievous star in influence.

Bestial signs, ♈, ♉, ♌, ♐ (the first half excepted), and ♑.

Besieged, is when a planet, fortunate by nature, is situated between two malevolent stars, as ♀ in 12° of ♋, ♄ in 15°, and ♅ in 10° of the same sign ; where she is in a state of "siege," and highly unfortunate. He whose significator it was, would be denoted thereby to be in "a great strait," and particularly "hemmed in" or surrounded with ill fortune.

Bicorporeal signs, ♊, ♐, and ♓, because each contains two different animals.

Biquintile, an aspect consisting of 144 degrees, or 4 signs 24 degrees, four-fifths of the whole diurnal arc.

Cadent houses, so called because they are cadent, that is, falling from the angles. These are the weakest of all the houses, and are the 3rd, 6th, 9th, and 12th.

Cazini, is when a planet is in the heart of the ☉, or within 15 minutes, or half a degree of his centre.

Cardinal Points, the north, south, west, and east points of heaven.

S represents the south, N, the north, E, the east, and W, the western points.

Cardinal signs, ♈, ♋, ♎, ♑.

Cancer, the Crab, one of the signs of the ecliptic, consisting of 83 stars, into which the Sun enters about the 21st of June, or upon our longest day. Tropic, cold, watery, phlegmatic, feminine, cardinal, northern, commanding, nocturnal, movable, and particularly fruitful sign, more so, perhaps, than any other sign in the zodiac, the house of the ☽.

Canis Majoris, a fixed star of the 2nd magnitude, in the 2nd face of ♋, the nature of ♀. Gives honour, renown and wealth.

Canopus, a star of the 1st magnitude, in the constellation Argo.

Capella, a fixed star of the 1st magnitude, in the left shoulder of the constellation Auriga, in the 4th face of ♊, the nature of ♂ and ☿, giving honours, eminence, renown, publicity, wealth, and eminent friends.

Capricornus, the Goat, consisting of 58 stars; into which the Sun enters about the 21st of December, or upon our shortest day. It is a cold, earthy, melancholy, arid, nocturnal, southern, obeying, movable, cardinal, quadrupedian, changeable sign, the house of Saturn.

Castor, a star of the 1st and 2nd magnitude, in the 4th face of ♋, the nature of ♂, ♀, ♄. Portends mischievousness and prone to violence.

Cauda Lucida (the Lion's Tail), a fixed star of the 2nd magnitude, in the constellation Virgo, 4th face, the nature of ♄, rather evil.

Caput Algol (Maduse), a star of the 2nd magnitude, in the 5th face of ♉, the nature of ♄ and ♃. The most unfortunate, violent, and dangerous star in the heavens.

Ceti (Lucida maxilla), MENKAR, a star of the 2nd magnitude, in the 3rd face of ♉, the nature of ♄. Denoting sickness, disgrace, and ill fortune, with danger from great beasts.

Capricorn, a fixed star of the 3rd magnitude, in the 1st face of ♒, nature of ♀ and ☿.

Circle of Position, an astronomical term used in calculating the polar elevation of any planet. They are small circles bearing the same relation to the meridian circle which the parallels of latitude do to the equator.

Collection of Light, when a planet receives the aspects of any two others which are not themselves in aspect. It denotes that the affair will be forwarded by a third person, described by that planet; but not unless they both receive him in some of their dignities.

Combustion, is when a planet is posited within 8° 30′ of the ☉, either before or after the ☉'s body. In horary questions, unless the ☉ be a chief significator, this is deemed unfortunate. The ☽ is singularly weak when so elongated.

Common signs, ♊, ♍, ♐, and ♓.

Conjunction, two planets being in the same longitude. If they be exactly in the same degree and minute, it is a partile conjunction, and very powerful; if within the half of the sum of their two orbs, it is a platic conjunction, and less powerful.

Constellation, a number of stars lying in the neighbourhood of each other, which Astronomers, for the sake of remembering with more ease, suppose to be circumscribed by the outlines of some animal or other figure.

Cosmical rising, or setting of a planet or star, is when it rises with the Sun in the morning, or sets with him in the evening.

Culminate, to arrive at the midheaven, meridian, or cusp of the 10th house.

Cusp, the beginning of any house. Thus the eastern horizon is the cusp of the 1st house, and the meridian, where the ☉ is at noon, is the beginning or cusp of the 10th house.

Cor Scorpio, a star of the 2nd magnitude, the nature of ♃ and ♂, in the 2nd face of ♐.

Crater (the Cup), in the 5th face of ♍, of the nature of ♀ and ♃, portending eminence, 4th magnitude.

Debilities, a planet in a weak and afflicted position, as fall, detriment, etc.

Decanate, ten degrees, the first ten degrees of a sign is the 1st decanate; from 10° to 20° the 2nd, and from 20° to 30° the 3rd decanate.

Declination, the distance any body is north or south of the equator. The ☉ has never more than 23° 28′ of declination, which happens only when he is in ♋ or ♑, and is caused by the pole of the Earth being inclined from the plane of the Earth's orbit.

Dichotominea, a term applied to the ☽ when she is in her headquarters, and appears only half illuminated.

Decile, an aspect consisting of 36°, or 1 sign 6 degrees.

Deneb, a star of the 2nd magnitude, in the 4th face of ♍, the nature of ♅; unfortunate, and publicly disgraceful.

Decreasing in light, when any planet is past the ☍ of ☉, it decreases in light; it is a testimony of weakness.

Decumbiture, a lying down; the figure erected for the time of any person being first taken ill and taking to their bed.

Degree, the 30th part of a sign in the zodiac, or the 360th part of any circle.

Descendant, the 7th house, or that space from the western horizon to one-third of the distance towards the meridian above the Earth.

Descension, the going down of any body from the meridian above the Earth to that below it; for though the ☉ is lost sight of at sunset, he still descends till he reaches the meridian at midnight, or the N., Fig. 4.

Descending in a figure, is when a planet is between the M.C. and 7th, or 7th and M.C.

Descension, Oblique, the reverse of Oblique Ascension.

Delation (or restoring of light), is when an inferior planet aspects a superior who is combust or retrograde, for then the higher planet restoreth to the inferior his virtue which he before sent him : this in angles, is good, in cadents with detriment.

Destruction, is when three planets shall be in one sign, of which one planet is ponderous, the other two more light: then one of the light planets should pass the ponderous, the other tends to a ☌ with the ponderous; but before that ☌ is made, the planet which passes the ponderous turns retrograde ; and is again joined to the ponderous, and from thence pass to the ☌ of the other light planet.

FIG. 5.

Diameter, a line passing through the centre of a circle, and dividing it into two equal parts ; as the line A B.

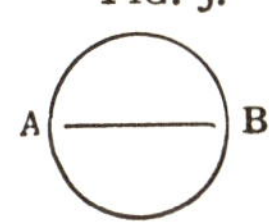

Dicotome (cut in two), the ☽ in 1st and 3rd quarters.

Detriment, the sign opposite the house of any planet; as ♂ in ♎ is in his detriment.   It is a sign of weakness, distress, etc.

Digit, in Astronomy, the 12th part of the ☉'s diameter, which is often used in the calculation of eclipses.

Dignities, these are either essential or accidental.   The former is when any planet is in its own house, exaltation, triplicity, joy; the latter is when any planet is in an angle, and well aspected, not afflicted, swift in motion, increasing in light, etc. The reverse of dignities are debilities.

Direct, as applied to planets, denotes their moving in the true order of the celestial signs, as from ♈ to ♉, etc.

Direction, the measuring the space between the bodies or aspects of any two planets, or that between any two parts of the heavens, to ascertain at what period of life the promised effect will appear. Their distance is a certain number of degrees of the A. R. of the ☉, which, when he has passed over, the direction is complete. It is called the Arc of Direction.

Direction, Secondary, the aspects formed by the ☉ or ☽ in the days immediately succeeding the birth. Each day between the birth and the time of the aspect is formed is equal to one exact year of life; thus, if the ☽ form a good aspect with ♃, exactly 21 days after birth, the native will feel his effects just about his 21st birthday.

Direct Motion, this is in reality converse motion, but is so called to distinguish the case of the promittors being carried towards the bodies or aspects of the ☉ or ☽, which directions are considered somewhat less powerful than those by converse motion.

Diurnal, of or belonging to the day; thus, the annual motions of the planets are the spaces they move through in a day.

Diurnal Arc, is the length of time that part of the heavens in which any planet is at birth is above the Earth; and it is usually measured by degrees.

Disc, of the ☉ or ☽, is its round face, which, on account of the great distance of the object, appears flat, or like a plain surface.

Diverging, going farther and farther asunder.

Dispose, Dispositor, a planet disposes of any other which may be found in its essential dignities. Thus, if ☉ be in ♈, the house of ♂, then ♂ disposes of ☉, and is said to rule, receive, or govern him. When the dispositor of the planet signifying the thing asked after is himself disposed by the lord of the ascendant, it is a good sign. To dispose by house is the most powerful testimony; then by exaltation, then triplicity, then term, and, lastly, face, which is a very weak reception.

Double-bodied signs, ♊, ♐, ♓.

Dorsa Leonis, a star of the 2nd magnitude, in the 2nd face of ♍, the nature of ♄ and ♀, unfortunate, causing unhappiness of mind and melancholy, or fear of poison. See Vindemiatrix.

Domal dignity, a planet in its own house.

Dragon's Head, thus marked, ☊, is the north node of ☽, or when she crosses the ecliptic into north latitude. It is always a good symbol, denoting success, a good disposition, etc.

Dragon's Tail, thus marked, ☋, is where the ☽ crosses the ecliptic into the south latitude, or her south node. It is very evil, and in all things the reverse of ☊, it diminishes the power of good, and increases that of evil planets.

Earthy signs, ♉, ♍, and ♑, which form the Earthy Triplicity.

Earth, ⊕, the globe which we inhabit, one of the eight Planets, and the third in order from the ⊙, and is always in ♊ to the orb of day.

Ecliptic (Celestial), a great circle of the sphere, in which the ⊙ always appears to move ; so called, because eclipses generally happen when the ☽ is on or near circle. The obliquity of the ecliptic is the angle it makes with the equator, which is now about 23° 28′.

Ecliptic (Terrestrial), the line round the Earth comprising the course of the ☽.

Elevation of the pole or star, is its height in degrees above the horizon.

Elections, are times chosen by art, for facilitating any noble performance.

Elevation by Latitude, is that planet which has most of two, either of south or north latitude ; but if the latitude be the same, he that has least declination is most elevated.

Elevation by Signs, is when a planet is distant from another according to the succession of the signs.

Elevation by House, is thus : a planet in the M.C. is elevated above another in 11th, 12th, or Ascendant, or in 9th, 8th, 7th, 6th, etc.: a planet in the 8th is elevated above another in the 7th, 6th, 5th, etc.

Equation of Time, owing to the irregular motion of the Earth round the ⊙, this latter body does not always come to the meridian exactly 24 hours after its last passage over that point ; but as all calculations in the old Ephemeres of the places of the planets are made for the time the ⊙ was on the meridian (or apparent noon), the watch is sometimes several minutes before or after the moment. The difference between the apparent noon, or that time shewn by the ⊙, being on the meridian, and the mean noon, or that shewn by a correct watch, is the Equation of time, which is the angular distance in time between the mean and the true Sun. The amount to be added to, or taken from, the time shewn by the watch is given in common Ephemereses for every six days ; but, in my Meteorologist, the Sun is given according to its sidereal time, and in this there needs neither subtraction nor addition ; and all the computations are according to mean time, and do not need this correction.

Elongation, the greatest distance ☿ or ♀ can be from the ⊙.

Embolismic, intercalatory. In every year there are twelve Moons of 29 days and a half each, and 11 days over, and when these odd days amount to 30 they make an additional, or Embolismic lunation. From these lunations the progression or process is formed, as every lunation answers to a year of the native's life.

Emersion, a planet coming from under the Sun beams so as to be seen. It is a term chiefly used in eclipses and occultations.

Enneatical, the ninth.   Every ninth year of a person's life, which being climacterial, is thought to bring with it a change of fortune. It also signifies the ninth day of a disease, when a change may be expected.

Ephemeris, a kind of almanack, containing the places of the Planets, etc.   The best is "Simmonite's Meteorologist," in which the Aspects are also calculated to the minute, an acquisition almost invaluable to the student of astrology, astronomy, and astro-meteorology.

Equator, a great circle which separates the northern from the southern hemisphere; and, being referred to the heavens, is called the Equinoctial.

Equatorial, of the equator, or a planet, etc., of the equator.

Equinox, equal night ; that time, or place, in the ecliptic where the days and nights are equal, which happens twice a year : when the ☉ enters ♈ and ♎.

Equinoctial signs, ♈ and ♎.

Exaltation, an essential dignity, next in power to that of the house.   If a planet be in that sign wherein he is exalted, you may consider him essentially strong.   If the significator be in his exaltation, and no ways impeded, but angular, it represents a person of a haughty condition, arrogant, assuming more to himself than is due.

Face, the sixth part of a sign, or five degrees.

Fall, a planet has its fall in the opposite sign to that in which it has its exaltation.   In horary questions, a planet in its fall denotes a person unfortunate, despised, and degenerated, mean, insolvent, or helpless ; and the thing signified by it is in a helpless state, except some good aspect by application, or some translation of light happen, which will relieve it quite unexpectedly.

Familiarity, any kind of aspect or reception.

Feminine signs, ♉, ♋, ♍, ♏, ♑, and ♓, these are the even signs. They are supposed to be weak and feminine on account of their active and passive qualities, coldness and moisture, and are supposed to render those they govern the same.

Feral, brutish, like a wild beast : such is said to be the dispositions of those whose ascendant is ♌, or the last half of ♐ ; or if the luminaries be in either of them, and the malefics in angles, it renders them fierce, cruel, and brutish, the ☽ is also said to be feral, when she is void of course, having separated from a planet, and applying to no other while she is in that sign.   There does not appear to be any ground for such an opinion, but this will be the best decided by experience.

Fiery signs, or Fiery triplicity, ♈, ♌, and ♐.

Figure, the diagram which represents the heavens at any time, it is called a scheme or horoscope.

Fomahaut, a star of the 1st magnitude, in the mouth of the South Fish, in the 2nd degree of ♓, of the nature of ♀ and ☿. Some say it is moderately beneficial, but others say it threatens bites of venomous creatures when joined to ♂; this is ridiculous, for it is too far south to be joined to any planet, or to do much evil or good in our hemisphere.

Fortitudes, influences of the planets made stronger by being well posited.

Fortunes, ♃ and ♀ and ☉, ☽ and ☿, if aspecting them, and not afflicted, are considered fortunate planets.

Fortunate signs, ♈, ♊, ♌, ♎, ♐, ♒. When one of these ascends in a nativity, the native is supposed more likely to be fortunate in his undertakings.

Fourfooted signs, ♈, ♉, ♌, ♐, ♑. Those born when they ascend are said to have the qualities of such animals, as being bold as the lion, lustful as the goat, etc.

Frustration, the cutting off, or preventing any thing shewn by one aspect by means of another. Thus, if ♀, lady of the ascendant, were hastening to the △ of ♂, lord of the 7th, in a question of marriage, it might denote that the match would take place; but if ☿ were to form an ☍ of ♂ before ♀ reached her △ of that planet, it would be a frustration, and would shew that the hopes of the querent would be cut off; and if ☿ were lord of the 12th, it might denote that it would be done by a private enemy; if the 3rd, by the means of relations, etc.

Fruitful signs, ♋, ♏, and ♓. In horary questions the Ascendant, the ☽, or lord of the Ascendant, in one of these signs, and strong, are symbols of children. Some consider this to be the case in nativities, and that the 5th, or its lord, being in a fruitful sign, is a symbol of children.

Geniture, the moment of time an infant is brought into the world.

Genethliacal, belonging to the Geniture, or the Doctrine of Nativities.

Geocentric, having the Earth for its centre, or the same centre as the Earth. All astrological positions are geocentric, because they relate wholly to the Earth.

Giver of Life, the Hyleg.

Horary Questions, so named from the Latin word hora, an hour, because the time of their being asked is noted, and the figure of the heavens for that time is taken by which to judge of the result.

Hydra's Heart, Alphard, or Cor Hydra, a fixed star of the 2nd magnitude, in the last face of ♌, of the nature of ♄ and ♀. It is said to cause drowning, or death by poison, when joined to ♂, and in evil aspect to the luminaries.

Heliacal Rising, is when a star that was hidden by the ☉'s rays becomes visible to the east of him, by getting clear of his rays.

Heliacal Setting, is when a star that before was visible is overtaken by the ☉ and lost in his rays. The ☽ is said to rise or set heliacally when 17° distant from the ☉, but other stars when a whole sign distant.

Heliocentric, having the ☉ for a centre.

Hircus, the Goat, called Capella, an eminent fixed star, of the 1st magnitude, in the 20th degree of ♊. It is of the nature of ♂ and ☿, and is said to give great martial honours and riches when culminating, for it is too far north to be with the lights, or to rise or set.

Horary Time, is the one-twelfth of the diurnal arc of a star, or one-sixth of its semidiurnal or seminocturnal arc.

Horoscope, the ascendant is sometimes so called; but it is more generally a term for the figure of the Heavens, used by astrologers for predicting by nativities, mundane astrology, and horary questions.

Houses, the twelve divisions or compartments into which the circle of the Heavens is divided; also the signs in which any planet is said to have most influence.

Human signs, ♊, ♍, ♒, and the first half of ♐. They are said, by Ptolemy, to give the native a humane disposition, when the lord of the geniture or the ascendant is in one, otherwise he will be brutish and savage. He also says, that the lord of an eclipse being in any human sign, its vile effects will fall on mankind.

Hyades, the first star in ♉, or the Bull's Head near Aldebaran, and the 1st face of ♊, the 3rd magnitude, of the nature of ♂ and the ☽.

Hyleg, see Apheta.

Hylegical Places, the 1st house, from 5° above to 25° below its cusp; 7th house, from 5° below to 25° above its cusp; the 9th house, from 5° outside its cusp to half way between the midheaven and the ascendant.

Hypogeon, under the Earth: a Greek name for the imum cæli, or 4th house.

Illumination, that period of the ☽ when she may be seen, which is 26 days and about 12 hours.

Impedited, this signifies being afflicted by evil stars. The ☽ is impedited in the highest degree when in ♂ with the ☉.

Imum Cœli, the lowest heaven. The 4th house, or north angle.

Inconjunct, a nonsensical phrase, and void of truth.

Increase in Light, when any planet is leaving the ☉, and is not yet arrived at the ☍; after which it decreases in light. The former is a good, the latter an evil testimony, especially as regards the ☽.

Increase in Motion, when any planet moves faster than it did on the preceding day.

Inferior Planets, ♀, ☿, and ☽; so called, because their orbit is inferior to that of the Earth.

Infortunes, ♅, ♄, and ♂; also ☿, when he is much afflicted.

Ingress, is the Sun's entrance into any sign, or other part of the ecliptic.

Intercepted, a sign which is found between the cusps of two houses, and not on either of them.

Joined to, being in any aspect, but especially a conjunction.

Latitude, the distance any star, etc., is north or south of the ecliptic. The ☉ never has any latitude. Latitude on the Earth is the distance any place is north or south of the equator.

Lights, ☉ and ☽.

Light of Time, the ☉ by day and ☽ by night.

Lion's Heart, a violent fixed star of the nature of ♅, in the 4th face of ♍. It is said to cause great martial honours, but they eventually end in ruin and violent death, particularly if it be joined to either of the luminaries.

Lion's Tail, Deneb, or Cauda Leonis, gives, it is said, riches and honours, which will end in trouble and disgrace. It is a star of the 2nd magnitude, in the 4th face of ♍.

Longitude, on the Earth, is the distance of any place east or west of Greenwich : in the Heavens, is the distance of any body from the first point of the zodiac, ♈, 0° 0′, measured on the ecliptic.

Lords, planets which have the most powerful effects in particular signs. Thus, if ♈ ascend any figure, ♂, who rules that sign, is the lord of the ascendant.

Luminaries, the ☉ and ☽.

Lunation, the ☌, □, or ☍ of ☉ and ☽ ; also the length of time in which the ☽ appears to move round the Earth: the time from New Moon to New Moon.

Malefic, ♅, ♄, and ♂, and ☿ in money, marriage, and law.

Markab, a violent star in the wing of Pegasus, in the 5th face of ♓, of the 2nd magnitude, the nature of ♂ and ♀. It is said to give honour and success, attended with great dangers and sufferings, and to threaten a violent death.

Masculine signs, they are odd signs, viz., ♈, ♊, ♌, ♎, ♐, ♒.

Matutine, appearing in the morning. The stars are called matutine when they rise before the ☉ in the morning, until they reach their first station, where they become retrograde. The ☽ is matutine until she has passed her first dicotome.

Mean Motion, when the diurnal motion of a planet is at a medium, neither faster nor slower than the average of the whole revolution.

Medium Cœli, the midheaven.

Medusa's Head, Cupot Algol : a violent fixed star of the 2nd magnitude, of the nature of ♄ and ♃, in the constellation of Perseus, in the 24th degree of ♉ : said, when found with the ☽, to cause beheading.

Meridian, a circle crossing the equator (from the poles at right angles). Every place has its own meridian passing through its zenith, where it forms the cusp of the midheaven, or the Sun's place at noon. From this to the horizon, either way, is the semi-diurnal arc of the ☉, or any star.

Meridian Distance, the distance any body is by A. R. from the meridian.

Midheaven (M. C.), the south angle or cusp of the 10th.

Moderators, the ☉, ☽, 10th and 1st houses, and ⊕. They are so called because each is said to have its own mode of operating on the native, according to its nature. Thus the 10th operates differently from the 1st, the ☉ differently from the ☽, and ⊕ differently from them all.

Movable signs, ♈, ♋, ♎, and ♑.

Mundane Aspects, distances in the world, measured by the semiarc wholly independent of the zodiac. Thus the distance of the 10th to the 12th is a ✶, although perhaps not 50° of the zodiac distant.

Mute signs, ♋, ♏, and ♓.

Mutilated degrees, another silly distinction, of certain degrees supposed to cause lameness, if they occupy the cusp of the ascendant.

Nadir, that point in the heavens which is directly opposite to the zenith, or the 4th house.

Nativity, the birth, the instant the native draws breath, or rather that when the umbilical cord is divided. It also signifies a figure of heaven from the time of birth.

Natural Day, the time of a complete revolution of the Earth on its axis.

Nebulæ, clusters of stars that appear like clouds. When ascending, or with the ☽, at birth, they are said to cause blindness, or some ocular defect, particularly when in an angle. Among these are included Presepe, the Pleiades, and even the Hyades.

Neomenium, the change of the Moon.

Nocturnal Arc, the distance or space through which the ☉ or a planet passes during the night. Also the time it takes from its setting to its rising again.

Nodes, the point where a planet crosses the ecliptic out of the south into the north latitude is called its north node, and where it crosses into the south latitude its south node. The Moon's north node is called the Dragon's Head, and marked ☊. Their motion is retrograde, about 3′ per day. (3′ 1770935 per day.)

Northern signs, ♈, ♉, ♊, ♋, ♌, ♍. They are also called commanding signs, because planets, in them, are said to command, and those in the opposite signs to obey.

Oblique Ascension, and *Oblique Descension* (see page 6).

Oblique Sphere, so called because all their ascensions and descensions are oblique, and all circles parallel to the equator are oblique to the horizon, and form acute angles with it. This is caused by one of their poles being more raised and the other more depressed, according to their distance from the equator.   All who inhabit between the poles and the equator live in an oblique sphere.

Occidental, falling down, killing ; western.   See " Oriental."

Occourses, or Occursors, promittors.

Opposition, is when two planets are distant 180°, or just half the distance of the zodiac apart, which places them in a diametrical radiation.   This is considered an aspect of perfect hatred.

Ophiucus, or Serpentarius, a northern constellation, consisting of 67 stars, in the 4th face of ♐, of the nature of ♄ and ♀, and said to produce wasteful characters.

Orion's Belt, in the 5th face of ♊, of the 2nd magnitude, the nature of ♃ and ♄ ; it gives notoriety.

Orb, the deferent of a planet, supposed by the ancients to fit into each other like the coats of an onion, and to carry the planets about with them.   The word is now used to describe the distance at which a planet may operate from a partile aspect before it quite loses its effects.   The orb of the cusp of any house, a fixed star, or ⊕, is 5°.

Oriental, planets found between the 4th house and the midheaven, rising, are in the eastern part of the figure, and said to be oriental. When they have passed the midheaven, and until they reach the 4th again, they are occidental.   In nativities, the ☉ and ☽ are oriental from the 1st to the 10th, and from the 7th to the 4th, and occidental in the opposite quarters.

Orion's Foot (Nigel), a benevolent star of the 1st magnitude, in the 3rd face of ♊, the nature of ♃ and ♂, said to cause great honours, and every degree of happiness, when rising or culminating.

Orion's Right Shoulder (Betelguese), a fixed star of the 1st magnitude, in the last face of ♊, the nature of ♂ and ☿, said to cause great martial honours and preferment.

Orion's Left Shoulder (Bellatrix), a star of the 2nd magnitude, in the 4th face of ♊, the nature of ♂ and ☿, said to cause great military honours, attended by eventual loss, danger, and ruin.   It causes blindness, by accidents, when joined to the luminaries.

Orion's Belt (Cingular Orionis), three stars, from 21° to 24° of ♊, of the 2nd magnitude, the nature of ♃ and ♄.   They are said to be fortunate.

Parallel, in the zodiac, are equal distances from the equator, or having the same declination, whether of the same name or opposite.   In the world, they are equal distances from the meridian, in proportion to the semiarcs of the planets which form them.   The student should pay very particular attention to the declination of the planets, as the zodiacal parallel is of more importance than any other aspect.   The effect of this position is exactly the same as that of a close conjunction, but more powerful.

Pars Fortunœ, the part of Fortune, ⊕.

Partile, an aspect is partile when it falls in the same degree and minute, both with respect to longitude and latitude. Thus ♃ would be in partile ☌ of ♂, if they were both in 3° 4′ of ♈. This can seldom happen, but a few minutes can make no difference. It is a perfect and powerful configuration, and, in horary questions, the business denoted is sure of completion, and near at hand, especially if it be by application.

Passive Stars, the ☉ and ☽.

Passive Qualities, moisture and dryness.

Perigree, that part of a planet's orbit where it is nearest to the ⊕.

Perihelion, the lower apsis of a planet or that point of its ellipse where it is nearest to the ☉.

Peregrine, a peregrine planet is one posited in a sign where it has no essential dignity of any kind. It is reckoned a debility of 5°. In questions of theft, a peregrine planet in an angle, or the 2nd house, is the thief. No planet is reckoned peregrine if it be in mutual reception.

Periodical Lunation, the time required by the ☽ in returning to her own place, viz., 27 d. 7 h. 41 m.

Phœnon, terrible, cruel : a Greek name of ♄, but more applicable to ♂.

Pisces, the house of Jupiter, the exaltation of Venus, is a moist, cold, watery, phlegmatic, nocturnal, bicorporeal, effeminate, sickly, southern, obeying sign.

Platic, wide, a ray cast from one planet, not to another, but to some place within its orb. Any aspect which is not partile, or exact, but only within orbs, or rather within moiety of the two planets' orbs. As if ♄ be in ♈ 10°, and ☽ in ♎ 20°, the ☽ is still in ☍ to ♄; because the half of their orbs being 10° 30′, she still wants 30′ of being clear of his ☍.

Pleiades, the (SEVEN STARS) in the (Bull's Neck), in 27° of ♉, all of which are of the 5th magnitude, except the middle star, which is of the 3rd. They are said, when rising, or with the luminaries, or when directed to the ascendant, to cause blindness from small-pox or measles, bad eyes, hurts in the face, sickness, disgrace, imprisonment, and every evil that can befall humanity.

Pole of the Horoscope, the latitude of the country.

Polar Elevation, or Pole, the pole of a country is its latitude; that of a body in the heavens is a certain elevation from the meridian towards the horizon. The word "pole" has caused some confusion; it is merely an abbreviation for "polar elevation."

Ponderable Planets, ♅, ♃, and ♂, so called because they move slower than the rest.

Pollux, a star of the 1st magnitude, in the 4th face of ♋, of the nature of ♂, said to produce renown and eminence.

Posited, situated in any place.

Præsepe, a nebulous cluster, in the 2nd face of ♌, of the nature of ♂ and the ☽, said to cause blindness when ascending or joined to either of the luminaries, particularly when the conjunction is in an angle. They are also said to cause diseases, disgrace, and every calamity.

Primum Mobile, the first mover, the 10th sphere of the Ancients. It was supposed to be beyond the sphere of the fixed stars, which was their 9th sphere, and by a motion of its own to whirl itself and all the subordinate spheres round the ⊕ every 24 hours.

Principal Places, five places where the luminaries are said to have the most beneficial effects in a nativity. The 10th, 1st, 11th, 7th, and 9th houses.

Process, the progression.

Procyon, a star of the 1st magnitude, in the 5th face of ♋, the nature of ♂ and ☿, and of course violent. It denotes activity, and sudden preferment by exertion, but generally causes evil in the end.

Profection, the progression.

Prohibition, the same as frustration. It indicates the state of two planets that are significators of some event, or the bringing of some business to an issue, or conclusion, and are applying to each other by conjunction ; but before such conjunction can be formed, a third planet, by means of a swifter motion, interposes his body, and destroys the expected conjunction, by forming an aspect himself; and this indicates that the matter under contemplation will be greatly retarded, or utterly prevented.

Promittor, that which promises to fulfil some event. Thus ♄ and ♂ are arnetic promittors, and promise to destroy the life of the native when the hyleg is directed to them; ♃ and ♀ are promittors of good, when directions to them are fulfilled. In horary questions the planet signifying the event is the promittor, as in a question of marriage the lord of the 7th is the promittor.

Propus, a star of the 4th magnitude, in the 29th degree of ♊, of the nature of ♂, thought to give eminence in life.

Prorogator, the apheta.

Pyrois, fiery, a Greek name of ♂.

Quadrants, the four quarters of heaven. The two oriental quarters are from the 1st to the 10th, and from the 7th to the 4th, and 4th to the 1st. In the zodiac the oriental quarters are from the beginning of ♈ to the beginning of ♋, and from the beginning of ♎ to the beginning of ♑. The reverse are the occidental quadrants.

Quadrantine Lunations, every □ , ☍ , and ☌ , of the ☉ and ☽. Their effects are good or evil according as they happen in good or evil aspect with the radical places of the fortunes or infortunes.

Quadratures, the ☽ dicotomes.

Quality and property of ♊ —it is an aerial, hot, moist, sanguine, diurnal, common or double-bodied human sign; the diurnal house of ☿ ; of the Airy triplicity, western, masculine.

Quartile, the □ ; a distance of 3 signs, or 90°. It is considered an evil aspect, but in a secondary degree.

Querent, is he or she who requires or asks the question, and desires the result of any event.

Quincunx, a new aspect, containing 5 signs, or 150°. Ptolemy, and most others consider it as an inconjunct. It is the opposite point of the semisextile, and those who hold it to be an aspect consider it a good one.

Quintile, is a benefic, but if to the evil planets is of no avail. It consists of 72° : thus, supposing a planet in 5° of ♒, and another in 27° of ♈, they are then in quartile aspect.

Radical ; Radix, the figure at birth is the radix or root from which everything is judged ; and the term radical refers to it.

Rapt Motion, the apparent diurnal motion of the heavens, occasioned by the real diurnal motion of ⊕. It was called rapt, or forcibly carried away, because the stars were supposed to be forcibly carried round by the motion of the Primum Mobile.

Rapt Parallel, parallels formed by the motion of the Earth on its axis, where both bodies are rapt or carried away by the same, until they come to equal distances from the meridian.

Rays, in the common acceptation of the word a ray is a beam of light emanating from a star or luminous body; but, in astrology, it signifies a beam of influence or sympathy, which accompanies such ray, and is supposed only to proceed from a planet. Thus, the doctrine that the fixed stars emit no rays does not mean that they emit no light, but that they have no distant influence by aspect, but only operate with a planet when joined to it, within from 5° to 2° of its body, according to the magnitude of the fixed stars.

Reception, is when two planets are mutually posited in each other's essential dignities ; as ♃ in ♈, and the ☉ in ♋, where ♃ being in the exaltation of the ☉, and the ☉ in the exaltation of ♃, both are in mutual reception ; or the ☉ in ♈, and in ♃ ♌, are in reception, one by house, the other by triplicity. This is accounted an aspect of singular amity and agreement.

Rectification, the method of bringing a nativity to its true time, as it is supposed that the inaccuracy of a clock or watch, or the mistake of those whose business it is to observe them, may cause an error in the time of birth, which requires to be rectified.

Refranation, is when two planets are applying to an aspect, but before the aspect can be completed one of them turns retrograde, which, in practice, is fatal to the success of the question.

Retrograde, when any planet is decreasing in longitude. It is a very great debility.

Retrograde Application, is when both planets are retrograde, and move contrary to the order of the signs of the zodiac, applying to each other.

Revolution, the moving round the ☉ by the Earth, which makes the ☉ appear to revolve and return to his place at birth once a year; very near the time of birth.

Rigel, see " Orion's Foot."

Right Ascension, any arc of the equator, reckoned from the beginning of ♈, and ending at that point which rises with any star or part of the ecliptic in a right sphere.

Right Descension, an arc of the equator that descends with any star or point of the ecliptic ; but this is only an unmeaning term, for the whole is right ascension from the first point of ♈, again including the whole circle of 360°.

Right Distance, the distance of any place from another by right ascension, and it is found by subtracting the right ascension of the preceding from that of the succeeding place, adding 360°, if subtraction cannot be made without.

Right Sphere, so called because all the circles parallel to the equator make right angles with the horizon, and the celestial bodies ascend and descend direct : hence it is called a *direct sphere*.

Ruminant Signs, signs that ruminate, or chew the cud: ♈, ♉, and ♑. It is well not to give medicine during the Moon's transit through these signs.

Sagittarius, is a hot, fiery, choleric, dry, masculine, diurnal, eastern, common, bicorporeal, quadrupedian, changeable, southern, obeying sign.

Satellites, attendants or guards ; a term applied in astronomy to those secondary planets or Moons that revolve round the primary as their Moon, or those of ♄, ♃, and ♅.

Saturn, see " Planets."

Scales, the north Scale is a star of the 2nd magnitude, of the nature of ♃ and ♂, in the 17° of ♏, said to be of a benefic nature ; and causing riches, honours, and happiness. The south Scale is said to be of a violent nature, and productive of every species of disease, and unfortunate. It is of the nature ♄ and ♀, and is posited in the 13th degree of ♏.

Scheme, see " Figure."

Scorpio is the house of Mars, and also his joy. It is termed a cold, moist, watery, phlegmatic, feminine, nocturnal, fixed, mute, southern, and extremely fruitful sign, of long ascension.

Scorpion's Heart (Antares), a violent fixed star of the 1st magnitude, in the 8th degree of ♐, of the nature of ☿ and ♂, said to cause rashness, enterprise, violence, and oppression, and productive of ultimate ruin and death.

Secondary Directions, those daily configurations to the luminaries and angles that happen after birth, every day of which is reckoned for a year, 2 hours for a month, 30 minutes for a week, and 4 minutes for a day.

Scorpii, a star of the 2nd magnitude, in the 1st face of ♐, the nature of ♄ and ♀, considered unfortunate.

Semi, half.

Semiarc, half a diurnal or nocturnal arc, and the half the arc a planet would form above the Earth if it remained fixed in the zodiac from the time of its rising until that of its setting, is called its semiarc diurnal. The half of the arc it would, in like circumstances, form under the Earth from its setting until its rising, is called its semiarc nocturnal.

Semicircle, half a circle, 180°.

Semiquartile, or Semisquare, this, whether found at birth, or formed by directional motion, is evil; but if benefics ♃ or ♀ form this aspect the evil influences are only very slight.

Semiquintile, half a quintile, containing 36° in the zodiac, or one-fifth of a diurnal or nocturnal arc in the world. It is said to be good because the quintile is good whence it is derived.

Semisextile, this aspect is found to be moderately fortunate and beneficial in influence. It consists of 30°, or *one sign* in the zodiac : thus, suppose ♃ in 4° of ♈, and ♀ in 4° of ♓, or ♉, they would then be in semisextile to each other.

Separation, when an aspect is past, the planets, etc., are said to be separating from that aspect ; and observe, that in a nativity the influence of any aspect to the moderators is more powerful if it be a few (4 or 5) degrees past, than if it be not yet formed. In Horary Astrology, when separating shows the influence is passing away, as application is the sign whereby events are denoted to take place, and separation denotes what has passed or taken place, whether good or evil.

Sesquiquadrate, this is unfortunate, and equal in all degrees to the semisquare. It is a ray of 135° : thus, supposing a star in 19° of ♑, and another in 4° of ♍, they are in sesquiquadrate aspect.

Sesquiquintile, 108° ; see " Tresile."

Sexagenary Tables, so called from Sexaginta, sixty : tables formed from the proportional parts of the number sixty, so as to give the product of two sexagenary numbers, that are to be multiplied, or the quotient of two to be divided.

Sextile (⚹), when two planets are two signs, or 60° distant from each other. In the world, it is two-thirds of a semiarc. It is also called an hexagon, and is supposed to be of the same nature as the △.

Schet Pegasi, a star of the 2nd magnitude, in the last face of ♓, of the nature of ♄, produces danger from drowning.

Sidereal Time, is the angular distance of the first point of ♈, or the true vernal equinox. It is, of course, the true right ascension on the meridian at noon, or that shewn by a good clock.

Significator, the significator of any party is that planet which rules, or has dominion by celestial house, over that part of the figure or scheme, peculiar to the business in hand. Thus, were the question about money, the lord of the 2nd house of heaven is the chief significator of the matter ; and his good or evil aspects must be well observed, ere the answer can be faithfully given. The lord of the ascendant is the general significator of the querent. The ☽ is, in general, his cosignificator.

Signs of the Zodiac, those groups of apparently neighbouring stars, lying within 9° on either side of the celestial ecliptic, and each group of which is classed under one name.

Signs of Long Ascension, ♋, ♌, ♍, ♎, ♏, ♐ ; so called because they take longer time in ascending than the others. Ptolemy says a ✶ in a sign of long ascension will have the same effect as a ☐.

Signs of Short Ascension, ♑, ♒, ♓, ♈, ♉, ♊ ; so called because they ascend in a shorter period of time than the others, from the diurnal motion of the Earth, being, when they ascend, nearly parallel with its orbit. A △, in a sign of short ascension, is, according to Ptolemy, equal to a ☐ in its effects ; but, long or short ascensions are mundane, and not zodiacal positions : for all signs occupy the same distance in the ecliptic, and the stars can only operate on each other according to their general positions, let Placidus say what he will.

Signs of Voice, ♊, ♍, ♎, ♒, and the first part of ♐, because, it is said, if any of them ascend, and ☿ be strong, the native will be a good orator.

Sinister Aspects, aspects to the left, according to the course of the signs. Thus, a slow planet in ♈ will cast a sinister ✶ to ♊.

Slow of Course, when a planet moves slower than its mean motion it is considered a great debility, and it may be so in some cases of horary questions.

Sol, ☉, the Sun.

Sirius, a star of the 1st magnitude, in the 2nd face of ♋, of the nature of ♃ and ♂, and produces glory and renown, or great wealth.

Sinistra, a star of the 3rd magnitude, in the 2nd face of ♎, of the nature of ☿.

Spica (Arista), a star of the 1st magnitude, in the 1st face of ♎, of the nature of ♂ and ♀, and produces riches, renown, and eminence.

Serpentis, a star of the 2nd magnitude, in the 4th face of ♏, of the nature of ♂ and ♀.

Southern Signs, ♎, ♏, ♐, ♑, ♒, and ♓, so called because they are to the south of the equator.

Speculum (a looking glass), a table, so called, which should be made out for every nativity, containing the ascensions, semiarcs, latitudes, declinations, poles, ascensional difference, etc., that the artist may always have them to refer to in bringing up directions.

Sphere, a globe, the deferent of a planet was also called its sphere, and was what is called at present its sphere.

Spheroid, a body resembling a sphere, but whereof one of the diameters is longer than the other.

Square, the quartile aspect, containing a quadrant or right angle. It consists in the zodiac of three signs, and in the world of a whole semiarc. Its effect as an aspect is evil, though somewhat less than an opposition.

Stations, those parts in the orbit of a planet where it becomes either retrograde or direct, because it remains for a while there stationary before it changes its course. The first station is where they become retrograde, but in the ☽, who is never retrograde, it is called her first dicotome. The second station is after they have passed their perigee, and from retrogradation become direct. This, in the ☽, is called her second dicotome. From these stations their orientality is reckoned. From their apogee to their first station they are called matutine, because they rise in the morning, before the ☽, and are in their first degree or orientality. From the 1st station to the lower apis or perigee, they are considered in their first degree of occidentality.

Stationary, when a planet is in its station and appears to stand still. The lights are never stationary.

Stellium, a crowd of planets in an angle. Persons having this in their radix have, at some period in the course of their lives, prodigious good or ill fortune. So far as my observation extends, a stellium of four or five planets in any part of the radix always produces in the course of the native's existence some tremendous catastrophe.

Strong Signs, ♌, ♏, and ♒, because they are said to give strong athletic bodies.

Succedent Houses, so called because they follow or succeed the angles. These houses are next in power to the angles, and are the 2nd, 5th, 8th, and 11th.

Superiors and Inferiors, ♅, ♄, ♃, and ♂ are called the former, being beyond the Earth; and ♀ and ☿ are called the latter, being between the Earth and the ☉. The former are more powerful and durable, in general, in their effects.

Sun Beams, a planet is accounted under the Sun beams till he be separated 17 degrees from him.

Swift in Motion, is when a planet moves more than his mean motion in 24 hours—and slow in motion when he moves less.

Synodical, see " Lunations."

Syzygies, the new and full Moon, also the ☌ or ☍ of any two planets, and is often used as a common term for familiarities of every description.

Table of Houses, these are necessary to erect a figure of the heavens.

Taurus, it is an earthy, cold, dry, melancholy, feminine, nocturnal, fixed, bestial sign, of the Earthy triplicity, and south.

Term, terms are certain degrees in a sign, supposed to possess the power of altering the nature of a planet to that of the planet in the term of which it is posited.

Terminus Vitæ, the termination of life, the fatal direction, or directions, that inevitably punish.

Testimony, having any aspect or dignity, etc., or being in any way in operation in the figure as regards the question asked.

Tetragonus, the square aspect.

Thema Cœli, a figure of the heavens.

Transits, these are the planets passing over the place of any moderator or planet, or their aspects, either in the radix, or revolution, etc., by any other body.

Translation of Light, the conveying the influence of one planet to another, by separating from the aspect of one and giving to the aspect of another. It is a very powerful testimony. Let ♄ be placed in 20° of ♈, ♃ in 13°, and ♂ in 14°, of the same sign; here ♂ separates from a ☌ with ♃, and translates the light and nature of that planet to ♄, to whom he next applies.

Triplicity, Trigon, an essential dignity. The zodiac is divided into four trigons or triplicities; the fiery ♈, ♌, ♐; the earthy, ♉, ♍, ♑; the airy, ♊, ♎, ♒; and the watery, ♋, ♏, ♓; agreeing with the four elements into which the ancients divide the natural world.

Trigonocrators, rulers of trigons. The ☉ and ♃ rule the fiery; ♀ and the ☽, the earthy; ♅ and ☿, the airy; and ♂ alone the watery, though the moderns have united ♀ and the ☽ with him in the watery triplicity.

Trimorian, the distance of three signs, or the square aspect.

Trine (△), a distance of four signs, or 120°, in the zodiac. In the Earth it is the whole of a semiarc and the third of another. It is reckoned the best aspect of the whole, though I own I have some doubts about this.

Tropical Signs, ♋ and ♑, so called, because they limit the course of the ☉, which after he has arrived at their first points, seems to turn and to diminish his declination; causing summer by the turn he makes in ♋, and winter by that which he makes in ♑.

True Moment of Birth, that wherein the child becomes independent of the mother, and the lungs are inflated.

Tresile, a quintile and a half, or 3 signs and 18° in the zodiac, or a whole semiarc and one-fifth of another in the world. It is said to be good, because the quintile is good on which it is founded.

Venus, this beautiful planet is situated nearer the ☉ than is the Earth. She goes round the ☉ in 32 weeks; and is very nearly the same size as our globe: her diameter is to the Earth as 0·975 to 1.

Vertical, directly overhead.

Vespertine, the reverse of matutine : when a planet sets in the evening after the ☉.

Via Combusta, the combust way ; the last half of ♎, and the whole of ♑, though others, the 1st 15° of ♏, so called from violent fixed stars, which they say render that place extremely unfortunate, particularly to the ☽, who suffers there as much as during an eclipse.

Violent Signs, those that are the houses or exaltations of the malefics, viz. ♈, ♎, ♏, ♑, and ♒. Also those signs are called violent where there are any remarkably violent fixed stars, as ♉ for caput Algol, etc.

Virgo, an earthy, cold, melancholy, barren, feminine, nocturnal sign; of the earthy triplicity.

Void of Course, forming no aspect in the sign the significator then is. When the ☽ is so, it denotes in general no success in the question.

Under the Sunbeams, when a planet is less than 17° from the ☉ It is reckoned four debilities. In horary questions it is reckoned fear, trouble and oppression, but not so bad as combustion.

Unfortunate Signs, ♉, ♋, ♑, ♏, and ♓. The natives are said to be unfortunate in the general tendency of the events of their lives. The most unfortunate of them all is ♑.

Vindematrix, a star of the 2nd magnitude, in the second face of ♍, the nature of ♄ and ♀, denotes mischief and unfortunate.

Ursa Major, the Great Bear, a northern constellation, consisting of 87 stars; sometimes called Charles's Wain.

Ursa Minor, the Little Bear, a northern constellation, near the pole, consisting of 24 stars.

Vulpes, the Fox, a northern constellation, consisting of 35 stars.

Watery Signs or Triplicity, ♋, ♏, and ♓.

Whale's Jaw (Menkar), a star of the 2nd magnitude, in the 3rd face of ♉, the nature of ♄, said to cause sickness when united to the luminaries, when in the midheaven disgrace, ruin, with danger from cattle.

Whale's Belly, a star of the 4th magnitude, in the 4th face of ♈, the nature of ♄, unfortunate, and giving falls and blows. See Ceti.

Whale's Tail (S. end), a star of the 2nd magnitude, in the 1st face of ♈, the nature of ♄, unfortunate,

Whole Signs, ♊, ♎, and ♒. Those born under these are said to be strong, robust, and not so liable to accidents.

Zenith, the point directly overhead. Thus, every place has its own zenith, and the nearer the planets are to that zenith the more powerful is their operation.

Zodiac, a kind of circle, or rather belt, 12° broad, with the ecliptic passing through the middle of it. It contains the 12 signs of the ecliptic. all of which being animals, it takes its name from them.

Modern astronomers consider it as 18° broad, on account of the extensive latitude of ♂ and ♀.

Zodiacal Aspects, aspects measured by the degrees of the zodiac. In this case the promittor's place is taken without latitude, instead of which the latitude is taken which the significator will have when it arrives at the place where the aspect is formed.

Zodiacal Parallels, see " Parallels."

N.B.—I recommend the student to study and digest the Terms, as a correct knowledge and explanation are indispensably necessary.

CHAPTER III.

GENERAL DESCRIPTIONS PRODUCED BY THE SIGNS.

OF ARIES, ♈.

Aries—ascending at birth, or time of question, produces a person of a dry, lean, spare body, rather tall, strong limbs, large bones, thick shoulders, long face, sharp piercing sight, dark eyebrows, reddish and wiry hair, swarthy complexion, and neck rather long.

9 *First face*, or from 1 to 5 degrees, on account of the fixed stars, produces a person of mean stature, not fat, rather low than tall, broad forehead, high cheeks, narrow chin, low hooked nose, reddish or dark hair, a little curling, swarthy, red complexion, and black eyes.

In this face are found the fixed stars Whale's Tail, South end, 1st degree, nature of ♄, generally unfortunate ; sometimes the body will be middle stature, especially if ♄, ♃, or ☿ be in this face, intellectual organs good, and rather quick perceptive development, journeys and frequent discord among herdsmen.

10 *Second face*, or from 5 to 10 degrees, shews a person of grave aspect, steady eye, not great stature, yet big boned, rather lean, brown or swarthy complexion, long visage, having a mole or mark upon the face, above the nose.

This face is dry and of the nature of ♂ and ☿, consisting of Algenib and Pegasi, of the 2nd magnitude, and if ♂ or ☿ be herein, the judgment will be more confirmed—Mercury in 14th degree, good and pleasant looking face.

11 *Third face*, or from 10 to 15 degrees, shews a moderately lean middle person, long visage, dark hair, grey hollow eyes, face good looking.

Venus and Jupiter rule this face, and is moist, Caput Andromedæ is in this face, and is powerful in influence, gains wealth, and conquers enemies, fond of dress of a gaudy colour. Venus here, the visage oval.

12 *Fourth face*, or from 15 to 20 degrees, shows a middle stature,

neat, well proportioned body, fresh, round face, light brown hair, and grey eyes.

Nature of ♃ and ♀, rather moist and fortunate; ♂ here, ruddy complexion; ☽, very changeable; ☉ here, high forehead; ☿ here, long face, freckled, light curling hair ; ♅ here, darker hair.

13 *Fifth face*, or from 20 to 25 degrees, shews a middle creature, dark hair and skin, long face, teeth distorted, which soon become decayed, legs bent, and indeed the whole native hooks forward.

It is dry, of the nature of ♄ generally, conceited and obstinate; ♂ here, strongly made—fierce and active—♂ in ♈, hollow eyes, quarrelsome—♄ in ♈, a strong hoarse voice, high forehead.

14 From 25 to 30 degrees shows one of good stature, rather tall than low, except the Moon be there, an austere countenance, thick eyebrows, black hair and curling, wide mouth, large nose, strong well set body, but the face seems manly, with some scar. Herschel on the 1st, denotes a long visage, and teeth rather large and some-what distorted.

This face is principally under ♂ and ♄, with Zona Andromedæ, of the nature of ♀ ; the face is, therefore, rather dry, and is generally fortunate, as sailors, chemists, and cattle keepers ; ♃ herein, pimples in the face; ☿ here, hollow cheeks, light eyelashes and eyebrows, flattish nose.

OF TAURUS, ♉.

Taurus—gives a short, full stout body, broad brows, large eyes, full face, thick lips, short neck, thick broad hands and shoulders, wide nose and mouth, dark curling hair, swarthy complexion.

15 *The first face*, or from 1 to 5 degrees, shews a low middle stature, black hair, a little curling, swarthy complexion, dark eyebrows.

This face is chiefly under the influence of ♄ and ♂, containing the ancient Ram's Head. The ☽ with ♄, ♅, or ♂, subject to quinsies. Makes an orator—but abrupt.

16 From 5 to 10 degrees, denotes a low middle stature, long face, broadish forehead, full cheeks, distorted teeth, dark brown hair, swarthy complexion, stooping in the shoulders, and melancholy appearance.

Under the power of ♄, consequently cold, denoting discord, and ill luck by buildings, mining. Makes epicures—large gustativeness.

17 From 10 to 15 degrees, gives a small stature, pale, swarthy complexion, little eyes, loooking downward, frowning eyebrows, large forehead, thick lips, almost flat nose, thin beard, unpleasant countenance, and broad stooping shoulders.

Under the influence of Stars of the nature of ♄, consequently dry and cold, consisting of Ceti. The 15th degree arising is fortunate, giving a high moral spirit and Herculean firmness, inclines the native to journey. The same if ☽ or ♀ be therein.

18 From 15 to 20 degrees, shews a middle stature, 5 feet 10 inches, proportionate, oval, pleasant face, seldom displeased, chestnut coloured hair, large forehead, grey eyes ; if a woman, she is generally a beauty.

Moist face, of the nature of ♀, gentle temper.

19 From 20 to 25 degrees, shews a short person, reddish complexion, pimples or other irruptions in the face; Saturn here, he gives the native a stinking breath, face rather oval, hair black, arms, hands, fingers, legs, and feet rather short, and the body fleshy.

It is temperate, of the nature of the ☽ and ♂ combined.

20 From 25 to 30 degrees, shews a robust person, square visage, brown complexion, generally a mark or scar in the face, low middle stature, 5 feet 9 inches, black hair.

This face is temperate, governed by ♂ and the ☽, Lucida Pleiadum in the 28th degree, defects in the eyes, and very probably small pox—rude in behaviour.

OF GEMINI, ♊.

Gemini—gives a tall, upright, well made body, strong and active, sanguine complexion, hazel eyes, very dark hair, smart active look, long arms, short fleshy hands and feet, quick step ; if a female, she has very fine eyes.

21 *The first face*, or from 1 to 5 degrees, shews a stiff person, long, thin, lean, red, swarthy face, dark or reddish hair, round shouldered, nimble tongued, and bow legged.

It is dry, of the nature of ♂, it shews huntsmen; and when this face rises, it is not well to take medicine. The 5th degree pockmarked, etc.

22 From 5 to 10 degrees, shows a spruce person, almost round visage, chestnut hair, and voluble tongue : altogether a good appearance.

Ruled by ♀ and ♂, consisting of Aldebaran and the Bull's South Eye ; 9th degree, dark complexion. Moon with ♄ or ♂, danger of hurts in the head or face.

23 From 10 to 15 degrees, gives a shortish person, red, round face, strong well composed body, short curled hair, almost black, the organ of language large, goggle eyes, distorted teeth, thick shoulders and short thick legs.

Of the nature of ♃ and ♂, contains Rigel in the 15th degree. The 12th degree fat. The ☽ with ♄ or ♂, danger of misfortune in the face.

24 From 15 to 20 degrees, portends a fullish stature, sandy hair, fresh countenance, rather corpulent, roundish visage, sparkling eyes, of a delicate composure in all respects ; teeth soon decay.

Bellatrix in the 19th degree, governed by ☿ and ♂, of a dryish nature, profitable marriage, gain of friends.

25 From 20 to 25 degrees, portends one of a good proportion,

but lean, black hair, long visage, narrow chin, brown complexion, black eyes, beard black, long slender legs, and looking as if consumptive.

Chiefly under the influence of ♂ and ♃, being dry.

26 From 25 to 40 degrees, shews a neat person, clean, oval visage, bright hair, whitish complexion.

It is temperate, of the nature of ♂ and ☿. Betelguese in its 27th degree, disgraceful person; 29th degree, dark.

OF CANCER, ♋.

Cancer—gives a small stature, strong and well set, fair and pale, round face, small features and voice, brown hair, grey eyes, bad teeth, the upper part of the body larger than the lower, slender arms, weak constitution, prolific.

27 *The first face*, or from 1 to 5 degrees, portends a middle stature, large, full, fleshy body, face between long and round, a little swarthy, brown hair, and indifferently handsome.

Governed by ☿ and ♀, temperate, danger of imprisonment; 4th degree, rather light and lower middle stature.

28 From 5 to 10 degrees, shews one of little stature, square visage, reddish swarthy complexion, dark brown hair and a little curling, strong voice, broad forehead, and a dimple in the chin.

Of the nature of ☿ and ♀.

29 From 10 to 15 degrees, portends one of middle stature, swarthy complexion, black hair, and if Mars be there curling, long, thin face and nose, slender body, looking as if in a consumption, shrill voice, and high cheek bones.

Ruled by stars of the influence of ♃, ♄, and ♂, containing the " Dog Star."

30 From 15 to 20 degrees, gives a lean, thin, black, swarthy visage, black hair, drawling speech, much affected though he speaks nonsense; crook legged, splay footed, heavy eyebrows and down looking.

This face is evil for female lovers, bringing dishonour upon them; 18th degree, lowish and dark.

31 From 20 to 25 degrees, signifies a lean visage, and boldness; great lips, high forehead, long hooked nose and chin, little beard hair either dark brown or sandy, slender legs, and incomposed body.

Influenced by Pollux and Procyon, of the nature of ☿ and ♂.

32 From 25 to 30 degrees, portends a long, freckled face, full forehead, large nose, full eyes, narrow chin, wide mouth, thin stooping body, low middle stature, broad shoulders, dark curling hair, if Sun or Mars be here, the hair is red or yellow.

It is dry, of the nature of ♄, ♂, and ☿, fond of dress and the water

LESSON SECOND.

QUESTIONS TO BE ANSWERED BEFORE THE STUDENT PROCEEDS.

What is Astrology; and what does it teach?

How many branches are there?

How many faces in a sign?

How many degrees in a face?

Why do faces vary the form and stature of a person?

Which are the fixed signs?

Which the movable?

Which the common?

Which the barren?

Which the fruitful?

What kind of a person does the 1st face of Aries produce?

The second? The third? The fourth? The fifth? The sixth?

When is a planet retrograde?

At what time does it signify?

Tell me the nature of each face in Aries.

When is a planet peregrine?

What is the corporature of the first face of Taurus?

What the second? The third? The fourth face of Taurus? The fifth? Tell me the sixth?

Mention the nature of the different faces of Taurus.

What is the general stature of Taurus?

What are the humane signs?

The bestial? The earthy? The airy? The watery? The fiery?

Which are the masculine signs?

The feminine?

Which are the double-bodied signs?

What is the general character of Gemini?

What do its different faces give?

Under what triplicity is Gemini?

What is the nature of Gemini's faces?

What is Cancer called?

What kind of person does Cancer generally produce?

What does the first face of Cancer produce?

The second? The third? The last?

What fixed stars are found herein?

Which are the Tropical signs?

Which the Equinoctial?

Which of the foregoing twenty-four faces produce red hair?

Which give brown?

Which tall persons?

Which of them produce low persons?

Which give black hair?

What do we mean by the Aspect?

Which are the Cardinal signs?

What do you mean by Zodiac?

What is the North Node?

What is the South Node?

OF LEO, ♌.

Leo—gives a large noble body, full, tall majestic stature, broad shoulders, austere, oval, ruddy fierce contenance, yellow bushy hair, large staring eyes, yet quick-sighted, strong voice, resolute, unbending, aspiring mind, bold and courageous.

33 *The first face*, or from 1 to 5 degrees, portends a short, thick, well-set body, square ruddy visage, brown hair, a little curling, all the features in good proportion, well made nose, pleasant eye, red lips, and nimble tongue, a strong, well-compact body.

The 2nd degree dark; 4th degree dark, pock-marked; 1st degree, stiff and plump; the 5th degree, light complexion, subject to dishonour if a female.

34 From 5 to 10 degrees, shews a middle stature, adorned with good features, clear skin, roundish visage, flaxen hair, grey eyes straight full body and breasts, in age grows fat.

The 8th degree largish; 9th degree, stiff.

35 From 10 to 15 degrees, produces a swarthy complexion, dark hair, large forehead, hanging eyebrows, black eyes, prominent cheek bones, distorted teeth, a mark near the left side of the chin, full stature, and consumptive appearance.

The 14th degree, tall; 10th and 11th degrees, rather stout, dark hair. Of the nature of Luna and Venus, fond of the water, and given to intemperance.

36 From 15 to 20 degrees, signifies a native tall, slender, high forehead, chestnut coloured hair, long face, pale complexion, slender legs, and a great eater, having gustativeness large.

The 17th degree, stiff; 19th degree, tallish, brown complexion; 16th degree, low and stiff; the 15th degree, exactly as the whole face. The nature of ♅, and the native is often of a fidgety disposition and haughty temper of mind.

37 From 20 to 25 degrees, signifies a comely, tall, lusty, full-faced person, brown hair, not curling, majestic carriage and deportment.

The 21st degree, stiff and lowish; 27th degree, middle stature, rather light—☽ here, giddy—they are generally profound in disputation, and philosophical in argumentation.

37 From 25 to 30 degrees, denotes a tallish, thin person, pock-marked, swarthy face, dark eyes and hair, broad shoulders, short arms and legs, and awry gait.

The 30th degree, dark and low; the 26th degree, tallish and light; 28th degree, rather low and moderate complexion; ☽ here, immodest; 27th degree, rather stout and darkish, but good looking. In the 28th degree is Cor Leo, agrees with ♂ and ♃, a prosperous face, and the natives are often aiming at honourable undertakings, and frequently raise themselves to power.

OF VIRGO, ♍.

Virgo—gives a middle stature, inclined to be tall, slender, brown, ruddy complexion, dark brown hair, round face, small shrill voice, round head, in short, a well composed body; sentimental organs well developed.

This first face is ruled generally by ☉ and ♄, consequently of a drying nature.

39 *The first face*, or from 1 to 5 degrees, shews a person rather tall, brown complexion, thin beard, brownish hair, broad forehead, the intellects good, Roman nose, narrow chin, long slender legs and feet.

The 4th degree, good stature; 1st and 2nd degrees, low and stiff; often tall.

This face appears to bring out egotists and great pretenders to science.   There is nothing else very remarkable.

40 From 5 to 10 degrees, signifies a tall stature, oval face, brown complexion, sometimes pale, pleasant countenance, in short, a good-looking person.

The bright star Vindematrix is in the 8th degree, nature of ♄ and Venus, rather unfortunate, but of an excellent disposition—often becomes widows, etc.

41 From 10 to 15 degrees, produces a comely person, full middle stature, roundish face, clear complexion, flaxen hair.

42 From 15 to 20 degrees, shews one rather tall, oval visage, broad forehead, large nose, wide mouth, full lips, swarthy complexion, slender waist, long legs, and sometimes a full dark eye.

This face is of the nature of ♅.   In the 20th degree, is Deneb, gives disgrace and ignominy, very busy in other men's matters.

43 From 20 to 25 degrees, shews one inclined to be tall, long thin visage, freckled face, narrow chin, high cheek bones, in a mean between fat and lean, black eyes, large nose and nostrils, thin lips.

44 From 25 to 30 degrees, shews a short person, full oval face, brown complexion, chestnut coloured hair, high forehead, and sometimes a Roman nose.

OF LIBRA, ♎.

Libra—tall and elegantly formed, round face, a beauty, rather slender, lank, auburn or flaxen hair, generally blue eyes, fine clear red and white complexion in youth, which, in old age, becomes pimpled.

45 *The first face*, or from 1 to 5 degrees, personates one rather tall, slender, oval visage, pale complexion, grey eyes, well formed nose and lips, chestnut hair, and a modest countenance.

This face is governed by Stars of the nature of ♂ and ☿ ; it is dry.

46 From 5 to 10 degrees, signifies a person much the same stature, and corporature with the former, except this is more corpulent, and clearer complexion.

Governed by ☿, consequently changeable.   Sinistra herein.

47 From 10 to 15 degrees, shews one of middle stature, longish visage, brownish complexion, broad forehead, full grey eyes, generally brown hair, a little curling, long arms and fingers, long nose, freckles in the face, yet generally good features.

48 From 15 to 20 degrees, shews a very comely creature, inclining to tallness, slender in the waist, roundish visage, clean white complexion, neat lips and nose, grey eyes, light or flaxen hair, long arms, hands and fingers, white soft skin, a most complete and lasting beauty.

49 From 20 to 25 degrees, shews one much like the former,

excepting a redder blush, or a more fresh countenance, but it generally exhibits a comely person and a perfect beauty.

Spica and Arcturus herein, the native becomes notorious in something, nature of ♂, ♃, ♀.

50 From 25 to 30 degrees, shews one much like the two former, excepting somewhat taller, but a beautiful body.

LESSON THIRD.

QUESTIONS TO BE STUDIED BEFORE THE STUDENT CAN PROCEED.

What is direct motion ?

What is converse motion ?

Which motion is the stronger ?

What do the faces of Leo produce ?

What kind of person does ♍ give ?

Tell the character of the first face—the second—the third— the fourth — the fifth — the sixth.

What is the stature of Libra ?

What does the second face produce ?

Which sign gives most beauty ?

What is the stature of the third face ?

Of the fourth face ? Of the fifth face ?   The sixth face ?

What does the word Libra mean ?

What is Arcturus ?

Where is Crater ?

Where is Deneb ?

Where is Cor Leo ?

Explain Prœcepe.

Which are strong signs ?

What is a transit ?

Explain the sign Virgo.

What are airy signs ?

What is apogee ?

What is meant by Cazimi ?

What is Capella ?

What is Castor ?

Which are common signs ?

What is disc ?

Which signs are fortunate ?

What is Hydra's Heart ?

Which are mute signs ?

Where is Orion's Belt ?

Where is Orion's Foot ?

Where is Pollux ?

Where is Procyon ?

What is Propus ?

Where is Sirius ?

Where is Spica ?

Which are violent signs ?

OF SCORPIO, ♏

Scorpio —gives a strong, robust, corpulent person, broad face, middle stature, dusky complexion, brown, curling, bushy hair, dark eyes, thick neck, coarse hairy legs, often bow-legged, active, often thoughtful, and reserved in conversation.

51 *The first face,* or from 1 to 5 degrees, shews one of middle stature, rather short, round full face, chestnut hair, not curling, pale complexion, grey eyes, well compact comely person, excellent features, and a good countenance.

Scorpio contains 46 stars.

52 From 5 to 10 degrees, shews one much like the former, but not so beautiful, thick in the waist, plumper visage, and thick short legs.

In the 10th degree is the North Crown—nature of ♀ and ☿.

53 From 10 to 15 degrees, shews one a little more slender, dark brown hair, brown complexion, greyish eyes, and broad forehead.

South Scale in the 13th degree, nature of ♄ and ♀, unfortunate in female figures.

54 From 15 to 20 degrees, shews a slender shortish person, broad shoulders, dark hair, a little curled, tawny or swarthy complexion, and a downward look.

North Scale in the 18th degree, nature of ♃ and ♂.

55 From 20 to 25 degrees, shews a little person, but more gross, oval face, pale complexion, dark hair, not curling, good features, and in all respects proportionately made.

Serpentis in the 20th degree, nature of ♄ and ♀.

56 From 25 to 30 degrees, shews a thick, well made person. square face, looking frowningly and surly, broad forehead and chin, thick eyebrows, hanging over, swarthy or ruddy complexion, sandy hair, inclining to red or yellow, and of a middle stature.

Last degree denotes a man having to do with books or science.

OF SAGITTARIUS, ♐.

Sagittarius,—endows the native with a strong, active, well formed body, rather tall, face rather long and handsome, fine clear eyes, ruddy or sunburnt complexion, chestnut coloured hair, growing off the temples, subject to.baldness, a Grecian nose.

57 *The first face,* or from 1 to 5 degrees, shews a tall body, broad shoulders, full breasted, thick waist, longish face, broad forehead, large eyebrows, yellowish complexion, and generally full of freckles, la ge nose and mouth, brown hair, a little curling at the end.

Mars herein, a mark or scar in the face, generally fortunate— Sagittarius contains 69 stars.

58 From 5 to 10 degrees, shews one of middle stature, pro- portionate body, full face, of a reddish blush or flesh colour, light brown hair, broad forehead, dark eyes, a neat mouth and nose.

Antares herein, nature of ☿ and ♂

59 From 10 to 15 degrees, shews one neither tall or low, full fat face and body, limbs well set, fair complexion, grey eyes, light eyebrows, light or flaxen hair, not curling, little mouth and lips, well proportionate body.

This face is of the nature ♄ and ♀, and not very fortunate.

60 From 15 to 20 degrees, shews a lusty, strong person, good stature, longish face, and freckled, brownish complexion, hollowish eyes, broad forehead, thick lips, brown hair, long arms, flattish nose, and modest countenance.

61 From 20 to 25 degrees, shews a middle, well-set proportionate body, clear complexion, oval face, light chestnut hair, large grey eyes, thin lips, and pleasant countenance.

1st degree, dark.

62 From 25 to 30 degrees, shews one rather tall, a pleasant

countenance, roundish face, clear skin, mixed red, and good features, hooked nose.

The last degree shews a worker in metals, smiths, etc.

OF CAPRICORN, ♑.

Capricorn—gives a tallish, slender person, long thin face, thin beard, dark hair, long neck, narrow chin and breast, weak knees, crooked ill-formed legs.

63 *The first face*, or from 1 to 5 degrees, gives a tallish person, thin face, pleasant countenance, dark hair, little mouth, and the face molested with freckles, a dark complexion.

This sign contains 60 stars.

64 From 5 to 10 degrees, gives a small stature, long face, pleasant look, brownish complexion, and sad hair, in every other respect like the first face.

Of the nature of ☉ and ♂ —self-esteem well developed.

65 From 10 to 15 degrees, shews a person much like the former, something taller, fatter, and whose presence carries along with it not only a greater awe and majesty, but a more imperious and commanding aspect.

66 From 15 to 20 degrees, gives a round-faced person, inclining to fatness, clear skin, brown hair, freckled, and neat mouth.

Saturn herein, dark and thin—plenty of cautiousness.

67 From 20 to 25 degrees, shews one fatter, taller, and fairer than the former, more beautiful, excellent features, and good proportion.

Saturn herein, dark and thin.

68 From 25 to 30 degrees, shews a yet more excellent than the former, middle stature, fairer and clearer complexion, flaxen hair, features of the body excellent proportion, admirable and beautiful.

Of the nature of ♅, fond of chemistry and lecturing.

OF AQUARIUS, ♒.

Aquarius—gives a person well set, stout, robust, strong, healthy, rather tall, never short, delicate or fair complexion, long face, clear but not pale, somewhat sanguine, hazel eyes, sandy or dark flaxen hair, generally an honest, benevolent disposition.

69 *The first face*, or from 1 to 5 degrees, denotes one rather tall, longish brown visage, long arms and legs, dark hair, wide mouth, Roman nose, and dark eyes.

This sign contains 110 stars, generally of the nature of ♀ and ☿ —containing Goat's Horn—large wonder and ideality.

70 From 5 to 10 degrees, gives one not so tall as the former, more slender, reddish face, rough skin, dark brown hair, longish visage, wide mouth and nostrils.

Mars therein, a mole on the top of the nose, between the eyes ; 8th degree, tall. This is dry—large secretiveness, and destructiveness sufficient.

71 From 10 to 15 degrees, denotes a tall, slender, thin person, thin visage, broad forehead, reddish face, narrow chin, hair curling.

This face is dry, large animal propensities—abusive secretiveness.

72 From 15 to 20 degrees, portends a thick middle stature, rather clear visage, full face, wide mouth and nostrils. chestnut hair, not curling, short arms and legs.

Jupiter herein, tall, good development of intellect ; ♀ herein, a seller of commodities; ♂ , a fiery appearance, with a mark in the face.

73 From 20 to 25 degrees, gives a lean person, thin visage, long nose, narrow forehead, high cheeks, the upper jaw hanging over the under.

Of the nature of ♄ , melancholy appearance, jealous minded, good perception, excessive love of approbation.

74 From 25 to 30 degrees, denotes a good-looking person, middle stature, good complexion, comely countenance, full face, roundish visage, and light hair.

This face is of the nature of ♅ , denoting a mechanic ; ♃ here, a kind-hearted person ; ♀ , a prodigal ; ♄ , a miser ; ♂ , a soldier ; ☉, a superintendent ; ☽, a washerwoman—moderate constructiveness.

OF PISCES, ♓ .

Pisces—this sign produces a short person, thick set, pale delicate complexion, flabby face and rather large, thick shoulders, stooping gait, clumsy step, dark hair, ill-shaped head, not very well made, sleepy eyes and large eyebrows, short arms and legs ; the native holds the head down when walking.

75 *The first face*, or from 1 to 5 degrees, produces one rather tall, middle proportion, broad shoulders, not fat, a longish face, dark brown hair, eyes sunken, high nose, large mouth, and narrow chin.

Mars herein, pock-marked ; Pisces contains 113 stars. A good organ of prophecy.

76 From 5 to 10 degrees, denotes one of a greater stature than the former, fuller visage and clear skin, a more pleasant look, lighter hair, large eyebrows, long legs, arms, fingers, and feet, and a wide mouth.

Mars near, pock-marked, yet the morals are good—a mesmeriser.

77 From 10 to 15 degrees, gives one more pleasant and neat, full oval face, clear skin, large and fair eyebrows, large forehead, brown hair, short stature, straight, but not very thick.

Saturn, Venus, or Dragon's Tail herein, gives the native a disposition to wantonness—prime regulating or moral powers moderate.

78 From 15 to 20 degrees, produces a strong middle stature, long visage, swarthy complexion, freckled, broad forehead, large eyebrows, little black eyes, narrow chin, black hair, seldom curling, short arms, legs, fingers, and feet.

This face is temperate, good moral region ; secretiveness moderate ; veneration tolerable.

79 From 20 to 24 degrees, gives an incomparable and delectable person, an excellent and proportionable stature, roundish visage, grey eyes, a neat well formed nose, dimpled chin, smiling countenance, and chestnut hair.

The 25th degree very good looking, pale—of the nature of ♂ and ♀, and in the 22nd degree is Markab—this degree rising is unlucky ; the organ of language large, benevolence good.

80. From 25 to 30 degrees, gives a little thin, consumptive, freckled or pimpled-faced person, tawny coloured skin, black hair ; if ever they grow fat, they become excessively so.

This face is of the nature of ♄, contains Schet Pegasi ; combativeness well developed.

LESSON FOURTH.

TO BE ANSWERED BEFORE THE STUDENT CAN PROCEED.

Explain Scorpio.

What is his general stature?

What does the 1st face shew?

Where is Markab?

What is the character of the second face of Scorpio?

Of the third? Of the fourth? Of the fifth? Of the sixth face?

What is the nature of the N. Crown?

Where is the South Scale?

Describe Sagittarius.

What is the first face?

The second? The third? The fourth? The fifth? The sixth face?

What is the nature of the first face?

How many stars does ♑ contain?

What kind of stature does Capricorn give?

What does the first face produce?

The second face? The third face?

The fourth? The fifth? The last face?

What fixed stars are in Capricorn?

How many stars do Pisces contain?

What is Altair?

Name the four-footed signs?

Where is Hircus?

Explain the first face of Aquarius.

The second. The third. The fourth. The fifth. The sixth face.

What are Hyades?

Which are mute signs?

What are Satellites?

Where is Schet Pegasi?

Tell the signs of voice.

Mention the strong signs.

What is the stature of Pisces?

Which of its faces gives large stature?

What is the character of stature of the first face of Pisces?

Of the second face? Of the third face? Of the fourth face?

Explain the fifth face. The sixth face of Pisces.

Which faces give the most benevolence?

Which produce combativeness?

Which faces give greatest combativeness?

Which faces produce secretiveness?

Tell the faces that portend love of Approbation.

Those which shew constructiveness.

CHAPTER IV.

DISPOSITION AND QUALITIES OF THE FACES.

OF ARIES, ♈

81 ASCENDING. *The first face*, or from 1 to 5 degrees, denotes audacity and boldness, a good orator, active and ingenious person, witty and inventive.

CULMINATING. Gives military preferment, and makes surgeons or the like; if he be an ordinary man, he proves a butcher, farrier but no preferment.

82 ASC. From 5 to 10 degrees, shews a lofty spirit, one extremely conceited, good orator, proud, sullen, spiteful: it is the face of jealousy, many sorrows and evils, and gives both good and evil fortune.

CUL. Gives rising to honour, glory, and renown, in the forepart of life: but the native may precipitate himself in his latter days ; it brings both frowns and favours of great men.

83 ASC. From 10 to 15 degrees, is the face of weariness, it gives a good rhetorician, counsellor, and able politician, sober and active wit.

CUL. Presages honour, and he will do well as a goldsmith, silversmith, jeweller, etc.

84 ASC. From 15 to 20 degrees, denotes a disposition affable, courteous, and pleasant; and will overcome foes.

CUL. Shews great honour, dignity and renown through government officers ; both military and civil : if Jupiter, Mars and Sun also culminate, the good and honour are durable ; but if Saturn be therein, he will be subject to be opposed and prejudiced ; Jupiter there, ecclesiastical preferments ; Mars, military advancement ; and Sun, makes him shine at court.

85 ASC. From 20 to 25 degrees, portends a stupid, deceitful, quarrelsome, and contentious person.

CUL. This face destroys the native's honour and respectability ; and he lives without popularity.

86 ASC. From 25 to 30 degrees, gives a courageous, confident, impudent, but fortunate person.

CUL. Gives martial preferment, but danger of being killed in battle.

OF TAURUS, ♉ .

87 ASCENDING. From 1 to 5 degrees, the native gains by his own industry ; being ingenious, serious, and resolute.

CULMINATING. Shews preferment by women ; if a poor man he becomes a town officer ; if a gentleman, a secretary ; if a scholar, a priest ; if a lawyer, he attains a barrister.

88 ASC. From 5 to 10 degrees, the native is discontented, unhappy, and subject to many evils ; but the Moon here, gain by common people.

CUL.   Shew honour by old men's means, and such as are devoted to a certain kind of sanctity ; if Saturn be there, or Mercury, the native's preferment will not be small.

89 Asc.   From 10 to 15 degrees, shews a slow, peevish, negligent person, ungrateful spirit, accepting kindness, but never returning, nor yet acknowledging those received.

CUL.   Gives shame, contempt, indignities, labour, care, and troubles ; if other configurations concur, the native will be poor.

90 Asc.   From 15 to 20 degrees, shews an affable disposition, one subject to wrongs, but never return any, expert in the art of loving ; in which faculty they may perform wonderful things, especially if Venus or Moon be there.

CUL.   Generally preferment through women ; and by the means of persons very honourable, and certain if Moon be there.

91 Asc.   From 20 to 25 degrees, portends a deceitful person, pretending one thing and intending another, no faith, trust, or honesty, and often given to railing, especially if either Moon or Mercury, or both be there.

CUL.   It is the face of impudence, treason, treachery, wickedness, and rising to a fading kind of honour, through some notorious action, or impudent prank.

92 Asc.   From 25 to 30 degrees, shews one quarrelsome, and mischievous disposition.

CUL.   Gives but little honour, sordid, till towards the latter years, and then significators concurring shew honour, yet full of trouble.

OF GEMINI, ♊.

93 ASCENDING.   From 1 to 10 degrees, shews an ill-humoured person, sometimes frantic, proud, disdainful, scornful disposition, and given to lying and thieving.

CUL.   Gives martial honour ; if a mean person, he oftentimes turns a highwayman, a thief ; or if education has altered him, he proves a surgeon, etc.; if Saturn, Mars, or Moon be there, he may be a butcher ; if a person of better quality, a captain, or the like, or one that gets a living by some idle way.

94 Asc.   From 5 to 10 degrees, shews one conceited of himself, proud and vain-glorious ; but if Mercury be here, Mars or Sun, the native has capacity and wit, and one that will not be fooled ; if Saturn, the capacity is full as large, penetrating, wily, deep, discerning, and crafty—very large secretiveness.

CUL.   It is the face of lasting martial or ecclesiastical honours, fame, glory, and repute ; but the native attains it by his own industry and labour.

95 Asc.   From 10 to 15 degrees, signifies a bold person ; one of an imperious, scornful disposition, magnifying himself, and despising others ; and if Mars be there, is proud and haughty, insulting,

talkative, and expecting that everyone should give him place and credit, though he often speaks lies ; if this place be fortified, or Mercury be there or in his dignities, one of great majesty.

CUL. It gives but mean preferment, rather makes the native a handicraft, mechanic, or artificer ; if Mercury be therein, he may be a clerk to an attorney, or some nobleman ; if Sun, it gives him court preferment, but not durable ; if Mercury, it prefers him more, and may, in his latter years, gives him the honour of an eminent and learned lawyer.

96 Asc. From 15 to 20 degrees, shews a bold, adventurous spirit, one aiming at all things, and undertaking anything (yet not often bringing things to perfection), of a free spirit and nimble tongue, rash, hasty, turbulent, humorous and conceited.

CUL. It gives the native the acquaintance and favour of captains, generals, military persons, and the estimation of scholars ; a good orator.

97 Asc. From 20 to 25 degrees, shews an indifferent temper, seeks the love of women, a little doting and lecherous, an apparent saint but a deceiver.

CUL. It shews preferment through his own ingenuity, and that he may through his craft, seeming sanctity, attain more than ordinary honour ; if a statesman, rises to kingly honour.

98 Asc. From 25 to 30 degrees, shews an affable, courteous, gentle disposition, ingenious active wit, skilled in most arts and sciences, and delights in those things which are ingenious, and profound quality.

CUL. It gives the native no extraordinary, or durable preferment from women.

OF CANCER, ♋,

99 Asc. From 1 to 5 degrees, shews a wise wary person, a good orator, deceitful, jealous of everybody, fearful, and always mistrusting the worst things.

CUL. It gives preferment to places of the highest trust in a kingdom, he is honourable, famous, beloved of princes ; and if Jupiter or Sun be herein, these judgments are without dispute ; if Moon or Venus, the native will attain those eminent honours chiefly by women of noble blood.

100 Asc. From 5 to 10 degrees, shews one of a good tongue, bold adventurous nature, yet doing all things with advice and consideration ; subject to affront everybody, but unwilling to receive any, a man conceited of his own wisdom and abilities, and to undervalue all others.

CUL. It seldom gives preferment, but if any, it is very mean ; yet if Jupiter be therein free from affliction, and in good aspect to Sun, Venus, or ruler of the first, it may signify preferment from the Church, which may be durable.

101 Asc. From 10 to 15 degrees, signify a good orator, one sober, serious, and of a melancholy disposition, crafty, subtle, and deceitful ; if Saturn be here, his craft is beyond measure ; if Mars, he is impudent in mischief ; if Sun, he accounts it his glory, yet Sun much meliorates the manners of the native, and makes him ambitious of doing worthy acts, not so much for the love as for the honour of them ; if Moon be here, the man is more worthy, but very mutable in his resolves ; if Jupiter, the man is honestly religious and sober.

Cul. It gives generally ecclesiastic preferment, according to the quality of the native ; if dull and mean, it makes him a preacher ; if of a more aspiring genius, it gives him some fat parsonage, or makes him capable of being partaker of the prebendary or deanery of some cathedral ; if Jupiter, Sun, or Moon be there, it unquestionably makes him a bishop, or some great prelate ; if Jupiter be in conjunction with Moon there, in England he may come to be an archbishop ; in the Papacy, a pope or cardinal.

102 Asc. From 15 to 20 degrees, it shews a melancholy person, envious, proud, stubborn, self-willed, not delighting to hear reason, but only what feeds and nourishes ill-humours ; of a sad and timorous disposition, yet outbraving the whole world.

Cul. The man may prove a merchant, a roguish fogger ; if the man be mean, he proves a sexton, or clerk to some priest ; or he may have the honour to be a hangman in a corporation.

103 Asc. From 20 to 25 degrees, gives the native boldness, impudence, a voluble tongue, proud, saucy, and malapert, thinking always too high of himself, and meanly of others, aiming at great things, but falling short of them through his own rashness ; great self-esteem.

Cul. Preferment in armies ; and makes a commander, the power of kings, princes, and great men ; and if Sun be there, honourable preferment at court ; but nothing durable, it is no sooner possessed than lost, and those honours and preferments are only a precipice to bring destruction : in war, shews danger of being killed ; at the court, the displeasure of his king, etc.

104 Asc. From 25 to 30 degrees, signifies an active, turbulent, spirited person, aiming at great things, through his own prudence, joined with an industrious and unwearied spirit, commonly attaining them, shews one serious but bold ; melancholy, yet undaunted, weighing matters, incredulous, believing nothing but what he knows, nor trusting farther than he tries.

Cul. One eminent in learning, of great parts, famous in those studies which he prosecutes ; he proves a good physician, surgeon, or chemist ; if Sun or Moon be there, he is preferred to the service of great men, and becomes eminently famous ; if Jupiter be there, he rises by the means of clergymen, and proves an honour to his benefactor ; if Venus, by the means of a lady ; but if Saturn be there, notwithstanding all his parts, and all his deserts, he falls under the frowns of fortune.

LESSON FIFTH.

QUESTIONS TO BE ANSWERED BEFORE THE STUDENT ENTERS ON

THE NEXT PORTION.

What do we mean by ascending ?

What does culminating mean ?

What do you mean by descending ?

Which are the horizons ?

Which do you call the meridians ?

What is the quality of the mind when the first face ascends ?

When it culminates ?

What does the second face when ascending portend ?

When culminating ?

Explain the disposition when the third face of Aries culminates.

When ascending.

What kind of disposition would a person have when the fourth face of Aries ascends ?

When it culminates ?

What is the character and honour of a person born under the fifth face of Aries ?

Explain the character of the last face of Aries.

Which of the faces of Taurus shew a native to rise by his own industry ?

Which shew preferment by women ?

Which shew a deceitful person ?

Which a quarrelsome person ?

Which denote a peevish person ?

Which portend honour by old men ?

Explain the effects of the fourth face.

What does the last face signify ?

What is the nature of Aries ?

Of Taurus ?

What are the properties of Gemini ?

What kind of honour does the first face give ?

What are the effects when the second face ascends and culminates ?

Explain the third face.

What kind of spirit and acquaintanceship does the fourth face portend ?

What is the temper of the fifth face ascending ?

Its preferment when culminating ?

What do you notice in the last face of Gemini ?

Tell me the nature of Cancer.

Explain its first face.

Give a description of the second face.

What kind of person does the third face shew when ascending ?

What honour when culminating ?

What kind of person when the fonrth face rises ?

What profession when it culminates ?

What is the disposition and preferment of the sixth face ?

What kind of spirit is shewn by the last face of Cancer rising ?

What is the native's ability of the sixth face culminating ?

OF LEO, ♌.

105 ASCENDING. From 1 to 5 degrees, shews a bold, daring, fearless, inconsiderate person, generally has no respect to honour, etc., but forms a bad opinion of all persons.

CUL. Gives martial honour, and preferment at court by means of ladies ; yet liable to lose honour by some person's enmity ; if Saturn be there, dishonour : if Mars, he precipitates himself ; if Sun or Jupiter, more durable : if of mean birth, he makes a good smith, farrier, chemist, or surgeon.

106 Asc. From 5 to 10 degrees, shews one kind, affable, courteous, obliging everybody, always returning good for evil, and kindness for ingratitude, easy to be entreated, yet changeable.

CUL. Shews the favour of women, queens, and great ladies ; if it be an ordinary person, a feminine kind of employment, a sempstress barber, or tailor, but what honour he gains, if Saturn be not there, it is durable and lasting.

107 Asc. From 10 to 15 degrees, produces a prudent, discreet person, unresenting any evil, but returns ill when an opportunity serves.

CUL. Gives martial honour ; if a soldier, he gets killed ; liable to the frowns of great personages ; if a woman's natus, she marries a soldier.

108 Asc. From 15 to 20 degrees, signifies a subtle person a wary cant, a religious hypocrite, and joins societies (like many others) for the sake of duping their brethren.

CUL. Portends favour of great persons, and make the native popular as a chemist, druggist, or physician ; yet he will be obnoxious to envy and slander.

109 Asc. From 20 to 25 degrees, makes a good orator, profound and serious ; constant, faithful, honest, courteous and upright.

CUL. Denotes honour, aiming at great things, a politician, lawyer, or divine. The native always rises higher in life than that in which he was born.

110. Asc. From 25 to 30 degrees, shews a hasty, envious, repining person ; rejoices at others losses, and contriving injuries.

CUL. Manifests slight fleeting honour ; he makes a draper, clerk, or weaver ; and if Mercury be there, he will make a pleader of causes, a runner for a bailiff, policeman, etc.

OF VIRGO, ♍.

111 ASCENSION. From 1 to 5 degrees, produces a bold, arrogant, proud, and conceited person ; a mixture of subtlety and craft.

CUL. Shews a person aiming at high things ; if Sun or Mercury be there, he attains preferment at court ; if Jupiter or Herschel be there, from the church, or law ; but if Mars be there, he turns out to be only a mechanic, engineer, etc.

112 Asc. From 5 to 10 degrees, denotes a sober, honest, courteous person; affecting nothing but what he is able to perform; if Jupiter, Sun, or Venus be on the 1st, this judgment will be confirmed.

Cul. No durable honor, or great preferment; if Herschel or Mercury be there, the native proves an orator; if Venus, scarcely anything above a tailor, draper, or some other fancy business; if Sun be there, he may be patronized by some nobleman.

113 Asc. From 10 to 15 degrees, gives a good temper, deep imagination, and seriousness.

Cul. Gives the favour of noble females; and if Dragon's Tail be there, eternal dishonor.

114 Asc. From 15 to 20 degrees, portends one wise, prudent, and a good speaker, but mutable disposition; inclined to learn the arts, sciences, and the like.

Cul. Makes the native's fortune very changeable.

115 Asc. From 20 to 25 degrees, denotes one affable, magnanimous, cheerful, hating all sordid actions, and a faithful friend; profound understanding, and a good speaker.

Cul. Gives martial honor, but not very eminent; if a poor person, he delights in fiddling.

116 Asc. From 25 to 30 degrees, marks a witty, active fancy, a newsmonger, and consequently a mischievous, lying busybody; backbiter, and intermeddler among neighbours, &c.

Cul. No great preferment, a petty lawyer; and it signifies a clerk, or writer.

OF LIBRA, ♎.

117 Ascending. From 1 to 5 degrees, portends a prudent, wise, sincere, honest, and wise understanding; a good tongue, and an admirable elocution.

Culminating. Gives slight honor, but durable; the native makes a good merchant, and profits by dealing with elderly persons, &c.

118 Asc. From 5 to 10 degrees, gives a wise, discreet, prudent, and serious person; as the last face.

Cul. Denotes honor from great personages, and the native will make a good secretary.

119 Asc. From 10 to 15 degrees, a serious, quick, thoughtful, fluent, studious person, one well qualified for business.

Cul. The native rises to honor by his own industry.

120 Asc. From 15 to 20 degrees, makes a brave, discreet, and prudent person, scientific, and much respected by men of talent.

Cul. Denotes benefits from eminent persons, and the native is brought to sit with honorable personages.

121 ASC. From 20 to 25 degrees, denotes a person much like the former face.

CUL. Like the former, this face gives a magnanimous spirit and honor.

122 ASC. From 25 to 30 degrees, signifies one wise, virtuous, noble, magnanimous, and honorable.

CUL. Gives a native the love of honorable ladies, ecclesiastical preferment, given to good actions, he is sure to rise higher in society than that in which he was born.

LESSON SIXTH.

QUESTIONS TO BE ANSWERED BEFORE THE STUDENT ENTERS ON THE NEXT PORTION.

Describe the qualities of Leo.

What do you notice when the first five degrees ascend ?

What kind of honor when culminating ?

What is the disposition of the second five degrees ascending?

What kind of favor when on M.C. ?

What does the third face produce ?

What kind of person does the fourth face ascending portend?

What is the effect when culminating ?

What kind of ability and honor does the fifth face give ?

What is the disposition of the last face of Leo ?

What is the character of persons born under the first face of Virgo ?

Of the second face ?

Repeat the third face.

Explain the fourth face.

What is the disposition and honor of the fifth face ?

What is the ability and profession of persons under the last face of Virgo ?

What is the meaning of Libra ?

Of Virgo ? Of Leo ? Of Cancer ? Of Gemini ? Of Taurus ? Of Aries ?

What is the ability of the first face of Libra rising ?

What kind of honor when culminating ?

Give a description of the second face.

Describe the third face.

What is the character of the fourth face?

What does the last face produce ?

Mention the character of the fifth face of Libra ?

OF SCORPIO, ♏.

123 ASCENDING. From 1 to 5 degrees, courteous, faithful, just, fond of learning, and in all respects an amiable person.

CULMINATING. Signifies favor of ladies, great men, and prelates ; honor and estimation by learning the arts and sciences.

124 ASC. From 5 to 10 degrees, portends a religious, zealous, generous disposition ; hating all base and sordid actions ; a lover of arts and sciences, and whatever is virtuous and useful.

CUL. Gives estimation by great ladies, princes, and great prelates, lawyers, and physicians.

125 Asc. From 10 to 15 degrees, a profound wit, clear judgment, brave and magnanimous; given to study, and able to learn all kinds of learning without a tutor.

CUL. Gives honor from princes, a clever professor of arts and sciences, and the native gains in all his undertakings.

126 Asc. From 15 to 20 degrees, makes a grave, noble, prudent, discreet person; fond of the arts and sciences, and of a good disposition, and an excellent elocutionist.

CUL. Is the face of honor, dignity, and exalts the native from mean conditions to glory and estimation.

127 Asc. From 20 to 25 degrees, in nature and disposition much like the last.

CUL. Like the last, the native is described as one honorable, &c.

128 Asc. From 25 to 30 degrees, portends a virtuous, just, worthy, and honorable disposition; altogether conscientious.

CUL. The native will be exalted by means of great persons; as prelates, noblemen, and princes.

OF SAGITTARIUS, ♐.

129 ASCENDING. From 1 to 5 degrees, denotes an honest, sober man, not of many words, pleasant, good disposition, loving peace and quietness, ready to do kindness, and to retaliate them, yet subject to melancholy when alone; and covetousness.

CULMINATING. Gives great honor and preferment in the world.

130 Asc. From 5 to 10 degrees, signifies one active, bold, daring, yet honest and just; a lover of religion, studious and ingenious.

CUL. Gives no very great honor, yet he may be a parson or physician.

131 Asc. From 10 to 15 degrees, gives a cheerful and merry person; aiming at honorable things; good health, active body, and lives to be old.

CUL. Derives benefit from the church and women, and has many friends.

132 Asc. From 15 to 20 degrees, portends a conceited person, seeking wordly applause; makes a gain of religion, and proves a complete hypocrite.

CUL. Signifies love or estimation among weak-minded women, which frequently proves his ruin, as well as the ruin of his fair admirer.

133 Asc. From 20 to 25 degrees, makes the native fickle, soon angry, soon pleased, talkative, precipitate, and blackguardish.

CUL. Produces many troublesome afflictions and sorrows from imprudence.

134 Asc. From 25 to 30 degrees, gives a mutable person, of an excellent disposition, just, sincere, and honest, faithful to his friend, pleasant in company, a little hasty and passionate, which is soon over,

CUL. Gives ecclesiastic and martial honor, makes the native oftentimes a churchman ; but it prefers to no high degree : the native proves many times a surgeon or chemist and druggist.

OF CAPRICORN, ♑.

135 Asc. From 1 to 5 degrees, denotes one of an excellent spirit, great thoughts, and lofty imaginations, true, just, sincere, modest, loving, and courteous ; hating every base and unworthy action, striving to serve and oblige every one.

CUL. Gives honor and preferment, but generally in the latter part of life, yet it prefers not the native so much in public affairs.

136 Asc. From 5 to 10 degrees, signifies a noble, brave, generous, just in all his actions, naturally delighting in change, mutable disposition, and ever desiring the company of ladies of inferior rank.

CUL. Shews one successful in affairs of state, in the acquaintance and society of great men, in learning, arts, sciences, and arms.

137 Asc. From 10 to 15 degrees, shews one of noble spirit, performing great actions with honor and glory, gives the native a good tongue, a rhetorician, the esteem and love of ladies, yet doing many things for vanity and ostentation's sake, kind even to enemies.

CUL. Gives no notable honor or preferment.

138 Asc. From 15 to 20 degrees, denotes one of an exceeding good humor, affable, courteous, and cheerful, thinking nor doing ill to any one : rather taking injuries and affronts than offering any.

CUL. May give the native some mean ecclesiastical preferment ; but if Jupiter be there, it may be extraordinary ; if Sun, the native is born to glorious actions ; if Saturn, Mars, or Venus, he meets with scorn, dishonor, and contempt ; if Herschel, no fast business.

139 Asc. From 20 to 25 degrees, shews a merry, jovial, magnanimous native, prepossessing and commanding.

CUL. Makes the native proud, stately, and majestical, but gives little preferment.

140 Asc. From 25 to 30 degrees, shews a wanton and effeminate disposition, delighting in women's company, if a man ; or in men's company if a woman ; very delectable, busied about some feminine matter, neat, trim and spruce, delighting in songs, music, plays, &c.

Cul. Shews preferment by women, and gives the native hope of great matters, which he will hardly find without much difficulty.

OF AQUARIUS, ♒.

141 Ascending. From 1 to 5 degrees, portends a crafty, subtil, self-willed, politic person, malicious, given to dissimulation, and to use deceit, and unjust actions.

Culminating. Shews sorrow, and of long expectations ; foreshews many troubles to the native, from Mercurial and Saturnine persons.

142 Asc. From 5 to 10 degrees, denotes a self-willed, hasty person, given to debaucheries, and incongruities ; full of dissimulation, craft and knavish policy, striving to outreach all men to accomplish his own ends, thinking none honest, incredulous, continually retaining an incredible covetous humour and disposition.

Cul. Shews contempt, unless the Sun, Jupiter, or Venus be there, the native seldom comes to any estimation in the world, but walks in obscurity.

143 Asc. From 10 to 15 degrees, denotes a wise, prudent person, swift, nimble, quick of apprehension, generous and pleasant; if Jupiter or Venus be here, the person is incomparably good, but Venus makes him a little effeminate ; if Mars be here, the native is more bold and daring ; if Mercury, more talkative ; if Herschel, eccentric.

Cul. Dignifies the native either with a sword or a pen.

144 Asc. From 15 to 20 degrees, gives not that clearness nor acuteness of wit which the former does, but makes the native affable, ready to do kindness, a lover of ingenuity, yet much conceited in his ways ; if he be a churchman, very zealous for the same, a strong stickler and defender of his own principles and way, let it be what it will.

Cul. Shews meanness of fortune and honor in the world.

145 Asc. From 20 to 25 degrees, shews one good-natured, yet sullen, given to suspicion, jealousy, and underhand dealings ; subtil, crafty, and studious of most kinds of literature, aiming to engross knowledge of all things, and one that may attain depth of knowledge and learning in several arts and sciences ; being very serious and studious, having a good elocution, though not with that grace and freedom which many have.

Cul. It is the face of despair, and signifies many sorrows.

146 Asc. From 25 to 30 degrees, signifies a good disposition, merry, jovial, free, honest and sincere ; healthy constitution, long life, of great prudence ; and if Jupiter be there, the more fortunate, wise, temperate, and courageous ; if Venus, one generous and a little prodigal ; if Saturn, one miserable, hard, and covetous, also

inclining to a consumption; if Mars, a bold and magnanimous mind, joined with deceit; if Herschel, very eccentric and a miser.

Cul. Gives a rising fortune, and signifies future honor and glory.

OF PISCES, ♓.

147 Ascending. From 1 to 5 degrees, signifies cunning, subtil, given to study, and learn arts and sciences, chiefly astrology, astronomy, geomancy; in which it is probable he will be very excellent, although of great subtilty, yet he proves just to his words and promises.

Culminating. Gives the native honor and estimation among common people, makes him famous for his skill among them; yet not without clamours and slanders; this judgment seldom fails if Dragon's Tail or Saturn be there, or Mars in opposition thereto.

148 Asc. From 5 to 10 degrees, shews a wise, discreet person, having a deal of prudence and understanding; honest, just, grave, sober, not easily provoked to anger, bearing all affronts; but in wrath not easily pacified without humble submission.

Cul. Signifies the native to continue in one condition almost all the days of his life; and only gives him a good repute among his neighbours,

149 Asc. From 10 to 15 degrees, gives a good temper and disposition, honest and just in conversation, except Dragon's Tail, Saturn, or Venus be there, and then the native becomes rather loose in character.

Cul. The native aims not at great things, except in things of an effeminate character.

150 Asc. From 15 to 20 degrees, shews an honest, virtuous, faithful, and friendly disposition; good understanding, profound judgment, studious of the arts and sciences.

Cul. Denotes ecclesiastical preferment; otherwise an eminent attorney, and becomes a government lawyer.

151 Asc. From 20 to 25 degrees, denotes a pleasant, cheerful, free, and loving disposition; kind to friends, harmless to foes, and wishes to be useful to himself and to society in general.

Cul. Gives honor, industry, preferment from women and parsons.

152 Asc. From 25 to 30 degrees, signifies a serious intellectual person; but of a rude disposition, given to contend with persons who are not of the same way of thinking with himself, in short, a coxcomb.

Cul. It is the face of sorrow, discontent, and adversity; and the native wades through trouble, calamities and misery.

LESSON SEVENTH.

TO BE ANSWERED BEFORE THE STUDENT PROCEEDS.

What is the meaning of Scorpio ?

What does the first five degrees produce ?

Is not the disposition of the second face good ?

Does the third face give honor and ability ?

What is the disposition of the fourth face ?

Like which face of Scorpio is the fifth face ?

What is the effect of the sixth face ascending ?

What is the effect when culminating ?

What do you mean by Sagittarius ?

Tell me what you have to notice on the first face of Sagittarius ?

Describe the second face.

Does the third face raise a native to honor ?

What is the disposition and honor of the fourth face ?

What kind of temper does the fifth face denote?

Explain the last face of Sagittary.

What does Capricorn signify ?

What does his first face signify ?

His second face?

What does his third face shew ?

Explain the fourth face.

What is the disposition of the fifth face, and how is the native raised to honor when culminating ?

Repeat the sixth face.

What is meant by Aquarius ?

What does its first face portend ?

What does the second face denote ?

What does the third face give ?

What is the ability of the person born under the fourth face ?

What is the nature of the disposition under the fifth face ?

Tell me what the sixth face signifies.

What does Pisces import ?

What is signified by Pisces's first face ?

What does the second face shew?

What is the temper and disposition of the third face ?

What does the fourth face denote ?

Repeat the fifth face.

Tell me what the last face of Pisces signifies.

CHAPTER V.

CORPORATURE AND TEMPERAMENT PRODUCED BY THE PLANETS.

153 HERSCHEL. When rising, or on the 10th house, gives a tall upright person, good looking, full face, light brown hair ; in other situations, a stiff corpulent person, strutting gait, stronger upper part of the body than the lower.

154 SATURN. Produces a full stature, yellowish complexion, dark hair, ordinary eyes, broadish chest, proportionate body, thickish lips and nostrils, broad shoulders, thin beard, and face rather of a melancholy aspect, looking downwards, good forehead, the perceptive faculties good, shuffling gait, temperament moist and cold, or what is called phlegmatic, bilious, nervous.

When OCCIDENTAL, he makes the personal figure more dark and thin, less hairy body, but tolerably shaped ; and if he is on the ecliptic, the body is not fleshy ; Great South latitude, the body is rather fleshy ; if North, rather stouter : temperament—bilious or melancholic.

155 JUPITER. Gives an upright tall stature, brown, ruddy, and good complexion, oval long visage, full and fleshy, high forehead ; benevolence and veneration large, conscientiousness and the moral region good ; large grey eyes, brown or soft auburn hair, much beard and whiskers, proportionate legs and thighs, long feet ; if in Cancer, Scorpio, or Pisces, fat and fleshy.

ORIENTAL. Skin more fair, honey coloured, sanguine temperament, large eyes, the body more fleshy, majestic appearance, generally a mole or scar on the right foot.

OCCIDENTAL. Fair complexion, but not so clear, shorter stature, nearly flaxen hair and smooth, bald about the temples and forehead.

156 MARS. Denotes a well-set but short stature, body lean and muscular, ruddy complexion, sharp hazel eyes, hooked nose, bright and red hair, fiery looking countenance, furred or in lines ; good head, combativeness large, healthy constitution, temperament—choleric.

ORIENTAL. The body simply ruddy, lower stature, little head, smooth body and less hairy, yellow hair, stiff and straight, temperament—dry.

The colour of the hair varies with the signs : If he be in ♉, ♍ or ♑, it is a sad brown ; if in ♋, ♏, or ♓, hair light and flaxen ; if in ♊, ♎, or ♒, curling or crisping ; if in ♈, ♌, or ♐, strong and wiry.

157 The SUN. Complexion obscure white, mixed with red, round face, short chin, good stature, proportionate; sometimes the complexion, yellowish or dark, but more generally sanguine, curling hair, tender skin, clear voice, large head, teeth rather distorted, slow of speech, large eyes, one that soon goes bald, and when in aspect to other planets, adds a greater nobleness of figure, and increases the healthiness of the constitution ; secretly vicious and lascivious.

158 VENUS. Persons under this planet have a fine round visage, full eye, ruddy lips, eyelids darker than the hair, the hair of different colours, soft and smooth, dimpled and smiling face, inclined to be rather short, but well shaped, amorous looking, eyes of an azure tint, sometimes a dark hazel or even black, sweet voice.

ORIENTAL. The body inclines to tallness, not corpulent, yet handsome.

OCCIDENTAL. The native is more short of stature, yet good looking and well made.

159 MERCURY. Describes a native tall, spare body, sallow complexion, long visage, high forehead, good intellect, dark or grey eyes, a thin, long and sharp nose, thin beard, hair of a dark auburn, slender body, small legs, nimble walk and active in his gait, long slender hands, plenty of hair on the head.

ORIENTAL. Makes the complexion yellowish, or like one sun-burnt, stature not very tall, but proportionate, small eyes, moderate growth of hair, temperament—chiefly hot.

OCCIDENTAL. A tawny visage, straight, dark hair, small slender limbs, hollow eyes, either sparkling or redish, with some squint or defect in them.

160 MOON. Varies her shape, her general character is to produce a round full face, complexion a perceivable mixture of red and white, but paleness predominates, grey eyes, short arms, hands and feet, hairy head and face, eyes appear odd ones ; in short, the Moon in aspect always gives greater delicacy of figure : in Cancer, Scorpio, or Pisces, freckled.

N.B.—The Planets, by their mixture and aspect with other Planets, vary their corporature, according to the predominating quality in the Ambient, and in judging the stature this must not be lost sight of.

LESSON EIGHTH.

TO BE ANSWERED BEFORE THE STUDENT PROCEEDS.

What kind of person does Herschel give ?

What is the stature produced by Saturn ?

What is the figure when Occidental ?

What kind of person does Jupiter give ?

What is the appearance when Jupiter is Oriental ?

When Jupiter is Occidental what is the bodily shape ?

What kind of a person does Mars denote ?

What when Oriental ?

Does the colour of the hair vary with the signs ?

What kind of complexion and figure does Sol produce ?

Describe a Venus person.

When she is Oriental.

When she is Occidental.

Describe a Mercurial person.

What is the personal appearance under Mercury Oriental ?

Declare a native under Mercury Occidental.

What is the appearance of Luna persons ?

What Planet produces the best looking person ?

CHAPTER VI.

QUALITIES OF THE DISPOSITIONS PRODUCED BY THE PLANETS.

OF HERSCHEL, ♅.

161 *Herschel* denotes an eccentric person, far from fortunate, always abrupt, and often violent in his manners.

When well dignified, he gives sudden and unexpected changes in life, of a beneficial character, yet changeable time of life; full of inventions and novelties.

When ill dignified, he causes remarkable and unlooked-for losses and misfortunes by public bodies.

OF SATURN, ♄.

162 *Saturn when well dignified*, is profound in imagination, in his acts severe, in words reserved, in speaking and giving very sparingly, in labour patient, in arguing or disputing grave, in obtaining the goods of this life studious and solicitous, in all manner of actions austere, a true friend, except when influenced by others.

When ill dignified, he is envious, covetous, jealous, mistrustful, timorous, sordid, outwardly dissembling, sluggish, suspicious, stubborn, a contemner of women, a liar, malicious, murmuring, never contented, and ever repining.

OF JUPITER, ♃.

163 *Jupiter when well dignified*, the native is magnanimous, faithful, bashful, honorably aspiring at high matters, in actions a lover of fair dealings, desiring to benefit all persons, doing glorious actions, honorable and religious, sweet, affable conversation, indulgent to his wife and children, reverencing age, reliever of the poor, full of charity, liberal, hating all sordid actions, just, wise, prudent, grateful and virtuous.

When ill dignified, he wastes his patrimony, suffers anyone to cozen him, is hypocritically religious, tenacious, and obstinate in maintaining false tenets in religion, ignorant, careless, not caring for the love of his friends, a gross dull capacity, systematical, abasing himself in company, insinuating and stooping where no necessity is, in order to gain and retain good opinions of others, a bad husband.

OF MARS, ♂.

164 *Mars when well dignified*, produces a fearless, violent, irascible, and unsubmitting person, naturally delighting in war, or contention, but, in other respects, prudent, rational, and even generous or magnanimous.

When unfortunately dignified, the native is wholly destitute of any virtue, prone to violence, boasting, quarrels, proud, treachery, robbery, murder, treason, and every species of cruelty and wickedness.

OF THE SUN, ☉.

165 *Sol when well dignified*, the disposition is noble, magnanimous, yet proud and lofty, but humane, a faithful friend, and a generous enemy, scorning to use advantages which may be given over to his opponents, generally of few words, but very pompous and magnificent, fond of dress, ornaments, and decorations of all sorts, extremely partial to costly jewels and splendid attire.

When ill dignified, the native is both proud and mean, arrogant and submissive, a tyrant, and yet a sycophant, empty, vain, a great talker, restless, vain boasting, uncharitable, despotical, unfeeling, selfish, ungenerous, unamiable, disliked on account of his arrogance and ignorant pomposity.

OF VENUS, ♀

166 *Venus when well dignified*, the temper is even, quiet, placid, graceful, engaging, fair spoken, sweet, merry and cheerful, amateurs in music, dancing and accomplishments, out of the ordinary way.

When ill dignified, the native is lewd, idle, profligate, shameless, timorous and lascivious, especially if in aspect to Mars or Dragon's Tail.

OF MERCURY, ☿.

167 *Mercury when well dignified*, represents a subtle-political brain and intellect, an excellent disputant or logician, arguing with learning and discretion, a searcher into mysteries and learning, sharp and witty, learning almost anything without a teacher, ambitious of being exquisite in every science, desirous to travel and see foreign parts, of unwearied fancy, curious in occult knowledge.

When ill dignified, the native is a phrenetic person, his tongue and pen against every man, wholly bent to fool his estate and time in loquacity and trying nice conclusions to no purpose, a great liar, boaster, prattler, busybody, newsmonger, false, a tale carrier, easy of belief, constant in no place or opinion, pretending all manner of knowledge, but void of learning, a trifler ; if the native prove a divine, then a mere verbal person, frothy, of no judgment, easily perverted, constant in nothing but idle words and bragging.

OF LUNA, ☽.

168 *Luna when well dignified*, the native has manners, a lover of sciences, a searcher and delighter in novelties, naturally inclined to remove his habitation, unsteadfast, caring for the present times,

timorous, prodigal, and easily frightened, loving peace, and to live free from the cares of life. If a mechanic, he learns many occupations, and tampers with many ways to trade in.

When ill dignified, the native is a vagabond, idle person, hating labour, a drunkard, of no forecast, delighting to live beggarly, carelessly, and discontented.

LESSON NINTH.

QUESTIONS TO BE ANSWERED BEFORE THE STUDENT PROCEEDS.

What is the disposition of an Herschel person?

What when well dignified?

What does he cause when ill dignified?

What is the temper of mind of a Saturnine person?

What does Saturn produce when evilly dignified?

Can you tell me the disposition of Jupiter?

What is the disposition of Mars?

What when ill dignified?

Mention the disposition of a Solar person when well dignified.

What when ill dignified?

Can you tell the disposition of Venus persons?

What is the disposition of Mercury when well situated?

What does Mercury signify when ill disposed?

What is the condition of Luna?

What if she be evil?

Which give changeable persons?

CHAPTER VII.

EMPLOYMENTS PRODUCED BY THE PLANETS.

HERSCHEL'S EMPLOYMENTS.

169 Antiquarians, astrologers, phrenologists, teachers, chemists, lecturers, sculptors, metaphysicians, mesmerisers, and all uncommon studies.

SATURN'S EMPLOYMENTS.

170 Saturn signifies husbandmen, clowns, and all employments of old men—curriers, bricklayers, miners, tinners, potters, plumbers, maltsters, sextons, scavengers, ostlers, carters, chandlers, gardeners, cowkeepers, shepherds, shoemakers, dyers, excavators.

JUPITER'S PROFESSIONS.

171 He signifies judges, senators, counsellors, lawyers, preachers, professors, doctors of the civil law, bishops, priests, ministers, cardinals, chancellors, clothiers, woollen-drapers.

MAR'S EMPLOYMENTS.

172 Mars signifies generals, colonels, captains, or any soldiers having command, all manner of soldiers, physicians, apothecaries,

surgeons, chemists, gunners, butchers, bailiffs, hangmen, thieves, smiths, bakers, armourers, watchmakers, tailors, cutlers, barbers, dyers, cooks, carpenters, tanners, gamesters, and according as Mars may be strong or weak.

SUN'S PROFESSIONS.

173 Sun signifies kings, princes, emperors, &c., dukes, marquesses, earls, barons, lieutenants, deputy lieutenants of counties, magistrates, gentlemen in general, courtiers, justices of peace, high sheriffs, constables, superintenders, stewards of noblemen's houses, the principal magistrate of a city, town, or country village, even a petty constable where no better is, goldsmiths, braziers, pewterers, coppersmiths, excisemen, and minters of money.

VENUS'S EMPLOYMENTS.

174 Venus signifies musicians, gamesters, silkmen, mercers, haberdashers, linen-drapers, painters, jewellers, players, embroiderers, lapidaries, women tailors, choristers, fiddlers, pipers ; when joined with the Moon ballad singers, perfumers, sempstresses, engravers, upholsterers, limners, glovers, and such as sell those commodities which adorn women, and those sold over a counter.

MERCURY'S PROFESSIONS.

175 Mercury, when well placed, astrologers, philosophers, mathematicians, secretaries, officers of state, merchants, travellers, sculptors, poets, lawyers, printers, teachers, divines, orators, ambassadors, commissioners, artificers, and all ingenious clever persons. When weak, he represents scriveners, clerks, pettifoggers, vile persons, cunning in acting mischief, thieves, carriers, messengers, footmen, servants, &c.

LUNA'S PROFESSIONS.

176 Luna signifies sailors, navigators, travellers, fishermen, fishmongers, brewers, publicans, letter carriers, coachmen, huntsmen, messengers, mariners, millers, maltsters, watermen, boatmen, navy officers, inferior servants, and dealers in all kinds of fluids, midwives, nurses, hackneymen.

LESSON TENTH.

QUESTIONS TO BE ANSWERED BEFORE THE STUDENT PROCEEDS.

What are the employments produced by Herschel ?

What are Jupiter's professions ?

What employments does Mars rule ?

What professions does Sol produce ?

What are the businesses of Venus ?

Tell me the professions of Mercury ?

Which generally produces writers ?

B

Which planet produces cattle keepers ?

Which planet produces the best mechanics ?

What does the Moon produce ?

Which produces the best surgeons ?

Which makes astrologers ?

CHAPTER VIII.

SICKNESSES PRODUCED AND RULED BY THE PLANETS.

HERSCHEL'S DISEASES.

177 *Herschel* rules all those complaints produced by bathings, sudden exposures to cold and dampness. By combining the effects of Mercury, Venus and Saturn, in the twelve signs, we shall come at a tolerable knowledge of Herschel's complaints.

The lord of 1st or 6th afflicted by Herschel, in Aries, gives demoniacal complaints brought about by bathing.

SATURN'S DISEASES.

Saturn gives all impediments in the right ear, toothache, agues, breakings out, consumption, tremblings, vain fears, rheumatic gout, jaundice, dropsy, apoplexies, too much flux of the hemorrhoids, and ruptures, if in Scorpio or Leo, in any ill aspect with Venus.

Saturn in Aries signifies rheum, melancholy, vapours, cold in the head, obstructions, stoppages in the stomach, pains in the teeth, deafness, &c.

Saturn in Taurus signifies swelling in the neck and throat, king's evil, scurvy, hoarseness, melancholy, chronic distempers about the neck and throat, and stoppage in the stomach, gouts.

Saturn in Gemini signifies infirmities incident to the arms and shoulders, consumption, black jaundice, and diseases proceeding from bad blood, pleurisies, dry belly-ache.

Saturn in Cancer denotes phthisis, ulceration in the lungs, asthma, obstructions and bruises in the breast, ague, scurvy, cancer in the breast, consumptions.

Saturn in Leo signifies the heart afflicted by grief or poison, consumption of the reins or inward parts, vapours, weakness and pains in the back, wasting of the liver, nervous affections.

Saturn in Virgo shews the blood corrupted, obstructions in the bowels, costiveness, weakness in the thighs, melancholy, gripings, stone, stoppage in the urine.

Saturn in Libra shows the blood corrupted, back and kidneys distempered, strangury, consumptive pains in the knees and thighs, rheumatism, sciatica, and gout.

Saturn in Scorpio denotes swellings or distempers of the secret parts, melancholy, piles, palsy, gout in the hands and feet, tumours in the groin, fistula.

Saturn in Sagittarius signifies weakness in the hips and thighs, old aches and bruises in those parts, and sciatica or gout.

Saturn in Capricorn denotes the gout in the lower parts, pains and obstructions in the head, ague, rheumatism, &c.

Saturn in Aquarius signifies disorders in the head and teeth, defects in the ears, pains in the joints, bruises, swelling in the legs, and sometimes a sore throat, deafness, cramps, &c.

Saturn in Pisces gives defluxions of rheum, king's evil, consumption, all distempers of the feet and toes, such as the gout, and illness by colds taken by wet feet, dropsy.

JUPITER'S DISEASES.

178 *Jupiter* gives all infirmities in the liver, pleurisies, inflammation of the lungs, palpitation and trembling of the heart, cramps, pain in the back bone, quinsies, flatulence ; all putrefaction in the blood, or fevers proceeding from too great abundance thereof.

Jupiter in Aries produces distempers in the head, a quinsey or swelling in the throat, chiefly from ill blood in the veins of the head, and causes strange dreams and imaginations, faintings or swoonings.

Jupiter in Taurus brings distempers in the throat, spasms, gripings in the bowels, and goutish humours in the hands and arms, flatulency.

Jupiter in Gemini produces pleurisy, or disorders of the reins and liver, too much blood.

Jupiter in Cancer gives the dropsy, the stomach affected, indigestion, corrupt blood, scurvy, surfeit, &c.

Jupiter in Leo indicates a fever, pleurisy, the heart affected, colic, gripings, &c.

Jupiter in Virgo indicates a consumption, obstructions of the lungs, melancholy, cold and dry liver, weakness in the back.

Jupiter in Libra shews the patient has too much blood, whence arise obstructions, corrupt blood, fevers, piles, surfeits, tumours, inflammations, &c.

Jupiter in Scorpio signifies the strangury, scurvy, piles, the blood discharged with watery humours, whence arise dropsy (lithiasis), &c.

Jupiter in Sagittarius denotes some choleric distemper, arising from putrefaction of the blood, tumours, fever, pains and swellings about the knees, disorders of the head and neck.

Jupiter in Capricorn, the patient is afflicted with melancholy, obstructions in the throat.

Jupiter in Aquarius portends the blood abounds too much, whence it is corrupted, and many diseases and flying pains afflict the body, lumbago, &c.

Jupiter in Pisces, the blood is too thin and waterish, swellings in the face, which breeds dropsy ; very frequently these diseases, under these significators, are incurable.

MAR'S DISEASES.

179 *Mars* portends the gall, tertian fevers, megrims in the head, carbuncles, the plague, scarlatina, and all plague sores, burnings, ringworms, blisters, phrensies, distempers in the head, yellow jaundice, bloody flux, fistulas, all wounds and diseases in men's genitals, the stone, both in the reins and bladder, small pox.

Mars in Aries signifies violent pains in the head, rheum in the eyes.

Mars in Taurus denotes pains in the throat and neck, king's evil weakness in the loins, and the gravel.

Mars in Gemini denotes that the blood is corrupted, itch, breakings out, surfeit, fever, pains in the arms and shoulders, disorders in the secret parts, strangury (dysuria).

Mars in Cancer gives pains in the breast and stomach, bilious dry cough, tumours in the thighs, accidents to the feet.

Mars in Leo denotes affliction at the heart, choleric humours, fever, gravel in the kidneys, pains in the knees.

Mars in Virgo signifies choleric humours, obstructions in the bowels, dysentery, bloody flux, worms in children, humours in the legs.

Mars in Libra produces diseases in the reins and kidneys, gravel, urine hot, lues, &c.

Mars in Scorpio produces some venereal distemper or ulcer in the secret parts, pains in the bladder, pains in the head, overflowing of courses, rheum in the eyes.

Mars in Sagittarius produces pain or ulcers in the hips and thighs, by humours settled in those parts, and an extreme heat in the mouth and throat.

Mars in Capricorn produces lameness in the knees, hands or arms, swellings, or a flying gout.

Mars in Aquarius signifies blood overheated, pains in the legs, surfeit, or intermittent fever, and other febrile indisposition.

Mars in Pisces produces lameness in the feet by corrupt humours settled there, sometimes the heart is afflicted, and pectoral affection.

DISEASES OF THE SUN.

180 *Sun* gives acne, palpitation, diseases of the brain and heart, infirmities of the eyes, cramps, tympanies, sudden swoonings,

diseases of the mouth and impure breath, catarrhs, putrid fevers, scrofula.

Sun in Aries produces sore eyes, megrims, headache, fevers.

Sun in Taurus produces tumours in the knees, quinsey or sore throat, breakings out and swellings in those parts.

Sun in Gemini produces inflamed blood, epidemic fevers, breakings out of the body, scurvy, pains and weakness in the legs.

Sun in Cancer produces measles or small pox, a disordered stomach, hoarseness, dropsy, and swelling in the feet.

Sun in Leo, violent pains in the head, madness, stone, pains in the back, plague, spotted fever.

Sun in Virgo produces humours in the bowels, obstructions in the stomach, bloody flux, sore throat, or swellings in the neck.

Sun in Libra, inflammation of the blood, pains in the arms and shoulders, stone and gravel, the venereal distemper.

Sun in Scorpio, distempers in the secrets, sharpness of urine, obstructions in the stomach, also phlegmatic dolens.

Sun in Sagittarius, the thighs are afflicted by hot humours, a fistula, fevers, swoonings.

Sun in Capricorn, lameness about the knees, bowels disordered, and a fever.

Sun in Aquarius, inflamed blood, breakings out, reins disordered, gravel, stone, strangury.

Sun in Pisces indicates the secret parts afflicted, strangury, and violent pains in those parts.

VENUS'S DISEASES.

181 *Venus's* diseases signify principally in the matrix and members of generation, in the reins, belly, back, navel, and those parts : the gonorrhœa, lues, venerea, or any disease of the genitals, kidneys, loins, heart-burn, priapism, impotency, hernias, diabetes, or an involuntary discharge of the urine.

Venus in Aries produces diseases in the head, from abundance of moist humours, lethargy, reins afflicted, and head disordered by cold.

Venus in Taurus produces pains in the head and secret parts, swellings in the neck, from moist humours in the head.

Venus in Gemini produces corrupted blood, scrofula, dropsy, and flux of rheum.

Venus in Cancer shews the stomach is much afflicted with cold, raw, undigested humours, many times with surfeit.

Venus in Leo produces ill affection of the heart, iliac passion, pains in the legs, of bad consequence.

Venus in Virgo, distemper in the bowels, flux, mucus in the bowels, pain in the private parts, and worms in children.

Venus in Libra produces a gonorrhœa, or surfeit by too much eating or drinking, also windy disorders, bilious flatulency.

Venus in Scorpio produces venereal distemper and pain in the private parts.

Venus in Sagittarius produces hip gout, surfeits, cold and moist humours.

Venus in Capricorn, gout in the knees and thighs, and swelling in those parts.

Venus in Aquarius, pains and swellings in the legs or knees from a cold, and the heart afflicted.

Venus in Pisces, lameness in the feet, swellings in the legs, flux, windy complaints.

MERCURY'S DISEASES.

182 *Mercury* produces vertigos, lethargies, or giddiness in the head, madness, phthisis, all stammering and imperfections in the tongue, vain imaginations, defects in the memory, hoarseness, dry coughs, too great abundance of spittle, snuffling in the head or nose, the hand and feet gout, dumbness, foul diseased tongue, convulsions.

Mercury in Aries shews the disease lies in the head and brain, vertigo and spasms in the head, and sometimes disorders in the womb.

Mercury in Taurus produces defects in the throat, swellings in the neck, hoarseness, and also pains in the feet.

Mercury in Gemini produces bilious flatulency, gouty pains in the head and arms.

Mercury in Cancer produces a cold stomach, gripings, spasms, distillation of rheum, lameness in the legs and knees from colds.

Mercury in Leo, tremblings, melancholy, pains in the back, occasioned by colds caught in the feet.

Mercury in Virgo produces much wind in the bowels, obstructions, pains in the head, short breath, and flatulent colic.

Mercury in Libra shews stoppage of urine, obstructions, disordered blood, breast, lungs, and reins afflicted.

Mercury in Scorpio denotes distempers in the secret parts, afflictions of the bowels, rheumatic pains in the arms and shoulders.

Mercury in Sagittarius shews distemper in the reins, weakness in the back, stoppage at the stomach, coughs, swellings in the hips and thighs.

Mercury in Capricorn denotes stoppage of urine, goutish humours above the knees, pains in the back, melancholy.

Mercury in Aquarius produces wind in the blood, running pains in different parts, fluxes, and disorders in the bowels, cholera.

Mercury in Pisces signifies pains in the head, weakness in the legs and feet, a gonorrhœa, or a distemper in the reins.

MOON'S DISEASES.

183 *Moon*, apoplexies, palsy, the colic, diseases in the left side, the bladder, and members of generation, the menstrues and liver iu women, dropsies, fluxes of the belly, cold rheumatic diseases, cold stomach, gout in the joints, sciatica, worms, hurts in the eyes, surfeits, coughs, convulsive fits, falling sickness, scrofula, abscess, small pox, measles, vertigo, and lunacy.

Moon in Aries signifies convulsions, defluctions of rheum from the head, lethargy, weakness in the eyes, and pains in the knees.

Moon in Taurus, pains in the legs and feet, swellings, stoppage in and sore throat.

Moon in Gemini, gout in the legs, arms, hands, and feet, surfeits, and obstructions.

Moon in Cancer, the stomach much afflicted, surfeit, small pox, convulsions, falling sickness, tympany, or dropsy (187).

Moon in Leo, the heart affected (carditis), sore throat, quinsey, king's evil (scrofula).

Moon in Virgo, pain and disorders in the bowels, cold blood, obstructions, weakness in the arms and shoulders.

Moon in Libra, the reins are distempered, dry belly-ache, weakness in the back, fluor albos, surfeits, pleurisy.

Moon in Scorpio, distemper in the secrets, small pox, dropsy, poison, the heart afflicted, swoonings.

Moon in Sagittarius, lameness, or weakness in the thighs, distemper in the bowels.

Moon in Capricorn, the stone, weak back, gout in the knees, whites in women.

Moon in Aquarius produces hysterics, swelling and pains in the legs and secret parts.

Moon in Pisces, cold taken in the feet, and body disordered thereby, swellings in the legs, dropsies, and the body overcharged with moist humours.

LESSON ELEVENTH.

QUESTIONS TO BE ANSWERED BEFORE THE STUDENT ENTERS ON THE NEXT PORTION.

What complaint does Herschel produce?

Tell me what diseases Saturn gives in the twelve signs.

What are the diseases of Jupiter alone?

Tell the complaints of Jupiter in each of the signs.

Mention the illnesses produced by Mars.

Which of the planets produce inflammatory complaints?

Tell me what Mars gives in each sign?

What kind of diseases does Sol denote?

What is the state of the blood under the Sun?

What does Sol produce in each sign?

What are the diseases of Venus?

What in each sign?

What afflictions does Mercury produce?

What does Mercury produce when afflicting in the twelve signs?

What does the Moon produce?

What afflicts the eyes?

Which planet and sign denote dropsy?

What does the Moon afflict in the zodiacal signs?

Which produces nervous fevers?

Which the small pox (variola)?

Which the measles (rubeola)?

Which the scarlet fever (scarlatina)?

Which planet produces gluttony?

Which gives flatulent indisposition?

What rules shingles (herpes zoster)?

What gives the dysentery?

Which shew the king's evil (scrofula)?

What produces pulmonary consumptions (phthisic)?

CHAPTER IX.

DISEASES RULED BY THE SIGNS.

ARIES'S DISEASES.

184 All gum boils, swellings, acne, small pox, hair lips, polypus, ringworms, epilepsy, falling sickness, apoplexies, megrims, toothache, headache, baldness, eruptions, measles.

TAURUS'S DISEASES.

185 The king's evil, sore throats, wens, fluxes of rheums falling into the throat, quinseys, abscesses, in those parts, croup.

GEMINI'S DISEASES.

186 Signifies accidents or infirmities in the arms, shoulders, and hands, corrupted blood, flatulency, distempered fancies, nervous diseases, brain fever, bilious complaints.

CANCER'S DISEASES.

187 Produces imperfections in the breast, stomach, and paps, weak digestion, asthma, phthisic, salt phlegms, rotten coughs, dropsical humours, imposthums, cancers, which are mostly in the breast, consumptions, and all pulmonary affections, pleurisy.

LEO'S DISEASES.

188 All sicknesses in the ribs and sides, as pleurisies, convulsions, syncopes, pains in the back, palpitation, small pox, inflammatory fevers, measles, sore eyes, epidemics, and jaundice.

VIRGO'S DISEASES.

189 The worms, wind, colic, all obstructions and croaking of the bowels, infirmities in the testicles, any disease in the belly, iliac passion, dysentery.

LIBRA'S DISEASES.

190 All diseases in the reins of the back and kidneys, heats in the loins or haunches, imposthumes or ulcers in the reins or bladder, debility, weakness in the back, corruption of the blood, wasting of the body (atrophia), syphilis.

SCORPIO'S DISEASES.

191 Produces the gravel, the stone, ruptures, fistulas, or the piles, priapisms, all afflictions in the private parts, defects in the matrix, lues, injuries, &c., to the spermatic cord, the groin, &c.

SAGITTARY'S DISEASES.

192 It rules the thighs and buttocks, all fistulous tumours or hurts falling in those members, gout, and generally denotes heated blood, fevers, endemics, falls, or hurts from four-footed beasts, also prejudice by fire, heat, and intemperateness in sports, rheumatism.

CAPRICORN'S DISEASES.

193 It has the government of the knees, and all diseases incident to those places, either by strains or fractures ; it denotes leprosy, itch, cutaneous complaints, hysterics, rheumatism, disorder of the chest and lungs.

AQUARIUS'S DISEASES.

194 It governs the legs, ankles, and all manner of infirmities incident to those members ; spasmodic and nervous diseases, cramps, wind, rheumatism, and all disorders produced from corrupted blood.

PISCES'S DISEASES.

195 Produces all diseases in the feet, as the gout, and all lameness and pains incident to those members, mucous discharges, itch, blotches, breakings out, boils and ulcers proceeding from corrupt blood, cold and moist diseases, and bowel complaints, caused by wet feet, corns.

196 TABLE,

Shewing what Parts of the Body each Planet signifies in the Twelve Signs.

SIGNS.	♄	♃	♂	☉	♀	☿	☽	♅
♈	breast arms	throat bowels	head bowels eyes	thighs	reins feet	secrets legs	head knees	head brain
♉	breast heart bowels	neck shoulders bowels	throat reins	knees	secrets head	thighs feet	throat legs	breast stomach
♊	bowels	breast reins	breast arms secrets	legs ankles	throat thighs	head knees	shoulders thighs	heart back
♋	reins	heart thighs	breast feet	feet	shoulders knees	eyes throat legs	head stomach	bowels
♌	reins secrets	bowels thighs knees	heart bowels	head	heart breast legs	throat arms feet	arms shoulders bowels	loins
♍	thighs secrets	reins knees	bowels	throat neck	stomach heart feet	heart breast	arms shoulders bowels	secrets
♎	knees thighs	head eyes secrets	reins feet	arms shoulders	head intestines	throat heart stomach	heart bowels	thighs
♏	legs	thighs feet	head secrets thighs	breast heart	throat reins	arms back bowels	stomach bowels	knees
♐	legs	head knees	throat hands	bowels	arms shoulders thighs	breast reins	back bowels thighs	ancles
♑	head feet	eyes neck legs	arms shoulders legs	back bowels	breast thighs	stomach secrets	reins thighs	feet
♒	neck head	arms breast feet	breast legs	reins	heart knees	heart bowels	secrets legs	head legs
♓	shoulders neck	head breast heart	heart bowels ancles	thighs	throat bowels	reins thighs	thighs feet	face

LESSON TWELFTH.

TO BE ANSWERED BEFORE THE STUDENT PROCEEDS.

What are the diseases of Aries?
What does Taurus rule?
Tell the diseases of Gemini.
Of Cancer. Of Leo. Of Virgo.
What rules the iliac action?
What produces syphilis?
What are Libra's diseases?
What does *Scorpio* rule?
What signs rule rheumatism?
What are the complaints of Sagittary?
What signs rule spasmodic action?

What are Capricorn's disorders?
What does Aquarius rule?
What disorders does Pisces produce?
What produce bowel complaints?
What produces scorbutic disorders?
What rules the breast, chest, and lungs?
What afflicts the knees?
What produces the bile?
What produces cancers?
Which give indigestion?

CHAPTER X.

A DIAGRAM OF THE TWELVE HOUSES.

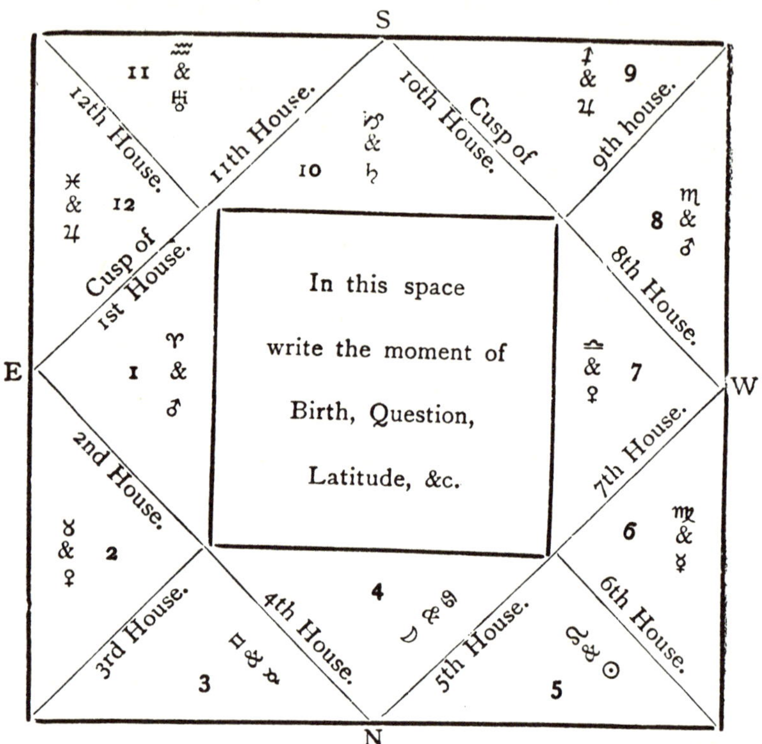

197 *Explanation of the above Diagram of the Twelve Houses.*

These houses are distinguished by figures, &c., and are either
ANGULAR, as E, S, W, and N, or by 1, 10, 7, and 4. SUCCEEDENT,
as 2, 5, 8, and 11. CADENT, as 3, 6, 9, and 12. At E the Sun
rises ; at S, the Sun souths, or is on the meridian ; at W, the Sun
sets, and is called the western angle ; at N, the Sun is on the nadir,
corresponding to midnight, being the opposite point the Sun
possesses at noon. Angles are of the greatest power ; the Succeedent, and lastly, Cadents are the weakest. The 10th is the
South angle, the 1st rhe East angle, the 7th the West angle, and
the 4th the North angle.

198 A Diagram, exhibiting the principal Significations of the Houses of the heavens in Nativities.

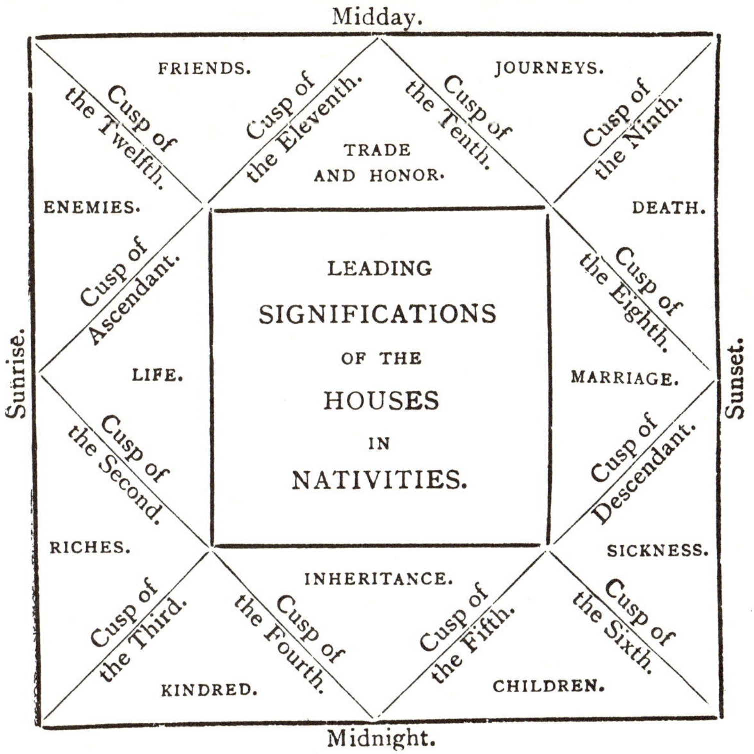

CHAPTER XI.

199 EFFECTS OF THE TWELVE HOUSES IN NATIVITIES.

THE FIRST HOUSE.

This influences the person's health, disposition, stature, &c.

THE SECOND HOUSE.

Influences his property in a pecuniary way, and money affairs in all matters.

THE THIRD HOUSE.

This influences the native's short journeys, brethren, near relations, and neighbours.

THE FOURTH HOUSE.

This influences the native's father, and his property in land or houses, his inheritance.

THE FIFTH HOUSE.

This affects his children, and the good or evil he may receive thereby, and speculations.

THE SIXTH HOUSE.

This will shew the nature of the disease to which the native is subject, servants and tenants.

THE SEVENTH HOUSE.

This has influence on the native's marriage, law suits.

THE EIGHTH HOUSE.

This points out, in part, the quality of the native's death, legacy.

THE NINTH HOUSE.

This has to do with the native's distant voyages, and pursuits in science, law, religion.

THE TENTH HOUSE.

This has much influence on his credit, and on his trade, profession, or employment, honor, and notoriety.

THE ELEVENTH HOUSE.

This will shew the character of his friends, whether true or false.

THE TWELFTH HOUSE.

This is the house of private enemies, and according to the quality of the planets therein, will the native meet with persons to do him secret mischief.

N.B.—Too great stress of dependence must not be put upon the symbolical signification of the houses, although you may judge to a great extent similar to examples. They have more signification and effects in Nativities than are generally allowed them.

LESSON THIRTEENTH.

TO BE ANSWERED BEFORE THE STUDENT PROCEEDS.

What does the first house influence?

Tell what the second house signifies.

What is the influence of the third house?

What does the fourth house presage?

What does the fifth house affect ?
What does the sixth house shew ?
Explain the power of the seventh mansion.
What does the eighth house point out ?
With what has the ninth house to do ?
What is the influence of the tenth house ?
What does the eleventh house show ?
What is the power of the twelfth house ?
In which house is the sun rise ?

What are the lines dividing the houses called ?
Which are the angular houses ?
In what house does the sun set ?
Mention the cadent houses.
Which are the East and the West horizon ?
How succeedent houses, and name them ?
Which is the nadir ?
Where is the Sun at midnight ?
Which is the Meridian ?
Which the Zenith ?
Which the West ?

CHAPTER XII.

QUALITIES AND EFFECTS OF THE ASPECTS.

The planetary orbs, in the course of their revolution through the ethereal fields of boundless space, perpetually form certain configurations or aspects with each other, by which their influence is not only hastened or impeded, but also modified or augmented, for some are malignant, and others benevolent.

200 The *Benefic Aspects* are the semisextile, the sextile, the quintile, the trine, the trecile, and the biquintile. When planets are situated at these distances from each other, they operate beneficially for the native ; and if the aspect be not yet complete at the birth, but may be wanting a few degrees, then the aspect is less powerful ; but it will be found to take effect at that period of life at which the arc of direction becomes complete. If the aspect be past, the planet which, by its more speedy motion, is separating from the other, will still retain the effect of the aspect until it has separated several degrees.

201 The *Malefic Aspects* are the semiquartile, the square, the sesquisquare, and the opposition.

When planets are found at the distances which constitute these aspects, they are evilly for the native. When the more speedy planet is wanting a few degrees completing a perfect aspect, then the influence is only approaching, and the more powerful effect will be felt when the angle is complete. But if the aspect be separating, then the influence is diminishing or passing away.

FIG. 6.

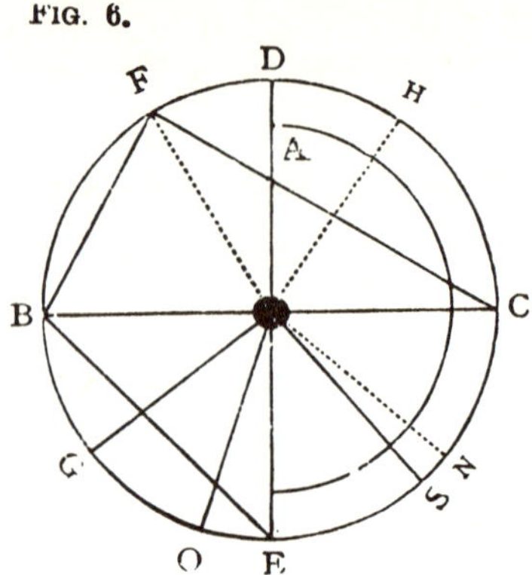

THE CONJUNCTION.

202 This is when two planets are in the same degree and minute of a sign.   This aspect is found to be good with good planets and good aspects (200), but evil with evil planets and evil aspects (201). Its effects are strong in all cases.   From D to A is a conjunction.

THE SEMISEXTILE, 30 DEGREES.

203 This is found to be moderately fortunate and of beneficial influence.   It consists of 30 degrees, one sign in the zodiac, or the space of one house in mundo, as the angle F ⊕ D, and this as a S ✶ from M.C., and a ✶ from F ⊕ B.

THE SEMIQUINTILE, 36 DEGREES.

204 This is half a quintile, 36 degrees in the zodiac, or the one-fifth of a diurnal or a nocturnal arc in the world, as the space between D ⊕ H.   This is an aspect to the midheaven as it stands in the preceding figure.

THE NONOGON, 40 DEGREES.

205 An aspect of some importance, forming a polygon of nine equal sides, as the angle N ⊕ C.

THE SEMISQUARE, 45 DEGREES.

206 This aspect, whether found at birth or formed by directional motion, is evil ; but if Jupiter or Venus form this aspect, the evil influence is only very slight ; the angle S ⊕ E is the space of the arc.

THE SEXTILE, 60 DEGREES.

207 This is a powerful benefic aspect, of 60 degrees, or two signs in the zodiac, or 2 houses in mundo, as the angle F ⊕ B.

THE QUINTILE, 72 DEGREES.

208 This is a benefic aspect, but if to evil planets is not important ; as the angle B ⊕ Q.

THE QUARTILE, SQUARE, OR QUADRATE, 90 DEGREES.

209 This is powerfully evil, it is 90 degrees in the zodiac, or 3 signs ; it is 3 houses in the world, and forms a figure of 4 equal sides, B ⊕ E.

THE SESQUIQUINTILE, OR TRECILE, 108 DEGREES.

210 This is a quintile and a half, containing 108 degrees in the zodiac, or a whole semiarc and one-fifth of another in the world ; it is good, because the quintile is good on which it is found.

THE TRINE, 120 DEGREES.

211 This is the most powerful of the good aspects. It is 120 degrees in the zodiac, and the space of 4 houses in the world ; the space of the great sphere from F round D and H to C.

THE SESQUISQUARE OR SESQUIQUADRATE, 135 DEGREES.

212 This is unfortunate, and equal in all respects to the semi-square (7), occupying the space from D round H and C to S.

THE BIQUINTILE, 144 DEGREES.

213 This is found to produce fortunate effects when with good planets, and when with evil planets its influence is not important (7).

THE QUINCUNX, 150 DEGREES.

214 This aspect is as powerful as the semisextile, good with good, and evil with evil planets ; it is the space of 5 houses, as from F round B to E.

THE OPPOSITION, 180 DEGREES.

215 This is most powerfully evil (7).   D A ⊕ to E or B ⊕ C.

THE ZODIACAL PARALLEL.

216 This signifies a parallel distance from the equator, or being in the same degree of declination, and whether of the same name, North or South, is of no different effect.   Thus, supposing a planet 13 degrees North and another 13 degrees South, they would be in parallel zodiacal.   Great attention must be paid to this aspect, for it is the most important and powerful, stronger than a conjunction in every respect.   (See page 18.)

LESSON FOURTEENTH.

QUESTIONS TO BE ANSWERED BEFORE THE STUDENT PROCEEDS.

How many aspects are there? (8.)

Name them.   (7.)

Name those that are real geometrical figures.

Which are the malefic aspects ?

Which the benefic ?

What is the effect of the conjunction ?

What is the nature of the semisextile ?

What is a semiquintile ?

What is a nonogon ?   Shew it me.

What is a semisquare ?   Shew it me.

What is a sextile ?   Shew it me.

What is the quality of the quintile ?

What is the square ?   Shew it me.

What is a trecile ?   Shew it me ?

What is the quality of the trine ?

What is a sesquisquare ?

What is a mundane trine ?

What constitutes a quincunx ?

Explain the opposition ?

What does the zodiacal parallel signify ?

How is the circle divided by a trecile ?

What is a platic aspect ?

CHAPTER XIII.

OF MUNDANE ASPECTS.

217 The next to be observed and duly considered is the mundane aspects, or those formed by the diurnal motion of the Earth round its axis, whereby every star is brought, at stated periods, to the cusp of each house, by which they are formed in due succession ; thus forming various aspects or configurations as well with each other as with the angles of the ascending or descending horizon, the zenith, nadir (197).   In order to explain them at one view to the attentive student, the following diagram is inserted, which will contain a complete exemplification of the mundane configurations or different aspects.   In nativities these are measured by the semiarcs of the planets.   Thus, a semisextile is one house, or one-third of a semiarc (203) ; a semiquintile is 1 one-fifth house, or two-fifths of a semiarc (204) ; a nonogon is 1 one-third house, or five-fifths of a semiarc (205) ; a semisquare, or 1½ house, or one-half of a semiarc (206) ; a sextile is 2 houses, or two-thirds of the semiarc (207) ; a quintile or four-fifths of the semiarc (208) ; a square, 3 houses, is the whole semiarc (209) ; a sesquiquintile, the whole semiarc and one-fifth of another (210) ; the trine, 4 houses or four-thirds of a semiarc (211) ; a sesquisquare, 4½ houses, nine-sixths, or 1½ semiarc (212) ; a biquintile is eight-fifths of the semiarc ; a quincunx is 5 houses five-thirds of the semiarc; the opposition, 6 houses. The mundane parallel is an equal distance from the meridian.

218 N.B.—When one mundane aspect is found, others may be derived therefrom, as the quintile may be found from the sextile, or from the square, as it is one-fifth of the sextile more than the sextile either way, and one-fifth of the square less than the square. Thus, if the sextile be 60 degrees, the quintile will be 72 degrees, which is one-fifth more; and if the square be 90 degrees, the quintile will be 72 degrees, which is one-fifth less.

219 The sesquisquare may be taken either from the trine or from the opposition, because if one-sixth of a semiarc more than the trine, and one-half of a semiarc less than the opposition.

220 The biquintile may also be found from the trine or the opposition; it is two-fifths of the sextile of that semiarc where the planet is posited more than the trine, and three-fifths of the same sextile less than the opposition, &c., &c.

221 If the planet has to pass over part of semidiurnal and semi-nocturnal arcs to form any of these aspects, take the original aspect behind it, and bring from the aspect required.

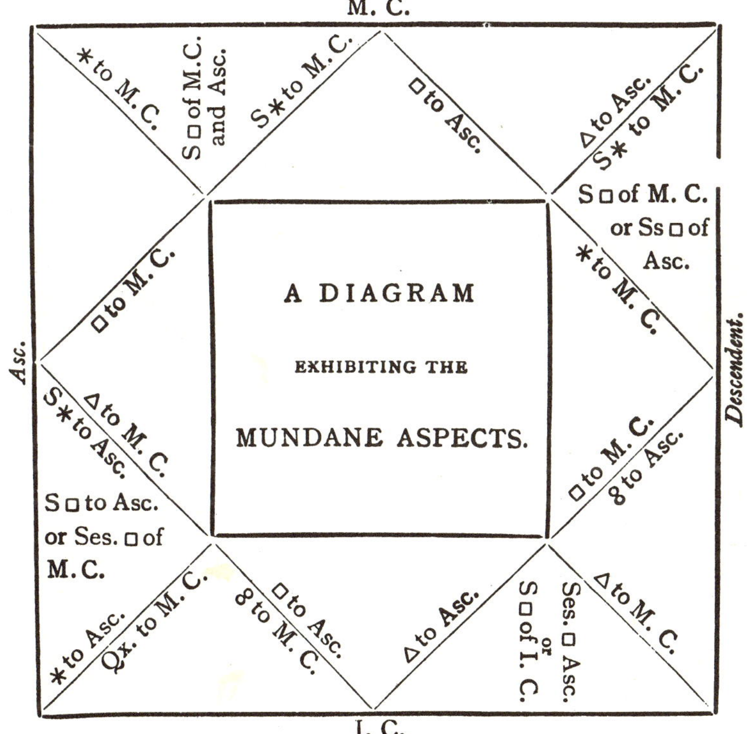

LESSON FIFTEENTH.

QUESTIONS TO BE ANSWERED BEFORE THE STUDENT PROCEEDS.

What is a mundane aspect?

How many mundane aspects are there?

How are they formed?

What are mundane parallels?

What house is in square with the M.C.?

With the I.C.?

What is a semisextile?

Which houses are in trine of the 6th, 8th, 12th, 4th, and 7th?

What points are in sesquisquare with the M.C. and Asc.?

Can these aspects be formed in any part of the heavens?

What geometrical figure does the trine form?

What mathematical figure is a sextile?

What is the polygon of a semisextile?

What is a trecile?

Explain the biquintile.

Which houses are in trine to M.C. and Asc.?

What portion of the semiarc does the semisquare require?

What does the square require?

What aspects do the M.C. and Asc. form to a planet in the middle of the 11th, 2nd, 5th, and 8th houses?

What is the geometrical figure of a semisquare? Of a square?

How can you form a biquintile?

How a quintile?   How a sesquisquare?

CHAPTER XIV.

A DESIDERATUM AND DEMONSTRATION OF THE ASPECTS.

222 The Equator is a Great Circle of the Sphere, and all circles, great or small, are divided into 360 degrees ; the space occupied by each degree is in proportion to the whole circle. The number may appear arbitrary, and might have been more or less than 360, but this number is nearly equal to the Sun's motion, a degree for a day, or a day for a year.

223 These 360 degrees are divided into 12 signs, which are not arbitrary, but irrevocably fixed by a certain unerring Law of Nature, which law was discovered by no other means than that of simultaneous observation. The Sun, the grand regulator of all time, makes his return to the first point of Aries once in little more than 365 days, and this number of days is the boundary of a year ; it was indispensably necessary that the great circle of the zodiac should be divided into larger portions, not only for the measure of but also for the notation of the planets' places. Those larger portions are made up by the number of degrees contained between two lunations. For the Moon occupies 27 days 7 hours and 43 minutes in moving from any certain degree of any sign, in conjunction with Sol, to reaching that degree again—the Sun, moving about a degree a day, will have gone nearly 28 degrees from the

degree of conjunction, so that the Moon will be nearly two days more ere she comes up to the Sun, during which time Sol will be gone two more degrees : hence, the Sun generally goes about 30 degrees during a lunation, of which there are twelve each year, and from which we have our twelve signs, as proportions for a convenient division of the Zodiac.

There is, perhaps, a danger in dwelling too exclusively on these laws, lest we should forget that, after all, they are only expressions of the mode in which the Creator is constantly acting on the universe. This tendency has shewn itself among all philosophers. It is sufficient, say they, to suppose matter endowed with certain properties for us to account for all its actions. This is true, so far as it goes ; but whence the properties? Whence matter itself? Their existence cannot be satisfactorily accounted for, except by regarding them as dependent upon the will of the Creator. And if that will underwent a change—if the supporting, guiding, and controlling hand were withdrawn but for an instant—the whole fabric of the universe must fall into confusion. The Deity has, by creating His materials, endued with certain fixed qualities and powers, impressed them in their origin with the spirit, not the letter, of His law, and made all their subsequent combinations and relations inevitable consequences of this first impression ; but the continued existence of these materials, and the various actions they perform, are but the manifestations of the continuance of the same mode of operation.

224 The next Division is the limitation of aspects, which are primarily in number five, namely, conjunction, sextile, square, trine, and opposition ; and inferior or new aspects, which are (Chap. I.) nine, namely, semisextile, decile, nonogon, semisquare, quintile, sesquiquintile, sesquisquare, biquintile, and quincunx. Most of the latter class of aspects were discovered by the immortal Kepler, one of the ablest astronomers that ever lived. Every aspect is either an exact angle, or supplemental angle, which may be inscribed in a spherical polygon. These are made from all parts of the zodiac, by the motion of the planets. These configurations have a direct reference to form only, and not so much respecting the straight beams of light which flow from every star, as how their beams arithmetically and geometrically meet at the Earth, and thus pour an influx of light and electric matter upon our atmosphere. Although in every degree of the circle the planets emit their rays to all other parts they behold, by which any two stars, intercepting an arc in the zodiac, and making an angle at the Earth, seem to make an aspect among themselves, independently of the Earth ; notwithstanding the ancients had respect only to the above five aspects.

225 To confirm the virtues and effects of these aspects, we need only consider what all philosophical and nature-acting physicians are taught by experience, namely, that the crisis of all acute

diseases has a palpable and extraordinary sympathy with all the major configurations of the Moon, made to her place at the beginning of the disease. Again, if the Moon's motion with respect to the tides; the spring tides, or high floods, at the conjunction and opposition to the Sun; the neaps and lowest tides are caused by her quarters; and it is equally remarkable that the seas, in their daily ebbing and flowing upon every coast, have respect only to such azimuthal circles as in quartile position when the Moon passes by them. Again, the Sun most evidently manifests great effects by the quartile aspects, since he modifies and governs the vicissitudes of seasons, for as when he enters Aries, the first equinoctial sign, the days and nights are equal all the world over, and increasing in our northern hemisphere; so when he re-enters they so happen again, so also when he reaches the opposite point—when he arrives at Cancer in square thereto, then occur our longest days and shortest nights, and vice versa when he arrives at the opposite degree in Capricorn.

We now hasten to shew, by geometrical demonstration, the reason why these nature-acting irradiations of the planets are more effecting-influential gravitating action than any other.

FIG. 7

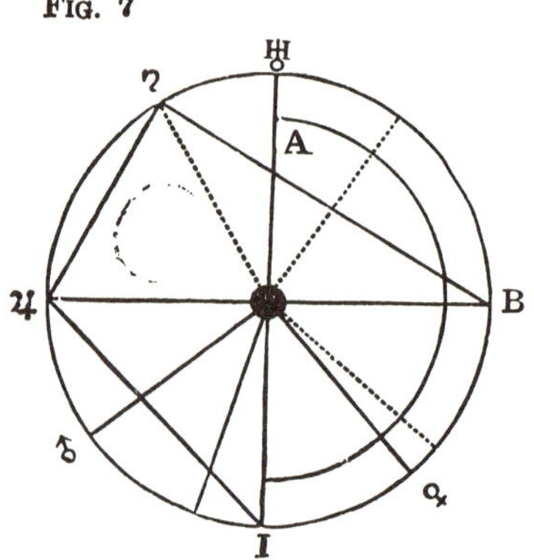

226 *Conjunction and Opposition demonstrated.* We take it for granted that an union of ray must either afford greater influence, or mitigate by amalgamation; it must be allowed that the conjunction and opposition are the most powerful configurations, shewn by the annexed figure, in which we find the beams, both incident and reflected, to be united.

Let A be in conjunction with Herschel, it is manifest that the beams flowing from Herschel to ⊕ must, of necessity, unite themselves with the rays sent from Herschel, and so jointly convey their virtue to ⊕. Secondly, in this we observe the beams ♅ A, or A ⊕, would come from the centre of the planets, reflects only into itself, as being perpendicular.

227 The conjunction is either good or evil, according to the inherent properties of the planets' atmospheres, whether they are inimical or coincident with each other ; if inimical, it is evil ; if coincident, it is good.   This may be demonstrated by almost every thing in nature, as the dictates of reason and experience corroborate. The union of rays that happen in an opposition is manifest, as the beams sent from A to ⊕ must meet with, and join, the beams of a planet at I, and so jointly convey, through ethereal space, their virtue to the ⊕, and this union is manifest that the beams sent from opposite points make one right line.

228 *The Sextile, Trine, and Semisextile demonstrated.*   These configurations have a concurrence of their beams at the ⊕, and a mutual reflection of the one into the other, and so an union by reflection is manifest.   Admit at the points placed ♅, ♄, ♃, and ♂ —then ♃ and ♄ in ✳ —then ♅ and ♃ in ◻ —and ♄ and ♅ in S ✳ ; then, forasmuch as ♄ ⊕ the beam incident of the ✳, falls obliquely in respect of ♅ ⊕, and makes an acute angle therewith, and ♄ reflects to ♅, and is united to ♄ ⊕, the incident of ♄, which is in trine to ♃ ; and ♄ strikes his beams to ♃, and then ♄ and ♃ strike down their rays to the ⊕, hence we are influenced by them reciprocally.

229 *The Square, Semisquare, Sesquisquare, &c., demonstrated.*   The square, ♅ ♃, is nothing more than the AB which cuts the reflective angle ♅ ⊕ ♃.   The right angular figure, ♅ ⊕ ♃, whose beams incident and opposite traverse the centre of the earth ; in the semisquare, B ♀ ⊕, the ray is reflected to ⊕ from ♀ ; and from ♅ to ♀, in the angle ♀ ⊕ ♅.   The inferior aspects are found and demonstrated as those are on which they are founded, and from which they are formed.   (See Fig. 6, &c.)

230 From the foregoing considerations, it is evident that the efficient power of the stars is deduced from their peculiar, proportional distances, and these effects are satisfactorily founded, both upon philosophical and mathematical principles, as well as by experimental facts, which, although apparently inexplicable, may easily be comprehended and thoroughly understood.   And I may be allowed to say, there are many simple things in nature, which are known from experience, that are inexplicable by man in the present stage of philosophy.   Metaphysicians agree that mind acts upon matter, but they cannot explain how it acts.   We know from experience that the mariner's needle always points to the North pole, but how or by what means we cannot tell.   We might offer an opinion, but in this work we forbear—Science may some day develop these present mysteries.

231 *A Table of the Essential Fortitudes and Debilities of the Planets, with their Nature and Qualities.*

	ESSENTIAL FORTITUDES.				DEBILITIES, NATURE, AND QUALITY.				
Signs.	House of Planets.	Exaltation.	Triplicities.	Powerful, or Joys in.	Detriment.	Fall.	Perigrine.	Nature of the Sign.	Quality.
♈	♂	☉	☉	☉	♀	♄	☽ & ♅	Fiery.	Movable.
♉	♀	☽	♀	♀	♂	♅	☉	Earthy.	Fixed.
♊	☿	☊	☿	☿	♃	☋	♀	Airy.	Common.
♋	☽	♃	♂	☽	♄	♂	☉	Watery·	Movable.
♌	☉		☉	☉	♅		☽	Fiery.	Fixed.
♍	☿	☿	☽	☿	♃	♀	♄	Earthy.	Common.
♎	♀	♄	♄	♄	♂	☉	♂	Airy.	Movable.
♏	♂	♅	♂	♂	♀	☽	☿	Watery.	Fixed.
♐	♃	☋	♃	♃	☿	☊	♄	Fiery.	Common.
♑	♄	♂	♅	♄	☽	ı	☿	Earthy.	Movable
♒	♅		♄	♅	☉		♂	Airy.	Fixed.
♓	♃	♀	♂		☿	☿	☽	Watery.	Common.

Explanation of the preceding Table.

1 The 1st column shews the twelve signs of the Zodiac.

2 LORDS OF HOUSES—In the 2nd column are the planets, and the sign opposite each denotes that the planet is lord or lady of that sign : where ♂ is placed denotes his house to be ♈ — ♀ lady and ♉, and so of the rest. Four of these planets, ♅, ♄, ☉, and ☽, have each one house, the other planets have each two houses. See page 16.

3 EXALTATION—The 3rd column shews in which each planet has its exaltation : thus, the ☽ in ♉ is exalted. See page 12 for exaltation.

4 TRIPLICITY—The 4th column tells you which planet governs each triplicity ; for if a planet be in any of those signs which are allotted him for his triplicity, he is also strong, but in a less degree. See page 26 for triplicity.

5 JOYS, OR VERY POWERFUL—The fifth column shews you in which sign each planet is most powerful. The efficacy of these have been proved by repeated experience, and they must be considered with attention. The foregoing are the essential dignities of the planets, and are good.

6 DETRIMENT—In the 6th column, over against ♈, is found ♀, being in ♈, is in an opposite sign to one of her own houses, and so is said to be in her detriment. This is an evil position. See page 10.

7 FALL—In the 7th column in juxtaposition, is found Jupiter, over his head "fall," that is, ♃, when in ♑, is opposite to his exaltation, and so is unfortunate, &c. When the lord of any question is in his detriment or fall, he is then very evil, and no good seldom comes of the matter in hand. See pages 12 and 13 for face.

The author rejects the distinctions of diurnal and nocturnal rule in houses or triplicities, as superfluous and void of truth.

The 8th column shews the nature, and the 9th the quality of the signs.*

LESSON SIXTEENTH.

QUESTIONS TO BE ANSWERED BEFORE THE STUDENT ENTERS ON THE NEXT PORTION.

How many houses are there?

What is meant by "lords of houses"?

Mention the house or sign of each planet?

Where will each planet have its fall?

Where its exaltation?

Where are the lords when in detriment?

In which sign have the planets their joy?

Tell me the triplicity of the planets.

When is a planet peregrine?

How many signs in a triplicity?

What are essential fortitudes?

Mention the debilities.

Tell the Fiery signs. The Earthy. The Airy. The Watery.

Which are the fixed signs?

Which the Movable?

Which the Common?

CHAPTER XV.

PRELIMINARY REMARKS.

232.—ORBS OF APPLICATION.

Orb is that distance round a planet to which its influence more particularly extends. We frequently make use of the term "within orbs," by which we mean that the aspect is not complete, but that the influence of the aspect is felt. The inferior planets apply to the superior; the superior never to the inferior, except the inferior be retrograde.

It is reasonable to expect the nearer an exact aspect the more powerful the effect, either good or evil; but as the aspect goes off it gradually becomes weaker till the aspect is at an end.

---

* For the explanation of these Terms, see Chap. II., for full and concise definitions, together with the foregoing Table.

It very seldom occurs that, at the time for which a figure is erected, all the aspects that appear are each perfectly composed of their exact number of degrees, in such case ; they are still in aspect as long as they continue within the moiety, or equal half part of their united orbs. This is called a Platic aspect, which is of less importance and powerful in influence than the exact aspect, which is termed a Partile or perfect aspect.

The number of degrees each planet extends an influence around its body is—

♅ 5 degrees,	♃ 9 degrees,	♀ 7 degrees,
♆ 7 degrees,	♂ 7 degrees,	☿ 7 degrees,
♄ 9 degrees,	☉ 15 degrees,	☽ 12 degrees.

Thus ♅, who is placed top of the table, applies to no planet except when retrograde ; ♄ applies only to ♅ and Herschel, and so of the rest in order, as before exemplified, where it may be seen that the ☽, being the last, applies to every other planet ; but no planet to her aspect unless retrograde.

It is necessary to observe in these platic aspects, whether the co-operation of the two planets is going off or coming on, as that will materially affect the matter under consideration. (201.)

RULE—Add the orbs of the two planets together, and one-half of the sum taken ; if the planets be beyond that distance, they are not even in platic aspect.

EXAMPLE—Suppose ♄ in 15 degrees of ♈ and ♀ in 10 degrees, they are then in platic aspect, for the orb of ♄ is 9° and that of ♀ 7° plus 9=16, the half of which is 8 degrees, so they are within orbs at 8 degrees distant, and in like manner of the other planets.

The Planet Neptune—This planet has only been known for a comparatively short time. From my own Radix I have found it to be very much after the nature of the planet Herschel, and to have a controlling influence over the minds of those who have to do much with persons who believe in the Art and Science of Astrology, dreams, inspirations, &c. Students will have a very good opportunity to watch the influence of Neptune during its progress through Gemini, the house of Mercury, which rules London and a great part of the United States as well as other places shewn by Simmonite's Prognostic Astronomy, or Horary Astrology. Taurus rules Ireland, and Dublin particularly. It is well known to the world what happened on May 6th, 1882, in Dublin, and the state of confusion that has reigned in Ireland generally since that time (see Raphael's Ephemeris for that date). Students, let your own study and observation be your guide with regard to the planet Neptune. I look forward to some notable inventions in arts and science being brought to light during the progress of Neptune through Gemini.

233 After due attention to the preceding indispensable instructions, the doctrine of the invaluable genethliacal prognostications
must be minutely and philosophically considered, for the sake of
order and perspicuity, in its successive heads of enquiry. It will
thus be found to present a mode at once feasible, practicable, com-
petent, and agreeable to nature.

THE DIFFERENT HEADS.

234 The question of enquiry subsequently to the birth relate—

1st.—To the Hyleg (page 5).

2nd.—To the Hylegical places (240).

3rd.—To the Anarata, or Taker of Life.

4th.—To the Duration of Life.

5th.—Signs of Death in Infancy.

6th.—Signs of Short Life.

7th.—Signs of Long Life.

8th.—Signs of a Violent Death.

9th.—To the Shape and Figure of the Body.

10th.—To the Hurts, Injuries, and Diseases of the Body.

11th.—Quality of Mind and Dis-positions.

12th.—The Mental Affections and Diseases of the Mind.

13th.—Riches, or Fortune and Wealth.

14th.—Signs of Wealth.

15th.—Signs of Poverty.

16th.—Notoriety, or Fortune of Rank.

17th.—Quality of Employment.

18th.—To Marriage.

19th.—To Children.

20th.—To Consentaneous Friendship.

21st.—To Travelling.

22nd.—To the Kind of Death.

23rd.—To the Parents.

24th.—To Brothers and Sisters.

25th.—Male or Female.

26th.—To Twins.

27th.—To Defective Birth.

28th.—To the effect of Aspects.

235 On each of the foregoing heads of enquiry, the doctrine and
precepts to be followed, are succinctly but thoroughly detailed ; all
idle conceits, promulgated by some professors without foundation,
are utterly avoided, in deference to the true mathametical and philosophical agencies derived from simple and harmonious primal
Nature herself.

ONENESS OF CAUSES AND EFFECTS.

236 It must be remembered that all causes, by which all effects,
whether general or particular, are produced and foreknown, are
essentially one and the same. The motion of the planets present
the operative causation of events which happen to any individual,
as well as to those which happen generally ; and the foreknowledge
of both may be obtained by the same accurate observation of the
distinct natures of the several substances, subjected to the influences of the heavenly bodies. Still, however, the causes of
general events are often more great than those of particular events.

GENERAL EVENTS.

237 In reference to general events, the data and origin are multifarious ; for all general events cannot always be traced to one origin, always considered by means of matter subjected to their operations, for it may also be established by circumstances occurring in the Ambient (page 4), and presenting the symbolical causation.

PARTICULAR EVENTS.

238 Particular events, however, which concern men individually, can be traced to one origin, on a single featured cause. Their origin is single, in respect to the primary composition of the nascent man ; but it is also manifold, in regard to other circumstances subsequently indicated by disposition in the Ambient, correlatively to the primary origin. In all particular events, the origin, or birth, of the subject-matter of itself, must, of course, be the primary origin ; and in succession thereto, the various beginnings of other subsequent circumstances are to be assumed. Hence, therefore, at the origin of the subject matter, all the properties and peculiarities of its contemperament must be observed ; then the subsequent events, which will happen at certain periods, sooner or later, are to be considered by means of the division of time, or arcs of directions.

EVENTS CONSISTENT.

239 Events are, from their commencement, always in conformity with the spiritual and corporeal faculties, and their occasional affections. In connection with man's body, these events are also applicable to his estate, and his conjugal cohabitations ; in connection with his spirit, these relate to his honor, rank, and notoriety.

CHAPTER XVI.

OF THE HYLEGICAL PLACES.

240 The Hylegical places are from 5 degrees above the 1st house to 25 degrees below, measured by oblique ascension—the whole of the 11th, 10th, and 9th houses—also from 5 degrees above the 8th to 5 degrees below the 7th, all calculated by oblique ascension.

241 No degrees under the earth are eligible to the rule of hylegical locus—consequently neither the limits of the 12th, 2nd, 3rd, 4th, 5th, 6th, or 8th house, are taken for the hylegical places.

OF THE HYLEG, OR GIVER OF LIFE.

242 The hyleg, or giver of life is, 1st, the Sun by day, if found in any of the hylegical places—2nd, the Moon by night, if she be so

found (240), when the Sun is not—3rd, the degree ascending *
becomes hyleg, if neither of the luminaries is in the hylegical
places—4th, if neither Sun nor Moon be so situated, that planet
will be hyleg which has most dignities in the last full Moon, provided it be in an Aphetical place ; but it must be dignified at least
three ways. If there be no such planet, and a new Moon last
preceded birth, take the degree ascending. If both the luminaries
be posited in a prorogatory place, then take that which appears
the most importantly situated.

N.B.—This last sentence scarcely needs be noticed ; because, if
the Moon be in any of the hylegical places by day, it will generally
be found that the Sun is also in one of those places ; and by night,
the Sun never can be in a hylegical place, because he is then under
the earth (241). Some may be ready to say that Herschel, Saturn,
nor Mars cannot be apheta, because they are generally anareta, or
the destroying planets—on this argument the Sun cannot, with
propriety, be chosen as both Giver of Life and Destroyer of Life,
and sometimes he is anareta (243).

OF THE ANARETIC PLANETS.

243 The Anaretic planets, by nature, are those of Herschel,
Saturn, and Mars ; but in some particular cases the Sun, Moon,
and Mercury will kill. The Sun in particular will kill when the
Ascendant or Moon is hyleg (246). The anaretic places are as
No. 241.

244 To occasion death, the hyleg must be afflicted by P. ☌, □,
or ☍, or any other evil aspect (201) to the anaretical stars, and
these must be afflicted of themselves, for life will be preserved, if,
at the same time, the hyleg be aspected by Jupiter, or within 12
degrees, or within 8 degrees of Venus. But the aspect of Venus or
Jupiter must be approaching. The opposition or square of Venus
or Jupiter will frequently save life when they fall amidst a train of
evil directions. In like manner will the life be preserved if the
anaretic planets have not the same latitude as the hyleg ; so also
if the killing planet have great latitude.

245 When there are two or more testimonies for death, and two
or more for life, then due observation must be made to ascertain
which party surpasses the other, in power as well as number.

The pre-eminence in number will be obvious ; but for pre-
eminence in power it must be seen whether the destroyers or
preservers are in places strong or weak ; and especially whether
those on the one side may be oriental, either with the Sun or of
the figure, and the other occidental. Oriental between 1st and
10th, Occidental between 10th and 7th.

---

* I have found the Sun, Moon, and Ascendant to be chief significators in
the prorogatory prerogatives, only I place them as above for the easy
reference of those who consider that the other significators have effect

246 No planet under the Sun's beams has power either to kill or save, unless when the Moon is hyleg, in which case, the place of the Sun being afflicted by a malefic planet joined to it, and receiving no help from Jupiter or Venus, will certainly produce death.   This rule must be particularly attended to, because, even though the Moon be not hyleg, the Sun becomes anaretic, if shackled by simultaneous presence of Saturn, Herschel, or Mars, and not restored to freedom of operation by Jupiter or Venus (244).

OF THE DURATION OF LIFE.

In order to complete the investigation of circumstances taking place simultaneously with the birth, or immediately consequent thereon, is, whether the child, then born, will be reared or not.

247 Of all events, which take place immediately after birth, the chief is the duration of life ; for it is useless to consider events contingent on the birth, if the duration of life is very short ; and the discussion of this enquiry is by no means simple and easy of execution.   This depends on the hylegical places, rulers thereof, and the disposition of the anaretic places.

248 See if the hyleg be strong and free from the malignant rays of Herschel, Saturn, or Mars ; for, according to the strength and fortitude of the hyleg, so will be the radical constitution and con-comitant effects.

249 If the hyleg be much afflicted, the child dies in its infantine state.   If either the Sun or Moon be angular, and if only one of the malefics be in conjunction of the Sun or Moon.   Or, if the malefic be in exactly equal zodiacal space between the Sun and Moon, while no benefic star partake in the configuration, and at the same time the rulers of the Sun and Moon be controlled by either Herschel, Saturn, or Mars, the child then born will die in its infancy, or under 5 years old (260).

250 Should not the configuration of the Sun or Moon and malefic planet exist precisely in the mode last mentioned, but that the rays of two of the malefics be bad to the Sun or Moon, or one malefic afflict both Sun and Moon, then, in these cases, no duration of life will be allotted to the child.

251 The Sun, Moon, and Ascendant all afflicted, the evil planets angular, their ill aspects close, and there be no assistance to the hyleg by the good planets, the child will die in infancy, except Jupiter be within 12 degrees, or Venus within 8 degrees of the anaretic point ; yet if the evil predominate, the constitution will be weak, and the first train of evil directions will destroy.

252 The child will be born almost dead if the malefics are in opposition, and the Sun and Moon in opposition, and the malefics being, at the same time, in square to both Sun and Moon, this is properly called a double opposition.   If a double opposition should exist, but the Sun and Moon separating, and the planets Jupiter and Venus preceding the Sun or Moon, the child will then live,

but will frequently be weakly, and the first ill aspect, between the hyleg and the anaretic, will kill.

253 Mars is exceedingly pernicious when succeeding the Sun, and Saturn when succeeding the Moon. But an opposite effect takes place when either Herschel, Saturn, or Mars is in opposition of the Sun or Moon, the malefics elevated above the lights ; for the Sun will then be afflicted by Saturn, and the Moon by Mars ; and more especially if the planets should have dignities in those signs in which the Sun, Moon, and Ascendant are.

254 The hyleg afflicted by aspect, and at the same time assisted by powerful rays of the benefics, life will be in danger under operating directions, but may be preserved by great caution.

255 The Sun or Moon in conjunction, P., Square, or opposition of Herschel, Saturn, or Mars, the native's constitution will be weak ; and if the malefics be joined with the hyleg, the native will be very liable to illness all through life. Saturn, in the 10th, in square to the hyleg, the native will suffer greatly from ill health, especially if Saturn receive ill aspects of Herschel or Mars ; except very powerful aspects of the benefics counteract, by aspecting both the hyleg and Saturn.

256 The hyleg being well aspected by Venus or Jupiter, and not afflicted by Herschel, Saturn, or Mars, then will the health be good, the constitution strong, and the native will live to a good old age.

257 Venus, ascending at birth, strengthens the constitution, but she gives such a strong inclination for pleasure that the native often injures his health in its pursuit.

251 The Moon, nearly in conjunction of the Sun, the native will be of a weakly constitution, and if not very well aspected and the hyleg not strong, of very short life. Persons born during an eclipse of the Sun, and Moon nearly in a direct line with the Sun, are invariably very weakly, and never live many years.

259 The Moon has, at all times, much to do with the stamina of the native's constitution ; and if she be much afflicted, health will rarely be good.

260 Children dying before 5 years of age are destroyed by the violent positions of the Sun and Moon at the time of birth—when both Jupiter and Venus are afflicted—and Herschel, Saturn, or Mars rule the places of the Sun and Moon, and afflict them (249). These are evil positions, they must kill.

The Moon in conjunction with Herschel ; Saturn and Mars in the 6th, 8th, or 12th houses ; or Herschel, Saturn, and Mars in the 1st. These are testimonies of a secondary nature.

The Dragon's Tail in conjunction with Herschel, Saturn, or Mars, in the 4th; or the Moon besieged by the Sun and Mars ; or between Saturn and Mars ; or between Herschel and Mars. I have frequently seen these destroy immediately after birth.

261 If the hyleg be joined with Jupiter or Venus, the constitution is strengthened thereby ; but if it be the Sun who is hyleg, his conjunction with Jupiter and Venus destroys the benefic's power to do good, in a great measure, and that benefic's favourable aspects to the Moon, M.C., ⊕, or ascendant, are of less avail.   If the hyleg, at birth, have Jupiter or Venus within 36 and 48 degrees, the health will be benefited.

262 The last aspect of the Sun and Moon with each other must be duly considered.

LESSON SEVENTEENTH.

TO BE ANSWERED BEFORE THE STUDENT PROCEEDS.

What do you mean by hyleg ?

Which are hylegical places ?

Which are admitted hylegs ?

When is the Sun hyleg ?

When is the Moon ?

What is hyleg by night ?

Are the degrees under the Earth ever hyleg ?

If both luminaries may be hyleg which do you take ?

When neither Sun nor Moon be hyleg what do you take ?

Which are anaretics ?

What will occasion death ?

Will Jupiter or Venus save ?

Does great latitude make a difference ?

What must be observed when there are equal testimonies for life and death ?

Which must prevail ?

What power has a planet combust ?

Upon what does duration of life depend ?

When is Sol anaretic ?

How do you judge of the radical constitution ?

Repeat (249).

What do you notice when the malefic is equally between the Sun and Moon ?

What are the effects of two of the malefics to the Sun and Moon ?

If two rays of malefic be cast evilly to the hyleg—what effect ?

Repeat (251).

When is the child born almost dead ?

What is the effect of a double opposition ?

When is Mars pernicious ?

What effect when the hyleg is afflicted, and also in good aspect of the benefics ?

What makes the constitution weak ?

What influence has Saturn in the 10th in square to the hyleg ?

What influence has Venus ascending ?

What the Moon nearly in conjunction with Sol ?

What effect when the native is under an eclipse ?

What kills children before five years of age ?

What strengthens the constitution ?

What do you notice in the last aspect of Sol and Moon previous to Birth ?

What effects have the conjunction of Sol with the benefics if he is hyleg ?

CHAPTER XVII.

OF THE FORM AND TEMPERAMENT OF THE PLANETS.

263 Consider the face ascending, and its FACE chiefly, for that will generally describe the native ; also notice the planets in the ascendant, and all those which throw an aspect to the cusp of the 1st, or its ruler, and make a judicious mixture.

264 Pay particular care to the Moon, how she is aspected—the parallels of declination will have an effect when within 5 degrees, especially if the swiftest planet is applying. For from the faces ascending the planets thereon, and the Moon, the conformation of the body is inferred.

265 Mark all planets in aspect to that which has dominion over the 1st, and all those which are aspecting the ruler of the 1st or the Moon ; but if no planet be in the 1st, nor aspect its ruler, then judge wholly by the face ascending.

266 If the ruler of the ascendant be R, or in detriment or fall, then consider him but very slightly. If two or more planets aspect the cusp of 1st, they must all be considered according to the sign in which they are posited, but the ruler of the 1st takes presidency with the face rising.

267 SATURN'S SHAPE IN SIGNS.

a Saturn in ♈, gives a dark ruddy complexion, spare and large boned, full face, high forehead, deep voice, dark hair, with little beard, a boasting, conceited, empty character, quarrelsome and ill-natured.

b Saturn in ♉, uncomely person, heavy, lumpy, awkward appearance, lobbing walk, dark hair, rough skin, and of a middle stature.

c Saturn in ♊, rather a tall stature, well proportioned, sanguine complexion, oval visage, dark brown or black hair.

d Saturn in ♋, gives a sickly looking person, thin, middle stature, meagre face, dark hair, languid eyes, stooping, and rather crooked, not at all well made (20).

e Saturn in ♌, moderately large stature, broad, round shoulders, large bones, wide chest, lightish stooping gait, eyes sunken (37).

f Saturn in ♍, represents a tall spare body, swarthy, dark hair, long head and face, solid countenance (43).

g Saturn in ♎, describes a person above the middle stature, comely, brown hair, oval face, large nose and forehead, clear complexion.

h Saturn in ♏, represents a person of mean stature, squat, thick, trussy body, broad shoulders, black or dark thick hair (54).

i Saturn in ♐, gives a person large, brown hair, good make, tolerable complexion, not stout, but raw boned.

j Saturn in ♑, personates a lean, raw boned body, dark hair, middle stature, sallow complexion, small eyes, long lean visage, and awkward stooping gait (63).

k Saturn in ♒, large stature, large head and face, corpulent, dark brown hair, clear complexion, sober and graceful deportment (70).

l Saturn in ♓, personates a middle stature, pale complexion, dark hair, large head and eyes, the teeth bad and distorted, active but waddling walk.

268.—JUPITER'S SHAPE IN SIGNS.

m Jupiter in ♈, gives a middle stature, but lean, light brown or flaxen hair, ruddy complexion, quick piercing eyes, oval face, high nose, and generally pimpled (12).

n Jupiter in ♉, personates a middle stature, stout, well set body, strong and compact, but not handsome, brown hair, and curling, swarthy complexion.

o Jupiter in ♊, personates a well compact body, rather tall, sanguine complexion, rather dusky, brown hair, and full expressive eyes.

p Jupiter in ♋, a middle stature, pale sickly complexion, oval face, dark brown hair, fleshy body, but disproportionate (27).

q Jupiter in ♌, represents a strong person, tall and well made, light brown or yellowish curling hair, ruddy complexion, full eyes.

r Jupiter in ♍, gives a full-sized person, well made and handsome, dark hair, ruddy complexion, not clear or fair, but well proportioned altogether (39).

s Jupiter in ♎, makes the native slender, tall, and handsome, upright, oval face, light brown hair, full eyes, and fair complexion, sometimes pimpled, but prepossessing (48).

t Jupiter in ♏, personates a stout compact body, middle stature, full face, dull complexion, and brown hair.

u Jupiter in ♐, personates a tall, upright, well made body, oval face, fine eyes, chestnut hair, and thick beard (45).

v Jupiter in ♑, personates a low middle stature, pale complexion, not much whiskers, thin face, a little head, dark brown hair, rather darker than the beard.

w Jupiter in ♒, personates a middle stature, well set, brown hair, a little red tinge, clear complexion, rather corpulent.

x Jupiter in ♓, represents a person of middle stature, full, fleshy body, dark complexion, brown hair.

269.—MARS'S SHAPE IN SIGNS.

a Mars in ♈, personates a middle stature, well set, large bones swarthy complexion, light or red curling hair, austere furrowed countenance, sharp hazel eyes (10).

b Mars in ♉, personates a low middle stature, dusky complexion, dark rough hair, broad face, wide mouth, and sometimes a scar or mark in the face (15).

c Mars in ♊, gives a tall person, well made, sanguine complexion, black or dark brown hair.

d Mars in ♋, gives a short, ill made and generally crooked body, with thick brown hair, not much whiskers (31).

e Mars in ♌, gives a well proportioned body, rather tall, light brown hair, oval face, sanguine or sunburnt complexion, large eyes, stout limbs, and a brisk cheerful aspect.

f Mars in ♍, personates a middle stature, well proportioned body, dark brown or black hair, swarthy complexion, and generally a mark or scar in the face.

g Mars in ♎, personates a tall stature, well proportioned body, oval face, sanguine complexion, light brown hair and soft, in the 1st face wiry and reddish (45).

h Mars in ♏, personates a well set middle stature, rather corpulent, broad face, swarthy complexion, and black curling hair.

i Mars in ♐, produces a tall, compact, well made body, oval face, brown hair, sanguine complexion, a quick penetrating eye, and cheerful in company (62).

j Mars in ♑, gives a small stature, lean body, thin face, little head, black lank hair, and bad complexion (64).

k Mars in ♒, personates a body well set, rather tall, and corpulent, fair complexion, sandy hair (74).

l Mars in ♓, represents a mean stature, rather short and fleshy, bad complexion, far from being handsome.

270.—SOL'S SHAPE IN SIGNS.

m Sun in ♈, personates a good stature, strong and well made, good complexion, though not very clear, yellow or flaxen hair, and large eyes.

n Sun in ♉, makes the native short and well set, rather ugly, dark complexion, wide mouth, broad face, and large nose—a strong athletic person (16).

o Sun in ♊, represents a well proportioned body, above the middle stature, sanguine complexion, and brown hair.

p Sun in ♋, gives a mean ill-formed body, unhealthy countenance, deformed face, and brown hair, affable disposition, and mild tempered.

q Sun in ♌, gives a strong, well made body, light brown or yellow hair, sanguine complexion, prominent eyes, full face, and sometimes a mark or scar in it, an excellent disposition (37).

r Sun in ♍, personates a tall, slender stature, well proportioned good complexion, much dark hair, cheerful and convivial (40).

s Sun in ♎, gives a straight, tall upright body, full eyes, light hair, oval face, ruddy complexion, and frequently a rash or pimples in the face (45).

t Sun in ♏, personates a square built, full fleshy person, broad face, cloudy complexion, dun or sunburnt, and brown hair.

u Sun in ♐, personates a tall, handsome, well proportioned body, oval face, sanguine complexion, and brown hair (62).

v Sun in ♑, represents a mean stature, ill made, spare thin body, oval face, sickly complexion, and lank brown hair ; in the 1st face light brown.

w Sun in ♒, personates a middle stature, well made, but corpulent, round full face, clear complexion and light brown hair (72).

x Sun in ♓, gives a short fleshy body, round face, and good complexion, with light brown or flaxen hair, especially in the 1st and 2nd faces.

VENUS'S SHAPE IN SIGNS.

a Venus in ♈, represents a middle stature, but slender, light hair, but in the 1st face, dark, good complexion, a pensive aspect, with a mark or scar in the face.

b Venus in ♉, gives a comely person, mean stature, fleshy body, well made, complexion ruddy, dark eyes, but not clear, and brown hair, and luxuriant in 1st and 2nd face, in 5th face, dark (18).

c Venus in ♊, gives a tall, slender, well made person, rather fair, brown or hazel eyes, and brown hair.

d Venus in ♋, personates a short, thick, fleshy body, round face, sickly complexion, and light hair ; Venus in last face, hair reddish, and a little hue in the face.

c Venus in ♌, personates a tall stature, well made, clear complexion, round face, full eyes, light flaxen or red hair, and face freckled.

f Venus in ♍, gives a tall, well proportioned body, dark complexion, oval visage, and sad brown, or dark hair.

g Venus in ♎, represents a tall, upright, elegant person, oval face, rather beautiful, sanguine complexion, often freckled, brown hair, and beautiful dimples (48).

h Venus in ♏, denotes a short, stout, well set, corpulent body, broad face, dusky complexion, and dark or black hair.

i Venus in ♐, personates a tall stature, well made, fair, sanguine complexion, oval face and brown hair (62).

j Venus in ♑, gives a mean, short stature, pale, thin, sickly visage, dark or black hair; and if in the 1st face, sad and brown.

k Venus in ♒, gives a handsome, well formed person, rather corpulent, clear complexion, with light brown or flaxen hair; in trine of Jupiter, a perfect beauty.

l Venus in ♓, personates a middle stature, rather plump and fleshy, full face, with a dimple in the chin, good complexion, and brown hair.

272.—MERCURY'S SHAPE IN SIGNS.

m Mercury in ♈, gives a thin, mean stature, oval face, light brown curly hair, and dull complexion; ill-disposed, thievish, and addicted to villainy.

n Mercury in ♉, gives a middle stature, corpulent, but well set, swarthy, sunburnt complexion, short, thick brown hair; slothful, gluttonous, and wanton, large gustativeness (16).

o Mercury in ♊, gives a person tall, upright, and well made, with brown hair, and good complexion; an orator, lawyer, or bookseller, self-interested.

p Mercury in ♋, gives a short squab figure, bad complexion, sad brown hair, thin face, sharp nose, and small eyes; dishonest, deceitful, and given to drinking.

q Mercury in ♌, gives a large body, swarthy complexion, brown hair, round face, full eye, and high nose; hasty, boasting, ambitious, and proud.

r Mercury in ♍, makes the body tall, slender, and proportioned; bad complexion, dark brown or black hair, long face, and austere look.

s Mercury in ♎, gives a tall, handsome person, but not thin; smooth light brown hair, sanguine complexion; just, virtuous, learned, and accomplished (46).

t Mercury in ♏, gives a mean stature, well set, broad shoulders, swarthy complexion, brown curling hair; one subtle, and careful of his own interest, fond of company and women.

u Mercury in ♐, personates a tall stature, well formed, not corpulent, rather spare, large boned, large nose, oval face, ruddy complexion; hasty tempered, but soon reconciled.

v Mercury in ♑, personates a mean stature, bow legged, thin face, often crooked, dusky complexion, brown hair, helpless, sickly and dejected; peevish and unfortunate.

w Mercury in ♒, personates a middle stature, rather fleshy, full face, clear complexion, and brown hair ; an ingenious, witty, kind humane character, possessing great invention (74).

x Mercury in ♓, gives a short squab figure, pale, sickly face, hairy body ; repining and peevish, addicted to women, very foppish and effeminate.

273.—THE MOON'S SHAPE IN SIGNS.

a Moon in ♈, personates a middle stature, rather plump, round face, light brown or flaxen hair, tolerably good complexion ; the mind rash, changeable, ambitious, and seldom fortunate.

b Moon in ♉, gives a strong corpulent, well set person, low middle stature, bad complexion, brown or black hair ; one gentle in manners, sober and kind.

c Moon in ♊, makes the native tall and well formed, upright and comely, brown hair, good complexion ; one subtle, crafty, and ingenious, ill-disposed and generally unfortunate.

d Moon in ♋, represents a middle stature, well proportioned, fleshy body, round full face, brown hair, pale dusky complexion ; pleasant, merry, easy disposition, harmless and free from passion, fortunate, and much respected, but changeable.

e Moon in ♌, personates a tall stature, strong, and large boned, large eyes, full face, sanguine complexion, light brown hair ; high minded, ambitious, and generally unfortunate.

f Moon in ♍, personates a tall stature, rather ruddy, oval face, dark brown or black hair ; an ingenious, reserved, covetous, melancholy person, seldom well-disposed, and generally unfortunate.

g Moon in ♎, gives a tall, well made person, with smooth, light brown hair, fine red and white complexion, handsome face; pleasant and merry, and very fond of amusement.

h Moon in ♏, gives an ill made, short, thick, fleshy body, dark brown or black hair, dark complexion ; ill-disposed, treacherous, malicious, brutish, and sottish. If a woman, she is generally infamous.

i Moon in ♐, gives a handsome person, oval face, sanguine complexion, brown hair ; open and generous disposition, rather hasty and ambitious, but honest and kind, fortunate, and much respected.

j Moon in ♑, personates a low stature, thin, small, weak body, thin face, bad complexion, dark hair, rather weak, and particularly in the knees ; idle, dull, imbecile, and generally a debauched character.

k Moon in ♒, represents a middle sized, corpulent person, well formed, brown hair, clear sanguine complexion ; ingenious, affable, kind, and inoffensive, possesses an active fancy, and ingenious.

l Moon in ✶, gives a short mean stature, but plump, pale countenance, and bright hair ; one idle, dull, evilly disposed, and unfortunate.

273A.—HERSCHEL'S SHAPE IN SIGNS.

m Herschel in ♈, or on the cusp of the house signifying the ascendant denotes one rather tall, auburn hair, thin in appearance, a little colour in the face, eccentric and hasty temper, and one that remembers an affront a long time, fond of learning, inquisitive, and one that does not marry early in life, given to novels and writing, a worker in wood, an artificer, inventor, and fond of farming and cattle.

n Herschel in ♉, represents a person of a mean stature, rather stout, not very handsome, dull complexion, and brown hair ; large gustativeness, grey eyes, one somewhat conceited, fond of money, in actions secret and eccentric.

o Herschel in ♊, personates a body tall, well proportioned, dull, sanguine complexion, brown or dark eyes, dark hair, oval face, intelligent looking countenance ; in manners blunt and prompt, especially if ♅ be not ill aspected by the ☽ ; the mind is somewhat scientific but not profound.

p Herschel in ♋, represents a short stature, dull pale complexion, sad brown hair, thin face, sharp nose, small eyes ; disposition jealous, slothful, eccentric, malicious, fond of recreations, and often puts the best side outwards, seems to be what he really is not, thievish, and other ill qualities, except ♃, ☾, ☿, or ♀ cast a good aspect to ♅. He confines himself to no fast employment.

q Herschel in ♌, portends a person of a rather upright genteel make, tolerably good complexion, high broad shoulders, strong bones, brown or auburn hair, fullish eye, and Roman nose, hasty temper, ambitious and proud. The qualities of the mind are philosophic, ingenious, learned, inquisitive, but eccentric, difficult to please, and secret.

r Herschel in ♍, represents a medium proportioned body, dark complexion, oval face, brown or black hair, good sized head, and austere countenance. The quality of the mind is clever, learned, acquiring knowledge by different means, though abrupt, and cares not for the foolery of fashion, generally employed in scholastic callings, such as teaching, writing, superintending, an excise officer, &c.

s Herschel in ♎, describes a person rather tall, upright stature, comely appearance, moderately stout, smooth brown hair, oval face, sanguine complexion, high forehead, grey eyes ; in disposition mild and kind, the quality of the mind learned and accommodating, faithful and trustworthy. He follows a clean light business.

t Herschel in ♏, portends a mean stature, well set, broad make, long face, dark complexion, dark hair and whiskers, broad shoulders;

disposition honourable, faithful, firm and conscientious. The mind ingenious, thoughtful, but reserved and fond of employment.

u Herschel in ♐, delineates a person tall or full sized, genteel make, fair complexion, brown hair, not fleshy, strong boned, and rather thin face, one hasty but soon reconciled, moderately careful, well disposed, and not covetous, rather proud, but strives after honourable things, fond of recreations, but no spendthrift, a sincere friend, but a perpetual foe to his opponents ; a joiner, modeller, architect, timber merchant, cabinet-maker &c.

v Herschel in ♑, gives a lean person, middle stature, dark or black hair, plenty of whiskers, thin face, dull complexion, little eyes, and stiving walk ; disposition reserved, secretiveness large, firm in his dealings and procedure, one that may be depended upon for his promises ; a farmer, or having to do with railways, butchers, and business that requires strength.

w Herschel in ♒, represents a middle stature, rather fleshy, clear complexion, a good sized head and face, and brown hair ; in disposition honourable, faithful and punctual to promises. The quality of the mind firm, ingenious, steady in speech, patient and industrious, yet one that does not marry early ; a mechanic, an inventor of items in machinery, and things connected with railways, &c.

x Herschel in ♓, personates one of a middle stature, pale complexion, oval face, dark brown curling hair, high forehead inclined to be plump or fleshy, and moderate beard and whiskers ; temper malicious, but not without cause, a lover of female company, and sometimes addicted to drinking ; disposition, just in his actions, rather fond of debate ; ingenious, but somewhat mutable in his resolves, and generally fortunate.   He does best in following a trade in which he sells articles of consumption, as beer, bread huckstering, fishmonger, and seller of all kinds of liquids.

Some writers say Neptune's signs and influences are to be taken much after Venus, but I take Neptune to be much after the nature of Herschel's influence, but slower in bringing things to pass, and in a milder way. A little time and study will soon prove its influence and effect.

CHAPTER XVIII.

PECULIAR TEMPERS, DISPOSITIONS, CHARACTERS, AND MANNERS.

274 *Herschel* is abrupt in manners, and cares not for the customs and fashions of society (161).

275 *Saturn* in ♈, ♉, ♊, and ♏, contentious, quarrelsome, morose, crafty, discontented, a retainer of anger, loquacious, but deliberate,

and this depends in a great measure how he is dignified and aspected, (162).   In ♋, morose and jealous disposition; in ♌, noble self-acting, generous, but somewhat courageous and malicious ; in ♍, subtle, studious, reserved and inclined to curiosity ; in ♎, fond of debate, and often overcomes, rather prodigal and regardless of wealth ; in ♐, a sincere friend, and merciful enemy, often makes promises which he finds impracticable to fulfil ; in ♑, a retainer of wrath, fearful, covetous, discontented, and melancholy ; in ♒, a searching fancy, profoundly philosophical, self-taught in most things, an able astro-philosopher ; in ♓, fickle.

276 *Jupiter* in ♈, ♉, ♊, ♌, ♎, ♐, ♒, and ♓, noble, free disposition, obliging, affable, admirer of females, magnanimous, industrious, and friendly (163).   In ♋, a busybody, loquacious, intermeddler with other men's affairs ; in ♍, a boaster, rather choleric, covetous, and rash ; in ♏, resolute, ill-natured, covetous, and subtle ; in ♑, peevish, helpless, indigent, and inactive.

277 *Mars* in ♈, ♌, ♎, ♏, ♐, ♑, bold, warlike, generous, free-spirited, conceited of his abilities, ready apprehension, active fancy, cheerful, penetrating, and often fortunate (164).   In ♉, ♊, ♋, ♍, ♒, or ♓, vicious drinking, and if he afflict ☽ or ☿, the native is inclined to dishonesty, unsettled, unfortunate ; in ♋, sottish, and meanly employed, especially if afflicted by ♄ or ☍ ; in ♍, revengeful and conceited ; in ♒, turbulent, and given to controversy ; and in ♓, a dissembler and debauchee.

278 *Sol* in ♈, ♉, ♋, ♌, ♍, ♎, ♏, ♐, and ♒, delights in warlike actions, noble, confident, majestic, ambitious, cheerful (165).   In ♊, affable, mild tempered ; in ♑, passionate ; and in ♓, prodigal, addicted to gaming and feasting to his detriment, harmless, and injures none but himself ; in ♋, ♏, and ♓, unfortunate.

279 *Venus* in ♈, ♍, and ♑, unfortunate and lewd ; in ♉, obliging ; in ♊, liberal and charitable ; in ♋, mutable and inconstant ; in ♌, soon angry, but quickly appeased ; in ♍, ingenious, but subtle ; in ♎, obliging and much beloved ; in ♏, debauched, contentious, and vicious ; in ♐, generous, but proud, good tempered, and fortunate ; in ♑, a lover of pleasure, and changeable ; in ♒, excellent disposition, and courteous, peaceful, and a lover of recreation ; in ♓, just and mild, peaceable and ingenious (166).

280 *Mercury* in ♈, ill-disposed and thievish, witty ; in ♉, slothful and fond of pleasure ; in ♊, of great understanding ; in ♋, a dissembler, sottish, thievish, except in good aspect to the ☽ and ♃ ; in ♌, hasty and bold, high spirit, ambitious, and contentious, not so persevering ; in ♍, ingenious and accomplished ; in ♎, just, virtuous, and prudent ; in ♏, subtile, and studious; in ♐, passionate, but soon appeased ; in ♑, peevish and discontented ; in ♒, ingenious and inventive ; in ♓, repining, disconsolate, addicted to women and drink.

281 *The Moon*, in ♈, ♋, ♎, or ♑, mutable, rash, debauched and mean ; in ♉, ♊, ♌, ♍, ♐, ♒, or ♓, mild, ingenious, obliging, rather proud, and peaceable ; in ♏, sottish, malicious, and treacherous.

LESSON EIGHTEENTH.

QUESTIONS TO BE ANSWERED BEFORE THE STUDENT PROCEEDS.

Which produce maliciousness ?

Which give pride and ambition ?

Which produce deceit ?

Which mutability ?

Which are given to drink ?

Which to women ?

Which to study ?

Which give slothful or idle persons ?

Which give virtue ?

Which give the best disposition ?

Which produces ingenuity ?

Where is Venus debauched ?

Which give prodigality in the above ?

In which signs is Sol unfortunate ?

Where is Venus unfortunate ?

What is meant by well dignified ?

By ill dignified ?

CHAPTER XIX.

THE QUALITY OF THE MIND AND DISPOSITION.

282 Mercury governs the intellectual endowments, Herschel the mental faculties, and the Moon the animal propensities.

RULE 1.—Consider the faces on the 1st and 10th, the lord of 1st, and the planets therein, and those planets which aspect the lord of the first ; and make a judicious mixture.

RULE 2.—Consider chiefly the Moon and Mercury, how they are situated, and how they are aspected ; before judging the effect of any planet upon the 1st, the Moon, or Mercury, observe how that planet is itself affected by aspects of other planets.

RULE 3.—Mark those planets which are rulers of Mercury, Herschel, and Moon, or those planets that have domal dignities in the signs in which Mercury, Herschel, and Moon are posited.

RULE 4.—Mark the strength of Herschel, Mercury and Moon ; and the aspects of each other, and with other planets, for the aspects bear powerful testimonies, the Moon receives various impressions of those stars with which she is configurated, as well by separation as by application. (Pages 23 and 5.) (292.)

283 The ☽, in extreme latitude, renders the mind various, versatile, and susceptible of change ; if in her nodes, the mind will be more acute, practical, and active (312). When in the 1st, rising, she gives great ingenuity, perspicuity, firmness ; but if under the

earth, she renders the mind more heavy, obtuse, variable of purpose more timid, and more obscure.

284 ♅, ☽, or ☿, void of aspect in ♈, ♋, ♎, or ♑, make the mind active in political matters, fond of distinction, busy in theology, ingenious, acute, inquisitive, inventive, speculative, ambitious and studious of astrology.

285 ♅, ☽, or ☿, in ♊, ♍, ♐, or ♓, and void of aspect, renders the mind variable, versatile, unsteady, acute feelings, deceitful, amorous, volatile, wily, repining, speculative, fond of music, careless, unhappiness in friendship and attachment, full of expedients, regretful, good conversation and manners.

286 ♅, ☽, or ☿, in ♉, ♏, ♌, or ♒, makes the person just, retentive memory, uncompromising, constant, firm, prudent, patient, industrious, strict, chaste, yet malicious, steady in pursuit, contentious, shrewd, ambitious, avaricious, pertinacious, thrifty, slow of speech, persevering, the organ of firmness good.

287 ♅, ☿, and the ☽, between the 1st and 10th, or 7th and 4th, especially in faces of their own nature, make the mind liberal, frank, self-acting, brave, ingenious, unreserved, strong, yet acute, undisguising.

288 Oriental positions, especially in the 1st or 10th house, make men reflective, of good memory, firm, prudent, magnanimous, inflexible, powerful in intellect, strict, judicious, active, hostile to crime, skilful in science, settled, constant, and fit to be depended on, penetrating, ardent, and persevering.

289 ♅, ☽, and ☿, and planets in aspect to them, between the 10th, 7th, and 4th, make men unsteady. irreverent, imbecile, impatient, doubting (if ☽ or ☿ are afflicted), boastful, lazy, slothful, intemperate, cowardly, wavering, and hard to rouse. If these three planets be well aspected among themselves, the natives are profoundly scientific; also ♅ on 12th in ✳ to M.C.

290 Those stars rising at the beginning of the night, and occidental (viz., those that ascend after sunset, and consequently in or near an opposition of the Sun), make the native wicked, unstable, weak, ambitious, boasting, yet dull, cowardly, mean, servile, and desperate.

291 Occidental positions, or between the 10th and 7th, or on the cusp of the 4th, or near it, and aspecting ♅, ☿, and ☽, or ☿ and ♀, rising, or at their greatest elongation, and rising or setting heliacally, make the native ingenious and prudent, but not capable of great recollection, nor fond of labour, yet inquisitive into occult matters, mechanical, inventive, studious of physical sciences, good mathematicians, philosophers, meteorologists, &c.

292 Planets ruling ♅, ☿, and the ☽, and in good aspect of each other, and in places in which the planets have dignities, the mental properties will still be good, more especially if the planets be con-

figurated with ♅, ☿, and the ☽, either by separation or application (page 5), and the best position is when ♅, ☿, and the ☽ are in good aspect of each other, either by application or separation (282).

293 ♅, ☿, and the ☽, not in good aspect, or afflicted by the malefics, or planets aspecting ♅, ☿, and the ☽, out of their essential dignities, then they will imprint the qualities of their natives; bu imperfectly, and in an obscure degree, not tending so much to the benefit and advancement of the native. They who are impressed by the malefics with evil dispositions, if a good aspect intervenes, have not the power to do the evil they otherwise would do, and even if they persevere, are so unfit for it that they are soon detected and punished.

294 The property of the planets ruling ♅, ☽, and ☿, will be powerfully impressed upon the mental energy, which energy is either strengthened or diminished, according to the force and action of subordinate configurations; for those who, by reason of strong malefic rays, are too prone to violence and injustice, have not their impulse to commit evil unrestrained, unless these evil rays are opposed by some contrary effect, as covetousness, hasty temper, meanness, and so on. But should a contrary condition oppose this familiarity of the malefics, the evil inclination is then proportionally corrected, and the mind is more easily brought to a proper sense of its intemperate pursuits, and is more likely to meet imposition or ill treatment.

295 Persons who are good and just, become so because born under a familiarity between the benefics and the places of ☿ and ☽, and more especially when no contrary influence of any planet in elevation interpose; the natives cheerfully perform good actions, never subject to injustice, but are fortunate from their honesty and virtue. But if a contrary familiarity should interpose, the mildness and humanity of these persons will operate to their disadvantage, exposing them to contempt and accusation, thus rendering them liable to be wronged by the designing multitude.

Thus we have considered the influence of Mercury and the Moon in a general way, unconnected with the operations and effects of any particular planet which may happen to assume the dominion, and thereby imprint its own peculiar influences upon the mental faculties, in proportion to its superiority over the other planets.

We shall now take cognizance of the effect of each distinct planet as is found to produce when it alone governs the mind at the time of birth.

296 ♅ ruling the ☽ and ☿, in his dignities, and elevated above Moon and Mercury, and in good aspect, makes men unsettled in life, partial to travelling, romantic, studious of antiquity, yet likely to strike out many novelties, astrologers, meteorologists, phrenologists, lecturers, chemists, and fond of new discoveries, especially in machinery; tutors, and professors of the physical sciences, and

the organ of constructiveness well developed. But badly situated, then the natives are enthusiastic, speculative, inventors of mischief, and plodders after business (169).

297 ♄ governing the ☽ and ☿, in elevation, and in good aspect, makes persons austere, profound in opinion, laborious, singular in their modes of thinking, original haters of crime, avaricious, accumulators of riches, envious ; but ♄, ☽, and ☿, badly situated, or badly aspected, debase the mind, making it bigoted, superstitious, cowardly, slovenly, ill disposed, solitary, envious, fretful, apt to cry, indiscriminately pusillanimous (162).

298 ♄ and ♃, in accordant familiarity, render the mind virtuous, benevolent, frugal, judicious, magnanimous, obliging, solicitous of good, mild, prudent, patient, philosophical, well intentioned, and magnanimously pursuing that which is of benefit to himself and mankind, affectionate in domestic ties. But in discordant familiarity or weak, the mind is incapable of learning, timorous, a dabbler in science, idle, superstitious, hypocritical, cunning, dull, misjudging, regardless of religion, foolish, cowardly, regretful, and cautiousness large, averse to children, and low philoprogenitiveness.

299 ♄ and ♂, in accordant configuration, render persons free in speech, boastful, proud, deceitful, laborious, inflexible, and collected, contemptuous, impatient to excel, able in office, vindictive, submitting to no opposition, turbulent, firm, watchful, bold, insidious, able in defence, tolerably successful, seditious, austere, and covetous. But in bad familiarity or position, makes men tyrannical, thievish, treacherous, infidels, mischievous, perjurous, adulterous, assassins, seekers of gain by their turpitude.

300 ♄ and ♀, in accordant familiarity, make men averse to women, fond of governing, prone to solitude, reserved, regardless of rank, envious, austere, unsociable, singular in opinion, addicted to religious service, and mysterious, desirous of being a preacher, reverential, sedate, studious of wisdom, faithful, reflective, circumspect, and rather scrupulous. But in bad familiarity, and Saturn out of all dignities, make persons licentious, practisers of lewdness, careless, obscene, treacherous to their family, quarrelsome, mean, slanderous, calumniators, adulterous, intemperate, and scoffers at religion.

301 ♄ and ☿, if in good position, and Saturn strong, free from affliction, incline the native to be inquisitive, loquacious, studious of law and of medicine, mystical, secretive, improvident in some things, quick in perception, vigilant, meditative, laborious, and tractable, petulant but acute. But Saturn and Mercury connected, and not well situated, then Saturn will make the native frivolous, vindictive, malicious, cruel, treacherous, thieves, swindlers, schedulers, forgers, house-breakers, runaway, and unsuccessful, base, and infamous.

302 When Jupiter alone has dominion over the mind, and gloriously situated, makes the native honourable, open, just, magnanimous, venerable, pious, courteous, noble, self-acting, benevolent, fond of learning, compassionate, calculated for government, and fortunate. But Jupiter, ruler of the mind, afflicted, the above qualities will be imposed upon the mind more faintly ; instead of generosity, profusion ; for piety, bigotry ; for modesty, timidity ; for nobleness, arrogance ; for courteousness, folly ; for elegance, voluptuousness ; for magnanimity, carelessness ; and for liberality, indifference ; proud, bashful, weak, and careless (163).

303 ♃ and ♂, well situated, the native will be bold, proud, contentious, impetuous, subordinate, hotheaded, active, fond of fighting, magnanimous, honourable, penetrating, judicious, courageous, successful, ambitious, dictatorial, free in speech, generous, irascible, and warlike. Jupiter and Mars configurated, but not well aspected, &c.; if Mars be ill aspected, the native will be cruel, seditious, arrogant, rash, rapacious, indiscreet, desperate, factious, stubborn, unstable, firmness low, lustful, faithless, dissatisfied, perverse, avaricious, prodigal, triflers, giving way to every impulse, and injudicious. The ☌ of ♂ and ♃ in ♌ is not good, often detrimental to the native's welfare (166).

304 ♃ conciliated with ♀, well disposed, the native is a person of taste, elegant, fond of pleasure, children, philoprogenitiveness well developed, partial to music, active, kind, affable, cheerful, ingenious, liberal, ambitious of love and admiration, scientific, a lover of poetry, sincere, sportive, affectionate, temperate, modest, and in all respects honourable and worthy. But evilly posited and ill disposed, the native will be sensual, addicted to pleasure, lustful, dissipated, fond of dress, show, and pleasure ; lasciviousness, talkative, yet not ill disposed ; affable, cheerful, free, effeminate, fond of dancing, dull, wasteful, observant, faithful, and liberal to misfortune (295).

305 ♃ and ☿ gloriously posited and in familiarity, he, ♃, disposes to business, and all kinds of learning, poetry, oratory ; he is sober, kind, cheerful, affectionate, wise, acute, temperate, politic, able in government, religious, philosophical, and dignified, but ill disposed, &c., produces contrary effects, the natives will be shallow, superficial, proud, stupid, trifling, enthusiastic, silly, credulous of falsehood, petulant, affectors of wisdom, arrogant, and vacillating, yet Jupiter will also produce men skilled in learning, strong memory, capable of imparting instruction (163).

306 ♂ alone, dominion of the mind, and well placed, makes the native bold, generous, brave, magnanimous, confident, rash, contemptuous, angry, violent, desperate, irascible, imperious, versatile, intellectual, careless, stern, and able in government (164). But unfortunated, the natives are cruel, bloody, drunken, furious, headstrong, turbulent, rapacious, luxurious, atheistical, extravagant,

precipitate, infidels, hostile to their families, and desperately mischievous.

307 ♂ and ♀ conciliated, and fortunately posited, then Mars renders the mind cheerful, merry, fond of music, dancing, and all kinds of amusement, circumspect, simple, good humoured, liberal, and friendly, but given to lust of every description, hasty tempered, brave, libidinous, extravagant, and jealous. Mars evilly posited and afflicting Venus, the natives will be proud, mischievous, liars, drunkards, treacherous, perjurers, rash, intemperate, very lascivious, adulterous, opprobrious, cheats, fickle, weak in mind, wasteful, fond of dress, audacious, and shameless.

308 ♂ connected with ☿, and placed in glory, or ☿ in ♈ or ♏, in good aspect of ☽, a deep understanding, and the native is bold, violent, laborious, witty, crafty, ready to invent mischief, ingenious, quick, treacherous, very active, eloquent, sophistical, inquisitive, fond of strife, good enough to those like himself, but mischievous to his enemies. But if Mercury be ill posited, in □ or ☍ of ♂, a sharp wit, but they will be prodigal, intemperate, cruel, liars, thieves, murderers, thief takers, parricides, assassins, forgers of writings, poisoners, bold, violent, regretful, vacillating, infidels, impostors, incendiaries, frequenters of theatres, jugglers, and deeply wicked.

309 ♀ alone, ruler of the mind, and well placed, renders it benignant, voluptuous, copious in wit, pure, gay, fond of dancing, music, and amusement, cheerful, kind, happy, charitable, refined in taste, complacent, well disposed, modest, easily reconciled, not fond of labour, and inclined to be jealous, fond of arts and sciences, and entirely amiable. But ill disposed, renders the mind dull, wanton, effeminate, lustful, profligate, timid, careless, obscene, amorous, indiscriminating, and ignominious (166).

310 ♀ and ☿ fortunate, and having familiarity over the mind, or in M.C. in ♂ in ♈, ♊, ♎, or ♏, then Venus makes persons learned, eminent, scientific and judicious, fond of law and divinity, eloquent, cheerful, fond of refined and delicate amusement, kind-hearted, well disposed, pleasing and courteous, magnanimous, yet given to contention where they think their rights invaded, polite, prudent, self-teaching, emulous, copious and agreeable in speech, serene, high-minded, and continent. But in bad familiarity they will be treacherous, crafty, subtle, unstable, liars, slanderers, perjurers, weak-minded, hypocritical, debauched, fond of personal adornment, intermeddlers, busybodies, and notoriously famous in all other propensities.

311 ☿ alone having dominion over the mind, and well posited, renders the mind prudent, clever, strong memory, scientific, inventive, poetical, logical, emulous, fond of mathematics, philosophy ; benevolent, accurate in judgment, mysterious, and generally well disposed. But ill disposed makes the mind precipitate, forgetful,

foolish, stupid, furious, trifling, covetous, knavish, deceitful, variable, avaricious, predisposed to error through a defect in judgment.

312 ☽ also contributes to the foregoing influence according to her position. When in her extreme latitude, North or South, she makes the mind more crafty and changeable, but when in ♌ or ♉ more acute, active and sprightly (283).

And when ☉ is conciliated with the ruler of the mind, angular or oriental, produces probity, industry, honour, and all laudable qualities. But ☉ occidently posited, or cadent, increases debasement, depravity, obscurity, cruelty, obstinacy, moroseness, and other dishonourable qualities.

313 ☿ ☌ ☉ makes the native fit for business, but when 20 or 30 degrees distant, more fit for learning ; ☿ R, natives are sceptics ; and when swift the native is unsettled and changeable ; under the Sun's beams, speculative ; in ☌ 3rd or 4th, skilled in physical science.

314 When ☿ and ☽ both form many aspects with planets, the native will be very unstable in disposition, resembling each planet by turns. The ☌, of △, ✳, of ☿ and ☽, shews ingenuity and great ability ; the □ shows wit, but often applied to evil purposes ; the ☍ shows one seditious, stubborn, impudent, and destructive ; also S □ astrologers.

315 ☽ and ☿, afflicted P. or ☌ □, ☍ of ♄, cause an impediment in speech, and bad to be understood. ☿ in ♈, ♊, ♍, or ♒ in good aspect with ♅, ♄, or ♂, shews a piercing wit and great understanding. ☉ and ♂ in the 1st, in Airy or Fiery signs, make proud, scornful, prodigal and conceited persons, boasters, mischievous and violent.

316 ☿ in ♍ or ♒, and in power and good aspects gives the native a speculative and inquisitive intellect ; if ☿ be in ♈ or ♏, especially ♈, the native will make an elocutionist ; or ☿ free from affliction where ♊, ♍, ♎, ♐, or ♒ ascend, a graceful speech and an elocutionist. And if ☿ be better dignified than the ☽, the reasoning faculties will be stronger than the sensitive.

LESSON NINETEENTH.

TO BE ANSWERED BEFORE THE STUDENT PROCEEDS.

Which planets are rulers of the mind ?

Which rules the mental faculties ?

Which rule the animal propensities ?

Which rules the perceptive faculties ?

Which rule the moral endowments ?

Which give benevolence ?

Which combativeness ?

Which the most politeness?
Which intemperance?
What does Herschel uninfluenced by other planets produce?
What does Saturn give?
What does Mercury and Venus well disposed produce?
Which give firmness?
Which produce the best philosophers?
Which rules prophecy?
What does Jupiter alone denote?

What Jupiter and Mercury happily disposed declare?
Which give gaiety?
Which make the best physicians?
Which make the best lawyers?
What is the effect of Mercury retrograde?
What is produced by Sol and Mercury in conjunction?
What does Sol produce when conciliated with the ruler of the mind?

CHAPTER XX.

ON THE DISEASES OF THE MIND.

317 Observe the position of ☿, ♅, ☽ and ascendant, for if ☽, ♅, and ☿ be unconnected with each other, or the 1st, or their rulers in ☍ to them and elevated above them, the mental qualities will then consequently become impregnated with various characters, ot which may be clearly known by the abilities of the stars thus controlling the places of ☽, ♅, ☿, and the 1st.

318 If ☽, ☿, ♅, and 1st be unconnected by good aspects, and be afflicted by ♄ or ♂, and these evil stars in angles and elevated above ☽, ♅, and ☿, and no assistance given by ♃ or ♀, the native born will be subject to epilepsy, idiopathy, madness, and insanity. If ♄ be so posited by day, and ♂ by night, the above diseases will occur; otherwise, when ♄ have ☌, □, or ☍ of Asc. by night; or ♂ by day, especially if in ♋, ♍, or ♓, the person born will become insane, or demoniac affections will be produced, especially under bad arcs.

319 The ☽ ☌ ☉, and they governed by ♄; or ☽ ☍ ☉, governed by ♂, and particularly in ♎, ♐, or ♓, the native will become demoniac, and afflicted with moisture of the brain and lunacy.

320 If ♄ or ♂ alone should rule ☿, ☽, or 1st, the disordered brain is incurable, although it be not very violent; but should ♃ or ♀ be well aspected, and posited between the 1st and 10th, while ♄ or ♂ may be in the 7th, then the disease, though violent, will be curable; if ♃ preside, curable by medical help; but if ♀, by the strength of the natural faculties. But should ♃ or ♀ be setting, or occidental, and ♄ or ♂ oriental and angular, the disorders become not only incurable, but also conspicuous, and the epileptic person will be subject to constant fits, and to danger of

death ; the insane become outrageous, unmanageable, wandering in nakedness; the demoniac, and those afflicted with moisture of the brain will become furious, uttering mysterious sayings, and wounding themselves.

321 If ☉ and ♂ rule ☿, ♅, ☽, or 1st, and the latter unconnected as above, the ☉ and ♂ contribute to insanity. If ♃ and ☿, they produce epilepsy ; if ♀ and ♅, produce fury of enthusiasm and eccentricity ; if ♄ and ☽, affections and moisture of the brain.

322 If instead of ☿, the ☉ be with the ☽, in masculine signs, with ♂ and ♀, then the male will possess propensities becoming his sex.

323 ♅ afflicting ☿ and ☽ at one time, especially if he be elevated above them, insanity at periods.

It is by such configurations as those just described that any morbid deviation, occurring in the active or reasoning faculties of the mind, is produced ; but a deviation of the passive, or merely sensitive faculties, is discernible chiefly in the excess and deficiency (as the case may be) of the masculine and feminine genders ; that is to say, in the superabundance or deficiency of the power of either gender to produce a confirmation agreeable to its own nature. (See on Children.)

CHAPTER XXI.

HURTS, INJURIES, AND DISEASES.

324 For the investigation of these circumstances the 1st, 7th, and 6th houses, and the planets affecting the hyleg, must be considered ; and judgment must be inferred from the general character.

325 If ♂, ♄, or ♅ be on the cusp of the 1st, 6th, or 7th ; or be in exact ☍, □ or S□ of these degrees, there will be external blemishes, or bodily infirmities, and more especially if ☉ and ☽ be in ☌ or ☍ in the 1st or 7th, or even if there be only one luminary with ♅, ♄, or ♂ in the 1st or 7th, infirmities will be produced in those parts of the body ruled by the signs on the 1st or 7th ; whether they be hurts, diseases, or both ; and those stars will also point out the cause and quality of the symptom (Chap. VII).

326 Blemishes and bodily hurts generally happen when ♅, ♄, or ♂ are oriental ; but disease, when occidental ; and as their cause is different, so also is their effect, for hurts or blemishes suffer pain only once, while disease is constant, or repeated at times, and planets R. have a tendency to cause disease.

327 The ☽ in the 1st or 7th, in exact ☌, S□, □, or ☍ of ☉, and afflicted by ♅, ♄, or ♂, or with any nebulous stars, such as the

Cloudy Spot of ♋, Pleiades, the Harrow of ♐, the Sting of ♏, the Mane of ♌, or the Urn of ♒ ; these cause the loss of one eye. If ♅, ♄, or ♂ be in ☌ or ☍ to both ☉ and ☽, and Luna in the 1st, 4th, or 7th, and in her decrease, and especially those that afflict the ☉ be oriental, or ascend before him, and those that afflict the ☽ be occidental, or ascend after her, then total blindness. Under these circumstances ♂ will cause blindness by fire, lightning, wounds, bruises, small pox ; and if with ♀, it will happen at play, or some amusement, or by some artifice, or private injury ; ♄ causes blindness by colds, cataracts, specks, gutta-serena, &c.; if ☿, it will proceed from reading, study, or mental exertion.

328 If ☉ be hyleg, and afflicted by ♄, in an angle, or posited in the 1st, the native will be consumptive ; if ☉ be setting in ♌, and afflicted, he will be liable to injury by fire or sword ; if ☽ be afflicted by ♂, and ♂ descending, the native will be in great danger of being burned to death, and if configurated by ☿ it comes from an accident in sport or by robbers.

329 Saturn and ☿ in ☌ of ☉, in the 1st or 7th, especially ☿ in the 7th, and behold ☽ with a P., □, or ☍, the native will have an impediment in his speech, and speak with difficulty, particularly if ☿ be in ♋, ♏, or ♓, it will be still worse. Should ♂ be with them it will remove the evil a little after the arc of ☽ to ☿ is passed over.

330 Mercury in Par., ☌ of ♄ or ♂, or □ to the ☽, from the 1st or 7th, causes the head to be very much diseased, and if both malefics concur, is apt to cause apoplexy. The ☽ in Par. of ♄ or ♂ will cause a humour or disease in the head ; and if ☿ be likewise afflicted by ♄ or ♂, the disease will be very severe.

331 Saturn or ♂ in ☌ in angles, and ☉ or ☽ in ☌ or ☍, or the luminaries directed to the malefics, or Luna, and if she be in her nodes or extreme latitude in hurtful signs, as ♈, ♉, ♋, ♏, and ♑, the native will be distorted, paralysed or lame. If ♄ or ♂ be in ☌ of the lights, the defect will be from the birth; but if in ☍ to them, or ♄ or ♂ be in the M.C., and in □ of ☉ or ☽, it will be by blows, falls from high places, stabs, robberies, shipwreck, and other accidents, by quadrupeds, &c.

332 If ☉ or ☽ are configurated together, and both in masculine signs (p. 15 and 16), both configurated with ♂ and ♀ in any way, males then born will have excessive virile members, and women will be hermaphrodites. If both ♂ and ♀ be also in masculine signs, men will have a mixture of sex, and females will be violently libidinous. If Venus be also in a masculine sign, they will be more discreet, and conceal their desires and practices in privacy.

333 If ☉ and ☽ are configurated together in feminine signs (p. 13), with ♂ and ♀, females will be of a masculine turn, and very salacious, but the men effeminate. If Venus be in a feminine sign alone, the native, if a male, will be nearly impotent, but lustful and licentious; but if a female, very lustful. If Venus be masculine,

and Mars feminine, males will have more shameless practices, with strength and vigour.   Mars and Venus being so configurated, when oriental and diurnal, make men more robust; but if occidental and nocturnal, they are more debilitated.   If Saturn be configurated with them all, they are more prone to violent, impure, obscene, and unnatural desires; Mercury adds to their lusts, mobility, notoriety, activity, and makes them fond of variety of contrivances, either male or female; but if Jupiter be configurated also, he moderates their desires, and renders them more circumspect.

334 The minor bodily disorders mostly occur on the Moon's being posited in ♈, ♉, ♊, cancers, eruptions in the face, and disorders arising from the white leprosy; in ♋, ♄, ♍, she causes ringworms, tetters, shingles, &c.; if Moon be in ♎, ♏, ♐, she causes scurvy, and a species of leprosy; in ♑, ♒, ♓, gives boils, eruptions of pimples, and other inconveniences, scabbed lips, and unsound legs, if the malefics are angular and occidental to the Moon, or oriental to the Sun, and in ♋, ♑, ♓, cause scurvy or scrofula; and, indeed, these in the 1st or 7th, in any sign ascribed to terrestrial animals and fishes, give these diseases, with putridity, tetters, excoriation, fistula, leprosy, and the like; while ♐ and ♊ produce diseases by falling fits, and epilepsy.   And if the planets happen to be posited in the latter degrees of the signs containing them, the extremities of the body will then be chiefly affected by the disease or hurt, which will arise from humours or accidents, producing leprosy, gout, or other infirmities in the hands, feet, &c., as cramp, rheumatisms.

335 The malefics in the angles occidental of the Sun, or oriental of the Moon, then Saturn will generally produce cold in the bowels, excessive phlegm, rheumatism, emaciation, sickliness, jaundice, dysentery, cough, obstructions, colic or scurvy; and in women, besides these diseases, he produces complaints of the womb (177). Mars wlll cause expectoration of blood, atrabilarious attacks, pulmonary complaints, sores and diseases in the privates and abdomen, such as fistula, hemorrhoids, or knots in the fundament, and also inflamed and putrifying ulcers, and other inflammatory affections (179).   In females, to these calamities he adds abortion, excision of the fœtus, or its mortification.   Mercury acting with Saturn, augments the coldness, and promotes the continuance of rheumatism, and disturbance of the fluids, especially in the chest, throat, and stomach.   If in familiarity with Mars, Mercury will tend to produce greater dryness, and will increase ulcers, abscesses, loss of hair, scarified sores, erysipelas, tetters, black bile, insanity, epilepsy, and similar disorders (320).   If none of the benefics are connected with the malefics which affect the evil, nor with the Sun and Moon in angles, these bodily diseases will be wholly incurable, and the blemishes never to be removed; and although the benefics be so configurated, the misfortune will still be incapable of remedy, if the malefics be well fortified and in elevation above them (318).

Should the benefics, however, be in elevation above the malefics, and hold tolerable situations, then the diseases will be mitigated, and the blemishes not so obvious, if more than barely discernible. The more angular or oriental the benefic or malefic may be, the more powerful will its effects be. Should Saturn be present in the configuration, the afflicted will move abroad to shew their maladies, and to complain ; and if Mercury be present, they will do so for the sake of deriving support and profit from the exhibition ; and very probably beg from door to door.

LESSON TWENTIETH.

TO BE ANSWERED BEFORE THE STUDENT PROCEEDS.

In judging the diseases of the mind, what do you notice first?

What is the effect when the rulers of the mind are unconnected?

What is the effect produced by ☌ of ☉ and ☽ ruled by Saturn ?

What is produced by Herschel afflicting Moon ?

What produces lunacy ?

What gives epilepsy ?

What is productive of insanity ?

What the producer of demoniacism ?

Which gives immoderate enthusiasm ?

When is the disease incurable ?

When curable ?

What produces outrageous disorganization ?

To what houses do you look for diseases, &c. ?

What produce external blemishes and disorders ?

What causes the loss of an eye ?

Which give total blindness ?

What gives blemishes in the face?

What causes impediments in speech ?

What gives apoplexy ?

What produces disease of the head ?

What produce lameness ?

What gives death by robbers ?

What by fire ?

What by suffocation ?

What by drowning ?

CHAPTER XXII.

RICHES, OR FORTUNE OF WEALTH.

336 Observe the position of the ⊕, ☽, and ☉, and the strength of the planet ruling ⊕, for if the dispositor of pars. be strong, dignified, and elevated, then the native will have considerable fortune in obtaining wealth, especially if the ☉ and ☽ give testimony, by being angular, or with eminent fixed stars, and well aspected by the benefics, the native will enjoy durable wealth.

337 *Saturn* gives wealth by means of buildings, navigation, agriculture, gardening, carting, butchering, and anything connected

with minerals.   Saturn, well configured, not in ☌ or Par. with ⊕ and ♃, or strong in the 4th, will cause riches by inheritance, legacy, particularly when angular and above the Earth, and ♃ occidental in double bodied signs, and receive the application of the ☽, the native will be adopted, and become the heir of others.

338 *Jupiter* has most power to give wealth.   If Jupiter be with ⊕, and in good aspect with the ☽, and angular, especially in the 1st, the native will become rich.   Jupiter contributes riches by the means of office, government, church preferment, law, legacy, patrimony, or by offices of trust.   If Jupiter be ill aspected by the luminaries, especially the ☽ in ☍ to ♃, he causes poverty through extravagance.

339 *Mars* in the same way, gives riches by means of warfare, military command.   The luminaries in bad aspect to Mars is highly unfortunate, but if Jupiter or Venus assist, the native will advance himself against all opposition.

340 *Mercury* gives riches by science and by trade ; but Mercury afflicted by Herschel, causes losses by public bodies, and by writing, and sudden accidents ; no success in books or business, and if Mercury be highly afflicted, gives imprisonment and poverty ; Mercury in good aspect of ⊕, ☽ and ☉, declares success in most things.

341 *Venus* being primary significator of riches, they come by the means of friends, by the dowry of wives, or by other gifts proceeding from women ; and being angular, unafflicted, gives preferment and good success, also if she be well aspected and not afflicted by position.

342 The best testimonies for riches are the ☉, ☽, and ⊕, angular, or with good fixed stars, in good aspect with each other, and one of them culminating, and especially the Moon ; all the planets above the Earth, and the benefics more angular (or in 10th, 11th, and 1st), than the malefics—many planets angular ; the ☊ is fortunate—☉ gives wealth by preferment, office, command, gifts, or dignity ; the ☽, by navigation, learning, the common people, and by women ; ☉ unafflicted △ ☽, rich.

343 Signs of poverty are the luminaries afflicted cadent, the ☽ combust or impeded by ☉, especially in the 2nd—all the planets under the Earth, many troubles in youth—many planets R., and the disposer of ⊕ afflicted—☍ in the 2nd or lord of 2nd R., or an unfortunate, weak in 2nd—♄ or ♂ angular, is naturally evil.   If there be a mixture of these circumstances, the native will have a middling portion of riches—♄ with the ☽, especially in an angle, is the worst of positions, and denotes poverty or ruin.

344 Should other planets, than those which rule the ⊕, exhibit testimonies of dominion, the wealth will be permanent ; but, on the other hand, if stars of an adverse condition should either be in

elevation above the ruling places, or ascend after them, the wealth will not continue. The general period of its duration, is, however, to be calculated by means of arcs of directions. The significators of riches oriental, swift, the native will be rich in youth, *et vice versa.*

LESSON TWENTY-FIRST.

QUESTIONS TO BE ANSWERED BEFORE THE STUDENT PROCEEDS.

How do you judge of wealth ?

Which produce most wealth ?

By what means do people become rich by Saturn ?

By Jupiter ?

By the Sun ?

By Mars ?

By Mercury ?

By Venus ?

What is productive of poverty ?

What shews insolvency ?

What will give legacy ?

What shews riches in youth ?

Which are bicorporeal signs ?

Which are the best testimony for riches ?

What do you mean by ascending after ?

What is meant by preascending ?

What produce mediocrity of wealth ?

CHAPTER XXIII.

NOTORIETY, OR FORTUNE OF RANK.

345 RULE.—The disposition of the luminaries and the respective familiarity (p, 13) exercised by the planets attending the ☉, ☽, and M.C., are to be considered as indicative of the degree of notoriety or fortune of rank or dignity.

346 Should Sun or Moon be found in masculine signs, well aspected, and in angles, or if only one of them, the Sun by day, or the Moon by night, be in an angle, and at the same time attended by three or more good stars, the Sun by oriental, but the Moon by occidental, and all these attendant stars in angles, or well configurated to the midheaven, and the luminaries in good aspect to each other, the native will become great, powerful, and mighty in the world ; and even yet more abundantly so, provided the configurations made by the attendant stars with the M.C. be dexter.

347 But when both luminaries may not be found in masculine signs, as before said (346), but the Sun only in a masculine, and the Moon only in a feminine sign, and only one, Sun or Moon, posited in the M.C., the other concomitant circumstances still existing in the mode above described, the natives will become governors, chief-magistrates, having absolute dominion and government, invested with the sovereignty of life and death.

348 The Sun and Moon angular, while the attendant stars should not be actually in angles, nor bear a good aspect to the M.C., the native will still enjoy eminence, yet will attain only some limited dignity or distinction ; such as that of a delegate or local governor, magistrate, commander of an army, or dignitary of the priesthood, yet will not be invested with absolute sovereignty.

349 If neither of the luminaries be in an angle, and it happen that most of the attendant stars be either themselves in angles, or well configurated with the midheaven, the native will then not attain to any very eminent rank, yet he will take a leading part in ordinary civil and municipal affairs ; but should the attendant stars have no configuration, happily, with the angles, the native will then remain altogether undistinguished, and without advancement (85).

350 Provided that the lights be not found situated in a masculine sign, nor angular, and the meridian have no good aspect of the Sun or Moon, nor be attended by any benefics, the native born gains no fame, but lives in complete obscurity, and often in adversity (152).

351 The general appearance of exaltation or debasement of rank is to be contemplated as the foregoing, but there are gradations intermediate the two extremes, and requiring observation of the particular interchanges or variations, incident to the Sun and Moon themselves, and their attendants, and also to the dominion of the planets which compose their doryphory. The condition in which the person is born must be taken into consideration, for that sometimes may destroy the most propitious configurations, and hinder the native from rising to the most princely dignities ; yet, when the natus is well and powerfully dignified, no evil rays can conspire to rob the native wholly of his prerogative of honour, but he shall be exalted to a degree of eminence and grandeur, infinitely beyond what could have been expected from the station of life in which he was born. Should the stars be benefic, and exercise chief dominion, the dignities to be acquired will be not only more important, but also more securely established ; on the other hand, if the chief ruler of the attendant stars be claimed by the malefics (343), the dignities will be more subordinate, and more dangerous and evanescent.

352 The best positions for rising in the world are ♃ in the M.C. and the ☉ and ☽ in ⚹ to each other, the ☽ △ ♃ — ☉ in 10th in ⚹ or △ to ⊕, or ☽ and ☌ —three or more planets in the same sign give a public name—two or more of the following in ♊, rising or culminating, ♃, ☉, ☽, ♀, ☿, or even ♂ —all the planets above the Earth in their dignities—☉, ♂, ♃, or ♀, in ⚹ M.C. from the 12th cusp—☽ rising in ⚹. △ of ☉, ♀, or ♃, or with fixed stars of their nature—the ☉ in ♋, the ☽ in ♏ in ☌ of ♃, or in △ with him from ♓—☉ or ☽ in ☌ of Regulus, or Arista, and ♃ in 10th, in △ to ☉, ☽, ♂, or ♀, rises to princely honour—favourites of nobles when

ruler of the Ascendant in $\ast$ or $\triangle$ of $\odot$, and oriental; or in $\triangle$ of ruler of M.C., ♂ in good aspect of $\odot$.

353 The species of dignity may be inferred by observing the peculiar qualities of the attendant ruling stars. And, if—

Saturn have chief dominion of the doryphory, the power and authority derived therefrom will lead to some wealth, but fleeting honour. If Saturn afflicts the M.C., the native meets with disgrace; and if in M.C., and not extremely well aspected, brings the native to shame and beggary (141). Saturn in square or opposition of M.C., Sun, or Jupiter, the honour will not be durable.

354 *Jupiter* ruler of the attendant stars (338), notoriety will come from gentlemen, by presents and honours. Jupiter in the 10th house, if not much afflicted, will alone cause the native to do extremely well in the world, and arrive at distinction and wealth.

355 *Mars* ruler of the doryphory, honour will consist in commanding armies (if there be honour in murder); however, the native is sure to become an " eminent scoundrel " in this (curse of nations) in obtaining victories, and in over-aweing the vanquished. If in the M.C., or on the cusp, the native will be a warlike character, and become eminent in chemistry, &c.

356 *Venus* ruler of the concomitant stars, will have the prerogative of giving the predilection to honour through ladies and feminine acquirements (341). If on M.C., she renders the native respectable, unless in ill aspect to Saturn, then mean and dissipated in privacy. She partakes very much with those planets to which she is in aspect, and a correct judgment of her effects can be formed only by taking this into full consideration; if ill aspected by Mars, the native is not chaste.

357 *Mercury*, honours proceeding from Mercury will be intellectual, superintending education and study, and directing the management of business, as foreman, manager, according as Mercury is strongly or (167) weakly situated.

358 *Herschel* ruler of the attendant stars, or chief governor of the dignity of honour, then the native rises by public bodies, a town or government officer, by science, or by engineering.

LESSON TWENTY-SECOND.

QUESTIONS FOR EXAMINATION BEFORE THE STUDENT PROCEEDS.

How do you judge of notoriety or rank?

Which is the house of honour?

Which is the strongest angle?

What have you to notice on the luminaries?

Which are masculine signs?

Which feminine?

When several stars claim prerogative in honour, which do you consider?

What happens when neither luminary is angular?

What does Jupiter produce?

What is the honour produced by Saturn ?

What is produced by Mars ?

What shews obscurity ?

What are the best positions for rising in the world ?

What is the effect of Saturn afflicting the midheaven ?

If Jupiter presides, what are the effects ?

What is the honour produced by Mars ?

What will occur when Venus is ruler of the concomitant stars ?

If she is afflicted by Mars ?

What are the honours of Mercury?

What does Herschel produce ?

What would the Sun produce ?

What the Moon ?

CHAPTER XXIV.

THE QUALITY OF EMPLOYMENT.

359 RULE 1.—The dominion of the employment, or profession, is claimed by the Sun, the sign on the M.C. or a planet in the M.C., and that planet which makes its oriental appearance nearest to the Sun, and especially when receiving the application of the Moon. If one planet be in the M.C., and also makes its nearest appearance before the Sun, it has at once the prerogative of employment.

360 RULE 2.—If, however, there should be one planet presenting its nearest appearance to the Sun, and another near the M.C., or configured happily thereto, or to the Moon, both then must be noticed ; and whichever of these claimants has greater rights of dominion, that which has greater sway must be preferred. But where there is not one near the Sun, nor in the M.C., nor in good aspect to the cusp of M.C., then take that which is ruler of the M.C., as lord of the employment ; it is, however, only some occasional occupation which can be thus denoted, because persons born under such a configuration most commonly remain at leisure, and unemployed.

361 If *Herschel* alone rule, causes employment out of the common course of life, whence he so generally conduces to the study of astrology, phrenology, geology, chemistry, astronomy (169).

362 *Saturn* has special influence on all businesses relating to ancient matters, buildings, architecture, agriculture, &c., and masons, and all those of a heavy, dirty, mean, or laborious occupation, and those wherein money is obtained with great difficulty (170).

363 *Jupiter*, sole ruler, denotes offices of trust, and honourable as well as lucrative occupations (171) ; he particularly denotes preferment either in the law or the church, and favour of the great (354).

364 *Mars* denotes all trades or occupations wherein fire, metals, or sharp instruments are used (172) ; the army, and military affairs relative to the army (164) ; also all ingenious and mechanical trades ; in ♋ or ♓, naval men.

365 *Venus* denotes all elegant occupations, and polite arts, whether relating to dress, decoration, jewels, ornaments, music, or such like, peculiar to the fair sex (166), or the luxuries of the great (174), dealers in grocery, botany, tinctures, aromatic waters, wines, cordials, and they make excellent medical doctors, and will be well to deal in the above.

366 *Mercury* is the author herein of all literary occupations, polite arts, and those of a scientific nature, students in law, physic, or divinity, or connected with writing, books, travelling, messages, papers (167), or nimble, active, but ingenious and light and easy occupations (175).

367 The *Moon* denotes various professions, according to the sign in which she is ; of her own nature, she denotes trades or professions where great changes or frequent alterations are necessary. In ♋, ♏, or ♓, she denotes those relating to the sea or naval occupations, dealing in fluids or liquids ; in other signs her nature is altered accordingly (168).

368 The *Sun* produces love of rule and dominion, and honourable employments, either under the state or under some public body of men (173).

MERCURY'S *signification when joined with others.*

369 Mercury and Saturn conjoined, persons then born will become managers of the affairs of others, or will be engaged in temples, for the sake of their fanaticism ; also lawyers, counsellors, stationers, dealers in antiquities, and those employed in the lower offices of state. ☿ S □, □, Ses □, ♄, denotes professed thieves, born to inherit the gallows, potters, turners. ☿ with ♂, sailors, shepherds, carvers, quarry masons, gravestone cutters, curriers, milk and cheese sellers.

370 Mercury ruler, and Jupiter conjoined, they will be painters, orators, pleaders in argument, barristers, bankers' clerks, and occupied with eminent personages, and parish clerks ; in ☌, very serious in religious professions, he may become an ambassador, excellent merchant.

VENUS, *mixed with other planets.*

371 Venus, ruler, and Saturn add his testimony to hers, he will cause persons to be employed in matters belonging to amusements, garments, apparel, and decoration (166); and will also produce

tailors, apothecaries, and learned tradesmen, publicans, jugglers, sorcerers, and charlatans, and all such as practise similarly ; both ill affected, they become harlots, &c.

372 Venus ruler, and Jupiter assist, persons attending exhibitions, mercers, priests, superintendents of religious ceremonies, haberdashers, bishops (171), and will be advanced in honour through female interest to some trust under government.

MARS *mixed with other planets.*

373 Mars ruler, and Sun being configurated, will produce persons who operate by means of fire ; in a nocturnal geniture, a soldier (172); especially if ☉ be in ♉ or ♌, or ☉ be near M.C., or aspect to M.C., also cooks ; huntsmen, as well as those who work in copper, brass, and other metals, founders, by mechanic melting, burning, and casting. If ♂ be separated from ☉, he will make shipwrights, smiths, agriculturalists, stonemasons, carpenters, and subordinate labourers; if in ☌ of ☉, carpenters of the highest order ; ☽ with ♂ make butchers, brewers, dyers, fishmongers.

374 Mars ruler, and Saturn bear testimony, persons will become mariners, workers in wells, vaults, or mines, plasterers, painters, whitewashers, keepers of beasts or cattle, cooks or butchers, tanners, and attendants on baths or exhibitions. Mars and Saturn afflicting each other, make sweeps, day-labourers, millers, bailiffs, charcoal burners, gas burners (170).

375 Mars ruler, and Jupiter join testimony, they will be soldiers, tobacconists, or mechanics, collectors of revenues, inn-keepers, toll-gatherers ; in conjunction, and Mars be the stronger, he may be a lawyer, and a professor of religion, or a parish clerk.

MERCURY *and* VENUS *co-mixed.*

376 Further, should it happen that two arbiters of employment may be found together, and provided they should be ☿ and ♀, will then produce musicians, melodists, dancers, poets, weavers, mimics, orators, actors, comedians, scholastic teachers, modellers in wax, painters, artists, musical instrument makers, and sculptors, if Mars aspect Mercury. If Venus be lady of the 2nd, gains a fortune by the above. And if Saturn join testimony with Mercury and Venus, the preparation of the sale of female ornaments, toymen, jewellers, will be added to the foregoing occupations; Jupiter in connection with Mercury and Venus, persons will become administrators of justice, magistrates, senators, instructors of youth, and more especially when ♊ or ♎ is on the M.C., and Mercury rises nearest before the Sun ; in the 12th, administers of public affairs. If Mercury be R. with Venus, they make excellent singers and music masters.

MERCURY *and* MARS *joint rulers.*

377 Mercury and Mars together be lords of the employment, persons will become statuaries, armour makers, carvers, gilders, engravers, sculptors, modellers of animals, wrestlers, boxers, duellists, surgeons, spies or informers, adulterers, busy in crime, and forgers. If Mercury be most powerful, they will be scientific; surveyors, printers, die-sinkers; and if Mars be strongest, they will be more violent or wickedly inclined, and cruel in their practices (164). If Saturn join Mercury and Mars, they will be thieves (especially if the Moon be in ill aspect to Mercury), and swindlers; if Saturn be in 7th, he will be hanged; if in the 12th, transported; if Moon be in ill aspect to Mars, they will be robbers or assassins, which is far worse if Venus, at the same time, assist in the malignancy of the configuration (164). If Jupiter join Mercury and Mars, he will engage persons in honourable warfare, and in industry, making them cautious and diligent in business, curious in foreign matters, and deriving profit from their pursuits. But Jupiter afflicted by Mercury and Mars, jangling attorneys, and encouragers of all undermining illegal proceedings.

MARS *and* VENUS *joint rulers of profession.*

378 Venus and Mars rule together, persons will become dyers, dealers in unguents, and perfumers, barbers, gardeners, workers in tin, lead, gold, and silver; also combatants, dancers in armour, dealers in medical drugs, agriculturalists, and physicians (174). Saturn with ♀ or ♂, will produce persons attendant on animals consecrated to religion, chapel keepers, also grave-diggers, sextons, and undertakers, curates, and fanatics occupied in religious ceremonies, lamentations and blood (170). If Jupiter add testimony to ♀ and ♂, the persons will become regulators of sacrifices, augurs, holders of sacred offices, governors placed over women, bastile or prison-keepers, and interpreters; and they will derive support from such occupations (171). If Herschel join with ♀ and ♂, bath-keepers, keepers of public establishments, police officers, constables, chemists, druggists, and philosophers (169). If Sun join testimony to ♀ and ♂, produce government office holders (173).

379 The Moon actually occupying the place regulating the employment, she causes many changes (168), and after the conjunction, continue in connection with ☿, and in ♉, ♊, ♋, ♐, ♑, or ♓, then she will produce sagacious and penetrating persons, astrologers, phrenologists, astronomers, and doctors. This is the more likely if ♅ be strong and aspected by ☿, or even the ☽. And if in ♎, ♈, or ♌, Luna will produce fanatics, and false religionists, enthusiastic preachers, and fills the mind with idle and immoderate ideas of gain by each respective business or avocation (281).

380 The properties of the signs, in which the lords of the employment may be posited, are also influential in varying the employment.

If in ♈, weak, he will make a good cattle-dealer, groom, farrier, grazier, &c. ; if strong, a coach-maker, veterinary surgeon, &c., where he has to do with cattle or horses in a respectable way.

381 If the significator be in ♉, then husbandry will best suit him, or gardening, corn dealing, grazing, &c., or if ♀ be the significator, such things as appertain to women's affairs, a soap boiler, fuller of cloth, scourer, and slubber.

382 If the significator be in ♊, he will make a writer, clerk, bailiff, &c., or a surveyor, painter, astronomer, astrologer, geometer, schoolmaster, traveller, &c.

383 If he be in ♋, he will be fitted for a variety of occupations ; but he will be likely to go to sea, or to deal in liquids, such as wines, beer, &c., and he will be fond of political distinction.

384 If he be in ♌, he will make a good horse-jockey, groom, cabman, or coachman ; a smith, watchmaker, glass-blower, huntsman, or cow doctor ; or to do with any trade which uses fire.

385 In ♍, he will make a good secretary to a person in power, a schoolmaster, accountant, stationer, printer ; he will be an excellent politician, or be a good astrologer, clever in whatever he takes up.

386 If in ♎, he will be a good poet or orator, singer or musician, silkman or linendraper, seller of commodities over the counter, confectioner, wine seller, &c.

387 If in ♏, he may prove a good surgeon, apothecary, or physician, or a brazier, founder, brewer, vintner, waterman, or maltster.

388 If in ♐, he will do very well to make a clergyman, to study chemistry, to buy and sell cattle, or to be a cook or butcher.

389 If he be in ♑, a good chandler, victualler, farrier, farmer, dealer in wool, lead, or farming commodities.

390 If he be in ♒, an excellent ship carpenter ; and if any planet aspect him out of a watery sign, he may prove a good sailor or ship-master, or a painter and ornamenter of ships, or a merchant, or bargeman, tide keeper, or waterman.

391 If he be in ♓, he makes a jester, singer, player, &c., brewer, fishmonger ; but generally the genius is dull, and the party given to sottishness.

392 From the foregoing rules, the various forms of employment are to be inferred, and its magnitude or importance will be manifested by the existing power of the ruling planets. For instance, if the said planets be oriental, or in angles, they will give the person eminence and authority in his employment ; but if occidental or cadent, they will render him subordinate. And should the benefics be in elevation, the employment will be important, lucrative, secure, honourable, and agreeable ; but on the other hand, if the malefics be in elevation above the lords of the employment, it will then be mean, disreputable, unprofitable, and insecure ; thus

♄ brings an adverse influence in coldness, indifference, or tardiness and in the composition or mixture of views and avocations ; and ♂ produces ill luck by audacity, presumption, and publicity in enterprise, and both ♄ and ♂ are alike hostile to proficiency and prosperity. Herschel well affected gives gain by a variety of extraordinary businesses.

393 The general period, at which any increase or diminution of the employment may take place, must, again, in this case also, be determined by the disposition of the stars, which operate the effect, towards the oriental and occidental angles. And the particular periods of success must be looked for from the arcs in active operation productive of success and honour. The general periods are to be judged as follows : the rules happily configurated in the eastern angle denotes the beginning of active business at 21 ; the midheaven, the middle portion of life, or from 30 to 45 years of age ; and the western angle, at the latter period of life, or from 40 to 55 years of age.

LESSON TWENTY-THIRD.

TO BE ANSWERED BEFORE THE STUDENT PROCEEDS.

What claim dominion of employment ?

When two planets claim sway over business, which do you take ?

What are Herschel's employments ?

What are Saturn's ?

What are Jupiter's?

What are Mars's ?

What are Venus's ?

What are Mercury's ?

What do the Moon's denote ?

What does the Sun produce ?

What does Mercury with Saturn produce?

What is the effect of Mercury and Jupiter in aspect ?

What are the effects of Jupiter and Venus combined ?

What do the Sun and Mars produce ?

What when Sol separates from Mars ?

What are the effects of Mars and Saturn ?

Of Mars and Jupiter ?

What produce musicians ?

What make the best physicians ?

What does Venus with Mars effect ?

What does Herschel with Venus and Mars produce ?

What the effects of the rulers of employment produced in each of the twelve signs ?

CHAPTER XXV.

ON MARRIAGE.

Men's Marriages.

394 RULE 1st.—Observe the position of the ☽ particularly. When the ☽ is oriental, or between the ☌ and 1st quarter,* or between the ☍ and last quarter, then men marry early in life, or to persons younger than themselves. 2nd. If the ☽ be between the last quarter and new, or between the first quarter and full, then men marry late in life, or to women older than themselves. Should the ☽ be in the latter situation, or in ☌ of ☉, afflicted by ♄, or ♅, men never marry, especially if they be stationary R. or in detriment, or if they marry, a very unhappy union. An early marriage from 17 to 21, late after 29.

395 RULE 2nd—Observe the planet assuming dominion over the 7th house and the state of ♀. 2nd. Venus in ♉, ♎, ♋, or ♌, is a small testimony of an early marriage. . If ♀ be in the same sign as the ☉, and not more than 18 degrees from his ☌, the testimony is stronger for marriage ; but the strongest testimony is ♀ or ☉ in △ or ✳ to ♂, chiefly when the aspect is separating. 3rd. When ♄ or ♅ assume dominion over the 7th house, does not conduce to an early marriage, not even if at the same time the (♅ or ♄) be well configurated to any planet, the ☉ and ☽ excepted.

Number of Wives.

396 If the Moon be oriental (394), and especially angular in ♊, ♐, or ♓, they become widowers, and marry more than once ; or ☽ in this situation, and in application to several planets, and they strong in one sign, marriage occurs twice or thrice. The ☽ in any other signs, and in application to only one planet, causes men to marry only once. Also many planets in the 1st or 7th give many lovers.

Quality of the Wives.

397 Mark the planet to which the Moon first applies, by aspect ; if to ♅, there will be little domestic comfort (161), and the wife will be of a hasty temper, yet fond of science (169). Herschel in 7th discord in both courtship and marriage, and more especially if ♅ be unassisted by the good aspects of ♃, ♀, ☿, or ☉.

398 If ♄ receives the Moon's application (162), the wives whom he provides are morose and grave. If ♄ be in 7th, not very comfortable ; but he being well affected, she will be industrious, but poor, sober aud careful, laborious, but not excellent health ; if ♄

---

* Old Authors say, Oriental from 75 degrees from conjunction to within 19 degrees of opposition to Sun ; Occidental the other portion. Also from the 4th to 10th eastward is Oriental, and Occidental from 10 to 4th westward.

be in detriment, one of low mean birth ; if ♄ afflict lord of 7th, immodestly inclined, and especially if lord of 7th be in 12th.

399 If ♃ first receive the Moon's application, the wives will be decorus, well conducted, and economical ; also great agreement if ♃ be in the 7th unafflicted (163) ; but ♃ afflicted, the wife may be virtuous, but her virtues are clouded (276).   In the 8th, rich wife.

400 If ♂ first receive the Moon's application, the wife will be bold and refractory, a true friend, but desirous of being master ; but being ill affected, she will be quarrelsome and proud ; and if ♂ afflict ♀ at the same time, then she will be licentious and lustful ; and if both ♂ and ♀ be configurated to ♃, and ♂ happen to be in ☌ of ☉, she will mingle in intercourse with servants, with persons inferior in rank to herself ; should it happen that ♀ be in ☌ of ☉, she will then connect herself with her superiors (164).   ♂ in the 8th, a fortune.

401 If ♀ receive the Moon's application, the wife will be cheerful, handsome, civil, good conditioned (166) ; but if ill affected, or in the 12th, she will be imprudent, prating, arrogant, prodigal, and lustful ; Venus in the 7th, unafflicted, a good housewife ; and if connected with ♃, ♄, or ☿, she will be provident, and attached to her husband and children ; but if ♀ be afflicted, unhappiness in love, or in □ or ☍ of ☽, or in aspect to ♂, irascible, unsteady, and indiscreet, (277) ; ♀ in good aspect with ♃ or ☿, the wife will be temperate, and control her desires, and escape all reproach (279). ♀ in 8th being its ruler, rich.

402 If ☿ receive the Moon's application (167), a clever, sensible woman ; but if ☿ be ill aspected, then she will be a lying, prating, inconstant woman (280).

403 The ☽ first applying to the ☉, he being well affected, the wife will be honourable, but proud ; generous, but dressy ; humane, but affecting high things.   Being ill affected, flashy and prodigal ; vain and domineering, idle and insulting, hypocritical and foolish (165).

Corporeal appearance of the Wife.

404 The planet either posited in the 7th, or to whom the ☽ first applies by aspect, will describe the wife's person and her condition.   Considering the sign in which the planet is (267), but more especially observe the face in which that planet is, as also the face on the cusp of the 7th (Chap. VII).

From where Marry, &c.

405 If the planet to which the Moon first applies be cadent, a stranger. If that planet be ♀, lady of the 9th, in the 1st or 10th, a person born at a long distance from him ; a stranger ♀ ☌ ☉ in the 7th ; should ♀ be in familiar concurrence with ♂, ♄, or ☿, and

she be in mutual reception (p. 21), she will effect marriages between kindred by blood, but jealous ; and provided also that ♀ in ☌ of ☽, will cause him to court two sisters or other near relations ; ♀ will produce entire love affection in the parties, and if ☿ also coincide with ☽ and ♀, such affections will become publicly manifest and profitable. Again, if ♀ be with ♄, the cohabitation will be established entirely in happiness and constancy. And if Mars be in mutual reception with ♀, ♄, and ☿, he will effect marriage between persons of equal age ; and if the said position happen in the 1st or 10th house, men will become connected with their maternal aunts. And if Venus be found occidental, men will connect themselves with low women and servants ; but Mars occidental, with women of respect and rank, else with women living with other men. But if Mars be separated from Venus and Saturn, but yet in good testimony with Jupiter, then men are decorous in sexual intercourse ; if Mars attach himself to Saturn only, men will be dull and careless ; if Saturn or Herschel and Mars be connected together, and Venus and Jupiter also configured with them, then men become easily excited to indecency, yet in a secret manner. But should Saturn or Herschel be absent, and Mars with Venus alone, then licentious.

Women's Marriages.

406 RULE 1.—The ☉ is to be taken and considered in all respects the same as the ☽ in the man's nativity. 2nd.—Also the 7th house, planets therein, ♀ and ♂ must be duly considered.

407 RULE 2nd.—Should the ☉ be posited between 4th and 1st, or between the 10th and 7th, women will marry either in their own youth, or to men younger than themselves ; but if ☉ be in the other quadrants, they will either marry late in life, or to men who have passed their prime, or some years their senior.

Number of Husbands.

408 If ☉ be orientally angular and in aspect to many oriental planets in ♊, ♐, or ♓, they marry more than once. Should the ☉ be in a sign of single form, or configurated with only one oriental planet, he will cause them to enter into matrimony only once. The time of marriage will be pointed out by the number of oriental planets to which ☉ applies, and the time of marriage is known by the arcs of direction.

Quality of the Husbands.

409 Mark the planet or planets to which the Sun first applies by par. or any aspect ; for the husbands will partake of the same nature and qualities of those planets to which the configurations are made. The 7th house in part shews the description of the husband ; Jupiter therein, an excellent husband ; Saturn and

Herschel therein, not lasting concord between them, annoyances in courtship and wedlock; Sun therein, rather proud, but majestic if well dignified (165); Mercury therein, of a romantic disposition, fond of addressing several lovers at one time, but this depends on his dignity (167); Moon herein, fond of change, and removes from places for the sake of employment. Venus therein, happiness; but ♂, discord.

410 If Herschel receives the Sun's application, the husband will be of a curious temper, fond of women's company; and if Sun be in ill aspect to Herschel, the female will be long ere she marries, and will have many lovers, and danger and disgrace in courtship, especially if Herschel be in the 5th, 7th, 10th, or 11th.

411 If Saturn first receives the Sun's application, he will provide husbands steady, advantageous, industrious, sober and grave, but cold and phlegmatic (398); Sun and Saturn in good aspect, happiness; Sun, Saturn, and Mercury well configurated, profitable marriage, and the husband tolerably well off.

412 If Jupiter receives the Sun's application, the husbands will be honourable, noble-minded, and generous (165); if he be afflicted, very likely a separation after marriage, and the husband is criminally connected with other women—this never fails if Jupiter be in ♓ in the 7th, just falling into the 6th.

413 If Mars receives the Sun's application, the husband will be severe, but not void of affection, rather intractable, passionate, and arbitrary. This depends on the aspect of ☉ and ♂, and ♂ dignities (164). If the Sun has no aspect with Mars, and Mars be weak in the figure, the female does not do well in marriage; and if, at the same time, Herschel or Saturn be in ill aspect of Sol, she will not marry, or she probably will live with a man unmarried. And if Moon be afflicted by Mars, unchaste, unless Jupiter assist in good aspect. If Sol be in conjunction of Mars, and Jupiter in ill aspect to either, then the woman is mean and sordid in her desires, more especially if these planets be in masculine signs (page 16); if the configuration happen in feminine signs, then her appetite will be more passive.

414 If the Sun first appears to Venus, well affected, the husband will be amiable and handsome; if Venus be in conjunction of Saturn or Herschel, or bad aspects to them, the husband will be dull and bad tempered, but ingenious and laborious; if with Jupiter, decorous, just and honest (412); if with Mars, hasty, lustful and adulterous; and if with Mercury, they will be immodest and wanton with young persons. If Venus be in good aspect to both Jupiter and Mercury at the same time, then women will be temperate, sober, and pure in their desires (401); but Venus in aspect with Mercury alone, they will be secretly sensual. ☿ ☌ ☉, husbands profitably employed.

LESSON TWENTY-FOURTH.

TO BE ANSWERED BEFORE THE STUDENT PROCEEDS.

What do you first notice on marriage ?

What is the second rule ?

How do you judge on the number of wives ?

How do you judge of the quality of wives ?

What kind of wife does Herschel produce ?

What the character of wife Saturn provides ?

What effect has Saturn or Herschel in the 7th ?

What kind of wife does Jupiter give ?

What if he be afflicted ?

What is the wife's character under Mars ?

What if he be afflicted ?

What is the effect of Mars afflicting Venus or the Moon ?

What is produced if Mars or Venus at the same time be conjoined with Sol ?

What is the character of wives under Venus ?

What kind if Venus be afflicted ?

What is produced by Venus unafflicted in the 7th ?

What if Venus be connected with Jupiter, Saturn, or Mercury ?

What kind of wife under Mercury ?

But if Mercury be afflicted ?

What kind of wife ruled by Sol ?

What effect if Sol be ill aspected ?

How do you judge on the corporeal appearance of the wife ?

How do you judge whence the wife will come ?

How do you know the wife will be a kindred ?

When will she be a stranger ?

When older ?

When younger ?

What cause men to cohabit with other men's wives ?

What makes them openly inconstant ?

What makes some men careless of marriage ?

What produces jealousy ?

What is the significator of women's births ?

What is the second rule ?

When is the Sun oriental ?

When occidental ?

What give plurality of husbands ?

How do you judge of the quality of the husband ?

What effect if Sol be afflicted by Saturn or Herschel ?

What effect if Jupiter or Venus be in the 7th ?

Of Sol in the 7th ?

Of Mercury in the 7th

Of the Moon in the 7th ?

What kind of husband does Herschel produce ?

What are his general effects ?

What is the character of husbands under Saturn ?

What kind of husbands under Jupiter ?

What is the effect of Mars and Sol having aspect to each other ?

What is produced by Sol being in ill aspect of Herschel or Saturn ?

If the Moon be afflicted by Mars what is the effect ?

What kind of husband under Venus ?

What are the effects of Venus in aspect with other planets ?

CHAPTER XXVI.

CHILDREN.

415 RULE.—Mark well the 10th and 11th houses, planets therein, and those casting an aspect to their cusps, and to planets therein, if any. But if none of these testimonies exist, then take notice of the 4th and 5th houses in the same way.

416 Planets, or ☋, in the 5th, in good aspect to Moon and Venus, signs of the ascendant and 5th, their rulers in fruitful signs show many children, and more especially when Jupiter and Venus are in good aspect to the Moon, or ruler of the 5th.

417 Herschel, Saturn, Mars, and ☋, deny children, or allow but few. Mercury acts according as he may partake with the fruitful or barren planets or signs, and gives children if he be oriental, but withholds when occidental.

418 If the planets which give progeny (416) be so posited as described (415), and placed singly, or unaspected, give but one child ; but should they be in bicorporeal or in feminine signs, they give twins ; so likewise if they be in watery signs, will produce two or more children at one birth. If they (415) are masculine, or in aspect to Sol, or in masculine signs, they cause males ; but otherwise, if femininely constituted, females.

419 If children are promised, yet Herschel, Saturn, Mars, and ☋ in the 5th, especially in ♌ or ♍, the native will lose children, and have much trouble by them. Saturn in 5th, stubborn ; Mars therein, bold and refractory ; Herschel makes the offspring very eccentric ; ☋, unhealthful ; Sol in the 5th, afflicted ; the Moon therein, afflicted by any planet in 8th or 12th, death to the children.

420 *Barrenness* is the result when the malefics and the Sun are rulers of offspring, and posited as before (417), and in barren signs, without the benefics concurring, or being most elevated, a total privation is indicated ; but should they (417) be in feminine or prolific signs, or supported by the testimony of the benefics, children will then be granted, yet they will be liable to disease and short lived. Sol in ill aspect to Herschel, or Saturn—or ruler of the 5th R, or conjunction of Sol in ill aspect to Mars or Saturn, and especially if these latter be peregrine. Except powerful testimonies to overpower the Moon in the husband's, and the Sun in the wife's nativity, both applying to Saturn, Herschel or ☋, in the 5th, they will have no family. The Moon in ♈, ♌, ♑, in evil aspect to Saturn, Mars, Sun, ☋, or Herschel, denotes barrenness to both parties.

421 If, however, planets of each condition should be configurated with, and have prerogative in prolific signs, there will happen a rejection of children, or will rear but very few ; in the same pro-

portion as they may be able by being oriental or angular ; more elevated or successively ascending (332 and 333).

422 When the rulers of the 10th and 11th are givers of offspring, and are oriental or in good places of the figure, the children will become respectable ; but if occidental, or in evil places of the figure, the children will be undistinguished and obscure. Moreover, should the said rulers be in concord with the $\oplus$ and with the 1st, the children will be amiable and beloved by their parents, and inherit their parents' substance ; but if these be unaspected, beneficially, the children vicious, incorrigible, losing their parents' esteem, and, probably ultimately, their inheritance of substance.

423 Should the givers of offspring be happily configured among themselves, they foreshow brotherly love and harmony, and they will mutually assist one another ; more especially if the 3rd house be possessed by good planets.   But if the significators afflict each other, they will excite in the family hatred, deceit, and treachery. The particular destiny of children can only be deduced by their own individual horoscopes.

LESSON TWENTY-FIFTH.

QUESTIONS TO BE ANSWERED BEFORE THE STUDENT ENTERS ON THE NEXT PORTION.

What is the rule for judging of children ?

Which are barren signs ?

Which are the fruitful ?

Which are the fruitful planets ?

Which are the barren ?

Which are the givers of offspring ?

Which testimonies give many children ?

Which give twins ?

Which are signs of barrenness ?

Which is the effect of Mercury ?

Which are the watery signs ?

Which are the masculine signs ?

Which the feminine ?

What are the effects of the malefics in the 5th ?

What give death to offspring ?

What are the signs of barrenness ?

What are the effects if the testimonies of children are conflicting in prerogative ?

What make children respectable?

What keep them undistinguished ?

What makes them amiable and agreeable ?

When are they vicious ?

What cause hatred in a family ?

CHAPTER XXVII.

ON CONSENTANEOUS FRIENDSHIP AND ENMITY.

With regard to friendship and enmity, it may be observed that great and lasting familiarities, or disagreements, are respectively called sympathies and antipathies ; while the smaller, such as arise occasionally, and subsist for a short time only, are denominated casual intimacies and strifes ; the whole are to be contemplated according to the following rules. Indications of great and lasting friendships or enmities may be perceived by observation of the ruling places exhibited in the respective nativities of both the persons between whom the friendship or enmity may exist.

Friendship.

424 RULE I.—Observe the Sun, the Moon, the Part of Fortune, and the Ascendant. Should all these be in the same sign, or in mutual reception, or the two ascendant be in the same sign, then there will be fixed and indissoluble friendship. If the above significators be in good aspect with the same significators in the other's nativity, then there will be minor friendship, or mere acquaintanceship. Fortunes in the 1st, 5th, 7th, 9th, and 11th houses, many friends. Many planets in good aspect of each other in the 11th, many friends.

425 Saturn and Jupiter transiting each other's place in the two nativities, produce friendship by agreements or engagements, relating either to building, agriculture, covetousness, or by the joint inheritance in fortune, or by meeting in societies or companies (170). Saturn and Venus, friendship on account of kindred, but it soon grows cold. Saturn and Mercury transiting each other's place, or good aspects of each other, produce friendship by conversation, business, profit, science, or confederacy.

426 Jupiter and Herschel cause friendship by meeting in one church, or by church discipline, meeting in public bodies, town offices, undertaking public concerns. Jupiter and Mars create friendship by means of dignities, combating against others. Jupiter and Venus create friendship by means of females, ecclesiastics, or attendant on charity and religious dealings. Jupiter and Mercury, friendship by means of science, painting, poetry, and philosophical inclinations (305). Public writers of every description should have Mercury unafflicted, and assisted by aspect of Jupiter and Venus, or they strive in vain to come at eminence, or to gain the public esteem.

427 Mars and Venus cause friendship by means of amours, dissipation to do wickedness (307). Venus and Mercury produce communion by means of the arts and sciences (310), by mutual interest in literature, or by females, also by being school-fellows.

428 Sol, in the place of any planet in another's nativity, makes friendship for honesty, honour (278). Jupiter, for utility (276). Venus, for pleasure. Moon, according to the conveniency of her nature as she may be affected with other planets. Venus, in one where the Moon is with the other native, sure and lasting friendship.

Enmities.

429 RULE.—Consider well the discordant positions of the malefics in each other's nativities, for if they are not in accordant familiarity (200) then great and lasting enmity between the natives whose nativities we investigate. If the places of the Sun, Moon, or Mercury be afflicted by conjunction or ill aspects (201) of Saturn, Mars, or Herschel, the native will have a rough, turbulent, and quarrelsome life, and many enemies.

430 Saturn and Mars produce enmity and contention, and often foreshow premeditated fraud and villainy. Jupiter and Mars produce enmity by politics, improper preferment, or interested measures of government. Mars and Mercury cause enmity by similar interest in business, or by the same parties following the same avocation. In these cases Mercury has great power, for wherever he is afflicted by aspect or position, the native is liable to much scandal, reproach, and vituperative abuse.

Power of their Friendship.

431 The greatest sympathies that can exist in two nativities, is by having Jupiter or Venus upon the place of the Sun, Moon, Part of Fortune, or Ascendant in each other ; and the luminaries of the latter upon the fortunes of the former. Jupiter, Sol, Venus, or Luna in the 11th, essentially strong, and in good aspect (200) with the ruler of the 1st, strong friendship. When Mercury or ☍ is in the 11th, false friends. The Sun and Moon, the Moon and Mercury, or the Sun and Mercury, posited in each other's places, the friendship is not very substantially fixed, the acquaintanceship will be fluctuating. If Saturn, Jupiter, Venus, Herschel, and Mars are in each other's places, there will be dissensions mixed with a kind of friendship ; and friendship seems to cease while the malefics of one is traversing the benefics of the other. He loves most whose ruler of the ascendant is a benevolent planet, or whose ruler of the 1st applies to good aspect of the other. They do not long agree whose sign ascending is the same sign on the 12th, 6th, or 8th of the other.

Power of their Enmity.

432 Ruler of the 12th ℞, or in detriment to the 6th, the native overcomes. Saturn or Mars in the 12th strong, argues the enemies die first. Who has ♊, ♐, or ♒ ascending, makes himself enemies. Saturn in the ascendant, or ruler thereof, in one nativity, being on the cusp of the 7th in another, then perfect hatred, and the latter will be the injured person. The greatest antipathy is where the infortunes in the one possess the place of the luminaries in the other ; and the luminaries in the latter possess the places of the infortunes in the former.

Their comparative intensity or relaxation of vigour is to be distinguished by the situation of the places which they occupy with regard to the four mentioned places (424).

LESSON TWENTY-SIXTH.

QUESTIONS TO BE ANSWERED BEFORE THE STUDENT PROCEEDS.

Repeat the rule which shows travelling.

What is the effect of fortunes in the 11th house?

What are the effects of Saturn and Jupiter transiting each other's place?

What the effects of Saturn and Venus? Of Saturn and Mercury?

What are the causes of friendship produced by Jupiter and Herschel? By Jupiter and Mars? By Jupiter and Venus? By Jupiter and Mercury?

What gains public writers friends?

What sort of friendship is produced by Mars and Venus? By Venus and Mercury?

What are the objects of Sol's friendship? What by Jupiter? By Venus? By the Moon?

Repeat the rule denoting enmity.

What give a quarrelsome life and many enemies?

What cause enmity between Saturn and Mars? Between Jupiter and Mars? Between Mars and Mercury?

What produce the greatest sympathies?

What is the effects of Mercury and ☋ in the 11th house?

What give fluctuating friendship?

What produce dissensions with friendship?

Who loves most?

What show short agreement?

Which enemy overcomes?

What produce the greatest antipathy?

How are you to judge of the intensity of enmity?

CHAPTER XXVIII.

ON TRAVELLING.

433 RULE.—Observe the power and position of the Sun, the Moon, Mars, and the Part of Fortune. If they are most of them cadent, and especially in ♈, ♋, ♎, or ♑, then the native will travel. The 9th, 3rd, 12th, or 6th, movable, are tokens of travelling, especially if the Sun and Moon are both cadent. The ⊕ alone cadent will cause many journeys. Mars descending, more particularly in the 9th, especially if he happen to be in square or opposition of Sun or Moon, produces tramping or itinerating.

434 The Moon descending from the 7th, 9th, or on the 1st or 10th, causes journeys and changes of residence, especially in ♈ or ♊ or ♐, and short journeys if in ♋, ♍, ♎, ♑, or ♓. The Moon

in any part of the figure, ♊, ♐, or ♓, causes frequent changes of residence, but usually these changes happen very unexpectedly, or in a strange and extraordinary way ; generally advantageous in ♓.

435 Mercury angular in movable or bicorporeal signs, gives restlessness of mind, and a predilection for travelling. If these, Mars, Mercury, and Moon be just setting in ♋, ♏, or ♓, cause voyages, or often travelling, long residence near the water. Also, the same, should Mercury and the Moon be in conjunction or reception, or both in the 1st, 3rd, or 9th, the native will travel long journeys.

The Good or Ill attending the Travelling.

436 Should Jupiter or Venus rule the places of the Sun and Moon, but more especially the Moon, and in good aspect thereto, they will render the journey agreeable, as well as free from danger, and the engagements abroad lucrative, and the return home speedy and unobstructed. And, provided Mercury also be present with Jupiter or Venus, utility, presents, and honour will likewise be derived from the journey.   Saturn in good aspect gives inheritance ; Mars, honours and office ; Herschel, a public situation.

437 The significators of travelling in ill aspect with Herschel, Saturn, Sun, Mars, and these a long distance from each other, or ascend after the other significators, then the journeys will be unfortunate, and the return replete with difficulties. Mercury in ill aspect, danger by piracy, imprisonment, or by poison ; Venus, unpleasant travelling.   The afflictor in the 12th, danger of imprisonment ; in the 2nd or 3rd, treachery by kindred or neighbours, and so on as the other houses signify (199). Being in ♋, ♏, or ♓, mischief by shipwreck, storms, drowning, or falling into desolate and inaccessible places ; in ♉, ♌, ♏, or ♒, by precipices, or tempests, or contrary winds ; in ♈, ♎, or ♑, by want of food and other necessaries, and through sickness ; in ♊, ♍, by the attack of robbers, pirates, or savages, especially if Mars or Mercury be the afflictors ; in ♐, by wild beasts and cattle. The particular times for good or ill luck are known by the Arcs of Directions.

Cause of Travelling.

438 The Sun or Moon in the 7th, or just setting, the native moves from different places for the gaining of situation, employment, and out of the way of public enemies. The significator of travelling, especially ♂ and ⊕, must be observed in what house they are posited, and of what house Mars is ruler, and so judge ; in the 2nd, he travels for the sake of gain ; in the 10th, for honour, trade, &c. (199); if in the 1st, he has an inclination to see fresh places. To judge further, take notice what kind of things the rulers of journeys signify, and say those are the things for which the peregrinator wishes to travel.

Whither he had better Travel.

439 The quarter of the globe to which he had better tend his steps is judged from the position of Sun and Moon. If the luminaries be placed in the 1st, the travels will take place in the eastern quarters of the world; if in the 10th, towards the south; if in the 7th, towards the west; if in the 4th, travel will then be prosecuted in the northern parts. And should the signs productive of travelling be ♊, ♐, or ♓, journeys will be constantly repeated; in the other signs, peregrinations will take place after retarded intervals. The countries to which he had better travel are chiefly those subjected to the signs of the 1st, 2nd, 9th, 10th, and 11th; or those signs in which Jupiter, Venus, ☊, or ⊕ are located at birth; but those in which the ☋, Herschel, Saturn, or Mars are placed must be avoided; as also those subjected to the sign of the 4th, 6th, 7th, 8th, or 12th houses.

LESSON TWENTY-SEVENTH.

QUESTIONS FOR EXAMINATION BEFORE THE STUDENT PROCEEDS.

What is the rule for producing travelling?

What does the Moon signify?

Where is she to be placed?

What is the effect of Saturn and Mars afflicting the significators of travelling?

What signs are productive of travelling?

Which of the houses produce travelling?

How do you judge for what the native travels?

To which quarters had he better go?

Which are ill houses for travelling?

What share has Mercury in travelling?

What are the effects when Jupiter and Venus have dominion over travelling?

And what when Mercury is present with them?

What effect has the Part of Fortune?

What has bicorporeal to do with journeys?

What the tropical? What the fixed signs? And what the humane?

CHAPTER XXIX.

THE KIND OF DEATH.

It remains to treat of the species of death, which are to be judged, in a great measure, by the Rules already laid down in CHAP. VII, whether death will ensue from an oriental or occidental position (245). The place of the meeting of the killing rays must be considered to point out the character of death to a certain extent (199).

The configuration of the stars, the properties of the aforesaid (241) anaretic places, and the nature of the signs, as in CHAP. IX, and of the faces, as in CHAP. IV, are, also, all of them co-operative.

440 RULE.—DEATH IS ALWAYS CREATED BY A TRAIN OF EVIL DIRECTION TO THE HYLEG AND OTHER VITAL POINTS. And remember, that if the hyleg be not afflicted, the life will not be destroyed, however evil the directions, and however much they may injure health (254). If the ascendant and the hyleg be well aspected, and if Jupiter, Venus, Moon, or Mercury, well aspected, be placed in the 8th house, the native dies a natural death. The nature of the death is to be judged of chiefly by the second direction in operation at the time :—

441 *Herschel* cannot kill by himself, but his ill aspects assist to destroy life ; and where they occur, will produce something sudden, singular, or extraordinary in the nature of the death (177), often by drowning, sometimes by machinery, which will often happen while the native is in his employment (450).

441A *Neptune* will help to destroy life when in ill aspects to the hyleg or the giver of life.

442 *Saturn* causes all cold diseases, colic, coughs, iliac passion, agues, rheumatism, consumption, dropsy, flux, &c. ; and if violent symptoms are perceived, he brings death by blows, falls, suffocation (451), the latter especially in Scorpio. Take notice also of the sign in which the planet is placed (177).

443 *Jupiter* brings death by quinsy, impure state of the blood, liver complaints, spasms, diseases of the lungs (178). If violence attend the death, it may be by sentence of a judge.

444 *Mars* causes death by fever, wounds, spitting of blood, erysipelas, childbirth, &c. If by violence, he kills by gun-shot or sword, suicide, or fire ; by breaking blood vessels, by bites of mad dogs, syphilis (179).

445 *Venus* produces death by cancer, ringworms, scurvy, dysentery, diabetes, or wasting away, fistulas, and putrid diseases. If violence attend, she causes poison (181).

446 *Mercury* produces death by fury, madness, melancholy, epilepsy, coughs, and obstructions. If violence attend, death is caused by accident, sport, or by robbers (462).

447 *The Moon.* When the ascendant or Sun is hyleg, the Moon will assist in causing death by cold phlegmatic diseases, and if she be placed in ♋, ♏, or ♓, by drowning (183).

448 *The Sun* will assist to cause death by his ill aspects to the ascendant or Moon if either be hyleg, and then he acts like Mars, and if in Leo will produce death by fire, if other testimonies accord (180).

On a Violent Death.

449 When the lords of death may fully possess their own peculiar and natural properties, and when Herschel, Saturn, Mars, may be in elevation above them, death will ensue in the modes above detailed, and in the ordinary course of nature. But a violent, or remarkable death happens when both the malefics attack both Sun and Moon, or have only one, and at the same time the ascendant be afflicted (250). If an evil planet be placed in the 8th house, it is an additional testimony of a violent death ; but if it be there when the other testimonies do not occur, then it merely shows a painful death. Saturn causes slow lingering deaths, and Mars and Herschel cause them to be more sudden.

450 *Herschel* by machine accidents, as on railways, drinking, bathing, shipwreck ; by the mob (441).

451 TO 461 If Saturn be in fixed signs, oriental, and in semi-square, square, sesquisquare, or opposition of Sun, he will produce death by suffocation, occasioned either by multitudes of people, or by hanging, or strangulation ; so likewise, should he be occidental, and the Moon be succeedent to him, he will operate the same effects. If he be posited in bestial signs, the native will be destroyed by wild beasts ; and if Jupiter also offer testimony, being at the same time afflicted, the death will then occur in public, by day. If Saturn be in the 1st, in opposition to the Sun or Moon when setting, will cause death in prison ; if Saturn be configurated with Mercury, and especially with Serpentis, in the 4th face of Scorpio, Saturn will produce death by venomous wounds or bites, and by reptiles and wild beasts ; and, should Venus also attach herself to Saturn and Mercury thus combined, death will ensue by poison or female treachery. If Saturn or Herschel be in ♋, ♍, ♏, or ♓, and evilly configurated with the Moon, he will operate death by means of water, intoxication, by drowning and suffocation ; and if found near Argo, by shipwreck. Should Saturn or Herschel be in ♈, ♋, ♎, or ♑, and the Sun or Mars in conjunction or opposition, death will be caused by the fall of houses or buildings ; and, if posited in the midheaven, death will happen by falls from heights or precipices ; if in the 4th, by being buried under the earth, &c.—These are the various effects of Saturn and Herschel, when configurated as described. Mars with the Pleiades, and Saturn with Regulus, denote danger of a violent death. Mars in conjunction, square, or opposition of Moon—and Saturn in the same aspect of the Sun from angles, show a violent death ; also, Sun or Moon in square, or opposition of Saturn or Mars from the 4th or 10th houses. Saturn or Mars with caput Algol, and Moon with Deneb, he dies by sentence.

462 *Mars* in ♊, ♍, ♒, and in the first half of ♐, and posited in square, or in opposition to the Sun or Moon, and Mars, eventually will operate death by slaughter, either by civil or foreign war. If

Mars be near Caput Algol, in the 5th face of Taurus (19), he will produce death by beheading, decapitation, or by mutilating a limb. If in ♏ or ♉, he will cause death by surgical amputation, burning, searing, or by spasms or convulsions. Should Mars be found in the 4th or 10th house, death will be inflicted by impalement or hanging, especially if Mars be within 5 degrees of Cepheus or Andromeda. If Mars be just setting, and especially in opposition or square of Sun or Moon (327), he will produce death by fire ; Mars with Aldebaran, by a stab ; in quadrupedal signs, by falls and fractures. Should Jupiter, however, bear testimony to Mars, and be at the same time afflicted, death will ensue from the wrath of rulers, and from judicial condemnation, or in an affair of honour, as duelling, chartering, &c. If Venus add testimony, death by women ; if Mercury, by robbers, pirates, &c.

463 If it happen that Herschel, Saturn, and Mars be in reception with each other, or in opposition from the 1st or 7th among themselves, or with the Sun or Moon, death will be more certain, but its species or quality, and its dominion, will depend upon that one malefic which may occupy anaretic places. And all, Herschel, Saturn, and Mars claim prerogative in the anaretic places (243) ; the bodies of persons who thus die will not have a churchal interment, but will be devoured by beasts and birds ; these circumstances will especially ensue when the malefics are found in signs similar in form to beasts and birds, and provided the benefics should neither offer testimony to the 4th house, nor to the anaretic places (224).

Lastly, death will occur abroad if the planets controlling the anaretic places be cadent, especially if the Moon be therein, and more especially if she be in square or opposition to the anareta.

464 One direction, however malevolent it may be, rarely kills, and in most nativities there is required a train of malevolent directions to concur to death ; where several malevolent directions concur so together without the aid or intervenings of the benevolents, they fail not to destroy life (244). In such train of directions, the fore most of the malevolent train is the killing place, and the second show the time of death ; but the following directions, though benevolent, show the quality. If the train fall altogether, and none follow, for the quality observe those which precede, though at a distance and benevolent also, for though the benevolent contribute to the preservation of life, yet they frequently specify the disease which is the cause of death (178 and 181). Notice the nature of the planets and the signs in which they are placed. In violent deaths, the genethliacal positions of the Sun and Moon are to be observed, and how the malefics affect them, and how the Sun and Moon are concerned by directions in the quality of death.

LESSON TWENTY-EIGHTH.

QUESTIONS TO BE ANSWERED BEFORE THE STUDENT PROCEEDS.

By what is death produced?

What is the nature of death produced by Herschel—by Saturn—by Jupiter—by Mars—by Venus—by Mercury—and by the luminaries?

When is a violent death produced?

Name the violent deaths produced by Herschel?

What are the effects of Saturn—of Saturn and Herschel—of Saturn and Mercury—and of Saturn and Mars?

What does Mars alone produce?

What when combined with the luminaries—if with Venus—and if with Mercury?

CHAPTER XXX.

OF THE PARENTS.

465 In conformity to nature, the Sun, 4th house, and Saturn represent the person of the father; and the Moon, 10th house, and Venus denote that of the mother. And, as these are found afflicted among themselves, or otherwise, we infer so will be the situation of the parents and their affairs. The planets which are configurated with the luminaries show what relates to their fortunes and possessions; for if they are surrounded, within 30 degrees, either before or after, by the benefics, and by such stars and planets as are of the same nature as themselves, their fortunes will be illustrious and splendid; particularly if the Sun be attended by the bodies which rise before him; or the Moon be followed within 30 degrees by bodies that rise after her. If Saturn and Venus be orientally posited, or in the M.C., they foreshow the prosperity according to the particular circumstances of each parent. If the Sun and Moon hold no good aspects with Jupiter and Venus, the adverse fortunes of the parents, their humble state, and obscurity are then denoted, especially if Saturn and Venus are debilitated. But if Sun and Moon are variously configurated with both good and evil stars, the parents are subjected to vicissitudes of fortune, never rising above the mediocrity, as, for instance, when Mars ascends next in succession to the Sun, or Saturn to the Moon; and the benefics weakly situated. If the ⊕, in the nativity, be found in a favourable position with the stars, configurated with the Sun and Moon, the affairs of the parents will then remain steady and secure; but if the positions be discordant, and situated in a bad place of the figure, with malefic stars, their affairs will be unproductive of good, and be unprofitable.

The probable Duration of Life to the Parents.

466 In reference to the father, a long life is presaged, if Jupitei or Venus be in any way configurated with Sol or Saturn—or, also, if Saturn be in sextile or trine, and strongly dignified in other respects.   But if Saturn be debilitated, or in square or opposition of Sol, and if both Saturn and Sun be in cadent houses, or Mars be elevated above or rise before Sol and Saturn, then the father is full of infirmities ; but, if in other houses, the father will die in the early part of his life, and suffer much sickness.   The shortness of his life is particularly intimated by the Sun and Saturn being in the 10th or 1st houses ; and affliction, if Sun or Saturn be in the 4th or 7th house.   If Mars be elevated above Sol, the father will die suddenly, or receive an injury in his face or eyes ; but should Mars be so aspected to Saturn, he will be afflicted by pains in the limbs (177).

467 In reference to the mother—should Jupiter be configurated to the Moon or Venus—or should Venus alone behold the Moon by conjunction, sextile, or trine, the mother will enjoy health and longevity.   But, if Mars be posited in any of the angular or succeedent houses in ill aspect to the Moon or Venus, or if Saturn be thus configurated with the Moon, retrograde, slow in motion, or cadent, adverse accidents and disease will attend the mother. Should Saturn or Moon, on the contrary, be swift in motion and angular, but in ill aspect, they portend that her life will be short, and frequently afflicted.   In the same manner, should Mars be thus aspected to the Moon, she oriental, the mother will be liable to hurts, injuries, and sudden death ; but if the Moon be occidental, death will be occasioned by miscarriage, in parturition, by inflammation, or by wounds.   Should Mars make these aspects to Venus, death will then take place from fever, or sudden sickness. Saturn afflicting the Moon when she is oriental, inflicts the mother, disease and death from extreme cold, or slow fevers ; but should the Moon be occidental, the danger arises from affections of the womb, or by consumption.

" In the investigation of all these circumstances, it is highly essential that the property of the signs, in which are situated the stars actuating the influence, should be also taken into consideration ; and that by day the Sun and Venus should be principally observed ;   and, by night, Saturn and Venus."   Thus, from the nativity of a child, may the principal concerns of the parents be ascertained ; such is the sympathy existing by this bond of nature and consanguinity, that little difference will be found, if compared with the proper nativity of each parent.

" If, however, after due attention has been paid to the foregoing principals, a more specific inquiry should still be demanded, it will then become necessary to assume the place allotted to the paternal or maternal condition, for an horoscope or ascendant, in order to pursue the investigation. In these, as in all other cases, the mode in which the influences are comixed must be carefully kept in view. Remember, that a star does not render a vigorous influence unless it was fully in communication at the time of birth."

468 RULES, 1.—In the figure erected for the father, if the nativity be diurnal, note the degree in which the Sun is posited in the child's nativity, and make that degree ascending upon the horoscope for the father ; and conformably to that, order the cusps of all the other houses by the rules herein laid down. 2.—If the figure be erected for the mother, then take the degree of Venus instead of the Sun, and proceed in the other respects the same. But if the nativity be nocturnal, take the degree of Saturn for the father, and that of the Moon for the mother. And in all these cases it must be observed that the nativity of the first-born is to be preferred, then that of the second, and so on ; and that whatever is prenoted in relation to the parents, from these figures, is only such as shall happen to them after the birth of the child, and not to anything before. 3.—The time in which any or each of these events shall happen is to be sought out by the arcs of direction, or distances, of that star which has the dominion in respect of the Sun and the angles of the world ; and this I shall make perfectly easy to the meanest understanding when I come to treat of directions in general (CHAP. XXXIII).

LESSON TWENTY-NINTH.

QUESTIONS TO BE ANSWERED BEFORE THE STUDENT PROCEEDS.

What are the significators of the native's father?

What of the mother?

What rules their fortunes?

Which show prosperity?

What indicate adversity?

What are the effects of the luminaries variously configurated?

What have you to notice cf the Part of Fortune?

How do you judge of the duration of life of the parents?

What does Saturn afflicted signify?

What afflicts the father?

What shows shortness of life?

What denote sudden death and sickness?

What give length of life to the mother?

What afflict her health?

How do you judge of what disease the mother will die?

Have the signs any effect in the foregoing affairs?

How would you erect a figure for the father out of the child's natus?

How the mother?

How do you judge of the time of any of the events affecting the parents?

CHAPTER XXXI.

OF BROTHERS AND SISTERS.

Under this head of enquiry, a general and cursory investigation only can be performed, and an attempt to dive into minute particulars would be fruitless, and would prove to be merely a vain search after things not open to philosophy.

469 The next consideration in the native's geniture is the place of brethren, and this is taken from the sign on the M.C. and the cusp of the 11th (416), and the maternal places, which is the position of Venus by day, and the position of the Moon by night. For, as this can only relate to children born of the same mother, this sign on M.C., and that which succeeds it being maternal, are considered as indicative of the mother and her children, the same is therefore properly allotted to brothers and sisters. Hence, provided this place be configurated with the benefics, there will be several brothers and sisters, the number of them depending upon the number and positions of such benefic stars (418), whether in bicorporeal signs or single form. If, however, the malefics (417) have superiority in number or power, or in the 4th, the brothers or sisters will be few in number, particularly if any of the malefics surround the Sun. Should the hostile configurations be from the ascendant, Saturn will then represent the first-born brother, and would destroy him by lingering sickness ; and Mars would destroy them all. If both Saturn and Mars be in the 1st or 7th show paucity of brethren.

470 Again, should the stars which promise brethren be well affected in the mundane situations, the fortunes of the brethren will be respectable and famous ; but humble and obscure if the contrary positions happen. If the malefics be elevated above (which is possible) those which give brethren, their constitution will be delicate, and their lives short. Stars constituted masculinely (418) represent brothers ; those femininely, sisters. The more oriental stars represent the elder born ; and those which are more occidental, the younger.

On the Agreement of the Brethren.

471 Should the stars which give brethren be harmoniously configurated (200) with that one which is ruler of the sign allotted to brethren, the brethren will be mutually friendly and affectionate ; and if the same planets be in good aspect to the ⊕, the brethren will live together in communion ; but if these stars be fouud in contrary positions (201), the brethren will then be at variance, practising enmity and fraud, the cause must be judged from those houses' signification (199) from which they cast their ill aspects. Rulers of the 1st and 3rd in good aspect, perfect agreement ; in ill

aspect, the contrary; or if the ☋, or Saturn, or Mars, be therein, peregrine, discord and variance.

LESSON THIRTIETH.

QUESTIONS TO BE ANSWERED BEFORE THE STUDENT PROCEEDS.

From what do you judge brethren?

What show many brethren?

What denote few brethren?

What are the effects if malefics rule?

If they are in the ascendant?

If in the 4th?

If in the 7th?

What portend short life to brethren?

How do you judge whether they will be brother or sister?

What foreshows the elder brethren?

What denotes agreement among brethren?

What disagreement?

What effect has the Part of Fortune?

CHAPTER XXXII.

MALE OR FEMALE.

The foregoing speculations are deduced from an investigation of the positions of the heavens at the time of birth; but in order to know whether the infant be male or female during the state of pregnancy, the time of conception only must be considered. For this purpose we must not rest on a single basis, nor can it be presumed on one direction alone, we must particularly—

472 Observe the situation of the ascendant, the Sun, and the Moon; and those stars which possess any prerogatives in those places, and of the mode in which the planets ruling them may be constituted. See whether the majority are masculinely or femininely situated; and prediction then must be regulated in conformity to their disposition. The masculine planets are the Sun, Herschel, Saturn, Jupiter and Mars. Also, Mercury is common to both genders, because at certain times he produces dryness; at other times moisture, and performs each in an equal ratio. The planets are also said to be masculine when they rise before the Sun, and between the 1st and 10th, and between the 7th and 4th. The feminine planets are the Moon and Venus, and especially when they set after the Sun, and between the 4th and 1st, or between the 10th and 7th. Also the nature of the signs are to be noticed, in which the planets are placed. The masculine signs are the odd signs; the feminine are the equal signs. Thus, from the sex chiefly prevalent, as observed by these rules, that of the native may be rationally inferred.

Of Twins.

With respect to the probability of the birth of twins, or more, at once, you must—

473 Observe again the ascendant, the Sun, and the Moon ; for when two or all three possess ♊, ♐ , and ♓, or many prolific stars cast good aspects to the same, that will be a plural conception. The number then generated is known from the planet which is connected with the ruling places ; and the sex or sexes are determined by the planets configurated with the Sun, Moon and ascendant. When both Sun and Moon are in the M.C., twins are procreated. When Saturn, Jupiter, and Mars have configuration with the 1st, Sun, and Moon, in Gemini, Sagittary, or Pisces, three males are generated ; but three females when Venus, Moon, and Mercury are configurated in the same way. When Saturn, Jupiter, and Venus are thus disposed, then two males and one female will be born ; but Venus, Moon, and Mars, then two females and one male, and so on.

In cases of the above kind, however, it most usually happens that the conception has not been complete, and that the children are born with some remarkable imperfection or deformity ; and these appear among the wonders of the day, although the cause has a radical foundation in nature, and can be accounted for by the Astral Philosopher.

Of Monstrous or Defective Birth.

474 When the Sun and Moon are cadent, without any good aspect to the 1st house, or the angles possessed by the malefics, then a monstrous or defective birth. In these cases observe the last full or new Moon, together with the ruler thereof, and the rulers of the Sun and Moon, for these unconnected with the preceding full or new Moon, what is then generated will be of unnatural conformation. And, if in addition to this absence of connection, the Moon and Sun be in ♈, ♉, ♌, ♐ , or ♑, with Herschel, Saturn, and Mars, in angles, what is then conceived will not be perfectly human shape ; but if Jupiter or Venus interpose their good aspects, and give testimonies to Sun and Moon, then what is conceived will not be of human conformation, but of a fierce and savage nature. If Mercury support the luminaries, the disposition will be agreeable to nature, but the form of the body will be unnatural (327) ; or, if Sun and Moon be in ♊, ♍, or ♒, and the ruling planets discordant, then the offspring will be of proper conformation, but monstrous in quality. If either Herschel, Saturn, or Mars give testimony in any of the foregoing positions, what is then generated will be irrational, or of ungovernable qualities ; but if Jupiter or Venus give testimony, the offspring will naturally possess the mental accomplishments, with an hermaphroditical conformation (332). If Mercury

alone give testimony to the aforesaid positions of the Moon and Sun, that which is procreated will be deaf and dumb, though intellectually well qualified and ingenious.

The foregoing refer to the time of conception, but what may befall the limbs after birth is judged by the figure of birth, and fully explained in CHAPTER XXI. and page 108.

Distinct from this species of conception, is that which though perfectly natural and well conformed, yet is void of stamina (259), and hence termed " an embryo not nourished." This kind of conception, is that which either Sun or Moon in an angle, is in conjunction with a malefic and that luminary giver of life (242) to such, no duration of life.

CHAPTER XXXIII.

TO JUDGE OF THE EFFECTS OF THE ARCS OF DIRECTIONS.

475 RULE 1.—The general nature of the Planets' aspects must be considered at the time of birth ; as also other Directions coming up at the same time, and then judge according to the native's situation in life.

476 RULE 2.—When direction is complete, the house in which the body directed falls will help to point out the character of the circumstance it will produce, as well as the signification of the house over which both bodies rule (199). The face in which the direction falls; thus, if Sun or Moon come to an ill aspect with Mercury in the 9th, or with Herschel (he being in ill aspect to Mercury at birth) may very probably denote a lawsuit (167). If ill directions fall in the Ascendant, they generally affect health ; if in the 2nd, his property, &c. A good direction gives prosperity from such things or persons as the Promissor signifies ; and also as the house over which he presides indicates.

477 RULE 3.—The extent and power of the directions are to be properly contemplated, according to the degree of angular power of the Promissor in the Radix, the sign in which it is posited, and its freedom from affliction; also the opposing influences are to be well considered, together with the subsequent direction. The effect of one direction will operate till another comes up. If the Significator be the stronger, the direction will operate with ease ; but if the Promissor be the stronger, the effects will fully operate. The ill directions of Sol and Saturn will not be so very evil if Sol be in good aspect of Jupiter at birth.

478 RULE 4.—If the Significator and Promissor be both weak in the Radix, and the direction falls in either debilities, the effects

of that direction will only be weak, which otherwise might have been very strong ; and if they be both weak in the Radix, or ill aspected, and the direction happens in a good house, and in the dignities of the Significator ; even then the effects will not be so strong, either for good or for evil, as if they had been essentially strong in the Radix. Observe, also, whether the direction falls near eminent fixed stars, and so judge, &c. If the nature of the star agrees in nature with the significator, then the effect of direction will be adjuvanted, *et vice versa*.

479 RULE 5.—In applying the effects of direction, you must always consider the Age, Position in Life, Gender of the native ; because their significations are always expressed according to the Ration of the years ; that direction which may signify marriage between 20 and 30 years of age, is very probable to come to pass ; but that same direction coming up at the age of 2 or 3, would have no effect upon the child, but it might denote marriage, &c., to some person in the family. Again, the directions in the child's nativity will fall more generally upon the parents than upon the native, till he have attained the age of 5 or 6 years.

480 RULE 6.—If two directions come up at one, or nearly one, and the same time, and the one good and the other evil (unless they be diametrically opposed to each other), the effects of both will appear ; but especially that which cohears with the revolution of the year, or that which appears the most powerfully posited, &c., at Birth (rule 4). If they agree in effect, then they are necessarily more powerful ; as also when both Significator and Promissor, shall sympathise together ; still keeping in mind the signification of the house at which the direction falls. Many conflicting events frequently occur at the same period, and a person may, at one and the same time, lose a kinsman, yet inherit his substance ; or be at the same time in ill health, yet prosperous and advantageously established in regard to fortune.

481 How long the effects of directions will operate is to be judged according to their strength or debility. The effects are often brought about by secondary direction and by transits. The effects of directions arise not simply from the impression made at the moment of birth, nor from the heavens alone, but from the homergene force of both, by the help of transits, by which the powers of direction, impressed at the time of birth, are converted into acts ; whence it is, that the effects of directions always happen not at the time precisely limited, but a little sooner or a little later.

482 Why do not the effects of directions appear at the birth ? Because the Promissor is not actually in the place of the Significator, but only in power ; consequently, their effects are afterwards brought into action by successive motion, and so many revolutions of years of the nativity, as the Promissor is distant from the Circle of Position of the Significator in degrees of the Equator. For there

is then a Union of Promissors' virtue, being both actually in the same circle of Position; and the time is marked out by the Arc of that motion, and then the same directions are brought to act by a secondary or renovated impression of their virtues upon the native, as an addition to the original and universal impression at the moment of birth. So that it appears there is a combination of general and particular influences upon the native, and a conjunction of powers and acts to produce the original impressed effects.

483 We direct the following five places and planets, which signify all persons and matters—

1st.—The horoscope or ascendant signifies all matters which affect the body or mind; or change of residence, travelling, sickness, health, birth, or death of children, &c. When it meets good directions of fortunate planets, or any others well dignified and aspected, then it shows health, prosperity, peace, and contentment; but with bad directions, sickness, mischief, crosses, adversaries, discontentment, and other afflictions of like kind. N.B.—All mundane directions act powerfully, and endure many weeks.

2nd.—The M.C. has signification of employment, friendship, possession of children, trade or profession; honour, credit, office, mother. Mundane directions, happening at birth, act all through life (217).

3rd.—The directions of the Sun have generally the most potent effects between 23 and 42 years of age. Authority of action is exercised in the mind, the career of life is entered upon, distinction and glory are desired, puerile irregularities are relinquished for more orderly conduct, and the pursuit of honour, preferment, and favour of the great. It also signifies the father and his affairs.

4th.—The Moon has the greatest effect in infancy, affecting both body and mind, also wealth and character, journeys, marriage, the estate of his wife, women, and near kinsfolk.

5th.—The part of fortune we direct to incidents affecting the substance or wealth, and family affairs.

484 We may direct Mercury for the intellectual faculties of the mind, journeys, scholarship, for the mind is aroused to discipline and instruction, imbibing the seed of learning, and developing, as it were, the elements and germs of genius and abilities, and their peculiar quality. Mercury has the most influence from 5 to 15 years of age. Venus signifies matrimony, love, pleasure, ornaments, maids, women, &c. From her, the movement of the seminal vessels originates, as well as an unrestrained impetuosity and precipitancy in amours. We direct Mars for animosity, war, the estate of brethren, for he induces austerity of life, together with vexation, care, and trouble, having most power between the age of 40 and 55. We direct Jupiter for glory, gravity, foresight, prudence, sagacity, honour, respect, privilege, children, religion, sobriety, &c.

We direct Saturn to signify ancestors, inheritance, fears, jealousies, mistrusts, &c., according as Saturn is well or ill affected. We direct Herschel to signify journeys, advancement, science and literature, inventions, discoveries, public bodies, deaths of distant relations, and public writers; also, trades connected with danger of loss of life therein.

484A I direct Neptune much after Herschel for inventions and discoveries of new lights in arts and sciences, for good or evil as it may be found at birth, or by directions and transits which may be found therein after birth (441A). Neptune will help to delay marriage, and cause separation if in or near the 7th house, or throwing evil influences to the Moon and Venus in the radix. Many things have come to pass which have not been accounted for by professors, who have closed their eyes to the same, or have been afraid to acknowledge the cause, or to dig deeper into it to try to give the student a knowledge of its influence and effects. Now, students, be your own professors in this matter, and try to have it opened to the new light upon a plan of improvement. Dip deeper into the science of Astrology, there is far too much of that skimming on the top, and dabbling with the science before getting any real knowledge of it. This may arouse the minds of some of our writers on the subject of Neptune in the future. The cause of this lack of knowledge may be through the want of a good work like this, and the day is not far distant in the womb of time when the doors of the treasure houses will be no longer locked to students, but will be unbarred and opened to give light to the mind of every seeker.

> But to insist on tedious proofs is vain,
> The art defends itself, the art is plain ;
> For art well grounded forces to believe,
> It cannot be deceived, nor can deceive.
> Events foretold fulfil the prophecy,
> What fortune seconds, how can man deny ?
> The proofs are sacred, and to doubt would be
> Not reason's action, but impiety.

Students, by having this book in your own study, many events will knock at your door. Open it, and let them enter to the seeker.

SPECIFIC RULES.

Ascendant to conjunction or ill aspect of Saturn.

485 *Saturn* oriental of the Sun, will impair the native's health, according to the sign in which Saturn is found at birth (177), especially if the Ascendant be hyleg (242), family affliction, mischief by elderly persons, or Saturnine affairs (170), accidents, falls, bruises, consumption—Saturn not being ruler of the 1st, danger of death ; if in the eighth, and near violent fixed stars, it is almost

sure to produce death. Saturn in ♋, ♏, or ♓, danger of drowning, dropsy, small-pox, measles; in ♏, danger of poisoning by women, gambling, drinking, or the treachery of enemies. In ♈, ♌, or ♐, danger of falls, blows, bruises, &c.; in ♈, a hurt or stroke in the head, especially if Saturn be in the Ascendant at birth; ♌ or ♐, danger by fire, and his property is likely to be destroyed by that element. Saturn in ♉, ♍, or ♑, accidents by being crushed, buried alive, &c. ; in ♉, danger of being harmed by a four-footed animal, probably a bull, &c. ; in ♑, defrauded, robbed, and other losses of property. Saturn in ♊, ♎, or ♒, danger of accidents from falls from heights; in ♎, unsuccessful in most pursuits, let him neither court nor marry, he is likely to be robbed, and if Saturn rules the first, he will be in danger of hazarding his life to rescue others from impending danger; many sorrows, and very melancholy. Saturn in the 2nd, or ruler thereof, afflicted on account of bonds, security, and such things, as the second house signifies. Saturn in the 3rd, at birth, the native suffers from neighbours, brethren, short journeys, death among his relations, and disagreement with his acquaintances. If ruler of the 4th, thoughts of changing residence, but to his disadvantage; danger of death to his father. Saturn, ruler of the 5th, a criminal intercourse; especially if Saturn be in ill aspect of Mars or Venus at birth, an illegitimate child will be laid to him. He is unsteady, given to drinking, gaming, and in danger of debilitating his constitution, more especially if ♏ be in the 5th. If Saturn be ruler of the 6th, ill health, bad servants (if any), loss by tenants and small cattle (if any), his paternal aunt or uncle will suffer, and be in danger of death, especially if the native be very young, say under 7 years of age. Saturn, ruler of the 7th, many public enemies, anxiety about wife or husband, fall out with many persons, danger of loss in law-suit, loss in trade, and if he be in partnership, disagreement and defrauding; if married, family broils, abuse, and danger of death to wife. If the man be unmarried, and engaged with a female in courtship, he breaks off his acquaintance, and acts very dishonour-ably, breaking his promise of marriage, and so on; danger of being robbed, is quarrelsome, and given to boasting and fighting. Saturn, ruler of the 8th, defrauded of property left him by the death of a relation, especially if Herschel be in ill aspect of Saturn at birth. If Saturn rule the 9th, suffers from pretended religious persons, especially if Jupiter or Saturn are in ill aspect in the radix; he must not travel, for in this he would be in danger of his life. If ruler of the 10th, unsuccessful in business, loses his honour, for if the Ascendant come to square of Saturn then the 10th would be afflicted, loss from mean disposed persons. If Saturn rule the 11th, false friends, disappointment in expectations, with loss of reputation. If ruler of the 12th, danger of imprisonment, much sorrow and trouble, unprofitable in large cattle and servants (if any), danger of suicide, with great anguish of mind, his maternal aunt or uncle will be in danger of death, many enemies.

If the Ascendant under these directions be afflicted, then the evils will be increased: but if the Ascendant be befriended, then these untoward events will be mitigated and diminished; also, if Saturn be occidental of the Sun at birth.

Ascendant to the good aspects of Saturn.

486 Render the native steady, honourable, favours from elderly men; if Saturn be strong, gain by agriculture, gardening, mines, colliers, buildings, will, or inheritance. It is said to be a good time, his engagements prosper, to let lands, or renew leases, build or speculate with Saturnine people, or things, and employments. If Saturn be ruler of the 8th, and in good aspect of Sun and Moon, or ruler of the 1st, he is likely to receive a legacy, or be benefited by the death of a person.

Ascendant to good aspects, parallel, or conjunction of Jupiter.

487 Produce prosperity, increase of wealth, inclined to be prosperous, new friends, cheerfulness, credit, honourable employment, the birth of children or their settlement in life, preferment (if a clergyman) and an improved state of health, and of much happiness, and, if capable, marriage. If lord of 8th, a bequest; to a scholar, some degree of preferment; if lord of 12th, gain, if a dealer in cattle. If Jupiter be strong in the radix, it is more beneficial, and produces greater prosperity; religious, if Jupiter is lord of 9th; if lord of 7th, marriage, to a farmer, excellent crops, and his cattle do well.

Ascendant to ill aspects of Jupiter.

488 Will cause quarrels with clergymen, magistrates, landlords, crosses, lawsuits, losses in trade, or by suretiship, or by travelling, or false friends; but except Jupiter be much vitiated at birth, the ill aspects by direction will not cause any lasting evil—diseases according to the sign in which Jupiter is placed, as (178). If the ☍ falls in ♒ or ♌, danger of pleurisy, or a passion of the heart.

Ascendant to conjunction, parallel, or ill aspects of Mars.

489 These are very evil directions, and indicate many miseries, and sometimes death; accidents by fire-arms, cuts, blows, injuries by animals; Mars afflicted in ♊ or ♍, falls and broken limbs, fevers, small-pox, madness, plague, boils, giddiness, pestilence, danger by robbers, horses, iron, stone, gunshot wounds, or swords; false accusation, it makes the native quarrelsome, death of friends, especially if the direction be to the hyleg; in Airy signs, he causes falls; in Fiery, fevers, duelling, hurts by fire, lightning and inflammations, it also causes imprisonments, danger to those who are imprisoned, murder, bloody flux; in Earthy, pestilential com-

plaints; in Watery, scalds, violent fluxes, and perils by waters, and inflammation of the pleura and intestines. Mars· in Pisces, afflicted by measles, small-pox, scabs, and cutaneous diseases, losses by military men, or persons in power, he brings various injuries; if Mars be lord of the M.C. it is attended with great infamy; and if lord of the 2nd, he wastes his substance peculiarly. While this direction lasts avoid all business and negociations. If Mars is anareta, it causes death; if Mars rules the 7th, many enemies, false friends.

Ascendant to good aspect of Mars.

490 Causes military advancement, the birth of children (generally males), journeys, and success in trade or employment, especially if a surgeon, mechanic, chemist, or dealer in metals; in a woman's nativity it frequently causes marriage, especially if Mars be lord of the 7th; if Mars be lord of the 2nd, it greatly augments the substance, gains by horse-racing; if a soldier, he will be promoted; if ruler of M.C., great glory and honour; if lord of 7th, marriage.

Ascendant to parallel or conjunction of Sun.

491 If Sol be well aspected at birth he gives dignity, office, fame and reputation, and success in all matters connected with power; if Sol be lord of the 10th, he is a favourite of a prince or nobleman; if Sol be ill aspected, he is likely to cause anxiety, diseases, pains in the head, and hurts in the right eye, especially if he be in Airy signs: in Fiery, or afflicted by Mars, fevers, or ophthalmia. They also say it causes all the actions of a man's life to be made public; makes him waste his substance, and quarrel with his brethren and sisters.

Ascendant to the good aspects of Sun.

492 Health of body, peace of mind, an increase of friends, &c.; also preferment and creditable employment, honourable journeys, &c., especially if Sol was in good aspect of Mars or Moon at birth; affairs generally successful; if Sol rules the 9th, much journeying; if the 10th, he arrives at dignity.

Ascendant to the bad aspects of Sun.

493 Troubles and diseases in the head, envy or ill treatment from a person in power, quarrels, enemies, lawsuits, prosecutions, &c., also decay of estate, deceit, and disrespect to the native, danger of shipwreck and imprisonment, complaints in the eyes, head, face, acute diseases, fevers, &c.; death or danger to the native's father, if lord of the 11th; if of the 8th, danger of death to the native.

Ascendant to parallel, or conjunction, or good aspects of Venus.

494 Pleasure and content, he is beloved of women, marries, especially if lady of the 7th, or has a daughter born if ruler of the 5th, or married; he purchases furniture, clothes, &c., and is generally given to luxury and pleasures, especially under the conjunction, where, if Venus be afflicted, he may suffer diseases accordingly; if Venus rules the 2nd, increase of wealth; if ruler of the 10th, honour, and prosperous business.

Ascendant to ill aspects of Venus.

495 Diseases by surfeit and excess, inclined to be wild, voluptuous, intemperate, and extravagant, vicious in pursuits, and is scandalized, many troubles by women, vexations in love matters, &c., jealousy and conjugal quarrels, health detrimented by unfortunate pleasures.

Ascendant to parallel, conjunction, or good aspects of Mercury.

496 This incites a desire to study, poetry, and mathematics, especially if ruler of the 1st or 9th; he takes a degree at the University, or enters some school or college, or goes apprentice, if a youth. It denotes a busy time with accounts, writings, law papers, &c., also journeys, and changes in situations. The whole good or evil according to the strength of Mercury in the radix. Monarchs contract leagues. It gives change of residence, promotion, improves his intellectual faculties, given to invention, and studious of arts and sciences, and makes bargains to his or her advantage; if Mercury be in good aspect of the Moon at birth, a journey advantageous.

Ascendant in evil aspect of Mercury.

497 This brings expenses by literary things and persons; if an astro-philosopher, he dabbles, ill tempered; a very unsettled time; disputes, quarrels, lawsuits, especially if Mercury is afflicted at birth, annoyances by young persons, and pilfering servants (if any), he may be arrested or questioned for some mistakes or fraud in accounts, or be libelled, or write some foolish book or libel, &c.; it also causes cutaneous disease, coughs, affections of the breath, &c. Much depends on the aspects to Mercury, if at birth he is in a good aspect of Jupiter or Venus, then the native prospers through the means of friends, relations, or neighbours.

Ascendant, parallel, or conjunction of the Moon.

498 Sudden benefits or reverses, changes, journeys, preferments, losses by the populace, death of the native's mother, &c., all depending on the strength of the Moon in the radix; it brings

marriage to males if ruler of the 7th, and sea voyages to all if ruler of the 9th; it causes lunar diseases, especially if the Ascendant be hyleg; if Luna is afflicted at birth, then danger of his life; if fortunate at birth, increase of health and wealth; journeys and bargains; preferment and happiness to the mother.

Ascendant to good aspects of the Moon.

499 Content of mind and body, much active business and employment, a journey, or sea voyage; it gives benefits by females, neighbours, mother, or kindred; new female friends, marriage, or the birth of a daughter, public esteem and prosperity.

Ascendant to bad aspects of the Moon.

500 Disputes and controversies, and the contrary to the last, especially with females and vulgar persons; death of a relation, misfortunes at sea, by robbery or fraud, danger to the left eye, loss of office, many public affronts, and open enemies, also lunar diseases, ill health, and also to some other of his female relatives, corrupt humours, cancers, &c. A general tendency to gluttony and intemperance, and the consequent distempers, stomachic complaints, and all according to the sign the Moon is in at birth (183). If married, husband and wife disagree on account of jealousy; Moon lady of the 8th, in a Watery sign, danger of being drowned.

Ascendant to conjunction, parallel, or ill aspect of Herschel.

501 Evil to health, relations, and from public bodies, editors, and so on. All Herschel's effects are unexpected and sudden; if ruler of the 2nd, loss in money matters; if of the 7th, discord in courtship and marriage, and very probably a separation. The Ascendant being hyleg, sudden dangers and extraordinary accidents.

Ascendant to good aspects of Herschel.

502 Unexpected benefits by means of public bodies and public writers, by machinery and liquids, by arts and sciences, by discovery and patent rights, by invention and lecturing, by exhibitions of antique curiosities, and by legacies, and by such things as are connected with paragraph 169 and so on.

Ascendant to the place of ☊.

503 Health, honour, prosperity, preferment, friends, satisfaction of mind, and new acquaintances; but to the place of ☋, sickness, measles, small-pox, flatulency, dyspepsia; if in the second, loss of money, overcharged with debts; if in the 3rd, bad for taking journeys, ill agreement between neighbours and relations; if in the 4th, loss of property and detriment to the father; in the 5th, bad speculations.

Ascendant to the place of Part of Fortune.

504 Increase of wealth (if Part of Fortune be well aspected and gloriously posited), and satisfaction of mind; if Herschel be in good aspect of Part of Fortune, he gains by discovery, as 361 describes; if Jupiter, by the church, office, or jovial men; if Sol, by the bounty and friendship of great men (173); if Venus, by ladies, wife, and by buying and selling merchandise (174); if Mercury, by writing and management, and by such persons as are denoted in 175; if in ill aspect with the above, then judge the contrary.

Ascendant brought to the Cusp of the 2nd house (217).

505 The native purchases household goods, gains by business, and pecuniary undertakings are prosperous and satisfactory; to the cusp of the 3rd house, which is two-thirds of a semiarc, good for journeys, and gains by relation and neighbours; to the cusp of the 4th, death.

Ascendant to Rigel, Orionis, Arcturus, or North Scale.

506 Inheritance by the dead, yet entangled in love matters, timid and melancholy, gains by the sword or the church, martial honour and preferment, gains by dealing in metals and in manufacturing articles out of steel, iron, &c.; a good direction for cutlers, smiths, smelters, ironmongers, railway contractors, and machine manufacturers.

Ascendant to the place of Ascelli, or Capricornus.

507 Danger of fever, inflammation in the eyes, hurts from beasts, many malicious enemies, yet to martial men preferment. As these stars are of the nature of Sol and Mars combined, danger from fire, fire-arms, scalds, and hot liquids. Cooling medicine should be taken during the influence of this direction.

Ascendant to the place of Stars of the nature of Mars.

508 To *Cor Leo*, honours, destruction of enemies, yet likely to enter into disputation, and much inflammatory action in the system —be careful what medicine is administered.

To *Aldebaron*, success in honourable pursuits and with men of honour and integrity.

To *Pollux*, popularity and perseverance in posts of honour, gaining reputation by natural tact and talent.

To *Regulus*, honours, yet the native will be obnoxious to a flow of blood to the head, and Apoplexy.

To *Arista*, often called *Spica*, preferment in ecclesiastical engagements, ingenious and industrious in the 5th face of Libra.

To *Propus*, or to the *Bull's N. Horn*, a degree of eminence, and advantages from eminent and high characters.

To *Hircus*, stirs the native up to valour, eminent in martial affairs, he vanquishes his enemies, often deals deceitfully to gain his ends, spoils his credit, spends his money, and sometimes takes to defrauding his creditors by taking advantage of the Bankruptcy Act.

To *Crator*, promotion, studious in divinity, ingenious and successful, health, happiness, and contentment.

To the *Pleiades*, *Hyades*, *Castor*, wounds or hurts in the eyes, danger from sharp instruments, and often deaths from fever.

To *Deneb*, worldly happiness, yet accompanied with melancholy, troubles, and discontent.

To *Markab*, danger from fever, and especially to females, with imprudent conduct.

To *Sirus*, health and wealth, especially to soldiers and persons working in iron, and where fire and metals are used.

To *Hydra's Heart*, danger of being drowned, or bites of animals.

MIDHEAVEN TO ASPECTS.

Midheaven to good aspects of Herschel.

509 Honour from public bodies, and from sciences. To evil aspects the contrary, with unexpected losses.

Midheaven, parallel, conjunction, or ill aspect of Saturn.

510 The anger of magistrates and employers is felt, loss of office and trade, disgrace and ruin may occur. Death of parents, &c., especially if Saturn is oriental of the Sun, and Sol be above the earth. He is apt to act discreditably, his servants do the same. Conspiracies against him, acts of violence, private enmity, &c., accusations and robberies. To a king it denotes tumults and discontent, breach of treaties, &c. And it rarely happens without lowering the native in rank and station; his parents suffer also by death or misfortune. If in the 10th, dishonour, except Saturn was strong in the radix; if ruler of the 6th, sickness, and liable to colds, and thievish servants. Mark well the house he rules.

Midheaven, parallel, or conjunction of Jupiter.

511 Preferment, employment, and numerous benefits by the favour of some person of rank, it raises in life, according to the situation of the native; it gives increase of wealth and honour, but

much depends on how the M.C. is aspected. In a married female's nativity, it benefits her husband; in children, their parents. Jupiter oriental of the Sun, and in good aspect of Sun or Moon in, the radix, then a lucrative employment, and often become parish officers; if in the 7th, or dignities therein, marriage; if in the 9th, religious.

Midheaven in good aspect of Jupiter.

512 This acts like the conjunction, but generally with less power. The trine by Jupiter coming to the cusp of the 2nd house gives great increase of wealth; to the 6th, improvement of health.

Midheaven to bad aspect of Jupiter.

513 Trouble by law, lawyers, gentlemen, and magistrates, the clergy, &c., losses in commerce and trade; accusations, &c., against the native, which rarely prevail, he suffers by persons pretending to religion. To a king it causes great disputes about law and privileges, &c., quarrels with the nobility, &c. If weak, he suffers by lawyers and parsons, and other pseudo-religionists; loss of credit, and is extravagant.

Midheaven, parallel, conjunction, or bad aspect of Mars.

514 Great mischances to life and fortune. The wrath of powerful men falls on the native, he suffers wrong or injury in various ways; if lord of the 12th, imprisonment, disgrace, &c.; loss by fire, theft, &c., if Mars is in Aries, Leo, or Sagittarius. To a king, it denotes war and bloodshed, violent conduct, &c.; to a soldier it gives military authority, but danger. It often shews a violent death, where the radix prenotes the same, especially if lord of the 8th. It kills or afflicts parents, &c. If lord of the 7th, lawsuits, which go against him, danger of being brought up for theft; if lord of 6th, thievish servants, loss of cattle (if any).

Midheaven to good aspects of Mars.

515 The native takes to military actions, fencing, shooting, riding, &c., and he may enter the army or receive promotion; to tradesmen, it denotes wealth, prosperity, good business; to kings, war or some increase in the army; if lord of the 7th, marriage.

Midheaven, parallel, or conjunction of Sol.

516 This elevates the native to dignity, wealth, and honour, makes him hold some public office, having command or control. It gives fame and reputation, and also benefits the native's parents; death of mother if Sol be ruler of the 5th; if a Member of Parliament, he receives a title, or is made an ambassador, &c.

Midheaven to good aspects of Sol.

517 Preferment, wealth, success, gifts, friendship, honours, &c., by means of persons of rank and power; it makes the native esteem himself higher, and lays the foundation for his farther advance in life. In female's nativity, it brings marriage, or if married, the birth of a son; to a king, it brings victory, peace, and popularity, or he makes a league, and he receives honour from foreign monarchs.

Midheaven to ill aspect of Sol.

518 This causes sudden disgrace, trouble, loss of office, enemies, employment, &c.; it causes imprisonment, the sentence of a judge, &c. To a tradesman, &c., it will bring losses by fire, and bankruptcy: it afflicts the parents, frequently by means of fire or public calamities; to a king, it brings loss of popularity, and many national evils and sufferings. And if Sol be lord of the 1st, 8th, or 12th, danger of sentence of death, &c.

Midheaven, parallel, conjunction, or good aspect of Venus.

519 Mirth, pleasure, gaiety, &c., to the native, who mixes in female society, falls in love, and may marry, if of proper age, &c.; also the birth of children, and their marriage when of age; prosperity in the family, new female friends, benefits by females, and general success; the going into new houses, buying furniture, &c.; health and happiness to the mother.

Midheaven to evil aspects of Venus

520 Scandal, disappointment in marriage, and disgrace by means of females, troubles, conspiracy, unfortunate wooings, dishonour, jealousy, contention, and delusion by women; loss of estate, death of a relation, and squandering of property; the opposition denotes a separation, &c., from a wife, and sometimes the death or misfortune of wife or sister, mother, &c.; if marriage occur, it is rash and unhappy. To a king, scandal about mistresses, &c.; if married, jealousy, difference with wife. If lady of the 2nd, loss in his estate; if of the 11th, by means of friends; if of the 6th, by means of servants or cattle; if of the 10th, by trade, &c.

Midheaven, parallel, conjunction, or good aspects of Mercury.

521 Preferment and credit by learning or literary productions; much active business, especially with accompts, lawyers, booksellers, merchandise, &c.; also the study of languages, geometry, astronomy, astrology, public speaking, &c.; youths go out into the

world, young men set up in business, take degrees, &c.; it brings new employments, journeys, profit by writings, &c. But if Mercury be weak or afflicted, the conjunction may give scandal, libels, informations, &c., against the native.

Midheaven to bad aspects of Mercury.

522 Trouble from Mercurial things, writings, clerks, lawyers, &c.; false accusations, not well to sign writings, false witnesses; if lord of the 11th, false friends; beware of forgery.

Midheaven, parallel, or conjunction of the Moon.

523 An unquiet and busy time, afflicted with a variety of matter and action, both in body and mind; a troublesome time, now well and now ill, full of business, sometimes getting, sometimes losing. All depends on the strength of the Moon at birth; if she be strong, it benefits greatly, bringing some new occupation of a public nature, office, trade or dignity, &c.; also journeys, if lady of 3rd, and sea voyages if lady of 9th, the latter especially, if Moon be in Watery signs. In a male nativity, if ruler of 7th, it promises marriage or female connection, and benefits by females.

Midheaven to good aspects of the Moon.

524 Increase of fortune, fame, and estimation, especially among the people, gifts and benefits by ladies, prosperity in the native's office or employment, a long sea voyage, &c., and sometimes public command, &c., according to the native's rank in life, changes and general prosperity. With a male, marriage, birth of children, male or female, as the Moon map be aspected. Family advancement.

Midheaven to ill aspects of the Moon.

525 Public disesteem, ill health, loss of good name and office, expense and waste of property by law or bad women, danger to the wife, mother, daughter, &c. Quarrels in the family, separations, punishment by the law, sentence by a judge, &c., for offences. The greatness of the evil depends on the Moon's aspects and the sign she occupies; fixed signs make it durable.

Midheaven to Cor Scorpio, Arista, Orionis, Rigel, or North Scale.

526 Chiefly these stars are of the nature of Jupiter and Mars, and they, as well as other stars of the same nature, produce honour, but with little profit, becomes acquainted with government officers, and preachers of the gospel, he is fond of sailing. Military men are prosperous.

Midheaven to Algenib, Bellatrix, Betalguse, Procyon, Antares, or any other Star of the nature of Mercury and Mars.

527 Many calamities, wranglings, adversaries, danger of imprisonment from writing, bonds, signings, forgery, or libelling.

Midheaven to Pleiades, or Lucida Pleiadum, Pollux.

528 Stabs, weak eyes, quarrels, and controversies, danger of imprisonment, or of some tragical end by means of women; success in martial affairs.

Midheaven to Aldebaron, Bull's S. Horn, Cor Leo, Arcturus, Spica, or Sirius.

529 Fortunate, ingenious, inventive, success in business, he gains a public office, a superintendent or overseer, he does well in water-works and gas-works, honour by the gentry, chemical and martial performances.

Midheaven to Algol, or Hydra's Heart.

503 Trouble, dishonour, riotous, murderous; he is turbulent, and it would be well to keep out of all danger of disputation, as he would be sure to be brought to justice, then transported for violent acts.

Midheaven to the Dragon's Head.

531 Honour and prosperity, popularity and preferment, gain and contentment, trade and respect. But to the Dragon's Tail, dishonour and losses, scandal and contempt, loss and infamy.

Midheaven arriving at the different Houses.

532 To the 11th house, new friends, and honourable acquaintance, advantage and preferment according to his hopes and wishes. To the 12th house, many private enemies, but not able to harm him; loss of cattle, with danger of imprisonment; secret sorrow and degradation. To the ascendant or its ruler, honour, glory, and dignity by his own application and industry. To the 2nd or its ruler, gain and honour, success and preferment. To the 3rd or its ruler, a journey, concord among brethren and neighbours, if the second ruler be a fortunate, *et vice versa.* To the 4th or its ruler, gains by means of his father, or by a mean occupation. To the 5th or its ruler, pleasure by means of children, and gain in speculations if he enters into them. To the 6th or its ruler, honoured by servants, preferment in office bearing. To the 7th or its ruler, courtship, marriage, and gain by wife or woman. To the 8th or

its lord, preferment by legacy, or marriage portion. To the 9th or its ruler, honour by arts, sciences, or by a long journey, and by merchandising.

THE SECOND HOUSE OR ITS RULER TO PROMITTORS.

To the parallel, conjunction, or ill aspects of Herschel.

533 Unexpected losses, disappointments, and he is cheated by his creditors; to his good aspects, benefit, gain, and unexpected advantages—much cash passes through his hands.

To the parallel, conjunction, or ill aspects of Saturn.

534 Much consumption of money, many expenses, much sorrow, and pecuniary disappointments. His good aspects, increase of money and credit, well to deal in mines, minerals, and agricultural pursuits, especially with Saturnine persons (170).

To the parallel, conjunction, or good aspects of Jupiter.

535 Increase of fortune by honourable pursuits, by the aid of gentlemen and the clergy; and by persons holding government offices, and by such persons and things as Jupiter denotes (171), and the house over which he presides (199). To his ill aspects, loss of honour and office, by such persons and means as those which raised him, his friends deceive him, loss in trade, many vexations by law matters.

To the parallel, conjunction or good aspects of Mars.

536 Loss by brothers, sisters, or servants, many quarrels with martial men, dogs, or other beasts, danger of lawsuit, fire, robbers, or controversy. The good aspects, then advantage by dealing in small cattle, in pigs or sheep, in iron or steel, in guns or cutlery, in iron-works and foundries, or in military employments and going to sea.

To the parallel, conjunction, or good aspects of Sol.

537 Gain by gentlemen, officers, and employments, gifts and preferment. To the ill aspects, wasteful and prodigal, loss and troubles by his superiors, false accusation and lawsuits by malicious men, and vain unnecessary expenses.

To the parallel, conjunction, or good aspects of Venus.

538 Advantage by women and feminine procedures, by gifts and by selling articles of consumption. To the ill aspects, loose habits,

dissipation, losses by women, wife extravagant, especially in bad aspect of Mars or Sol at birth.

To the parallel, conjunction, or good aspect of Mercury.

539 Gain by travel, sea voyages, inventions, buying and selling light commodities, pleadings, writings, and learning may now be attended to. Studious of arts and sciences. To the ill aspects, contention in lawsuits, bonds, with false witnesses, counterfeit writings, loss by merchandise, and by men of learning; under this aspect it will be well not to enter into any new business, neither to take journeys in getting in debts, &c.

To the parallel, conjunction, or good aspect of the Moon.

540 These aspects denote good, increase of substance by means of females, esteem and gain by the common people, and well to take journeys, seek in debts, &c. To the ill aspects, loss by means of women, voyages, suits at law, and the hatred of wife's mother, or slander by a female, much controversy and loss of credit.

To the Moon's Nodes.

541 To the North Node, ☊, profit, credit, by faithful dealings, religious, and charitably inclined. To the ☋, loss of substance, and the reverse of the above, danger of being cheated, and the native is given to dissembling and falsehood; he is knavish and selfish, and is very obnoxious to perplexity and mourning, in the 2nd, extravagant.

DIRECTION OF THE SUN TO PROMISSORS.

The Sun to parallel, conjunction, or ill aspect of Herschel.

542 Death of relations, generally those most distant in the family—yet it may be the father, if ruler of the fourth, or if he be posited therein at birth, especially the square aspect—it is likely to be the mother if located in the 10th, or is ruler thereof. If Sol be hyleg, and Herschel rule the 8th, or is anareta (243), or is in the anaretic places (241), then death, or sudden danger, and extraordinary accidents. The parallel often gives the death of aunts, and strange conduct, much trouble by public bodies, the church, from clubs, committees, &c. If ruler of the 2nd, or 7th, loss in pecuniary affairs; if of the 6th, liable to suffer from bathing or water; if of the 9th or 10th, by machinery and inventions, and often accidents in his employment (441).

Sol to good aspects of Herschel.

543 Unexpected benefits from relations, inventions, or from public bodies; also popular in his writings (if engaged therein),

studious of the arts and sciences (169), and he gains both money and popularity, especially if on the 12th, or in the 9th at birth; and if near the 12th, so as to be in mundane sextile of the M.C., then popular in astrology, and other uncommon studies. If ruler of the 2nd, money matters go well; if of the 3rd, neighbours, relations, and short journeys, are advantageous; if of the 7th, gain in lawsuits, &c.; and so judge of the effects as he may be situated in houses (199).

The Sun parallel, conjunction, or ill aspects of Saturn.

544 If the Sun be hyleg, danger of severe and fatal illness; death of relations. Much weakness of body, colds, melancholy, chronic diseases, especially in the head, heart, back, and stomach, or other parts, according to the sign Saturn is in at birth; the eyes are likely to suffer (177), danger of falls from buildings, of being crushed, &c., also the native's father suffers, if lord of the 4th, he may die. Much trouble by Saturnine persons, especially such as are in power, noblemen, landlords, &c.; danger in travelling, loss by storms, shipwreck, &c., separation of the native's parents, destruction to his fame and credit, loss of business and good name, &c., he is robbed and cheated by servants, tenants, &c., if lord of the 6th especially, and is full of heavy thoughts, and suffers much vexation, and may be tempted to commit suicide. Envy and malice are active against the native, and more especially if ruler of the 10th. If an eclipse happen at the time on the place of the conjunction, the effect is violent, and generally of a public nature. To a king, defeat, especially if he be in the 7th or 10th house.

The Sun in good aspect of Saturn.

545 Some marks of esteem, and promotion from an aged gentleman or person in power, he gains in lawsuits, the native is preferred, and manages his affairs prosperously, receiving honour, gifts, &c.; it imports wealth by husbandry, legacy, architecture, or some inheritance; it inclines to gravity and severity, laborious studies or works; the native succeeds with elderly persons, and in all matters under the influence of Saturn, such as masonry, minerals, metals, coals (170).

The Sun parallel, conjunction, or good aspect of Jupiter.

546 Health of body, peace of mind, increase of wealth, victory over adversaries, and enjoyment of the goods of fortune, preferment, office, dignity, employment, &c., according to the native's situation in life; church preferment, inclined to be religious, benefits by lawyers, magistrates, merchants, especially if Jupiter is fortified at birth, &c.; to a king, it denotes peace and tranquillity, commerce flourishing, yet the clergy grasping at power, &c. The

native may have a son born, or preferred, or a legacy left from a deceased friend, or, if capable, he will either court or marry.

The Sun in ill aspect of Jupiter.

547 The native suffers by lawyers, magistrates, clergymen, and professors of religion, who cause him expenses, more especially if either Sol or Jupiter is ruler of the 2nd, yet he usually overcomes and recovers all : to a king, it shews a discontented clergy and nobility, breach of laws and privileges of the realm, mercantile sufferings, injury to bankers, &c. (171). The native suffers by private enemies if Jupiter is lord of the 12th : if ruler of the 7th, by public enemies, both in fortune and credit ; if Sol or Jupiter be ruler of the 1st, then health will be repaired.

The Sun parallel, conjunction, or ill aspect of Mars.

548 Acute diseases, fevers, accidents by fire, iron, or hot water, &c., also kicks by horses, bites by dogs, &c., according to the sign Mars is in (179). In a martial nativity, the conjunction gives preferment ; in Watery signs, these directions denote fluxes, apoplexy, and in all cases some loss of blood ; the native is rash and violent, he does nothing prudently, losses by thieves, lawsuits ; let him, therefore, beware of disputes with superiors and men of rank, and let him avoid any new work, for he will have no success, let him shun quarrels and the company of soldiers, especially if the Sun be hyleg ; also let him beware of fevers if ruler of the 6th, and inflammation, and live temperately (270) ; if Mars be ruler of the 4th, 8th, or 12th, great danger of death, especially if he be the killing planet (243).

The Sun to good aspects of Mars.

549 These bring martial friends and preferment ; marriage if ruler of the 7th, also an inclination to shoot, hunt, ride, &c., more than formerly. Soldiers act daringly and meet promotion, if ruler of the 10th. It causes a journey, and much trotting and trudging about ; if in a lawsuit or fight, he overcomes ; in arts and sciences he gains by study, lecturing, &c. ; a physician or surgeon does well under this direction, and he may make a useful discovery.

The Sun parallel, conjunction, or good aspects of Venus.

550 Stirs up a desire for music, plays, and merriment ; all kinds of Venus's pleasures ; the native makes love, or marries, and spends his time and money among the ladies. If Venus be weak, the conjunction causes unlawful affections. The body is now healthy and mind cheerful ; all things succeed, estate increased, female children born, and the native respected. In female nativities,

marriage. If Sun or Venus be rulers of the 2nd, gain by employment, is witty and ingenious ; if Venus rule the 6th, healthful, and
servants agree.

The Sun to bad aspects of Venus.

551 A barren time, no issue, the native given to impure conduct
and sordid actions, he incurs contentions, discredit, and scandal.
If Sun be hyleg, he suffers Venus's diseases, according to the sign
Venus is in at birth. He has differences with females, is refused
marriage, quarrels with his wife, his daughter elopes, &c., and he
suffers by scandalous adversaries, and probably by law, if it fall
in the 7th ; drinking and disorderly if in the 5th or 11th. The
opposition seldom occurs in a person's life time.

The Sun conjunction, parallel, or good aspects of Mercury.

552 Much active business, studious, and inclination to literary
things and persons, gain by literature, or dealing in books, new
employments, &c., occupied with accompts and writings, he gains
fame thereby, or by some invention, if Mercury be strong ; it brings
an inclination to travel, and benefits by young persons, also, the
conjunction brings controversies and disputes, thefts, lawsuits,
and unprofitable journeys, or prejudiced by false witnesses, or lies
being spoken, &c., of the native ; and if the Sun be hyleg, serious
diseases, hurts, &c., according as Mercury is aspected ; he is
generally changeable in his fancy, and unsettled in his studies.

The Sun in bad aspects to Mercury.

553 Accusations and suits against the native, character im-
pugned, or he may be guilty of some deceit or knavery, and be
thereby much disgraced ; he suffers by forgery and fraud, bad
bills, &c., and unsuccessful journeys, and is greatly annoyed by
lawyers and young persons, his mind is afflicted, and loses his
employment, bad trade, &c., probably by decision of a court
against him. Young persons run away from their employers, are
rusticated from college, &c., it gives an averseness to learning,
and the native is often unjustly aspersed ; his health suffers
according to the sign Mercury is in, and the planets which aspect
him. The last two aspects seldom occur.

The Sun to parallel or conjunction of the Moon.

554 This impairs the health, brings humours, &c., in the head,
weak eyes, blindness, &c., the native is unsettled, travels, removes,
wastes his property by idle courses and improvidence. The Moon
being strong, gives preferment, and may give marriage, but the
wife will be proud and imperious, striving for mastery ; if weak,
inconstancy.

The Sun parallel, or good aspects of the Moon.

555 Favour and friendship of powerful persons, rich ladies, &c., who employ the native, or benefit him by preferment. It gives journeys of a profitable and honourable kind, and public employments, he is much occupied with females, and may marry a rich wife if Moon be strong; it increases his friends, and may give the birth of children, or their settlement in life to the native's content.

The Sun in ill aspects of the Moon.

556 An unhappy time, full of losses, bad trade, and crosses, many powerful men are provoked against the native, he wrangles with his wife, and may separate, quarrels occur in the family, his parents separate, his children die or act amiss. The native lives intemperately, mixes with low company, loose women, &c., and has ill health. If Moon be hyleg, he suffers grievous disease, according to the sign the Sun is in. It produces fevers, sore eyes, and blindness, the small-pox, measles, worms, &c., it lowers the native's credit and character, and renders him unpopular. If the direction falls in the 8th, or Sun or Moon rule the 8th, and radically afflicted by Saturn or Mars ruler of the 8th, very likely a sickness ending in death.

The Sun conjunction, parallel, or good aspects of the Part of Fortune.

557 Honourable disbursements, the native more liberal than formerly, waste of estate and prodigality, according to the house in which the ⊕ falls. Profit and advantage by persons of rank, many friends above his rank in life, profit but expenditure, not much saving.

The Sun in ill aspect of the Part of Fortune.

558 Damage by lawsuits, waste of property by the envy of great persons, false and scandalous accusations, loss of office, &c.

The Sun to the Moon's Nodes.

559 The Sun to the North Node brings honour, credit, gain by business, if in the 10th; legacy if in the 8th; in the 11th, many friends, and the native gains in his wishes; if in the 4th or 5th, good for speculations, and attendant upon pleasure, lecturers have good audiences, parsons full congregations, and more especially if Sol is ruler of the 9th at birth; if in the 12th, his enemies are unable to do him any important harm. ✕ To the South Node just the contrary effects may be expected, loss of substance, office, and friends, danger of sickness by fevers, endemic and epidemic contagion, pains and weakness in the eyes, melancholic or rheumatic affections, many losses and bad bargains—at this period it would be well not to speculate.

The Sun brought to the Cusps of Houses.

560 To the 1st House, honour, preferment, health, respect, new agreeable acquaintances, private enemies and he are reconciled, servants obedient and industrious, purchases fortunate, and his domestic affairs go well—yet danger by large cattle. To the 2nd, many unnecessary expenses, yet if Venus or Jupiter be therein, he augments his pecuniary affairs. To the 3rd, he takes short journeys to see friends and kindred, and relations are favourable to him. To the 4th, if the fortunes aspect the cusp of the 4th, gain by lands, buildings, minerals, &c., but if Saturn casts his square or opposition, it portends loss by servants, and may be cheated by his father, loss by old persons, servants, tenants, and by fire. To the 5th, good to his children, fond of feasting, pleasure, and speculating, and if the Sun be unfortunate in the 5th, losses by pleasure, feasting, and so on. To the 6th, gain by cattle, servants, uncles, yet sickness to him or to his father. To the 7th, an inclination to marry, court, and combat; he overcomes his public foes, but is very liable to sickness. To the 8th, gain by the wife or husband, he fears his own death, and is perplexed by concurring inheritance. To the 9th, inclined to travel if the cusp of the 9th be Cancer, Scorpio, or Pisces, then he may take a short voyage, but in this case if Herschel, Saturn, or Mars afflict the 9th, then danger of shipwreck, and the journeys will be unfortunate; church preferment if an ecclesiastic. To the 10th, gain by trade, honour, office, merchandise, yet if the 10th be afflicted it threatens imprisonment or transportation. To the 11th, many good friends, much esteem from his creditors, and he succeeds according to his moderate wishes. To the 12th house, many enemies, and they privately malign his character; much displeasure will arise from some acts of deceit. He thrives by dealing in cattle.

NOTE.—The Sun being radically strong and well posited, and brought to the cusps of these houses, will signify all these, and also when directed to good aspects of these houses; but the contrary, if Sol be unfortunate or directed to the evil aspects of these points.

The Sun directed to his own aspects.

561 To his ill aspects (201), signify infamy, contempt, loss, mischief by those things and persons signified by that house in which it falls (199). Sickness and malady, according to the sign in which the Sun is, and in which the aspect falls. The square brings sure death. To his good aspects (202), dignity, honour, prosperity, happiness, by those things and persons signified by that house in which the direction falls. The sextile is sure to be fortunate (476), but it should fall in a good house. To his own parallel, preferment, pleasure, &c., according to his dignity (477).

The Sun directed to the fixed Stars.

562 *Sol to Rigel,* boldness, insolency, surliness of temper, makes himself enemies, and precipitates into animosities and entrapments.

To Orionis, will have the same effect; culminating, prosperity in business, and martial preferments.

To Cor Scorpio, honour if the native is mindful, yet danger of inflammation in the eyes, the blood is heated, and danger of feverish action throughout the whole system.

To Sirius, military preferment, and workers in metal do well, yet they may have some competitions against which they will have to contend, but will conquer.

To Cor Leo, some preferment, but death of a male in the family, the parents indisposed, tradesmen do well, and they act honourably, new friends.

To Arcturus, pecuniary gain, and the native acts honourably.

To the Asselli, a fever, loss of honour, he is obnoxious to censure; to a dissipated character, imprisonment.

To the North Scale, rather fortunate.

To Præsepe, Pleiades, Hyades, Castor, Pollux, and other stars of the nature of the Moon and Mars combined, will cause blindness of one or both eyes, and if Præsepe be on the Ascendant or with Sun or Moon in an angle, certainly blindness.

To Aldebaron, fortunate in his affairs yet much indisposed, in other respects he acts like Mars.

To Spica advancement and contentedness.

To Antares, and all other stars of the nature of Mercury and Mars combined, presages sickness, with a disposition to haughtiness and ignorant pride.

To Deneb, and all others of the nature of Herschel, unfortunate, and publicly disgraced.

To Cauda, great turmoil in connection with the native's respectability, yet he may raise himself to some degree of eminence, but it is generally brought about by fraudulent procedure.

To the Cratch, in the breast of the Crab, in the 6th degree of Leo, danger to the head and eyes, injury by means of gunshot, or by machinery, or by falls or bruises.

To Hircus, advancement, and fortunate when culminating.

For a farther judgment on the Fixed Stars, look in the " Definition of Terms " for the nature and position of those distant bodies.

THE MOON TO ASPECTS.

The Moon to the body, bad aspect, or parallel of Herschel.

563 Unexpected public disesteem, and if the Moon is hyleg, death in the family, and extraordinary accidents—not well to speculate—keep from all precipices, railways, and machinery—it is dangerous to bathe, or even to go near water—affliction in the head, and the native acts very eccentrically; if in the 10th or 2nd, sudden loss; if in the 9th or 3rd, disputation among brethren and neighbours—bad for travelling, or taking scientific expeditions, or for making religious adventures; if in the 11th or 5th, ill luck to his children, and no success in speculations; if in the 7th, discord in the hymeneal tie, and he is liable to suffer from open enemies; in the 12th, danger of imprisonment, with other secret sorrows; in the 8th, death in the family; in the 6th, sickness, or treacherous servants, and to a farmer this brings loss in his stall in the 2nd, unlooked for anxiety.

The Moon to good aspects of Herschel.

564 Benefits by means of public bodies and public writers; in the 2nd, a profitable money period; in the 3rd, take journeys; in the 4th, speculate in buildings; in the 5th, benefit to children; in the 6th, health, he may trade in cattle, hire servants, &c.; in the 7th, becomes friends with his public foes; in the 8th, an expected legacy will be obtained; in the 9th, travel, study, and purchasing books; in the 11th, many good friends, benefits to his children (if any); in the 12th, reconciliation between him and his foes, he does well in large cattle. In these directions take into consideration what that house signifies in which Herschel is found, as 476 and 479.

The parallel, conjunction, and ill aspect of Saturn.

565 Many chronic, cold, and moist diseases arise, with humours abounding, and general ill health. If Moon be hyleg, it gives agues, and low fever, pains in the eyes, colic, palsy, dropsy, rheumatic affections, coughs and influenza, gout, apoplexy, &c., all lingering diseases, according to the nature of Saturn, and the sign he occupies. These directions bring mental troubles, discontent and afflictions, public adversaries and lawsuits, fears and anxieties, loss of property, lying informations, thieves and aspersions of character by low vulgar people, servants, and the mob; he quarrels with female relations, loses by the sea or seamen, becomes bankrupt or insolvent, &c.; if the direction falls in the 12th or 8th houses, it may be productive of imprisonment or death of himself, or some aged female of his family; in the 6th, sickness is sure; in the 7th, jealousy between husband and wife.

The Moon in good aspects of Saturn.

566 Gifts and rewards from elderly persons, honourable acquaintances, especially females, respect from the lower classes, much
popularity, friendship of Saturnine persons, benefits by dealing in
Saturnine commodities, as lead, coals, tillage, cattle, wool, &c.,
and by buildings, farming, &c., also legacies.   If a merchant, he
does best by dealing with elderly persons, and such like as are
described in 267.

The Moon parallel, conjunction, or good aspects of Jupiter.

567 Health, content, wealth and honour occur according to the
situation in life of the native, prosperity and success in journeys,
lawsuits and speculations, he conquers his enemies.   Office,
employment, marriage, command, new business, &c.   University
degrees, clerical advancement or law preferments, many friends.
To kings, peace, flourishing revenues, ambassadors sent abroad to
good purpose.

The Moon to ill aspects of Jupiter.

568 Difficulties in his employment or office; lawyers and religious people, magistrates, &c., annoy him; losses of property by
waste, cheats, thieves, and extravagance; by his own virtue and
exertions he may overcome all attempts against him, and those
who were his enemies will become his friends; he may be likely to
quarrel with his landlord, or some petty lawyer or churchman, or
about church matters, especially if he be in church fellowship, yet
no lasting evil need be apprehended, the blood becomes corrupt,
and hence diseases of the liver, and particularly if Jupiter be in
Leo, or the 6th house.

The Moon parallel, conjunction, or ill aspect of Mars.

569 Abundance of sorrows, enmity, accidents, and misfortunes,
imprisonment, loss of property, thefts, squandering on the part of
his wife, &c. ; active enemies start up against him, and he suffers
strange anxieties; he has diseases according to the sign Mars is in,
and accidents (179) ; he is in danger of fever and of death if Moon
be hyleg, by fire, cuts, wounds, bites, kicks, or gunshot: and if
Venus throw an ill aspect, by poison, or treachery of females; he
is choleric, and quarrelsome, very much inclined to bear arms, or
associate with martial men, and becomes addicted to vices,
according to the sign Mars is in; if in the house of Herschel,
curious temper; if in the house of Saturn, he is dogged; if that of
Jupiter, he becomes hypercritical; that of the Sun, proud and
haughty ; his own house, very quarrelsome; that of Venus, loose ;
that of Mercury, fraudulent; that of the Moon, unsettled.   If Mars
be aspected by Saturn or Sol, and he in Leo, especially near

Ascelli, Bull's Eye, or Cor Scorpio, affliction to the eyesight, he may die of pestilence or fire. He receives disdain and insults by women, if he has a good wife she may die, it causes injuries to the face or eyes, also the small-pox, stone, gravel, and gonorrhœa, &c. If he marry under the conjunction, it is very unfortunate. To a king, war, bloodshed, and losses.

The Moon to good aspect of Mars.

570 It gives a desire to martial and manly exercises, as riding, shooting, gambling, carding, dicing, and the native takes delight in horses, the company of military men, and warlike affairs. Preferment and profit, birth of a son, or if single, he may marry, yet he may expect losses by women, and by dealing in horses, unless Mars be well aspected. If Mars be weak, and the nativity denote it, he takes to drinking, gaming, or loose conduct. To a king, it denotes increase of the army, and if at war, great battles, victories, &c. To a merchant, dealings at sea, and good returns; to a tradesman, much business and success in his trade; to a farmer, increase of stock, and he will be made constable, or some other parish officer.

The Moon to conjunction of Sun.

571 It causes fevers and affections of the eyes, &c., and if the Moon be hyleg, it may cause death. Much anxiety of mind, many mutations and expectations in his affairs, reverses, &c. In many cases it denotes marriage. To merchants, &c., good trade, yet some slur on their credit, it causes generally some great change in the life and affairs of the native; if Sol be strong and fortunate, beneficial; if otherwise, the reverse.

The Moon to good aspects of the Sun.

572 Profitable and honourable friends, popularity, especially among females of rank, &c., he has good health, and receives some office or employment. Journeys or voyages beyond the sea, especially if it fall in the 9th house and in a watery sign, much gain thereby, the native should exert himself under this influence to rise in life; he is strongly inclined to marry, and if he does, it is prosperous; if married, he may expect a child, unless Sol be afflicted. To merchants, reputation, it brings prosperous trade; to a king, removal of leagues, victory, honourable peace; to farmers, good luck in cattle, and his crops are favourable.

The Moon to bad aspects of the Sun.

573 Extreme danger and affliction of body and mind, it converts the love of some female to hatred, it causes injury by popular tumult, &c., and the dissembling friendship of some man of rank, loss of office, by which the native suffers. If the aspect fall near

nebulous stars, there is danger of hurts or diseases to the eyes. It produces fevers, coughs, colics, fluxes, &c., according to the nature of the sign and house the significator and promittor are in (180). To a nobleman, it shows popular dislike—loss of honour; to a farmer, an ill landlord, who wrongs him; to a poor man, danger of the treadmill, &c. It brings contentions and quarrels, and oppressions from men in power, and is an ill time to speculate; it generally endures for five or six months.

The Moon conjunction, or good aspects of Venus.

574 A pleasant, healthful, contented and happy period, the native inclines to be merry and jocund, fond of entertainment, and addicted to pleasure, which will be legitimate or otherwise as Venus is well or ill aspected. He receives gifts and favours from females; if a female servant, then perquisites from ladies, is inclined to love-making and marriage (if capable), and free from all care. To the married, it denotes children, chiefly females, and also the marriage and settlement of children; to merchants, good success; to farmers, profit by Venus matters, small cattle, poultry, &c. Generally happy marriage, obedient children, domestic felicity, and prosperity by means of females. To kings, peace and new allies.

The Moon in ill aspect of Venus.

575 Much trouble by wandering affections, illicit amours, scandal, disrepute, and infamy in consequence. Many crosses, annoyances, and controversies through women. Waste of estate by improvidence, bad contracts, and intemperance. If the native marries under these directions, it is unhappy, and to one whom he loves not, and one who will not be obedient and affectionate. It produces Venus diseases, and, in children, if Venus be afflicted in a watery sign, measles, small-pox, &c.; in women, irregular and abundant courses, diseases of the matrix, especially if Moon or Venus be in the 5th, or ruler thereof, or in Scorpio (183), or in Taurus (181).

The Moon in conjunction of Mercury.

576 This direction brings journeys or voyages, the latter if Mercury be in Cancer in the 9th. It engages him in causes and controversies sometimes, brings him much active business, is very energetic, manages his business well, and is given to study, writing, public speaking, &c. If Mercury is afflicted at birth, the native is then given to lying, dissembling, cozening. To a merchant, much business, journeys; to a factor, many accompts. All depends on how Mercury is aspected; as, if afflicted at birth, he gives troubles by frauds, bankrupts, thefts, also sickness and accidents, according to the sign. To a king, foreign news, active exertions among his allies, sends ambassadors, &c.

The Moon to good aspects of Mercury.

577 Success to the native in his employments, he is inclined to pursue accompts, mathematical studies, &c. It gives delight in music or mechanical devices, a propensity to travel and make changes in his abode, he has the friendship of some lady of rank, or receives an employment, secretary, librarian, literary, or as a messenger, traveller, or ambassador, he has pleasure in his children, may have a child born, or married, apprenticed. Succeeds in law, or with young people.

The Moon in ill aspects of Mercury.

578 An averseness to study, books, science, is felt. If Mercury is ruler of the 12th, 4th, or 8th, danger of imprisonment. He is frowned on by the vulgar, suffers by popular tumult, questioned by some fraud or forgery, according as Mercury is aspected at birth. Many scandals, libels, false charges, swindling, and fraudulent attempts by cunning attorneys, &c., against the native, injuries by law and lawyers, ministers, thefts; he is annoyed by his children, who are unfortunate and imprudent, and by young persons generally; he may lose a child. There is sometimes danger of delirium and madness.

The Moon to Dragon's Head or to the Dragon's Tail.

579 To the Dragon's Head, the forerunner of a thriving year, increasing the native's estate, with honour, tranquillity of mind, health of body. To the Dragon's Tail, the native has strange distempered fancies, and afflicted by the envy of Saturnine and martial persons, with whom he has variance; generally brings a melancholic disease, proceeding from phlegm; also an impediment in one of the eyes, generally the left, often endangers the native's life by poison, or a sudden fall.

The Moon to conjunction or good aspects of the Part of Fortune.

580 Friendship and gain by females, much action for and with the common people, by whom the native profits. He may undertake long journeys or voyages, and he will have full employment.

The Moon to bad aspect of the Part of Fortune.

581 Losses by bargains, contracts, &c., by trade with the lower classes, by sea voyages or sailors. Hatred by some respectable female; many lawsuits and heavy debts.

The Moon to the Twelve Houses.

582 To the 1st, if Moon be ruler of the 7th, marriage; if of the 6th, sickness, loss by servants, cattle, &c. To the 2nd, gain,

especially if Jupiter or Venus be near the cusp. To the 3rd, a short journey, visiting among relations and neighbours. To the 4th, inheritance, gain by farming, loss of honour, &c. (525). To the 5th, delight in children, mirth, pastime, play, sport and pleasure. To the 6th, thefts by servants, loss in small cattle, an ill habit of body—of the effects as in 524. To the 7th, troubled with enemies, disagrees with wife or sweetheart, a lawsuit, or has difference with his landlord; if ruler of the 1st, marriage—other events as in 525, also 500. To the 8th, death, disagreement connected therewith, slight danger to the native's life, some good, as in 524. To the 9th, a journey by land, if Taurus, Virgo, or Capricorn be on the cusp, then a journey on water. To the 10th, as 524. To the 11th new friends, and benefit from them and by their means, and he receives the fruits of his anticipations. To the 12th, loss, contempt, sorrows, mischief, private enemies; if Mars or Saturn be thereon, fear of death or imprisonment, loss in great cattle, if a farmer; if good planets be on the 12th, then judge as in 524.

The Moon to the fixed Stars.

583 *Moon to Rigel*, danger of sickness and even death to his wife, mother, or other elderly female relation.

To *Aldebaron*, popularity, gain of wealth, honour, and respectability.

To *Algeneb*, dishonour, public disesteem, unfortunate in writings, accompts, and mercantile pursuits.

To *Medusæ*, unfortunate, violent and dangerous, of the nature of Jupiter and Saturn.

To *Caput Andromedæ*, of the nature of Jupiter and Venus, fortunate, producing riches and honour.

To *Antares*, much active business and popularity.

To *Arcturus*, riches and respectability, preferment and health.

To *Arista* or *Virgin's Spike*, increase of wealth by invention, gains honour and public estimation.

To *Bellatrix, Betalguese, Cæpella, Crater, Procyon*, all these are prognostic of military honour, and workers in iron gain by their business. Bellatrix, blindness by accident when joined with the lights.

To *Hydra's Heart*, trouble, through women, and ill fortune, well not to purchase, danger of losing office or employment.

To *Bull's South Eye*, fortunate in all affairs ruled by Venus.

To *Lucida, Pleidum, Presæpe, Hyades, Pollux, Ascelli, Deneb,* and other stars of the nature of Moon and Mars combined, denote great defect in the sight, often blindness, and more especially if the luminaries are with any nebulous stars at birth. The Moon in the 22nd degree of Gemini, afflicted, is productive of the loss of one eye. The Moon with Pleiades with Mars, and Saturn with Regulus, shew the loss of one or both the eyes.

To *Cor Scorpio*, many enemies, yet he rises above them all, death of wife or mother, or some female friend and acquaintance; danger from cattle and falls from vehicles.

To the *Bull's Horns*, danger from intoxication, and other furious and beastly procedure; inflammatory action, surfeit, blotches, dysuria, fever, venereal distempers, with pains in the arms and shoulders.

To *Canis Majoris*, pleasure and health, and the love of females.

To *Capella, Crater, Nigel, Orion's Belt*, prosperity in business, publicity and many friends, especially when culminating or on the ascendant.

To *Casta, Cauda, Lucida, Caput Algol*, portends mischief and great anxiety, fortunate in new undertakings.

To *Ceti*, sickness, disgrace, ill fortune, danger from falls and great cattle.

To *Deneb*, public disgrace, misfortunes from water and vehicles of conveyance.

To *Hercules*, the native is proud, unhealthful, damage to his wife, mother, or daughter (if any).

THE PART OF FORTUNE TO ASPECTS.

To the parallel, conjunction, or ill aspects of Herschel.

584 This is extremely detrimental to all pecuniary procedures, bargains are bad made under these aspects, the native suffers from bonds, clubs and speculations. He is very likely rogued out of some legacy, or has disputations about wills or debts; no money affairs will be successful. The good aspects are reversed in effects, producing a good period for getting in his debts, his speculations are prosperous, and he may have a relation who promises him a legacy or property—he is fortunate in clubs, bonds, and in railways if he wish.

The Part of Fortune to the aspects of Saturn.

585 The ill aspects, waste of property, he is robbed, if he bets or gambles he is sure to be a loser, he has many calls for money which he is not able to pay, and if a tradesman, he has trouble in obtaining his debts. The good aspects, he has gain by aged persons, and by agricultural pursuits, and by those persons and things mentioned in 362 and 170.

The Part of Fortune to the aspects of Jupiter.

586 The good aspects, gifts, rewards, benefits, patronage, success in business, and gain therein, especially by those persons and things as in 171, and he ought to follow after distinction (354). The bad aspects, loss by means of gentlemen, religious persons, law-suits and vexations, falling off in trade or income, disappointment in receiving money (338).

The Part of Fortune to the aspects of Mars.

587 To his bad aspects, loss by thievish servants, or robbery by thieves or soldiers, or by fires, by gaming or betting wagers, by idle courses, lawsuits, quarrels, backbiting (164). His good aspects signify augmentation of wealth by means of martial persons and things, as in 172, he may trade safely in cattle, and in maritime articles, &c., his merchandise turns out well, and he may now make negotiations connected with trade and traffic, especially in those articles spoken of in 364.

The Part of Fortune to the aspects of Sol.

588 To the good aspects, honourable disbursements, he is chari-table, the conjunction gives prodigality and consumption through indifference and thoughtless expenses, many friends above his own rank, yet does not save much money, he has many friends and active employment. The ill aspects, danger of lawsuits, the envy of great persons, many false accusations, and it is the forerunner of the loss of office.

The Part of Fortune to the aspects of Venus.

589 The good aspects, gifts from a lady, he purchases furniture, clothes, &c.; tradesmen do well, and merchants have good fortune. The bad aspects produce unnecessary expenses, occasioned by women, he has much strife, and falls into dishonour and disgrace through females, he is extravagant and riotous, jealous of his wife, and is given to drink and pleasure.

The Part of Fortune to the aspects of Mercury.

590 To his good aspects, increase of fortune by bargains, con-tracts, accompts, learning, law, and by all witty inventions; he might gain by voyages, commerce; to a scholar, he gains degrees at college, and advances his fortune by a literary publication. His ill aspects denote much turmoil to lawyers, false witnesses, bonds, writings and unjust accompts, he is disposed to act unjustly, and his credit is questioned; if in a lawsuit, he loses, and his children trouble him; not well to speculate in writings, neither is it well to have anything to do with disputations.

The Part of Fortune to the Moon's Nodes.

591 To the good aspects of Moon's North Node, which is the Dragon's Head, produces gain by means of friends, and having a multiplicity of occupations, &c., he advances his fortune by means of jovial persons, as in 171.   To the Dragon's Tail, waste of estate, by fire, fury, war or disputation ; if in lawsuit, he loses, and his enemies overcome him.

Note.—The Part of Fortune can have no effect with the Fixed Stars, except it is in conjunction with them at birth.   It may have some effect by being brought to the cusp of the Houses.   To the 1st, gain by his own industry ; to the 2nd, increase of wealth ; to the 3rd, by kindred and short journeys ; to the 4th, he may gain by agricultural pursuits, or by purchasing minerals or property ; to the 5th, rewards, and gain to his children ; to the 6th, gain by cattle and servants ; to the 7th, damage by lawsuits and public enemies ; to the 8th, gain by the dead, or by the means of the wife ; to the 9th, success, and gain by long journeys, literature, &c.; to the 10th, gain by friends in trade and authority ; to the 11th, many friends to the native's advantage ; to the 12th, he may deal in large cattle, and he will gain by horse racing and other transactions in cattle.

THE PLANETS TO THEIR OWN ASPECTS.

592 The Moon to her own good aspects, produce profitable changes, and removals to the native's advantage, friendship of females, and benefits from their influence, journeys will be prosperous.   But the Moon to her own ill aspects, produce troubles, losses, unfortunate changes, and the enmity of women and the populace ; thieves are taken when the Moon is in semisquare with her own place in their nativities.

Herschel to aspects of his own place or to the Planets.

593 To his own good aspects, unexpected benefits and profitable changes, according to the house over which he rules, &c. (476).   To his bad aspects, unlooked-for misfortune of a public character, danger of falls, bruises, and other accidents.   To unfortunate aspects of Saturn, danger of falls from heights and drowning, imprisonment for neglect of family, and he may expect annoyances from parish officers ; the fortunate aspects will give some benefits, especially if the native be then connected with minerals and other things, as 362.   The ill fortune angles with Jupiter, disrespect from religionists, loss of public office, and detriment from the populace ; if a religionist, he is brought before the officers of the church to answer for some misdemeanour, and is very likely to be cast out of church fellowship—many false accusations ; to fortunate angles,

the reverse, great respect among preachers, and in the church, he is a popular preacher, and does well in business among those persons to whom he is joined in society.   To Mars by evil aspect, obnoxious to hurts, injuries, and diseases; to good aspects, he will then do well to trade in metals, or anything mentioned in 172.   The conjunction of Sol, or to his ill aspects, inflammatory indisposition, according to the sign Herschel was in at birth; if ruler of the 10th, unexpected losses in trade; ruler of the 2nd, unwelcomed annoyances about money, and so judge of the rest of the houses.   The good transits or aspects of Herschel to the Sun portend sudden benefits, and public approbation, if he is a person of any notoriety; if ruler of the 3rd, and passing there, or is ruler, then a journey to visit friends; if ruler of the 9th, or passing there, or its lord, the native is studious, religiously disposed, and if a literary character, he gets promoted.   To the good aspects of Venus, marriage, or benefits from females, or such things as are noted in 174, or gain by dealing in such things as are mentioned in 365; the bad aspects of Herschel to Venus give disputation with his wife or lover, it may be with his mother if in the 10th, or Venus rule that house; if she rule the 3rd, it will be with his sister.   To the good aspects of Mercury it is excellent for writing, public speaking, or for advancing himself in learning, or for obtaining an office of trust, especially if Mercury was strong at birth.   To bad aspects of Mercury, then the reverse of the foregoing, danger of loss from writings, bonds, lawsuits, controversy, trade, or office.   To the place or bad aspects of the Moon, danger of sickness, not well to take journeys, especially if either of them rules the 3rd or 9th; disputation with wife or female foes, if she rules the 7th; death to a female if she rules the 8th, or be on its cusp; to the good aspects of the Moon, advantages from females, also by speculations in those things found in 176.   To the Dragon's Head, by bad aspect, unexpected adversity; but the good aspects produce unlooked-for prosperity; the bad aspects of the Dragon's Tail is bad, bringing disagreement with some of his acquaintance; but the good aspects are of very little importance.

Saturn to his own aspects, or to those of other Planets.

594 Saturn to his own good aspects is powerful in producing good according to the power he has at birth; if ruler of the 1st or 6th, health generally good; if ruler of the 2nd, pecuniary affairs are prosperous; if of the 10th, business is permanently good, with Saturnine honour; his ill aspects act the reverse, producing sickness or loss, or other calamities, according to the house Saturn rules.   To the body or good aspect of Jupiter, slight honour, health, wealth and dignity from the favour of the great; to his ill aspects, slight dishonour and indisposition, with some loss if either of them is ruler of the 10th or 2nd: bad for journeys, if ruler of the 3rd or

9th.   Saturn to the good aspects of Mars, and Mars be well affected, then martial preferment, the native will do well with metals; yet he is given to dissemble, especially if ruler of the 12th or 8th; and the bad aspects produce danger among thieves; if ruler of the 7th or 6th, bad servants; if ruler of the 8th or 4th, danger of falls or bruises, during these effects it will be well for the native to be as little busied as possible with any new undertaking.   To the body or bad aspects of the Sun, dishonour and loss in trade, if ruler of the 10th or 2nd, his expectations are frustrated; sickness if the Sun is hyleg, or either of them rule the 6th, or 8th, or 1st; their good aspects, not anything important beyond the native being thoughtful, sparing, and may attempt to obtain some office of trust ($\odot$ to $\hbar$).   Saturn to the body or good aspects of Venus, the native is inclined to be immodest, given up to pleasure and company.   The ill aspects are productive of disputation with females, or with his wife if rulers of the 7th.   To the body or ill aspect of Mercury, the native is subtile, crafty, knavish, vexed by words or writings, his fancy perplexed, children disobedient if ruler of the 5th, dull of apprehension, and he will affect gravity; the good aspects, he is conceited, full of whims, loves curiosity, and is studious and reserved.   The body or bad aspects of the Moon makes him changeable, he is plagued with coughs, colds, and rheumatisms, if the Moon is hyleg, or ruler of the 6th or 8th; he disagrees with his wife if in the 7th, or with the governess thereof; subject to enemies if ruler of the 12th; the good aspects produce gain by all agricultural pursuits, and at this time farmers, masons, (170), &c., are fortunate.   Passing the 10th, trouble and difficulty by or through connections formed at that time, especially if R. Passing the 4th, evil effects, except counteracted by favourable configurations or circumstances in operation at the same time. Passing the 2nd, generally some great change in the native's pursuits in the world, often leading him into important speculations. Common sign on this cusp at birth, and Saturn therein, confer a restless, unsettled, speculative turn of mind, constantly removing or changing his business or pursuits, fond of travelling.   Passing the 11th or 5th, lasting friendship.   To the ☌, honour and happiness; to ☍, dishonour, contempt, malice, shame, enemies.   To ⊕, increase of fortune if he was strong at birth.

Jupiter to his own aspects, or Transits to other Planets.

595 To his own place, or good aspect of others, much benefit, good health, an increase of acquaintances, respect and estimation. To Herschel, popularity and gain; but the ill aspects, disrepute, and loss of honour; to Saturn, if Saturn be good in the radix, an augmentation of good; and if Jupiter rule the 1st, or come to bad aspect of Saturn, danger to the native, sorrow, implacable adver-

saries, and lingering indisposition, especially if Saturn rule the 1st, 6th, or 8th; but in the 12th, many secret sorrows; to the good aspect of Mars, profit by travel, commerce, kindred, and honourable men; but to the ill aspects, the reverse; to the body or bad aspect of Sol, denotes no good; prejudice from persons of character; but the good aspects, the reverse. Over the place of Venus, happiness, health of body, content of mind, with pecuniary advantages; the bad aspects are of but little moment, yet slight dishonour from a female or lover. Benefits when transiting the angles, except when they are occupied by the sign Gemini, Virgo, or Capricorn. To the body or good aspect of Mercury, ingenious, studious, and associates with good men. Transiting the body of the Moon, popularity, health, wealth, and honour by the commonalty, or by a lady, he may have a child born if married, especially if in the 5th house; if in the 3rd, a journey, and visiting among neighbours and relations. Transiting the ☊, good fame and gain; but the ☋, shame and contempt; transiting the ⊕, augmentation of property. Passing the 10th, honour and good trade; the 11th, friends, and gain by trade; the 12th, to a farmer, great good, and to others, less anxious fears.

Mars to his own place or Transiting others.

596 Mars to Herschel, a fever or inflammatory dealings; to Saturn, many sorrows, controversy, and sickness, intends short journeys, which will be attended with annoyance and disappointment; death in the family of an aged person; to Jupiter, advantages from profession and professional characters; to his own place, danger by fire, he forms new acquaintances, and may gain by martial procedures; to the Sun, imprisonment is threatened, and the disapprobation of some great man; yet, if well situated, it may give him a chance of advancement. To Venus, an infamous course of life, disputation with lover, wife, or mistress, given to gluttony and drunkenness. To Mercury, predisposes him to lying and cheating, with deception in his transactions, except Mercury be in the house of Venus. To the Moon, he associates with bad company, fond of women and wandering. To the ☊, success in war, quarrels and duels; to the ☋, rashness, cowardice, and liable to perils. To the ⊕, profit in trade, good for speculating. To his own good aspects, he does well in business; his bad aspects the reverse; over the cusp of the 1st, disputation and rash proceedings, indisposed, fretful, well not to undertake any new business, neither form any new acquaintanceships; to the 2nd, or its ruler, danger of bad bargains, neither buy nor trust; to the 3rd, disputations with relations, go no short journey; to the 4th, of little effect, except to the native's father; to the 5th, or its ruler, bad time for speculating and to his children, take no species of pleasure; to the 6th, or its ruler, danger of sickness, and loss from thievish servants; to the

7th, or its lord, ill agreement with wife or lover, danger of lawsuit; if R, bustle and contention, danger of loss of situation, and has many public enemies; to the 8th, death in the family; to the 9th, bad long journeys, and sickness to the father; to the 10th, loss of honour; and if R, trouble and difficulty, well not to form any new connections; to the 11th, hasty procedures; if R, violent and hasty; to the 12th, many enemies.

Venus to her own aspects, or Transiting others.

597 To the body of Herschel, some unexpected and sudden evil from females; to the ill aspects of Saturn, a libidinous course of life, trouble and crosses, disagrees with wife or husband, especially in the 7th; to Jupiter, the good aspects, an increase of wealth, virtue, and pleasure, visits his kindred and friends, profits from persons in rank, feels disposed to be pious and useful; to the body of Mars, marriage, given to pleasure and debauchery, keeps ill company and fond of gaming; to the Sun, honour, pleasure, favour of respectable persons; if Sun be ill dignified, then evil attends the native, jealous of his wife or lover; to her own place, all things succeeded, enjoys health, given to pleasure, music, dancing, &c.; to the place of Mercury, if both Venus and Mercury were well situated at birth, gives honour and gain by literature, he studies poetry and science; to the Moon, the native is changeable, obtains new acquaintances, and seeks female company; passing the cusp of the angles is good; the other houses of little importance; to the ☊, makes him happy; to the ☍, gives him disgrace by lewd courses; to ⊕, gain, especially from women, and from all commodities signified by Venus (174).

Mercury to his own aspects, or Transiting others.

598 To Herschel, gain by writings and science (169); to Saturn, profit by husbandry, buildings, old persons, but inclines the native to knavery (162); to Jupiter, a good time for gaining office, he gains by trade, and is honourably employed; to Mars, inclined to all things brave and magnanimous (164); but Mars weak, inclined to lying, cheating, wrangling with relations, and he falls into quarrels; to Sol, honour and preferment; but the bad aspects, busy in controversy, and meets with disappointments, bills of all descriptions should be avoided; to Venus, given to pleasure, carding, yet healthful and agreeable; to his own place, preferment; passing the angles, look well to his accounts; to the Moon, business, journeys, changes, new friends, and many advantages; if the Moon was strong at birth, then very good; if ill dignified, the reverse (578): to ☊, credit from business; to ☍, loss and damage, with many little annoyances and disadvantages; to ⊕, gain by Mercurialists (175), and some trades.

Moon's Transits.

599 To Herschel, sudden good or ill, as Herschel is dignified (565); to Saturn, the native is low-spirited, pensive, meets with crosses, and is contentious about property, or with old persons; to Jupiter, health, contentment, good company, journeys by land, to the married, increase of family, or pleasure from those born; to Mars, sickness, controversy, danger in travelling, much wrangling with servants, and danger to the eyesight; to Venus, pleasure, according as Venus is situated at birth; beware of scandal under bad aspects; to the Sun, frowns or injuries, changes of residence; to Mercury, journeys, gain by merchandise, a good period for buying and selling; to ☊, credit and repute, especially among females; to ☋, loss of credit and estate, vexation from females; to ⊕, profit, but if badly situated at birth, then loss and disappointment.

600 I have always observed those times to be unfortunate to a native, when the luminaries are transiting the conjunction, square, or opposition of the radical place of Herschel, Saturn, or Mars, especially if Sol or Luna happen to square their own place at the same time, or if the preceding lunation was in an evil place. Some remarkable evil event is generally at hand when the Sun is in opposition, or the Moon is square at the same time to a radical malefic.

CHAPTER XXXIV.

OF SECONDARY OR PROGRESSIVE DIRECTIONS.

601 All the directions hitherto contemplated and perspicuously explained are called PRIMARY DIRECTIONS, because they operate sometimes several weeks (481). SECONDARY DIRECTIONS are weaker than primary, and are those configurations and familiarities of the planets which arise daily from their Geocentric Longitude in the zodiacal signs, and their parallels of declination. All aspects to the planets or to the angles, that happen on the first day after birth, correspond to the first year, those of the second, to the second year, and so on. The nature of the event may be very clearly pointed out by paragraphs 593 to 600. These directions endure only a few weeks; the aspects of the Sun and Moon operate about two months; Saturn and Herschel, three months; those of Mars are soon over, but are very effective. Parallels falling in the sign Capricorn or Cancer continue a great length of time in operation. The aspects of the Moon with other planets are soon over. To

judge more particularly, we must take into consideration the effects—

OF PERIODIC REVOLUTIONS.

602 Each of the planets has a complete period of its own, entirely distinct from every other motion which it may acquire, either in the zodiac or in the world; and a problem is prepared for the working of these important periodic aspects. And here follow—

The effect of the periodic direction of Saturn.

603 Saturn directed to the radical place of the Sun is evil according to the house in which it falls (146), causing discredit, loss of honour, makes the native changeable, weakness of sight, sickness, especially if the Sun be hyleg, or ruler of the 6th or 8th; the good aspects not much effect; to the Moon, evil, deaths among relations; to Venus, trouble through women, he keeps company with imprudent persons, and is dishonoured by the same, and if Venus be lady of the 7th, prejudice to the wife, and disappointment through love affairs, &c.; to Mercury, troubles in business, through writings, youthful persons, children disobedient (if any), he is dull of apprehension, &c.; to Mars, accidents, danger among thieves; but the good aspects and Mars well affected, short journeys, gain by military or martial preferment; to Jupiter, loss of money; the good aspects, slight honour, dignity from persons in power.

The effects of Mars by periodic revolution.

604 Mars produces a variety of evil, but the effects are soon over. To Herschel, danger of sickness, pain in the head, under this the native must not bathe, danger from thieves, falls, fire gunshot, &c.; if in the 6th, 4th, or 8th, danger of fractures from falls; if in the 9th or 3rd, very dangerous on railways—do not speculate; to Saturn's ill aspects, death to some distant relation; if in the 10th, loss of office; if in the 7th, controversy or law, with affliction to his enemies; to Jupiter, gain by kindred, the clergy, great cattle, lawyers, &c.; if ill aspects, then the reverse; to Venus, love intrigues, or marriage, especially if these were in good aspect with each other, or with the Sun; surfeit and infamy if in bad aspects; to Mercury, by body or bad aspect, inclined to dissemble, quarrel, evil speaking, bad for writings, bonds, lawsuits, old debts; to the Moon, given to drink, ill company, short journeys, slander from females, &c. (569). When Mars returns to his own place at nineteen years of age, and then is in good aspect of Sol or Venus, the native either marries or is engaged in love.

The effects of Jupiter by periodic revolution.

605 Over the Sun's place, friendship, prosperity, and honourable acquaintances, health and gain; the bad aspect, sickness, loss of office or honour (547); over the Moon, marriage, or gain by a woman, healthful and popularity, reputation from the common people, he takes a journey, or may have a child born, if married (567); passing over the place of Mercury, gain in business, he seeks the company of learned persons, he is ingenious and inclined to science; over Mars, in a male natus, friends; in a female horoscope, courtship or marriage, profits by travelling, but danger of indisposition, by commerce and by kindreds; over Saturn, renewal of old acquaintance, esteem may be anticipated; but if Saturn be ill aspected, many sorrows, enemies, &c.; over Herschel, or his good aspects, gain, studious if either rule the 9th, inventive, and sudden benefits; to bad aspects, the reverse.

The effects of the Sun by periodic revolution.

606 The Sun is an active significator of honour, credit, and accidentally of life and health. His good aspects to Herschel, sudden honours and advancements, the ill aspects, dishonour and pecuniary losses, death to a distant relation; his bad aspects to Saturn (544) or to Mars (548) is decidedly dangerous. Every one who has the Sun afflicted at birth, has an illness or peculiar trouble every 10th year. The good aspects of Jupiter (546), or of Venus (550), is very fortunate, according to the house ruled (476). Coming to the M.C., benefits in profession or business, but if in bad aspect of Mars at the time, then evil may occur; to good aspects of Mercury, journeys, removals, active business, and successful lawsuits (552): his bad aspects, troubles by similar means, frauds from young persons, servants, &c. (553); to good aspects of the Moon, preferment, or an important change in circumstances, marriage or courtship (555); his ill aspects, sickness, extravagant, fickleness, &c. (556).

The effects of the Moon by periodic revolution.

607 The Moon is powerful, producing numerous inferior events, which, however light they may appear, do not fail to cause much passing annoyance or transitory benefit; her effects are frequently anticipated nearly three weeks, but seldom prolonged. To Herschel, a sudden journey, or public office; to Saturn by ill aspect, loss and annoyances; to good aspect, benefits (556); to Jupiter, generally good (567); to Venus, benefits by females, marriage, or children (574 and 575); to Mercury, sudden slight changes (577 and 578); to Mars, advancement (570); his ill aspects, loss by frauds, disease, and death of relations (569).

The effects of Venus by periodic revolution.

608 Venus's effects are transient, but generally good and agreeable (484); over the Sun, marriage, health, an inclination to enjoy pleasure and amusement (550); her ill aspect cause trouble by females, and by free living, producing disease and discredit, disappointment in marriage, slander, and many vexations (551); her aspects to Jupiter are good or ill according to Jupiter's power in the figure at birth; to Saturn or Mars, evil, disappointment, and sickness; to Herschel, benefits in the family; to Mercury, fond of study and science; to the Moon, or M.C., honour, pleasure, and prosperity (571); to ill aspect, sickness and sorrow, produced from previous pleasure.

The effects of Mercury by periodic revolution.

609 Over Herschel, turmoil with money and bills, the native's creditors are unjust, and his debtors are dilatory. The situation of Mercury must be particularly noted, especially those planets with which he is in parallel, as he partakes strongly of the nature of those planets with which he is connected by aspect, and will act accordingly. If evil at birth, and come to ill aspect of the Moon, or the hyleg, mental diseases, epilepsy, &c., may be expected. His good aspects generally give journeys, removals, much activity in business, and general success.

The effects of Herschel by periodic revolution

610 Whatever good he may produce, when aspecting, will be of a sudden description, and out of the common course of things. His evil aspects to the hyleg are very evil, bringing death into the family; in ill aspect to Moon, Sun, or Venus, decidedly evil in domestic affairs, disorder and turmoil; he is equally evil in love, and peculiarly inimical to the fair sex; over Saturn or Mars, very evil, great care must be taken in health and wealth, matrimony and business.

611 Upon delivering judgment on any of these species of directions, it is absolutely necessary to pay the greatest attention to the nature and quality of the aspects, for it often happens that a primary direction may import much good, when, at the same time, a malignant secondary, or a periodic configuration may come up of so strong and powerful a nature as to frustrate all beneficial effects portended by the former. The want of attending to this has frequently confounded our modern practitioners, who, confiding in the benignant tendency of some extraordinary good aspect in the zodiac, have promised an advance of fortune to the native, which has never come to pass, because of counter-aspects of this latter order. Hence it must appear to every rational mind, and experi-

mental astral student, that the strictest caution, and the utmost deliberation are necessary in forming our opinions on the directions upon a nativity, for, if at least we err in this, all our labour is lost, and the unfortunate enquirer is deluded with vain expectations of a happy run of good fortune, or fearful of some dreadful catastrophe, neither of which by the nature of the stars, was ever intended to happen.

As the planet Neptune is one of an almost unknown character, so far as its influence is concerned, we must class it in the same category as Herschel, as I consider its influence is very similar (page 146).

CHAPTER XXXV.

We do not consider any more kinds of directions than the two following, namely, 1st—

OF REVOLUTIONARY FIGURES.

612 A revolutionary figure is the exact position of the Heavens at the moment the Sun returns to the same degree and minute he possessed the moment the native was born. The judgments of a revolution are easy to be understood, by considering in what house and sign in the revolution the radical significators are posited, for according to the cordant or discordant positions and configurations, so must we judge. If the radical figure be unfortunate, the native will reap but little benefit from a promising revolution, for a radical evil can never be eradicated by an accidental good, though the evil may be necessarily mitigated.

613 Compare the figure of the revolution with that of birth, and observe how the cusp of the houses and significators agree, or are disposed, for upon these the judgment depends. If the revolutional Ascendant and M.C. be in good aspect with the radical, or be the same with the angles, signify good health, prosperity, and an increase of substance, especially if the lords of the Ascendants be well dignified. If the Ascendant of the revolution be in bad aspect with the angles of the radix, then evil will be felt that year, according to the signification of the revolutionary Ascendant did signify in the radix.

614 If the planets are returned to their radical place, or in sextile, trine, parallel, or any good aspect thereto, shew a good revolution. If the planets are in bad aspect to their radical situation, then evil may necessarily be anticipated.

615 If the sign of the radical 6th, 7th, or 12 be the 1st of the revolution, in that year may be expected sickness, open foes,

imbecility of body, and such things as those houses signify, and more especially if those houses or their lords were evilly disposed at birth. The sign of the 7th in the radix being the 1st, of the revolution, shows contentions, animosities, lawsuits, the native either marries or desires to do so.

616 Whenever you find the lord of the radical 2nd, Part of Fortune, or Jupiter, in the revolution 2nd, the native shall be pecuniarily advantaged, and augmention of patrimony by things or persons signified by that house, &c. If the lord of the 2nd of the radix be in the 3rd, of the revolution, denotes gain by short journeys, kindreds, or neighbours; and if lord of the 2nd be also in sextile or trine, with the lord of the 3rd in the radix, the above effects will be felt. If with the lord of the 4th, by a father, prosperity. If in the 5th, or in sextile or trine to its lord, gain by children, speculation, gaming, sports, selling of spices, liquors. If in the 6th, or in sextile or trine with its radical lord, gain by servants, workmen, small cattle, tenants. Proceed in this way through all the houses, and if the significators be evil, then judge ill from the above portentions, &c.

617 So that it appears, that the significators of substance in a revolution is not the lord of the 2nd in the revolution, but the lord of the 2nd in the radix; the same understand of the rest of the houses. The revolution is firmer if the same sign ascend as that which ascended at birth; the same, if those planets which were lords of the house in the radix be lords of the same in the revolution, though they possess not the same sign. If in the revolution any of the planets behold the radical places of Sun, Moon, Jupiter, Part of Fortune, or Venus, by good aspects, are very good signs; and so much the more if they behold them in the revolution with fortunate aspects. But the contrary effects will be felt if the aspects are evil, as 201.

618 In every revolution in which the planets are contrarily disposed to those in the radix, though of themselves be tolerably situated, yet they signify evil, as if at birth all the planets were above the earth and the revolution, any planets well aspected below the earth, they will have but little portention to good, &c. Ill may be expected when Herschel, Saturn, Mars, or ☷ passes over the Ascendant or M.C. of the revolutional figure.

619 Observe in what house the Sun is posited, and of what he is ruler, and accordingly those things which he signifies will be either good or evil, honourable or dishonourable, joy or sorrow, according as the Sun is well or ill placed in the revolution, and the good or evil may be known from the house in which the Sun is posited at the revolution, and by the nature of the impediting planet.

620 The planets of a revolution have no relation to the native, as lord of the houses of the revolution, but only from their radical

position and domination, for the 1st of a revolution is not the native Ascendant, but only an accidental Ascendant.

621 The transit of body or conjunction is much more powerful than any aspect; and Sun or Moon transiting Herschel, Saturn, or Mars, or their opposition, especially if the luminaries be rulers of the Ascendant will prove inimical, death or sickness if the hyleg be afflicted by direction. If Herschel, Saturn, Mars, or Mercury, was radically unfortunate, although they transit the angles; the places of Jupiter, Venus, Sun, or Moon, signify no good, but losses, crosses, troubles, quarrels, and ill management of affairs, the same also when they pass their square or opposition; but when they pass their sextile, or trine, are adjuncts of good if they have dignities in those places. We are to take great care of the transits, as we have before noticed their effects in part, together with the ingresses and Problems are provided for them. As for the—

LUNATIONS.

622 They are the full and new Moon immediately preceding any important event, which generally show, by the position of the luminaries, as regards the planets' places in the radix, and at the revolution the nature of the events to follow.

OF TRANSITS OF PLANETS.

623 Transits are the planets' passing over important places of a radical figure, its Asc., M.C., and other parts of primary significa-tion; also of the eratics aspecting the place of a planet, or the passing of one body over the place of another in both nata and revolutions. Transits of good planets signify good, but by evil places and aspects they denote evil; transits of Herschel, Saturn, and Jupiter are of great importance, for they never pass without sensible effects. Transits of the planets are easily perceived by SIMMONITE'S EPHEMERIS, in which the aspects are also calculated to the very moment when they take place. Observe the day on which any of the planets by body or aspect, good or evil, pass any of the cusps of the houses of the natus, or that degree wherein the planets possessed at birth.

624 In all transits observe the inherent properties of the tran-sitor, the radical determination of the transit, and the state, capacity, or condition of the native at the time of the transit, as the transition may be strong or weak—fortunate or unfortunate—as to the planet or place transited. If Herschel, Saturn, Mars, or Mercury was radically unfortunate, although they transit the body or good aspect of the angles or planets, they signify no good, but the contrary. If one bad transit is speedily succeeded by another evil one, and more especially the same place or body, during a

coherent direction or revolution, presages a duplication of the signified evil, and consequently augments danger and misfortune.

625 The actual transit of the Moon continues about 6 days—that of the Sun, 12 days—that of Jupiter, 20 days—that of Saturn, 30 days—that of Mars, about 9 days—that of Mercury, 6 days—that of Venus, 9 days—and the effect of Herschel's transits, not less than 40 days. The transits of Luna discover the almost daily occurrences of life, and she must be particularly attended to. See on what day she casts a good aspect to the cusp of the 2nd or its ruler, or a planet near its cusp, or to the ⊕, and say that is a good day, and profitable for getting in money, or transacting any bargain ; but the evil aspects to these act contrarily.

626 If good planets, or the lord of the Ascendant, transit the M.C. or place of its lord, or its good aspects (200), good for seeking orders in business, situations, &c., as the 10th house signifies. The ruler of the 1st, then health if a benefic ; sickness if a malefic ; to the 2nd, gain, &c. ; to the 3rd, by good aspect, a journey, friendship among brethren, &c., and so judge of the rest.

END OF BOOK ONE.

ARCANA

OF

PRACTICAL ASTRAL PHILOSOPHY.

BOOK THE SECOND.

ON THE DOCTRINE OF THE SPHERE AND ASTRO-MATHEMATICS.

1 By the Doctrine of the Sphere is meant the Solution of such Problems as relate to the Heavens, or Concavity of the visible World ; in measuring the Circles thereof, the Angles they make with each other, I shall show in a method more concise and methodical than any other. I here combine Spherical Geometry, Spherical Trigonometry, Astronomical Problems, and the use of Logarithms, which are inseparably connected therewith.

2 A Sphere, commonly called a globe, is a round body, having every point on its surface equal distance from a point within, called the centre.

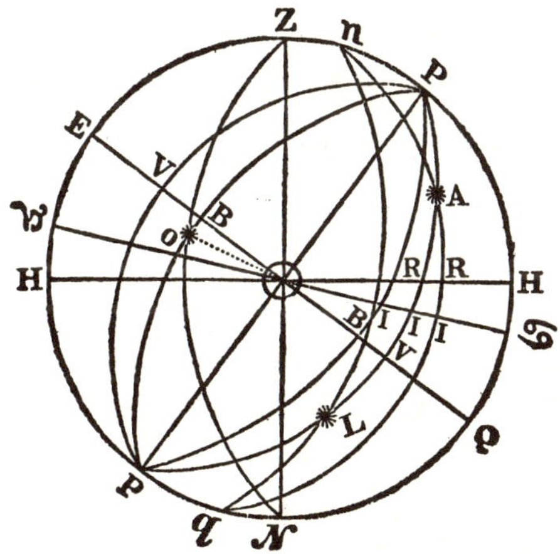

3 If on a clear night you place yourself in a situation in which the view of the horizon is uninterrupted, and attentively observe the heavens, you will see the stars, as fixed in a concave spherical surface, which surface is everywhere bespangled with an innumerable multitude of shining stars, which are continually changing their places.

Some stars rise above the horizon towards the east, some disappear towards the west, and others never reach the horizon, all these performing their motions, whilst their relative positions remain the same.

There are various methods of the construction of the sphere, but the most simple, and most generally employed, is the stereographic, in which all the circles of the sphere are represented by straight lines or circles. Suppose a transparent globe, on whose surface is the representation of the heavens, and the eye placed in any part of that surface viewing the opposite side, the lines should then appear as is represented by this projection.

4 To project an object of the sphere in plano, is a true geometrical declination of the circles of the sphere, or any assigned part of them upon the plane of some one great circle, as on the horizon, meridian, equinoctial, ecliptic, colours, or on the tropics, &c., and we delineate this Stereographic Projection, which supposes the eye to be but 90 degrees distant from, and perpendicular to the plane of the projection. That plane, upon which the object is projected or delineated, is called the plane of projection, or primitive; and the point in which the eye is situated is called the projecting point, or the point of sight.

To Project the Sphere Stereographically upon the Plane of the Meridian.

5 The foregoing stereographic projection of the sphere is that in which a great circle is assumed as the plane of the projection, and the opposite equinox as the projecting point.

CONSTRUCTION.—With the chord of 60 degrees describe the circle H, Z, H, N, and draw the diameter H, H, and Z, N, at right angles with each other; then will H, H, represent the equator, and Z, N, the polar axis. Lay off from the same line of chord 23° 28′ the obliquity of the ecliptic (12), setting one foot of the compass upon E ♑, Q ♋, and make *n* and *q* perpendicular thereto. From ⊕ to B lay the tangent of 30 degrees, and from ⊕ to V that of 60 degrees, through which points P and P (7), describe the circles P B P, P V P, &c. The meridians of celestial longitude (15), *n* A *q*, and *n* I * *q*, are described in a similar manner, laying the tangent of the required number of degrees, which, in the foregoing projection, are 45° and 75° from ⊕ on the line ♋ ⊕ ♑ towards ♋.

H H are the Horizon (25),
P P are the Poles (7),
E Q are the Equator (8),
Z is the Zenith (9),
N is the Nadir (10),
♋ ♑ are the Ecliptic (11),
P *n* the obliquity of Ecliptic (12),

H P are the elevation of the Poles (13),
⊕ B the Right Ascension (15),
⊕ O the Declination (16),
P ✳ the Latitude (17),
⊕ O the Longitude (15).

Of the Sphere and its Circles.

6 H H represent the equinoctial line, is a plane of the terrestrial equator, extending to the fixed stars; and if the axis of the earth be produced in like manner, they will be the poles of the celestial equator. This is also the horizon.

7 P P, the poles of a sphere are the extremities of the axis, as P P are the poles of the circle P B P. The poles of great circles are each 90 degrees from the circumference of the circles. In the figure (2) the arcs P V P, P B P, between the great circle and its pole, P, are arcs of 90 degrees.

8 E Q, Equator, a great circle which separates the northern from the southern hemisphere.

9 Z, the Zenith, which is the summit of the celestial dome above us, or perpendicularly over our heads, 90 degrees from the horizon, the pole of the horizon. The prime vertical passing through 0 degrees of Aries. The Sun arrives here about mid-day, or noon. This is also Medium Cœli, or Mid-heaven, that degree of the ecliptic which is upon the meridian at any time of our day, also called Upper Meridian.

10 N, the Nadir (an Arabic term), is the point of the heavens directly under the feet of the observer, and diametrically opposite to the zenith. The Sun arrives here at mid-night. This point is also called the Imum cœli, or under-heaven; being the cusp of the fourth house.

11 ♋ ♑, the Ecliptic. The apparent great circle in the heavens in which the Sun appears to move in the course of the year, *n* shows its north pole, and *q* its south pole. It intersects the equator into two points, called the vernal and autumnal equinoxes, because, when the Sun is in these points, the days and nights are equal all over the earth. It is called the ecliptic, because all the eclipses of the luminaries must necessarily happen in this line (22).

12 P *n*, the Obliquity of the Ecliptic. The ecliptic and equator, being great circles, must bisect or equally divide each other, and their inclination, or difference, is called the obliquity of the ecliptic, or the Sun's greatest declination.

13 H P, Elevation of the pole or star is its height, in degrees, between the pole and the horizon, or equal to the latitude of the place at birth, or country, observatory, &c.

14 P V P, P O P, P A L *q*, are meridians of terrestrial longitude which are the halves of great circles drawn round the earth through its poles and passing the latitude of any place in its meridian. Longitude, on the earth, is the distance of any place east or west of Greenwich, according to British computation.

15 *n*, A, I, *q—n*, l, *, *q*, &c., are meridians of celestial longitude, and is the distance of any heavenly body from first point of the zodiacal sign Aries, o° o, measured on the ecliptic. The Longitude and Right Ascension are measured in this direction. In the right-angled triangle ⊕ B O, the line ⊕ O is the Sun's longitude, or an arc of the ecliptic, from the first point of Aries. ⊕ B, the Sun's Right Ascension, or an arc of the equator, from the first point of Aries (20).

16 ⊕ O, on the ecliptic, in the right-angled triangle, is the Sun's declination, and the angle B ⊕ O is the obliquity of the ecliptic, measured by the arc Q ♋, E ♑.

N.B.—When the Sun, or any other heavenly body, is in that part of the ecliptic which is Q ♋ towards the north pole, the declination is called north, and when in that part which is E ♑ towards the south pole, the declination is south.

17 P * represent the circle of latitude; *n* A, the complement of the star's latitude; I A, when the star is on the north side of the ecliptic, it is called north latitude; but if on the southern side, then it is called south latitude. P A, the complement of the star's declination B A.

18 The angle P *n* A, the complement of the star's longitude. The supplement of the angle *n* P A, measured by the arc V Q, equals the complement of the star's right ascension (151).

All spheres are divided into two, great and small circles.

19 A Great Circle of a sphere is a circle drawn upon its surface, whose plane passes through the ⊕ centre of the sphere, as P B P, Z O N, are great circles. Every section of a sphere is a circle. A Small Circle of a sphere is a circle drawn upon its surface, whose plane does not cut the centre of the sphere. Two Great Circles of the sphere crossing each other, into two equal parts or semicircles, as both the great circles, P ⊕ P, Z O N, divide each other into two equal parts or semicircles.

20 A great circle passing through the Sun and the poles will intersect the equator in a point which represents the place of the Sun referred to the equator. The arc of the equator intercepted between this point and the vernal equinox, is called the Sun's

right ascension (15). The arc of the ecliptic intercepted between the Sun and the same equinox, is denominated the Sun's longitude. And the arc of the great circle intercepted between the Sun and its place referred to the equator, is called the Sun's declination.

21 The Tropics are two small circles, parallel to the equator, at 23 degrees 28 minutes distance from the equator; that to the north is called the tropic of Cancer, and where the Sun reaches in declination about the longest day; and that to the south, the tropic of Capricorn, where the Sun arrives about the shortest day.

22 Solstitial Points are the first point of ♋, and the first point of ♑, being the most extreme north and south points in the ecliptic. At these points, the Sun seems to stand still, or be at the same height in the heavens, at noon, for several days together (11). The extent of the obliquity of ecliptic.

23 The Axis is the diameter about which it rotates, which does not shift its position, while the other parts describe circles around it.

24 Azimuth, or vertical circles, are great circles of the sphere passing through the zenith and nadir, and are perpendicular to the horizon. Let a person stand at ⊕, and let H H be his horizon, then the circle Z O N is a vertical or azimuth circle. Azimuth of any celestial object is an arc of the horizon, contained between the east and west point of the heavens, and a vertical circle passing through the centre of that object (2).

25 The Horizon is a great circle (19) perpendicular to the vertical, or 90 degrees distant from the nadir and zenith, thus dividing the world into two equal parts, or hemispheres; it is the diameter of the sphere, as H H. The eastern, or left hand H, is the ascendant, or 1st house; the western H is the descendant, or 7th house (9 and 10).

THE CIRCLE, AND TRIGONOMETRICAL LINES.

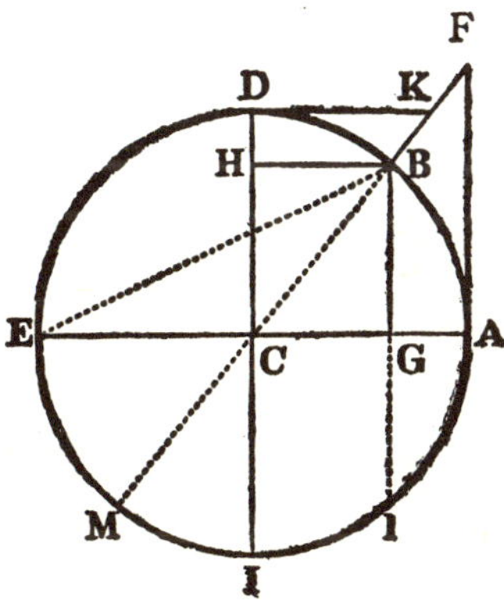

26 A Circle is a plane figure bounded by one line, called the circumference, every point of which is equally distant from a certain point within the figure, called its centre.

In the figure, C is the centre, E D A I is the circumference, which is sometimes called the periphery.

27 The Diameter of a Circle is a line drawn through the centre, and terminated at both ends by the circumference, as A E is a diameter.

28 Every diameter is double the radius, and divides the circle into two equal parts. The terminating points of the diameter are sometimes called its poles, as D and I.

29 The Radius of a circle is a line drawn from the centre C to the circumference, as C A ; also E C and D C are called radii.

30 A Semicircle is a segment cut off by the diameter, or half the area of the circle, and contains 180 degrees, as I D A.

31 A Chord of a Circle is a straight line joining the two extremities of an arc, as B G L, thus cutting the circle into two unequal parts.

32 A Quadrant is the half of a semicircle, or quarter of the whole circle, consisting of 90 degrees, as E D C.

33 All circles, great or small, are divided into 360 equal parts, called degrees; each degree into 60 minutes; each minute into 60 seconds, and so on. The degrees may be great or small, according to the size of the circle.

34 An Arc of a circle is any part of the circumference.

35 A Segment of a circle is the arc cut off by a straight line, as B A L is a segment.

36 A Tangent to a circle is a straight line, which touches the circle, and on being continued, does not cut it, as A F is a tangent.

37 The Sine B G of an arc A B is a straight line drawn from B, one of its extremities, perpendicular to the diameter A E, which passes through the other.

38 The Versine A G of an arc A B is that portion of the diameter A E upon which the sine is perpendicularly intercepted between the sine and the arc.

39 The Secant C F of an arc A B is a straight line drawn from C, the centre, to F, the farthest extremity of the tangent.

40 The sine, versine, tangent and secant, of an arc A B, are called the sine, versine, tangent, and secant, of the angle A C B, measured by the arc, to the radius A C.

41 The Complement of an arc A B, or angle A B C, is what it wants of a quadrant, or aspect of 90 degrees. Thus, B D, or B C D is the complement of A B, or A C B.

42 The Supplement of an arc A B, or of an angle A C B, is what it wants of a semicircle, or 180 degrees. Thus, B E, or A M, is the supplement of A B, and B C D, or A C M the supplement of A C B.

43 The Explement of an arc A B, or of an angle A C B, is what it wants of the whole circumference, or of four right angles. Thus, B D E M L A is the explement of A B, or of A C B.

An arc, or angle, and its supplement, have the same sine, tangent, and secant, for B G is the sine of B E, or B C E, A F the tangent of A M, or A C M, and C F the secant of A M or A M C. B C E the supplement to two right angles. The radius is equal to the sine, or versine of 90 degrees, and to the tangent, or cotangent of 45 degrees.

Observation.

I have considered it would be better and more expeditious to commence calculations with a perspicuous Elementary Series of Practical Problems in Genethliological Mathematics, easy to be understood even by the merest tyro in Arithmetic, after which I intend entering more minutely into the Mathematical Treatises of Spherical Geometry, Spherical Trigonometry, and Astronomical Problems, illustrating by diagrams the Anatomy of the Sphere. By these means the philosophy of Aspects and the natural divisions of the Heavens will be fully demonstrated.

Instructions in erecting an Horoscope of the Heavens, for any latitude, at any moment of time.

PROBLEM I.

44 To find the Geocentric Longitude of the Sun or planets, at any given moment of time.

RULE 1st.—Find the amount of longitude in the zodiac traversed by each planet, or other heavenly bodies, between the noon preceding and that which follows the given time or moment at birth. 2nd.—Then say, if 24 hours give that amount, what will that time for which the figure is intended from the preceding noon give? 3rd.—Add the result to the planet's longitude at the preceding noon, and the amount is its true place.

NOTE.—If the planet be retrograde, then SUBTRACT the result from the planet's place from the preceding noon.

What is the Sun's longitude May 24th, at 4h. 4m. 35s. A.M. 1819.

EXAMPLE.

	°	′	″
On the noon of the 24th day is......	2	25	32
The Sun at noon on the 23rd is......	1	27	53
Moved in 24 hours.....................	0	57	39

Worked by Diurnal Logarithms.

Add logarithm of ☉'s longitude in 24h. 0° 57′ 39″ = 1·4025
To time since noon 23rd is............16h. 4m. 35s. = ·1740

0° 38′ 22″ = 1·5765

Thus we see, after making all necessary equations, the result for the time given is 2 degrees 6¼ minutes for the Sun's place. See Problem xvi for finding logarithms for degrees, minutes, and seconds.

By rule of proportion it may be found thus :—If 24 hours give 57 minutes 39 seconds, what will 16h. 4m. 35s. give ?

Ans. 0° 38′ 22″

Add the Sun's place on the 23rd ...... 1 27 53 of ♊

The Sun's true place is .... 2 6 15   ♊

Observe.—For regular practice say the Sun is in 2 degrees 6 minutes of Gemini, as the 15 seconds will not make any visible or material difference.

EXERCISES.

What is Herschel's longitude at the above time ?	Ans. 23 ♐ 20
Find Saturn's longitude.	Ans. 28 ♓ 46.
What is Jupiter's longitude ?	Ans. 16 ♒ 57.
What is the Moon's longitude ?	Ans. 3 ♊ 33.
What is Mercury's longitude ?	Ans. 8 ♉ 55.
What is Sol's longitude October 10th, 2h. P. M., 1830 ?	Ans. 16 ♎ 44.
Where was the Moon at that time ?	Ans. 6 ♌ 40.
Where was Mercury in the zodiac, 1844, March 17th, 2h. 34m. P. M. ?	Ans. 8 ♓ 23.
What is Mar's longitude 9th November, 1841, at 10h. 48m. A. M. ?	Ans. 12 ♑ 14.
November 9th, 1841, at 10h. 48m. A. M., what was the longitude of the Moon?	Ans 29 ♍ 26.

PROBLEM II.

45 Given the Sun's geocentric longitude and greatest declination (23° 27′ 40″) to find his Right Ascension.

RULE.—Add the cosine of Sol's greatest declination (9·96253) to the tangent of Sun's longitude, and the sum will be the tangent of the Sun's Right Ascension.

What is the A. R. of the Sun, May 24th, 4h. 4m. 35s. A.M., 1819?

EXAMPLE.

Add cosine of 23° 28′ nearly .... 9·96253
To tangent of Sol's longitude 2 ♊ 6 = 62° 6′ = 10·27616

The Right Ascension of the ☉ = 60° 0′ = 10·23869

EXERCISES.

1.—What was the A. R. of Sol November 29th, 6h. 30m. P.M., 1824? Ans. 245° 44′
2.—What was Sol's A. R. March 17th, 1844, 2h. 34m. P.M.? Ans. 327° 23′
3.—What A. R. had Sol 10th October, 2h. P.M., 1830? Ans. 192° 22′

46 Mark well.—If the Sun or star be in ♈, ♉, or ♊, the arc thus found, after adding the sine and tangent, will be the A. R. But if the star be in ♋, ♌, or ♍, the result must be subtracted from 180°. If in ♎, ♏, or ♐, the A. R. must be added to 180°. If in ♑, ♒, or ♓, then the arc must be subtracted from 360 degrees.

PROBLEM III.

47 To convert time into degrees and minutes.

RULE.—Multiply the hours by 15 and divide the minutes of time by 4, which will give degrees; then multiply the odd minutes over by 15, and divide the sum by 4 for minutes and seconds, and the result will be the answer.

EXAMPLE.

What are the degrees of an arc of 16 hours, 4 minutes, 32 seconds of time? Ans. 241° 8′ 42″

	°	′	″
16h. × 15 =	240	0	0
4m. ÷ 4 =	1	0	0
32 seconds ÷ by 4 =	0	8	45
Ans. 16h. 4m. 32s. =	241	8	45

A more expeditious method will be by the following Table.

For turning Degrees and Minutes into Time, and the contrary.

D M	H M (M S)	D	H M (M S)	D	H M (M S)	D	H M (M S)	D	H M (M S)	D	H M (M S)	M S (S T)	M (Sec. Thi.)
1	0. 4	61	4. 4	121	8. 4	181	12. 4	241	16. 4	301	20. 4	0 15	1
2	0. 8	62	4. 8	122	8. 8	182	12. 8	242	16. 8	302	20. 8	0 30	2
3	0.12	63	4.12	123	8.12	183	12.12	243	16.12	303	20.12	0 45	3
4	0.16	64	4.16	124	8.16	184	12.16	244	16.16	304	20.16	1 0	4
5	0.20	65	4.20	125	8.20	185	12.20	245	16.20	305	20.20	1 15	5
6	0.24	66	4.24	126	8.24	186	12.24	246	16.24	306	20.24	1 30	6
7	0.28	67	4.28	127	8.28	187	12.28	247	16.28	307	20.28	1 45	7
8	0.32	68	4.32	128	8.32	188	12.32	248	16.32	308	20.32	2 0	8
9	0.36	69	4.36	129	8.36	189	12.36	249	16.36	309	20.36	2 15	9
10	0.40	70	4.40	130	8.40	190	12.40	250	16.40	310	20.40	2 30	10
11	0.44	71	4.44	131	8.44	191	12.44	251	16.44	311	20.44	2 45	11
12	0.48	72	4.48	132	8.48	192	12.48	252	16.48	312	20.48	3 0	12
13	0.52	73	4.52	133	8.52	193	12.52	253	16.52	313	20.52	3 15	13
14	0.56	74	4.56	134	8.56	194	12.56	254	16.56	314	20.56	3 30	14
15	1. 0	75	5. 0	135	9. 0	195	13. 0	255	17. 0	315	21. 0	3 45	15
16	1. 4	76	5. 4	136	9. 4	196	13. 4	256	17. 4	316	21. 4	4 0	16
17	1. 8	77	5. 8	137	9. 8	197	13. 8	257	17. 8	317	21. 8	4 15	17
18	1.12	78	5.12	138	9.12	198	13.12	258	17.12	318	21.12	4 30	18
19	1.16	79	5.16	139	9.16	199	13.16	259	17.16	319	21.16	4 45	19
20	1.20	80	5.20	140	9.20	200	13.20	260	17.20	320	21.20	5 0	20
21	1.24	81	5.24	141	9.24	201	13.24	261	17.24	321	21.24	5 15	21
22	1.28	82	5.28	142	9.28	202	13.28	262	17.28	322	21.28	5 30	22
23	1.32	83	5.32	143	9.32	203	13.32	263	17.32	323	21.32	5 45	23
24	1.36	84	5.36	144	9.36	204	13.36	264	17.36	324	21.36	6 0	24
25	1.40	85	5.40	145	9.40	205	13.40	265	17.40	325	21.40	6 15	25
26	1.44	86	5.44	146	9.44	206	13.44	266	17.44	326	21.44	6 30	26
27	1.48	87	5.48	147	9.48	207	13.48	267	17.48	327	21.48	6 45	27
28	1.52	88	5.52	148	9.52	208	13.52	268	17.52	328	21.52	7 0	28
29	1.56	89	5.56	149	9.56	209	13.56	269	17.56	329	21.56	7 15	29
30	2. 0	90	6. 0	150	10. 0	210	14. 0	270	18. 0	330	22. 0	7 30	30
31	2. 4	91	6. 4	151	10. 4	211	14. 4	271	18. 4	331	22. 4	7 45	31
32	2. 8	92	6. 8	152	10. 8	212	14. 8	272	18. 8	332	22. 8	8 0	32
33	2.12	93	6.12	153	10.12	213	14.12	273	18.12	333	22.12	8 15	33
34	2.16	94	6.16	154	10.16	214	14.16	274	18.16	334	22.16	8 30	34
35	2.20	95	6.20	155	10.20	215	14.20	275	18.20	335	22.20	8 45	35
36	2.24	96	6.24	156	10.24	216	14.24	276	18.24	336	22.24	9 0	36
37	2.28	97	6.28	157	10.28	217	14.28	277	18.28	337	22.28	9 15	37
38	2.32	98	6.32	158	10.32	218	14.32	278	18.32	338	22.32	9 30	38
39	2.36	99	6.36	159	10.36	219	14.36	279	18.36	339	22.36	9 45	39
40	2.40	100	6.40	160	10.40	220	14.40	280	18.40	340	22.40	10 0	40
41	2.44	101	6.44	161	10.44	221	14.44	281	18.44	341	22.44	10 15	41
42	2.48	102	6.48	162	10.48	222	14.48	282	18.48	342	22.48	10 30	42
43	2.52	103	6.52	163	10.52	223	14.52	283	18.52	343	22.52	10 45	43
44	2.56	104	6.56	164	10.56	224	14.56	284	18.56	344	22.56	11 0	44
45	3. 0	105	7. 0	165	11. 0	225	15. 0	285	19. 0	345	23. 0	11 15	45
46	3. 4	106	7. 4	166	11. 4	226	15. 4	286	19. 4	346	23. 4	11 30	46
47	3. 8	107	7. 8	167	11. 8	227	15. 8	287	19. 8	347	23. 8	11 45	47
48	3.12	108	7.12	168	11.12	228	15.12	288	19.12	348	23.12	12 0	48
49	3.16	109	7.16	169	11.16	229	15.16	289	19.16	349	23.16	12 15	49
50	3.20	110	7.20	170	11.20	230	15.20	290	19.20	350	23.20	12 30	50
51	3.24	111	7.24	171	11.24	231	15.24	291	19.24	351	23.24	12 45	51
52	3.28	112	7.28	172	11.28	232	15.28	292	19.28	352	23.28	13 0	52
53	3.32	113	7.32	173	11.32	233	15.32	293	19.32	353	23.32	13 15	53
54	3.36	114	7.36	174	11.36	234	15.36	294	19.36	354	23.36	13 30	54
55	3.40	115	7.40	175	11.40	235	15.40	295	19.40	355	23.40	13 45	55
56	3.44	116	7.44	176	11.44	236	15.44	296	19.44	356	23.44	14 0	56
57	3.48	117	7.48	177	11.48	237	15.48	297	19.48	357	23.48	14 15	57
58	3.52	118	7.52	178	11.52	238	15.52	298	19.52	358	23.52	14 30	58
59	3.56	119	7.56	179	11.56	239	15.56	299	19.56	359	23.56	14 45	59
60	4. 0	120	8. 0	180	12. 0	240	16. 0	300	20. 0	360	24. 0	15 0	60

N. B.—It is particularly requested and highly recommended that the student study every Problem perfectly, and every Exercise worked in each Problem, before he proceeds to the subsequent Problem, by which means he will become complete master of the calculations.

EXAMPLES.

Look opposite the 16 hrs. 4 mins. on the left hand, we have 241 0 0
Look in the last column and you have opposite on left hand for 35s.................................... .... 0 8 45

Ans. 16h. 4m. 35s.= 241 8 45

EXAMPLE 2.

Convert 15h. 43m. 27s. into degrees, minutes, &c. Ans. 235° 51′ 45″

Look for 15h. 40m. in the 8th column, equal to 235 0 0
Then 3m. in the last column is..................... 0 45 0
And 27s. in the last column, equal to............. 0 6 45

Ans. for 15h. 43m. 27s.= 235 51 45

3.—Convert 8 hours into degrees.   Ans. 120 degrees.
4.—Turn 13 hours into degrees.   Ans. 195 degrees.
5.—Convert 12 hrs. 16 min. into degrees, &c.   Ans. 148 degrees.
6.—Convert 20 hours 40 minutes 30 seconds
    into degrees, &c.   Ans. 317° 30′

PROBLEM IV.

48 To turn degrees and minutes of an Arc into time.

RULE 1.—Look in the column marked degrees (D) and minutes (M) for the number of degrees required, and opposite to them, in the next column to the right hand, will be the hours and minutes.

Rule 2.—For the minutes of a degree look in the same column and opposite to the minutes on the right hand will be the minutes and seconds of time.

EXAMPLE.

1.—What is the time answering to 57 degrees, 26 minutes ?

	h.	m.	s.
The number opposite 57 degrees is	3	48	0
The number opposite 26 minutes is	0	1	44
Ans.	3	49	44

2.—What time answers to 64° 21′ ?   Ans. 4h. 17m. 24s.
3.—What time answers to 99° 47′ ?   Ans. 5h. 59m. 8s.

PROBLEM V.

*49 To find the Right Ascension of the Midheaven, in any latitude
at any given time.*

RULE 1.—Add the Sun's sidereal Right Ascension to the time
past the preceding noon, and the sum will be the A. R., in time, of
the M. C.

RULE 2.—Convert this time into degrees and minutes, and if the
time exceed 24 hours, or 360 degrees, take the excess for the answer.

EXAMPLE.

1.—What is the A. R. of M. C. in Queen Victoria's natus.   Born
May 23rd, 16h. 4m. 35s., 1819, latitude 51° 32′ ?

	h.	m.	s.
The ☉ A. R. at noon of 23rd =	4	0	0
Time afternoon is	16	4	35
A. R. of the M. C. is 301° 8′	20	4	35 Ans.

EXERCISES.

2.—What is the A. R. of the M. C. November 29,
6½h. P. M., 1824?   Ans. 345° 59′

3.—What is the A. R. of M. C. May 13d. 2h.
25m. P. M., 1825 ?   Ans. 86° 17′

4.—What is the A. R. of M. C. March 17d. 2h. 34m.
P. M., 1844 ?   Ans. 33° 48′

5.—What is the A. R. of M. C. Sept. 29d. 10h.
45m. A. M., 1827 ?   Ans. 168° 45′

PROBLEM VI.

50 *The Obliquity of the Ecliptic and the R. A. of the M. C. given to find the degree of the Ecliptic, on the 10th House, or Meridian.*

RULE.—To the cosine (9·962526) the obliquity of the ecliptic, add the cotangent of the R. A. of the M.C. from the nearest equinox, ♈ or ♎ (46), and the Sun is the cotangent of its longitude from the same equinoctial point.

EXAMPLE.

1.—In Queen Victoria's natus, the A. R. of the M. C. is 201° 8′, its nearest equinoctial point is Aries.

	°	′
From the whole circle	360	0
Subtract the A. R. of M. C.	301	8
	58	52

	°	′	
To cosine of obliquity of Ecliptic 23° 28′ nearly			9·962526
Add the cotangent of	58	52	9·781060
Cotangent from Aries	61	0	9·743586

Thus 61 degrees from Aries will leave 29 degrees ♑ upon the cusp of the 10th House.

Found thus, 61 added to 180 equals 241, and this subtracted from 360 leaves 119 degrees because the M. C. is found in Capricorn (46).

EXERCISES.

2.—What degree of the Ecliptic is on the M. C. when Right Ascension is 8° 21′? Ans. 9° ♈ 6′.

3.—What sign and degree culminate when the A. R. of M. C. is 214° 38′? Ans. 7 of Scorpio.

4.—What is the cusp of the 10th when its A. R. is 72° 27′? Ans. 14° ♊ 38′.

5.—What is culminating when the M. C. has 321° 15′ of A. R.? Ans. 19 Aquarius.

6.—What is culminating when the M. C. has 345° 59′ of A. R.? Ans. 14° ♓ 46′.

PROBLEM VII.

51 *To find the Oblique Ascension of the Six Eastern Houses.*

RULE—Add 30 degrees to each House from the Mid-heaven, and take the sum, rejecting 360 degrees if it exceed that number.

In the Queen's natus A. R. of 10th House is...... 301 8
For the Oblique Ascension for the 11th ......add   30 0
                                                  ———————
                 Oblique Ascension of 11th. 331 8
For the Oblique Ascension of the 12th ....add   30 0
                                                  ———————
                                             361 8
                                  Rejecting 360 0
                                                  ———————
         Oblique Ascension of the 12th =   1 8
For the Oblique Ascension of the Ascendant...add 30 0
                                                  ———————
          Oblique Ascension of the 1st =   31 8
For the Oblique Ascension of the 2nd...........add 30 0
                                                  ———————
          Oblique Ascension of the 2nd =   61 8
For the Oblique Ascension of the 3rd...........add 30 0
                                                  ———————
     Oblique Ascension of the 3rd House =   91 8

PROBLEM VIII.

52 *To find the Oblique Descension of the Six Western Houses.*

RULE.—Add 180 degrees to the Oblique Ascension of the opposite Houses, and the sum is the Descension required.

EXAMPLES.

In Queen Victoria's Nativity we find—

Oblique Ascension of 10th to be 301 8 add 180 equal 121 8 for 4th.
Oblique Ascension of 11th to be 331 8 add 180 equal 151 8 for 5th.
Oblique Ascension of 12th to be   1 8 add 180 equal 181 8 for 6th.
Oblique Ascension of 1st to be 31 8 add 180 equal 211 8 for 7th.
Oblique Ascension of 2nd to be   61 8 add 180 equal 241 8 for 8th.
Oblique Ascension of 3rd to be   91 8 add 180 equal 271 8 for 9th.

The above are the Oblique Ascensions and Descensions under their own Poles. And as these are so simple we need give no further exercises.

PROBLEM IX.

53 *To find the Sun's Ascensial Difference or of the Houses of any Horoscope.*

RULE.—Add the tangent of the Obliquity of the Ecliptic (9,637496) to the tangent of Latitude of Birth Place, and the sum will be the sine of the Ascensial Difference of the House.

EXAMPLE.

1.—What is the Sun's Ascensial Difference in Latitude 51° 32′ ?
Tangent of the Obliquity of the Ecliptic 23° 38′ nearly = 9,637496
Add the tangent of the Latitude .... 51° 32′   10,099914

Give sine of Ascensial Difference .... 33° 7′   = 9,737410

45 Observe.—The Ascensial Difference in a given latitude (or Polar Elevation) is exactly that which any body has, as determined by its distance from the meridian; Ascensial Difference being in both cases the difference between Right and Oblique Ascension. We say the Sun because it is the same as House.

EXERCISES.

2.—What is the Ascensial Difference of Sol in the
  latitude 54 degrees, 18 minutes ?   Ans. 37° 10′.
3.—What is the Ascensial Difference of Sol for the
  latitude 53 degrees, 26 minutes ?   Ans. 35° 48′.

Problem X.

55 *To find the Pole of the 11th, 5th, 3rd, and 9th Houses.*

RULE.—Add the sine of one-third of the Sun's Ascensial Difference to the cotangent (10,362504) and the sum will be the tangent of the Pole.

EXAMPLE.

1.—What is the Pole of these Houses in Queen Victoria's Nativity ?
  The Sun's Ascensial Difference is 33° 7′ and $\frac{1}{3}$ is 11° 2$\frac{1}{3}$′
      The sine of 11° 2′ is 9,281897
  The cotangent of the Ecliptic is 10,362504

Tangent required is 23° 48′ = 9,644401

EXERCISES.

2.—What is the Pole of the 11th house in Latitude 53°?   Ans. 53° 6′.
3.—What is the Pole of 5th house in Lat. 48°?   Ans. 21° 3′.
4.—What is the Pole of 3rd house in Lat. 53° 26′?   Ans. 25° 29′.

Problem XI.

56 *To find the Pole of the 12th, 6th, 2nd, and 8th Houses.*

RULE.—Add the sine of two-thirds of the Ascensial Difference to the tangent of 10,362504.

EXAMPLE.

Find the Pole of the 12th house in the latitude of London.
The Sun's Asc. Diff. is 33° 7′, and two-thirds of 33° 7′
  is 22° 5′, the sine is.................................. = 9,575136
                    Cotangent of Ecliptic boundary is = 10,362504
                    ____
          Tangent of the Pole required is 40° 54′ = 9,937640

EXERCISES.

2.—What is the Pole of the 12th house in the latitude
    of Scarborough, 54 degrees, 18 minutes ?   Ans. 44° 0′
3.—What is the Pole of the 6th house in latitude of
    Sheffield, 53 degrees, 26 minutes ?   Ans. 42° 59′.
   A more expeditious plan, and equally correct, may be obtained
by the following Table.

TABLE II.

Of the Poles of the Houses for every degree, from 1 degree to 60
degrees, and every half degree of Latitude in Great Britain.

Lat.	Pole of 11th and 5th, 3rd and 9th.		Pole of 12th and 6th, 2nd and 8th.		Lat.	Pole of 11th and 5th, 3rd and 9th.		Pole of 12th and 6th, 2nd and 8th.		Lat.	Pole of 11th and 5th, 3rd and 9th.		Pole of 12th and 6th, 2nd and 8th.	
1	0	21	0	42	25	8	54	17	22	49	21	46	38	12
2	0	41	1	22	26	9	17	18	5	50	22	33	39	14
3	1	0	2	0	27	9	43	18	52	50½	22	57	39	46
4	1	21	2	41	28	10	8	19	37	51	23	21	40	18
5	1	41	3	23	29	10	32	20	21	Lond.	23	48	40	54
6	2	0	4	0	30	10	59	21	9	52	24	12	41	24
7	2	21	4	40	31	11	26	21	56	52½	24	44	41	58
8	2	41	5	21	32	11	54	22	46	53	25	6	42	32
9	3	2	6	2	33	12	23	23	36	Sheffi.	25	30	42	59
10	3	23	6	43	34	12	51	24	25	53½	25	33	43	6
11	3	43	7	24	35	13	26	25	15	54	26	1	43	39
12	4	4	8	5	36	13	51	26	5	54½	26	30	44	13
13	4	24	8	45	37	14	8	26	55	55	26	59	44	48
14	4	45	9	26	38	14	52	27	48	55½	27	29	45	24
15	5	7	10	10	39	15	24	28	40	56	28	1	45	59
16	5	29	10	50	40	15	56	29	32	56½	28	33	46	36
17	5	49	11	30	41	16	29	30	25	57	29	6	47	14
18	6	12	12	14	42	17	5	31	20	57½	29	40	47	50
19	6	34	12	57	43	17	42	32	18	58	30	15	48	27
20	6	57	13	41	44	18	20	33	15	58½	30	47	49	5
21	7	20	14	24	45	18	58	34	13	59	31	29	49	44
22	7	43	15	7	46	19	37	35	10	59½	32	8	50	24
23	8	5	15	50	47	20	19	36	10	60	32	48	51	4
24	8	30	16	36	48	21	3	37	12					

57 EXPLANATION OF THE TABLE OF POLES OF HOUSES.

The first column shows the Poles of the 1st and 7th houses, which is always the latitude of the country; the second column shows the Poles of the 3rd, 5th, 9th, and 11th houses; and the third column the Poles of the 2nd, 6th, 8th, and 12th houses. If the latitude of the place be anywhere between an even degree and half a degree, a proportion may be readily calculated for the difference, thus, if the latitude be that of Sheffield 53° 25', and it be required to find the pole of the 12th house, say, as 30 miles are to the difference between the poles of the 12th, for 53° and 53° 30', which is 33 minutes, so is the difference of latitude 25 to the difference of pole 27½', to be added to the pole of the 12th for 53 degrees. Hence, the pole of the 12th, at Sheffield, is 42° 59½', which is correct with that found by trigonometry to within ½ a minute, its true pole being 42° 59'.

58 *To find the sine, cosine, &c., answering to any given arc expressed in degrees and minutes.*

RULE.—If the number of degrees is less than 45, find the number at the top of the page, and the minutes in the left hand column; opposite to the minutes, and under the word sine, cosine, &c., is the logarithm required. If the degrees are 45, or upwards, find the number required at the bottom of the page, and opposite the number of minutes in the right hand column, and under the proper title, will be found the logarithm required.

EXAMPLES.

1.—To find the log. sine of 35° 45.'

Under the word sine, in the page marked 35° at the top, and opposite 45' in the left hand column, is found 9,766598, the log. sine required.

2.—Required the log. sine of 23° 28'.

Under the word sine in the page marked 23° at the top, and opposite 28' in the left hand column, is 9,600118, the sine required.

3.—To find the log. tan. of 57° 16'.

Above the word tan. in the page marked 57° in the bottom, and opposite 16' in the right hand column, is found 10,191917, the log. tan. required.

4.—What is the cotangent of 55° 57'?

In the page marked 55° at the bottom, and opposite 57' in the right hand side column, is 9,829805, the cotangent of 55° 57'.

PROBLEM XIII.

59 *To find the logarithmic number, between 90 degrees and 180 degrees.*

RULE 1.—Subtract the given degrees and minutes from 180 degrees, and take the logarithm of the difference; or if 90 degrees be subtracted from the given sine, then take the cosine of the remainder, which will give the same.

RULE 2.—To find the cosine of an arc above 90 degrees, reject 90 degrees and take the sine of the remainder. The same method may be followed for tangents and secants, cotangents and cosecants.

EXAMPLES.

1.—Find the sine 94 degrees 33 minutes.

Take 180 degrees 0 minutes, and subtract 94° 33′ therefrom, and the remainder 85 degrees 27 minutes work by the cosine of this remainder, and the proper result will be brought out.

2.—Find the tangent of 104 degrees 16 minutes. Subtract the given number from 180° and the remainder is 75° 44′ of the cotangent.

PROBLEM XIV.

60 *To find the logarithmic number between 280 degrees and 270 degrees.*

RULE.—Subtract the given number from 270 degrees and take the log., sine, tangent, &c., of the remainder.

EXAMPLES.

1.—What is the log. sine of 189 degrees?
Diminish 189 by 180 equals the log. sine of 9 degrees.
2.—What is the log. tangent of 214 degrees 11 minutes?
Subtract 214° 11′ from 270° 0′ and the remainder is the tangent 55° 49′.

PROBLEM XV.

61 *To find the logarithmic number between 270 and 360 degrees.*

RULE.—Subtract the given number from 360 degrees and the remainder will be the log. sought.

EXAMPLE.

What is the sine of 284 degrees 44 minutes?
Take 284° 44′ from 360°, remain 75° 16′, which is the cosine. If it was the tangent, the cotangent would be the answer, and so on of the rest in this Problem.

PROBLEM XVI.

62 *To find the log., sine, tangent, &c., of any arc expressed in degrees, minutes, and seconds.*

RULE.—Find the log., sine, tangent, &c., corresponding to the given number of degrees and minutes, as directed in the three last Problems, and take the difference between it and that answering to the next greater minutes ; multiply this number by the given number of seconds, and divide the product by 60, then add the quotient to the log., sine, tangent, &c., but subtract it from the log. cos., log. cot., &c. of the given degrees and minutes and the sum or difference will be the log. required.

EXAMPLES.

1.—Required the log. sine of 23° 27′ 40″

$$\text{Log. sine of } 23° \ 27' \text{ is } 9{,}599827$$
$$23° \ 28' \text{ is } 9{,}600118$$

| Difference | 291 |
| Seconds | 40 |

$$60)11640$$
$$194$$

| Log. sine of 23° 27′ | = 9,599827 |
| Proportional part for 40″ | 194 |

Log. sine of 23° 27′ 40″ is 9,600021

2.—Find the log. cos. of 24° 16′ 26″.

$$\text{Log. cos. for } 24° \ 16' = 9{,}959825$$
$$\text{Log. cos. for } 24° \ 17' = 9{,}959768$$

| Difference | 57 |
| Seconds | 36 |

$$60)2052$$

$$34$$

| Log. cos. of 24° 16′ | = 9,959825 |
| Subtract Proportional part for 36′ | = 34 |

Log. cos. 24° 16′ 36″ = 9,959791

3.—What is the sine of 26 degrees, 28 minutes, and 32 seconds ?   Ans.   9,649155.

4.—What is the cosine of 32 degrees, 18 minutes,
26 seconds ?   Ans. 9,926956.

5.—Required the tangent of 47 degrees, 18
minutes, 20 seconds.   Ans. 10,034989.

6.—What is the cotangent of 36 degrees, 29
minutes, 17 seconds ?   Ans. 10,130980.

7.—What is the sine of 136 degrees, 15 minutes,
24 seconds ?   Ans. 9,839747.

8.—Required the cosine of 284 degrees, 16 minutes,
12 seconds ?   Ans. 9,391713.

9.—What is the tangent of 220 degrees, 15 minutes, 10 seconds ?   Ans. 9,927702.

10.—What is the cotangent of 108 degrees, 16
minutes, 20 seconds.   Ans. 9,518751

PROBLEM XVII.

63 *To find the Arithmetical Complement of a Logarithm.*

RULE.—Subtract the Logarithm from 10, an integer, or subtract the right hand figure from 9.

EXAMPLE.

1.—What is the Arithmetical complement of the proportional logarithm of 24 degrees, or 24 hours ?

Place, according to rule 10,0000
Proportional logarithm of 24 is   ,8751

Arithmetical complement of 24 is =   9,1249

EXERCISES.

2.—What is the Arithmetical complement of the
tangent of 17 degrees 18 minutes ?   Ans.   ,506590.

3.—What is the Arithmetical complement of the
sine of 24 degrees 11 minutes ?   Ans. 0,387579.

4.—What is the Arithmetical complement of
2,730459 ?   Ans. 7,269541.

5.—What is the Arithmetical complement of the
circle 360 degrees ?   Ans. 7,443697.

PROBLEM XVIII.

64 *To find the log., sine, tangent, &c., of an arc less than 3 degrees,*
and also of one greater than 87 degrees.

RULE 1.—To find the sine. Add the constant number 4,685475
to the log. of the arc in seconds, and subtract one-third of the

arithmetical complement of the log. cosine from the sum, the remainder will give the log. sine of the given arc.

RULE 2.—To find the tangent. To the constant number 4,685575 add the log. of the arc in seconds, and also two-thirds of the arith. metical complement of cosine; the sum is the log. tangent of the given arc.

Note.—For the log. cos., and cot., take the log. sine, and tan. of the complement of the given arc.

EXAMPLES.

1.—To find the log. sine of 1 degree, 2 minutes, 12·5 seconds:

$$\begin{aligned}
\text{Constant number} &= 4,685575 \\
\text{Log. of } 3732{\cdot}5 \text{ sec.} &= 3,572000
\end{aligned}$$

$$8,257575$$

⅓rd arith. com. cos. 1 deg. 2 min. 12·5 sec.   24

Log. sine of 1 deg. 2 min. 12·5. sec = 8,257551

2.—To find the log. tan. of 0 degree 24 minutes, 15.3 seconds.

$$\begin{aligned}
\text{Constant number} &\quad 4,685575 \\
\text{Log. of } 1455{\cdot}3 \text{ sec.} &= 3,162952
\end{aligned}$$

⅔rds Arith. com. cos. 24 min. 15'3 sec. = 0,000007

Log. tan. of 0 deg. 24 min. 15·3 sec. = 7,848534

PROBLEM XIX.

65 *To find the degrees, minutes, and seconds answering to any given log. sine or tangent.*

RULE—In its respective column find its nearest sine, tangent, &c., to that given, and take the degrees from the top or bottom of the page, according as the quantity is found in a column, with the proper title at the top or bottom, and the minute is found in the same horizontal line, in the left or right hand marginal columns, according as the quantity is found in a column titled at the top or bottom of the page (78, 79 and 80).

EXAMPLES.

1.—Required the arc or degrees and minutes corresponding to the log. sine 9,584665.
This is found in a column marked sine at the top under 22 degrees, and opposite 36 minutes, or 1 hour 30 minutes, and 24 seconds of time.

2.—What are the degrees, minutes, and seconds answering log. tangent 9·538764.

Given log. tangent 9,538764
Log. tangent 19° 4′ = 9,538611

9,538611
153 Log. tangent 19° 5′ = 9,539020

409

Then 153 × 60 ÷ 409 = 9180 ÷ 409 = 22·4. Hence 9,538764 is the log. tangent of 19° 4′ 22·4″

3.—To find the degrees, minutes, and seconds answering to log. cosine 9,568421.

Given log. cosine   9,568421
Log. cosine 68° 17′ = 9,568222

9,568222
... 199 Log. cosine 68° 16′ = 9,568539
Multiply by   60

317

317)11940(37·7
951

2430
2219

·2110

∴ 9,568421 is the log. cosine answering to 68° 17′—37 7″ = 68° 16′ 22·3″.

Note.—Instead of taking the log. cosine or log. tangent next less, we may take the next greater, when the seconds, found as before, must be added to the arc, thus—

Log. cosine 68° 16′ = 9,568539   = 9,568539
Given log. cosine = 9,568421
... 118
Multiply by 60   Log. cosine 68° 17′ = 9,568222

317)17080   317
Hence 68° 16′ 22·3 the arc as
22·3   before.

EXERCISES.

4.—What is the arc answering to log. sine
9,574486?   Ans. 22° 2′ 47·7″.
5.—Required the arc of log′ cosine 9,534876?   Ans. 69° 57′ 37·3″.
6.—What is the log. tangent of 1c,400864?   Ans. 68° 19′ 52·7″.
7.—Required the cotangent of 10,076543.   Ans. 39° 58′ 36·6″.
8.—What is the log. cosine of 9,823456?   Ans. 48° 14′ 35·1″.

PROBLEM XX.

66 *To find the degrees, minutes, and seconds, answering to the logarithmic sine or tangent of an arc under 3 degrees and above 87 degrees.*

RULE 1.—To find the arc answering to a given logarithmic sine. Add together the given logarithmic sine, the constant number 5,314425, and one third of the supplement of the corresponding cosine, the sum will be the logarithm of the number of seconds in the required arc.

RULE 2.—To find the arc corresponding to a given logarithmic tangent. Add together the given logarithmic tangent and the constant number 5,314425, and from the sum take two-thirds of the supplement of the corresponding cosine, the remainder is the logarithm of the arc in seconds.

Note.—For the arc answering to the logarithmic cosine and cotangent, take the complement of the arc answering to the logarithmic sine and tangent.

1.—To find the arc whose log. sine is 8,257551
Constant number 5,314425
⅓rd Arith. com. cosine 9,999929   = 0,000024

3732·5″ log. = 3,572000
Or 1° 2′ 12·5″.

2.—To find the arc whose log. tan. is 7,848534
Constant number 5,314425

3,162959
⅔rd Arith. com. cosine 9,999989 = 0,000007

1455·3″ log. 3,162952
Or 0° 24′ 15·3″.

PROBLEM XXI.

67 *To perform Multiplication by Logarithms.*

RULE 1.—Add the logarithm of the multiplier and multiplicand, and the sum is the logarithm of the product.

Multiply 76	Log. = 1,88081	Multiply 98	Log. = 1,99123
by 54	Log. = 1,73239	by 76	Log. = 1,88081
Product 4104	= 3,61320	7448 Log.	3,87204

Multiply 76,4 Log. = 1,88309 | Multiply 7825 Log. = 3,893484
   by   5,4 Log. = 0,73239 | by   873 Log. = 2,941014

   412·56   = 2,61548 | Log.6831218·8   = 6,834498 sum. (their)

Observe.—The correct product is 6,831225, or 6·2 greater than that found by the logarithms; but when there are various operations, the final error is scarcely appreciable, as the slight inaccuracy of one operation generally balances that of another.

RULE 2.—A negative index must be subtracted when the logarithm is added, and added when the logarithm is subtracted.

Multiply 786 by ·0073.

Log.   786 = 2,895423 or 2,895423
Log. ·0073 = 3,863323   7,863323

            0,758746   0·758746

RULE 3.—When the positive index is used, in adding we reject 10 from the index, but in subtracting we borrow 10.

EXERCISES.

Multiply 78,36 by 8,5.   Ans. 666.06.
Multiply 486,95 by 2,0087.   Ans. 978,1364.
Multiply 210,4 by 00372.   Ans. 7826875.
Multiply 21896 by 274,35   Ans. 6007166,7.

PROBLEM XXII.

68 To perform Division by Logarithms.

RULE.—From the logarithm of the dividend subtract the logarithm of the divisor, the remainder is the logarithm of the quotient.

EXAMPLES.

1.—Divide 78634   Log. = 4,895610
   by   27   Log. = 1,431364

Quotient 2912,37   Log. = 3,464246 difference.

2.—Divide 5486 by 96.
   Dividend 5486   Log. = 3,739256
   Divisor   96   Log. = 1,982271

Quotient 57,146   1,756985
                 40

                 45

3.—Divide 0,07856 by 0,003482

Dividend = 0,07856   Log. = 2,895201

Divisor = 0,00342   Log. = 3,541829

Quotient 22,5617   1,353372

39

33

19

14

4.—Divide 7856 = 3,895201 or 3,895201

by ,0053 = 3,724276 or 7,724276

Quotient 1482263   6,170925 or 6,170925

Problem XXIII.

To work a Proportion, or the Rule of Three by Logarithms.

Rule.—Add together the Arithmetical complement (63) of the Logarithm of the first term, and the Logarithms of the second and third terms, the sum is the Logarithm for the Answer.

Example.

1.—If 27 give 45 what will 63 require ?

As : Log. of 27 Arithmetical complement = 8,568636

is to :: Log. of 45   .... = 1,653213

so is : Log. of 63   .... = 1,799341

Ans. Log. 105 = 2,021190

Exercises.

2.—If 12 require 16 what will 24 require ?   Ans. 8.

3.—If 36 require 84 what will 112 require ?   Ans. 48.

Problem XXIV.

70 To find the degree of the Ecliptic on the 11th, 12th, 1st, 2nd, 3rd Houses in any Latitude.

Rule 1.—Add the cosine of the Oblique Ascension of the cusp of the house to the cotangent of the Pole of the House ; the sum is the cotangent of the first angle, which call the angle A.

RULE 2.—If the Oblique Ascension of the House be less than 90 degrees, or more than 270 degrees, add 23 degrees 28 minutes to angle A, and the sum will be the second angle, or angle B: When these are added and exceed 90 degrees then subtract it from 180 degrees. But if the Oblique Ascension of the House exceed 90 degrees, or be less than 270 degrees, then subtract 23 degrees 28 minutes, and the remainder is angle B. When angle B is less than 90 degrees, the longitude must be reckoned from the same equinoctial point from which the Oblique Ascension was taken.

RULE 3.—Add together the Arithmetical complement of the cosine of B; the cosine of A and the tangent of the Oblique Ascension of the House; the sum is the tangent of its longitude, from the equinoctial point Aries or Libra, according as it was nearest to either by Oblique Ascension. If between Cancer and Libra subtract from 180 degrees (46).

EXAMPLE I.

What is the cusp of the 11th house on the 24th of May, 4h. 4m. 35s. A.M., 1819?

According to Problem VIII, you find the Oblique Ascension of the 11th house 331° 8′ from Aries, being more than 270° subtract this from 360 degrees, the remainder is 28° 52′ from Aries (46).

To the cosine of Ob. Asc. of 11th	28 52 =	9,942378
Add cotangent of Pole of 11th house	23 48 =	10,355510

Cotangent of angle A	26 44 =	10,297888
Being nearest Aries add	23 28	

The second angle, or angle B 50 12

Add cosine of angle B	50 12 (Arith. com.) =	0,193746
To cosine of angle A	26 44	= 9,950905
And tang. of Ob. Asc. from ♈	28 52	= 9,741365

Sum is tang. of long. from ♈	37 34	= 9,886016

As the Angle B was less than 90 degrees we must subtract this from the first of Aries, from which we took it, which leaves 22 ♒ 26 for the cusp of the 11th house.

EXAMPLE 2.

What degree of the Ecliptic occupies the 12th house?

According to Problem VIII, the Oblique Ascension of the 12th is 1° ♈ 8′.

Cosine of Oblique Ascension 1   8 = 9,999915
Cotangent of Pole of 12th   40 54 = 10,062368

Cotangent of angle A 40° 54′   =   10,062283
Being nearest ♈ add 23 28

Cosine of angle B 64 22 (Ar. co.) = 0,364903
Cosine of angle A 40 54   = 9,878438
Tang. of Ob. Asc. 12th 1 ♈ 8   = 8,296292

Tangent of 1 degree 59 minutes of Aries = 8,539633

As both the Oblique Ascension of the house and angle B are less than 90 degrees, we take the tangent of Rule 3rd from the 1st point of Aries (46), because the Oblique Ascension of the cusp of the 12th is nearest Aries.

<h3 style="text-align:center">EXAMPLE 3.</h3>

What degree of the Ecliptic occupies the Ascendant whose Oblique Ascension is 31° 8′

Cos. of the Oblique Asc. of the Ascendant 31° 8′ = 9,932457
Add cot. of Pole of Ascen. 51 32 = 9,900087

Cot. of the angle A 55 47   =   9,832544
Add 23 28

Angle B 79 15

Cos of Angle B 79° 15′ (Ar. co.) = 0,279265
Cos of Angle A 55   47   = 9,749987
Tang. Obl. Asc. of 1st 41   8   = 9,781060

Tangent of Long. of the Asc. 61° 14′ = 10,810312
On the Ascendant 61° 14′ equal to 1 ♊ 14.

<h3 style="text-align:center">EXAMPLE 4.</h3>

What point of the Ecliptic occupies the 2nd House, its Pole being always the same as the 12th, 2nd its Oblique Ascension being 61 degrees 8 minutes?

Cos. of 61° 8′ = 9,683743
Add cot. of the 2nd Pole 40 55 = 10,062368

Cot of the angle A 60 52 = 9,746111
Add 23 28

Cos. of angle B 84 20 (Ar. co.) 1,005503
Cos. of angle A 60 52   9,687389
Tan. of Obl. Asc. of 2nd 61   8   10,258635

                         83 37   = 10,951527
On the 2nd is 83° 38′ equal to 23 ♊ 37.

EXAMPLE 5.

What point of the Ecliptic occupies the 3rd House, whose Pole is always the same as the 11th House?

Note.—The pole of the 3rd house is 23° 48′, its oblique ascension is 91° 8′, as may be seen in problem 7, and as it falls nearest to Libra it must be worked from that point, according to the 2nd part of the rule, 2nd in this problem 91,8—108 = 88° 52′, from the first point of Libra (46).

EXAMPLE.

To the cosine of Obl. Asc. from ♎ 88° 52′ = 8,296207
Add cotang. of pole of 3rd 23 48 = 10,355510

Cotang. of angle A 87 26 = 8,651717
Subtract when nearest ♎ 23 28

Angle B 63 58
As cosine of angle B 63° 58′ = (Ar. co.)   357640
Is to cosine of angle A 87 26 =   8,651102
So is tangent of Obl. Asc. 3rd 88 52 =   11,703708

Tang. of long. from ♎ 79 0 =   10,711450

Or the 3rd is 79° 0′ equal to 11 ♋ 0, when subtracted from 180 degrees 101° or 11 ♋ 0, or the cusp of the 3rd house, or the point of the ecliptic where the circle of position cuts it.

Thus have I given the method of erecting a Figure by the Doctrine of Triangles. You need only to calculate for the six houses herein shown; for the cusps of the other six are always the same degree and minute of the opposite sign. The figure of heaven at the birth of Queen Victoria.

The foregoing rules will serve for South latitude by adding 23° 26′ instead of subtracting; and subtracting where it requires adding in North Latitude, or by putting the opposite signs in the opposite houses.

PROBLEM XXV.

71 *To erect a Figure of the Heavens by the "* TABLE *of* HOUSES *"
at any given moment.*

RULE 1.—Find the Sun's Right Ascension the previous noon to the time given, in hours, minutes, and seconds. (After proportion is made for the Sun's A. R.)

RULE 2.—To this A. R. add the time given from the preceding noon, this sum will be the A. R. of M. C. for the hours which have elapsed since noon preceding.

Note.—If the result exceed 24 hours, take the excess of 24 hours, and find that for the M. C., &c.

RULE 3.—Find the longitude answering to the R. A. in the column of the " Table of Houses," for the latitude of Birth, headed, "time from noon," thus found the number required, in the next right hand column will be the degree occupying the 10th house.

RULE 4.—In the line with this is found the longitudes on the cusps of the first six houses, namely, the 11th, 12th, 1st (asc.), 2nd, and 3rd.

Having thus completed the six eastern houses, find the signs and degrees, exactly opposite to each of them, and enter the degrees on the cusps of the opposite, or western six houses. The opposite houses and signs to these (which are always the same) are—

HOUSES.		HOUSES.	SIGNS.		SIGNS.
10th	opposite	4th	♈	opposite	♎
11th	do.	5th	♉	do.	♏
12th	do.	6th	♊	do.	♐
1st	do.	7th	♋	do.	♑
2nd	do.	8th	♌	do.	♒
3rd	do.	9th	♍	do.	♓

What is the face of the heavens, December 14th, 3h. 25m. P.M., 1844, for the latitude of Sheffield ? (See the Table of Houses for Sheffield and same Latitude at the end of this book).

	h.	m.	s.
The Right Ascension of Sun, noon 14th =	17	33	1
Add the time after noon =	3	25	0
The Right Ascension of Midheaven =	20	58	1

The longitude nearly equal to this, casting away the odd second, is 12° ♒, which I place on the 10th house, and the same degree of the opposite sign 12° ♌ on the 4th.

In the (3rd) next column, I find 9° ♓ , which must be placed on the 11th house, and the same degree of the opposite sign 9° ♍, on the 5th.

In the 4th column I find 26° of ♈, place this on the 12th, and the opposite 26° ♎, on the 6th house.

In the 5th column I find 20 ♊ 27, on the 1st, and then 20 ♐ 27 on the 7th or opposite house.

In the 6th are 7° of ♋, on the 2nd, and 7° ♑ place on the 8th.

In the 7th column I see 23° ♋ on the 3rd house, and 23° ♑ must be placed on the 9th house.

The Figure now exhibits the Signs of the Zodiac at the afore-mentioned time of Birth

SOL in ARIES and TAURUS.

Time from Noon.	10 ♈	11 ♉	12 ♊	Ascen. ♋		2 ♌	3 ♍
h. m.	°	°	°	°	′	°	°
0 0	0	9	22	26	37	12	3
0 4	1	10	23	27	18	13	3
0 7	2	11	24	27	58	14	4
0 11	3	12	25	28	37	15	5
0 15	4	13	25	29	17	15	6
0 18	5	14	26	29	55	16	7
0 22	6	15	27	0 ♌	34	17	8
0 26	7	16	28	1	14	18	8
0 29	8	17	29	1	55	18	9
0 32	9	18	♋	2	33	19	10
0 36	10	19	1	3	14	20	11
0 40	11	20	1	3	54	20	12
0 44	12	22	2	4	33	21	13
0 48	13	23	3	5	12	22	14
0 51	14	24	4	5	52	23	15
0 55	15	25	5	6	30	23	15
0 59	16	26	6	7	9	24	16
1 3	17	27	6	7	50	25	17
1 6	18	28	7	8	30	26	18
1 10	19	29	8	9	9	26	19
1 14	20	♊	9	9	48	27	19
1 18	21	1	10	10	28	28	20
1 21	22	2	10	11	8	28	21
1 25	23	3	11	11	48	29	22
1 29	24	4	12	12	28	♍	23
1 33	25	5	13	13	8	1	24
1 36	26	6	14	13	48	1	25
1 40	27	7	14	14	28	2	25
1 44	28	7	15	15	8	3	26
1 48	29	8	16	15	48	4	27
1 52	♉	9	17	16	28	4	28
1 55	1	10	18	17	8	5	29
1 59	2	11	19	17	48	6	♎
2 3	3	12	19	18	28	7	1
2 7	4	13	20	19	9	8	2
2 11	5	14	21	19	49	9	3
2 15	6	15	22	20	29	9	3
2 19	7	16	22	21	10	10	4
2 23	8	17	23	21	51	11	5
2 26	9	18	24	22	32	11	6
2 30	10	19	25	23	14	12	7
2 34	11	20	25	23	55	13	8
2 38	12	21	26	24	36	14	9
2 42	13	22	27	25	17	14	10
2 46	14	23	28	25	58	15	11
2 50	15	24	29	26	40	16	12
2 54	16	25	29	27	22	17	12
2 58	17	26	♌	28	4	18	13
3 2	18	26	1	28	46	18	14
3 6	19	27	2	29	28	19	15
3 10	20	28	3	0 ♍	12	20	16
3 14	21	29	3	0	54	21	17
3 18	22	♋	4	1	36	22	18
3 22	23	1	5	2	20	22	19
3 26	24	2	6	3	2	23	20
3 31	25	3	7	3	45	24	21
3 35	26	4	7	4	28	25	22
3 39	27	5	8	5	11	26	23
3 43	28	6	9	5	54	27	24
3 47	29	7	10	6	28	27	25

SOL in GEMINI and CANCER.

Time from Noon.	10 ♊	11 ♋	12 ♑	Ascen. ♍		2 ♍	3 ♎
h. m.	°	°	°	°	′	°	°
3 51	0	8	11	7	21	28	25
3 55	1	9	12	8	5	29	26
4 0	2	10	12	8	49	♎	27
4 4	3	10	13	9	33	1	28
4 8	4	11	14	10	16	2	29
4 12	5	12	15	11	2	2	♏
4 16	6	13	16	11	46	3	1
4 21	7	14	17	12	30	4	2
4 25	8	15	17	13	15	5	3
4 29	9	16	18	14	0	6	4
4 33	10	17	19	14	45	7	5
4 38	11	18	20	15	30	8	6
4 42	12	19	21	16	15	8	7
4 46	13	20	21	17	0	9	8
4 51	14	21	22	17	45	10	9
4 55	15	22	23	18	30	11	10
4 59	16	23	24	19	16	12	11
5 3	17	24	25	20	3	13	11
5 8	18	25	26	20	49	14	13
5 12	19	25	27	21	35	14	14
5 16	20	26	28	22	20	15	14
5 21	21	27	28	23	6	16	15
5 25	22	28	29	23	51	17	16
5 29	23	29	♍	24	37	18	17
5 34	24	♌	1	25	23	19	18
5 38	25	1	2	26	9	20	19
5 43	26	2	3	26	55	20	20
5 47	27	3	4	27	41	21	21
5 51	28	4	4	28	27	22	22
5 56	29	5	5	29	13	23	23
6 0	♋	6	6	0 ♎	0	24	24
6 4	1	7	7	0	47	25	25
6 9	2	8	8	1	33	26	26
6 13	3	9	9	2	19	27	27
6 17	4	10	10	3	5	27	28
6 22	5	11	10	3	51	28	29
6 26	6	12	11	4	37	29	♐
6 31	7	13	12	5	23	♏	1
6 35	8	14	13	6	9	1	2
6 39	9	15	14	6	55	2	3
6 44	10	16	15	7	40	2	4
6 48	11	16	16	8	26	3	4
6 52	12	17	16	9	12	4	5
6 57	13	18	17	9	58	5	6
7 1	14	19	18	10	43	6	7
7 5	15	20	19	11	28	7	8
7 9	16	21	20	12	14	8	9
7 14	17	22	21	12	59	8	10
7 18	18	23	22	13	45	9	11
7 22	19	24	22	14	30	10	12
7 27	20	25	23	15	15	11	13
7 31	21	26	24	16	0	12	14
7 35	22	27	25	16	45	13	15
7 40	23	28	26	17	30	13	16
7 44	24	29	27	18	15	14	17
7 48	25	♍	28	18	59	15	18
7 52	26	1	28	19	43	16	19
7 56	27	2	29	20	27	17	20
8 0	28	3	♎	21	11	18	20
8 5	29	4	1	21	56	18	21

SOL in LEO and VIRGO.

Time from Noon.		10 ♌	11 ♍	12 ♎	Ascen. ♎		2 ♏	3 ♐
h.	m.	°	°	°	°	′	°	°
8	9	0	5	2	22	40	19	22
8	13	1	5	3	23	24	20	23
8	17	2	6	3	24	7	21	24
8	21	3	7	4	24	50	22	25
8	25	4	8	5	25	34	23	26
8	29	5	9	6	26	18	23	27
8	34	6	10	7	27	1	24	28
8	38	7	11	8	27	44	25	29
8	42	8	12	8	28	26	26	♑
8	46	9	13	9	29	8	27	1
8	50	10	14	10	29	50	27	2
8	54	11	15	11	0 ♏	32	28	3
8	58	12	16	12	1	15	29	4
9	2	13	17	12	1	58	♐	4
9	6	14	18	13	2	39	1	5
9	10	15	18	14	3	21	2	6
9	14	16	19	15	4	3	2	7
9	18	17	20	16	4	44	3	8
9	22	18	21	16	5	26	4	9
9	26	19	22	17	6	7	5	10
9	30	20	23	18	6	48	5	11
9	34	21	24	18	7	29	6	12
9	38	22	25	19	8	9	7	13
9	41	23	26	20	8	50	8	14
9	45	24	27	21	9	31	9	15
9	49	25	28	22	10	11	9	16
9	53	26	28	23	10	51	10	17
9	57	27	29	23	11	32	11	18
10	1	28	♎	24	12	12	12	19
10	5	29	1	25	12	53	12	20
10	8	♍	2	26	13	33	13	20
10	12	1	3	26	14	13	14	21
10	16	2	4	27	14	53	15	22
10	20	3	5	28	15	33	16	23
10	24	4	5	29	16	13	16	24
10	28	5	6	29	16	52	17	25
10	31	6	7	♏	17	32	18	26
10	35	7	8	1	18	13	19	27
10	39	8	9	2	18	52	20	28
10	42	9	10	2	19	31	20	29
10	46	10	11	3	20	11	21	♏
10	50	11	11	4	20	51	22	1
10	54	12	12	4	21	30	23	2
10	57	13	13	5	22	9	24	3
11	1	14	14	6	22	49	24	4
11	5	15	15	7	23	28	25	5
11	9	16	16	7	24	8	26	6
11	12	17	17	8	24	47	27	8
11	16	18	17	9	25	27	28	9
11	20	19	18	10	26	6	29	10
11	23	20	19	10	26	45	♑	11
11	27	21	20	11	27	25	0	12
11	31	22	21	12	28	5	1	13
11	34	23	22	13	28	44	2	14
11	38	24	23	13	29	24	3	15
11	42	25	23	14	0 ♐	3	4	16
11	45	26	24	15	0	43	5	17
11	49	27	25	15	1	23	5	18
11	53	28	26	16	2	3	6	19
11	56	29	26	17	2	43	7	20

SOL in LIBRA and SCORPIO.

Time from Noon.		10 ♎	11 ♎	12 ♏	Ascen. ♐		2 ♑	3 ♒
h.	m.	°	°	°	°	′	°	°
12	0	0	27	17	3	23	8	21
12	4	1	28	18	4	4	9	22
12	7	2	29	19	4	45	10	24
12	11	3	♏	20	5	26	11	25
12	15	4	1	20	6	7	12	26
12	18	5	1	21	6	48	13	27
12	22	6	2	22	7	29	14	28
12	26	7	3	23	8	10	15	29
12	29	8	4	23	8	51	16	♓
12	33	9	5	24	9	33	17	2
12	37	10	6	25	10	15	18	3
12	40	11	6	25	10	57	19	4
12	44	12	7	26	11	40	20	5
12	48	13	8	27	12	22	21	6
12	51	14	9	28	13	4	22	7
12	55	15	10	28	13	47	23	9
12	59	16	11	29	14	30	24	10
13	3	17	11	♐	15	14	25	11
13	6	18	12	1	15	59	26	12
13	10	19	13	1	16	44	27	13
13	14	20	14	2	17	29	28	15
13	18	21	15	3	18	14	29	16
13	21	22	16	4	19	0	♒	17
13	25	23	16	4	19	45	1	18
13	29	24	17	5	20	31	2	20
13	33	25	18	6	21	19	4	21
13	36	26	19	7	22	6	5	22
13	40	27	20	7	22	54	6	23
13	44	28	21	8	23	42	7	25
13	48	29	21	9	24	31	8	26
13	52	♏	22	10	25	20	10	27
13	55	1	23	11	26	10	11	28
13	59	2	24	11	27	2	12	♈
14	3	3	25	12	27	53	14	1
14	7	4	26	13	28	45	15	2
14	11	5	26	14	29	36	16	4
14	15	6	27	15	0 ♑	29	18	5
14	19	7	28	15	1	23	19	6
14	22	8	29	16	2	18	20	8
14	26	9	♐	17	3	15	22	9
14	30	10	1	18	4	11	23	10
14	34	11	2	19	5	9	25	11
14	38	12	2	20	6	7	26	13
14	42	13	3	20	7	6	28	14
14	46	14	4	21	8	6	29	15
14	50	15	5	22	9	8	♓	17
14	54	16	6	23	10	11	2	18
14	58	17	7	24	11	15	4	19
15	2	18	8	25	12	20	6	21
15	6	19	9	26	13	27	8	22
15	10	20	9	27	14	35	9	23
15	14	21	10	27	15	43	11	24
15	18	22	11	28	16	52	13	26
15	22	23	12	29	18	3	14	27
15	26	24	13	♑	19	16	16	28
15	31	25	14	1	20	32	17	29
15	35	26	15	2	21	48	19	♉
15	39	27	16	3	23	8	21	2
15	43	28	17	4	24	29	22	3
15	47	29	18	5	25	51	24	5

SOL in SAGIT. and CAPRICORN.							SOL in AQUARIUS and PISCES.						
Time from Noon.	10 ♐	11 ♐	12 ♑	Ascen. ♑		2 ♓	3 ♉	Time from Noon.	10 ♒	11 ♒	12 ♈	Ascen. ♊		2 ♊	3 ♋
h. m.	°	°	°	°	′	°	°	h. m.	°	°	°	°	′	°	°
15 51	0	18	5	27	15	26	6	20 9	0	24	4	2	45	25	12
15 55	1	19	6	28	42	28	7	20 13	1	25	5	4	9	26	13
16 0	2	20	7	0 ♒ 11		♈	9	20 17	2	27	7	5	32	27	14
16 4	3	21	8	1	42	2	10	20 21	3	28	9	6	53	28	15
16 8	4	22	10	3	16	3	11	20 25	4	29	11	8	12	28	16
16 12	5	23	11	4	53	5	12	20 29	5	♓	12	9	27	29	16
16 16	6	24	12	6	32	7	14	20 34	6	2	14	10	43	♋	17
16 21	7	25	13	8	13	9	15	20 38	7	3	16	11	58	1	18
16 25	8	26	14	9	57	11	16	20 42	8	4	18	13	9	2	19
16 29	9	27	15	11	44	12	17	20 46	9	6	19	14	18	3	20
16 33	10	28	16	13	34	14	19	20 50	10	7	21	15	25	4	21
16 38	11	29	18	15	26	16	20	20 54	11	8	23	16	32	5	22
16 42	12	♑	19	17	20	18	21	20 58	12	10	24	17	39	6	23
16 46	13	1	21	19	18	20	22	21 2	13	11	26	18	44	7	24
16 51	14	2	22	21	22	21	23	21 6	14	13	28	19	48	8	24
16 55	15	3	23	23	29	23	25	21 10	15	14	29	20	51	8	25
16 59	16	4	24	25	36	25	26	21 14	16	15	♉	21	53	9	26
17 4	17	5	26	27	46	26	27	21 18	17	16	2	22	53	10	27
17 8	18	7	27	30	0	28	28	21 22	18	17	4	23	52	11	28
17 12	19	8	28	2 ♓ 19		29	29	21 26	19	19	5	24	51	12	29
17 16	20	9	29	4	40	♉	♊	21 30	20	20	7	25	48	13	29
17 20	21	10	♒	7	2	2	2	21 34	21	21	8	26	44	13	♌
17 25	22	11	1	9	26	3	3	21 38	22	22	10	27	40	14	1
17 30	23	12	2	11	54	5	4	21 41	23	24	11	28	34	15	2
17 34	24	13	4	14	24	7	5	21 45	24	25	12	29	29	16	3
17 38	25	14	5	17	0	8	6	21 49	25	26	14	0 ♋ 22		17	4
17 43	26	15	6	19	33	10	7	21 53	26	28	15	1	15	18	5
17 47	27	16	8	22	6	11	9	21 57	27	29	17	2	7	18	5
17 51	28	17	9	24	40	13	10	22 1	28	♈	18	2	57	19	6
17 56	29	18	11	27	20	15	11	22 5	29	1	19	3	49	20	7
18 0	♑	19	12	30	0	16	12	22 8	♓	3	21	4	38	21	8
18 4	1	20	14	2	39	19	13	22 12	1	4	22	5	28	22	9
18 9	2	21	15	5	19	21	14	22 16	2	5	23	6	17	22	10
18 13	3	22	17	7	55	22	15	22 20	3	7	24	7	5	23	10
18 17	4	23	19	10	29	24	16	22 24	4	8	26	7	53	24	11
18 22	5	24	20	13	2	25	17	22 27	5	9	27	8	42	25	12
18 26	6	25	22	15	36	26	18	22 31	6	10	28	9	29	25	13
18 30	7	26	23	18	6	28	19	22 35	7	12	29	10	16	26	14
18 35	8	27	25	20	34	29	20	22 39	8	13	♊	11	2	27	15
18 39	9	28	27	22	59	♊	21	22 42	9	14	1	11	47	28	16
18 44	10	29	28	25	22	2	22	22 46	10	15	2	12	31	28	16
18 48	11	♒	♓	27	42	3	23	22 50	11	17	4	13	16	29	17
18 52	12	2	2	29	58	4	24	22 54	12	18	5	14	1	29	18
18 57	13	3	3	2 ♉ 13		6	25	22 57	13	19	6	14	45	♌	19
19 1	14	4	5	4	24	7	26	23 1	14	20	7	15	28	1	19
19 5	15	5	7	6	30	8	27	23 5	15	21	8	16	11	2	20
19 9	16	7	9	8	36	9	28	23 8	16	23	9	16	54	3	21
19 14	17	8	10	10	40	11	29	23 12	17	24	10	17	39	3	22
19 18	18	9	12	12	39	12	♋	23 16	18	25	11	18	20	4	23
19 22	19	10	14	14	35	13	1	23 20	19	26	12	19	3	5	24
19 27	20	11	16	16	28	14	2	23 23	20	27	13	19	45	6	24
19 31	21	13	18	18	18	15	3	23 27	21	28	14	20	26	6	25
19 35	22	14	19	20	3	16	4	23 31	22	29	15	21	8	7	26
19 39	23	15	21	21	48	17	5	23 34	23	♉	16	21	50	8	27
19 44	24	16	23	23	29	18	6	23 38	24	2	17	22	31	8	28
19 48	25	18	25	25	9	19	7	23 42	25	3	18	23	12	9	28
19 52	26	19	27	26	45	20	8	23 45	26	4	19	23	53	10	29
19 56	27	20	28	28	18	22	9	23 49	27	5	20	24	34	11	♍
20 0	28	21	♈	29	49	23	10	23 53	28	6	21	25	15	11	1
20 5	29	23	2	1 ♊ 19		24	11	23 56	29	8	22	25	56	12	2

PROBLEM XXVI.

72 To find the Planets' places at any given time from the Ephemeris. (44).

RULE 1.—Find, in the Ephemeris, the amount of longitude the Planet moves from the preceding noon and succeeding noon.

RULE 2.—Then look in Diurnal Logarithms for the log. answering to that daily motion, and add the log. of the time given, and the sum will give the log. of longitude for that time.

RULE 3.—Add the result to that planet's longitude at the preceding noon, and the amount is its true place.

Note.—If the planet be retrograde SUBTRACT the result from the planet's place at the preceding noon.

What is the Moon's place in the Queen's Nativity, on May 23rd, 16 hours 5 minutes, 1819?

EXAMPLE.

May 23rd the Moon in 25° ♉ 12′
On the 24th she moved to 7° ♊ 39′ 37   39

Moon moved in 24h. = 12   27

Add log. of Moon's longitude in 24h. 12° 27′ = 28504
To time since noon 16h. 5m. = 17384

Moved in 16h. 5m. = 8° 21′ = 45888

Noon of 23rd   25 ♉ 12
Add   8   21

Amount   33   33—30 = 3° ♊ 33′

EXERCISES.

1.—What is the longitude of Sol, May 24th, 4h. 5m., A.M., 1819?   Ans. 2° ♊ 6′

2.—The longitude of Herschel?   Ans. 23° ♐ 20′ R.

3.—The longitude of Saturn?   Ans. 28° ♓ 46′

4.—The longitude of Jupiter?   Ans. 16° ♒ 57′

5.—The longitude of Mars?   Ans. 17° ♈ 38′

6.—The longitude of Venus?   Ans. 26° ♈ 35′

7.—The longitude of Mercury?   Ans. 8° ♉ 55′

PROBLEM XXVII.

73 To find the Planets' Latitude in the Ephemeris at any given time.

This is given in the Ephemeris for every day at noon for the Moon, and the proportional part may be found as the longitudes.

The Sun is never considered to have latitude. The other Planets' latitude is given for every sixth day, and the proportion may be found by the golden Rule of Three.

EXAMPLE.

Mercury on May 19th, 1819, is   3° 17′
On the 25th of May   3   38

Difference   0   21

As 6 days by Diurnal log. (Ar. Com.)   9,3979
Is to 21′, the 6 days' motion   1,8361
So is 4 days 16 hours   ,7501

Movement to add 0° 15′   1,9841
Add on the 19th   3   17

Mercury's latitude of 3 s 32 on the 24th day.

Generally only the Moon, Mercury, and Venus, will need calculating, the other planets may be seen by inspection.

Observe.—If the planets pass from North to South, or from South to North, so that they cross the ecliptic, add the amount of motion to find the difference.

EXERCISES.

1.—What is Herschel's latitude?   Ans. 0 deg. 8 min. South.
2.—What is the latitude of Saturn?   Ans. 2 deg. 6 min. South.
3.—What is the latitude of Jupiter?   Ans. 0 deg. 39 min. South
4.—What is the latitude of Mars?   Ans. 1 deg. 10 min. South.
5.—What is the latitude of Venus?   Ans. 1 deg. 56 min. South.
6.—What is the latitude of the Moon?   Ans. 3 deg. 33 min. North.

PROBLEM XXVIII.

74 To find the Declination of the Planets from the Ephemeris,
when they are given daily.

RULE.—Find the distance they move from one period to another, and equate as you did in the latitude for the declination at the given time (73.)

EXAMPLE.

What is the Sun's declination in the Queen's nativity at birth?
Sun on the 24th day (increasing) is 20° 40′
Sun on the 23rd day is 20 29

Sun moved in 24 hours 0 11

By Diurnal Logarithms, 11 min. give 2,11697
Add the log. of 16 hrs. 5 min. afternoon 17384

The sum of log. give 0° 7′ = 2,29081
Add Sun's dec. on 23rd 20 29

Sun's dec. required = 20 36

EXERCISES.

1.—What is the declination of Herschel? Ans. 23 deg. 26 min. South.
2.—What is Saturn's declination ? Ans. 2 deg. 26 min. South.
3.—What is Jupiter's declination ? Ans. 16 deg. 24 min. South.
4.—What is the declination of Mars ? Ans. 5 deg. 51 min. North.
5.—What is the declination of Venus ? Ans. 8 deg. 28 min. North.
6.—What is the declination of Luna ? Ans. 24 deg. 23 min. North.
7.—What is the declination of Mercury? Ans. 11 deg. 19 min. North.

PROBLEM XXIX.

75 *To find the Declination of a Star from the Ephemeris, when
given at intervals of days.*

RULE.—Find the distance the body moves, and equate by Proportional Logarithms for the time required.

EXAMPLE.

What is Mercury's declination in Queen Victoria's horoscope?
Mercury on the 25th of May is 11° 18′
Mercury on the 19th of May is 10 40

6 days. 0 33

By Proportional Logarithms.

As 6 days by Diurnal Log. (Ar. com.) 9,3979
Is to 33 minutes, the 6 days' motion 1,6398
So is 4 days 16 hours 0,7501

Movement to add 0° 24′ = 1,7878
Add on the 19th 10 45

Mercury's declination 11 9 on the 24th.

2.—What is Jupiter's declination in the Queen's horoscope ?

Jupiter on the 19th day is 16° 26′
Jupiter on the 25th day is 16 23

Moved in 6 days o 3

As 6 days by Diurnal Log. (Ar. Co.) 9,3979
Is to 3 minutes, the 6 days' motion 2,6812
So is 4 days 16 hours 0,7501

Answer, 2 minutes nearly = 2,8292

These two minutes to be subtracted from 16° 26′ equal 16 degrees 24 seconds.

PROBLEM XXX.

76 To find the declination of a Star from the " Tables " prepared for that purpose.

RULE.—Find the proportional part for the Longitude and Latitude by the Rule of Three.

EXAMPLE I.

The Sun is in 2 degrees 6 minutes of Gemini, the declination of 2 degrees is 20° 35′, that of 3° is 20° 47′, difference 12 minutes; then say, as 6o minutes are to 6 minutes, so are 12 minutes to 1 minute, which added to the declination of 2 degrees, as the Sun is increasing in declination, and the Sun's declination will be 20 degrees 36 minutes, and as he is in a northern sign the declination is north.

EXAMPLE 2.

Find the declination of the Moon in Queen Victoria's nativity.

The Moon is in 3° 33′ of ♊, with 3° 33′ of north latitude. Under 3° of Gemini, opposite 3 degrees of longitude, are found 23° 42′; and in the same column opposite, 4 degrees of longitude, are found 23° 54′, the difference is 12 minutes, then say, 6o : 22 :: 33 : 7′ plus. Next look for the difference between 3 deg. and 4 deg. of latitude, and 4 degrees opposite the 3 deg. of long. is 24° 41′, then say, as 6o is to 59, the difference between 3° and 4° lat., so is 33 minutes to 31, plus.

Note.—As both corrections are plus we must add them thus, for 3° longitude and latitude 23° 42′

For the 33 minutes more add o 7
And for 33 minutes more of latitude add o 31

The Moon's declination is 24 20

77 Observe.—If both corrections be plus, or both minus, add them together to find the true correction, which if plus add to, and if minus take from the number opposite to the even degrees of longitude and latitude which the planet has just passed (82).

EXERCISES.

In the Queen's Nativity.

1.—What is the declination of Herschel?   Ans. 23 S 26.
2.—What is the declination of Saturn?   Ans. 2 S 26.
3.—What is the declination of Jupiter?   Ans. 16 S 24.
4.—What is the declination of Mars?   Ans. 5 N 51.
5.—What is the declination of Venus?   Ans. 8 N 28.
6.—What is the declination of Mercury?   Ans. 11 N 9.

PROBLEM XXXI.

78 To find the Declination of the Planets without latitude by Trigonometry.

RULE.—To the sine log. 9,600002 add the sine of the planet's distance from the nearest equinoctial point (46), and the sum is the sine of the declination required.

EXAMPLE.

What is the Sun's declination in the Queen's Nativity, the Sun is in 2 ♊ 6, or 62° 6′ from ♈.

$$\text{To the sine } 23° \; 28′ = 9,600002$$
$$\text{Add the sine } 62 \quad 6 = 9,946337$$

$$\text{Sum is sine of dec. } 20 \quad 36 = 9,546339$$

EXERCISES.

1.—Require the declination of Saturn in the Queen's natus.   Ans. 2 S 26.
2.—What is Herschel's declination in the Queen's natus?   Ans. 23 S 26.
3.—Obtain Jupiter's declination in the Queen's natus.   Ans. 16 S 24.
4.—Find the declination of Mars in the Queen's natus.   Ans. 5 N 51.
5.—What is the declination of Venus in the Queen's natus?   Ans. 8 N 28.
6.—What is the declination of Mercury in the Queen's natus?   Ans. 11 N 9.

PROBLEM XXXII.

79 *Given the Latitude and Longitude of a Star to find its Declination.*

RULE 1.—Add the sine of the Star's longitudinal distance from ♈ or ♎ to the log. 9,637496 and the sum is the tangent of angle A.

RULE 2.—If the latitude and longitude be of one denomination, subtract the Star's latitude from 90. But if latitude and longitude be of different denominations the latitude must be added to 90 degrees, subtract the first angle A (70) from the sum or remainder, and it will give the second angle.

RULE 3.—Add the cosine of first angle to the log. 9,962526, and the sum is sine of declination.

RULE 4.—If latitude and longitude be of one denomination the declination will be the same; but if of different names, and the declination less than the latitude, it will be the same as the latitude; but if declination be greater than the latitude, the declination will be of the same name as the sign in which the star is (5). The first six signs are North, the others South.

Required the declination of Saturn in the Queen's natus.

Saturn's longitudinal distance is found to be 1° 14′ from ♈.
Saturn's latitude is 2   6 South.

EXAMPLE.

Saturn's longitude 1° 14′ its sine = 8,332924
Add log. tangent of 23° 28′   = 9,637496

Tangent of first angle 0° 32′ 7,970420

From 90 subtract Saturn's lat. 2° 6′ = 87° 54′
From which subtract first angle, or angle A =   0 32

Angle B, or second angle = 87 22

Then as cosine of first angle   0° 32′ (Ar. Com.) 0,000019
Is to cosine of second angle 87 22   = 8,662230
So is cosine of Obliq. of ecliptic 23 28   = 9,962526

To sine of Saturn's declination 2 S 25   = 8,624775

The Declination may be more readily found by the Table.

EXERCISES.

1.—What is the declination of Jupiter in 2 ♏ 15
    and latitude 1 N 8 ?   Ans. 11 S 12.
2.—What is the declination of 7 ♐ 5 latitude
    0 N 4 ?   Ans. 21 S 35.

3.—What is the declination of 20 ♈ 26 and latitude 0 N 25?   Ans. 8 N 23.

4.—What is the declination of 8 ♒ 36 and latitude 0 S 51?   Ans. 18 S 57.

5.—What is the declination of 0 ♐ 32 and latitude 1 N 11?   Ans. 19 S 7.

PROBLEM XXXIII.

80 To find the Planets' Right Ascension without latitude by Trigonometry.

RULE.—Add the cosine of its longitudinal distance from the nearest equinoctial point, to the Arithmetical Complement of the cosine (or its whole secant) of declination, the sum will be the cosine of its Right Ascension from that point whence the distance was taken (46).

If the Star be in Aries, Taurus, or Gemini, the arc thus found will be the R. A. But if it be in Cancer, Leo, or Virgo, it must be subtracted from 180 degrees. If in Capricornus, Aquarius, or Pisces, the arc thus found must be subtracted from 360 degrees (46).

EXAMPLES.

1.—What is the Sun's Right Ascension in Queen's natus, the Sun being in 2 ♊ 6, his declination 20° N. 36'?

To the cosine 20° 26' (Arith. Com.) or secant = 0,028697
Add cosine longitudinal distance 62° 6' = 9,670181

The sum is cosine R. A. 60 0 = 9,698878

Observe, these may be found also as in Problem ii (page 195).

2.—Find the Right Ascension of Saturn in the Queen's natus.

To the cosine of 2° S. 26' his declination (Arith. Com.) = 0,00039
Add cosine of Saturn's distance from ♈ 1° 14' = 9,99990

The sum is cosine of Right Ascension 359° 41' = 10,00029

EXERCISES.

1.—What is the Right Ascension of Jupiter?   Ans. 319° 38'.

2.—What is the Right Ascension of Mars?   Ans. 16 38.

3.—What is the Right Ascension of Venus?   Ans. 25 22.

4.—What is the Right Ascension of Mercury?   Ans. 37 3.

PROBLEM XXXIV.

81 *Given the Latitude, Longitude, and Declination, to find the Right Ascension of any Heavenly Body.*

RULE.—Add together the Arithmetical Complement of cosine, or the whole secant, of declination and cosine of longitudinal distance (46) and the cosine of latitude, and the sum will be the cosine, of the Right Ascension of the body from Aries or Libra (46).

EXAMPLES.

1.—What is Mercury's Right Ascension, his longitude 63° 25′, latitude 3° 45′, and his declination 17° 11′ ?

Add
{
Cosine of declination 17° 11′ its secant   0,01983
Cosine of longitude 63 25 its log.   9,65079
Cosine of latitude   3 45 its log.   9,99907
}

The sum is cosine of Mercury's Right Ascension 62° 8′ = 9,66969

Note.—As this 62 degrees 8 minutes is less than 90 degrees, it is in the first quadrant (32) of the heavens, we have no need either to add or subtract, but merely to take the result of the cosine found.

2.—What is Saturn's Right Ascension in the Queen's natus, being in 28° ♓ 46′, with south latitude 2° 6′, and the declination 2° 25′ ?

Saturn's being nearest Aries we subtract 358° 26′, which are equal to 28 degrees 46 minutes of Pisces. Here 360, from which take 358° 26′ equal to 1° 14′.

Add
{
Saturn's cosine of declination   2° 25′ (Arith. Com.). 0,000386
Cosine of longitudinal distance 1 14 from ♈   9,999899
Cosine of latitude   2   6 its log.   9,999708
}

The sum of log. cosine is 0° 19′ the A. R. from ♈ = 9,999993

This 0° 19′ must be subtracted from 360° and it will leave the A. R. of Saturn to be 359° 41′.

3.—The Right Ascension of Herschel is required in the Queen's natus.

As cosine of Herschel's declination 23° 26′ (Ar. Com.) 0,03738
Is to cosine of his longitude 83 20 from ♎   9,06401
So is cosine of his latitude 0 S 8 its log.   9,99999

The sum is the cosine from ♎ Herschel's A. R. 82° 44′ = 9,10138

This must be added to 180 degrees, the distance 82° 44′, and the sum is 262 degrees 44 minutes the Right Ascension of Herschel.

PROBLEM XXXV.

82 *Given the Longitude and Latitude of a Star to find its Right Ascension by the Tables.*

RULE.—Find the A. R. of the Planet for the equal degree of longitude and latitude, then take the proportional parts of the odd minutes; observing if the R. A. be less than 180 degrees the latitude ought to be North, if more than 180 degrees, then it is generally South (76.)

EXAMPLE.

1.—What is the Right Ascension of Venus when in 26 degrees 35 minutes of ♈, with 1 degree 56 minutes South latitude?

Look in the Tables of R. A. under one degree of latitude, and opposite to 26 degrees of Aries are 24° 28′, and under the same latitude, opposite to 27 degrees are 25° 25′, the difference is 57 minutes. Then say, as 60′ : 57′ : : 35′ : 33¼′ plus, as the A. R. is increasing. Next look for the difference between 1 and 2 degrees of latitude, which is 32 minutes plus: then say, as 60′ is to 32′ so is 56′ to 21′ the answer.

Found thus, for 26 degrees of Aries are   24° 28′

And for 35 minutes add   0 33

For the plus of latitude add   0 21

The sum is the Right Ascension of Venus = 25 22

PROBLEM XXXVI.

83 *Given a Star's Right Ascension and the Right Ascension of the Midheaven to find its Meridian Distance.*

RULE 1.—Take the difference between the star's R. A. and the R. A of the M. C., but in this the star must be above the earth, and the difference is the star's meridian distance.

RULE 2.—If the star be below the earth, then the difference between the I. C. or 4th house and its Right Ascension will be the star's meridian distance.

Note.—The Right Ascension of the 4th is always found by adding 180° to the A. R. of the Midheaven or 10th house, and if it exceed 360 degrees take that number from the sum or plus of 360.

EXAMPLES.

1.—What is Saturn's meridian distance in the Queen's horoscope?

	°	′
Saturn's Right Ascension is	359	41
Right Ascension of the M. C. is	301	8

The Meridian distance of Saturn is = 58 33 or M.C. ♂ ♄

2.—What is the Sun's Right Ascension below the earth ?

	°	′
Right Ascension of the 4th house	121	8
From which subtract the R. A. of Sol	60	8

The Sun's Meridian distance = 61 0 or M.C ☍ ☉

3.—Herschel's Meridian distance.

	°	′
The Right Ascension of the Midheaven is	301	8
The Right Ascension of Herschel with lat.	262	44

Herschel's Meridian distance = 38 24 or M. C. ♂ ♅

4.—Mar's Meridian distance

	°	′
The A. R. of Mars with the whole circle	376	42
The Right Ascension of the M. C.	301	8

Mar's Meridian distance = 75 34 or M.C. ♂ ♂

Problem XXXVII.

84 To find a Star's Ascensional Difference under the Pole of Horoscope.

RULE.—Add the tangent of the latitude of the given place (or birth place) to the tangent of the star's declination, and the sum will be the sine of the Ascensional difference under the Pole of the country.

EXAMPLE.

1.—What is the Sun's ascensional difference his declination being 20° N. 36′ and the latitude of London 51° 32 ?

Tangent of Sun's declination being 20° 36′ =		9,575044
Add the tangent of 51 32 =		10,099913

Ascensional difference sine 28   14 =   9,674957

EXERCISES.

In the Queen's nativity.

2.—What is the ascensional difference of Herschel?   Ans. 33° 4'.
3.—What is Saturn's ascensional difference?   Ans.   3 4.
4.—What is Jupiter's ascensional difference?   Ans. 21 42.

Proceed till all the ascensional differences are obtained.

☞ Now get out all the sines of their ascensional difference.

PROBLEM XXXVIII.

85 *To find the Semi-diurnal Arc of a Star above the Earth.*

RULE.—If the star be above the Earth in North declination, add the ascensional difference to 90 degrees; but if it be South declination subtract the ascensional difference from 90 for its semiarc.

EXAMPLES.

1.—What is Mar's semidiurnal arc?

	°	′
Set down	90	0
Add Mar's ascensional difference North	7	23
Sum is Mar's semidiurnal arc =	97	23

2.—What is Saturn's semidiurnal arc?

	°	′
Set down the degrees	90	0
Subtract the asc. diff. as the dec. is south	86	56
Saturn's semidiurnal arc =	3	4

PROBLEM XXXIX.

86 *To find the Semi-nocturnal Arc of a Star when below the Earth.*

RULE.—If in north declination subtract the ascensional difference from 90 degrees. But if in South declination add the ascensional difference to 90 for the semiarc.

Note.—Subtract the acquired arc from 180 degrees, and the remainder is the contra-semiarc.

EXAMPLES.

1.—The Sun's semiarcs.

o   ,

From the given degrees 90 0
Subtract the Moon's ascensional difference = 28 14

Sol's semi-nocturnal arc = 61 46
Thus found, subtract it from 180 0

Sol's semi-diurnal arc = 118 14

2.—The Moon's semiarcs.

o   ,

From the given degrees 90 0
Subtract the Moon's ascensional difference 24 42

The Moon's semi-nocturnal arc = 55 18
Thus found, subtract it from 180 0

Moon's semi-diurnal arc = 124 42

☞ Now get out all the contrary semiarcs and their proportional logs., which reserve in the speculum.

PROBLEM XL.

87 To find the Semiarcs without the Ascensional Difference.

RULE.—Add the tangent of the Latitude of Birth Place to the tangent of the Star's declination, and the sum will be the cosine of the Semiarc.

Care.—If the latitude of the country be North and the declination South, the result will be the semi-diurnal arc. But if the latitude of the country be of the same name, North or South, as the declination, the sum will be the semi-nocturnal arc. The latitude will always be N. in this hemisphere.

EXAMPLE I.

What is the semiarc of Jupiter in the latitude of London with 16 degrees 52 minutes South latitude?

Tangent of 51 degrees 32 minutes = 10,099914
Tangent of declination 16 deg. 22 min. = 9,467880

Cosine of this is 68 deg. 18 min. = 9,567794

The result is Jupiter's semi-diurnal arc, 68 degrees 18 minutes.

EXAMPLE 2.

What is Mars's semiarc in the Queen's natus?

Tangent of latitude 51 degrees 32 min. = 10,099914
Tangent of declination 5 deg. 51 min. =   9,010546

The cosine is semi-nocturnal arc 82° 35′ =   9,110460

Work all the semiarcs in the Queen's natus.

3.—What is Herschel's semi-diurnal arc?   Ans.   56 deg. 56 min.
4.—What is Saturn's semi-diurnal arc?   Ans.   86 deg. 56 min.
5.—What is the Sun's semi-diurnal arc?   Ans. 118 deg. 14 min.
6.—What is Venus's semi-diurnal arc?   Ans. 100 deg. 48 min.
7.—What is Mercury's semi-diurnal arc?   Ans. 104 deg. 3 min.
8.—What is the Moon's semi-diurnal arc?   Ans. 124 deg. 42 min.

The Part of Fortune's semiarc is always 90 deg.   The contrary arc may be seen in the speculum; therefore we have no need to work them by way of example.   For when the semiarc of a planet is found, that planet's contrary semiarc may be found by subtracting the semiarc already obtained from 180 degrees, and the remainder will be the semiarc required.

PROBLEM XLI.

88 *To find the Logarithm of a Planet's Circle of Position.*

RULE.—Add the Arithmetical Complement of the Planet's semiarc (63) to the proportional Logarithm 90 (3010), and the sum is the Logarithm of Circle of Position.   The Logarithm must be preserved in the speculum, for future calculations.

EXAMPLES.

1.—The Circle of Position of Herschel.

Semiarc of Herschel is 56° 56′ (Ar. Co.) is 9,5001
Proportional Ar. of 90 degrees is 0,3010

Logarithm of Circle of Position = 9,8011

2.—The Circle of the Position of Saturn.

The semiarc of Saturn 86° 56′ = 9,6839
Proportional arc of 90 degrees = 0,3010

Logarithm of Saturn's Circular Position = 9,9849

3.—The Circle of Position of Jupiter.

The semiarc of Jupiter 68° 18′ (Ar. Co.) = 9,5791
Add the Logarithm of 90 degrees = 0,3010

Logarithm of Jupiter's Circular Position = 9,8801

4.—The Circle of Position of Venus.

The semiarc of Venus is 100° 48′ (Ar. Co.) = 9,7481
Add the Logarithm of 90 degrees = 0,3010

Logarithm of the Circle of Position of Venus = 0,0491

5.—The Circle of Position of Mercury.

The semiarc of Mercury is 104° 3′ (Ar. Co.) = 9,7619
Add Logarithm of 90 degrees = 0,3010

Logarithm of Mercury's Circular Position = 0,0629

6.—The Circle of Position of the Part of Fortune.

The semiarc of Pars 90 degrees (Ar. Co.) = 9,6990
Add Logarithm of what you borrowed = 0,3010

The Circle of Part of Fortune is always this 0,0000

PROBLEM XLII.

89 *To find a Planet's difference of Circle of Position or Second
Meridian Distance in any Figure.*

RULE.—Add together the Logarithm of the Circle of Position to
the Logarithm of the Planet's Meridian Distance, and the sum
will be the proportional Logarithm of the difference of the Circle
of Position, or the Planet's second Meridian Distance.

EXAMPLES.

1.—The difference of circle of position of Herschel.

The logarithm of circular position of Herschel is 9,8011
Meridian distance of Herschel is 38° 24′ its prop. log. = 0,6709

Difference in circular position of Herschel is 60° 42′ = 0,4720

2.—The difference of circular position of Saturn.

The logarithm of circular position of Saturn is 9,9849
Meridian distance of Saturn 58° 33′ proportional diff. = 0,4877

Difference in circle of position of Saturn is 60° 37′ = 0,4726

3.—The difference of circular position of Jupiter.

The logarithm of circular position of Jupiter is 9,8801
Meridian distance of Jupiter 18° 30′ proportional log. =   0,9881
____
Difference in circle of position of Jupiter is 24° 23′ =   0,8682

4.—The difference of circle of position of Luna.

The logarithm of circular position of the Moon is 0,1416
Meridian distance of the Moon 119° 37′ proportional log. = 0,1775
____
Difference in circle of position of Luna 86° 20′ = 0,3191

5.—The difference of circular position of Mercury.

Mercury's logarithm of circle of position is   ,0629
Meridian distance of Mercury 95° 55′ its proportional log. =   ,2734
____
Mercury's difference of circle of position 82° 58′ =   ,3363

6.—The difference of circle of position of the Part of Fortune.

The Part of Fortune's logarithm is equal to 0,0000
The logarithm of its meridian distance must be added 0,3236
____
The diff. of circle of position of Part of Fortune is 85° 26′ = 0,3236

7.—The difference of circle of position of Mars is 69 degrees 5 minutes.

8.—The difference of circle of position of Sol is 80 degrees 5 minutes.

9.—The difference of the circle of position of Venus is 75 degrees 14 minutes.

90.   The circle of position of all the planets between the meridian and the horizon are analogous to the circles of latitude, which are small circles of the sphere (13), having their planes parallel with the plane of the meridian.   The circle of position of a planet, &c., has a certain point where it and the pole of the planet intersect the equator.   The circle of position being obtained by Problem 41, we have only to find the difference between it and the distance of the planet itself, and we obtain the ascensional difference of the planet under its own pole, as by the 44th Problem.

____

PROBLEM XLIII.

91   *To find a Planet's Ascensional Difference under its own Pole.*

RULE.—The difference between the Planet's Meridian Distance and the difference of its Circle of Position is the Ascensional Difference under its own Pole.

EXAMPLE.

1.—What is Mars's Ascensional Difference under his own pole, in the Queen's nativity?

o   ,

Mars's meridian distance is 75 34
Difference in circle of position = 69 50

Mars's Ascensional difference under his own pole   5 44

EXERCISES.

2.—What is the Ascensional difference of
      Jupiter under his own pole?   Ans. 5 deg. 53 min.
3.—Required the Ascensional difference of
      Herschel under his own pole?   Ans. 22 deg. 17 min.
4.—What is the Ascensional difference of
      Saturn under his own pole?   Ans. 3 deg. 5 min.
5.—Required the Ascensional difference of
      the Moon under her own pole?   Ans. 33 deg. 17 min.
6.—What is the Ascensional difference of
      Mercury under his own pole?   Ans. 12 deg. 55 min.
7.—Required the Ascensional difference of
      Sun under his own pole?   Ans. 27 deg. 58 min.
8.—What is the Ascensional difference of
      Venus under her own pole?   Ans. 9 deg. 0 min.

PROBLEM XLIV.

92 *To find the Pole of any Star in any Figure.*

RULE.—To the sine of the Ascensional Difference, last found add the cotangent of its Declination, and the sum will be the tangent of its pole.

EXAMPLE.

1.—Find Mars's pole in the Queen's nativity.
      Sine of Ascensional difference 5° 44′ = 8,999560
      Add cotangent of Mars's dec. 5   51 = 10,989454

      Tangent of the pole of Mars 44   21 = 9,989014

EXERCISES.

2.—What is the pole of Herschel in the
      Speculum?   Ans. 41 deg. 12 min.
3.—What is the pole of Saturn in the Queen's
      natus?   Ans. 40 deg. 19 min.

4.—What is the pole of Jupiter ?   Ans. 19 deg. 14 min.
5.—What is the pole of the Sun ?   Ans. 51 deg. 16 min.
6.—What is the pole of Venus ?   Ans. 46 deg. 28 min.
7.—What is the pole of Mercury?   Ans. 49 deg. 17 min.
8.—What is the pole of the Moon ?   Ans. 50 deg. 31 min.
9.—What is the pole of the Part of Fortune ? Ans. 49 deg. 55 min.

PROBLEM XLV.

93 *To find a Planet's Oblique Ascension or Oblique Descension under its own pole.*

RULE 1.—Add the Ascensional Difference to its Right Ascension if the declination be South; but subtract the Ascensional Difference if the declination be north from the Right Ascension, and the result is the Answer.

RULE 2.—If the Star have north declination add the Ascensional difference to the Right Ascension; and if south subtract it, the result is the oblique Descension.

N.B.—Oblique Ascension is wanted when the star is between the 4th rising towards the Ascendant up to the 10th. Oblique Descension from the 10th past the 7th to the 4th house.

EXAMPLES.

1.—What is Mars's Oblique Ascension in the nativity of Queen Victoria ?

	o	'
Mars's Right Ascension is	16	42
Subtract Mars's Ascen. Diff. as he is north	5	44
Mars's Oblique Ascension is	10	58

2.—What is Herschel's Oblique Descension in the horoscope ?

	o	'
Herschel's Right Ascension is	262	44
Subtract ♅'s Asc. Diff. under his own pole S.	22	17
Herschel's Oblique Descension is	240	27

Remark:—We have subtracted the Ascensional Difference, in both examples, from the Right Ascension; although the Declinations are one north, and the other south; but then you will perceive, according to Rule, that when the Declination is north, we take the difference for the Oblique Ascension; also the difference for Oblique Descension is south, *et vice versa.*

EXERCISES.

3.—What is Sol's Oblique Ascension in the
Queen's natus ?   Ans. 32 deg.   3 min.

4.—It is required to find Jupiter's Oblique
Ascension.   Ans. 325 deg. 31 min.

5.—Required   the   Oblique   Ascension   of
Venus.   Ans. 16 deg. 21 min.

6.—Find the Oblique Ascension of the Moon.   Ans. 27 deg. 28 min.

7.—What   is   the   Oblique   Ascension   of
Mercury ?   Ans. 24 deg. 8 min.

8.—Required   the   Oblique   Ascension   of
Saturn ?   Ans. 1 deg. 45 min.

9.—The Oblique Ascension of the Part of
Fortune is required.   Ans. 26 deg. 34 min.

PROBLEM XLVI.

94 *To bring a Star to the Cusp of any of the Celestial Houses when above the Earth.*

RULE.—To bring it to the Cusp of the 1st house subtract the
whole semi-diurnal arc from its Meridian Distance, or the difference
between them.   To the Cusp of the 12th, the difference between
its Meridian Distance and two-thirds of semiarc—if to the Cusp of
the 11th the difference between the Meridian Distance and one-
third of semiarc ; if to the 10th, the Meridian Distance is the arc.
If to the 9th, add one third of the semiarc ; if to the 8th, add two-
thirds ; if to the 7th, add the whole semi-diurnal arc to the Meridian
Distance, and the sum will be the respective distance of each
Planet required.

EXAMPLES.

1.—To bring the Moon to the cusp of the 1st in the Queen's
natus.   o   ′

The whole semi-diurnal arc of the Moon is 124 42
The Moon's distance from the 10th is 119 37

The Moon's distance from cusp of the 1st above   5   5 or M.C.☐ ☽.

---

95 On account of the Moon's great latitude she is actually 5
degrees 5 minutes above the Ascendant, although she appears by
her geocentric longitude to be below the earth.   Found by another
method—Take one-third of the Moon's semi-diurnal arc, which is
the space of one house.   Her semiarc diurnal is 124 degrees 42
minutes, and one-third is 41 degrees 34 minutes, subtract from this
36 degrees 29 minutes distant from the cusp of the 12th.   PROOF.—

Take two-thirds of the Moon's semiarc, 83 degrees 8 minutes from the Meridian distance 119 degrees 37 minutes, remain 36 degrees 29 minutes as before; so here you see she is above the earth. The Moon's square to M. C. is 5 degrees 5 minutes, her sextile to M. C. is 36 degrees 29 minutes; her sextile to Asc. is 78 degrees 3 minutes or distance from the cusp of the 11th, which is a semi-sextile to the M. C.; found—add one-third of semiarc 41 degrees 34 minutes to M.C. sextile Moon 36 degrees 29 minutes equal 78 degrees 3 minutes; or subtract one-third of semiarc 41 degrees 34 minutes from her Meridian distance 119 degrees 37 minutes leave 78 degrees 3 minutes, as before.

2.—Bring Mars to the cusp of 11th house.

Mars's semi-diurnal arc is 97° 25′, and ⅓rd is 32° 28′
    Taken from Mars's Meridian distance 75   34

♂'s distance from 11th or Asc. to the ✶ of ♂ = 43   6 or M.C. S. ✶ ♂.

3.—Bring Saturn to the 10th, which will be his Meridian distance, or M. C. ☌ ♄

    The Right Ascension of Saturn is 359°41′
The Right Ascension of the 10th house or M. C. 301   8

Saturn's distance from the 10th house, or M.C.= 58 33 or M.C. ☌ ♄.

Note.—This aspect of Saturn is the conjunction of M. C. Saturn; the same 58 degrees 33 minutes is the Asc. square Saturn—and the Mid. dist. of Saturn. All the Mundane aspects to the Ascendant and Mid-heaven can be obtained by this method.

PROBLEM XLVII.

96 *A Planet below the Earth, to bring it to the Cusp of any of the Houses.*

RULE.—If to the cusp of the 6th or 2nd, subtract two-thirds of its semi-nocturnal arc from its Meridian distance, or take the difference if subtraction cannot be made. If to the 5th or 3rd, the difference between one-third of semiarc and Meridian distance. If to the 4th, its Meridian distance.

EXAMPLE.

1.—Bring the Sun to the cusp of the 2nd houses.
    The Sun's Meridian distance from the I.C. is 61° 8′
Sol's semi-noct. arc is 61° 46′, and two-thirds are 41 11

Sol's distance from the cusp of the house = 19 57 or M.C. △ ☉

PROBLEM XLVII.

*97.   To find the Pole and Oblique Ascension or Oblique Descension
of a Star in any Figure.*

RULE 1.—Add the Logarithms of Circle of Position to the Log. of Meridian Distance; the sum will be the Planet's second distance (89).

RULE 2.—Add or subtract the second distance to or from the Meridian Distance as the declination may be south or north, and the sum or difference will be the oblique ascension or descension of the planet under its own Pole (93).

RULE 3.—Take the difference between the Right Ascension of the Planet and its Oblique Ascension and Oblique Descension, which is its ascensional difference under its own Pole.

RULE 4.—For the Pole.—From the sine of ascensional difference subtract the tangent of its declination, and the remainder is the tangent of its Pole (91).

EXAMPLE.

In Queen Victoria's nativity the Moon's declination is 24° 23′, her semi-diurnal arc is 124° 42′; her Meridian distance 119° 37′, and her Right Ascension 60° 45′—required her Oblique Ascension and her Pole.

Add Log. of Circle of Position, which is 0,1416
To the Meridian distance of the Moon 119° 37′   1775

The sum is the 2nd dist. of the ☽ from the Mid. 86° 20′ = 0,3191 as P. 89.
To 86° 20′ add the R. Asc. of the Meridian = 301 8

The sum   387 28
As 387° 28′ is more than the circle, we take 360   0

The true Obl. Asc. of the ☽ under her pole is = 27 28

The difference between her Oblique Ascension and Right Ascension is the Ascensional Difference under her own Pole, therefore, 27° 28′ from 60° 45′ her A. R. will leave 33° 17′.

The sine of Ascensional Difference 33° 17′   = 9,739398
Subtract tangent of Moon's declination 24   20 = 9,655348

Remains the tangent of Moon's Pole 50   31 = 10,084050

N.B.—This Problem serves for Paragraphs 89, 90, 91, 92, and 93.

PROBLEM XLIX.

98 *To find the place of the Part of Fortune.*

RULE.—From the Oblique Ascension or Descension of the Moon under her own Pole, subtract the Sun's Oblique Ascension or Oblique descension under his own Pole, and to the difference add the Oblique Ascension of the Ascendant, and the sum will be the required distance from the Oblique Ascension or Descension of the House to which it falls the nearest.

EXAMPLE.

In the Queen's nativity find the place of the Part of Fortune·

Oblique Ascension of the Moon under her own pole is $27° 28'$ we must add the circle to this or subtraction cannot be made,

<pre>
                                then we have 287° 28'
Subtract Sun's Oblique Ascension under his pole   32   2
                                                 ───────
                                                 355 26
   Add Oblique Ascension of the Ascendant   31   8
                                                 ───────
Gives Oblique Ascension of the Part of Fortune   386 34
   Subtract the Oblique Ascension of the 12th   361   8
                                                 ───────
</pre>

Remains Part of Fortune distant from the 12th inside 25 26 or $4° 34'$ from the cusp of the Ascendant answering to $1° ♊ 57'$ in the zodiac.

After finding the distance of the Part of Fortune from a House by this method, then I allow it a semiarc of 90 degrees, and it will work the direction correct, according to the true mundane distance of the Moon from the Sun.

N.B.—The Part of Fortune is never moved or directed like the Planets—it is the Planets that are directed to the Part of Fortune's mundane aspects.

The Part of Fortune is always the same distance from the Ascendant, in the order of the signs, as the Sun is from the Moon ; to prove this being correct, here follows the calculation—

<pre>
        The Oblique Ascension of the Sun 32° 2'
        The Oblique Ascension of the Moon 27 28
                                          ───────
        The luminaries from each other   4 34
                                          ───────
Again {The Oblique Ascension of Ascendant   31   8
      {The Oblique Ascension of the Part of Fortune 26 34
                                          ───────
Distance of Part of Fortune from the Ascendant   4 34
                                          ───────
</pre>

This proves our method of calculation to be correct.

If we wish to have the A. R. of the Part of Fortune, which is of no use, here is the calculation. We have found its Oblique Ascension to be 26 degrees 34 minutes. Find its Pole of Position, thus—

Pole of the Ascendant 51° 32′, pole of the 12th 40° 53′ difference 10° 39′. Then as 30, the space of a house, give 10° 39′ what will the Part of Fortune's distance from the 1st give, 4° 34′. Ans. 1° 37′, which taken from 51° 32′ leave 49° 55′, and this tangent is—

$$
\begin{array}{r}
10,074904 \\
\text{The } \oplus\text{'s declination as the } \mathcal{D}\ 24°\ 20' =\quad 9,655348 \\
\hline
\end{array}
$$

It gives sine of Asc. Diff. $\mathcal{D}$'s under pole 32 30= 9,730252
Add 32° 30′ to Obl. Asc. of $\oplus$ under pole 26 34

This gives the A. R. of Part of Fortune= 59 4

Allowing it the same latitude as the Moon, it shows its place to be in the zodiac in 1° ♊ 57′.

INFORMATION.

" These are the only data required to proceed to calculate the arcs of direction, by which not only the nature of the events which shall befall the native may be foreseen, but also the period when they shall occur (to within a few days) may be undoubtedly ascertained." (For further information see Arcana, Problems 142 and 143.)

A direction, or an arc of direction, is the pathway or track described in the heavens by any planet that is significator, or that assumes the dominion or government of life, or any other accident or event peculiar to the native, from the moment of birth to its meeting or forming an aspect with the anaretas or promittors, at which time the event, be it what it may, that is indicated thereby, comes to pass. For as all the heavenly bodies constantly move in circles, their progress, whether for a long or short time, will necessarily form arches, the content or degrees of which, being accurately found, and measured, are equated by the solar motion, will describe the length of time, whether it be years, months, or days, which the significator will be in forming the arc of direction which produces the event.

99 If the planet directed should pass the horizon in forming aspects, that is if the arc of direction should be longer than the planet's distance from the horizon, then its other semiarc must be used for those aspects which fall beyond the horizon. Great care is to be taken to avoid errors by taking the wrong semiarc ; this may be done by observing that if the aspect occur above the earth,

the SEMI-DIURNAL ARC is to be taken ; and if below the earth, the SEMI-NOCTURNAL ARC of that planet which is directed, must be taken.

100 Directions in mundo.—In all cases if the secondary distance of a planet be on the same side of the cusp whence the primary was taken, when the aspect is completed, SUBTRACT the primary and secondary distance from each other, and the difference will be the arc of direction. But if the primary and secondary distance be on different sides of the cusp whence the primary was taken, then add them, and the sum will be the arc of direction.

101 Mundane parallels are formed when two planets are equidistant from the angles of a figure, and are, like all other mundane aspects, measured by the semiarcs of the planets ; thus a star on the cusp of the second house would be in mundane parallel to another on the cusp of the 6th, because they are both two houses distant from the 4th ; a star on the cusp of the 9th is in the same parallel with another on the cusp of the 11th, because they are equidistant from the midheaven, &c.

102 Zodiacal Aspects.—If the Sun or Moon be exactly on the meridian, then it has no pole, and the arc of direction must be found by Right Ascension. If the Sun or Moon be exactly on the horizon, it will have the polar elevation of the horizon itself, which is always the latitude of the Birth place. The Ascendant, when it is directed in the zodiac, must always be directed under the pole or latitude of the place of birth.

THE NATIVITY OF QUEEN VICTORIA.

A. R. of M. C. 301° 8′.

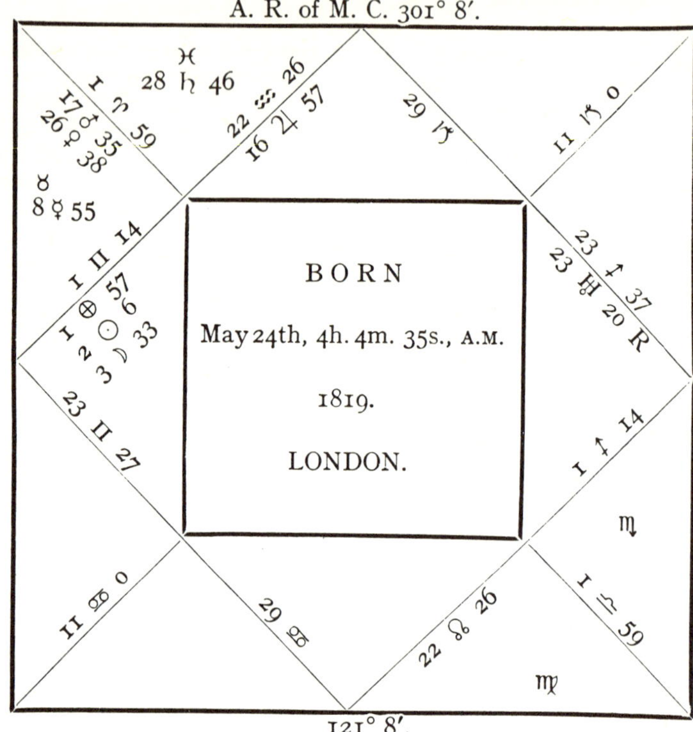

Plan- ets.	Lati- tude.		Decli- nation.		Tangent of Declina.	Cotangent of Declina.	A. R.		Mid. Dist.		Its Log.
	°	′	°	′	°	°	°	′	°		
♅	0 s 8		23 s 26		9,636919	10,3631	262	44	38	24	6709
♄	2 s 6		2 s 26		8,62834	11,3717	359	41	58	33	4877
♃	0 s 39		16 s 24		9,468814	10,5312	319	38	18	30	9881
♂	1 s 10		5 N 51		9,01055	10,9894	16	42	75	34	3769
☉	.. ..		20 N 36		9,57504	10,4250	60	0	61	8	4690
♀	1 s 56		8 N 28		9,17277	10,8272	25	22	84	14	3298
☿	3 s 32		11 N 9		9,29468	10,7053	37	3	95	55	2734
☽	3 N 33		24 N 20		9,655356	10,3446	60	45	119	37	1775
⊕	.. ..		.. ..		.. ..	.. ..	59	4	85	26	3236

NOTE.—Some give the time of Birth, May 24th, 4 h. 4 m. 55 s., and if this time be correct it will prolong the life of Her Majesty by some few years than the time given in the Figure, which will be shown by the arc of direction, which comes up a little later in life than the time shown.

Planets.	Semi-diurnal Arc.	A.C. of Pro. Log. of S. Arc.	Semi-nocturnal Arc.	A.C. of Pro. Log. of S.N.A.	⅓ of the Planet's S.D.A.	Proport. Log. of S.D.A.	Log. of Semiarc.	Ascens. Difference Horosope.	Sine of Ascensional Difference.	Poles.	Tangent of Pole.	Log. of Circle of Position.	Asc. diff. under the Plt's Pole.	Ob. Asc. and Obl. Dec. under its Pole.
	° '		° '		° D '			° '		° '			° '	° '
♅	56 56	9,5001	123 4	9,8379	18 D 59	9768	4999	33 4	9,7369	41 12	9,9422	9,8011	22 17	240 D 27
♄	86 56	9,6839	93 4	9,7135	28 D 59	7931	3161	3 4	9,7283	40 19	9,9287	9,9849	3 5	1 A 45
♃	68 18	9,5791	111 42	9,7927	22 D 46	8980	4209	21 45	9,5687	19 14	9,5428	9,8801	5 53	325 D 31
♂	97 25	9,7333	82 35	9,6616	32 D 28	7438	2666	7 25	9,11046	44 21	9,98901	0,0343	5 44	10 A 58
☉	118 14	9,8175	61 46	9,5354	39 D 25	6600	1825	28 14	9,67492	51 16	0,09585	9,8364	27 58	32 A 3
♀	100 48	9,7481	79 12	9,6434	33 D 36	7290	2518	10 48	9,27268	46 28	0,0222	0,0491	9 0	16 A 21
☿	104 3	9,7619	75 57	9,6252	34 D 41	7152	2380	14 22	9,39459	49 17	0,06518	0,0629	12 55	24 A 8
☽	124 42	9,8406	55 18	9,4874	41 D 34	6365	1594	34 41	9,75526	50 31	0,08405	0,1416	33 17	27 A 28
⊕	90 0	9,6990	90 0	9,6989	30 0	7782	3010			49 55	0,0750	0,0000	0 0	26 A 24

Directions.—1.—After getting the Planets' Declination, then get their tangents and co-tangents.

2.—When the Mid. distance is obtained, then look for all their proportional Logs.

3.—When the semiarcs are worked out, then find at once all their Arith. Com.

4.—To this Arith. Com. of the semi-arc add 3010 and the sum is the Circle of Position which now get at.

5.—Add the Log. of Circle of Position and the Proportional Log. of Mid. distance immediately after the Circle of Position is found.

PROBLEM L.

103 *To direct the M. C. to the conjunction of a Planet in mundo when above the Earth.*

RULE.—The difference between the R. A. of M. C. and the Planets R. A. with lat. is the Arc required.

Note.—This is the star's distance from the M. C. or Mid-distance. If the planet be between the 10th and 1st, this is a square to Asc. ; if between the 7th and 10th, then it is an opposition to the Asc.

EXAMPLE.

When will the M. C. form a conjunction of Jupiter in Victoria's nativity ?

The Right Ascension of Jupiter is 319° 38′
The Right Ascension of the Mid-heaven 301 8
                                    —————
                                       18 30

EXERCISES.

1.—Find the conjunction of Jupiter to the Medium
Cœli.   Ans. 18° 30′.
2.—What is the arc of M. C. to the conjunction of
Saturn ?   Ans. 58 33.
3.—What is the arc of the M. C. to the body of Mars ? Ans. 75 34.

PROBLEM LI.

104 *To direct the M. C. to a Semisextile of any Planet above the Earth.*

RULE.—Take the difference between the Planet's Meridian Distance and one-third of its semi-diurnal arc.

EXAMPLE.

Jupiter's semiarc is 68° 18′, and one-third of this is 22° 46′
Jupiter's Meridian Distance is to be subtracted=18 30
                                               —————
Arc of the M. C. to semisextile of Jupiter= 4 16

Note.—When the Planet falls between the 10th and 1st Houses this direction is a sextile to the ASCENDANT in all figures. But if the Planet is between the 7th and 10th, then it is a trine to the Asc.

EXERCISES.

1.—How far is Saturn from the semisextile of the
Midheaven ?   Ans. 29° 51′.
2.—Find Mars's semisextile to the Midheaven.   Ans. 43   6.
3.—How far is the Midheaven from the semisextile
of the Planet Venus ?   Ans. 50 38.

PROBLEM LII.

105 *To direct the M. C. to a semiquintile of a Planet above the Earth.*

RULE.—Take the difference between the Planet's Meridian Distance and two-fifths of the Semi-diurnal Arc for the Arc of Direction.

EXAMPLES.

1.—What is the arc of the M. C. to a semiquintile of Jupiter ?
Jupiter's semi-diurnal arc is 68° 18' and two-fifths are 27° 11'
Subtract Jupiter's Mid. dist. 18 30

M. C. to the semi-quintile of Jupiter= 8 41

2.—What is the arc of the Midheaven to the semi-quintile of Venus ?
Venus's Meridian distance is 84° 14'
Venus's semi-diurnal arc is 100° 48', and two-fifths are 40 21

The M. C. to the semi-quintile is arc=43 53

PROBLEM LIII.

106 *To find the arc of M. C. to the nonagon of a Planet.*

RULE.—Take the difference between the Planet's M. D. and four-ninths of its semi-diurnal arc, and the remainder is the Arc of Direction.

EXAMPLE.

What is the arc of the M. D. to the nonagon of Jupiter ?
Jupiter's semi-diurnal arc is 68° 18', and four months is 29° 3'
Subtract Jupiter's Mid. dist. 18 30

M. C. to the nonagon of Jupiter=10 33

These are worked the same as the foregoing Problems, only care must be taken in getting out the four-ninths of the semi-diurnal arc.

PROBLEM LIV.

107 *To direct the M. C. to the semi-quartile of a Planet.*

RULE.—The Planet must be above the Earth, and the difference between half the Planet's semi-arc diurnal and its Mid. dist. is the Arc of Direction.

Note.—If the Planet falls between the 10th and 1st houses, this arc is the semi-square of the Asc. If the Planet lies between the 10th and 7th houses, this arc is the semi-square to the Asc. (218).

EXAMPLE.

What is the arc of the M. C. to semi-square of Jupiter ?

Jupiter's semi-diurnal arc is 68° 18′, the half is 34° 9′
Subtract the Mid. dist. of Jupiter 18 30
____

M. C. to the semi-square of Jupiter=15 39

N.B.—This is the semi-square of the Ascendant to Jupiter, as it falls between the 10th and 1st houses. Herschel semi-square M. C. will be the sesquisquare of Ascendant.

EXERCISES.

1.—Find the arc of the midheaven to the semi-square of Mars.   Ans. 26° 51′.

2.—What is the arc of the semi-square of Mercury to the Midheaven ?   Ans. 43 53.

PROBLEM LV.

108 *To direct the M. C. to the sextile of a Star.*

RULE.—The Star must be above the Earth, and the difference between the Star's Mid. Dist. and two-thirds of its semi-diurnal arc is the Arc of Direction (207).

Observe.—Any Planet brought to the Cusp of the 12th or 8th houses will be the M. C. to sextile of that Planet.

EXAMPLE.

What is the arc of the M. C. to the sextile of Jupiter ?

Jupiter's semi-arc is 68° 18′ and two-thirds=45° 32′
Subtract Jupiter's Meridian distance 18 30
____

M. C. to the sextile of Jupiter=27 2

EXERCISES.

1.—Find the Midheaven to the sextile of Venus.   Ans. 17° 2′.

2.—What is the arc of Midheaven to the sextile of Mercury ?   Ans. 26 33.

PROBLEM LVI.

109 *To direct the M. C. to the quintile of a Star.*

RULE.—Take the difference between four-fifths of the Star's semi-diurnal arc and its Mid. Dist. for the Arc of Direction.

Note.—For this direction the Star may be below the Earth, but then it must be taken with semi-diurnal arc, and its Mid. Dist. must also be taken from the 10th house, and this can be found by subtracting its Mid. Dist. of the 4th house from 180 degrees. This must be particularly attended to.

EXAMPLE 1.

For Jupiter in the Queen's Nativity above the Earth.

Jupiter's semi-diurnal arc is 68° 18′, and four-fifths=54° 39′
From which subtract his Mid. Dist.   18   30

M. C. quintile of Jupiter=36   9

EXAMPLE 2.

Find the quintile of the Sun.

The Sun is below the Earth, consequently his Mid. Dist. has been taken from the 4th, subtract his Mid. Dist. 61° 8′ from 180° and there remain 118° 52′ from the 10th house.

Here Sol's Mid. Dist. from the 10th=118° 52′
His semi-diurnal arc 118° 14′, and four-fifths= 94   36

M. C. to the quintile of Sol= 24   16

EXERCISES.

1.—What is the Midheaven to the quintile of Mercury ?   Ans. 12° 21′.
2.—What is the arc of the Midheaven to the quintile of the Sun ?   Ans. 24   16.

PROBLEM LVII.

110 *To direct the M. C. to the square of a Planet.*

RULE.—The difference between the Planet's M. D. and the whole semi-arc is the Arc of Direction.

Note.—If the Planet fall between the 10th and 2nd eastward, this aspect is a conjunction to the Ascendant ; but if it fall between the 10th and 6th westward, then the arc thus found is the opposition to the ascendant.

EXAMPLE.

Find the square of M. C. to Jupiter.

Jupiter's semi-arc is 68° 18′
Jupiter's M. D. is 18   30

M. C. to the square of Jupiter=49   48

EXERCISES.

1.—What is the arc of the Midheaven to the square
   of Mercury ?   Ans. 8° 8′.
2.—What is Herschel's arc to the square of the
   Midheaven ?   Ans. 18 32.

PROBLEM LVIII.

111 *To direct the M. C. to a trecile of any Planet.*

RULE.—The difference between the Star's M. D. or 10th house
and six-fifths of its semi-diurnal arc for the Arc of Direction.

Note.—If the Planet fall between the 10th and 4th westward,
this is a quintile of the Ascendant.

EXAMPLES.

1.—Take Jupiter's for example.
   Jupiter's semi-diurnal arc is 68° 18′ and six-fifths=81° 57′
         Subtract Jupiter's distance from M. C.=18 30

         The M. C. are to the trecile of Jupiter=63 27

2.—What is the arc to the Midheaven of the trecile
   of Mercury ?   Ans. 28° 56′.
                     Found as follows :
         Mercury's semi-diurnal arc is 104° 3′
             which is divided by 5)104 3
                     add them 20 48 is one-fifth.

         The amount is the six-fifths = 124 51
             Take Mercury's Mid. Dist. 95 55

   Remains the arc of direction=28 56 the M. C. trecile ☿.

PROBLEM LIX.

112 *To direct the M. C. to the trine of any Planet.*

RULE.—If the Planet be above the Earth add one-third of its
semi-nocturnal arc to its own arc, from which subtract its M. D.,
and the remainder is the Arc of Direction ; or, add one-third of its
semi-nocturnal arc to the square already found, and the sum will
be the Arc of Direction.

EXAMPLES.

The whole semi-diurnal arc of Herschel is 56° 56′
His semi-nocturnal arc is 123° 4′, and one-third is 41   1

$$\begin{array}{rr} & 97 \; 57 \\ \text{From which subtract his M. D.} & 38 \; 24 \\ \hline \end{array}$$

M. C. to the trine of Herschel 59 33

Second way.

The M. C. to the square of Herschel is 18° 32′
Add one-third of semi-nocturnal arc 41   1

M. C. trine of Herschel by the second way 59 33

If originally under the Earth.

RULE.—Take the difference between two-thirds of its semi-nocturnal arc and distance from 4th cusp, and the remainder is the arc of direction.

EXAMPLE.

The Sun under the Earth.

Sol's Mid. Dist. from I. C. is 61° 8′
His semi-nocturnal arc is 61° 46′, and two-thirds= 41 11

M. C. to the trine of the Sun= 19 57

N.B.—In the former of these two Examples Herschel is brought to the cusp of the sixth, which forms a quinqunx of the ascendant, which is always the case if the Planet is posited between the 10th and 4th westward. But if between the 10th and 4th eastward, the trine is a semi-sextile to the ascendant, or sextile to the 4th house or I. C., and it is also the planet's distance from the second house.

PROBLEM LX.

113 *To direct the M. C. to the sesquisquare of any Planet.*

RULE.—If above the Earth add one-half of the semi-nocturnal arc to the whole diurnal, from which subtract the Planet's M. D.

EXAMPLE.

Mercury's whole semi-diurnal arc is 104° 3′
Semi-nocturnal arc is 75° 57′, the one-half is 37 58

$$\begin{array}{rr} & 142 \; 1 \\ \text{Subtract Mercury's M. D.} & 95 \; 55 \\ \hline \end{array}$$

M. C. to the sesquisquare of Mercury 46   6

A second way.

RULE.—Add one-half of the Planet's semi-nocturnal arc to the square, and the sum is the arc of direction.

EXAMPLE.

Mercury's square to M. C. is 8° 8'
Semi-diurnal arc is 75° 57', the one-half is 37 58
____

M. C. Sesquisquare of Mercury as before 46   6

A third way.

RULE.—If in the 2nd subtract one-sixth of the semi-nocturnal arc from the trine, or if it is in the 5th, add one-sixth of the semi-nocturnal arc to the trine, and this is a sesquisquare to the ascendant.

EXAMPLE.

M. C. trine of Mercury is 33° 27'
Mercury's semi-nocturnal arc is 75° 57' and one-sixth=12 39
____

M. C. sesquisquare of Mercury=46   6

Another way.

RULE.—If originally below the Earth, the difference between one-half of its semi-nocturnal arc and its M. D. is the arc of direction.

Note.—Let this direction be found between the 7th and 4th, it will be the sesquisquare to both the M. C. and the ascendant. It is also one-half of the semi-nocturnal arc of the square of ascendant, or opposition of M. C. (Art. 219). When formed between the Ascendant and 4th, it is a semi-square to the ascendant.

PROBLEM LXI.

114 *To direct the M. C. to the biquintile of a Planet above the Earth.*

RULE.—Add three-fifths of the Planet's semi-nocturnal arc to its whole semi-diurnal arc, from which sum subtract its M. D.

EXAMPLE.

Thus, Herschel biquintile to M. C.
The whole of his semi-diurnal arc 56° 56'
His semi-nocturnal arc 123° 4' and three-fifths=74 52
____

131 48
Subtract Herschel's M. D. 38 24
____

M. C. biquintile of Herschel 93 24

Originally below the Earth.

RULE 1.—If between the 4th and 7th, then add one-tenth of the semi-nocturnal to the sesquisquare first obtained, and the sum is the arc of direction.

RULE 2.—If between the 1st and 4th subtract one-tenth of the semi-nocturnal arc from the sesquisquare, and the remainder will be the arc of direction.

EXAMPLE.

The Sun to biquintile of M. C. in the Queen's nativity.

The M. C. to sesquisquare of Sol 30° 15′
Subtract one-tenth of 61° 46′   6   11

M. C. biquintile of the Sun = 24   4

PROBLEM LXII.

115 *To direct the M. C. to the quincunx of a Planet when under the Earth.*

RULE.—Add one-third of the semi-nocturnal arc to the trine first found, or two-thirds of the semi-arc to the square, and the sum will be the arc of direction ; or the difference between one-third of the semi-arc and its M. D.

Note.—If the Planet fall between the 10th and 4th, this is a sextile to the ascendant ; but if it fall between the 7th and 4th, this aspect is a trine to the ascendant.

EXAMPLES.

Sol's semi-nocturnal arc is 61° 46′, and two-thirds = 41° 11′
Add M. C. □, or Asc. ☌ of Sol   0   37

M. C. quincunx of the Sun = 41   48

PROBLEM LXIII.

116 *To direct the M. C. to the opposition of a Planet under the Earth.*

RULE.—The difference between the Planet's Right Ascension and the A. R. of the 4th house, or I. C. is the arc of direction.

Note.—This is the Star's nocturnal Mid. Dist., which is also a square to the Ascendant.

EXAMPLE.

Find the M. C. opposition of the Sun.

$$\begin{array}{lr}
\text{Right Ascension of the I. C.} = & 121^\circ \ 8' \\
\text{Sol's Right Ascension is} & 60 \quad 0 \\
\hline
\text{The M. C. } \mathrm{\textit{8}} \text{ of } \odot, \text{ or Asc.} \square, \text{ or } \odot\text{'s M. D.} & 61 \quad 8 \\
\hline
\end{array}$$

OBSERVATIONS.

117 Whenever an aspect is measured between two planets, any other aspect may be ascertained, if it fall in the same hemisphere, by merely taking the relative proportion of the semi-arc (Ar. 218) of the planet to be directed. Thus, if we know the distance between two planets, that is, the arc of direction to the conjunction, then one-half of the semi-arc of the planet which is directed, added to that, will give the arc of direction to the semi-quartile (219) ; by adding one-sixth part of the semi-arc to this we have the arc of direction to the sextile ; one-third more of the semi-arc will give the square, and another third the trine ; to which add one-sixth for the sesqui-quadrate, &c.

118 To direct the Midheaven to the opposition of a star, bring it to the cusp of the 4th house ; to the trine, bring it to the second or 6th house ; for the quartile, to the Ascendant or seventh ; to the sextile, it must be brought to the cusp of the 12th or 8th ; the sesqui-quadrate falls in the middle of the 2nd and 5th houses. All aspects in mundo are measured by the semi-arc of the promittor (Ar. 221).

EXAMPLES.

We will direct the Sun to the different aspects it will form with the M. C. ; if we subtract his distance from the Imum Cœli 61° 9' from his semi-arc nocturnal 61° 46' we have his distance from the cusp of the 1st 0° 37', which is the arc of direction, M. C. $\square$ $\odot$; as the next aspect falls above the Earth, we must use his semi-diurnal arc, which is 118° 14', one-fifth of which is 23° 32', which add to the distance below, the first produces 24° 16' the arc of direction of M. C. Q. $\odot$, add two-fifths more of the Sun's space of a house 39° 25', two-fifths of which is—

$$\begin{array}{lr}
 & 15^\circ \ 46' \\
\text{Add the other arc of direction} & 24 \quad 16 \\
\hline
\text{The arc of direction M. C. } \ast \ \odot \text{ mundo} & 40 \quad 2 \\
\text{Add half the space of a house} & 19 \quad 42 \\
\hline
\text{And we have arc of direction M. C. S. } \square \ \odot \text{ mundo} & 59 \quad 44 \\
\hline
\end{array}$$

TO DIRECT THE ASCENDANT IN MUNDO.

PROBLEM LXIV.

119 *To direct the Ascendant to the conjunction of any Star.*

RULE.—The Planet must be between the 4th and 10th eastward, then the difference between its semi-arc and Meridian distance is the Arc of Direction.

EXAMPLE.

Mercury above the Earth, his semi-diurnal arc 104° 3'
Subtract Mercury's Mid. Distance 95 55

Ascendant to the conjunction of Mercury 8 8

Observe.—This is Mercury's square of the M. C. ; had Mercury been in the 4th, then it would have been in opposition to the M. C.

EXERCISES.

1.—What is the arc of Mars to the conjunction of the
Ascendant ?   Ans. 21° 51'.
2.—Bring the Sun to the cusp of the Ascendant.   Ans. 0 37.

Some Professors will undoubtedly object to Mercury, Mars, and similar positions being brought to the cusp of the Ascendant ; the reason I use that method is, because I have proved it to have very powerful effect ; therefore, I unhesitatingly adopt similar directions.

PROBLEM LXV.

120 *To direct the Ascendant to the semi-sextile of a Planet.*

RULE.—When above the Earth the sextile to M. C. is the arc of Direction ; if below the Earth the trine of M. C. to that Planet is the arc of Direction.

Another Rule.—Bring to the cusps of the 12th and 2nd for the Arc of Direction by Problems 46 and 47.

EXAMPLES.

Mars's semi-sextile Ascendant.
Mars's Mid. distance 75° 34'
Mars's semi-arc is 97° 25', and two-thirds=64 57

Ascendant to Semi-sextile of Mars 10 37

Ascendant to semi-sextile Sol.

Sol's Mid distance 61° 8'
Semi-nocturnal arc 61° 46', and two-thirds=41 11

———

Ascendant to the semi-sextile of Sol 19 57

———

As these directions are so simple I need not work any more; because, while working the Midheaven to aspects, most of the Arcs of Directions to the Ascendant are obtained.

———

PROBLEM LXVI.

121 *To direct the Ascendant to the semi-square of any Planet, anywhere between the 10th and 4th eastward.*

RULE.—If it fall between the 10th and 1st, its semi-square is the semi-square to the M. C. If it fall between the 1st and 4th, the sesquisquare to the M. C. is the Arc of Direction.

These need no example.

———

PROBLEM LXVII.

122 *To direct the Ascendant to the sextile of any Planet.*

RULE 1.—If above the Earth, bring the Planet to the cusp of the 11th ; or, the difference between one-third of its semi-diurnal and its M. D. is the Arc of Direction ; which is the M. D. semi-sextile of the star.

RULE 2.—If below the Earth, bring it to the cusp of the 3rd house (96) ; or, the difference between one-third of its semi-nocturnal arc and its M. D. is the Arc of Direction ; which is the M. C. to qx. of the Planet. Or—

RULE 3.—If below the Earth, subtract one-third from its square to Ascendant. If between the 1st and 10th, subtract one-third of its semi-diurnal arc from the conjunction of M. C. and the Planet and the remainder is the Arc of Direction.

EXAMPLE.

Mercury's conjunction of M. C. 95° 55'
Mercury's semi-arc 104° 3', and one-third=34 41

———

Ascendant to the sextile of Mercury=61 14

———

PROBLEM LXVIII.

123 *To direct the Ascendant to the quintile of a Star.*

RULE.—The difference between the Planet's M. D. and one-fifth of its semi-arc, either above or below the Earth, is the Arc of Direction.

EXAMPLES.

Mars's Meridian Distance is	75°	34′
Mars's semi-diurnal arc 97° 25′, and one-fifth is	19	29
Ascendant to the quintile of Mars	56	5

Herschel's nocturnal Mid. Distance	38°	24′
Herschel's semi-arc 123° 4′, and one-fifth is	24	57
Ascendant to quintile Herschel	13	27

PROBLEM LXIX.

124 *To direct the Ascendant to the square of any Planet.*

RULE.—The Planet's Meridian Distance, either above or below the Earth, is the Arc of Direction.

EXAMPLE.

Right Ascension of Midheaven	301°	8′
Herschel's Meridian Distance	262	44
Ascendant square Herschel	38	24

PROBLEM LXX.

125 *To direct the Ascendant to the trine of any Planet.*

RULE.—If between 1st and 4th, or between 1st and 10th, add one-third of the semi-arc to the M. D. ; but if between the 7th and 4th, or 10th and 7th, subtract one-third for the Arc of Direction.

EXAMPLE.

Sol's Mid. distance is	61°	8′
Sol's semi-arc is 61° 46′, and one-third of this is	20	35
Ascendant to the trine of Sol is	81	43 the Arc.

PROBLEM LXXI.

126 *To direct the Ascendant to the sesquisquare of any Planet.*

RULE.—If the Star be originally between the 10th and 7th, or 7th and 4th, the difference between its M. D. and half of its semi-arc is the Arc of Direction.

EXAMPLE.

Ascendant sesquisquare of Herschel.

Herschel's Mid. distance is 38° 24′
Semi-arc is 56° 56′, the half is 28 28

Ascendant sesquisquare Herschel 9 56

PROBLEM LXXII.

127 *To direct the Ascendant to the biquintile of any Planet.*

RULE 1.—If between the 12th and 10th add three-fifths of its semi-arc to its M. D.; from the 10th to the middle of the 8th, subtract two-thirds of its semi-arc from its M. D.; if between the middle of the 8th and cusp of the 7th, add one-tenth of its semi-arc to the sesquisquare for the Arc of Direction.

RULE 2.—If it fall in the 5th house, subtract one-tenth of semi-nocturnal arc from the sesquisquare of the M. C. for the Arc of Direction.

Note.—A Planet, to form a biquintile aspect to an angle, must be further distant than the sesquiquadrate by one-tenth of its whole semi-arc.

EXAMPLES.

What is the Ascendant to the biquintile of Jupiter ?

Jupiter between the 12th and 10th, the three-fifths of 68° 18′ his semi-arc is 41° 0′, add his Mid. distance 18° 30′, equals 59° 30′, the Arc. Or, secondly—

His sesquisquare is 52° 39′, then add to this one-tenth of his semi-arc which is 6° 51′, the amounts is 59° 30′, the Arc, as before.

PROBLEM LXXIII.

128 *To direct the Ascendant to the opposition of a Planet.*

RULE.—The Planet must be between the 10th and 4th westward ; then the difference between the M. D. and its semi-arc is the Arc of Direction.

N.B.—The shortest way is to find one direction to the Ascendant or M. C., and then add or subtract the portion of the Planet's semi-arc to find the others.

We will direct Jupiter to the different aspects of the Ascendant and M. C., and the first is the quintile to the Ascendant ; if we take Jupiter's distance past the 11th, 4° 16′ from two-fifths the space of his house 22° 46′—two-fifths are 9° 6′, remains 4° 50′, the Arc of Direction Asc. Q. ☉.

His Mer. distance 18° 30′ is the Arc of Direction Asc.□☉, it is also M. C. ☌ ☉ add to his Mer. distance 18° 30′
The space of Jupiter's house 22 46
______

We have Arc of Direction Asc. △ ♃ M. 41 16
Again, add half the space of a house 11 23
______

Gives Arc of Direction Asc. sesqui-□♃ and M. C.△ ♃ 52 39
Add to this one-tenth of Jupiter's whole arc 6 50
______

Gives Arc of Direction Asc. B. Q. ♃ M. 59 29
______

ZODIACAL ASPECTS.

TO DIRECT THE M. C. AND ASCENDANT TO ASPECTS IN THE ZODIAC.

PROBLEM LXXIV.

129 *To direct the M.C. to aspects of Planets.*

RULE.—The difference between the A. R. of the aspect without latitude and the A. R. of the M. C. is the Arc of Direction.

EXAMPLES.

1.—Direct the M. C. to the □ of ☉ zodiac.
The □ of ☉ falls in 2 ♓ 6, its R. A. is 334° 7′
Subtract the R. A. of M. C. 301 8
______

Remainder is Arc of Direction M. C.□☉ zod. 32 59
______

2.—The Midheaven to the sextile of Mars.
The sextile falls in 26 ♓ 35, its R. A. 320° 50′
Subtract the R. A. of the Midheaven 301 8
______

Arc of Direction of the M. C. ⚹ ♂ in zod.= 19 42
______

M. C. ♂ of ♃, the conjunction falls in 16 ♒ 57, its R. A. is 319° 26', from which take 301° 8', Arc 18° 18'.

M. C. ⚹ ☉, the sextile falls in 2 ♈ 6, its R. A. is with 360°, and as the aspect and the M. C. are in different hemispheres 361° 55', take 301° 8', Arc of Direction is 60° 47'.

PROBLEM LXXV.

130 *To direct the Ascendant to aspects in the Zodiac without latitude.*

RULE 1.—Find the declination of the place of aspect without latitude by problem 31, or by Problem 30. I prefer the Tables of Declination.

RULE 2.—Find the A. R. of that longitude without latitude by the table of Right Ascension.

RULE 3.—To the log. tangent of the Pole of the Ascendant, or latitude of Birth, add the log. tangent of the Declination of the Aspects ; the sum will be the log. sine of its Ascensional Difference.

RULE 4.—Take this Ascensional Difference from the A. R. if the declination be north, or add it thereto if the declination be south ; the result is the Oblique Ascension of the Aspect under the Pole of the country.

RULE 5.—Subtract the Oblique Ascension of the aspect, and the remainder is the Arc of Direction.

EXAMPLE.

Direct the Ascendant to □ ♄ in the zodiac.

The square of Saturn falls in 28° ♊ 46', the declination of which is 23° 28', and the R. A. 88° 40'.

To the log. tang. of Pole of 1st 51° 32' = 10,099913
Add log. tangent of Declination 23 28 = 9,637611

It gives log. sine of Ascensional Difference 33° 7' = 9,737524

From the A. R. of the aspect 88° 40'
Take the Asc. Difference, the declination being North 33 7

It gives the Oblique Ascension of the aspect 55 33
From this take Oblique Ascension of Ascendant 31 8

The Arc of Direction Ascendant □ ♄ zodiac 24 25

EXERCISES.

The Ascendant to Aspects in the zodiac.

Trine Jupiter falls in 16♊57, this declination is 22 N. 52, its A. R
75° 49'.

Sextile Mars falls in 17♊38, this declination is 22 N. 59, its A. R.
76° 55'.

Sextile Venus falls in 26♊35, this declination is 23 N. 28, its R. A.
86° 15'.

Sextile Mercury falls in 8 ♋ 55, this declination is 23 N. 16, its R.
A. 99° 0'.

Opposition Herschel falls in 23♊20, this declination is 23 N. 21,
its R. A. 82° 44'.

Proceed in this manner till all the aspects, as above, are gathered
out, then find the tangent of all the declinations, which reserve for
easy reference in the computation.

PROBLEM LXXVI.

131 *To direct the M. C. to the parallel of declination without
latitude.*

RULE 1.—That place in the ecliptic must be found where the
Sun acquires the declination of the Star, either north or south, to
whose parallel the M. C. is directed.

RULE 2.—Then, from this A. R. of the Sun subtract the A. R.
of the M. C. for the Arc of Directions.

EXAMPLE.

Jupiter's declination is 16° 22'.
Sol acquires 16° 22' in 15 ♒ 3, the Right Ascension 317° 32'
A. R. of the Midheaven 301   8

M. C. parallel of Jupiter   16   24

PROBLEM LXXVII.

132 *To direct the Ascendant to the parallel of any Planet's
declination.*

RULE 1.—Any place in the Ecliptic in which the Sun meets the
declination of the star to whose parallel the Ascendant is directed.

RULE 2.—Then find the Oblique Ascension of the Sun, by
Problem 45, under the pole of the Birth place, from which subtract
the Oblique Ascension of the Ascendant for (51) the arc of direction.

EXAMPLES.

The Sun's declination is 20° 36′.
Sol acquires 20° 36′ in 28 ♋ 5, R. A. of which is 120° 12′
Sol's Ascensional difference   28   14
———
Oblique Ascension of the Parallel   91   58
Subtract the Oblique Ascension of the Ascendant =   31   8
———
Arc of Direction   60   50
———

Venus's declination is 8° 28′ N.
Sol acquires the 8° 28′ in 8 ♍ 37, this Right Ascension is 116° 15′
Take from this the Oblique Ascension of the Ascendant   31   8
———
The Ascendant to parallel of Venus in zodiac   85   7
———

PROBLEM LXXVIII.

133 To direct the Sun, Moon and Planets to aspects of their own places in Mundo.

RULE.—Take the proportional part of their own semi-arcs for the Arcs of Direction.

EXAMPLE.

The Sun to his own semi-square.
Sol's semi-arc is 61° 40′ ; the half is 30° 50′, the Arc of Direction.
Sol's sextile, take two-thirds of 61° 40′, equal ☉ ✶ ☉, 41° 6′.
The Moon to her sextile—her semi-arc is 61° 46′, two-thirds ☽✶☽, 411° 11′ Arc of Direction.

PROBLEM LXXIX.

134 To direct all the Planets to their own aspects, also the time of aspect as they from by their daily or secondary motion.

RULE 1.—Look to the Ephemeris when the Planet directed passes the degrees and minutes of the slower Planets.

RULE 2.—Subtract the place of the swifter Planet from that of the slower on the noon previous to the formation of aspect, which difference retain.

RULE 3.—Then subtract the place of the slower Planet from that of the swifter on the noon after aspect ; add the two differences together ; the sum call the second distance.

RULE 4.—Then, by diurnal logarithms, take out the first difference, from which subtract the 2nd, and the remainder will be the log. time of aspect.

RULE 5.—Account one day's motion a year ; two hours a month ; four minutes a day.

EXAMPLE.

When will Mars arrive at the square of Jupiter by Ephemeral motion, which is 16 ♒ 57 ?

Now, Mars moves to 16 ♉ 57 at 12 minutes past midnight of July 2nd, which is equal to 38 days, 20 hours, 12 minutes after birth, the time answering to this is 38 years, 10 months, 3 days, or March 28th, 1858.

Mars, from noon, July 2nd, to 3rd, moves 43 minutes, and before he comes to 16 ♉ 57, has to move 22 minutes.

The diurnal log. of 22 minutes is   1,8159
Subtract Mars's log. of daily motion, 43 minutes 1,5249
____
This log. answers to 12 hours, 16 minutes ,2910
____

PROBLEM LXXX.

135 *To direct the Sun or Moon to parallel in mundo, direct direction.*

RULE 1.—Take that Star's Meridian distance which moves conversely, and call it the primary distance.

RULE 2.—Add the Arithmetical Complement of the Proportional Log. of the Sun or Moon's semi-arc and the Proportional Log. of the Sun or Moon's Meridian distance to the Log. of the Planet's semi-arc, and the sum of the three lines will be the Planet's second distance.

RULE 3.—The difference between the Planet's M. D. and its second distance ; or, if the Planet pass the Meridian to form the parallel, their sum will be the Arc of Direction.

EXAMPLE I.

Find the arc of ☉ Par. ♅ D. D.

N.B.—As the ☉ is below the Earth ♅ will form the parallel below, therefore ♅'s semi-nocturnal arc must be used.

As the ⊙'s S. N. A. 61° 46′ log. Ar. Com. 9,5355
Is to ⊙'s dist. below the Earth   0 37 log.   2,4652
So is ♅'s S. N. A. 123   4 log.   0,1657
———
To second dist. of ♅ below the Earth   1 14   12,1658
Add ♅'s distance from 18 32   ———

Arc of Direction ⊙ Par. ♅ D. D. 19 46

EXAMPLE 2.

Find the Arc of ☽ Par. ♅ D. D.
As the ☽'s S. D. A. 124° 42′ log. Ar. Com. 9,8406
Is to ☽'s Mer. distance 119 37   ,1775
So is ♅'s S. D. A.   56 56   ,4999
———
To ♅'s 2nd dist. from Mer.   54 36   10,5180
Sub. ♅'s true Meridian dist.   38 24   ———

Arc of Direction ☽ Par. ♅ D. D.   16 12

PROBLEM LXXXI.

136 *To direct the Sun or Moon to Mundane Parallels (converse).*

This is reversing the operation of the last Problem.

RULE 1.—Add together the Prop. Log. (Ar. Co.) of the Planet's semi-arc and the Log. of the Planet's M. D. to the Sun or Moon's semi-arc, and the sum call the second distance of Sun or Moon from the Meridian.

RULE 2.—The difference between the Sun or Moon's Meridian Distance and Second Distance is the Arc of Direction ; or if it pass the Meridian to form the parallel, the sum must be taken.

EXAMPLE.

Direct ⊙ to the Par. of ♅ converse.
As the semi-diurnal arc of ♅   56° 56′ log. (Ar. Co.) 9,5001
Is to ♅'s Mer. dist. 38 24 log.   ,6709
So is ⊙'s S. D. A. 118 14 log.   ,1825
———
To ⊙'s second distance from 10th house 79 45   10,3535
Subtract from ⊙'s distance from 4th 118 51   ———

Arc of Direction ⊙ P. ♅ con.   39   6

PROBLEM LXXXII.

137 *To direct the Sun or Moon to any Aspect in Mundo, direct Direction.*

When the Sun or Moon are supposed to remain fixed in the place they were at birth, and the planets Herschel, Saturn, Jupiter, Mars, Venus, or Mercury are moved on to form the aspects, according to the regular motions of the heavens, the direction is called direct direction.

RULE 1.—Add together the Pro. Log. (Ar. Co.) of Sun or Moon, semi-arc and the Log. of the distance of Sun or Moon from the cusp of the preceding or succeeding house, to the log. of semi-arc of the planet, and the sum is the second distance of that Planet.

RULE 2.—Add or subtract it from the Planet's primary distance, as (100).

EXAMPLE I.

Direct the ☉ to the □ of ♃ by Direct Direction.

As ☉'s semi-nocturnal Arc 61° 46′ Prop. log. (Ar. Co.)			9,5355
Is to ☉'s distance inside 1st	0	37	2,4652
So is ♃'s semi-diurnal Arc 68	18		,4209
To ♃'s 2nd distance from 10th	0	41	2,4216
Subtract from ♃'s Meridian dist.	18	30	
Arc of Direction ☉ □ ♃ D. D.	17	49	
Add ⅓rd ♃'s semi-diurnal Arc	22	46	
Arc of ☉ △ ♃ D. D.	40	35	

Thus you may obtain, by adding or subtracting, as the case may be, the Proportional part of the Semi-arc of the Planet directed, all the other directions after one direction is obtained.

EXAMPLE 2.

Find the Arc of ☽ ✶ ♄ D. D.

As ☽'s semi-diurnal arc 124° 42′ Prop. log. (Ar. Co.)			9,8406
Is to ☽'s dist. outside 1st	5	5	1,5491
So is ♄'s semi-diurnal Arc	86	56	,3161
To 2nd distance of ♄ from 11th	3	33	1,7058
Add Arc of Asc. ✶ ♄	29	35	
Arc of Direction ☽✶♄ D. D.	33	8	
Subtract ½ the space of ♄'s S.D.A.	14	29	
Leaves Arc of Direct. ☽S□♄ D.D.	18	39	
To this add ½ of ♄'s semi-arc	43	28	
Gives Arc of Direction ☽□♄ D.D.	62	7	

EXAMPLE 3.

Direct the Moon to the opposition of Herschel, Direct Direction.

N.B.—When Herschel comes to the opposition of the Moon's direct motion in this Nativity, he will be below the Earth, consequently his semi-nocturnal arc must be used.

As the ☽'s semi-nocturnal arc	124° 42′		(Ar. Co.)	9,8406
Is to ☽'s distance outside 1st	5	5		1,5491
So is ♅'s semi-nocturnal arc	123	4		,1651
To ♅'s 2nd distance below the 7th	5	1		1,5548
Add arc of Asc. ☍ ♅	18	52		
Arc of ☽ ☍ ♅ D. D.	23	53		

PROBLEM LXXXIII.

138 *To direct the Sun or Moon to any aspect in mundo (converse).*

When the Sun or Moon, above the Earth, is moved onward to form the aspect, from the East towards the West, or below the Earth, from the West towards the East, it is termed a Converse Direction.

RULE 1.—Add together the Pro. Log. (Ar. Co.) of semi-arc of the Planet to which the Sun or Moon is directed, to that Planet's distance within or without a certain house (94 and 96), and the semi-arc of the Sun or Moon, and the sum is the second distance of Sol or Luna from the house which forms the required aspect.

RULE 2.—If this second distance be on the same side of the cusp whence the primary was taken, the difference will be the Arc of Direction ; but if the Sun or Moon pass the cusp to form the aspect, the sum will be the Arc of Direction (100).

EXAMPLE 1.

Required the Arc of ☉ △ ♅ converse.

As the semi-arc of ♅	56° 56′		Prop. log. Ar. Co.	9,5001
Is to ♅'s distance from 8th outside	0	26		2,6184
So is ☉'s semi-diurnal arc	118	14		,1825
To ☉'s 2nd distance outside the 12th	0	54		
Add ☉'s distance from 12th	40	2		2,3010
Arc of Direction ☉ △ ♅ con.	40	56		
Sub. half space of ☉'s Diurnal house	19	42		
Arc of ☉'s sesquisquare ♅ con.	21	14		
Add half ☉'s semi-arc	59	7		
Arc of ☉ □ ♅ con.	80	21		

Thus you will perceive, that having worked one direction, others may be generally obtained from it, by the proportional parts of the semi-arc of that luminary directed.

N.B.—That semi-arc, whether diurnal or nocturnal, must be taken where the planet or luminary is, when the aspect is completed. The Sun at the Queen's birth was under the Earth, but when he formed the above aspects converse with Herschel he was above the Earth, consequently his semi-diurnal arc must be taken.

EXAMPLE 2.

Direct Moon to sesquisquare Sun converse.

As the semi-nocturnal arc of ☉	61° 46′	log. Ar. Co.	9,5355
Is to ☉'s distance inside 1st	0 37		2,4652
So is ☽'s semi-diurnal arc	124 42		,1594
To ☽'s second distance	1 15		2,1601

If we subtract this second distance from the arc of Asc. semi-square Moon mundo 57° 16′, it leaves the arc of direction Moon semi-square Sun converse 56° 1′, it is also Sun semi-square Moon direct direction, and by adding the proportional parts of Moon's semi-arc, the other aspect's arcs may be found as we did with the Sun's.

———

PROBLEM LXXXIV.

139 To direct the Sun, Moon, or any Planet, to any aspects of the Part of Fortune.

From the manner in which we have taught the calculation of this mundane point, and what we have before spoken about it, it will be seen, that as the degrees of distance from the Part of Fortune from a house are those on the Equator, it may justly be allowed 90 degrees for its semi-arc in all cases, and it will bring out the corrections correctly (98).

RULE 1.—Add the log. 9,6990 (Ar. Co. of 90 degrees) to its distance from any house it may be near, and the log. of the semi-arc of the planet directed, and the sum will be the log. of the Planet's second distance.

RULE 2.—Add or subtract the second distance (100).

EXAMPLE.

Required the arc of ⊕□♃, in Queen Victoria's nativity.

As Prop. Log. of 90°, its Ar. Co. 9,6990
Is to ⊕ dist. from 1st   4° 34′ Prop. log. 1,5957
So is ♃'s semi-arc 68 18   ,4209

To ♃'s dist. past 10th   3 28   1,7156
Add ♃'s Mer. dist. 18 30

Arc of Direction ⊕□♃ 21 58

EXERCISES.

1.—What is the Part of Fortune to the body of Sol ?   Ans. 6° 36′.
2.—What is the Part of Fortune to the semi-square
    of Saturn ?   Ans. 19 31.
3.—What is the Part of Fortune to the semi-square
    of Mars ?   Ans. 31 48.
4.—What is the Part of Fortune to the semi-square
    of Venus ?   Ans. 37 57.
5.—What is the Part of Fortune to the sextile of
    Mars ?   Ans. 48   2.
6.—What is the Part of Fortune to the square of
    Saturn ?   Ans. 62 59.

PROBLEM LXXXV.

140 *To direct any Planet to the parallel of the Part of Fortune.*

RULE 1.—Add the log. 9,6990 (Ar. Co. of 90 degrees) to log. of pars. M.D., and the log. of Planet's semi-arc, and the sum will be the log. of the second distance from the Meridian.

RULE 2.—Take the second distance from the Planet's M.D., or add it to for the Arc of Direction (100).

EXAMPLE.

Direct ⊕ to parallel of ♅.

As Prop. log. of 90°, its Ar. Co. 9,6990
Is to ⊕ Meridian distance 85° 26′ Prop. log. ,3236
So is semi-arc of Herschel 56 56   ,4999

To ♅'s 2nd distance from Meridian 54   3   ,5225

From Herschel's 2nd distance from Meridian 54   3
Subtract Herschel's true Meridian distance 38 24

Arc of Direction ⊕ Par. ♅ 15 39

PROBLEM LXXXVI.

141 *To direct the Sun or Moon to Rapt Parallels in Mundo.*

Rapt Parallels—meaning being carried away—are the joint approach of two Stars conversely to the 10th and 4th houses—an arc of extraordinary strength, even where life and death are concerned.

RULE 1.—Add the semi-arcs together, diurnal if above the Earth, and nocturnal if below, of the Sun or Moon and Planet, and take half—as the sum may not exceed 180 degrees.

RULE 2.—Take half the difference between the A. R. of the Sun or Moon and that of the Planet—as the parallel is always formed by Right Ascension.

RULE 3.—Take half of the semi-arc of the body that applies to the Meridian when the parallel is formed, which is the primary distance.

RULE 4.—Add the log. (Ar. Co.) of the sum of half the semi-arcs and the body applying to the Meridian ; and half the difference of their A. R. and the sum will be the second distance of the body applying to the Meridian ; which double.

RULE 5.—From the distance of the applying body from the Meridian subtract the second distance, which will be the Arc of Direction (100).

EXAMPLE I.

Bring the ⊙ to the Rapt Parallel of Herschel in the Queen's Nativity.

Add S.D.A. of ⊙	118° 14′	R.A. ⊙ +360° = 420°	0′
To semi-arc of ♅	56 56	R.A. ♅ 262	44

Then, as 175   10 : 118 14 : : difference R.A. 157 16

As Prop. log. of sum semi-arc (Ar. Co.) 175 10 = 9,9882
Is to Prop. log. of ⊙'s semi-diurnal arc 118 14 = ,1825
So is difference of Right Ascension 157 16 = ,0586

To second distance of ⊙ from 10th 106 10   ,2293
Take from ⊙'s distance from 10th 118 52   ——

Arc of Direction ⊙ R. P. ♅   12 42

EXAMPLE 2.

Direct the Moon to the Rapt Parallel of Jupiter.

To S.D.A. of ♃	68° 18	R.A.☽+360°=420° 45′	
Add ☽'s S.D.A.	124 42	R.A. ♃ =319 38	

Then, as 2)193 0 : 124 42 :: difference R.A. 2)101 7

As 96 30   50 33

As the first of those three terms is greater than the Prop. logarithms extend, since they only go up to 180 degrees, we will take half the first and third terms, and the result will be the same.

Then, as Prop. log. of half 1st terms 96° 30′ Ar. Co.=9,7293
  Is to Prop. log. of 2nd term 124 42   ,1594
  So is Prop. log. of half 3rd term 50 33   ,5516

To Prop. log. of 2nd distance from Meridian 65 18   ,4403
  Which take from ☽'s Meridian distance 119 37

  Arc of Direction ☽ R.P.♃ 54 19

EXERCISES.

1.—What is the R. P. of Moon and Herschel ?   Ans. 11° 8′.
2.—What is the R. P. of Sun and Herschel ?   Ans. 12 42.
3.—What is the R. P. of Sun and Jupiter ?   Ans. 55 15.

Another Problem.

There is a Rapt Parallel which is sometimes formed by one Planet being above the Earth and another below, when it is formed ; but as both semi-arcs must be worked of one denomination, viz., either both diurnal or both nocturnal, then, in such cases, we have to work with one of the Planets exactly as though it was in its opposite place.

EXAMPLE.

As there is not such a position in the Queen's nativity to illustrate the Rule, we must imagine one.

Suppose Herschel, in the Queen's nativity, had been in 23 ♊ 20′ with 0° 8′ North latitude, but the Sun and all the other positions the same as they are ; then the Rapt Parallel would still have been exactly the same as it is, and we should have calculated it in the same way as we have done in the last Problem.

PROBLEM LXXXVII.

142 *To find the Place of the Zodiacal Aspects of the Sun,
and his declination at that place.*

RULE.—Find, as in a Speculum, the aspects the Sun can form
during a lifetime, and mark his declination at that Zodiacal point
where the aspect falls, by either Problems 30, or 28, or 31.

The Sun to the

Semi-square of Mars falls in 2♊38, R.A. 60° 33′, its Dec. 20° 46′,
its tangent 9,57886.

Semi-square of Venus falls in 11♊35, R.A. 70° 2′, its Dec. 22° 15′,
its tangent 9,661184.

Trine of Jupiter falls in 16♊57, R.A. 75° 49′, its Dec. 22° 53′, its
tangent 9,62538.

Sextile of Mars falls in 17♊58, R.A. 76° 33′, its Dec. 22° 57′, its
tangent 9,62679.

Semi-square of Mercury falls in 23♊15, R.A. 82° 39′, its Dec.
23° 21′, its tangent 9,63518.

Opposition of Herschel falls in 23♊20, R.A. 82° 44′, its Dec.
23° 21′, its tangent 9,63518.

Sextile of Venus falls in 26♊36, R.A. 86° 17′, its Dec. 23° 28′,
its tangent 9,63761.

Parallel of Herschel falls in 27♊0, R.A. 86° 44′, its Dec. 23° 26′,
its tangent 9,63962.

Square of Saturn falls in 28♊46, R.A. 88° 40′, its Dec. 23° 28′,
its tangent 9,63761.

Sesquisquare of Jupiter falls in 1♋57, R.A. 92° 62′, its Dec.
23° 28′, its tangent 9,63761.

PROBLEM LXXXVIII.

143 *To direct the Sun to any conjunction, parallel, or aspect
of any Planet in the Zodiac, direct.*

RULE 1.—If the birth be between midnight and noon, find the
Oblique Ascension of Sol under his own pole ; or, if birth took
place between noon and midnight, find his Oblique Descension
under his pole.

RULE 2.—Find the declination of the place of the aspect—add
the tangent of dec. to the tangent of Sol's pole. The sum is the
sine of the aspect's asc. difference under that pole, by which asc.
diff. find its oblique ascension or oblique descension. Work by
Table of Asc. Difference.

RULE 3.—Subtract that of the Sun from that of the aspect for the arc of direction.

EXAMPLE.

Direct the ☉ to a ☐ of ♄ in the zodiac in Queen Victoria's nativity.

Saturn is in 28♓46, the ☉ comes to his ☐ in 28♊46, by the Tables the R.A. of that place is 88° 40', its declination is 23° 28'.

To the tangent of 23° 28'=9,637611
Add tangent of ☉'s pole 51 16 =0,095852

Sum is sine of Asc. Diff. 32 46 =9,733463

As we want the Oblique Ascension, and the Declination is North, we subtract the Asc. Diff. from the Right Ascension 88° 40'

Subtract Ascensional Difference 32 46

Oblique Ascension under ☉'s pole 55 54
Subtract ☉'s Oblique Ascension 32   2

Arc of Direction ☉☐♄ zod. 23 52

By the following method the Sun may be directed in the Zodiac without having recourse to Tables of R.A., Declination, &c.

RULE.—Note the longitude of the aspect and take its longitudinal distance from the nearst equinox, add its tangent to the cosine of Obliquity of Ecliptic, the sum is the tangent of Right Ascension. Then to the sine of R.A. add the tangent of Obliquity, also the tangent of Sun's pole : the sum of these three Logarithms gives the sine of Ascensional Difference, which apply as before taught.

EXAMPLE.

Direct the ☉ to the sesquisquare of ♃ in the zodiac.
The sesquisquare falls in 1 ♋ 57, its distance from that ♎88° 3'

To the tangent of ♎ 88° 3'=1,467920
Add cosine Obl. of Ecliptic 23 28 =9,962508

Sum is tangent of R.A. from ♎ 87 52 =1,430428

Then, to the sine of R.A. 87 52 =9,999699
Add {tangent Obliq. of Ecliptic 23 28 =9,637611
     {tangent of ☉'s pole   51 16 =0,095852

Sum is sine of Asc, Diff. under ☉'s pole 32 45 =9,733162

Then, by subtracting 87° 52' from 180° we have the

$$
\begin{array}{lr}
\text{R.A. at } 2\!\!\!/\text{'s sesquisquare aspect} & 92° \ 8' \\
\text{Subtract, as declination is North} & 32 \ 45 \\
\hline
\text{Ob. Asc. of aspect under } \odot\text{'s pole} & 59 \ 23 \\
\text{Subtract } \odot\text{'s Oblique Ascension} & 32 \ \ 2 \\
\hline
\text{The Arc of Direction } \odot \text{ sesquisquare } 2\!\!\!/ \text{ zod.} & 27 \ 21 \\
\hline
\end{array}
$$

PROBLEM LXXXIX.

144 *To direct the Sun to Parallels in the Zodiac.*

RULE 1.—Find where the Sun meets with the Declination of the Planet in the Radix, by Problem 20, or the two last rules.

RULE 2.—Find the A.R. of the longitude the Sun is in at that declination without latitude, by Problem 26.

RULE 3.—Add the tangent of the declination to the tangent of Sun's pole, and the sum is the sine of Asc. Difference of the aspect under that pole. Hence, you see, all you want is the Asc. Diff.

RULE 4.—Find the Ob. Asc., or Ob. Dec., as before ; from which subtract that of the Sun for the arc of Direction.

EXAMPLE.

Direct the Sun to the Zodiacal parallel of Herschel, in the nativity of Queen Victoria.

Note.—The Sun will touch the parallel of Herschel twice, once before he arrives at his greatest Declination, which is 23° 28', and once after. We will work the first by the first rules, and the second by the other. The Sun will touch the first Par. in 27♊0, its R.A. is 86° 44', then to the tangent of Declination add tangent of Sol's pole, sum is sine of Ascensional Difference.

$$
\begin{array}{lr}
\text{Tangent of Declination } 23° \ 26' = & 9,636919 \\
\text{Add tangent of } \odot\text{'s pole } 51 \ \ 16 = & 0,095892 \\
\hline
\text{Sum is sine of Ascensional Diff. } 32 \ 43 = & 9,732771 \\
\hline
\end{array}
$$

$$
\begin{array}{lr}
\text{From R.A. of Par. Decl. of } \rlap{\text{♅}} 86° \ 44' \\
\text{Subtract the Asc. Diff. under } \odot\text{'s pole} \quad 32 \ 43 \\
\hline
\text{Oblique Asc. of } \rlap{\text{♅}} \text{ Par. Decl.} \quad 54 \ \ 1 \\
\text{Subtract Oblique Asc of } \odot \text{ under his pole} \quad 32 \ \ 2 \\
\hline
\odot \text{ Par. of } \rlap{\text{♅}} = 21 \ 59 \\
\hline
\end{array}
$$

The next Par. we shall calculate by the other rules of the last problem.

To the tangent of ♅'s decl. 23° 26′ = 9,636919
Add the cotangent of 23 28 = 0,362389

Gives sine R.A. from ♎ 86 46 = 9,999308

Then, to sine R.A. 86 46 = 9,999308
Add { tangent of Obl. of Ecliptic 23 28 = 9,637611
{ tangent of ☉'s pole   51 16 = 0,095892

Gives sine of Asc. Diff. 32 43 = 9,732771

Then, from 180° subtract the distance in R.A. from ♎ 86° 46′, it leaves the R.A. of Par. ♅ 93° 14′.

From this R.A. 93° 14′
Subtract the Asc. Diff. 32 43

Leaves Ob. Asc. of Par. ♅ under ☉'s pole 60 31
Subtract Obl. Asc. of ☉   ditto.   32   2

☉ Par. of ♅ 28 29

———— ————

PROBLEM XC.

*145 To direct the Moon in the Zodiac to any Aspect except
a Parallel.*

RULE.—Find the Oblique Ascension or descension of the aspect under the pole of the Moon ; and subtract the Moon's Oblique Ascension or Descension from it, the remainder is the Arc of Direction.

N.B.—The latitude of the Moon in the aspect must be observed to find her true R.A. and declination therein.

EXAMPLE.

Direct the Moon to the sextile of Mercury in the Zodiac.

The sextile falls in 8 ♋ 55, where the Moon, according to the Ephemeris, will have 5° 0′ north latitude, and the declination answering to that longitude and latitude is 28° 12′, its R.A. is 99° 21′.

Then, to the tangent Decl. 28° 12′ = 9,729323
Add tangent of ☽'s pole 50 31 = 0,084050

Sum is sine of Asc. diff. 40 36 = 9,813373
Subtract from R.A. 99 21

Obl. Asc. of ⚹ of ☿ under ☽'s pole 58 45
Subtract ☽'s Obl. Asc. ditto 27 28

Arc of Direction ☽ ⚹ ☿ zod. 31 17

EXERCISES.

1.—Find the Moon square of Mars zod.   Ans. 43° 42′.
2.—Find the Moon square of Venus zod.   Ans. 56 30.
3.—Find the Moon trine Saturn zod.   Ans. 59 49.

PROBLEM XCI.

146 *To direct the Moon to Parallels of Declination.*

RULE 1.—Look in the Ephemeris for the days succeeding the Birth, and see at what time the Moon falls on the declination you require ; then calculate, by Proportion, the Latitude and Longitude she will have at that time.

RULE 2.—Find the R.A. for that Latitude and Longitude, and take from, or add to it, the Ascensional Difference given by the tangent of the required declination and the tangent of the Moon's added as before ; the result will be Oblique Ascension or Descension of the aspect. The Moon's Oblique Ascension or Descension taken from it will leave the Arc of Direction.

EXAMPLE.

Direct the Moon to a parallel of Herschel's declination in Queen Victoria's nativity.

I find on the 28th of May, 1819, the Moon's declination is 25° 59′, and on the 29th it is 23° 2′, difference in 24 hours of 2° 57′ ; then, if the difference 2° 57′ is equal to 24 hours, what will the difference at noon, on the 28th, 25° 59′, and the declination of Herschel 23° 25′, which is 2° 33′, amount to ? Ans. 20 hrs., 45 min. after noon of the 28th ; at which time I find the Moon is in longitude 6 ♌ 12 with 4° 53′ north latitude—the R.A. answering to this longitude and latitude is 129° 56′.

To the tangent of ♅'s declination 23° 26′ = 9,636919
Add tangent of ☽'s pole 50 31 = 0,084050

Sum is sine of Ascensional diff. 31 44 = 9,720969

Subtract from R.A. 129 56

Oblique Ascension of aspect 98 12
Subtract oblique Ascension of ☽ 27 28

Arc of Direction ☽ P. ♅ zod. 70 44

———

PROBLEM XCII.

147 To direct the Sun or Moon to Zodiac Aspects.

RULE.—Observe in these Directions the Planets are directed under their Pole to the Bodies or Aspects of the Sun or Moon.

N.B.—The Latitude of the Planet in the place of the Aspect must be observed in the same way as the Moon's in order to find its true R.A. and declination therein.

EXAMPLE.

Direct ♂ to the ☌ of ☉ in the Queen's nativity.

I find, by the Ephemeris, when Mars arrives at the Sun's place 2 ♊ 6 he has 0° 38′ south latitude; the declination answering to that longitude and latitude is 19° 59′, and R.A. 60° 7′. I find, by the rules before laid down, that Mars Obl. Asc., under his own pole, is 10° 57′, and the tangent of his pole 9,990270
To which add tangent of decl. 19° 59′ = 9,560673

Sum is sine of Asc. diff. 20 50 = 9,550943

From R.A. of place of conjunction 60° 7′
Subtract Ascensional difference 20 50

Oblique Asc. of place of ☌ 39 17
Subtract Obl. Asc. of ♂ under his pole 10 57

Arc of Direction ☉ ☌ ♂ zod. con. 28 20

PROBLEM XCIII.

148 *To direct the M.C., the Ascendant, and the Part of Fortune to Promissors.*

RULE 1.—Note the Promissor either backwards or forwards, and see when it meets with the M.C., Asc., or Part of Fortune.

RULE 2.—Then, for every day, add 1 year ; for every 2 hours, a month ; for 30 minutes, a week ; and for 4 minutes, a day ; and the sum is the Arc of Direction (134).

EXAMPLE.

When does Mars come to the square of the M.C. ?
Mars arrives at 29 degrees of ♈ on June 7th 20h. 43m.
The time after birth in May is 7 days 7h. 55m.

Arc of Direction 15 4 38

These 15 days are equal to 15 years, and 4 hours are equal to 2 months, and 38 minutes equal to 8 days.

PROBLEM XCIV.

149 *To direct the Planets to their Periodic Aspects in the Zodiac.*

RULE.—Look at the Table for the time each Planet, by direction, takes in forming a periodical aspect, either with its own place or any Star, accounted from Birth.

TABLE.

Planets.	Celestial Periods.	Motion per Year.		Motion per Month.		Time each planet, by direction, takes forming an Aspect, either with its own Place, or with any other Star, accounted from birth.									
						S □		✳		□		△		☍	
	Yrs.	deg.	m.	deg.	m.	yr.	m.	yr.	m.	yr.	m.	yr.	m.	yr.	m.
♅	84	7	0	0	35	10	6	14	0	21	0	28	0	42	0
♄	30	12	0	1	0	3	9	5	0	7	6	10	0	15	0
♃	12	30	0	2	30	1	6	2	0	3	0	4	0	6	0
♂	19	19	0	1	35	2	4½	3	2	4	9	6	4	9	6
☉	19	19	0	1	35	2	4½	3	2	4	9	6	4	9	6
♀	8	45	0	3	45	1	0	1	4	2	0	2	8	4	0
☿	10	36	0	3	0	1	3	1	8	2	6	3	4	5	0
☽	4	3 signs.		7	30	0	6	0	8	1	0	1	4	2	0

EXAMPLE.

When does Jupiter arrive at the conjunction of Saturn ?

Saturn in 28 ♓ 46, and Jupiter in 16 ♒ 57, shows that Jupiter has 41° 49′ to go before he reaches the place of Saturn ; and as Jupiter moves 2° 30′ per month, he will arrive at 41° 49′ in 18 months 3 weeks after birth, which would be in December of 1820 ; and as Jupiter's celestial period is 12 years, he would come at Saturn in December, 1832—again, by adding 12 years more, he arrived at the body of Jupiter in December, 1844—by adding 12 years more, Jupiter will arrive at 28 ♓ 46, in 1856, by celestial period—when the Queen will be very popular and much esteemed.

☞ I should rather trust to transits than to this method of calculating.

Dates of Transits :—♃ to ♄'s place is February 23rd, 1821 ; February 4th, 1833 ; May 25th, 1844. R. and Ret., January 12th, 1845 ; May 2nd, 1856 ; March 28th, 1880, and March, 1892.

PROBLEM XCV.

150 *To direct the M.C., or the Cusp of a House, to the Cusp of any other House.*

RULE.—Look in the " Table of Houses," under 10th or any other House, for the Time occupied by them, against which observe the hours and minutes under the " Time from Noon," then, under the same house, observe the hours and minutes ; subtract the former time from this remainder converted into degrees and minutes, by Problem 4, for the Arc of Direction.

EXAMPLE.

Find the time between the 10th and 12th houses.

		h.	m.
The 12th house has ♈ 2° equal		0	7	upon it.
add		24	0
The Midheaven has 29 ♑ equal		20	5
Their difference is 61° 45′, or		4	2

PLACIDUS MEASURE OF TIME.

PROBLEM XCVI.

151 *To convert the Arcs of Directions into Time.*

RULE.—To the R.A. of Sun, at Birth, add the Arc of Direction, which will be the R.A. of Sun when the Aspect is complete.   Find in how many days and hours after birth the Sun acquires this R.A., and allow, for each day, one year of life, and each two hours, one month. To find this time, look in the Ephemeris for the longitude answering to this R.A., and from the day and hour when the Sun reaches this longitude, take the day and hour of birth; the difference is the number of days and hours after birth, which are to be turned into years and months, to know the age at which the direction will operate.

EXAMPLE.

Required the time of life when the direction of ☽ ☍ ♅ d. d. in the Queen's nativity will operate.

The Right Ascension of Sun at birth 60° 0′
The Arc of direction ☽ ☍ ♅ d. d. 23 33

R.A. of Sun when the aspect is complete 83 33

The longitude answering to this R.A. is 24 ♊ 5, and the Sun arrived at this longitude at about 15 hours after noon on the 15th of June. Then, as the birth was in the month previous, add the days in that month :—days 31 0 hours.
To the day and hour when the Sun arrives 15 15

Total from which 46 15
Take the day and hour of birth 23 16

There remains 22 23

Which, at the rate of 1 year for 1 day, and 1 month for 2 hours, is very near the age of 23 years—22 years, 11 months, and 2 weeks —which would fall the second week in May of 1841. See my Method of Timing.

PROBLEM CXVII.

152 To find the time of the Arc of Direction by Naibod's Measure of Time.

EXAMPLE.

yrs. dys. hrs.
Convert 18 dgs. 18 mns. into time ; thus, 18 dgs. give 18 96 0
and 18 minutes give 0 111 4

18 207 4

Measure of Time for Degrees.									Measure of Time for Minutes.				
Deg	Yrs.	Dys.	Deg	Yrs.	Dys.	Deg	Yrs.	Dys.	Min	Dys.	Hrs.	Min	Dys.	Hrs.
1	1	5	31	31	166	61	61	326	1	6	4	31	191	11
2	2	10	32	32	171	62	62	330	2	12	8	32	197	16
3	3	16	33	33	177	63	63	337	3	18	13	33	203	20
4	4	21	34	34	181	64	64	342	4	24	17	34	210	0
5	5	26	35	35	186	65	65	347	5	30	21	35	216	4
6	6	32	36	36	192	66	66	353	6	37	1	36	222	9
7	7	37	37	37	197	67	67	358	7	43	6	37	228	13
8	8	43	38	38	202	68	68	364	8	49	10	38	234	17
9	9	48	39	39	208	69	69	4	9	55	14	39	240	21
10	10	53	40	40	213	70	70	9	10	61	18	40	247	2
11	11	59	41	41	218	71	71	15	11	67	23	41	253	6
12	12	64	42	42	224	72	72	20	12	74	3	42	259	10
13	13	69	43	43	229	73	73	25	13	80	7	43	265	14
14	14	74	44	44	234	74	74	30	14	86	11	44	271	18
15	15	80	45	45	240	75	75	36	15	92	16	45	277	23
16	16	85	46	46	245	76	76	41	16	98	20	46	284	3
17	17	90	47	47	250	77	77	46	17	105	0	47	290	7
18	18	96	48	48	256	78	78	52	18	111	4	48	296	11
19	19	101	49	49	261	79	79	57	19	117	9	49	302	16
20	20	106	50	50	266	80	80	62	20	123	13	50	308	20
21	21	112	51	51	272	81	81	68	21	129	17	51	315	0
22	22	117	52	52	277	82	82	73	22	135	21	52	321	4
23	23	122	53	53	282	83	83	78	23	142	1	53	327	9
24	24	128	54	54	288	84	84	84	24	148	6	54	333	13
25	25	133	55	55	293	85	85	89	25	154	10	55	339	17
26	26	138	56	56	298	86	86	94	26	160	14	56	345	21
27	27	144	57	57	304	87	87	100	27	166	18	57	352	2
28	28	149	58	58	309	88	88	105	28	172	23	58	358	6
29	29	154	59	59	314	89	89	110	29	170	3	59	364	10
30	30	160	60	60	320	90	90	116	30	185	7	60	370	14

SIMMONITE'S NAIBOD MEASURE OF TIME.

PROBLEM XCVIII.

153 To every nativity there must be a Table formed for the Minutes of any equated Arc. In the first column on the left hand enter with the degree under the degree of Arc of Direction, and against it, in the same column, under equated Minutes (under E.M.), which minutes are to be added to the Arc of Direction.

RULE 2.—Then, with the minutes of this equated Arc, enter Tables II, look for the minutes over the equated degrees, and you will find the day of the month agreeing on which the direction will be completed.

RULE 3.—Enter with the degree of the same Arc under Table III, and against that degree will be found the Year of our Lord in which the said direction will operate.

To form the Second Table of Nativities.

RULE.—Against every minute in first column add six days preceding it from the day of birth, beginning at one minute and continuing to sixty.

Remark.—At 11, 22, 34, 45, and 57 minutes, to each you must add 7 days to recompense the hours proportional.

EXAMPLE.

In the Queen's natus, when did M.C. sextile Venus operate?

Arc of Direction $17°$ $2'$
Equation added   o 15
____
Equated Arc is 17 17
____

This Arc answers to the 5th of September, 1836.

Again, Arc of Direction $\odot \, \circ \, ♀$ $20°$ $3'$
Equation added   o 17
____
Equated Arc is 20 20
____

Would answer to 3rd September, 1839.

Mark.—As no event of the nature of these aspects occurred at the time, we consider this measure is erroneous for all nativities. When the Sun is moving from 59 to 60 minutes per day, then these Tables will answer.

TABLE I.

	E.M.		E.M.		E.M.
1	1	31	27	61	53
2	2	32	28	62	54
3	3	33	29	63	55
4	3	34	30	64	56
5	4	35	31	65	57
6	5	36	32	66	58
7	6	37	32	67	59
8	7	38	33	68	60
9	8	39	34	69	60
10	9	40	35	70	61
11	10	41	36	71	62
12	11	42	37	72	63
13	11	43	38	73	64
14	12	44	39	74	65
15	13	45	40	75	65
16	14	46	40	76	66
17	15	47	41	77	67
18	16	48	42	78	68
19	17	49	43	79	69
20	17	50	44	80	69
21	18	51	45	81	70
22	19	52	45	82	71
23	20	53	46	83	72
24	21	54	47	84	73
25	22	55	48	85	74
26	23	56	49	86	75
27	24	57	50	87	75
28	25	58	51	88	76
29	25	59	52	89	77
30	26	60	53	90	78

TABLE II.

1	May.....31	31	Nov......29
2	June 1	32	Dec. 5
3	,, ...12	33	,, ...11
4	,, ...18	34	,, ...17
5	,, ...24	35	,, ...24
6	,, ...30	36	,, ...30
7	July 6	37	Jan. 5
8	,, ...12	38	,, ...11
9	,, ...18	39	,, ...17
10	,, ...24	40	,, ...23
11	,, ...31	41	,, ...29
12	Aug. 6	42	Feb. 4
13	,, ...12	43	,, ...10
14	,, ...18	44	,, ...16
15	,, ...24	45	,, ...22
16	,, ...30	46	Mar. 1
17	Sept. 5	47	,, ... 7
18	,, ...11	48	,, ...13
19	,, ...17	49	,, ...19
20	,, ...23	50	,, ...25
21	,, ...29	51	,, ...31
22	Oct. 6	52	April 6
23	,, ...12	53	,, ...12
24	,, ...18	54	,, ...18
25	,, ...24	55	,, ...24
26	,, ...30	56	,, ...30
27	Nov. 5	57	May 6
28	,, ...11	58	,, ...12
29	,, ...17	59	,, ...18
30	,, ...23	60	,, ...24

TABLE III.

Years.	A.D.	Years.	A.D.	Years.	A.D.
1	1820	21	1840		1860
2	1821	22	1841	42	1861
3	1822	23	1842	43	1862
4	1823	24	1843	44	1863
5	1824	25	1844	45	1864
6	1825	26	1845	46	1865
7	1826	27	1846	47	1866
8	1827	28	1847	48	1867
9	1828	29	1848	49	1868
10	1829	30	1849	50	1869
11	1830	31	1850	51	1870
12	1831	32	1851	52	1871
13	1832	33	1852	53	1872
14	1833	34	1853	54	1873
15	1834	35	1854	55	1874
16	1835	36	1855	56	1875
17	1836	37	1856	57	1876
18	1837	38	1857	58	1877
19	1838	39	1858	59	1878
20	1839	40	1859	60	1879

SIMMONITE'S METHOD OF EQUATING ARCS OF DIRECTIONS.

PROBLEM XCIX.

154 To every Nativity there must be a Table formed from the Sun's Right Ascension in Degrees and Minutes. But as the Ephemerides do not contain the Sun's Right Ascension in Degrees, Simmonite's Astronomical Ephemerides will, for the future, contain it. For the sake of the Students, I here insert the Sun's Right Ascension for Equating the Arcs in the Queen's nativity.

The Sun's Right Ascension from May 23rd to the end of July, 1819.

May.	☉'s A.R.		June.	☉'s A.R.		June.	☉'s A.R.		July.	☉'s A.R.	
	°	′		°	′		°	′		°	′
23	59	19	10	77	41	28	96	26	16	114	54
24	60	20	11	78	43	29	97	28	17	115	55
25	61	21	12	79	45	30	98	30	18	116	55
26	62	22	13	80	47	July.	99	32	19	117	55
27	63	22	14	81	49	2	100	33	20	118	55
28	64	23	15	82	51	3	101	35	21	119	55
29	65	24	16	83	54	4	102	37	22	120	55
30	66	25	17	84	56	5	103	39	23	121	55
31	67	26	18	85	58	6	104	41	24	122	54
June.	68	27	19	87	1	7	105	42	25	123	54
2	69	28	20	88	4	8	106	44	26	124	53
3	70	29	21	89	7	9	107	45	27	125	53
4	71	30	22	90	10	10	108	47	28	126	52
5	72	31	23	91	13	11	109	48	29	127	51
6	73	33	24	92	15	12	110	49	30	128	50
7	74	35	25	93	18	13	111	51	31	129	49
8	75	37	26	94	21	14	112	52	Aug.	130	47
9	76	39	27	95	23	15	113	53	2	131	46

PROBLEM C.

155 *To Rectify a Nativity by Personal Accidents.*

RULE I.—Erect the Figure, and place in the Planets at the estimated time of Birth, and learn at what time some two or three important events took place.

RULE 2.—Turn the age at which any event happened into degrees and minutes by the Table of Equating Arcs, in the last problem, then find the Arc of Direction nearest corresponding with the event —find the difference between this and the true Arc, and convert that difference into minutes and seconds by the Table (page 196), which difference will show the correct time of Birth.

Observe.—The best directions by which to rectify the estimated time of birth are those of the M.C. to Mars or the Sun, the Sun to parallels of Mars or the angles, as their effects do generally answer very closely to the time of direction. Marriage, accident, and death of parents, are safe events by which to rectify. Take two accidents, especially if they come near likely Arcs, and correct by both. As the Queen's natus has been rectified, I have given a figure, as an example, in the *easy abbreviated method of working Nativities.*

OF THE FIXED STARS.

Although the fixed stars are very numerous, only few of them are found to have a visible effect in nativities, for the following reasons :—

First.—No star can either rise or set when its declination exceeds the co-latitude of the country for which a figure is erected ; hence, they can never affect the Ascendant.

Secondly.—The reason they are omitted, because when near the horizon, the greatness of their latitude prevents us having a correct idea of their mundane station. For instance, Rigel, which is in 15 degrees of Gemini, rises with 27 degrees of Cancer, and sets with the 14th degree of Taurus ; consequently it is a folly to place fixed stars in a horoscope, except they be truly computed, and then placed in their proper mundane station ; for when the 17th degree of Gemini ascends, which is the ecliptic longitude of Rigel, then it is far below the cusp of the 2nd house ; consequently will not arrive at the Ascendant in less than three hours after.

Modern professors never name them, or even notice them, for no other reason than because of the difficulty of knowing their mundane stations ; hence the liability to err in judgment, in cases in which these stars intervene. The Fixed Stars have influence, of this the Ancients were aware, not that a single star was of great power, but the whole combined ; for there is not a degree rising, setting, or culminating, which is not accompanied by several stars.

The stars can affect the Planets only by body and zodiacal parallels, and the latter aspect will be most powerful. Therefore, planets about the middle of Scorpio and Aquarius will be afflicted by Sirius ($16\frac{1}{2}$ degrees south declination). The Star's conjunction will have no visible effect on the Sun, Moon, or Planets, if they differ, in latitude more than 5 degrees, yet may have the same longitude. If we do admit the aspects of the fixed stars, they must be in opposition both in latitude and in longitude, within 5 degrees, or they are void of effect.

Although Sirius has no effect on the planets in conjunction, yet its effects, when on the angles, is as great as that of Antares, which is 35 degrees nearer the ecliptic; consequently, when on the angles with the planets, has powerful effects.

If the stars' aspects are considered of important effect, then their latitudes will not alter their effect. My conviction is, that neither the aspects of the planets nor the fixed stars can be as powerful as a conjunction.

If it was not the difference of latitude which diminishes the power of the Aspects, then the place of a sextile would not be 60 degrees in longitude measured in the ecliptic, but from the place of each body. The latitude is the perpendicular of a spherical triangle, the longitude its base, and 60 degrees the hypothenuse; then we have the following proportions :—

As the co-sine of the latitude,
Is the co-sine of 60 degrees,
So is the radius of the co-sine of their difference of longitude of the place of the sextile from the place of the fixed star when measured on the ecliptic; but the square will always be 90 degrees, because then the base and the hypothenuse are equal.

SCHOLIUM.—The above proportions are very simple, as the sum of the logarithms of the 2nd and 3rd terms will always be 19,6990, from this take the co-sine of latitude, and we have the co-sine of longitude; then add this longitude to the stars' longitude, and it will give the sinister sextile, and the opposite point will be its trine.

SECOND.—Now subtract the distance required from the stars' longitude and the remainder will be the dexter sextile, and the opposite point of the zodiac will be its trine.

EXAMPLES.

Required the place where the sextile of Sirius falls, its latitude being 39° S. 32′.

From the constant logarithms 19,6990
Take the co-sine of the latitude of Sirius 39° 32′ = 9,8872
                                                    ———
And we have the distance required 49 35 = 9,8118
Add Sirius' longitude 11° ♋ 51′ or 101 51   ———
                                           ———
                                151 26, or, 1 ♍ 26, and its
                                ———trine falls in 1 ♓ 26

Required to find where its dexter aspect sextile will fall.

Sirius' longitude is 11° ♋ 54′, or 101° 54′
Take the found distance 49 35
                         ———
Difference 52 19
            ———

This remainder falls in 22 ♉ 19, and its opposite point will be
22 ♏ 19, or its trine.

EXPLANATION OF THE TABLES.

TABLE 1.—This contains 60 remarkable Stars, arranged according to the order of the Sign, with their name, longitude, latitude, declination, magnitude, and nature.

TABLE 2.—This contains the rising, setting, and culminating, arranged according to the advancement in time of the M.C. With this number, in the narrow column to the left with the letters a (ascending or rising), c (culminating), s (setting).

Those with a are ascending when the Right Ascension (R.A.) of the M.C. is the same as the time with the letter ; the c denotes culminating ; the s shows the Star's setting. All this in Sidereal Time.

This Table is of great importance, not only in seeing at one view what star is ascending at birth, but also in directing the angles of the fixed stars.

EXAMPLES.

A person born January 17th, 3h. 40m. P.M., 1847—what stars are rising, setting, and culminating ?

```
                                         h.  m.  s.
The Right Ascension of Medium Cœli at noon is =  19  45  9
                    Add the time past noon      3  40  0
                                               ____________
        The Right Ascension of the M.C. is     23  25  9
                                               ____________
```

Then look for the nearest correspondent in Table 2nd, and you find 23h. 27m. 12s. a, and opposite, in the narrow left-hand column, stands No. 13. Now refer to Table 1st, and you will find No. 13 to ORION'S BELT, which is in 20♊7, of the 2nd magnitude, of the nature of ♃ and ♄. Again, we find nearly the same R.A., viz., 23h. 35m. 21s. a. Then, by looking at Table 2, we find the No. 15th star, which, in Table 1, we find ORIONIS (middle star) which is in 21♊13, of the 2nd magnitude, of the nature of ♃ and ♂. And because each of them has a attached, it signifies they are ascending.

2nd.—When will COR LEO come to the Ascendant by direction ?

By Table 1, we find Cor Leo No. 31, for which number we look in Table 2, and with it stands 2h. 58m. 32s. a, which shows Cor Leo to ascend when the M.C. is 2h. 58m. 32s.

Now subtract the R.A. of M.C. at birth from the star's R.A. (after 24 hours have been added, when subtraction cannot be made) and the difference will be the Arc required.

```
                                              h.  m.  s.
Thus, from the R.A. of M.C. when Cor Leo ascends  2  58  32
            Take the R.A. of M.C. at birth       23  25   9
                                                ____________
            This gives the Arc required.          3  33  23
                                                ____________
```

Convert 3h. 33m. 23s. into degrees by Problem iv. in Table 1, page 196.

```
                                               o   '   "
Look opposite 3h. 32m., on the left hand and you find  53   0   0
            Then 1 minute in the last column is    0  15   0
            And 23 seconds in the last column is   0   5  45
                                                  ____________
            The Arc of Direction is               53  20  45
                                                  ____________
```

When will the Ascendant come to a conjunction of Sirius ?

By Table 1, we find Sirius No. 21, for which number
we look in Table 2, and find opposite to it............ 2 12 56
From which take the R.A. of M.C. 23 25 9
———————
This gives the Arc required 2 47 47
———————

Convert 2h. 47m. 47s. into degrees, and it gives 41° 56′ 45″.   Ans.

TABLE I.

A TABLE OF SIXTY EMINENT FIXED STARS.

No.	The Names of the Stars.	Long. (° ′)	Lat. (° ′)	Dec. (° ′)	Mag.	Semidiurnal Arc. (° ′)	Nature of
1	Whale's Tail (S. end)	0 ♈ 18	2 S 47	18 S 51	2	62 52	♄
2	Algenib	6 35	13 N 35	14 S 20	2	70 3	♂ ☿
3	Caput Andromedæ ..	12 4	25 N 41	28 N 15	1	136 43	♃ ♀
4	Zona Andromedæ ..	28 8	25 N 56	34 N 46	2	160 7	♀
5	Ram's Head..	5 ♉ 25	9 N 57	22 N 44	2	123 29	♄ ♂
6	Ceti ..	12 4	12 S 37	3 N 29	2	94 56	♂
7	Lucida Pleiadum ..	27 45	4 N 1	23 N 38	3	126 23	♂ ☽
8	1st Star, Hyades, in ♉	3 ♊ 42	5 S 56	15 N 28	3	112 0	♂
9	Bull's South Eye ..	6 13	2 S 36	18 N 50	3	117 30	♀
10	Aldebaron ..	7 32	5 30	16 N 11	1	113 10	♂
11	Rigel ..	14 35	31 10	8 S 23	1	78 29	♃ ♂
12	Bellatrix ..	18 43	16 31	6 N 6	2	98 20	☿ ♂
13	Orion's Belt ..	20 7	23 36	0 S 25	2	89 17	♃ ♄
14	Bull's North Horn ..	20 19	5 N 21	28 N 28	2	137 17	♂
15	Orionis ..	21 13	24 S 33	1 S 18	2	68 14	♃ ♂
16	Bull's South Horn ..	22 33	2 S 13	20 N 1	3	119 35	♂
17	Betalguse ..	29 30	16 S 4	7 N 22	2	109 5	♂ ☿
18	Geminorium ..	1 ♋ 12	0 S 56	22 N 31	3	124 11	☿ ♀
19	Geminorium (m) ..	3 3	1 S 51	22 N 35	3	124 17	☿ ♀
20	Bright Foot of Gemini	6 52	6 S 47	16 N 34	2 & 3	113 46	☿ ♀
21	Sirius..	11 54	39 S 32	16 N 31	1	66 20	♃ ♂
22	Geminis ..	12 45	2 S 5	20 S 50	3	58 58	♄
23	Canis Majoris ..	8 17	51 S 43	28 S 46	2	41 54	♀
24	Castor ..	18 1	10 N 4	32 N 13	1 & 2	148 40	♂ ♀ ♄
25	Pollux ..	21 1	6 N 39	28 N 23	1	132 52	♂
26	Procyon ..	23 36	15 S 58	5 N 37	1	97 40	♀ ♂
27	North Ascellus ..	5 ♌ 18	3 N 10	22 N 2	4	123 16	♂ ☉
28	South Ascellus ..	6 29	0 N 4	18 N 36	4	117 9	♂ ☉
29	Hydra's Heart ..	25 3	22 S 25	7 S 59	2	79 3	♄ ♀
30	Leo's Neck ..	27 20	8 N 47	22 N 10	2	123 28	♄

TABLE I. CONTINUED.

A TABLE OF SIXTY EMINENT FIXED STARS.

No.	The Names of the Stars.	Long. ° ′	Lat. ° ′	Dec. ° ′	Mag.	Semidiurnal Arc ° ′	Nature of
31	Cor Leo (*Regulus*)	27 37	0 N 27	12 N 43	1	107 52	♂
32	Vindemiatrix	7 ♍ 3	14 N 9	21 N 23	2	122 3	♄ ♀
33	Deneb	19 25	12 N 17	15 N 26	1	111 43	♅
34	2nd Star in Libra	2 ♎ 37	1 N 22	0 N 15	3	90 20	♂ ☿
35	Sinistra	7 38	2 N 49	2 N 9	3	87 5	☿
36	Spica Virgo	21 36	2 S 2	10 N 22	1	75 41	♂ ♀
37	Arcturus	21 59	31 N 0	19 N 59	1	119 34	♃ ♂ ☿ ♀
38	North Crown	10 ♏ 1	44 N 21	27 N 14	2	134 16	♀ ☿ ♀
39	South Scale	12 51	0 N 22	15 S 23	2	68 7	♄ ♀ ♂
40	North Scale	17 8	8 N 8	8 S 48	2	77 40	♃ ♂
41	Serpentis	19 49	25 N 32	6 N 55	2	99 30	♄ ♀
42	Frons Scorpio	0 ♐ 18	1 S 57	22 S 7	2	56 35	♄ ♂
43	Scorpii	0 58	1 N 5	19 S 22	2	61 23	♄ ♀
44	Cor Scorpio	5 24	4 S 0	25 S 9	2	50 19	♃ ♂
45	Antares	7 25	4 S 32	26 S 5	1	48 25	☿ ♂
46	Ophinci's Knee	15 45	7 N 14	17 S 10	3	65 17	♄ ♀ ☿ ♀
47	Ophinci	19 10	1 S 48	24 S 52	3	51 15	♄ ♀ ♀ ♂
48	Ophinci's Head	20 11	35 N 58	11 N 40	2	107 48	♄ ♀ ♀ ♂
49	Capricornus	10 ♑ 8	3 S 35	26 S 34	3	47 12	⊙ ♂
50	Altair	29 28	29 N 19	8 N 28	1	101 52	♅
51	Goat's Horn	1 ♒ 37	6 N 58	13 S 1	3	71 16	♀ ☿ ♀
52	Capricorn	1 48	4 N 37	15 S 20	3	68 11	♀ ☿
53	1st Star in Goat's Tail	19 33	2 S 31	17 S 14	3	65 11	♄
54	Aquarius	21 10	8 N 39	6 S 17	3	81 25	♅
55	Goat's Tail	21 28	2 S 33	16 S 51	3	65 47	♄
56	*d* Aquari	26 29	2 N 4	10 S 46	3	75 12	♅
57	Fomalhaut	1 ♓ 34	21 S 5	30 S 26	1	37 9	☿ ♀ ♀
58	*a* Aquari	9 21	0 N 23	7 S 46	3	79 22	♄ ♃ ♀
59	Markhab	21 15	19 N 25	14 N 23	2	110 18	♂ ♀
60	Schet Pegasi	27 8	31 N 8	27 S 10	2	45 55	♄

TABLE II.

THE RISING, SETTING, AND CULMINATING OF SIXTY FIXED STARS.

No.	H	M	S	No.	H	M	S	No.	H	M	S	No.	H	M	S	No.	H	M	S
3	0	0	17c	14	5	16	22c	15	11	21	18s	41	15	36	12c	43	20	2	12s
2	0	5	10c	13	5	24	0c	13	11	21	48s	59	15	38	46a	60	20	6	2a
27	0	19	40a	16	5	24	57c	8	11	34	15s	52	15	49	14a	14	20	7	10a
1	0	33	42c	15	5	28	17c	33	11	41	2c	42	15	50	22c	51	20	9	20c
48	0	38	53s	17	5	46	40c	4	11	41	33s	43	15	56	20a	52	20	11	58c
52	0	44	42s	18	6	4	57c	12	11	50	0s	54	15	57	20a	40	20	20	0s
28	0	46	34a	37	6	10	14a	43	11	50	0a	44	16	11	16a	57	20	20	24a
51	0	54	24s	34	6	12	42a	10	11	58	35s	56	16	13	0a	1	20	22	16a
22	0	58	28a	19	6	13	27c	7	12	3	52s	45	16	19	52c	9	20	25	2a
26	1	1	24a	59	6	15	35s	42	12	4	20a	36	16	19	31c	6	20	32	25a
4	1	1	56a	36	6	19	40a	9	12	5	15s	28	16	23	46s	8	20	38	15a
57	1	17	36s	20	6	28	24c	34	12	14	2c	25	16	27	10s	10	20	54	15a
5	1	58	28c	38	6	31	8a	17	12	27	0s	27	16	45	48s	47	20	56	32a
30	1	58	10a	21	6	38	16c	35	12	33	24c	46	17	1	0c	46	21	22	0s
53	1	58	20s	35	6	45	6a	46	12	40	0a	47	17	12	12c	54	21	23	17c
55	2	1	38s	23	6	52	26c	44	12	50	0a	55	17	15	2a	16	21	26	37a
21	2	12	56a	22	6	54	20c	22	12	50	12e	53	17	17	16a	24	21	29	45a
60	2	13	38s	24	7	24	25c	50	12	55	39a	24	17	19	5s	53	21	38	0c
50	2	30	33s	26	7	31	4c	45	13	6	12a	31	17	21	28s	55	21	38	10c
56	2	44	36s	25	7	35	42c	16	13	16	55c	58	17	21	48a	56	21	43	10c
54	2	49	20s	27	8	32	44c	46	13	23	17s	48	17	27	38c	18	21	48	13a
6	2	51	9c	28	8	35	10c	47	13	27	52a	5	17	44	20a	49	21	50	23s
32	2	57	34a	41	8	58	0a	26	14	1	44s	34	18	15	22s	19	21	56	3a
31	2	58	32a	3	9	7	20s	20	14	3	28s	35	18	24	44s	37	22	6	46s
7	3	38	20c	31	9	10	0c	37	14	8	30c	30	18	25	4s	41	22	14	22s
58	3	56	44s	6	9	10	53s	4	14	20	37a	49	18	41	7c	38	22	39	16c
29	4	3	40a	29	9	19	52c	18	14	21	41s	36	18	59	0s	12	22	42	4a
23	4	5	20a	23	9	40	32s	14	14	25	34s	35	19	8	0s	25	22	44	14a
8	4	6	15c	40	9	57	54a	19	14	30	51s	32	19	14	0s	20	22	53	20a
33	4	14	0a	39	10	9	44a	39	14	42	14c	39	19	14	28s	58	22	56	58c
10	4	26	55c	30	10	11	12c	29	14	36	29s	7	19	14	48a	59	22	57	11c
1	4	45	10s	5	10	16	26s	3	14	53	14a	2	19	25	10a	17	23	6	2a
2	4	45	10s	48	10	16	26a	40	15	8	34c	44	19	32	32c	60	23	10	8c
58	4	46	44s	11	10	21	2s	51	15	24	16a	45	19	33	32s	13	23	27	12a
11	5	7	2c	21	11	21	2s	38	15	28	2c	42	19	36	42s	15	23	35	21a
12	5	16	6c	32	11	5	53c	49	15	31	50a	50	19	43	7c	11	23	53	6a

THE NATURE AND EFFECTS OF THE FIXED STARS.

Of ♅.—*Ascending*, gives eccentricity, and gain by learning.

Culminating, makes the native eminent in arts, science, mechanism, curious inventions, and learned.

Of ♄.—*Ascending*, the native is grave, thoughtful, and solicitous about building, mines and minerals ; full of care, vexation, and melancholy ; subject to disgrace.

Culminating, shows strife, and vexation from aged men, loss of character, troubles, imprisonment, and losses in trade, and deceitful associates.

Of ♃.—*Ascending*, the native born will be sober, grave, and patient, and gain by gifts, church preferment, and legacies.

Culminating, gives honour, glory, preferment, also success in trade, or religious preferment.

Of ♂.—*Ascending*, gives wealth and power, ingenuity, and a noble mind ; courageous and generous. He rises to authority, and is inclined to martial services, by which he is elevated ; yet is subject to cuts and other wounds ; some sore on the face, or pain of the head, and feverish complaints.

Culminating, the native will be successful in trade, and chiefly in metals ; he shall hold some office of martial eminence, according to his quality of birth.

Of ♀.—*Ascending*, good fortune, inheritance, worldly happiness, and the love of women ; gifts, or legacy preferment.

Culminating, gives honour, and makes much by dealing with women, apparel, &c.

Of ♃ and ♄.—*Ascending*, give legacies, inheritance, also gain by jovial men, and gain an eternal name ; but foolish in love matters, and the dupe of Venus.

Culminating, show honour and preferment.

Of ♄ and ♂.—*Ascending*, show loss by land estates, the health indisposed by cold temperament, the native poor, and he will have but few friends. If the stars be of the first magnitude, he may rise by usury and other unfair means.

Culminating, the native will bear a bad name, will rise by trade and fall again to disgrace and ruin ; frequently in an unexpected way.

Of ♄ and ♀.—*Ascending*, the native will gain by industry and by marriage, will be of a good temper, healthful, and live in estimation, the Virgin's Spixe appears to be of this nature (508).

Culminating, if of the first magnitude rises to fame, by men above the native's own rank, with an improved state of health.

Of ♃ and ♂.—*Ascending*, if of the first magnitude, as of Sirius, give martial preferment and honour ; study well the paragraph 508, pages 152 and 153.

Culminating, prosperity in business, and martial preferment, especially if the star be Rigel, Arcturus, and the North Scale (529).

Of ♂ and ☽.—*Ascending*, give wantonness, sore and inflammatory and accidents to the eyes, weak sight, liable to trouble and loss by women.

Culminating, the native is often in disgrace, and sometimes brought to imprisonment ; Lucidum, Pleiadum, and other nebulus stars are of this character.

Of ♂ and ☉.—*Ascending*, give preferment to workers in iron, steel, and at the fire ; iron masters have good success ; soldiers are called into active exercise.   When stars of this nature are *Culminating*, as the North and South Ascelli and Capricornus, the natives prosper in all martial undertakings, and hardware businesses.

Of ☿ and ♀.—*Ascending*, imprint on the mind a ready apprehension, given to poetry, learning, painting, and teaching.

Culminating, the natives ought to follow the calling of printer, bookseller, clerk, lawyer, and such-like, in which the pen and mind have to be in active exercise.

Of ♂ and ☿.—*Ascending*, give a rash disposition, often very obstinate, and the native is sometimes ruined by some foolhardy procedure, setting at defiance the advice of his friends, and acts according to his precipitate and foolish fancy.

Culminating, he is changeable in his business, and is never long satisfied, although he succeeds tolerably well, he must be trying some other calling in life.

ABBREVIATED METHOD OF WORKING NATIVITIES.

156 After erecting the Figure, as directed (page 281), rectify by the Rules there given.   " When angles are significators they will meet with a number of aspects, which, when compared together with the time of accidents, will be so exactly alike in error that the true time cannot be mistaken."

157 *Rectification of a Nativity.*

The time of this nativity was not exactly known, but was stated to be about 10h. 45m. A.M., 27th November, 1812, for which time a figure was erected, and the planets' places inserted.   The native had a fall into a deep well at 4 years and 2 months old.

The estimated time of Birth 27th November, 10h. 45m. A.M.
which is equal to 26 days, 22h. 45m., equal to 341° 16'
The Sun's Right Ascension at Birth estimate 243   7

Right Ascension 584 23
Subtract the Circle, as it is more than 360   0

The Right Ascension of the Midheaven at Birth 224 23

Looking over the figure of the heavens I find that Saturn would afflict the Ascendant by conjunction about that age ; and, indeed, according to page 146, and paragraph 485, that would be a very powerful arc to indicate a fall and other accidents. From

Saturn's Meridian distance false M.C.   127° 25'
Add the Arc of the Asc. ☌ of Saturn mundo   4 25

The Meridian Distance of Saturn 131 50
Saturn's Semi-nocturnal Arc is 126 31

This shows the false M.C. to be too much   5 19

The Right Ascension of the Imum Celi for the
estimate time with the circle is 405° 23'
Subtract Saturn's Right Ascension 276 58

Again we have found Saturn's M.D. 127 25
Subtract Saturn's Semi-nocturnal Arc 126 31

This is what Saturn is above the Ascendant   0 54
To which add the Arc for 4 years and 2 months= 4 25

5 19

This 5° 19' is the distance Saturn has to be cast below the Ascendant to make the Arc of Direction of Saturn to the conjunction of Ascendant at the time the native fell into the well.

The false M.C. is 224° 23'
Which is too much by   5 19

The true Right Ascension of M.C. 219   4

The 5° 19' must be turned into time, which give 21 minutes and 20 seconds sooner for the time of birth.

h. m. s.
The estimate time given 22 45   0
From which Subtract   0 21 20

The native was born 26th November, 1812, at 22 23 40

Abbreviated Method.

This is according to Problems 57 and 64, and for the Ascendant to be brought to Saturn's body in mundo, Saturn must be brought below the earth 4 degrees 25 minutes, but we find him above the estimate time 54 minutes of an Arc, so we find the M.C. in error 5 degrees 19 seconds, or the time of birth too late by about 22 mins.

CALCULATION.—Right Ascension of Saturn is 276° 58'
Right Ascension of the M.C. estimate 224 23

Saturn's Mid dist. is 52 35
Saturn's S.D.A. is 53 29
Saturn's Mid. dist. is 52 35

Saturn is above the Ascendant= 0 54
Add the Arc for 4 yrs. 2 months 4 25

The M.C. too much by 5 19
This subtract from 224 23

The true Right Ascension of M.C. 219 4
R.A. 219° 4'.

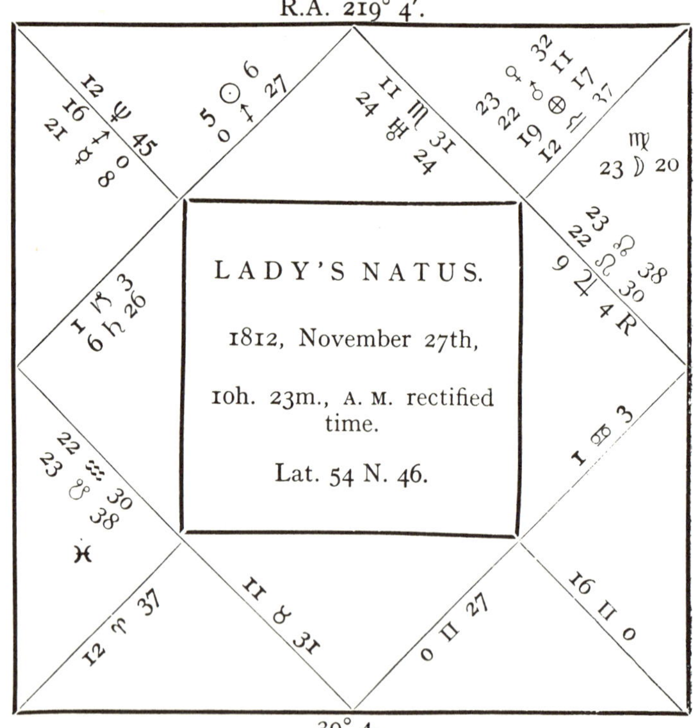

39° 4.

	♅	♄	♃	♂	☉	♀	☿	☽
Lat.	0 N 14	0 N 31	0 N 31	1 N 3	...	... 2 N 6	2 S 15	2 N 31
Dec.	18 S 40	22 S 48	18 N 30	7 S 40	21 S 11	7 S 11	25 S 24	4 N 58

Sol and Mars to Aspects in Mundo.

1st.—Find the ☉'s R.A. in 5 ♐ 6 by the Tables of R.A. equal 243° 9'.

2nd.—☉'s Mid. distance, its R.A. is 243° 9', take R.A. of M.C. 219° 4' equal 24° 5'.

Problem 37.—Tangent of ☉'s Dec. 21 S 11 = 9·58831 Cot. 10·41168
Add Tangent of Birth place 43 46 = 10·15101

Asc. Diff. Sine 33 17 = 9·73932
Problem 38.—Take ditto from 90 0

☉'s S.D.A. = 56 43 = ⅓rd 18 55
☉'s Mid dist., or M.C. ☌ ☉ mundo = 24 5 Log. 8735

Prob. 46.—☉ from the 11th, or M.C.S. ⚹ ☉ mun. = 5 10 Log. 1·5420
Problem 41.—The Prop. Log. of 90 degrees = 3010
The Prop. Log. of 56° 43' = 9·4985 Arith. Comp.

Log. of Circle of position 9·7995
Problem 42.—Log. of ☉'s Mid. dist. 8736

☉'s difference of Cir. Pos. 6731 = 38° 12'
Sol's Mid. dist. 24 5

Problem 43.—☉'s Asc. diff. under his own pole 14 7 Sine 9·38721
Problem 45.—Sol's Right Asc. to be added 243 9

Sol's Oblique Ascension 257 16
Problem 44.—Sine of ☉'s Asc. diff. 14° 7' = 9·38721
Cotangent of ☉'s Dec. 21 11 = 10.41168

Tangent of the ☉'s Pole 32 11 = 9.79889

This completes the Speculum for the Sun, besides producing the Ascendant ⚹ ☉ and M.C.S. ⚹ ☉ 5° 10', and the M.C. ☌ ☉ and Asc. □ ☉ 24° 5'. Place your results as you obtain them in a Speculum, and the different Logarithms as they come out, and place your Arc of Direction in their appropriate places. We will now find all the necessaries for Mars in the same way.

Mar's Preliminaries.

Prob. 35.—Mars in 22 ♎ 11 with 1 N 3 Lat. its R.A. is 200° 53'
Right Ascension of M.C. is 219 4

Problem 36.—Log. of Mars's Mid distance = 18 11 M.D.

Prob. 37.—Tangent of Mars's Dec. 7s40= 9·12909=Cot. 10·87091
Add Tangent of Birth Place 54 46=10·15101

Ascen. diff. sine 10° 59′= 9·28010
Problem 38.—Subtract 90   0

Mars's S.D.A.=79° 1′ its Log. 3571 ⅓rd Arc 26 20
Mars's Mid. distance is 18 11
Probs. 46 & 70th.—Mars's true Asc. and Dis. from 9th 8 9

Problem 41.—The Prop. Log. of 90° 0′   3010
The   do.   do. of 79 1 =96429 Ar. Comp.

Log. of Circle of Position 9·9439
Problem 42.—Log. of Mars's M.D.   9956

Mars's diff. of Cir. Pos.   9395   20° 41′
Mars's Mid. distance   18 11

Problem 43.—Mars's Asc. difference under the pole   2 30
Mars's R.A. subtracted 200 53

Mars's Oblique Descension 198 23

Problem 44.—Sine of Mars's Asc. diff.   2° 30′= 8·63968
Cot. of Mars's Decli.   7s 40 =10·87091

Tangent of Mars's pole 17 57 = 9·51059

The Sun to the Sextile of Mars direct.

Problem 71.—First find a constant Log. ; that is, by adding the Arithmetical complement of the Sun's semi-diurnal Arc to his distance from the 11th cusp, which will give a constant Log.
As ☉'s S.D.A. 56° 43″   Arith Comp. 9·4985
Is to his distance from 11th cusp 5° 11′   1·5406

Constant Log. 1·0391
So is Mars's semi-diurnal Arc 79·1=   3575

Mars's secondary distance from 9th 7° 13′=13966
Mars's primary distance from 9th 8 11   ——

☉'s ⚹ ♂ d.d. mundo   0 58
Add one-third of semi-arc 26 20

This is the ☉□ of ♂ d.d. 27 18
Add one-third semi-arc more 26 20 for the ☉△♂

This is the ☉ △ ♂ d.d. 53 38

$$\odot \ \square \ \mars \text{ is } 27°\ 18'$$

Take one-fifth semi-arc 79.1 = 15 48

Remains ⊙ qu. ♂ = 11 30

By the same process we find the other aspects to the Sun in mundo direct.   Let us work the Sun to Venus.   The preliminaries of Venus will be found for the Speculum as those of Sol and Mars before.

The Sun to the aspects of Venus Direct.

The Sun's constant Log. was found 1.0391
Add the Log of Venus's S.D.A. 79° 43'   3537

Venus's second distance from 9th   7° 17′=1.3928
Venus's primary   do.   do.   10   4 = ♀ from the 9th cusp.

Sun ✳ Venus   2 47
Add one-third of Venus's S.D.A.== 26 34

Sun square of Venus 29 21
Add one-third more 26 34

Gives ⊙ trine of Venus 55 55

The square is 29 21
From which take ⅕th of S. A. which is 15 57

Sun quintile Venus 13 24

We might reverse these directions, but as there can be only a semisquare of the Sun to Venus or Mars, we will take the aspects of Sun and Jupiter by converse, which is performed as the others, only we must make Jupiter stand still upon the cusp of the 8th till we bring the Sun down to him.   We must find the constant Log. of Jupiter.

Thus Jupiter's S.D.A. is found to be 118° 17'   Arith. Comp. 9.8177
Add the dist. Jupiter is from the 8th   8 39   1.3183

Constant Log. of Jupiter from 8th= 1.1360
Sol's semi-arc is 56° 43' Log.   5015

Sol's second distance from the 11th 4 9   1.6375
Add Sol's primary dis. from 11th 5 9

Jupiter square Sol 9 18
Add one-fifth of Sun's S.D.A 56° 43' = 11 21

Jupiter quintile Sun = 20 37

To the ♃ square ☉ add one-third of 56° 43′ = 18° 54′
Add the Square 9 18

This gives the ⚹ 28 12
Add one-half more for S☐ 28 21

Jupiter S☐ Sol converse 56 33

When many directions are found to one Planet I always keep a standing or constant Log., for it facilitates the Arcs of Directions. We shall proceed to show how the angles may be easily directed.

THE ANGLES TO ASPECTS IN MUNDO.
Midheaven to Aspects in the World.

I have, in the Problems, shown how the Midheaven may form aspects, and the Planets shall have passed that meridian point in mundo. I have proved from experience their effects, and I would call such aspect mundane or meridian antecedentia, otherwise say the planet directed to the angles. For instance, Venus is past the Meridian, and some Professors would say the M.C. cannot form a conjunction with Venus, but I would say Venus to the conjunction of M.C., or the M.C. itself comes down to the place of Venus. In all cases when a Planet is above the Earth, Problem 50, that Planet's mid. distance is the conjunction to the M.C. But to be after the manner of the other Professors the Planet must be between the 1st and 10th cusps; then, in this case, subtract the R.A. of the M.C. from the Planet's R.A., and the difference is the Arc. Right Ascension of Mercury 260 deg. 10 min., take Right Ascension of M.C. 219 deg. 4 min., difference, 41 deg. 6 min., Arc of Direction M.C. conjunction Mercury.

PROBLEM 51.—*M.C. to semi-sextile.* The Planet must be between the cusps of the 1st and 11th, and 10th and 9th, bring the Star to the cusp of these houses by Problem 46. The Planet must be between the 11th and 1st, 10th and 9th, the difference between one-third of semi-arc and Mid. distance will be the M.C. S⚹☉. Thus Mercury's M.D. is 41° 6′ from which take one-third of 47° 45′ which is 15° 55′, and the difference is 25° 11′ for the Arc. As this is brought to the cusp of the 11th, it is also the Ascendant to the sextile of Mercury; according to NOTE 104. We will bring Venus to the M.C. semisextile; one-third of her S. A. is 26° 34′, from which take 16° 31′, leave 10° 3′ for M.C. S⚹♀, or Ascendant trine of ♀. See Note 104.

PROBLEM 54.—*The Midheaven to the Semi-square.* In this case the Planet must be between the Ascendant and the middle of the 11th, or between the middle of the 8th and cusp of the 10th. Then the difference between one-half the semi-arc and the Planet's Mid. distance will be the Arc of Direction. Thus one-half of Mercury's S.D.A. is 23° 53′ and M.D. 41° 6′, the difference 17° 13′ Or for Venus, her S.D.A. is 79° 43′, and the one-half is 39° 51′, M.D. 16° 31′, difference, 23° 20′. M.C. or Ascendant Sesquisquare of ♀. See Note 167.

PROBLEM 55.—*The M.C. to sextile.* The star must be below the cusp of the 12th, and between the 10th and 8th cusps; then the difference between the Planets M. D. and two-thirds of its semi-diurnal arc. Two-thirds of Mercury's Semi-arc 31° 50′ taken from 41° 6′, leaves the Arc M. C. ✱ ☿ 9° 16′. For Mars, two-thirds of Mars S.D.A. is 52° 41′, his M.D. 18° 11′, arc M.C. ✱ ♂ 34° 30′.

PROBLEM 56.—*The M.C. to quintile.* See 109. In this case the planet must be below the 12th and between the 10th and 7th cusps. Then the difference between four-fifths of semi-diurnal arc and M.D. For M.C. quintile Saturn his S.D.A. is 53°29′, and four-fifths 42° 47′ take his distance from 10th, 57° 54′ difference 15° 7′ is the arc of M.C. qu. ♄. For Mars his M.D. is 18° 11′ and four-fifths of 79° 1′ are 63° 13 and take 18° 11′ leave 45° 2′ for M.C. quintile ♂.

PROBLEM 57.—*The M.C. to square.* This Problem will also answer for Problems 64 and 73. In this the Planet must be below the 10th and 7th and the 4th and 1st cusps. Then the difference between the Mid. distance and the Planet's semi-arc will be the Arc of Direction. For Saturn, his semi-arc is 126° 31′, from which take his M.D. 122° 6′, the arc 4° 25′ of M.C. □ ♄, or Asc. ☌ ♄. See Note 110. For Mars, his S.A. 79° 1′, and his M.D. 18° 11′, the difference 60° 50′, is M.C. □ ♂, or Asc. ☍ ♂. See Note 110.

PROBLEM 59.—*The M.C to trine.* Mark—The Planet must be between the cusps of the 8th and 6th, or the 4th and 2nd, or brought to those positions, else it will be no use, as the arc would be very great. Work by the directions laid down in Problem 59, which cannot be abbreviated. The other Problems connected with the Mid-heaven are as succinct and plain as they can be made.

A Shorter Method.

The method I follow, in my practice, is first to look out the last aspect before birth the M.C. might form with any Planet, I then merely add or subtract the proportional parts of the star's semi-arc. In this natus I would first obtain Saturn's square to M.C.

<pre>
            Saturn's semi-arc 126° 31′
            Take M.D.   122   6
                               ─────────
        M.C. □ ♄   4 25 or Asc. ☌ ♄
 Add one-third S.D.A. 17 50
                     ─────────
        M.C. ✱ ♄   22 15 or Asc. S ✱ ♄.
 Add one-sixth more   8 55 half of ⅓rd of semi-arc.
                     ─────────
        M.C. S □ ♄ 31 10 or Asc. S □ ♄.
 Add half of a house 8 55
                     ─────────
        M.C. S ✱ ♄ 40 5 Asc. ✱ ♄.
 Add one-third S.A. 17 50
                     ─────────
        M.C. ☌ ♄   57 55 Asc. □ ♄.
</pre>

As one result depends upon another, great care must be taken not to add or subtract incorrectly, else every subsequent result will be in error.

Venus to aspect of M.C.

Right Asc. of M.C. is	219° 4′	
Venus's Right Asc.	202 33	
	———	
Venus's M.D.	16 31	M.C. ☌ ♀.
One-third S.A. is	26 34	
	———	
M.C. S ✶ ♀	10 3	Asc. △ ♀.
Add half of one-third S.A.	13 17	
	———	
M.C. S □ ♀	23 20	Asc. Ss □ ♀.
Add the half again	13 17	
	———	
M.C. ✶ ♀	36 37	
Add one-third of S.A.	26 34	
	———	
M.C. □ ♀	63 11	Asc. 8 ♀.
	———	

Ascendant to Aspect in Mundo.

PROBLEM 64.—To bring a Star to the conjunction of the Ascendant the Planet must be between the 4th and first cusps.

PROBLEM 65.—For the semisextile the Planet must be between the cusp of the 1st and 12th, or the 4th or 2nd, then follow out the Rule.

PROBLEM 66.—The Ascendant to Semisquare, the Star must be between the 4th cusp and middle of the 2nd, then the difference between half its S.N.A. and Meridian distance, if below the Earth. If above the Earth, the star must be between the 1st and middle of the 12th, then the difference between its M.D. and half its S.D.A. for the Arc of Direction.

PROBLEM 67.—The Ascendant to the sextile of a planet, which must be between the cusps of the 11th and 1st, or between the 3rd and 6th, and then proceed as No. 122.

PROBLEM 68.—As is directed in 123, only the planet must be between the 4th and 3rd, or between the 10th and 9th.

PROBLEM 69.—As directed in 124, which cannot be abbreviated.

PROBLEM 70.—This Problem answers only when the planet is between the first and 9th, or between the 7th and 5th, and then proceed as No. 125.

PROBLEMS 71, 72, and 73, must be worked as there directed. We have given an example of Abbreviations in Problem 73, which must be adhered to.

ZODIACAL ASPECTS.

PROBLEM 74 is as clear and succinct as we can possibly make it. Bearing in mind, that if the M.C. is nearly at the end of the Zodiac, say Aquarius or Pisces, then the planet to which the M.C. is directed may be in Aries, Taurus, &c. Then in such cases, 360 degrees must be added to the planet's Right Ascension, if subtraction cannot otherwise be made.

PROBLEM 75.—In working the Problems connected with the Ascendant, I recommend the student to frame Oblique Ascensions for the latitude of birth places. Then proceed as in Rules 1, 2, and 5 of this Problem, which is as brief as can be conveniently made.

PROBLEM 76.—To direct the M.C. to parallel of Declination in the Zodiac, without latitude. RULE 1.—That place in the ecliptic must be found where the Sun acquires the declination of the planet, either north or south, to whose parallel the M.C. is directed, which retain.

Mark well.—To get out the Right Ascension and Declination of aspect, is also obtaining the place which will serve for the Sun's parallel that is wanted in Problem 89. This also serves for Problem 76, and 77, and 89 which should be worked together; for Rule 1 of Problem 76, 77, and 89, are all worked alike.

PROBLEMS 78, 79, 80, 81, 82, 83, 84, 85, 86, must be worked as I have directed in their respective operations.

PROBLEM 81.—This is a short Problem and easily understood, and the examples I have given are sufficient to make it plain.

The residue of the Problems remain as they are, for we cannot make them either shorter or plainer.

SIMMONITE'S METHOD OF TIMING ARCS OF DIRECTIONS.

According to Problem 99 make a Table for the Sun's Daily regular Motion (not his Mean Motion), and add each day's motion together for as many days as you calculate years for.

Example.—The Queen was born 23rd May, 16h. 4m., at the noon of that day set down 0° 0', and by looking how far the Sun has moved in Right Ascension, which is from 59° 19' to 60° 20', which is 1° 1', which is equal to one year of life. Again, add the next daily motion, which is 1° 1', to the last 1° 1' and they make 2° 2', equal to two years of the native's life. For 20 years of the Queen's life requires 20° 26' of an arc. Table II. serves for equating the minutes of a degree, but if you wish to know the day of the month you must frame a Table like that of page 280, and proceed as in Table III. of that page

U

The M.C. to the trine of the Sun is 19° 57' turned into time. Opposite with 19 years I find 19ᶜ 24', which I find is 33 minutes short of the full arc 19° 57', and these 33 minutes I apply to Table II., and find it to fall in December, and adding the years after birth, 19, I apply it to Table III., page 280, and find it to correspond with 1838, so the arc of M.C. trine Sun came up in December, 1838. If I wished to find out the day on which the arc was completed, I apply the 33 minutes to Table III., page 280, and find it December 11th, 1838.

Table I.

Yr	°	'	Yr	°	'	Yr	°	'	Yr	°	'
0	0	0	17	17	20	34	35	2	51	52	31
1	1	1	18	18	22	35	36	5	52	53	32
2	2	2	19	19	24	36	37	7	53	54	33
3	3	3	20	20	26	37	38	9	54	55	34
4	4	4	21	21	28	38	39	11	55	56	34
5	5	5	22	22	30	39	40	12	56	57	34
6	6	6	23	23	33	40	41	14	57	58	34
7	7	7	24	24	35	41	42	16	58	59	34
8	8	8	25	25	37	42	43	18	59	60	34
9	9	9	26	26	40	43	44	20	60	61	34
10	10	10	27	27	43	44	45	21	61	62	33
11	11	11	28	28	46	45	46	23	62	63	33
12	12	12	29	29	49	46	47	24	63	64	32
13	13	13	30	30	52	47	48	26	64	65	32
14	14	14	31	31	54	48	49	27	65	66	31
15	15	16	32	32	57	49	50	28	66	67	30
16	16	18	33	34	0	50	51	30	67	68	29

Table II.
24th of each Month.

Min.		
0	May	0
5	June	1
10	July	2
15	August	3
20	September	4
25	October	5
30	November	6
35	December	7
40	January	8
45	February	9
50	March	10
55	April	11
60	May	12

Arcs of Directions in the Queen's Nativity.

Aspects.	°	'	y.	m.	Aspects.	°	'	y.	m.
☉ half square Mars zod.	0	26	0	5	☽ sextile Mars zod.......	10	6	10	0
M.C. sextile Saturn ...	0	36	0	7	M.C. sextile Jupiter ...	10	33	10	5
Asc. body of Sol	0	37	0	7	M.C. sextile Mars	10	37	10	6
Pars. body of Moon ...	1	15	1	3	☽ rapt par. Herschel ..	11	8	11	0
Asc. trine Jupiter	4	16	4	3	☉ trine Jupiter zod.......	12	7	12	0
☽ half square Venus z....	5	23	5	4	M.C. quintile Mercury	12	11	12	3
Sol conjunction ☽, con.	5	26	5	4	☉ rapt par. Herschel ...	12	42	12	7
☽ conjunction Sol, d.d.	5	26	5	4	☉ sextile Mars, zod. ...	12	45	12	7
Pars. conjunction Sol.	6	37	6	6	☉ half square ♄, d.d. .	14	13	13	11
☉ half square Venus zod.	7	26	7	4	☽ half square Mercury, z.	15	6	14	9
☉ sextile Jupiter, con....	8	0	7	11	...oppositon ♅, z.	15	10	14	10
M.C. trine Mercury......	8	7	9	0	...conjunction Venus, c.	15	25	15	1
☽ trine Jupiter zod.......	9	32	9	6	Part of Fortune P. ♅...	15	39	15	4
☉ conjunction ☿ con. ...	9	52	9	9	M.C. semisquare Jupiter	15	39	15	4

Aspects.	°	'	y.	m.
☽ par. Herschel, d.d. ...	16	13	15	11
M.C. square Venus......	16	34	16	3
☽ ssq. Herschel, con. ...	16	39	16	4
M.C. sextile Venus......	17	2	16	8
☉ square Jupiter, d.d....	17	49	17	6
...opposition ♅, d.d. ...	17	55	17	7
...half square ☿, z.	18	8	17	9
...opposition ♅, z.	18	13	17	10
☽ sextile Venus, zod. ...	18	21	17	11
M.C. conjunction ♃	18	30	18	1
......square Herschel ...	18	32	18	1
Asc. opposition ♅	18	32	18	1
☽ semisquare ♄, d.d. ...	18	39	18	3
☉ par. Herschel	19	11	18	9
Part of Fortune S□♄	19	31	19	1
M.C. sextile Mars, zod.	19	42	19	3
☉ conjunction of ♀, z.	20	3	19	7
☽ square Saturn, zod....	20	36	20	1
☉ sesq. Herschel. con.	21	14	20	9
☽ square Venus, zod. ...	21	31	21	1
M.C. square Mars, mun.	21	51	21	4
Part of fortune □ Jupiter	21	58	21	5
☉ par. Herschel, zod....	22	20	21	9
☽ conjunction Mars,con.	22	53	22	4
...half square ♃, con....	23	29	22	11
...opposition ♅, d.d. ...	23	33	23	0
☉ square Saturn, zod....	23	52	23	3
☽ ssq. Jupiter, zod. ...	24	2	23	5
M.C. quintile Sol. mun.	24	16	23	7
⊕ opposition Herschel	24	47	24	2
☉ half square Mars, d.d.	25	53	25	2
M.C. sextile Mercury...	26	33	25	10
......semisquare Mars ..	26	51	26	1
......sextile Jupiter	27	2	26	3
☉ conjunction ♂ con. ...	27	8	26	4
..ssq. Jupiter zod	27	22	26	7
...half square ♃, con....	27	42	26	11
...par. Herschel zod. ...	28	33	27	10
...sextile Saturn, d.d. ..	28	42	28	0
M.C. tre. Mercury, mun.	28	56	28	2
Asc. sextile Saturn	29	35	28	10
M.C. ssq. Sol	30	15	29	5
☽ semisquare Mars, d.d.	30	49	30	0
☉ half square Sol.........	30	50	30	0
☽ sextile Venus, zod. ...	31	25	30	6
⊕ half square Mars......	31	48	30	11
☉ semisquare ♀, d.d. ..	32	49	31	11
M.C. square Sol. zod....	32	59	32	1
☽ sextile Saturn, d.d. ...	33	8	32	3
M.C. trine Mercury ...	33	27	32	7
.. ...half square Venus	33	50	32	11
⊕ sextile Saturn	34	0	33	0
☉ sextile Mercury zod.	34	37	38	7
☽ par. Herschel, con. ...	35	32	34	6
...conjunct Saturn, con.	35	38	34	7
M.C. sextile Moon	36	29	35	5
☽ trine Herschel	37	26	36	4
...semisquare ♀, d.d. ...	37	57	36	10
⊕ half square Venus ...	38	57	37	9
☉ P. Herschel, con. ...	39	8	37	11
.. conjunc. Saturn, con.	39	13	38	0
M.C. sextile Sol	39	2	38	10
☉ quintile Saturn, d.d.	40	18	39	1
Asc. square Jupiter,d.d.	40	34	39	4
☉ trine Jupiter, d.d. ...	40	34	39	4
...trine Herschel, con.	40	56	39	8
...sextile Sol, mundo ...	41	6	39	10
☽ sextile Moon, mundo	41	11	39	11
Asc. trine Jupiter	41	16	40	0
☉ sextile Mars, d.d. ...	42	7	40	10
...half square ♃ d.d. ...	42	50	41	6
Asc. sextile Mars	43	5	41	9
☽ trine Mars, zod.	43	42	42	4
M.C. half square ☿	43	53	42	6
☽ trine Jupiter, d.d.	44	3	42	8
☉ semisquare Sol, zod.	44	38	43	3
☽ Q. Saturn	44	44	43	4
⊕ trine Jupiter..........	44	44	43	4
...quintile Sol	45	36	43	4
☉ square Mars, zod. ...	46	20	44	11
☽ sextile Mars, d.d.......	47	3	45	8
☉ semisquare ☽, zod ...	46	29	46	1
⊕ sextile Mars...........	48	2	46	7
☽ semisq. Mercury, d.d.	48	8	46	8
⊕ half square Mercury	49	10	47	8
☉ sextile Venus, d.d. ...	49	37	48	2
Asc. sextile Venus	50	38	49	8
☉ sesq. Jupiter, d.d. ..	51	58	50	6
Asc. sesq. Jupiter ...	52	39	51	2
...quintile Mars	52	49	51	4
☽ rapt. par. Jupiter......	54	19	52	9
...sextile Venus, d.d. ...	54	45	53	2
☉ Q. Mars, d.d.	55	6	53	6
...rapt par. Jupiter... ..	55	15	53	8
☽ sesq. Jupiter..........	55	26	53	11
Part of Fortune ✱ ♀ ...	55	45	54	3

Aspects.	°	′	y.	m.	Aspects.	°	′	y.	m.
☉ half square Moon, d.d.	56	1	54	6	D Q. Mars, d.d.	60	2	58	6
D semisquare ☉, con. ...	56	1	54	6	☉ sextile Mercury, d.d.	60	11	58	8
⊕ ssq. Jupiter	56	7	54	7	Asc. Q. Venus	60	43	59	2
D square Venus, zod. ...	56	30	55	0	M.C. sextile Sol, zod....	60	47	49	3
☉ square Venus, zod. ..	57	12	55	8	☉ trine Saturn, zod. ...	61	10	59	7
Asc. half square Moon	57	16	55	9	Asc. sextile Mercury ...	61	14	59	8
☉ square Saturn, d.d....	57	41	56	2	D square Saturn, d.d. ...	62	7	60	7
⊕ quintile Mars	57	46	56	3	...semisquare D, mun....	62	21	60	10
☉ half square Sol, mun.	58	32	57	0	⊕ trine Saturn............	62	59	61	5
M.C. conjunction Saturn	58	33	57	0	Bq. Jupiter	62	57	61	5
Asc. square Saturn......	58	33	57	0	☉ Q. Venus, d.d..........	63	3	61	6
☉ Bq. Jupiter, d.d.	58	48	57	3	⊕ sextile Mercury	63	36	62	1
M.C. trine Herschel ...	59	33	58	0	M.C. sextile Jupiter ...	64	2	62	6
Asc. semisquare Sol ...	59	44	58	2	......Q. Venus	64	4	62	6
D trine Saturn, zod......	59	49	58	3	D sextile Mercury, d.d.	65	29	64	0
☉ par. Sol, zod.	60	2	58	6	...Q. Venus, d.d..........	68	11	66	9

LADY'S NATUS, Page 292.

R. A. 219° 4′.

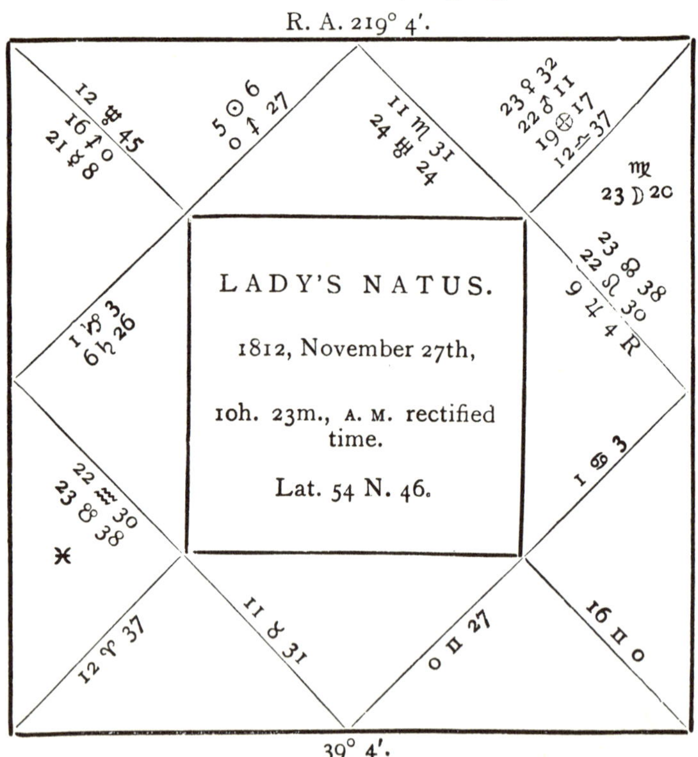

39° 4′.

Pla.	Lat.	Decli.	R. A.	M. D.	S. Arc	O.A. & O.D.	Poles.
	° ′	° ′	° ′	° ′	° ′	° ′	° ′
♅	0 N 14	18 s 40	232 5	13 1	61 25	238 A 8	17 20
♄	0 N 31	22 s 48	276 58	122 6	126 31	312 A 13	53 56
♃	0 N 31	18 N 30	131 40	87 24	118 17	152 D 34	46 50
♂	1 N 3	7 s 40	200 53	18 11	79 1	198 D 21	18 11
☉	... ...	21 s 11	243 9	24 5	56 43	257 A 16	32 11
♀	2 N 6	7 s 11	202 33	16 31	79 43	200 D 25	16 27
☿	2 s 15	25 s 24	260 10	41 6	47 45	296 A 33	51 19
☽	2 N 31	4 N 58	174 53	44 11	97 4	178 D 6	32 51
⊕	... ..	... ...	226 32	7 28	62 2	229 A 54	10 30

Arcs of Directions.

Aspects.	°	′	y.	m.	Aspects.	°	′	y.	m.
Moon ✶ Herschel, d.d.	0	2	0	0	☽ sextile of ♃, zod.......	11	27	10	7
Sun quin. Moon, zod.	0	17	0	3	Part of Fort. semisq. ☿	11	28	10	7
☽ semisquare Jupiter, z.	0	34	0	6½	☉ quintile Mars, d.d. ...	11	29	10	7
☉ sextile of Mars, d.d.	0	57	0	10½	☽ square Sun, converse.	11	40	10	9
☽ trine of Mercury, con.	1	41	1	7	☉ square Moon, d.d. ...	11	40	10	9
☉ semisquare ♂ zod. ...	2	27	2	4	☽ semisq. ♅, zod........	11	41	10	9
...sextile of Venus, d.d.	2	47	2	7	☉ semisquare Mars... ..	11	49	10	11
...sextile of Saturn, con.	3	11	3	0	...conj. Herschel, con.	12	4	11	2
Part of Fortune ✶ ☿ ...	3	31	3	4	...sextile Moon, conv.	12	6	11	2
☉ semisquare ☿, con. ...	3	37	3	5	...parallel Venus, con.	12	20	11	5
.. semisquare Venus, z.	4	3	3	10	Mid-heaven ♂ ♅	13	1	12	0
Asc. conjunction ♄, m.	4	25	4	2	☉ sextile of ☿, con. ...	13	4	12	1
☉ quintile of Moon, con.	4	32	4	3	...parallel Saturn, zod.	13	45	12	8
☽ quintile of Sun, d.d.	4	32	4	3	☽ square Mercury, d.d.	15	5	13	10
☉ trine of Jupiter, zod.	4	40	4	4	☉ parallel of Mars, d.d.	15	21	14	1
Asc. ✶ of Sun, mun. ...	5	11	4	10	Part of Fort. ✶ Saturn	15	49	14	6
Asc. conj. Saturn, zod.	5	33	5	2	Part of Fort. □ Jupiter	16	39	15	3
Part of Fort. ♂ Herschel	5	38	5	3	Part of Fort. ♂ of Sun...	17	16	15	10
Sun rapt par. of Venus	7	12	6	8	☉ parallel of Venus, d.d.	17	19	15	11
Sun rapt par. of Mars	7	25	6	10	☉ sesquisquare of ♃, z.	17	32	16	1
Sun semisquare ♀ con.	7	29	6	11	☉ semisquare ♅, d.d....	17	39	16	2
Asc. trine Mars, mun.	8	9	7	7	☽ conjunction Mars, d.d.	17	47	16	4
Sun semisq. Saturn, d.d.	8	28	7	11	Asc. semisquare ☉, zod.	17	49	16	5
Sun semisq. Mars, con.	8	47	8	2	☽ sesquisquare ☿, con.	17	51	16	5
Part of Fort. ✶ of Moon	8	50	8	3	☉ conjunction ☿, zod....	18	43	17	2
Midheaven ✶ of ☿	9	16	8	8	☉ rapt parallel Uranus	18	46	17	3
Sun square of ♃, con...	9	17	8	8	Asc. square Mars, zod.	19	6	17	6
Moon square of ♄, zod.	9	30	8	10	☽ parallel Mercury, d.d.	19	22	17	9
Asc. trine of ♀, mun....	10	3	9	4	☽ semisquare ☉, zodiac	19	29	17	10
☽ semisquare ♅, d.d....	10	16	9	6	...conjunction of ♀, d.d.	19	46	18	1
☉ quintile of ♄, con. ..	10	45	9	11	☉ sextile Mercury, zod.	19	53	18	3
☽ trine of Saturn, d.d....	10	56	10	1	Asc. trine of ☽, zodiac	19	56	18	4
☉ parallel of Mars, con.	11	2	10	2	...square Venus, zodiac	20	5	18	5

Aspects.	°	'	y.	m.
⊙ trine of Jupiter, d.d.	20	6	18	5
☽ sextile of Mercury ...	20	15	18	7
Part of Fort. parallel ♅	20	24	18	9
Midheaven ✶ ☽, mun.	20	31	18	10
⊙ quintile Jupiter, con.	20	37	18	11
⊙ quintile Mercury, con.	20	38	18	11
Asc. ✶ of Herschel, zod.	20	41	18	11
⊙ conjunction ☿, d.d....	20	50	19	1
☽ conjunction Mars, z.	21	1	19	3
⊙ square of Moon, zod.	21	12	19	5
Mid. semisqu. ♂, mun.	21	19	19	6
⊙ sextile Venus, zod....	21	25	19	7
⊙ semisquare ☽, con. ...	21	33	19	9
☽ rapt parallel Saturn...	21	38	19	10
Part of Fort. quintile ☽	21	46	19	11
☽ conjunction Venus, z.	21	55	20	1
⊙ square Saturn, con....	22	6	20	3
Midheaven ✶ Saturn, m.	22	15	20	4
☽ quintile Saturn, zod.	22	39	20	8
Midheaven semisq. ♀ m.	23	20	21	4
Asc. square Sun	24	5	22	0
Midheaven conj. ⊙	24	5	22	0
⊙ ✶ Saturn, zod. con....	24	24	22	4
☽ semisq. Venus, con....	24	28	22	4
...quintile Jupiter, zod.	24	36	22	6
Part of Fort. semisq. ♄	24	44	22	7
Part of Fort. ✶ of Mars	24	59	22	10
Asc. ✶ Mercury, mun. ..	25	11	23	0
☽ sextile ♀, zod. con. ...	25	36	23	5
... ☌ Jupiter, zod. con...	25	37	23	5
...sextile ♂, zod. con....	26	41	24	4
...semisquare ♂, con....	26	41	24	4
Part of Fort. sextile ♀	27	2	24	8
⊙ square of Mars, d.d.	27	17	24	11
☽ conjunc. Jupiter, con.	27	31	25	1
...biquintile ☿, con......	27	33	25	1
⊙ biquintile Jupiter, z.	27	36	25	2
Asc. sextile ⊙, zod ..	27	36	25	2
⊙ sextile Uranus, d.d.	27	53	25	5
sextile Jupiter, con...	28	11	25	8
Asc. semisq. Mercury..	28	13	25	9
⊙ semisquare ⊙, mun.	28	21	25	11
☽ square Saturn, d.d....	28	46	26	4
⊙ square Venus, d.d....	29	21	26	9
Asc. sesquisquare ☽, z.	29	29	26	11
☽ △ Mercury, zod. con.	29	31	26	11
Asc. opposition ♃, zod.	29	53	27	3
Asc. opposition ♃, mun.	30	53	28	3

Aspects.	°	'	y.	m.
Part of Fort. parallel ⊙	30	54	28	
☽ sextile Mercury, d.d.	31	0	28	
Asc. semisq. ♄, mun. ...	31	10	28	
☽ semisqu. Mercury, z.	31	22	28	
...sextile Saturn, zod....	31	37	28	1
⊙ sextile Jupiter, zod. c.	31	37	28	1
⊙ square Mercury, con.	31	58	29	
...quintile Mars, zod....	32	1	29	
☽ square Herschel con.	32	17	29	
...semisquare ☽, zod. ...	33	6	30	
⊙ rapt parallel Mercury	33	19	30	
Midheaven quintile ☽...	33	27	30	
Asc. trine ♅, mun.......	33	29	30	
☽ parallel Saturn, d.d.	33	33	30	
...square Jupiter, zod...	33	48	30	
Asc. quintile Sun, zod.	33	57	30	1
......biquintile ☽, zod....	34	4	31	
Midheaven ✶ ♂, mun...	34	29	31	
⊙ quintile Venus, zod..	34	32	31	
...conjunction ♄, d.d....	35	12	32	
Part of Fort. con. ☿ ...	35	21	32	
⊙ conjunction Saturn, z.	35	29	32	
Part of Fort. quin. ♂ ...	35	31	32	
⊙ sesquisquare ♃, d.d...	35	33	32	
...conjunc. Venus, con.	35	50	32	
Asc. sextile Mercury, z.	35	51	32	
......semisquare ♄ zod...	36	0	32	
⊙ quintile ♅, d.d.	36	4	32	1
Part of Fort. semisq. ♅	36	20	33	
Asc. trine Mars, zod....	36	23	33	
Midheaven sextile ♀ ...	36	37	33	
Asc. trine Venus, zod.	37	3	33	
Asc. conj. Dragon's Tail	37	6	33	
⊙ conjunction ♂, con....	37	8	33	
Asc. square ♅, z.	37	23	34	
⊙ semisquare ♃, con....	37	38	34	
Part of Fort. qu. Venus	37	40	34	
⊙ sextile Sun, mundo...	37	48	34	
☽ sextile Jupiter, d.d....	38	24	35	
...semisquare ☿, d.d. ...	38	57	35	
⊙ sextile ☿, zod. con....	39	14	35	
☽ rapt parallel Jupiter...	39	27	35	1
...quintile Saturn, d.d.	39	28	35	1
Asc. sextile Saturn, m.	40	5	36	
⊙ semisquare ♅, con....	40	25	36	
☽ sextile Venus, con. ...	40	38	36	1
⊙ square ♄, zod. con....	40	49	37	
☽ conjunction ♅, d.d....	40	58	37	

Aspects.	°	′	y.	m.
☉ trine Saturn, converse	41	0	37	3
Midheaven ♂ Mercury	41	6	37	4
Part of Fort. ☐ Moon ...	41	11	37	5
☉ rapt parallel, Saturn	41	30	37	9
...biquintile ♃, d.d.......	41	43	37	11
...semisq. ♃, zod. con...	41	43	37	11
☽ sesquisq. ☿, zod. con	41	43	37	11
Asc. square Sun, zod...	41	47	38	0
......sextile Saturn, zod.	42	19	38	6
☉ parallel Saturn, zod.	42	23	38	8
Asc. sesqui. Mars, zod.	42	47	38	11
☽ sextile Mars, con. ...	42	51	39	0
Asc. trine Sun, mundo	42	59	39	1
......sesquisq. Venus, z.	43	8	39	3
☽ semisq. Saturn zod....	43	29	39	7
Midheaven semis. ♅, m	43	43	39	9
☉ trine Moon, d d.	44	1	40	0
☽ trine Sun, con	44	1	40	0
Part of Fort. trine ♃	44	2	40	0
☉ semisq. Mercury, d.d.	44	42	40	8
... ♂ Mars, zod. con. ...	44	55	40	10
☽ sextile Moon, zod. ..	45	2	40	11
☉ quintile Sun, mundo	45	22	41	3
Part of Fort. semisq. ☉	45	37	41	6
☽ conjunction ♅, zod...	45	49	41	8
⊕ sextile Herschel	46	34	42	4
☽ sextile Saturn, d.d. ...	46	36	42	4
Asc. biquintile Venus, z.	46	36	42	4
☽ ☍ Saturn, zod. con. ...	48	3	43	8
☉ parallel Sun, mundo	48	10	43	9
...square Herschel, d.d.	48	21	43	11
☽ semisqu. Moon, mun.	48	32	44	1
Asc. oppo. Moon, zod.	48	35	44	2
......sesquisq. ♃, zodiac	48	50	44	5
☉ semisquare Sun, zod.	49	12	44	8
☽ oppo. Saturn con. ...	49	28	44	11
☉ sextile Herschel, con.	49	52	45	4
...conjunct. Moon con.	49	54	45	4
☽ conjunct. Sun, d.d....	49	54	45	4
☉ sesquisq. Saturn, con.	50	27	45	11
...trine Mercury, con.	50	52	46	4
Asc. biquintile ♅, mun.	51	4	46	6
☉ square Mars, zodiac	51	11	46	7
Part of Fort. square ♂	51	19	46	9
Midheaven △ Jupiter, m.	51	27	46	10
Part of Fort. ♂ Saturn	51	28	46	10
☉ trine Moon, zodiac	52	16	47	8
Midheaven smsq. ☉, m.	52	26	47	10
☉ square Venus, zod....	52	27	47	10
...sextile Mercury, d.d.	52	40	48	0
Asc. trine ☉, zodiac......	52	42	48	0
......oppo. Moon, mun.	52	53	48	2
☉ trine Saturn, z. con.	53	11	48	5
Asc. square Saturn, z.	53	12	48	5
☉ sextile Herschel, con.	53	14	48	6
☽ quintile Venus, con.	53	29	48	9
☉ trine Mars, d.d.	53	37	48	10
Part of Fort. ☐ Venus...	53	37	48	10
☉ parallel Mercury, con.	53	59	49	2
Asc. trine Jupiter, zod.	54	9	49	3
Part of Fort. S ☐ Jupiter	54	19	49	5
Part of Fort. quintile ♅	54	45	49	10
☽ conjunct. Sun, zodiac	55	14	50	3
...quintile Mars, con....	55	23	50	5
... ☐ Venus zod. con. ...	55	27	50	6
...semisqu. Saturn, d.d.	55	31	50	7
...parallel Saturn, con.	55	47	50	10
☉ trine Venus, d.d.......	55	55	51	0
... ☐ Mercury, zod. con.	55	55	51	0
...biquintile ♄, con......	56	7	51	2
☽ square Mars, z. con.	56	23	51	5
☉ square Sun, mundo	56	43	51	9
...rapt parallel Jupiter	56	53	51	11
☽ semisquare Mars. zod.	56	53	51	11
...rapt parallel Mars	56	57	51	11
Asc. △ Mercury, mun....	57	1	52	0
☽ semisquare Mars, d.d.	57	17	52	3
☉ quintile ♅, d.d.	57	26	52	5
Midheaven ♂ Saturn ...	57	54	53	1
☽ semisq. Venus, zod....	58	6	53	2
Asc. sesquisq. Sun, zod.	58	10	53	2
☽ rapt parallel Venus...	58	10	53	2
...trine Jupiter, zod. ...	58	33	53	7
Asc. trine Mercury, z.	58	35	53	7
☽ oppo. ☿, zod. con. ...	58	40	53	8
.. square Jupiter, d.d....	58	58	54	0
☉ quintile Mercury, d.d.	59	2	54	0
Asc. oppo. Mars, zod....	59	2	54	0
Part of Fort. S ☐ ☿ ...	59	13	54	2
Asc. oppo. Venus, zod.	59	32	54	5
☽ semisqu. Venus, d.d.	59	37	54	6
☉ sesquisquare ☿, con.	60	19	55	2
Part of Fort. biquin. ♃	60	29	55	4
Asc ☍ Mars, mundo......	60	50	55	4
......biquintile Sun, z....	61	43	56	8
Midheaven sesquisq. ♃	61	44	56	8

Aspects.	°	′	y.	m.		Aspects.	°	′	y.	m.
Midheaven sextile Sun.	61	53	56	9		☉ opposition ♃, d.d. ...	66	24	61	0
☉ semisquare ♄, d.d....	61	56	56	9		Part of Fort. □ ♅	67	2	61	7
...sesquisquare ☽, d.d....	62	9	56	11		Part of Fort. sextile ☿	67	10	61	8
☽ sesquisquare Sun, con.	62	9	56	11		☉ semisquare ♂, d.d. ...	67	37	62	1
Part of Fort. quintile ☉	62	37	57	4		...square Mercury, d.d.	68	35	63	1
☉ sextile Sun zodiac ...	62	45	57	5		...square Herschel, con.	68	46	63	3
☽ conjunction ☿, d.d....	62	50	57	6		.. trine Herschel, d.d.	68	49	63	3
...trine Herschel, con.	62	57	57	7		☽ square Venus, con. ...	70	4	64	6
...sextile Moon, mundo	63	0	57	8		...biquintile Sun, con...	70	27	64	11
Asc. oppo. Venus, mun.	63	12	57	10		☉ biquintile Moon, d.d.	70	27	64	11
☉ sesquisquare ☿, zod.	63	38	58	3		Part of Fort. trine ☽ ...	70	33	65	0
...semisquare ♀, con....	64	10	58	9		☉ sesquisq. Venus, d.d.	70	49	65	3
Part of Fort. parallel ♄	64	20	58	11		...sextile Saturn, d.d....	70	51	65	4
☽ opposition ☿, con. ...	64	26	59	0		☽ S □ Herschel, d.d. ...	71	38	66	1
...parallel Jupiter, d.d.	64	30	59	1		...square Mars, con. ...	71	58	66	6
Asc. sesquisq. ☿, zod.	64	44	59	4		Asc. sesquisq. ♄, zod ...	72	16	66	9
Asc trine Saturn, zod.	64	51	59	5		☉ biquintile Moon, zod.	72	41	67	3
Midheaven semisq. ☿ ..	64	58	59	6		Midheaven sextile ☿ ...	72	56	67	6
☉ sesquisquare, ☽, zod.	65	27	60	0		☉ sextile Venus, con....	74	7	68	6
...semisquare ♂ con. ...	65	29	60	1		☽ parallel Jupiter, con.	74	33	68	11
Asc. sesquis. ☽, zod ...	65	44	60	4		☉ sextile Mercury, zod.	75	37	70	9
☉ conjunct. ♃, con. ...	65	59	60	7		...trine Mars, zodiac ...	76	25	70	0
...biquintile ☿, con....	65	59	60	7		...trine Venus, zod.......	77	27	71	10
...opposition ♃, zod. ...	66	4	60	8		...oppo. Saturn, con. ...	78	48	73	2
Asc. square ♃, zod.......	66	4	60	8						

END OF BOOK II.

ERRATA.

PAGE.

19.—Ponderable Planets ♅, ♃, and ♂, should be ♆, ♅, ♄, ♃.

31.—No. 26, from 25 to 40 degrees should be 25 to 30 degrees.

82.—In Table head line 3, Exalt ♌ in ♊ should be ☊ in ♊.

82.—In Table head line 7, Fall, ☿ in ♑ should be ♃ in ♑.

216.—Table, head line 11, ♑ under ↑↓, should be ♌.

221.—Exercises, line 7, ☿, Ans. 11 deg. 19 min. North, should be Ans. 11 deg. 9 min. North.

238.—Problem XLVII should be XLVIII.

239.—Example, line 4, 287° 28′ should be 387° 28′.

Mathematical
and
Astronomical Tables

For the use of Students of Astro-Mathematics
Practical Astronomers, Astrologers,
and Astro-Meteorologists,

WITH AN

INTRODUCTION, CONTAINING AN EXPLANATION
AND USE OF THE TABLES.

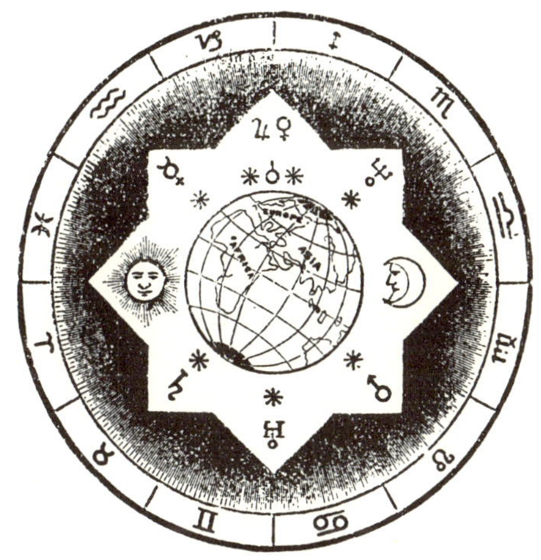

COPYRIGHT.

*"Nature, which is the timevesture of God, and reveals
Him to the wise, hides Him from the foolish."*

—CARLYLE.

LONDON :

W. FOULSHAM & CO., LTD., 10/11, RED LION COURT, FLEET STREET, E.C. 4.

TABLES

FOR

CALCULATING NATIVITIES.

INTRODUCTION.

The 1st Table is for converting CLOCK TIME into equivalent SIDEREAL TIME to find the true Right Ascension of the Meridian perpetually. To the Sidereal time at noon, given in the Ephemeris, add the Clock time and then add the amounts in the table corresponding to the Clock time, and the result will be the Sidereal time of Right Ascension of the Meridian.

Example,—Required the Right Ascension on the Meridian at 34 minutes past 10 o'clock at night, of January 27th, 1901.

	h	*m.*	*s.*
Sidereal Time, at noon, Ephemeris 1901, January 27th	20	24	17
Add the clock time	10	34	0
Add for 10 hours	0	1	39
And then add for the 34 minutes	0	0	6
	31	0	2
N.B,—When the Right Ascension, after adding, amounts to more than 24 hours, as in this example, deduct the	24	0	0
Right Ascension on the Meridian =	7	0	2

The 2nd Table is the Poles of the Houses from the Equator to 60 degrees of Latitude, and they are so simple that we need not give any examples, only say that the first column shows the Poles of the first and 7th houses, which are always the elevation of the pole, or latitude of the country; the second column shows the poles of the 3rd, 5th, 9th, and 11th houses; and the third column the poles of the 2nd, 6th, 8th and 12th houses. If the latitude of the place be anywhere between an even degree you have only to equate for the proportionate plus over the equal degree.

For example, suppose a place of birth should be 52 degrees 15 minutes, find the difference between 52 and 53 degrees; for 52 degrees the pole is 24 degrees 12 minutes, and for 53 degrees 25 degrees 5 minutes, difference 0 degree 53 minutes; hen say, by the Rule of Proportion, 60 : 53 :: 15 : 13, which add to the pole of

52 degrees 24 degrees 12 minutes, amount 24 degrees 25 minutes for the pole of the 11th and 5th, 3rd and 9th houses, under 53 degrees 15 minutes North latitude. Or work by Proportional Logarithms, Problem 23rd.

The third table is of incalculable worth in many problems; for instance, in finding the place, either in latitude, longitude, declination, right ascension, and so on, for any interval of time between the noons of any day throughout the whole year.

Example.— Required the Sun's place for 12th of March, 1849, at 20 hours 46 minutes.

Add together $\begin{cases}\text{Time required 20h. 46m. the D. Log.} \dots\dots\dots & 0629 \\ \text{Change of longitude in 24 hours, 1 degree Log.} & 1.3802\end{cases}$

$$\text{Proportional part 20h. 46m.}\quad 0°\ 52' = \quad 1.4431$$
$$\text{Sol's longitude preceding noon } 21 \Upsilon 50$$

$$\text{Sol's place 46m. past 8h. \textsc{a:m.}, March 13th} = 22\quad 42$$

Observe.—These Diurnal Logarithms will do for any number of degrees up to 24 the same as the following Proportional Logarithm.

Table 4th is for turning degrees and minutes into time, and the contrary. For instance, 4 degrees of an arc are equal to 16 minutes of time; or, 4 minutes are equal to 16 seconds of time. The Table is very simple, and needs no further examples.

Table 5th is for deducing Longitude and Latitude from the given Right Ascension and Declination of the Planets, Fixed Stars, and Comets, as given in the Nautical Almanack. In this Table the Obliquity of the Ecliptic is assumed $= 23°\ 27'$, and in most cases the difference that is caused by variations in the obliquity may be neglected; but when requisite, the changes may be thus allowed for; take the tenth of the difference of two consecutive terms, subtract 16 from it, the remainder will be the variation produced by an augmentation of $173''\ 6'''$ upon the obliquity of the ecliptic. If this quantity be diminished by its 25th part, and the remainder multiplied by o 6, we shall have the variation that corresponds to an augmentation of $100'$ to the obliquity of the ecliptic. The logarithm of the fractions are increased by 10, agreeably to the ordinary usage in Tonometrical tables. The first argument o·oo, is, therefore, really —10. Also, at the commencement, the variations of log. A being almost equal to the increments of the argument, the diff. between those two quantities is given in the two columns of the first page of the table, which are headed Ar. Diff. arithmetical comp. of the diff.

The Argument of this table is = log. Rt. Ascens. + log. cot. declin. : with this argument we take log. A. and log. B., and thus—
      Log. Tan. Longitude = Log. tan. Rt. Acs. + log. A.
      Log. Sine Latitude = Log. Sin. Declin. + log. B.

But to be more plain, excluding "Axiums," and all other ums, we institute the more philosophic rules, more philosophic because better understood than all the abbreviated symbols given in Algebraical jargon.

*When the Right Ascension is between 0 hours and 6 hours,
or between 12 and 18 hours.*

RULE.—*For the longitude*—Add together the sine of the body's
Right Ascension, when turned into degrees and minutes, and the
cotangent of its Declination, and the sum will be the Argument A,
which argument add to the tangent of Right Ascension, and the
sum will be the tangent of the Longitude required.

For the latitude—Add together the sine of the body's Declination
and the argument of log B, and the sum will be the sine of the
Planet's Latitude required.

1st N.B.—If the R.A. be North and the Declination South, read the argu
ments from the bottom of the page.

2nd N.B.—When the Argument does not exceed 0·36 the Latitude of a Planet
is of the same name as the declination.

Example.—What is the longitude and latitude of Neptune on the 1st of Jan.,
1901, whose R.A. is 5h. 49m. 14s., equal to 87° 18·5', and declination
22° 10·75' N. ?

R. Asc. 87° 18·5' sine 9·99952	Tang R. Asc. 11·32778
Declin. 22° 10·75' cota. 10·38969	Argum. A. 0·03335
Arg. A. 0·03335 = 0·38921	27 II 30 = 11·36113

Latitude.

Sine of Neptune's declination 22° 10·75' = 9·57692
Arg. of log. B   8·76118

Sine of latitude 1°S. 15' = 8·33810

*When the Right Ascension is between 6 and 12 hours, or between
18 and 24 hours.*

RULE.—Proceed as in last Rule, but instead of Sine take Co-sine
of Right Ascension, Cotangent as in the last in the declination,
and instead of the results being Tangent take Cotangent for the
Longitude required.

Example.—What is the longitude and latitude of Jupiter on the 31st of January,
1901, whose Right Ascension is 18h. 11m. 1·51s. and Declination 23° 9·4'S. ?

Right Asc. 2° 45·4' Cosine 9·99950	Cot. R.A. 11·31741
Declination 23° 9·4' Cotang. 10·36885	Arg. A. 0·03656
Arg. A. is 0·03656 = 0·36835	2 ♑ 32 = 11·35397

Sine of Jupiter's declination = 9·59467
Arg. of Log. B. = 8·07662

Sine of Jupiter's Lat. 0 N, 16 = 7·67129

When the Arguments do not fall at the equal number of Argument, take the difference between the number more and number less than the required, multiply that difference by the other figures in the Argument, and divide by 1000, and that result add or subtract as the Argument is increasing or decreasing.

Example.—In finding the Argument A. in the above example, we find the Argument A. 0·36835, now under 0·36 we find 0·39787, and opposite 0·37 we find 0·03630 the difference is 0·00157, which, multiply by 835, which are the next three figures of decimals, and divide by 1000, and the quotient is 0·00131, subtracted from 0·03787, as the Argument is decreasing, and the true Argument of 0·36835 is 0·03656.

When the Right Ascension is North and the Declination South

or vice versa.

RULE.—*For the Longitude.*—Add together the sine of the Planet's Right Ascension—when reduced from time into degrees and minutes by Table IV.—and the cotangent of Declination, and the Sum will be the Argument A, which Argument add to the tangent of Right Asc., and the sum will be the tangent of the Longitude required.

N.B.—The Argument is read from the bottom of the page.

For the Latitude.—Add together the sine of the Planet's Declination and the Argument of Log. B, and the sum will be the sine of the Planet's Latitude required.

What are the longitude and latitude of Mercury on 16th April, 1901 ?

The R.A. being 2° 4·5′ and the Dec. 1° 58 S.

2° 4.5′ sine	8·55880	Tan. R.A.	8·55909
1 58 cot.	1·46422	Arg. A.	9·73233
	10·02302	1° ♈ 7′	8·29142

Sine dec.	8·53552
Arg. B.	0·12614
Sine 2° 38 S.	8·66166

A new way of finding Latitude.

To find the Geocentric Latitude of the Planets. RULE.—Add the log. of the Planet's Rad. Vect. to the tang. of its Heliocentric latitude, from which subtract the log. of the Planet's true distance from the Earth, and the remainder will be the tang. of the Planet's Geocentric latitude.

What is the latitude of Neptune 1st January, 1901?

Tangent of Neptune heliocentric latitude is 1° 12·5′ = 8·32412
Log, of Radius Vector   ..   ..   1·47534

9·79946

Neptune's log. of true distance from the Earth   1·46117

Neptune's lat. 1 S. 15 tangent   ..   ..   ..   8·33829

This Table will also abbreviate the calculation of a correct Horoscope for any latitude by trigonometry.

Rule 1.—Add the co-sine of the oblique Ascension of the cusp of the house to the cotangent of the pole of the house, and the sum is the Log. of Argument A. To this Log. Arg. A. add the cotangent of the Oblique Ascension of the pole of the house, and the sum is the cotangent of the cusp of the house, or that point of the ecliptic which is cut by the cusp.

Rule 2.—When the Oblique Ascension falls in ♈, ♉, or ♊, or in ♑, ♒, or ♓, the Argument is found from the bottom of the page, and the Argument is taken from the first point of ♈.

Example.—What point of the Ecliptic ascends whose cusp is 31° 8′, and the pole of the house 51° 32′?

The co-sine of Obl. Asc. of the Ascendant = 31° 8′ = 9·93246
The cotangent of the Pole of the Ascen. 51 32 = 9·90009

This gives the Argument 9·52205 = 9·83255
The cotangent of Obl. Asc. of Ascen. = 31° 8′ = 10·21894

This cotangent gives 61 9 = 9·74099

Mark well.—The Ob. Asc. of ♈, ♉, and ♊ are found the same as the Ob. As. of ♎, ♏, and ♐, only taking the last signs from the first point of Libra instead of Aries in the former.

Rule 3.—When the Oblique Ascension is more than 90 degrees we subtract it from 180, and then, instead of reading Argument A from the bottom, read from the TOP, and proceed as in Rule 1.

Rule 4.—When the Oblique Ascension is in ♋, ♌, or ♍, subtract its Oblique Ascension from 180, and then proceed; but if in the opposite signs subtract from 360, and then proceed as Rule 1.

Example.—What point of the Ecliptic ascends whose cusp is 125° 38′ in latitude 51° 32′?

The Oblique Ascension is more than 90 degrees, therefore we subtract its Obl. Asc. from 180° and 54° 22′ its Obl, Asc. from the first point of Libra remains.

To the co-sine of Obl. Acs. from ♎ 54° 22′ = 9·76537
Add cotangent of Pole 51 32   9·90009

Argument A. 0·24973 = 9·66546
Add the cotang of 54 22 = 9·85540

Cotangent 38° 8′ = 10·10513

This 38° 8′ must be taken from 180, as the Oblique Ascension is taken from ♎ and the remainder is 51° 52′, and reckoning 30 degrees for each sign, we have 21° ♌ 52′ for the ascendent. Or if, instead of taking the cotangent we take the tangent of the above results, we shall have the same 51° 52′ beyond 90 degrees, as the Oblique Ascension is between 90 and 180 degrees, according to Rule 2 page 311, of the Astronomical Tables. See also paragraph 46 of those Problems.

Table V. may be applied to the Astronomical Problems 24, 32, 75, 88, and many others in Astronomy.

Use of Table VI. Proportional Logarithms. This Table is chiefly used for facilitating the method of finding any proportional number. The Table is very useful in calculations where sexagesimal divisions are employed. In finding a proportional number we have only to find the Arith. Comp. of the first term, then add it to the 2nd and 3rd terms, and the sum will be the Log. for the Answer.

Use of Table VII.—Contains the logarithmic sines, cosines, tangents, and cotangents for each degree and minute of the quadrant in the usual way. This Table is so frequently referred to that we need not give any examples, being so simply understood. Suffice it to say, that the degrees are numbered at the top of the Table in a direct order, from 0° to 44° and, at the bottom of the Table in a retrograde order, from 45° to 90°. The minutes are contained in two of the marginal columns. The minutes in the left-hand column belong to the degree at the top of the page, and those in the right-hand column belong to the degree at the bottom.

Use of Table VIII. is for easily obtaining the Oblique places of Planets for the latitude of Sheffield.

For Example.—Suppose I wish to know the Oblique Ascension of Saturn in 28° 30′ of Gemini, I look for 28 degrees, I find .... 52° 3′
For 29 degrees 53 7

The difference is   1   4 for the 1 degree or 60 minutes, then 30 minutes give the half of 1° 4′, namely, 32 minutes, which I add to 52° 3′, and the Oblique Ascension of 28° 30′ of Gemini in the latitude of Sheffield is 52° 35′.

To find the Oblique Descension for 28° ♊ 30′, look in the Tables of Right Ascension and find the difference between its Oblique Asc. and this Right Asc., which difference will be its Ascensional Difference, which from ♈ to ♎ must be added, and subtracted from ♎ to ♈.

Example—Right Ascension of 28 ♊ 30 is 88° 22'
Oblique Ascension of dit o is 52 35
____
The Ascensionai Difference is 35 47
As ♊ is in the first 6 signs I add the **A.R.** 88 22
____
See Problem 93.   The Oblique Des. of 28 ♊ 30 = 124   9
____

Table IX. contains Sexagenary Tables, serving to multiply, divide, and find out the Proportional Parts for any number under 60, very useful where all time is connected with hourly motion.

Example.— If 60° give 24°, what will 16 require?
I look for the column headed 16, and find it gives 6° 24'.

This Table is so simple that I need not give any examples. They are nearly allied in use and utility to the " Proportional Logarithms.'

Table X. contains the exact Latitude and Longitude (in Time) from Greenwich, very useful for finding the Latitude of the place of Birth, and the Latitude and Longitude of any other adjacent place to those named in the List of Latitude.   A minute of Latitude is equal to about a mile **Geographical.**

For example, Sheffield is 53 N. 25 latitude, and Rotherham is about 5 miles North of Sheffield (although it is 6 miles N.E. but not more than 5 miles direct North).   I should add the 5 miles, or 5 minutes of a degree to 53 N 25, and the amount is 53 N. 30, the latitude for Rotherham.

Table XI. shows the difference in Time for every **Ten** English Miles East or West throughout Great Britain.   Explanation.— To find the exact Longitude, or Difference in Time, between Greenwich and any other place in Britain   obtain the number of miles the given place is east or west from any town in Table X. ; then refer to the number of seconds of difference of Time in Table XI. in ten English miles in the Latitude nearest to that of the town so found ; record the number of seconds in the distance of the given place, and ADD the amount, if the town be to the east, or subtract if the town be to the west, in west Longitude, and the contrary if in east Longitude.

Example.—Find the difference of Time between Doncaster and Greenwich. Doncaster lies in about Latitude 53° N, 30, and is about 17 miles east of Sheffield. Then, as 10 miles in that latitude give 59 seconds.   17 miles by Proportional Logarithms give 100 seconds, or 1 minute 40 seconds, which subtract from the longitude of Sheffield, 6m. 0s., and you have 4m. 20s. for the longitude, or " Difference of Time." between Doncaster and Greenwich.

Table XII. is for finding the **Right Ascension** of a Planet or Star, for which enter the left-hand column of the Table, and under the sign and degree of latitude at the top of the columns, and in the angle of meeting is the Right Ascension required.

Example.—Suppose a planet to be found in 10 degrees of Aries, and to have 2 degrees North latitude ; enter this Table of R.A. with 10 degrees of Aries, in the left-hand column ; and in the angle of meeting, under 2 degrees of North latitude will be found 8° 2' for the Right Ascension thereof.   X

Example 2.—Suppose a planet is in 28≏6 with 2 degrees 24 minutes South latitude, what is its Right Ascension ?

Here 28° give, under 2° of latitude, 205° 16', and I perceive that the R.A. has moved 57 minutes from 28 to 29 degrees of Libra.   Then if 60 give 57, what will 6, the odd minutes give ?   Ans.—6 to which I add 205° 16' amount to 205° 22' for the exact 28≏6 of 2 degrees South latitude ; but we want for 24 minutes more, and I find between 2 and 3 degrees latitude, the difference is less 22 minutes. Then say, if 60 give 22, what will 24 require ?   Ans.—9 minutes, and as the Right Ascension decreases as the latitude increases, we subtract the 9 minutes from 205° 22' and leaves 205° 13' for the Right Ascension of 28≏6 with 2° 24' south latitude. Study well Problem 35 of the Arcana. (Page 227).

Table XIII. is for finding the Declination of a Star, according to its place in degrees and minutes in the signs, with any particular latitude up to 6 degrees.

This Table will also be found nearer correct than depending on the Declinations which are given in the general Ephemeres, which are " Apparent Declinations."

Example 1.—What is the declination of a planet in 27 degrees of ♌ with 4° north latitude ?   Enter the column at 27 degrees and you will find at the common angle of meeting 12° 32', the declination required.

Example 2.—What is the declination of 12° of Taurus, south latitude 4° 20' ? I find under 4 degrees of latitude and opposite 12° of longitude 11° 39', for the odd 20 minutes take the difference between the columns 4 and 5 which amounts to 57'. Then say, if 60 give 57 what will 20 give ?   Ans.—19°, which add to 11° 39' make 11° 58'.

The latitudes in these Tables go only to 6 degrees, which is the utmost any planet goes, except Venus and Mars sometimes.   When these happen, you must perceive what difference of Declination one degree of latitude creates opposite to the longitude required. For example, suppose Venus be in 20° of Virgo, with 7° of north latitude, required the difference between 5° and 6° opposite 20° of Virgo, which difference is 55'.   I subtract this from the Declination of 6°, namely, 9° 29', the difference is 8° 34' for 7° latitude in 20° of V rgo

Caution.—Care must be taken not to confuse the Latitudes and Declinations by taking the Table of South for North Latitude and *vice versa*, as is common among young beginners, and if this mistake be avoided, there is none other can happen.   Each page serves for 8 signs, 4 of them South, and 4 of them North, reading both downwards and upwards ; but the common angles of meeting for the Latitudes are the same.

The junction of the different declinations where the North ends and the South begins, is marked across the page by black lines, and should the fractional parts so happen as to be one part North and the other South, and *vice versa*, they must both be added ; the sum of these is called the difference, from which find the proportional parts for the minutes, and if they are less than the first angle's declination, subtract them from it.

Example.—What is the declination of a star in 9 degrees 10 minutes of Libra with 4 degrees north latitude? In the angle of meeting opposite 9 degrees is 0° 6′ north declination, and opposite 10° is 0° 18′ south declination, these added make 24, which is called the difference. If 60 minutes of longitude give 24 minutes what will the odd 10 minutes give? Ans.—4 minutes; which being less than the first angle's declination, 6 minutes, subtract 4 from 6 and the remainder is the true declination of 0° 2′ north. Had the number found been greater than the first angle's declination, the latter must have been subtracted from it; the remainder would have been the true declination south.

Example.—Suppose the longitude to be 9° 40′ of Libra, with 4 degrees north latitude, what is its declination? Proceed as before described—the fourth term found for the odd 40 minutes is 16 minutes, which being greateer than the 6 minutes found in the common angle the latter 6 minutes must be subtracted from it, and the remainder is the true declination 0° 10′ south.

Table XIV. contains the Ascensional Difference, for finding the Oblique Ascension and Oblique Descension of the Planets, from any Latitude or Polar Elevation, from 1 degree to 60 degrees.

Example.—Take the declination of the star or place of the Ecliptic, and enter the Table of the Ascensional Difference under the pole of the Planet, or Place of Birth, as occasion may require, and in the common angle of meeting will be found the Ascensional Difference.

Example 1.—If a star, or any part of the Ecliptic, has 16 degrees of Declination in the latitude of 53 degrees, what will be its Ascensional Difference? Look in the first column for 16 degrees, and in the next column—on the top of which is the Pole's elevation, 53 degrees—will be found 22 degrees 22 minutes for the Ascensional Difference.

Example 2.—If a star has 19 degrees 20 minutes declination in the latitude of London 51° 32′, what is the Ascensional Difference? In the common angle of meeting 19 degrees and 51 degrees, we find, as before, 25 degrees 10 minutes, and for the remaining 20 minutes of declination say, if 60′ give 1° 33′, or 93 minutes— the difference between the declination for 19 degrees and 20 minutes—what will 20 minutes give? Ans.—31 minutes—which add to the 25 degrees 10 minutes, and the amount is 25° 41′. There yet remains 32 minutes difference in the pole's elevation. We therefore say, if 60° give 59′ what will 32 minutes give? Ans.— 31 minutes—which add to the 25° 41′ make the Ascensional Difference complete 26° 12′.

A great portion of these Tables may be worked or equated mentally, or by Sexagenary Tables.

Example.—If 60 : 1° 33′ : : 20° 31′
Add 25 10

Amount for the declination = 25 41

Look in Sexagenary Tables for 32′ of a degree of the pole

Thus, if 60 : 59 : : 32 31′ 0 31

26 12

By Sexagenary Tables.

I look under 93′ for 2° minutes give 0 31′
And for the 59 see the top and side for 32 = 0 31

For the equated minutes the amount is = 1 2
The Declination of 19° 20′ = 25 10

The Answer as before = 26 12

I should recommend students to find the Ascensional Difference for the Latitudes of the Place of Birth, and the Poles of the Sun and Moon, for every nativity which they calculate, and which may be easily done by the Sexagenary Tables. Then, by that means, the Oblique Ascensions, and the Semiarcs are much facilitated. See the Tables which follow the Table of Declinations.

On some occasions the Moon's Declination will exceed 28°, the limits of the Table of Ascensional Difference; but the difference between 27° and 28° being found, and the proportion allowed for the next degree, will give the Ascensional Difference of the Moon sufficiently near.

Example.—What is the Ascensional Difference of the Moon when 28° 16′ north Declination in latitude 53°? The difference between 27° and 28° of Declination is 2° 20′, or 140 minutes. Look in the Sexagenary Table for 140 minutes, or 2° 20′, and in the common angle of meeting at 16 is the Answer, 37m. which, added to 44° 24′, the Ascensional Difference, for 28° Declination give the Ascensional Difference required; namely, 45° 1′

The Tables of Houses are very simply understood. You have only need to work as under Table I. to find the Right Ascension of the Midheaven or Meridian ; when found, look in the column headed " Time from Noon," and proceed on the columns horizontally, and you will have the degrees occupying the six eastern houses, and the opposite signs must be placed on the six western houses.

Table XV. is a " Table of Houses " for the Latitude of 53 degs. North, which will serve for all England, especially for Horary Astrology. I have given the use of Table of Houses in Problem XXV. ; but to make the explanations complete—

Suppose a child be born December 25th, 1901, at 4h. 10m. afternoon, at Nottingham, which is 53 degrees North latitude, what is the face of the heavens ?

<pre>
                                                      h. m. s
Example.—The Sun's R.A. at noon, 25th December, is 18   3 13
                   Time elapsed since noon is   4 10   0
    According to Table I. this 4h. 10m. give R.A. add 0   0 41
                                                     ───────────
</pre>

At 4h. 10m. P.M., December 25th, 1901, the R.A. of M.C. is 22 35 54

The longitude answering to this in the Tables is nearly 4 degrees of ♓ on the cusp of the 10th; 8 degrees of ♈ on the 11th house ; 27 degrees of ♉ on the 12th cusp and 9° ♋ 34′ on the Ascendant ; 25 degrees of ♋ on the 2nd house ; and 12 degrees of ♌ on the 3rd cusp—and the same degrees must be placed on the opposite house with the opposite signs.

Table XVI. is for reducing Minutes and Seconds of Time into Degrees and Minutes of Longitude, which will be a ready Table for finding the Longitude of any place from Greenwich by having the difference of time given.

For example, Sheffield is 6m behind Greenwich, and the clocks at Sheffield to be correct must be 6m behind Greenwich to be correct Solar Time.—Then I look in Table XVI. and find 6 minutes of Time give 1° 30′, which is the longitude west of Sheffield from Greenwich. The table is so simple that we need no other example. The Student must well understand the Rules.

To convert CLOCK TIME *into equivalent* SIDEREAL TIME *to find the* TRUE *Right Ascension of the Meridian* PERPETUALLY.

Clock Time.	Sidereal Time to add.		Clock Time.	Sidereal Time to add.		Clock Time.	Sidereal Time to add.
hour.	*min.*	*sec.*	*hour.*	*min.*	*sec,*	*min.*	*sec.*
1	0	10	13	2	8	4	1
2	0	20	14	2	18	10	2
3	0	30	15	2	28	16	3
4	0	39	16	2	38	22	4
5	0	49	17	2	48	28	5
6	0	59	18	2	57	34	6
7	1	9	19	3	7	40	7
8	1	19	20	3	17	46	8
9	1	29	21	3	27	52	9
10	1	39	22	3	37	58	10
11	1	48	23	3	47	60	10
12	1	58	24	3	57		

TABLE II.

Of the Poles of the Houses from the Equator to 60 *degrees of Latitude.*

Ascendant	Pole of 11 & 5 3 & 9 Houses.		Pole of 12 & 6, 2 & 8 Houses.		Ascendant.	Pole of 11 & 5, 3 & 9 Houses,		Pole of 12 & 6, 2 & 8 Houses.		Ascendant.	Pole of 11 & 5, 3 & 9 Houses.		Pole of 12 & 6, 2 & 8 Houses.	
lat.	*de.*	*m.*	*de.*	*m.*	*lat.*	*de.*	*m.*	*de.*	*m.*	*lat.*	*de.*	*m.*	*de.*	*m.*
1	0	20	0	40	22	7	42	15	7	43	17	42	32	17
2	0	40	1	20	23	8	6	15	51	44	18	19	33	14
3	1	0	2	0	24	8	29	16	35	45	18	57	34	11
4	1	20	2	40	25	8	53	17	20	46	19	37	35	10
5	1	40	3	21	26	9	18	18	5	47	20	19	36	10
6	2	1	4	1	27	9	43	18	51	48	21	2	37	10
7	2	21	4	41	28	10	8	19	37	49	21	46	38	12
8	2	41	5	21	29	10	34	20	23	50	22	33	49	15
9	3	2	6	2	30	11	0	21	10	51	23	21	40	19
10	3	22	6	42	31	11	26	21	57	London	23	48	40	53
11	3	43	7	23	32	11	54	22	46	52	24	12	41	24
12	4	4	8	4	33	12	22	23	35	53	25	5	42	30
13	4	24	8	45	34	12	50	24	23	Sheffield	25	28	42	59
14	4	46	9	27	35	13	19	25	13	54	26	1	43	39
15	5	7	10	8	36	13	49	26	4	55	26	59	44	48
16	5	28	10	50	37	14	19	26	55	56	28	1	45	59
17	5	50	11	32	38	14	51	27	46	57	29	6	47	12
18	6	12	12	15	39	15	23	28	39	58	30	15	48	27
19	6	34	12	57	40	15	56	29	32	59	31	29	49	44
20	6	57	13	40	41	16	30	30	26	60	32	48	51	4
21	7	19	12	23	42	17	5	31	21					

TABLE III.—Diurnal Logarithms.

Min.	Hour. 0	Hour. 1	Hours. 2	Hrs. 3	Hrs. 4	Hrs. 5	Hrs. 6	Hrs. 7	Hrs. 8	Hrs. 9	Hrs. 10	Hrs. 11
0	3,1584	1,3802	1,0792	9031	7781	6812	6021	5351	4771	4260	3802	3388
1	3,1584	,3730	,0756	07	63	6798	09	41	62	52	3795	82
2	2,8573	,3660	,0720	8983	45	84	5997	30	53	44	88	75
3	,6812	,3590	,0685	59	28	69	85	20	44	36	80	69
4	,5563	,3522	,0649	35	10	55	73	10	35	28	73	62
5	2,4594	1,3454	1,0614	8912	7692	6741	5961	5300	4726	4220	3766	3355
6	,3802	,3388	,0580	8888	74	26	49	5289	17	12	59	49
7	,3133	,3323	,0546	65	57	12	37	79	08	04	52	42
8	,2553	,3258	,0511	42	39	6698	25	69	4699	4196	45	36
9	,2041	,3195	,0478	19	22	84	13	59	90	88	38	29
10	2,1584	1,3133	1,0444	8796	7604	6670	5902	5249	4682	4180	3730	3323
11	,1170	,3071	,0411	73	7587	56	5890	39	73	72	23	16
12	,0792	,3010	,0378	51	70	42	78	29	64	64	16	10
13	,0444	,2950	,0345	28	52	28	66	19	55	56	09	03
14	,0122	,2891	,0313	06	35	14	55	09	46	49	02	3297
15	1,9823	1,2833	1,0280	8683	7518	6600	5843	5199	4638	4141	3695	3291
16	,9542	,2775	,0248	61	01	6587	32	89	29	33	88	84
17	,9279	,2719	,0216	39	7484	73	20	79	20	25	81	78
18	,9031	,2663	,0185	17	67	59	09	69	11	17	74	71
19	,8796	,2607	,0154	8595	51	46	5797	59	03	09	67	65
20	1,8573	1,2553	1,0122	8573	7434	6532	5786	5149	4594	4102	3660	3258
21	,8361	,2499	,0091	52	17	19	74	39	85	4094	53	52
22	,8159	,2445	,0061	30	01	05	63	29	77	86	46	46
23	,7966	,2393	,0030	09	7384	6492	52	20	68	79	39	39
24	,7782	,2341	1,0000	8487	68	78	40	10	59	71	32	33
25	1,7604	1,2289	0,9970	8466	7351	6465	5729	5100	4551	4063	3625	3227
26	,7434	,2239	,9940	45	35	51	18	5090	42	55	18	20
27	,7270	,2188	,9910	24	18	38	06	81	34	48	11	14
28	,7112	,2139	,9881	03	02	25	5695	71	25	40	04	08
29	,6960	,2090	,9852	8382	7286	12	84	61	16	32	597	01
30	1,6812	1,2041	0,9823	8361	7270	6398	5673	5051	4508	4025	590	3195
31	,6670	,1993	,9794	41	54	85	62	42	4499	17	83	89
32	,6532	,1946	,9765	20	38	72	51	32	91	10	77	83
33	,6398	,1899	,9737	00	22	59	40	23	82	02	70	76
34	,6269	,1852	,9708	8279	06	46	29	13	74	3995	63	70
35	1,6143	1,1806	0,9680	8259	7190	6333	5618	5003	4466	3987	3556	3164
36	,6021	,1761	,9652	39	74	20	07	4994	57	79	49	57
37	,5902	,1716	,9625	19	59	07	5596	84	49	72	42	51
38	,5786	,1671	,9597	8199	43	6294	85	75	40	64	35	45
39	,5673	,1627	,9570	79	28	82	74	65	32	57	29	39
40	1,5563	1,1584	0,9542	8159	7112	6269	5563	4956	4424	3949	3522	3133
41	,5456	,1540	,9515	40	7097	56	52	47	15	42	15	26
42	,5351	,1498	,9488	20	81	43	41	37	07	34	08	20
43	,5249	,1455	,9462	01	66	31	31	28	4399	27	01	14
44	,5149	,1413	,9435	8081	50	18	20	18	90	19	3495	08
45	1,5051	1,1372	0,9409	8062	7035	6205	5509	4909	4382	3912	3488	3102
46	,4956	,1331	,9383	43	20	6193	5498	00	74	05	81	3096
47	,4863	,1290	,9356	23	05	80	88	4890	65	3897	75	89
48	,4771	,1249	,9330	04	6990	68	77	81	57	90	68	83
49	,4682	,1209	,9305	7985	75	55	66	72	49	82	61	77
50	1,4594	1,1170	0,9279	7966	6960	6143	5456	4863	4341	3875	3455	3071
51	,4508	,1130	,9254	47	45	31	45	53	33	68	48	65
52	,4424	,1091	,9228	29	30	18	35	44	24	60	41	59
53	,4341	,1053	,9203	10	15	06	24	35	16	53	35	53
54	,4260	,1015	,9178	7891	00	6094	14	26	08	46	28	47
55	1,4180	1,0977	0,9153	7873	6885	6081	5403	4817	4300	3838	3421	3041
56	,4102	,0939	,9128	54	71	69	5393	08	4292	31	15	35
57	,4025	,0902	,9104	36	56	57	82	4799	84	24	08	28
58	,3949	,0865	,9079	18	41	45	72	89	76	17	01	22
59	,3875	,0828	,9055	00	27	33	61	80	68	09	3395	16

Min.	Hrs. 12	Hrs. 13	Hrs. 14	Hrs. 15	Hrs. 16	Hrs. 17	Hrs. 18	Hrs. 19	Hrs. 20	Hrs. 21	Hrs. 22	Hrs. 23
0	3010	2663	2341	2041	1761	1498	1249	1015	0792	0580	0378	0185
1	04	57	36	36	56	93	45	11	88	77	75	82
2	2998	52	30	32	52	89	41	07	85	73	71	79
3	92	46	25	27	47	85	37	03	81	70	68	75
4	86	41	20	22	43	81	34	0999	77	66	64	72
5	2980	2635	2315	2017	1738	1476	1229	0996	0774	0563	0361	0169
6	74	29	10	12	34	72	25	92	70	59	58	66
7	68	24	05	08	29	68	21	88	66	56	55	63
8	62	18	00	03	25	64	17	84	63	52	52	60
9	56	13	2295	1998	20	60	13	80	59	49	48	57
10	2950	2607	89	1993	1716	1455	1209	0977	0756	0546	0345	0153
11	45	02	84	88	11	51	05	73	52	42	42	50
12	38	2596	79	84	07	47	01	69	49	39	39	47
13	33	91	74	79	02	43	1197	65	45	35	35	44
14	27	85	69	74	1698	38	93	62	42	32	32	41
15	2921	2580	2264	1969	1694	1434	1189	0958	0738	0529	0329	0138
16	15	75	59	65	89	30	85	54	34	25	26	35
17	09	69	54	60	85	26	82	50	31	22	22	32
18	03	64	49	55	80	22	78	47	27	18	19	29
19	2897	58	44	50	76	17	74	43	24	15	16	25
20	2891	2553	2239	1946	1671	1413	1170	0939	0720	0511	0313	0122
21	85	47	34	41	67	09	66	35	17	08	09	19
22	80	42	29	36	63	05	62	32	13	05	06	16
23	74	36	23	32	58	01	58	28	09	01	03	13
24	68	31	18	27	54	1397	54	24	06	0498	00	10
25	2862	2526	2213	1922	1649	1393	1150	0920	0702	0495	0296	0107
26	56	20	08	17	45	88	46	17	0699	91	93	04
27	50	15	03	13	40	84	42	13	95	88	90	01
28	45	09	2198	08	36	80	38	09	92	85	87	0098
29	39	04	93	03	32	76	34	05	88	81	83	94
30	2833	2499	2188	1899	1627	1372	1130	0902	0685	0478	0280	0091
31	27	93	83	94	23	68	26	0898	81	74	77	88
32	21	88	78	90	19	63	23	94	78	71	74	85
33	16	83	73	85	14	59	19	91	74	68	71	82
34	10	77	68	80	10	55	15	87	70	64	67	79
35	2804	2472	2164	1875	1605	1351	1111	0883	0667	0461	0264	0076
36	2798	67	59	71	01	47	07	80	64	58	61	73
37	93	61	54	66	1597	43	03	76	60	54	58	70
38	87	56	49	62	92	39	1099	72	56	51	55	67
39	81	51	44	57	88	35	95	68	53	48	51	64
40	2775	2445	2139	1852	1584	1331	1092	0865	0649	0444	0248	0061
41	70	40	34	48	79	27	88	61	46	41	45	58
42	64	35	29	43	75	22	84	57	42	37	42	55
43	58	30	24	38	71	18	80	54	39	34	39	52
44	53	24	19	34	66	14	76	50	35	31	35	48
45	2747	2419	2114	1829	1562	1310	1072	0846	0632	0428	0232	0045
46	41	14	09	25	58	06	68	43	29	24	29	42
47	36	09	04	20	53	02	64	39	25	21	26	39
48	30	03	2099	16	49	1298	61	35	21	18	23	36
49	24	2398	95	11	45	94	57	32	18	14	20	33
50	2719	2393	2090	1806	1540	1290	1053	0828	0614	0411	0216	0030
51	13	88	85	02	36	86	49	24	11	08	13	27
52	07	82	80	1797	32	82	45	21	08	04	10	24
53	02	77	75	93	28	78	41	17	04	01	07	21
54	2696	72	70	88	24	74	37	14	01	0398	04	18
55	2691	2367	2065	1784	1519	1270	1034	0810	0597	0394	0201	0015
56	85	62	61	79	15	66	30	06	94	91	0197	12
57	79	56	56	74	10	61	26	03	90	88	94	09
58	74	51	51	70	06	57	22	0799	87	84	91	06
59	68	46	46	65	02	53	18	95	83	81	88	03

D M	H M / M S	D M	H M / M S	D M	H M / M S	D M	H M / M S	D M	H M / M S	D M	H M / M S	D M / M S / ST	M / Sec. Thi.
						For turning Degrees and Minutes into Time, and the contrary.							
1	0. 4	61	4. 4	121	8. 4	181	12. 4	241	16. 4	301	20. 4	0 15	1
2	0. 8	62	4. 8	122	8. 8	182	12. 8	242	16. 8	302	20. 8	0 30	2
3	0.12	63	4.12	123	8.12	183	12.12	243	16.12	303	20.12	0 45	3
4	0.16	64	4.16	124	8.16	184	12.16	244	16.16	304	20.16	1 0	4
5	0. 20	65	4.20	125	8.20	185	12.20	245	16.20	305	20.20	1 15	5
6	0. 24	66	4.24	126	8.24	186	12.24	246	16.24	306	20.24	1 30	6
7	0. 28	67	4.28	127	8.28	187	12.28	247	16.28	307	20.28	1 45	7
8	0. 32	68	4 32	128	8.32	188	12.32	248	16.32	308	20.32	2 0	8
9	0. 36	69	4.36	129	8.36	189	12.36	249	16.36	309	20.36	2 15	9
10	0.40	70	4.40	130	8.40	190	12.40	250	16.40	310	20.40	2 30	10
11	0.44	71	4.44	131	8.44	191	12.44	251	16.44	311	20.44	2 45	11
12	0.48	72	4.48	132	8.48	192	12.48	252	16.48	312	20.48	3 0	12
13	0.52	73	4.52	133	8.52	193	12 52	253	16.52	313	20.52	3 15	13
14	0.56	74	4.56	134	8.56	194	12.56	254	16.56	314	20.56	3 30	14
15	1. 0	75	5. 0	135	9. 0	195	13. 0	255	17. 0	315	21. 0	3 45	15
16	1. 4	76	5. 4	136	9. 4	196	13. 4	256	17. 4	316	21. 4	4 0	16
17	1. 8	77	5. 8	137	9. 8	197	13. 8	257	17. 8	317	21. 8	4 15	17
18	1.12	78	5.12	138	9.12	198	13.12	258	17.12	318	21.12	4 30	18
19	1.16	79	5.16	139	9.16	199	13.16	259	17.16	319	21.16	4 45	19
20	1.20	80	5.20	140	9.20	200	13.20	260	17.20	320	21.20	5 0	20
21	1.24	81	5.24	141	9.24	201	13.24	261	17.24	321	21.24	5 15	21
22	1.28	82	5.28	142	9.28	202	13.28	262	17.28	322	21.28	5 30	22
23	1.32	83	5.32	143	9.32	203	13.32	263	17.32	323	21.32	5 45	23
24	1.36	84	5.36	144	9.36	204	13.36	264	17.36	324	21.36	6 0	24
25	1.40	85	5.40	145	9.40	205	13.40	265	17.40	325	21.40	6 15	25
26	1.44	86	5.44	146	9.44	206	13.44	266	17.44	326	21.44	6 30	26
27	1.48	87	5.48	147	9.48	207	13.48	267	17.48	327	21.48	6 45	27
28	1.52	88	5.52	148	9.52	208	13.52	268	17.52	328	21.52	7 0	28
29	1.56	89	5.56	149	9.56	209	13.56	269	17.56	329	21.56	7 15	29
30	2. 0	90	6. 0	150	10. 0	210	14. 0	270	18. 0	330	22. 0	7 30	30
31	2. 4	91	6. 4	151	10. 4	211	14. 4	271	18. 4	331	22. 4	7 45	31
32	2. 8	92	6. 8	152	10. 8	212	14. 8	272	18. 8	332	22. 8	8 0	32
33	2.12	93	6.12	153	10.12	213	14.12	273	18.12	333	22.12	8 15	33
34	2.16	94	6.16	154	10.16	214	14.16	274	18.16	334	22.16	8 30	34
35	2.20	95	6.20	155	10.20	215	14.20	275	18.20	335	22.20	8 45	35
36	2.24	96	6.24	156	10.24	216	14.24	276	18.24	336	22.24	9 0	36
37	2.28	97	6.28	157	10.28	217	14.28	277	18.28	337	22.28	9 15	37
38	2.32	98	6.32	158	10.32	218	14.32	278	18.32	338	22.32	9 30	38
39	2.36	99	6.36	159	10.36	219	14.36	279	18.36	339	22.36	9 45	39
40	2.40	100	6.40	160	10.40	220	14.40	280	18.40	340	22.40	10 0	40
41	2.44	101	6.44	161	10.44	221	14.44	281	18.44	341	22.44	10 15	41
42	2.48	102	6.48	162	10.48	222	14.48	282	18.48	342	22.48	10 30	42
43	2.52	103	6.52	163	10.52	223	14.52	283	18.52	343	22.52	10 45	43
44	2.56	104	6.56	164	10.56	224	14.56	284	18.56	344	22.56	11 0	44
45	3. 0	105	7. 0	165	11. 0	225	15. 0	285	19. 0	345	23. 0	11 15	45
46	3. 4	106	7. 4	166	11. 4	226	15. 4	286	19. 4	346	23. 4	11 30	46
47	3. 8	107	7. 8	167	11. 8	227	15. 8	287	19. 8	347	23. 8	11 45	47
48	3.12	108	7.12	168	11.12	228	15.12	288	19.12	348	23.12	12 0	48
49	3.16	109	7.16	169	11.16	229	15.16	289	19.16	349	23.16	12 15	49
50	3.20	110	7.20	170	11.20	230	15.20	290	19.20	350	23.20	12 30	50
51	3.24	111	7.24	171	11.24	231	15.24	291	19.24	351	23.24	12 45	51
52	3.28	112	7.28	172	11.28	232	15.28	292	19.28	352	23.28	13 0	52
53	3.32	113	7.32	173	11.32	233	15.32	293	19.32	353	23.32	13 15	53
54	3.36	114	7.36	174	11.36	234	15.36	294	19.36	354	23.36	13 30	54
55	3.40	115	7.40	175	11.40	235	15.40	295	19.40	355	23.40	13 45	55
56	3 44	116	7.44	176	11.44	236	15.44	296	19.44	356	23.44	14 0	56
57	3.48	117	7.48	177	11.48	237	15.48	297	19.48	357	23.48	14 15	57
58	3.52	118	7.52	178	11.52	238	15.52	298	19.52	358	23.52	14 30	58
59	3.56	119	7.56	179	11.56	239	15.56	299	19.56	359	23.56	14 45	59
60	4. 0	120	8. 0	180	12. 0	240	16. 0	300	20. 0	360	24. 0	15 0	60

For Deducing Longitude and Latitude from Right Ascension and Declination.

Arg.	Log. A.	Log. B.		Arg.	Log. A.	Log. B.	
0.00	9.59983	9.96256	10.00	8.38	1.24321	9.95801	1.62
1.00	8.59983	56	9.00	39	23378	791	61
2.00	7.59983	56	8.00	8.40	1.22428	9.95781	1.60
3.00	6.59983	56	7.00	41	21483	70	59
4.00	5 59983	56	6.00	42	20540	5S	58
5.00	4 59984	56	5.00	43	19598	46	57
6.00	3.59993	54	4.00	44	18657	35	56
7.00	2.60083	37	3.00	8.45	1.17717	9.95722	1.55
10	50109	32	2.90	46	16779	10	54
20	40141	26	80	47	15842	697	53
30	30182	18	70	48	14906	84	52
40	20234	08	60	49	13972	71	51
7.50	2 10298	9.96196	2.50	8.50	1.13039	9 95657	1.50
60	00379	81	40	51	12108	43	49
70	1.90482	61	30	52	11178	28	48
80	80610	37	20	53	10259	13	47
90	70771	06	10	54	09322	598	46
8.00	1.60973	9.96067	2.00	8.55	1.08397	9.95582	1.45
8.01	59996	62	1.99	56	07474	66	44
02	59019	58	98	57	06552	50	43
03	58043	53	97	58	05631	33	42
04	57067	48	96	59	04713	16	41
8.05	1.56092	9.96044	1.95	8.60	1.03796	9.95499	1.40
06	55118	39	94	61	02881	81	39
07	54144	34	93	62	01968	63	38
08	53171	28	92	63	01056	44	37
09	52198	23	91	64	00147	25	36
8.10	1.51226	9.96018	1.90	8.65	0 99239	9.95406	1.35
11	50254	12	89	66	98333	9.95386	34
12	49283	06	88	67	97429	65	33
13	48313	01	87	68	96528	44	32
14	47344	9.95965	86	69	95628	23	31
8.15	1.46375	9.95989	1.85	8.70	0.94731	9.95301	1.30
16	45407	82	84	71	93835	9.95278	29
17	44440	76	83	72	92942	55	28
18	43473	70	82	73	92051	32	27
19	42507	63	81	74	91162	08	26
8.20	1.41542	9.95956	1.80	8.75	0.90276	9.95184	1.25
21	40577	49	79	76	89383	59	24
22	39613	42	78	77	88511	33	23
23	38651	34	77	78	87632	07	22
24	37689	27	76	79	86755	9.95080	21
8.25	1.36728	9.95919	1.75	8.80	0.85881	9.95052	1.20
26	35768	11	74	81	85009	23	19
27	34809	03	73	82	84140	9.94994	18
28	33850	9.95895	72	83	83274	64	17
29	32892	87	71	84	82414	33	16
8.30	1.31936	9.95878	1.70	8.85	0.81549	9.94902	1.15
31	30980	69	69	86	80690	9.94870	14
32	30026	60	68	87	79835	37	13
33	29073	51	67	88	78982	03	12
34	28120	41	66	89	78132	9.94768	11
8.35	1.27169	9.95832	1.65	8.90	0.77285	9.94733	1.10
36	26219	22	64	91	76442	697	09
37	25269	11	63	92	75601	660	08
38	1.24321	9.95801	62	93	0.74764	9.94623	07
	Log. B.	Log. A.	Arg.		Log. B.	Log. A.	Arg.

Deducing Longitude and Latitude from Right Ascension and Declination.

Arg.	Log. A.	Log. B.		Arg.	Log. A.	Log. B.	
8.93	0 74764	9.94623	1.07	9.47	0.35523	9.90308	0.53
94	73930	584	06	48	34931	159	52
8.95	0.73098	9.94544	1.05	49	34344	9.90006	51
96	72270	504	04	9.50	0.33762	9.89849	0.50
97	71445	462	03	51	33186	688	49
98	70624	419	02	52	32616	523	48
99	69807	375	01	53	32052	353	47
9.00	0.68992	9.94330	1.00	54	31494	178	46
01	68181	285	0.99	9.55	0.30941	9.88998	0.45
02	67374	239	98	56	30393	813	44
03	66570	191	97	57	29851	623	43
04	65770	141	96	58	29315	428	42
9.05	0.64974	9.94090	0.05	59	28786	228	41
06	64181	038	94	9.60	0.28263	9.88023	0.40
07	63392	9.93984	93	61	27745	9.87812	39
08	62607	929	92	62	27233	595	38
09	61826	873	91	63	26726	371	37
9.10	0.61049	9.93816	0.90	64	26224	141	36
11	60276	757	89	9.65	0.25727	9.86904	0.35
12	59507	697	88	66	25237	660	34
13	58742	636	87	67	24753	409	33
14	57981	574	86	68	24275	150	32
9.15	0.57225	9.93510	0.85	69	23803	9.85884	31
16	56473	444	84	9.70	0 23336	9.85610	0.30
17	55725	376	83	71	22875	328	29
18	54982	307	82	72	22420	9.84037	28
19	54243	236	81	73	21970	737	27
9.20	0.53508	9.93163	0.80	74	21526	429	26
21	52778	088	79	9.75	0.21087	9.84112	0.25
22	52053	93011	78	76	20654	83785	24
23	51332	932	77	77	20227	448	23
24	50615	852	76	78	19806	100	22
9.25	0.49903	9.92770	0.75	79	19390	82740	21
26	49196	686	74	9.80	0.18980	9.82368	0.20
27	48494	599	73	81	18575	81984	19
28	47797	510	72	82	18176	1581	18
29	47105	419	71	83	17782	1173	17
9.30	0.46417	9.92325	0 70	84	17394	0751	16
31	45734	229	69	9.85	0.17012	9.80325	0.15
32	45056	131	68	86	16635	79874	14
33	44384	030	67	87	16263	407	13
34	43717	91926	66	88	15897	78924	12
9.35	0 43055	9.91820	0.65	89	15534	525	11
36	42398	711	64	9.90	0.15180	9,77910	0.10
37	41746	599	63	91	14829	376	09
38	41099	484	62	92	14484	76822	08
39	40458	367	61	93	14144	247	07
9.40	0.39823	9.91247	0.60	94	13809	75650	06
41	39192	123	59	9.95	0.13479	9 75030	0 05
42	38566	90996	58	96	13154	74386	04
43	37946	865	57	97	12834	73717	03
44	37332	730	56	98	12519	73023	02
9.45	0.36724	9.90593	0.55	99	12209	72303	01
46	36121	452	54	0.00	0.11904	9 71555	0.00
47	35523	308	53	0.01	0.11604	9.70773	9 99
	Log. B.	Log. A.	Arg.		Log. B.	Log. A.	Arg.

For Deducing Longitude and Latitude from Right Ascension and Declination.

Arg.	Log. A.	Log. B.		Arg.	Log. A.	Log. B.	
0.01	0.11604	9.70773	9.99	0.56	0.01157	9.72219	9.44
02	11309	69958	98	57	052	74905	43
03	11018	69108	97	58	00949	77494	42
04	10732	68221	96	59	847	79990	41
0.05	0.10451	9.67293	9.95	0.60	0.00748	9.82404	9.40
06	10175	66323	94	61	651	84747	39
07	09903	65307	93	62	555	87012	38
08	636	64243	92	63	462	89218	37
09	373	63126	91	64	371	91365	36
0.10	0 09114	9.61953	9 90	0.65	0.00282	9 93458	9.35
11	0s860	60719	89	66	194	95499	34
12	610	59419	88	67	108	97494	33
13	365	58046	87	68	0.00024	9.99445	32
14	124	56595	86	69	9.99941	0.01354	31
0.15	0.07887	9.55058	9.85	0.70	861	0.03224	9.30
16	654	53427	84	71	782	05058	29
17	425	51693	83	72	705	06858	28
18	200	49843	82	73	630	08626	27
19	06980	47865	81	74	556	10362	26
0 20	0.06763	9.45742	9.80	0.75	9.99483	0.12071	9.25
21	550	43458	79	76	412	13753	24
22	341	40989	78	77	343	15408	23
23	135	38309	77	78	275	17040	22
24	05934	35383	76	79	209	18648	21
0.25	0.05736	9.32170	9.75	0.80	9.99144	0.20234	9.20
26	542	28614	74	81	080	21798	19
27	351	24648	73	82	018	23344	18
28	164	20176	72	83	98957	24871	17
29	04980	15067	71	84	897	26380	16
0.30	0.04800	9.09129	9.70	0.85	9.98839	0.27872	9.15
31	623	9.02080	69	86	782	29347	14
32	450	8.93435	68	87	726	30806	13
33	279	8.82353	67	88	671	32250	12
34	112	8.67018	66	89	617	33680	11
0.35	0.03948	8.42349	9.65	0.90	9.98565	0.35095	9.10
36	787	7.76022	64	91	514	36497	09
37	630	8.18988	63	92	464	37887	08
38	475	8.57068	62	93	415	39264	07
39	323	8.77413	61	94	367	40630	06
0.40	0.03175	8.91485	9.60	0.95	9.98320	0.41984	9.05
41	029	9.02315	59	96	274	43327	04
42	02886	11162	58	97	229	44660	03
43	746	18667	57	98	185	45983	02
44	608	25198	56	99	142	47297	01
0.45	0.02473	9.30998	9.55	1.00	9.98101	0.48601	9.00
46	342	36229	54	01	060	49896	8 99
47	212	40997	53	02	020	51183	98
48	085	45390	52	03	97981	52462	97
49	01261	49466	51	04	942	53732	96
0.50	0.01839	9.53277	9.50	1.05	9.97904	0.54994	8.95
51	719	56860	49	06	867	56249	94
52	602	60241	48	07	831	57497	93
53	487	63450	47	08	796	58738	92
54	375	66504	46	09	762	59971	91
0.55	265	9.69422	45	1.10	728	0.61198	8.90
0 56	0.01157	9.72219	9.44	1.11	9 97695	0.62420	8.89
	Log. B.	Log. A.	Arg.		Log. B.	Log. A.	Arg.

TABLE V. *(Continued.)*

For Deducing Longitude and Latitude from Right Ascension and Declination.

Arg.	Log A.	Log. B.		Arg.	Log. A.	Log. B.	
1.11	9.97695	0.62420	8.89	1.64	9.96686	1.21627	8.36
12	662	63636	88	1.65	9.96676	1.22682	8 35
13	631	64845	87	66	66	23736	34
14	600	66048	86	67	57	24788	33
1.15	9.97570	0 67245	8.85	68	48	25839	32
16	541	68437	84	69	39	26889	31
17	512	69624	83	1.70	9.96630	1 27938	8.30
18	484	70806	82	71	22	28986	29
19	456	71983	81	72	14	30033	28
1.20	9.97429	0.73156	8.80	73	606	31078	27
21	403	74325	79	74	598	32122	26
22	377	75489	78	1.75	9 96590	1.33165	8.25
23	352	76648	77	76	82	34208	24
24	327	77803	76	77	74	35249	23
1.25	9.97303	0 75953	8.75	78	67	36289	22
26	279	80099	74	79	60	37328	21
27	256	81242	73	1.80	9 96553	1.38366	8.20
28	234	82382	72	81	46	39403	19
29	212	83518	71	82	39	40439	18
1.30	9 97190	0.84651	8.70	83	33	41475	17
31	169	85780	69	84	27	42510	16
32	149	86906	68	1.85	9.96521	1.43544	8.15
33	129	88028	67	86	15	44577	14
34	109	89147	66	87	09	45610	13
1.35	9 97090	0.90263	8.65	88	503	46642	12
36	071	91376	64	89	497	47673	11
37	053	92487	63	1.90	9 96492	1.48703	8.10
38	034	93595	62	91	87	49733	09
39	019	94700	61	92	82	50762	08
1.40	9.97000	0.95802	8.60	93	77	51790	07
41	83	96902	59	94	72	52817	06
42	66	97999	58	1.95	9.96467	1.53845	8.05
43	50	99094	57	96	62	54870	04
44	34	1.00186	56	97	57	55895	03
1.45	9.96919	1 01276	8.55	98	52	56920	02
46	904	02363	54	99	48	57945	01
47	889	03449	53	2.00	9.96444	1.58970	8.00
48	75	04533	52	10	01	69180	7.90
49	62	05615	51	20	370	79346	80
1.50	9.96848	1.06695	8.50	30	50	89468	70
51	35	07773	49	40	31	99582	60
52	22	08849	48	2.50	9.96315	2.09666	7.50
53	09	09823	47	60	303	19730	40
54	796	10995	46	70	293	29794	30
1.55	9.96784	1.12065	8.45	80	85	39824	20
56	72	13134	44	90	79	49856	10
57	60	14202	43	3.00	9.96274	2 59882	7.00
58	49	15267	42	4.00	58	3.59983	6.00
59	38	16331	41	5.00	56	4.59982	5.00
1.60	9.96727	1.17393	8.40	6.00	56	5.59983	4.00
61	16	18454	39	7.00	9.96256	6.59983	3.00
62	06	19513	38	8,00	56	7.59883	2.00
63	696	20571	37	9.00	56	8 59983	1.00
64	9.96686	21627	8.36	10.00	9.96256	9.59983	0.00
	Log. B.	Log. A.	Arg.		Log. B.	Log. A.	Arg.

" s	h. m. 0'	h. m. 1'	h. m 2'	h. m. 3'	h. m. 4'	h. m. 5'	h. m. 6'	h. m. 7'	h. m. 8'	h. m. 9'
0		2.25527	1.95424	1.77815	1 65321	1.55630	1.47712	1.41017	1.35218	1.30103
1	4.03342	24809	064	575	141	486	592	40914	128	023
2	3.73239	24103	94706	335	64961	342	472	811	038	29942
3	55630	23408	352	097	782	198	352	708	34948	862
4	43136	22724	000	76861	603	055	232	606	858	782
5	33445	22051	93651	625	426	54912	113	503	768	703
6	25527	21388	305	391	249	770	46994	401	679	623
7	18833	20735	92962	158	073	629	876	300	589	544
8	13033	20091	621	75927	63897	487	758	198	500	464
9	07918	19457	283	696	722	347	640	097	411	385
10	3.03342	2.18833	1.91948	1.75467	1.63543	1.54206	1.46522	1.39996	1.34323	1.29306
11	2.99203	18217	615	239	375	066	405	895	234	227
12	95424	17609	285	012	202	53927	288	794	146	148
13	91948	17010	90957	74787	030	788	171	694	058	070
14	88730	16419	632	562	62859	649	055	593	33970	28991
15	85733	15836	309	339	688	511	45939	493	882	913
16	82930	15261	89988	117	518	374	824	394	794	835
17	80297	14693	670	73896	349	236	708	294	707	757
18	77815	14133	354	676	180	100	593	195	619	679
19	75467	13580	041	457	012	52963	478	096	532	601
20	2.73239	2.13033	1.88730	1.73239	1.61845	1.52827	1.45364	1.38997	1.33445	1.28524
21	71120	12494	420	023	678	692	250	899	359	446
22	69100	11961	114	72807	512	557	136	800	272	369
23	67170	11435	87809	593	347	422	022	702	186	292
24	65321	10914	506	379	182	288	44909	604	099	215
25	63548	10400	206	167	018	154	796	506	013	138
26	61845	09893	86907	71956	60854	021	684	409	32927	061
27	60206	09390	611	745	691	51888	571	312	842	27984
28	58627	08894	316	536	529	755	459	215	756	908
29	57103	08403	024	328	367	623	347	118	671	831
30	2.55630	2.07918	1.85733	1.71120	1.60206	1.51491	1.44236	1.38021	1.32585	1.27755
31	54200	7438	445	70914	045	360	125	37925	500	679
32	52827	6964	158	709	59885	229	014	829	415	603
33	51491	6494	84873	504	726	098	43903	733	331	527
34	50194	6030	590	301	567	50968	793	637	246	451
35	48936	5570	309	099	409	838	683	541	162	376
36	47712	5115	030	69897	251	708	573	446	077	300
37	46522	4665	83752	696	094	579	463	351	31993	225
38	45364	4220	477	497	58938	451	354	256	909	150
39	44236	3779	203	298	782	322	245	161	826	075
40	2.43136	2.03342	1.82930	1.69100	1.58627	1.50194	1.43136	1.37067	1.31742	1.27000
41	42064	2910	660	68903	472	067	028	36972	659	26925
42	41017	2482	391	707	317	49940	42920	878	575	850
43	39996	2060	124	512	164	813	812	784	492	776
44	38997	1639	81858	318	011	687	704	691	409	701
45	38021	1223	594	124	57858	560	597	597	326	627
46	37067	0812	332	67932	706	435	490	504	244	553
47	36133	0404	071	740	554	309	383	411	161	479
48	35218	0000	80811	549	403	184	276	318	079	405
49	34323	1.99600	554	359	253	060	170	225	30997	331
50	2.33445	1.99203	1.80297	1.67170	1.57103	1.48936	1.42064	1.36133	1.30915	1.26257
51	32585	8810	043	981	56953	812	41958	040	833	184
52	31742	8421	79790	794	804	688	853	35948	751	110
53	30915	8035	538	607	656	565	747	856	670	037
54	30103	7652	287	421	508	442	642	765	588	25964
55	29306	7273	039	236	360	320	538	673	507	891
56	28524	6897	78791	051	213	197	433	582	426	818
57	27755	6524	545	65868	067	076	329	491	345	745
58	27000	6154	300	685	55921	47954	225	400	264	672
59	26257	5788	057	503	775	833	121	309	183	600
	0	1	2	3	4	5	6	7	8	9

'' s	h. m. 10'	h. m. 11'	h. m. 12'	h. m. 13'	h. m. 14'	h. m. 15'	h. m. 16'	h. m. 17'	h. m. 18'	h. m. 19'
0	1.25527	1.21388	1.17609	1.14133	1.10914	1.07918	1.05115	1.02482	1.00000	0.97652
1	455	322	549	077	863	870	070	440	0.99960	614
2	383	257	489	022	811	822	025	397	920	576
3	311	191	429	13966	760	774	04980	355	880	538
4	239	126	369	911	708	726	935	312	839	500
5	167	060	309	855	657	678	890	270	799	462
6	095	20995	249	800	05	630	845	228	759	424
7	024	930	189	745	554	582	800	185	719	386
8	24952	865	129	690	503	534	755	143	679	348
9	881	800	070	635	452	486	710	101	640	310
10	1.24809	1.20735	1,17010	1.13580	1.10400	1.07438	1.04665	1.02059	0.99600	0.97273
11	738	670	16951	525	349	391	620	017	560	235
12	667	605	891	470	298	343	576	01974	520	197
13	596	541	832	415	247	295	531	932	480	159
14	526	476	773	360	197	248	486	890	441	122
15	455	412	714	306	146	200	442	848	401	084
16	384	348	655	251	095	153	397	806	361	047
17	314	284	596	197	044	105	353	764	322	009
18	244	219	537	142	09994	058	308	723	282	96972
19	173	155	478	088	943	011	264	681	243	934
20	1.24103	1.20091	1.16419	1.13033	1.09893	1.06964	1.04220	1.01639	0.99203	0.96897
21	033	028	361	12979	842	916	175	597	164	859
22	23963	19964	302	925	792	869	131	556	124	822
23	894	900	243	871	741	822	087	514	085	784
24	824	837	185	817	691	775	043	472	045	747
25	754	773	127	763	641	728	03999	431	006	710
26	685	710	068	709	591	631	955	389	98967	673
27	616	647	010	655	540	634	911	348	928	635
28	546	584	15952	601	490	588	867	306	888	598
29	477	520	894	548	440	541	823	265	849	561
30	1.23408	1.19457	1.15836	1.12494	1.09390	1.06494	1.03779	1.01223	0.98810	0.96524
31	339	395	778	440	341	447	735	182	771	487
32	271	332	721	387	291	401	691	141	732	450
33	202	269	663	333	241	354	647	100	693	413
34	133	206	605	280	191	308	604	058	654	376
35	065	144	548	227	142	261	560	017	615	339
36	22997	081	490	173	092	215	516	00976	576	302
37	928	019	433	120	042	168	473	935	537	365
38	860	18957	375	067	08993	122	429	894	498	228
39	792	895	318	014	943	076	386	853	459	191
40	1.22724	1.18833	1.15261	1.11961	1.08894	1.06030	1.03342	1.00812	0.98421	0.96154
41	657	771	204	908	845	05983	299	771	382	117
42	589	709	147	855	796	937	256	730	343	081
43	521	647	090	802	746	891	212	689	304	044
44	454	585	033	750	697	845	169	648	266	007
45	386	523	14976	697	648	799	126	607	227	95971
46	319	462	919	644	599	753	083	567	189	934
47	252	400	863	592	550	707	039	526	150	897
48	185	339	806	539	501	662	02996	485	111	861
49	118	278	750	487	452	616	953	445	073	824
50	1.22051	1.18217	1.14693	1.11435	1.08403	1.05570	1.02910	1.00404	0.98035	0 95788
51	21984	155	637	382	355	524	867	363	996	751
52	918	094	581	330	306	479	824	323	958	715
53	851	033	524	278	257	433	781	282	919	678
54	785	17973	468	226	209	388	739	242	881	642
55	718	912	412	174	160	342	696	202	843	606
56	652	851	356	122	112	297	653	161	805	569
57	586	790	300	070	063	251	610	121	766	533
58	520	730	244	018	015	206	568	080	728	497
59	454	669	189	0966	07966	161	525	040	690	460
	10	11	12	13	14	15	16	17	18	19

'' s	h. m. 20'	h. m. 21'	h. m. 22'	h. m. 23'	h. m. 24'	h. m. 25'	h. m. 26'	h. m. 27'	h. m. 28'	h. m. 29'
0	95424	93305	91285	89354	87506	85733	84030	82391	80811	79287
1	388	271	252	323	476	704	002	364	786	262
2	352	236	219	292	446	675	83974	337	760	238
3	316	202	186	260	416	646	946	311	734	213
4	280	168	154	229	386	618	919	284	708	188
5	244	133	121	197	356	589	891	257	682	163
6	208	099	088	166	326	560	863	230	657	138
7	172	065	055	135	296	531	835	204	631	113
8	136	030	023	103	266	502	808	177	605	088
9	100	92996	90990	072	236	473	780	150	579	063
10	95064	92962	90957	89041	87206	85445	83752	82124	80554	79039
11	028	928	925	010	176	416	725	097	528	014
12	94992	894	892	88978	146	387	697	070	502	78989
13	956	860	859	947	116	358	670	044	477	964
14	921	825	827	916	086	330	642	017	451	939
15	885	791	794	885	056	301	614	81991	425	915
16	849	757	762	854	026	272	587	964	400	890
17	813	723	729	823	86996	244	559	938	374	865
18	778	689	697	792	967	215	532	911	349	840
19	742	655	664	761	937	187	504	884	323	816
20	94706	92621	90632	88730	86907	85158	83477	81858	80297	78791
21	671	587	599	699	877	129	449	832	272	766
22	635	554	567	668	848	101	422	805	246	742
23	600	520	535	637	818	072	394	779	221	717
24	564	486	502	606	788	044	367	752	195	693
25	529	452	470	575	759	015	339	726	170	668
26	493	418	438	544	729	4987	312	699	144	643
27	458	385	406	513	699	958	285	673	119	619
28	423	351	373	482	670	930	257	647	094	594
29	387	317	341	451	640	902	230	620	068	570
30	94352	92283	90309	88420	86611	84873	83203	81594	80043	78545
31	317	250	277	390	581	845	175	568	017	521
32	281	216	245	359	552	816	148	541	79992	496
33	246	183	213	328	522	788	121	515	967	472
34	211	149	181	297	493	760	094	489	941	447
35	176	115	148	267	463	732	066	463	916	423
36	141	082	116	236	434	703	039	436	891	398
37	105	048	084	205	404	675	012	410	865	374
38	070	015	052	175	375	647	82985	384	840	349
39	035	91981	020	144	346	619	958	358	815	325
40	94000	91948	89988	88114	86316	84590	82930	81332	79790	78300
41	93965	915	957	083	287	562	903	305	764	276
42	930	881	925	052	258	534	876	279	739	252
43	895	848	893	022	228	506	849	253	714	227
44	860	815	861	87991	199	478	822	227	689	203
45	825	781	829	961	170	450	795	201	663	179
46	791	748	797	930	140	421	768	175	638	154
47	756	715	766	900	111	393	741	149	613	130
48	721	682	734	870	082	365	714	123	588	106
49	686	648	702	839	053	337	687	097	563	081
50	93651	91615	89670	87809	86024	84309	82660	81071	79538	78057
51	617	582	639	778	85995	281	633	045	513	033
52	582	549	607	748	965	253	606	019	488	009
53	547	516	575	718	936	225	579	80993	463	77984
54	513	483	544	687	907	197	552	967	437	960
55	478	450	512	657	878	169	525	941	412	936
56	443	417	481	627	849	141	498	915	387	912
57	409	384	449	597	820	114	471	889	362	888
58	374	351	417	566	791	086	445	863	337	863
59	340	318	386	536	762	058	418	837	312	839
	20	21	22	23	24	25	26	27	28	29

s	30'	31'	32'	33'	34'	35'	36'	37'	38'	39'
0	77815	76391	75012	73676	72379	71120	69897	68707	67549	66421
1	791	368	74990	654	358	100	877	688	530	402
2	767	344	967	632	337	079	857	668	511	384
3	743	321	944	610	316	058	837	648	492	365
4	719	298	922	588	294	038	817	629	473	347
5	695	274	899	566	273	017	797	609	454	328
6	671	251	877	544	252	70997	777	590	435	310
7	647	228	854	523	231	976	756	570	416	291
8	623	205	832	501	209	955	736	551	397	273
9	599	181	809	479	188	935	716	531	378	254
10	77575	76158	74787	73457	72167	70914	69696	68512	67359	66236
11	551	135	764	435	146	894	676	49	340	217
12	527	112	742	413	125	873	656	473	321	199
13	503	089	719	392	103	852	636	454	302	180
14	479	065	697	370	082	832	616	434	283	162
15	455	042	674	348	061	811	596	415	264	143
16	431	019	652	326	040	791	576	395	245	125
17	407	75996	629	305	019	770	557	376	226	106
18	383	973	607	283	71998	750	537	356	207	088
19	359	950	585	261	977	729	517	337	188	070
20	77335	75927	74562	73239	71956	70709	69497	68318	67170	66051
21	311	903	540	218	935	688	477	298	151	033
22	288	880	517	196	914	668	457	279	132	014
23	264	857	495	174	892	647	437	259	113	65996
24	240	834	473	153	871	627	417	240	094	978
25	216	811	450	131	850	606	397	221	075	959
26	192	788	428	109	829	586	377	201	056	941
27	169	765	406	088	808	566	358	182	038	923
28	145	742	383	066	787	545	338	163	019	904
29	121	719	361	044	766	525	318	143	000	886
30	77097	75696	74339	73023	71745	70504	69298	68124	66981	65868
31	074	673	317	001	724	481	278	105	962	849
32	050	650	294	72980	703	464	258	086	944	831
33	026	627	272	958	682	443	239	066	925	813
34	002	604	250	936	662	423	219	047	906	794
35	76979	581	228	915	641	403	199	028	887	776
36	955	559	205	893	620	382	179	008	869	758
37	931	536	183	872	599	362	159	67989	850	739
38	908	513	161	850	578	342	140	970	831	721
39	884	490	139	829	557	321	120	951	812	703
40	76861	75467	74117	72807	71536	70301	69100	67932	66794	65685
41	837	444	095	786	515	281	080	912	775	666
42	813	421	072	764	494	260	061	893	756	648
43	790	398	050	743	473	240	041	874	737	630
44	766	376	028	721	453	220	021	855	719	612
45	743	353	006	700	432	200	002	836	700	594
46	719	330	73984	678	411	179	68982	816	681	575
47	696	307	962	657	390	159	962	797	663	557
48	672	285	940	636	369	139	942	778	644	539
49	649	262	918	614	349	119	923	759	625	521
50	76625	75239	73896	72593	71328	70099	68903	67740	66607	65503
51	602	216	874	571	307	078	884	721	588	484
52	578	194	852	550	286	058	864	702	570	466
53	555	171	830	529	265	038	844	682	551	448
54	531	148	808	507	245	018	825	663	532	430
55	508	126	786	486	224	69998	805	644	514	412
56	485	103	764	465	203	977	785	625	495	394
57	461	080	742	443	183	957	766	606	477	376
58	438	058	720	422	162	937	746	587	458	357
59	414	035	698	401	141	917	727	568	439	339
	30	31	32	33	34	35	36	37	38	39

''	h. m. 40'	h. m. 41'	h. m. 42'	h. m. 43'	h. m. 44'	h. m. 45'	h. m. 46'	h. m. 47'	h. m. 48'	h. m. 49'
0	65321	64249	63202	62180	61182	60206	59251	58317	57403	56508
1	303	231	185	164	166	190	236	302	388	493
2	385	214	168	147	149	174	220	287	373	478
3	267	196	151	130	133	158	204	271	358	463
4	249	178	133	113	116	142	189	256	343	449
5	231	161	116	096	100	126	173	241	328	434
6	213	143	099	080	083	110	157	225	313	419
7	195	125	082	063	067	094	141	210	298	404
8	177	108	065	046	051	078	126	194	283	390
9	159	090	047	029	034	061	110	179	268	375
10	65141	64073	63030	62012	61018	60045	59094	58164	57253	56360
11	123	055	013	61996	001	029	079	148	238	345
12	105	038	62996	979	60985	013	063	133	223	331
13	087	020	979	962	969	59997	047	118	208	316
14	069	002	962	945	952	981	032	102	193	301
15	051	63985	945	929	936	965	016	087	178	287
16	033	967	927	912	920	949	000	072	163	272
17	015	950	910	895	903	933	58985	056	148	257
18	64997	932	893	878	887	917	969	041	133	243
19	979	915	876	862	871	901	954	026	118	228
20	64961	63897	62859	61845	60854	59885	58938	58011	57103	56213
21	943	880	842	828	838	870	922	57995	088	199
22	925	862	825	812	822	854	907	980	073	184
23	907	845	808	795	805	838	891	965	058	169
24	889	827	791	778	789	822	875	949	043	155
25	871	810	774	762	773	806	860	934	028	140
26	853	792	757	745	756	790	844	919	013	125
27	835	775	739	728	740	774	829	904	56998	111
28	818	757	722	712	724	758	813	888	983	096
29	800	740	705	695	708	742	798	873	968	081
30	64782	63722	62688	61678	60691	59726	58782	57858	56953	56067
31	764	705	671	662	675	710	766	843	938	052
32	746	688	654	645	659	694	751	827	923	037
33	728	670	637	628	642	678	735	812	908	023
34	710	653	620	612	626	663	720	797	893	008
35	692	635	603	595	610	647	704	782	879	55994
36	675	618	586	579	594	631	689	767	864	979
37	657	601	569	562	578	615	673	751	849	964
38	639	583	552	545	561	599	658	736	834	950
39	621	566	535	529	545	583	642	721	819	935
40	64603	63548	62518	61512	60529	59567	58627	57706	56804	55921
41	586	531	501	496	513	551	611	691	789	906
42	568	514	484	479	496	536	596	675	774	892
43	550	496	468	463	480	520	580	660	759	877
44	532	479	451	446	464	504	565	645	745	862
45	514	462	434	429	448	488	549	630	730	848
46	497	444	417	413	432	472	534	615	715	833
47	479	427	400	396	416	457	518	600	700	819
48	461	410	383	380	399	441	503	584	685	804
49	443	392	366	363	383	425	487	569	670	790
50	64426	63375	62349	61347	60367	59409	58472	57554	56656	55775
51	408	358	332	330	351	393	456	539	641	761
52	390	340	315	314	335	378	441	524	626	746
53	373	323	298	297	319	362	425	509	611	732
54	355	306	282	281	303	346	410	494	596	717
55	337	289	265	264	286	330	395	479	582	703
56	320	271	248	248	270	314	379	463	567	688
57	302	254	231	231	254	299	364	448	552	674
58	284	237	214	215	238	283	348	433	537	659
59	267	220	197	198	222	267	333	418	522	645
	40	41	42	43	44	45	46	47	48	49

" s	h. m. 50'	h. m. 51'	h. m. 52'	h. m. 53'	h. m. 54'	h. m. 55'	h. m. 56'	h. m. 57'	h. m. 58'	h. m. 59'
0	55630	54770	53927	53100	52288	51491	50708	49940	49184	48442
1	616	756	913	086	274	478	696	927	172	430
2	601	742	899	072	261	465	683	914	159	418
3	587	728	885	059	248	452	670	902	147	405
4	572	714	871	045	234	438	657	889	135	393
5	558	699	857	031	221	425	644	876	122	381
6	543	685	843	018	208	412	631	864	110	369
7	529	671	830	004	194	399	618	851	097	356
8	515	657	816	52991	181	386	605	838	085	344
9	500	643	802	977	167	373	592	826	072	332
10	55486	54629	53788	52963	52154	51360	50579	47813	49060	48320
11	471	614	774	950	141	346	566	800	047	307
12	457	600	760	936	127	333	554	788	035	295
13	442	586	746	922	114	320	541	775	023	283
14	428	572	732	909	101	307	528	762	010	271
15	414	558	719	895	087	294	515	750	48998	258
16	399	544	705	882	074	281	502	737	985	246
17	385	530	691	868	061	268	489	724	973	234
18	370	516	677	855	047	255	476	712	960	222
19	356	501	663	841	034	242	464	699	948	210
20	55342	54487	53649	52827	52021	51229	50451	49687	48936	48197
21	327	473	636	814	007	215	438	674	923	185
22	313	459	622	800	51994	202	425	661	911	173
23	299	445	608	787	981	189	412	649	898	161
24	284	431	594	773	967	176	399	636	886	149
25	270	417	580	760	954	163	387	623	874	136
26	255	403	567	746	941	150	374	611	861	124
27	241	389	553	732	927	137	361	598	849	112
28	227	375	539	719	914	124	348	586	836	100
29	212	361	525	705	901	111	335	573	824	088
30	55198	54347	53511	52692	51888	51098	50322	49560	48812	48076
31	184	332	498	678	874	085	310	548	799	063
32	169	318	484	665	861	072	297	535	787	051
33	155	304	470	651	848	059	284	523	775	039
34	141	290	456	638	835	046	271	510	762	027
35	127	276	442	624	821	033	258	498	750	015
36	112	262	429	611	808	020	246	485	737	003
37	098	248	415	597	795	007	233	472	725	47990
38	084	234	401	584	781	50994	220	460	713	978
39	069	220	387	570	768	981	207	447	700	966
40	55055	54206	53374	52557	51755	50968	50194	49435	48688	47954
41	041	192	360	543	742	955	182	422	676	942
42	026	178	346	530	729	942	169	410	663	930
43	012	164	332	516	715	929	156	397	651	918
44	54998	150	319	503	702	916	143	385	639	906
45	984	136	305	489	689	903	131	372	626	893
46	969	122	291	476	676	890	118	360	614	881
47	955	108	278	462	662	877	105	347	602	869
48	941	094	264	449	649	864	092	334	590	857
49	927	080	250	436	636	851	080	322	577	845
50	54912	54066	53236	52422	51623	50838	50067	49309	48565	47833
51	898	052	223	409	610	825	054	297	553	821
52	884	038	209	395	596	812	041	284	540	809
53	870	024	195	382	583	799	029	272	528	797
54	855	011	182	368	570	786	016	259	516	785
55	841	53997	168	355	557	773	003	247	503	772
56	827	983	154	342	544	760	49991	234	491	760
57	813	969	141	328	530	747	978	222	479	748
58	799	955	127	315	517	734	965	209	467	736
59	784	941	113	301	504	721	952	197	454	724
	50	51	52	53	54	55	56	57	58	59

" / s	h. m. 1 0	h. m. 1 1	h. m. 1 2	h. m. 1 3	h. m. 1 4	h. m. 1 5	h. m. 1 6	h. m. 1 7	h. m. 1 8	h. m. 1 9	h. m. 1 10	h. m. 1 11
0	47712	46994	46288	45593	44909	44236	43573	42920	42276	41642	41017	40401
1	700	982	276	582	898	225	562	909	266	632	007	391
2	688	971	265	570	887	214	551	898	255	621	40997	381
3	676	959	253	559	875	203	540	887	244	611	986	371
4	664	947	241	547	864	191	529	877	234	600	976	361
5	652	935	230	536	853	180	518	866	223	590	966	350
6	640	923	218	524	841	169	507	855	213	579	955	340
7	628	911	206	513	830	158	496	844	202	569	945	330
8	616	899	195	501	819	147	485	833	191	559	935	320
9	604	888	183	490	808	136	474	823	181	548	924	310
10	47592	46876	46171	45478	44796	44125	43463	42812	42170	41538	40914	40300
11	580	864	160	467	785	114	452	801	159	527	904	289
12	568	852	148	456	774	102	441	790	149	517	894	279
13	556	840	137	444	762	091	431	780	138	506	883	369
14	544	828	125	433	751	080	420	769	128	496	873	259
15	532	817	113	421	740	069	409	758	117	485	863	249
16	520	805	102	410	729	058	398	747	106	475	852	239
17	508	793	090	398	717	047	387	737	096	464	842	228
18	496	781	078	387	706	036	376	726	085	454	832	218
19	484	769	067	375	695	025	365	715	075	443	821	208
20	47472	46758	46055	45364	44684	44014	43354	42704	42064	41433	40811	40198
21	460	746	044	353	672	003	343	693	053	423	801	188
22	448	734	032	341	661	43992	332	683	043	412	791	178
23	436	722	020	330	650	981	321	672	032	402	780	168
24	424	710	009	318	639	969	310	661	022	391	770	157
25	412	699	45997	307	627	958	300	651	011	381	760	147
26	400	687	986	295	616	947	289	640	000	370	749	137
27	388	675	974	284	605	93	278	629	41990	360	739	127
28	376	663	962	273	594	925	267	618	979	350	729	117
29	364	652	951	261	583	914	256	608	969	339	719	107
30	47352	46640	45939	45250	44571	43903	43245	42597	41958	41329	40708	40097
31	340	628	928	238	560	892	234	586	948	318	698	087
32	328	616	916	227	549	881	223	575	937	308	688	076
33	316	604	905	216	538	870	212	565	927	298	678	066
34	304	593	893	204	526	859	202	554	916	287	667	056
35	292	581	881	193	515	848	191	543	905	277	657	046
36	280	569	870	182	504	837	180	533	895	266	647	036
37	268	557	858	170	493	826	169	522	884	256	637	026
38	256	546	847	159	482	815	158	511	874	246	626	016
39	244	534	835	147	470	804	147	500	863	235	616	006
40	47232	46522	45824	45136	44459	43793	43136	42490	41853	41225	40606	39996
41	220	510	812	125	448	782	126	479	842	214	596	985
42	208	499	800	113	437	771	115	468	832	204	585	975
43	196	487	789	102	426	760	104	458	821	194	575	965
44	185	475	777	091	414	749	093	447	811	183	565	955
45	173	464	766	079	403	738	082	436	800	173	555	945
46	161	452	754	068	392	727	071	426	789	162	544	935
47	149	440	743	057	381	716	060	415	779	152	534	925
48	137	428	731	045	370	705	050	404	768	142	524	915
49	125	417	720	034	359	694	039	394	758	131	514	905
50	47113	46405	45708	45022	44347	43683	43028	42383	41747	41121	40503	39895
51	101	393	697	011	336	672	017	372	737	111	493	885
52	089	382	685	000	325	661	006	362	726	100	483	874
53	077	370	674	44988	314	650	42995	351	716	090	473	864
54	066	358	662	977	303	639	985	340	705	080	463	854
55	054	346	651	966	292	628	974	330	695	069	452	844
56	042	335	639	955	280	617	963	319	684	059	442	834
57	030	323	628	943	269	606	952	308	674	048	432	824
58	018	311	616	932	258	595	941	298	663	038	422	814
59	006	300	605	921	247	584	931	287	653	028	412	804
	60	61	62	63	64	65	66	67	68	69	70	71

" s	h. m. 1 12	h. m. 1 13	h. m. 1 14	h. m. 1 15	h. m. 1 16	h. m. 1 17	h. m. 1 18	h. m. 1 19	h. m. 1 20	h. m. 1 21	h. m. 1 22	h. m. 1 23
0	39794	39195	38604	38021	37446	36878	36318	35765	35218	34679	34146	33619
1	784	185	594	011	436	869	309	755	209	670	137	611
2	774	175	585	002	427	859	299	746	200	661	128	602
3	764	165	575	37992	417	850	290	737	191	652	119	593
4	754	155	565	983	408	841	281	728	182	648	111	585
5	744	145	555	973	398	831	271	719	173	634	102	576
6	734	136	545	963	389	822	262	710	164	625	093	567
7	724	126	536	954	379	812	253	700	155	616	084	558
8	714	116	526	944	370	803	244	691	146	607	075	550
9	704	106	516	934	360	794	234	682	137	598	066	541
10	39694	39096	38506	37925	37351	36784	36225	35673	35128	34589	34058	33532
11	684	086	497	915	341	775	216	664	119	581	049	524
12	674	076	487	905	332	766	207	655	110	572	040	515
13	664	066	477	896	322	756	197	646	101	563	031	506
14	653	056	467	886	313	747	188	636	092	554	022	498
15	643	046	458	877	303	737	179	627	083	545	014	489
16	633	037	448	867	294	728	170	618	074	536	005	480
17	623	027	438	857	284	719	160	609	065	527	33996	471
18	613	017	428	848	275	709	151	600	056	518	987	463
19	603	007	419	838	265	700	142	591	047	509	978	454
20	39593	38997	38409	37829	37256	36691	36133	35582	35038	34500	33970	33445
21	583	987	399	819	246	681	123	573	029	491	961	437
22	573	977	389	809	237	672	114	563	020	483	952	428
23	563	968	380	800	227	663	105	554	011	474	943	419
24	553	958	370	790	218	653	096	545	002	465	935	411
25	543	948	360	781	208	644	086	536	34993	456	926	402
26	533	938	351	771	199	634	077	527	984	447	917	393
27	523	928	341	761	189	625	068	518	975	438	908	385
28	513	918	331	752	180	616	059	509	966	429	899	376
29	503	908	321	742	171	606	050	500	957	420	891	367
30	39493	38899	38312	37733	37161	36597	36040	35491	34948	34411	33882	33359
31	483	889	302	723	152	588	031	481	939	403	873	350
32	473	879	292	713	142	578	022	472	930	394	864	341
33	464	869	282	704	133	569	013	463	921	385	856	333
34	454	859	273	694	123	560	003	454	912	376	847	324
35	444	849	263	685	114	550	35994	445	903	367	838	315
36	434	839	253	675	104	541	985	436	894	358	829	307
37	424	830	244	665	095	532	976	427	885	349	820	298
38	414	820	234	656	085	522	967	418	876	340	812	289
39	404	810	224	646	076	513	957	409	867	332	803	281
40	39394	38800	38215	37637	37067	36504	35948	35400	34858	34323	33794	33272
41	384	790	205	627	057	494	939	391	849	314	785	263
42	374	781	195	618	048	485	930	381	840	305	777	255
43	364	771	186	608	038	476	921	372	831	296	768	246
44	354	761	176	599	029	467	911	363	822	287	759	237
45	344	751	166	589	019	457	902	354	813	278	750	229
46	334	741	156	579	010	448	893	345	804	270	742	220
47	324	731	147	570	001	439	884	336	795	261	733	211
48	314	722	137	560	36991	429	875	327	786	252	724	203
49	304	712	127	551	982	420	865	318	777	243	715	194
50	39294	38702	38118	37541	36972	36411	35856	35309	34768	34234	33707	33186
51	284	692	108	532	963	401	847	300	759	225	698	177
52	274	682	098	522	953	392	838	291	750	217	689	168
53	264	673	089	513	944	383	829	282	741	208	681	160
54	254	663	079	503	935	374	820	273	732	199	672	151
55	245	653	069	494	925	364	810	264	723	190	663	142
56	235	643	060	484	916	355	801	254	715	181	654	134
57	225	633	050	474	906	346	792	245	706	172	646	125
58	215	624	040	465	897	336	783	236	697	164	637	117
59	205	614	031	455	888	327	774	227	688	155	628	108
	72	73	74	75	76	77	78	79	80	81	82	83

"	1 24	1 25	1 26	1 27	1 28	1 29	1 30	1 31	1 32	1 33	1 34	1 35
s	h. m.	h. m.	h. m.	h. m.	h. m.	h. m.	h. m.	h. m.	h. m.	h. m.	h. m.	h. m.
0	33099	32585	32077	31575	31079	30588	30103	29623	29148	28679	28214	27755
1	091	577	069	567	071	580	095	615	141	671	207	747
2	082	568	061	559	063	572	087	607	133	663	199	740
3	073	560	052	550	054	564	079	599	125	656	191	732
4	065	551	044	542	046	556	071	591	117	648	184	724
5	056	543	035	534	038	548	063	583	109	640	176	717
6	048	534	027	525	030	539	055	575	101	632	168	709
7	039	526	019	517	021	531	047	567	093	625	161	702
8	030	517	010	509	013	523	039	560	086	617	153	694
9	022	509	002	501	005	515	031	552	078	609	145	686
10	33013	32500	31993	31492	30997	30507	30023	29544	29070	28601	28138	27679
11	005	492	985	484	989	499	015	536	062	593	130	671
12	32996	483	977	476	980	491	007	528	054	586	122	664
13	987	475	968	467	972	483	29999	520	046	578	114	656
14	979	466	960	459	964	475	991	512	038	570	107	648
15	970	458	951	451	956	466	983	504	031	562	099	641
16	962	449	943	442	948	458	975	496	023	555	091	633
17	953	441	935	434	939	450	967	488	015	547	084	626
18	944	432	926	426	931	442	958	480	007	539	076	618
19	936	424	918	418	923	434	950	472	28999	531	068	610
20	32927	32415	31909	31409	30915	30426	29942	29464	28991	28524	28061	27603
21	919	407	901	401	907	418	934	456	984	516	053	595
22	910	398	893	393	898	410	926	448	976	508	045	58
23	902	390	884	384	890	402	918	441	968	500	038	580
24	893	381	876	376	882	393	910	433	960	493	030	572
25	884	373	867	368	874	385	902	425	952	485	022	565
26	876	365	859	360	866	377	894	417	944	477	015	557
27	867	356	851	351	857	369	886	409	937	469	007	550
28	859	348	842	343	849	361	878	401	929	462	27999	542
29	850	339	834	335	841	353	870	393	921	454	992	534
30	32842	32331	31826	31326	30833	30345	29862	29385	28913	28446	27984	27527
31	833	322	817	318	825	337	854	377	905	438	976	519
32	824	314	809	310	817	329	846	369	897	431	969	512
33	816	305	801	302	808	321	838	361	890	423	961	504
34	807	297	792	293	800	313	830	354	882	415	953	497
35	799	288	784	285	792	305	822	346	874	407	946	489
36	790	280	775	277	784	296	814	338	866	400	938	481
37	782	271	767	269	776	288	806	330	858	392	930	474
38	773	263	759	260	768	280	798	322	851	384	923	466
39	765	255	750	252	759	272	790	314	843	376	915	459
40	32756	32246	31742	31244	30751	30264	29782	29306	28835	28369	27908	27451
41	747	238	734	236	743	256	775	298	827	361	900	444
42	739	229	725	227	735	248	767	290	819	353	892	436
43	730	221	717	219	727	240	759	282	811	346	885	429
44	722	212	709	211	719	232	751	275	804	338	877	421
45	713	204	700	203	710	224	743	267	796	330	869	413
46	705	195	692	194	702	216	735	259	788	322	862	406
47	696	187	684	186	694	208	727	251	780	315	854	398
48	688	179	675	178	686	200	719	243	772	307	846	391
49	679	170	667	170	678	192	711	235	765	299	839	383
50	32671	32162	31659	31161	30670	30184	29703	29227	28757	28292	27831	27376
51	662	153	650	153	662	175	695	219	749	284	824	368
52	654	145	642	145	653	167	687	211	741	276	816	360
53	645	136	634	137	645	159	679	204	733	268	808	353
54	636	128	625	128	637	151	671	196	726	261	801	345
55	628	120	617	120	629	143	663	188	718	253	793	338
56	619	111	609	112	621	135	655	180	710	245	785	330
57	611	103	600	104	613	127	647	172	702	238	778	323
58	602	094	592	095	605	119	639	164	695	230	770	315
59	594	086	584	087	596	111	631	156	687	222	763	308
	84	85	86	87	88	89	90	91	92	93	94	95

'' s	h. m. 1 36	h. m. 1 37	h. m. 1 38	h. m. 1 39	h. m. 1 40	h. m. 1 41	h. m. 1 42	h. m. 1 43	h. m. 1 44	h. m. 1 45	h. m. 1 46	h. m. 1 47
0	27300	26850	26405	25964	25527	25095	24667	24244	23824	23408	22997	22589
1	293	843	397	956	520	088	660	237	817	401	990	582
2	285	835	390	949	513	081	653	229	810	395	983	575
3	278	828	382	942	506	074	646	222	803	388	976	569
4	270	820	375	934	498	066	639	215	796	381	969	562
5	262	813	368	927	491	059	632	208	789	374	963	555
6	255	805	360	920	484	052	625	201	782	367	956	548
7	247	798	353	913	477	045	618	194	775	360	949	542
8	240	790	346	905	469	038	610	187	768	353	942	535
9	232	783	338	898	462	031	603	180	761	346	935	528
10	27225	26776	26331	25891	25455	25024	24596	24173	23754	23339	22928	22521
11	217	768	323	883	448	016	589	166	747	333	922	515
12	210	761	316	876	440	009	582	159	740	326	915	508
13	202	753	309	869	433	002	575	152	734	319	908	501
14	195	746	301	861	426	24995	568	145	727	312	901	494
15	187	738	294	854	419	988	561	138	720	305	894	488
16	180	731	287	847	412	981	554	131	713	298	888	481
17	172	723	279	840	404	973	547	124	706	291	881	474
18	165	716	272	832	397	966	540	117	699	284	874	467
19	157	709	265	825	390	959	533	110	692	278	867	461
20	27150	26701	26257	25818	24383	24952	24526	24103	23685	23271	22860	22454
21	142	694	250	810	376	945	518	096	678	264	854	447
22	135	686	242	803	368	938	511	089	671	257	847	440
23	127	679	235	796	361	931	504	082	664	250	840	434
24	120	671	228	789	354	923	497	075	657	243	833	427
25	112	664	220	781	347	916	490	068	650	236	826	420
26	105	656	213	774	339	909	483	061	643	229	819	413
27	097	649	206	767	332	902	476	054	636	223	813	407
28	090	642	198	759	325	895	469	047	629	216	806	400
29	082	634	191	752	318	888	462	040	623	209	799	393
30	27075	26627	26184	25745	25311	24881	24455	24033	23616	23202	22792	22386
31	067	619	176	738	303	874	448	026	609	195	785	380
32	060	612	169	730	296	866	441	019	602	188	779	373
33	052	605	162	723	289	859	434	012	595	181	772	366
34	045	597	154	716	282	852	427	005	588	175	765	359
35	037	590	147	709	275	845	420	23998	581	168	758	353
36	030	582	140	701	267	838	413	991	574	161	752	346
37	022	575	132	694	260	831	405	984	567	154	745	339
38	015	567	125	687	253	824	398	977	560	147	738	333
39	007	560	118	680	246	817	391	970	553	140	731	326
40	27000	26553	26110	25672	25239	24809	24384	23963	23546	23133	22724	22319
41	26992	545	103	665	231	802	377	956	539	127	718	312
42	985	538	096	658	224	795	370	949	533	120	711	306
43	977	530	088	650	217	788	363	942	526	113	704	299
44	970	523	081	643	210	781	356	935	519	106	697	292
45	962	516	074	636	203	774	349	928	512	099	690	286
46	955	508	066	629	196	767	342	921	505	092	684	279
47	947	501	059	621	188	760	335	914	498	086	677	272
48	940	493	052	614	181	752	328	908	491	079	670	265
49	932	486	044	607	174	745	321	901	484	072	663	259
50	26925	26479	26037	25600	25167	24738	24314	23894	23477	23065	22657	22252
51	917	471	030	592	160	731	307	887	470	058	650	245
52	910	464	022	585	152	724	300	880	464	051	643	239
53	902	456	015	578	145	717	293	873	457	044	636	232
54	895	449	008	571	138	710	286	866	450	038	629	225
55	887	442	000	563	131	703	279	859	443	031	623	218
56	880	434	25993	556	124	696	272	852	436	024	616	212
57	872	427	986	549	117	689	265	845	429	017	609	205
58	865	419	978	542	109	681	258	838	422	010	602	198
59	858	412	971	534	102	674	251	831	415	004	596	192
	96	97	98	99	100	101	102	103	104	105	106	107

″ s	h. m. 1 48	h. m. 1 49	h. m. 1 50	h. m. 1 51	h. m. 1 52	h. m. 1 53	h. m. 1 54	h. m. 1 55	h. m. 1 56	h. m. 1 57	h. m. 1 58	h. m. 1 59
0	22185	21785	21388	20995	20605	20219	19837	19457	19081	18709	18339	17973
1	178	778	381	988	599	213	830	451	075	702	333	966
2	171	771	375	982	593	207	824	445	069	696	327	960
3	165	765	368	975	586	200	818	439	063	690	321	954
4	158	758	362	969	580	194	811	432	056	684	315	948
5	151	751	355	962	573	187	805	426	050	678	308	942
6	145	745	349	956	567	181	799	420	044	672	302	936
7	138	738	342	949	560	175	792	413	038	665	296	930
8	131	732	335	943	554	168	786	407	032	659	290	924
9	125	725	329	936	547	162	780	401	025	653	284	918
10	22118	21718	21322	20930	20541	20155	19773	19395	19019	18647	18278	17912
11	111	712	316	923	534	149	767	388	013	641	272	906
12	105	705	309	917	528	143	761	382	007	634	266	900
13	098	698	303	910	522	136	754	376	000	628	259	894
14	091	692	296	904	515	130	748	369	18994	622	253	887
15	084	685	289	897	509	123	742	363	988	616	247	881
16	078	678	283	891	502	117	735	357	982	610	241	875
17	071	672	276	884	496	111	729	351	976	604	235	869
18	064	665	270	878	489	104	723	344	969	597	229	863
19	058	659	263	871	483	098	716	338	963	591	223	857
20	22051	21652	21257	20865	20476	20091	19710	19332	18957	18585	18217	17851
21	044	645	250	858	470	085	704	325	951	579	210	845
22	038	639	243	852	464	079	697	319	944	573	204	839
23	031	632	237	845	457	072	691	313	938	567	198	833
24	024	626	230	839	451	066	685	307	932	560	192	827
25	018	619	224	832	444	060	678	300	926	554	186	821
26	011	612	217	826	438	053	672	294	920	548	180	815
27	004	606	211	819	431	047	666	288	913	542	174	809
28	21998	599	204	813	425	040	659	282	907	536	168	803
29	991	592	198	806	418	034	653	275	901	530	162	797
30	21984	21586	21191	20800	20412	20028	19647	19269	18895	18523	18155	17790
31	978	579	184	793	406	021	640	263	888	517	149	784
32	971	573	178	787	399	015	634	257	882	511	143	778
33	964	566	171	780	393	009	628	250	876	505	137	772
34	958	559	165	774	386	002	621	244	870	499	131	766
35	951	553	158	767	380	19996	615	238	864	493	125	760
36	944	546	152	761	373	989	609	231	857	487	119	754
37	938	540	145	754	367	983	602	225	851	480	113	748
38	931	533	139	748	361	977	596	219	845	474	107	742
39	924	526	132	741	354	970	590	213	839	468	100	736
40	21918	21520	21126	20735	20348	19964	19584	19206	18833	18462	18094	17730
41	911	513	119	728	341	958	577	200	826	456	088	724
42	904	507	112	722	335	951	571	194	820	450	082	718
43	898	500	106	715	328	945	565	188	814	443	076	712
44	891	493	099	709	322	938	558	181	808	437	070	706
45	884	487	093	702	316	932	552	175	802	431	064	700
46	878	480	086	696	309	926	546	169	795	425	058	694
47	871	474	080	690	303	919	539	163	789	419	052	688
48	864	467	073	683	296	913	533	156	783	413	046	682
49	858	460	067	677	290	907	527	150	777	407	040	676
50	21851	21454	21060	20670	20284	19900	19520	19144	18771	18400	18033	17669
51	844	447	054	664	277	894	514	138	764	494	027	663
52	838	441	047	657	271	888	508	131	758	388	021	657
53	831	434	041	651	264	881	502	125	752	382	015	651
54	824	427	034	644	258	875	495	119	746	376	009	645
55	818	421	028	638	251	869	489	113	740	370	003	639
56	811	414	021	631	245	862	483	106	733	364	17997	633
57	805	408	015	625	239	856	476	100	727	357	991	627
58	798	401	008	618	232	849	470	094	721	351	985	621
59	791	395	001	612	226	843	464	088	715	345	979	615
	108	109	110	111	112	113	114	115	116	117	118	119

" s	h. m. 2 0	h. m. 2 1	h. m. 2 2	h. m. 2 3	h. m. 2 4	h. m. 2 5	h. m. 2 6	h. m. 2 7	h. m. 2 8	h. m. 2 9	h. m. 2 10	h. m. 2 11
0	17609	17249	16891	16537	16185	15836	15490	15147	14806	14468	14133	13800
1	603	243	885	531	179	830	484	141	801	463	127	795
2	597	237	879	525	173	825	479	135	795	457	122	789
3	591	231	873	519	168	819	473	130	789	451	116	784
4	585	225	868	513	162	813	467	124	784	446	111	778
5	579	219	862	507	156	807	461	118	778	440	105	773
6	573	213	856	501	150	802	456	113	772	435	100	767
7	567	207	850	496	144	796	450	107	767	429	094	761
8	561	201	844	490	138	790	444	101	761	423	088	756
9	555	195	738	484	133	784	439	096	755	418	083	750
10	17549	17189	16832	16478	16127	15778	15433	15090	14750	14412	14077	13745
11	543	183	826	472	121	773	427	084	744	407	072	739
12	537	177	820	466	115	767	421	079	738	401	066	734
13	531	171	814	460	109	761	416	073	733	395	061	728
14	525	165	808	454	103	755	410	067	727	390	055	723
15	519	159	802	449	098	749	404	061	722	384	049	717
16	513	153	796	443	092	744	398	056	716	379	044	712
17	507	147	791	437	086	738	393	050	710	373	038	706
18	501	141	785	431	080	732	387	044	705	367	033	701
19	495	135	779	425	974	726	381	039	699	362	027	695
20	17489	17129	16773	16419	16068	15721	15375	15033	14693	14356	14022	13690
21	483	123	767	413	063	715	370	027	688	251	016	684
22	477	117	761	407	057	709	364	022	682	345	011	679
23	471	111	755	402	051	703	358	016	676	339	005	673
24	465	105	749	396	045	697	353	010	671	334	000	668
25	459	099	743	390	039	692	347	005	665	328	13994	662
26	453	093	737	384	034	686	341	14999	659	323	988	657
27	447	087	731	378	028	680	335	993	654	317	983	651
28	441	082	725	372	022	674	330	988	648	311	977	646
29	435	076	720	366	016	669	324	982	643	306	972	640
30	17429	17070	16714	16361	16010	15663	15318	14976	14637	14300	13966	13635
31	423	064	708	355	005	657	312	971	631	295	961	629
32	417	058	702	349	15999	651	307	965	626	289	955	624
33	411	052	696	343	993	646	301	959	620	284	950	618
34	405	046	690	337	987	640	295	954	614	278	944	613
35	399	040	684	331	981	634	290	948	609	272	938	607
36	393	034	678	325	975	628	284	942	603	267	933	602
37	387	028	672	320	970	623	278	937	598	261	927	596
38	381	022	666	314	964	617	272	931	592	256	922	591
39	375	016	660	308	958	611	267	925	586	250	916	585
40	17369	17010	16655	16302	15952	15605	15261	14919	14581	14244	13911	13580
41	363	004	649	296	946	599	255	914	575	239	905	574
42	357	16998	643	290	941	594	250	908	569	233	900	569
43	351	992	637	284	935	588	244	902	564	228	894	563
44	345	986	631	279	929	582	238	897	558	222	889	558
45	339	980	625	273	923	576	232	891	553	217	883	552
46	333	974	619	267	917	571	227	886	547	211	878	547
47	327	968	613	261	912	565	221	880	541	205	872	541
48	321	963	607	255	906	559	215	874	536	200	866	536
49	315	957	602	249	900	553	210	869	530	194	861	530
50	17309	16951	16596	16243	15894	15548	15204	14863	14524	14189	13855	13525
51	303	945	590	238	888	542	198	857	519	183	850	519
52	297	939	584	232	883	536	192	852	513	177	844	514
53	291	933	578	226	877	530	187	846	508	172	839	508
54	285	927	572	220	871	525	181	840	502	166	833	503
55	279	921	566	214	865	519	175	835	496	161	828	497
56	273	915	560	208	859	513	170	829	491	155	822	492
57	267	909	554	203	854	507	164	823	485	150	817	486
58	261	903	549	197	848	502	158	818	480	144	811	481
59	255	897	543	191	842	496	153	812	474	138	806	475
	120	121	122	123	124	125	126	127	128	129	130	131

" s	h. m. 2 12	h. m. 2 13	h. m. 2 14	h. m. 2 15	h. m. 2 16	h. m. 2 17	h. m. 2 18	h. m. 2 19	h. m. 2 20	h. m. 2 21	h. m. 2 22	h. m. 2 23
0	13470	13142	12817	12494	12173	11855	11539	11226	10914	10605	10298	09994
1	464	137	811	489	168	850	534	221	909	600	293	989
2	459	131	806	483	163	845	529	215	904	595	288	984
3	453	126	801	478	157	839	524	210	899	590	283	978
4	448	120	795	472	152	834	518	205	894	585	278	973
5	442	115	790	467	147	829	513	200	889	580	273	968
6	437	109	784	462	141	824	508	195	883	575	268	963
7	431	104	779	456	136	818	503	189	878	569	263	958
8	426	099	774	451	131	813	497	184	873	564	258	953
9	421	093	768	446	125	808	492	179	868	559	253	948
10	13415	13088	12763	12440	12120	11802	11487	11174	10863	10554	10247	09943
11	410	082	757	435	115	897	482	169	858	549	242	938
12	404	077	752	430	110	792	476	163	852	544	237	933
13	399	071	747	424	104	787	471	158	847	539	232	928
14	393	066	741	419	199	781	466	153	842	534	227	923
15	388	061	736	414	094	776	461	148	837	528	222	918
16	382	055	730	408	088	771	456	143	832	523	217	913
17	377	050	725	403	083	765	450	137	827	518	212	908
18	371	044	720	397	078	760	445	132	821	513	207	903
19	366	039	714	392	072	755	440	127	816	508	202	898
20	13360	13033	12709	12387	12067	11750	11435	11122	10811	10503	10197	09893
21	355	028	703	381	062	744	429	117	806	498	192	887
22	349	023	698	376	056	739	424	111	801	493	186	882
23	344	017	693	371	051	734	419	106	796	487	181	877
24	338	012	687	365	046	729	414	101	791	482	176	872
25	333	006	682	360	041	723	408	096	785	477	171	867
26	328	001	677	355	035	718	403	091	780	472	166	862
27	322	12995	671	349	030	713	398	085	775	467	161	857
28	317	990	666	344	025	708	393	080	770	462	156	852
29	311	985	660	339	019	702	387	075	765	457	151	847
30	13306	12979	12655	12333	12014	11697	11382	11070	10760	10452	10146	09842
31	300	974	650	328	009	692	377	065	754	446	141	837
32	295	968	644	323	003	686	372	059	749	441	136	832
33	289	963	639	317	11998	681	367	054	744	436	131	827
34	284	957	634	312	993	676	361	049	739	431	126	822
35	278	952	628	307	987	671	356	044	734	426	120	817
36	273	947	623	301	982	665	351	039	729	421	115	812
37	267	941	617	296	977	660	346	034	724	416	110	807
38	262	936	612	291	972	655	340	028	718	411	105	802
39	257	930	607	285	966	650	335	023	713	406	100	797
40	13251	12925	12601	12280	11961	11644	11330	11018	10708	10400	10095	09792
41	246	920	596	275	956	639	325	013	703	395	090	787
42	240	914	590	269	950	634	320	008	698	390	085	782
43	235	909	585	264	945	629	314	002	693	385	080	777
44	229	903	580	259	910	623	309	10997	688	380	075	772
45	224	898	574	253	935	618	304	992	682	375	070	766
46	218	892	569	248	929	613	299	987	677	370	065	761
47	213	887	564	243	924	608	294	982	672	365	059	756
48	207	882	558	237	919	602	288	977	667	360	054	751
49	202	876	553	232	913	597	283	971	662	355	049	746
50	13197	12871	12548	12227	11908	11592	11278	10966	10657	10349	10044	09741
51	191	865	542	221	903	587	273	961	652	344	039	736
52	186	860	537	216	897	581	267	956	646	339	034	731
53	180	855	531	211	892	576	262	951	641	334	029	726
54	175	849	526	205	887	571	257	945	636	329	024	721
55	169	844	521	200	882	566	252	940	631	324	019	716
56	164	838	515	195	876	560	247	935	626	319	014	711
57	158	833	510	189	871	555	241	930	621	314	009	706
58	153	828	505	184	866	550	236	925	616	309	004	701
59	148	822	499	179	860	545	231	920	610	304	09999	696
	132	133	134	135	136	137	138	139	140	141	142	143

s	h. m. 2 24	h. m. 2 25	h. m. 2 26	h. m. 2 27	h. m. 2 28	h. m. 2 29	h. m. 2 30	h. m. 2 31	h. m. 2 32	h. m. 2 33	h. m. 2 34	h. m. 2 35
0	09691	09390	09092	08796	08501	08209	07918	07630	07343	07058	06775	06494
1	686	385	087	791	496	204	913	625	338	053	770	489
2	681	380	082	786	491	199	908	620	333	049	766	485
3	676	375	077	781	486	194	904	615	329	044	761	480
4	671	370	072	776	482	189	899	610	324	039	756	475
5	666	365	067	771	477	184	894	606	319	034	752	471
6	661	361	062	766	472	179	889	601	314	030	747	466
7	656	356	057	761	467	175	884	596	310	025	742	461
8	651	351	052	756	462	170	880	591	305	020	738	457
9	646	346	047	751	457	165	875	586	300	016	733	452
10	09641	09341	09042	08746	08452	08160	07870	07582	07295	07011	06728	06447
11	636	336	037	741	447	155	865	577	291	006	724	443
12	631	331	033	736	442	150	860	572	286	001	719	438
13	626	326	028	732	438	146	855	567	281	06997	714	433
14	621	321	023	727	433	141	851	562	276	992	709	429
15	616	316	018	722	428	136	846	558	272	987	705	424
16	611	311	013	717	423	131	841	553	267	982	700	419
17	606	306	008	712	418	126	836	548	262	978	695	415
18	601	301	003	707	413	121	831	543	257	973	691	410
19	596	296	08998	702	408	116	827	539	253	968	686	405
20	09591	09291	08993	08697	08403	08112	07822	07534	07248	06964	06681	06401
21	586	286	988	692	398	107	817	529	243	959	677	496
22	581	281	983	687	394	102	812	524	238	954	672	391
23	576	276	978	682	389	097	807	519	234	949	667	387
24	571	271	973	678	384	092	802	515	228	945	663	382
25	566	266	968	673	379	087	798	510	224	940	658	377
26	561	261	963	668	374	083	793	505	219	935	653	373
27	555	256	958	663	369	078	788	500	215	931	648	368
28	550	251	953	658	364	073	783	496	210	926	644	364
29	545	246	948	653	359	068	778	491	205	921	639	359
30	09540	09241	08943	08648	08355	08063	07774	07486	07200	06916	06634	06354
31	535	236	939	643	350	058	769	481	196	912	630	350
32	530	231	934	638	345	053	764	476	191	907	625	345
33	525	226	929	633	340	049	759	472	186	902	620	340
34	520	221	924	628	335	044	754	467	181	898	616	336
35	515	216	919	624	330	039	750	462	177	893	611	331
36	510	211	914	619	325	034	745	457	172	888	606	326
37	505	206	909	614	320	029	740	453	167	883	602	322
38	500	201	904	609	316	024	735	448	162	879	597	317
39	495	196	899	604	311	020	730	443	158	874	592	312
40	09490	09191	08894	08599	08306	08015	07726	07438	07153	06869	06588	06308
41	485	186	889	594	301	010	721	433	148	865	583	303
42	480	181	884	589	296	005	716	429	143	860	578	298
43	475	176	879	584	291	000	711	424	139	855	574	294
44	470	171	874	579	286	07995	706	419	134	850	569	289
45	465	166	869	575	282	991	702	414	129	846	564	284
46	460	161	865	570	277	986	697	410	124	841	560	280
47	455	156	860	565	272	981	692	405	120	836	555	275
48	450	151	855	560	267	976	687	400	115	832	550	271
49	445	147	850	555	262	971	682	395	110	827	545	266
50	09440	09142	08845	08550	08257	07966	07678	07391	07105	06822	06541	06261
51	435	137	840	545	252	962	673	386	101	817	536	257
52	430	132	835	540	248	957	668	381	096	813	531	252
53	425	127	830	535	243	952	663	376	091	808	527	247
54	420	122	825	530	238	947	658	371	087	803	522	243
55	415	117	820	526	233	942	654	367	082	799	517	238
56	410	112	815	521	228	937	649	362	077	794	513	233
57	405	107	810	516	223	933	644	357	072	789	508	229
58	400	102	805	511	218	928	639	352	068	785	503	224
59	395	097	800	506	213	923	634	348	063	780	499	219
	144	145	146	147	148	149	150	151	152	153	154	155

" / s	h. m. 2 36	h. m. 2 37	h. m. 2 38	h. m. 2 39	h. m. 2 40	h. m. 2 41	h. m. 2 42	h. m. 2 43	h. m. 2 44	h. m. 2 45	h. m. 2 46	h. m. 2 47
0	06215	05937	05662	05388	05115	04845	04576	04308	04043	03779	03516	03256
1	210	933	657	383	111	840	571	304	038	774	512	251
2	206	928	652	378	106	836	567	300	034	770	508	247
3	201	923	648	374	102	831	562	295	030	766	503	243
4	196	919	643	369	097	827	558	291	025	761	499	238
5	192	914	639	365	093	822	553	286	021	757	495	234
6	187	910	634	360	088	818	549	282	016	753	490	230
7	182	905	629	356	084	813	544	277	012	748	486	225
8	178	900	625	351	079	809	540	273	008	744	482	221
9	173	896	620	347	075	804	536	269	003	739	477	217
10	06168	05891	05616	05342	05070	04800	04531	04264	03999	03735	03473	03212
11	164	887	611	337	066	795	527	260	994	731	469	208
12	159	882	607	333	061	791	522	255	990	726	464	204
13	155	877	602	328	056	786	518	251	986	722	460	199
14	150	873	597	324	052	782	513	246	981	717	455	195
15	145	868	593	319	047	777	509	242	977	713	451	191
16	141	864	588	315	043	773	504	237	972	709	447	186
17	136	859	584	310	038	768	500	233	968	704	442	182
18	131	854	579	306	034	764	495	229	963	700	438	178
19	127	850	575	301	029	759	491	224	959	696	434	173
20	06122	05845	05570	05297	05025	04755	04486	04220	03955	03691	03429	03169
21	117	841	565	292	020	750	482	215	950	687	425	165
22	113	836	561	288	016	746	478	211	946	682	421	160
23	108	831	556	283	011	741	473	206	941	678	416	156
24	104	827	552	278	007	737	469	202	937	674	412	152
25	099	822	547	274	002	732	464	198	933	669	408	147
26	094	818	543	269	04998	728	460	193	928	665	403	143
27	090	813	538	265	993	723	455	189	924	661	399	139
28	085	808	533	260	989	719	451	184	919	656	395	134
29	080	804	529	256	984	714	446	180	915	652	390	130
30	06076	05799	05524	05251	04980	04710	04442	04175	03911	03647	03386	03126
31	071	795	520	247	975	706	437	171	906	643	381	121
32	067	790	515	242	971	701	433	167	902	639	377	117
33	062	785	511	238	966	697	429	162	897	634	373	113
34	057	781	506	233	962	692	424	158	893	630	368	108
35	053	776	501	228	957	688	420	153	889	626	364	104
36	048	772	497	224	953	683	415	149	884	621	360	100
37	043	767	492	219	948	679	411	144	880	617	355	096
38	039	762	488	215	944	674	406	140	875	612	351	091
39	034	758	483	210	939	670	402	136	871	608	347	087
40	06030	05753	05479	05206	04935	04665	04397	04131	03867	03604	03342	03083
41	025	749	474	201	930	661	393	127	862	599	338	078
42	020	744	470	197	926	656	388	122	858	595	334	074
43	016	739	465	192	921	652	384	118	853	591	329	070
44	011	735	460	188	917	647	380	114	849	586	325	065
45	006	730	456	183	912	643	375	109	845	582	321	061
46	002	726	451	179	908	638	371	105	840	578	316	057
47	05997	721	447	174	903	634	366	100	836	573	312	052
48	993	717	442	170	899	629	362	096	832	569	308	048
49	988	712	438	165	894	625	357	091	827	564	303	044
50	05983	05707	05433	05161	04890	04620	04353	04087	03823	03560	03299	03039
51	979	703	429	156	885	616	348	083	818	556	295	035
52	974	698	424	151	881	612	344	078	814	551	290	031
53	970	694	419	147	876	607	340	074	810	547	286	026
54	965	689	415	142	872	603	335	069	805	543	282	022
55	960	684	410	138	867	598	331	065	801	558	277	018
56	956	680	406	133	863	594	326	061	796	534	273	014
57	951	675	401	129	858	589	322	056	792	530	269	009
58	947	671	397	124	854	585	317	052	788	525	264	005
59	942	666	392	120	849	580	313	047	783	521	260	001
	156	157	158	159	160	161	162	163	164	165	166	167

'' s	h. m. 2 48	h. m. 2 49	h. m. 2 50	h. m. 2 51	h. m. 2 52	h. m. 2 53	h. m. 2 54	h. m. 2 55	h. m. 2 56	h. m. 2 57	h. m. 2 58	h. m. 2 59
0	02996	02739	02483	02228	01974	01723	01472	01223	00976	00730	00485	00242
1	992	734	478	223	970	718	468	219	972	726	481	238
2	988	730	474	219	966	714	464	215	968	722	477	234
3	983	726	470	215	962	710	460	211	964	718	473	230
4	979	721	465	211	958	706	456	207	960	714	469	226
5	975	717	461	206	953	702	452	203	955	709	465	222
6	970	713	457	202	949	698	447	199	951	705	461	218
7	966	709	453	198	945	693	443	195	947	701	457	214
8	962	704	448	194	941	689	439	190	943	697	453	210
9	958	700	444	190	937	685	435	186	939	693	449	206
10	02953	02696	02440	02185	01932	01681	01431	01182	00935	00689	00445	00202
11	949	692	436	181	928	677	427	178	931	685	441	197
12	945	687	431	177	924	672	422	174	927	681	436	193
13	940	683	427	173	920	668	418	170	923	677	432	189
14	936	679	423	168	916	664	414	166	918	673	428	185
15	932	674	419	164	911	660	410	161	914	669	424	181
16	927	670	414	160	907	656	406	157	910	665	420	177
17	923	666	410	156	903	652	402	153	906	660	416	173
18	919	662	406	152	899	647	398	149	902	656	412	169
19	915	657	402	147	895	643	393	145	898	652	408	165
20	02910	02653	02397	02143	01890	01639	01389	01141	00894	00648	00404	00161
21	906	649	393	139	886	635	385	137	890	644	400	157
22	902	644	389	135	882	631	381	133	886	640	396	153
23	897	640	385	130	878	627	377	128	881	636	392	149
24	893	636	380	126	874	622	373	124	877	632	388	145
25	889	632	376	122	869	618	368	120	873	628	384	141
26	884	627	372	118	865	614	364	116	869	624	380	137
27	880	623	368	114	861	610	360	112	865	620	376	133
28	876	619	363	109	857	606	356	108	861	616	372	129
29	872	615	359	105	853	601	352	104	857	611	367	125
30	02867	02610	02355	02101	01848	01597	01348	01100	00853	00607	00363	00121
31	863	606	351	097	844	593	344	095	849	603	359	117
32	859	602	346	092	840	589	339	091	845	599	355	113
33	854	597	342	088	836	585	335	087	840	595	351	109
34	850	593	338	084	832	581	331	083	836	591	347	105
35	846	589	334	080	827	576	327	079	832	587	343	101
36	841	585	329	076	823	572	323	075	828	583	339	097
37	837	580	325	071	819	568	319	071	824	579	335	093
38	833	576	321	067	815	564	315	067	820	575	331	089
39	829	572	317	063	811	560	310	062	816	571	327	085
40	02824	02568	02312	02059	01806	01556	01306	01058	00812	00567	00323	00080
41	820	563	308	054	802	551	302	054	808	563	319	076
42	816	559	304	050	798	547	298	050	804	559	315	072
43	811	555	300	046	794	543	294	046	799	554	311	068
44	807	551	295	042	790	539	290	042	795	550	307	064
45	803	546	291	038	785	535	286	038	791	546	303	060
46	799	542	287	033	781	531	281	034	787	542	299	056
47	794	538	283	029	777	526	277	029	783	538	295	052
48	790	533	278	025	773	522	273	025	779	534	290	048
49	786	529	274	021	769	518	269	021	775	530	286	044
50	02781	02525	02270	02017	01764	01514	01265	01017	00771	00526	00282	00040
51	777	521	266	012	760	510	261	013	767	522	278	036
52	773	516	262	008	756	506	257	009	763	518	274	032
53	769	512	257	004	752	501	252	005	759	514	270	028
54	764	508	253	000	748	497	248	001	754	510	266	024
55	760	504	249	01995	744	493	244	00997	750	506	262	020
56	756	499	245	991	739	489	240	992	746	502	258	016
57	751	495	240	987	735	485	236	988	742	497	254	012
58	747	491	236	983	731	481	232	984	738	493	250	008
59	743	487	232	979	727	476	228	980	734	489	246	004
~	168	169	170	171	172	173	174	175	176	177	178	179

′	Sine.	Cosine.	Tang.	Cotang.	Sine.	Cosine.	Tang.	Cotang.	′
		0 DEGREE.				1 DEGREE.			
0	0.000000	10 000000	0.000000	Infinite.	8.241855	9.999934	8.241921	11.758079	60
1	6.463726		6.463726	13 586274	9033	32	49102	50897	59
2	764756		764756	285244	56094	29	56165	43835	58
3	940847		940847	059153	63042	27	63115	86885	57
4	7.065786		7 065786	12.934214	9881	25	9956	30044	56
5	162696		162696	837304	76614	22	76691	23309	55
6	241877	9.999999	241878	758122	83243	20	83323	16677	54
7	308824		308825	691175	9773	18	9856	10144	53
8	366816		366817	33183	96207	15	96292	03708	52
9	417968		417970	582030	302546	13	302634	697366	51
10	463725	999998	463727	36273	08794	10	8884	91116	50
11	7.505118	9.999998	7.505120	12.494880	8.314954	9.999907	8.315046	11.684954	49
12	42906	7	542909	57091	21027	05	21122	78878	48
13	77668	7	77672	22328	7016	02	27114	2886	47
14	609853	6	609857	390143	32924	899	33025	66975	46
15	39816	6	39820	60180	8753	97	8856	1144	45
16	67845	5	67849	32151	44504	94	44610	55390	44
17	94173	5	94179	05821	50181	91	50289	49711	43
18	718997	4	719003	280997	5783	88	5895	4105	42
19	42477	3	42484	57516	61315	85	61430	38570	41
20	64754	3	94761	35239	6777	82	66895	3105	40
21	7.785943	9.999992	7.785951	12.214049	3 372171	9.999879	8.372292	11.627708	39
22	806146	1	806155	193845	7499	76	77622	2379	38
23	25451	0	25460	74540	82762	73	82889	17111	37
24	43934	89	43944	56056	7962	70	8092	1908	36
25	61662	8	61674	38326	93101	67	93234	06766	35
26	78695	8	78708	21292	8179	64	8315	1685	34
27	95085	7	95099	04901	403199	61	403338	596662	33
28	910879	6	910894	089106	8161	58	08304	1696	32
29	26119	5	26134	73866	13068	54	13213	86787	31
30	40842	3	40858	59142	7919	51	8068	1932	30
31	7.955082	9.999982	7 955100	12.044900	3.422717	9 999848	8.422869	11.577131	29
32	68870	1	68889	31111	7462	44	7618	2382	28
33	82233	0	82253	17747	32156	41	32315	67685	27
34	95198	79	95219	04781	6800	38	6962	3038	26
35	8.007787	7	8.007809	11.992191	41394	34	41560	58440	25
36	20021	6	20045	79955	5941	31	6110	3890	24
37	31919	5	31945	68055	50440	27	50613	49387	23
38	43501	3	43527	56473	4893	23	5070	4930	22
39	54781	2	54809	45191	9301	20	9481	0519	21
40	65776	1	65806	34194	63665	16	63849	36151	20
41	8.076500	9.999969	8.076531	11.923469	3.467985	9.999812	8.468172	11.531828	19
42	86965	8	86997	13003	72263	09	72454	27546	18
43	97183	6	97217	02783	6498	05	6693	3307	17
44	107167	4	107202	892797	80693	01	80892	19108	16
45	16926	3	16963	83037	4848	797	5050	4950	15
46	26471	1	26510	73490	8963	93	9170	0830	14
47	35810	59	35851	64149	93040	90	93250	06750	13
48	44953	8	44996	55004	7078	86	7293	2707	12
49	53907	6	53952	46048	501080	82	501298	498702	11
50	62681	4	62727	37273	5045	78	5267	4733	10
51	8.171281	9.999952	8.171328	11.828672	8.508974	9.999774	8.509200	11.490800	9
52	79713	0	79763	20237	12867	69	12098	86902	8
53	87985	48	88036	11964	6726	65	6961	3039	7
54	96102	6	96156	03844	20551	61	20790	79210	6
55	204070	4	204126	795874	4343	57	4586	5414	5
56	11895	2	11953	88047	8102	53	8349	1651	4
57	19581	0	19641	80359	31828	48	32080	67920	3
58	27134	38	27195	72805	5523	44	5779	4221	2
59	34557	6	34621	65379	9186	40	9447	0553	1
60	41855	4	41921	58079	42819	35	43084	56916	0
′	Cosine.	Sine.	Cotan.	Tang.	Cosine.	Sine.	Cotan.	Tang.	′
		89 DEGREES.				88 DEGREES.			

′	Sine.	Cosine.	Tang.	Cotang.	Sine.	Cosine.	Tang.	Cotang.	′
		2 Degrees.				3 Degrees.			
0	8.542819	9.999735	8.543084	11.4569 6	8.718800	9.999404	8.719396	11.280604	60
1	6422	31	6691	3309	21204	538	1806	78194	59
2	9995	26	50268	49732	3595	91	4204	5796	58
3	53539	22	3817	6183	5972	84	6588	3412	57
4	7054	17	7336	2664	8337	78	8959	1041	56
5	60540	13	60828	39172	30688	71	31317	68683	55
6	3999	08	4291	5709	3027	64	3663	6337	54
7	7431	04	7727	2273	5354	57	5996	4004	53
8	70836	699	71137	28863	7667	50	8317	1683	52
9	4214	94	4520	5480	9969	43	40626	59374	51
10	7566	89	7877	2123	42259	36	2922	7078	50
11	8.580892	9.999685	8.581208	11.418792	8.741536	9.999329	8.745207	11.254793	49
12	4193	80	4514	5486	6802	22	7479	2521	48
13	7469	75	7795	2205	9055	15	9740	0260	47
14	90721	70	91051	08949	51297	08	51989	48011	46
15	8948	65	4283	5717	3528	01	4227	5773	45
16	7152	60	7492	2508	5747	294	6453	3547	44
17	600332	55	600677	399323	7955	86	8668	1332	43
18	3489	50	3839	6161	60151	79	60872	39128	42
19	6623	45	6978	3022	2337	72	3065	6935	41
20	9734	40	10094	89906	4511	65	5246	4754	40
21	8.612823	9.999635	8.613189	11.386811	8.766675	9.999257	8.767417	11.232583	39
22	5891	29	6262	3738	8828	50	9578	0422	38
23	8937	24	9313	0687	70970	42	71727	28273	37
24	21962	19	22343	77657	3101	35	3866	6134	36
25	4965	14	5352	4648	5223	27	5995	4005	35
26	7948	08	8340	1660	7333	20	8114	1886	34
27	30911	03	31308	68692	9434	12	80222	19778	33
28	3854	597	4256	5744	81524	05	2320	7680	32
29	6776	92	7184	2816	3605	197	4408	5592	31
30	9680	86	40093	59907	5675	89	6486	3514	30
31	8.642563	9.999581	8.642982	11.357018	8.787736	9.999181	8.788554	11.211446	29
32	5428	75	5853	4147	9787	74	90613	09387	28
33	8274	70	8704	1296	91828	66	2662	7338	27
34	51102	64	51537	48463	3859	58	4701	5299	26
35	3911	58	4352	5648	5881	50	6731	3269	25
36	6702	53	7149	2851	7894	42	8752	1248	24
37	9475	47	9928	0072	9897	24	800763	199237	23
38	62230	41	62689	37311	801892	26	2765	7235	22
39	4968	35	5433	4567	3876	18	4758	5242	21
40	7689	29	8160	1840	5852	10	6742	3258	20
41	8.670393	9.999524	8.670870	11.329130	8.807819	9.999102	8.808717	11.191283	19
42	3080	18	3563	6437	9777	094	10683	89317	18
43	5751	12	6239	3761	11726	86	2641	7359	17
44	8405	06	8900	1100	3667	77	4589	5411	16
45	81043	00	81544	18456	5599	69	6529	3471	15
46	3665	493	4172	5828	7522	61	8461	1539	14
47	6272	87	6784	3216	9436	53	20384	79616	13
48	8863	81	9381	0619	21343	44	2298	7702	12
49	91438	75	91963	08037	3240	36	4205	5795	11
50	3998	69	4529	5471	5130	27	6103	3897	10
51	8.696543	9.999463	8.697081	11.302919	8.827011	9.999019	8.827992	11.172008	9
52	9073	56	9617	0383	8884	10	9874	0126	8
53	701589	50	702139	297861	30749	02	31748	68252	7
54	4090	43	4646	5354	2607	8993	3613	6384	6
55	6577	37	7140	2860	4456	84	5471	4529	5
56	9049	31	9618	0382	6297	76	7321	2679	4
57	11507	24	12083	87917	8130	67	9163	0837	3
58	3952	18	4534	5465	9956	58	40998	59002	2
59	6383	11	6972	3028	41774	50	2825	7175	1
60	8800	04	9396	0604	3585	41	4644	5356	0
′	Cosine.	Sine.	Cotan.	Tang.	Cosine.	Sine.	Cotang.	Tang.	′
		87 Degrees.				86 Degrees.			

′	4 Degrees.				5 Degrees.				′
	Sine.	Cosine.	Tang.	Cotang.	Sine.	Cosine.	Tang.	Cotang.	
0	8.843585	9 998941	8.844644	11.155356	8.940296	9.998344	8.941952	11.058048	60
1	5387	32	6455	3545	1738	33	3404	6596	59
2	7183	23	8260	1740	3174	22	4852	5148	58
3	8971	14	50057	49943	4606	11	6295	3705	57
4	50751	05	1846	8154	6034	00	7734	2266	56
5	2525	896	3628	6372	7456	289	9168	0832	55
6	4291	87	5403	4597	8874	77	50597	49403	54
7	6049	78	7171	2829	50287	66	2021	7979	53
8	7801	69	8932	1068	1696	55	3441	6559	52
9	9546	60	60686	39314	3100	43	4856	5144	51
10	61283	51	2433	7567	4499	32	6267	3733	50
11	8.863014	9.998841	8.864173	11.135827	8.955894	9.998220	8.957674	11.042326	49
12	4738	32	5906	4094	7284	09	9075	0925	48
13	6455	23	7632	2368	8670	197	60473	39527	47
14	8165	13	9351	0649	60052	86	1866	8134	46
15	9868	04	71064	28936	1429	74	3255	6745	45
16	71565	795	2770	7230	2801	63	4639	5361	44
17	3255	85	4469	5531	4170	51	6019	3981	43
18	4938	76	6162	3838	5535	39	7394	2606	42
19	66 5	66	7849	2151	6893	28	8766	1234	41
20	8285	57	9529	0471	8249	16	70133	29867	40
21	8.879949	9.998747	8.881202	11.118798	8 969600	9.998104	8.971496	11.028504	39
22	81607	38	2869	7131	70947	092	2855	7145	38
23	3258	28	4530	5470	2289	80	4209	5791	37
24	4903	18	6185	3815	3628	68	5560	4440	36
25	6542	08	7838	2167	4962	56	6906	3094	35
26	8174	699	9476	0524	6293	44	8248	1752	34
27	9801	89	91112	08888	7619	32	9586	0414	33
28	91421	79	2742	7258	8941	20	80921	19079	32
29	3035	69	4366	5634	80259	08	2251	7749	31
30	4643	59	5984	4016	1573	996	3577	6423	30
31	8.896246	9.998649	8.897596	11.102404	8.982883	9 997984	8.984899	11.015101	29
32	7842	39	9203	0797	4189	72	6217	3783	28
33	9432	29	900803	099197	5491	59	7532	2468	27
34	901017	19	2398	7602	6789	47	8842	1158	26
35	902596	09	3987	6013	8083	35	90149	09851	25
36	4169	599	5570	4430	9374	22	1451	8549	24
37	5736	89	7147	2853	90660	10	2750	7250	23
38	7297	78	8719	1281	1943	897	4045	5955	22
36	8853	68	10285	89715	3222	85	5337	4663	21
40	10404	58	1846	8154	4497	72	6624	3376	20
41	8.911949	9.998548	8.913401	11.086599	8.995768	9.997860	8.997908	11.002092	19
42	3488	37	4951	5049	7036	47	9188	0812	18
43	5022	27	6495	3505	8299	35	9.000465	10.999535	17
44	6550	16	8034	1966	9560	22	1738	8262	16
45	8073	06	9568	0432	9.000816	09	3007	6993	15
46	9591	495	21096	78904	2069	797	4272	5728	14
47	21103	85	2619	7381	3318	84	5534	4466	13
48	2610	74	4136	5864	4563	71	6792	3208	12
49	4112	64	5649	4351	5805	58	8047	1953	11
50	5609	53	7156	2844	7044	45	9298	0702	10
51	8.927100	9.998442	8.928658	11.071342	9.008278	9.997732	9.010546	10.989454	9
52	8587	31	30155	69846	9510	19	1790	8210	8
53	30068	21	1647	8353	10737	06	3031	6969	7
54	1544	10	3134	6866	1962	93	4268	5732	6
55	3015	399	4616	5384	3182	80	5502	4498	5
56	4481	88	6093	3907	4400	67	6732	3268	4
57	5942	77	7565	2435	5613	54	7959	2041	3
58	7398	66	9032	0968	6824	41	9183	0817	2
59	8850	55	40494	59506	8031	28	20403	79597	1
60	40296	44	1952	8048	9235	14	1620	8380	0
′	Cosine.	Sine.	Cotan.	Tang.	Cosine.	Sine.	Cotan.	Tang.	′
	85 Degrees.				84 Degrees.				

	6 Degrees.				7 Degrees.				
′	Sine.	Cosine.	Tang.	Cotang.	Sine.	Cosine.	Tang.	Cotang.	′
0	9.019235	9.997614	9.021620	10.978380	9.085994	9.996751	9.089144	10.910856	60
1	20435	C1	2334	7166	6922	35	0187	9813	59
2	1632	588	4044	5956	7947	20	1228	8772	58
3	2825	74	5251	4749	8970	04	2266	7734	57
4	4016	61	6455	3545	9990	688	3302	6698	56
5	5203	47	7655	2345	91008	73	4336	5664	55
6	6386	34	8852	1148	2024	57	5367	4633	54
7	7567	20	30046	69954	3037	41	6395	3605	53
8	8744	07	1237	8763	4047	25	7422	2578	52
9	9918	493	2425	7575	5056	10	8446	1554	51
10	31089	80	3609	6391	6062	594	9468	0532	50
11	9.032257	9.997466	9.034791	10.965209	9.097065	9.996578	9.100487	10 899513	49
12	3421	52	5969	4031	8066	62	1504	8496	48
13	4582	39	7144	2856	9065	46	2519	7481	47
14	5741	25	8316	1684	100062	30	3532	6468	46
15	6896	11	9485	0515	1056	14	4542	5455	45
16	8048	397	40651	59349	2048	498	5550	4450	44
17	9197	83	1813	8187	3037	82	6556	3444	43
18	40342	69	2973	7027	4025	65	7559	2441	42
19	1485	55	4130	5870	5010	49	8560	1440	41
20	2625	41	5284	4716	5992	33	9559	0441	40
21	9.043762	9.997327	9.046434	10.953566	9.106973	9 996417	9.110556	10 889444	39
22	4895	13	7582	2418	7951	00	1551	8449	38
23	6026	299	8727	1273	8927	384	2543	7457	37
24	7154	85	9869	0131	9901	68	3533	6467	36
25	8279	71	51008	48992	10873	51	4521	5479	35
26	9400	57	2144	7856	1842	35	5507	4493	34
27	50519	42	3277	6723	2809	18	6491	3509	33
28	1635	28	4407	5593	3774	02	7472	2528	32
29	2749	14	5535	4465	4737	285	8452	1548	31
30	3859	199	6659	3341	5698	69	9429	0571	30
31	9.054966	9.997185	9.057781	10.942219	9.116656	9.996252	9.120404	10.879596	29
32	6071	70	8900	1100	7613	35	1377	8623	28
33	7172	56	60016	39984	8567	19	2348	7652	27
34	8271	41	1130	8870	9519	02	3317	6683	26
35	9367	27	2240	7760	20469	185	4284	5716	25
36	60460	12	3348	6652	1417	68	5249	4751	24
37	1551	098	4453	5547	2362	51	6211	3789	23
38	2639	83	5556	4444	3306	34	7172	2828	22
39	3724	68	6655	3345	4248	17	8130	1870	21
40	4806	53	7752	2248	5187	00	9087	0913	20
41	9.065885	9.997039	9.068846	10.931154	9.126125	9.996083	9.130041	10.869959	19
42	6962	24	9938	0062	7060	66	0994	9006	18
43	8036	09	71027	28973	7993	49	1944	8056	17
44	9107	6994	2113	7887	8925	32	2893	7107	16
45	70176	79	3197	6803	9854	15	3839	6161	15
46	1242	64	4278	5722	30781	998	4784	5216	14
47	2306	49	5356	4644	1706	80	5726	4274	13
48	3366	34	6432	3568	2630	63	6667	3333	12
49	4424	19	7505	2495	3551	46	7605	2395	11
50	5480	04	8576	1424	4470	28	8542	1458	10
51	9.076533	9.996889	9.079644	10.920356	9.135387	9.995911	9.139476	1.0860524	9
52	7583	74	80710	19290	6303	894	0409	859591	8
53	8631	58	1773	8227	7216	76	1340	8660	7
54	9676	43	2833	7167	8128	59	2269	7731	6
55	0719	28	3891	6109	9037	41	3196	6804	5
56	81759	12	4947	5053	9944	23	4121	5879	4
57	2797	797	6000	4000	40850	06	5044	4856	3
58	3832	82	7050	2950	1754	788	5966	4034	2
59	4864	66	8098	1902	2655	71	6885	3115	1
60	5894	51	9144	0856	3555	53	7803	2197	0
′	Cosine.	Sine.	Cotan.	Tang.	Cosine.	Sine.	Cotang.	Tang.	′

83 Degrees.   82 Degrees.

	8 Degrees.				9 Degrees.				
′	Sine.	Cosine.	Tang.	Cotang.	Sine.	Cosine.	Tang.	Cotang.	′
0	9.148555	9 995753	9.147803	10.852197	9.194382	9.994620	9.199713	10.800287	60
1	4153	35	8718	1282	5129	00	200529	799471	59
2	5349	17	9632	0368	5925	580	1345	8655	58
3	6248	699	50544	49456	6719	60	2159	7844	57
4	7136	81	1454	8546	7511	40	2971	7029	56
5	8026	64	2363	7637	8302	19	3782	6218	55
6	8915	46	3269	6731	9091	499	4592	5408	54
7	9802	28	4174	5826	9879	79	5400	4600	53
8	50686	10	5077	4923	200666	59	6207	3793	52
9	1569	591	5978	4022	1451	38	7013	2987	51
10	2451	73	6877	3123	2234	18	7817	2183	50
11	9.153330	9.995555	9.157775	10.842225	9.203017	9.994398	9.208619	10.791381	49
12	4208	37	8671	1329	3797	77	9420	0580	48
13	5083	19	9565	0435	4577	57	10220	89780	47
14	5957	01	60457	39543	5354	36	1018	8982	46
15	6830	482	1347	8653	6131	16	1815	8185	45
16	7700	64	2236	7764	6906	295	2611	7389	44
17	8569	46	8123	6877	7679	74	8405	6595	43
18	9435	27	4008	5992	8452	54	4198	5802	42
19	60301	09	4892	5108	9222	33	4989	5011	41
20	1164	390	5774	4226	9992	12	5780	4220	40
21	9.162025	9.995372	9.166654	10.833346	9.210760	9.994191	9.216568	10.783432	39
22	2885	53	7532	2468	1526	71	7356	2644	38
23	3743	34	8409	1591	2291	50	8142	1858	37
24	4600	16	9284	0716	3055	29	8926	1074	36
25	5454	297	70157	29843	3818	08	9710	0290	35
26	6307	78	1029	8971	4579	087	20492	79508	34
27	7159	60	1899	8101	5338	66	1272	8728	33
28	8008	41	2767	7233	6097	45	2052	7948	32
29	8856	22	3634	6366	6854	24	2830	7170	31
30	9702	03	4499	5501	7609	03	3607	6393	30
31	9.170547	9.995184	9.175362	10.824638	9.218363	9 993982	9.224382	10.775618	29
32	1389	65	6224	3776	9116	60	5156	4844	28
33	2230	46	7084	2916	9868	39	5929	4071	27
34	3070	27	7942	2058	220618	18	6700	3300	26
35	3908	08	8799	1201	1367	897	7471	2529	25
36	4744	089	9655	0345	2115	75	8239	1716	24
37	5578	70	80508	19492	2861	54	9007	0993	23
38	6411	51	1360	8640	3606	32	9773	0227	22
36	7242	32	2211	7789	4349	11	80539	69461	21
40	8072	13	3059	6941	5092	789	1302	8698	20
41	9.178900	9.994993	9.183907	10.816093	9.225833	9.993768	9 232065	10.767935	19
42	9726	74	4752	5248	6573	46	2826	7174	18
43	80551	55	5597	4403	7311	25	3586	6414	17
44	1374	35	6439	3561	8048	03	4345	5655	16
45	2196	16	7280	2720	8784	681	5103	4897	15
46	3016	896	8120	1880	9518	60	5859	4141	14
47	3834	77	8958	1042	230252	38	6614	3386	13
48	4651	57	9794	0206	0984	16	7368	2632	12
49	5466	38	90629	09371	1714	594	8120	1880	11
50	6280	18	1462	8538	2444	72	8872	1128	10
51	9.187092	9.994798	9.192291	10.807706	9.233172	9.993550	9.239622	10.760378	9
52	7903	79	3124	6876	3899	28	40371	59629	8
53	8712	59	3953	6047	4625	06	1118	8882	7
54	9519	39	4780	5220	5349	484	1865	8135	6
55	90325	19	5606	4394	6073	62	2610	7390	5
56	1130	00	6430	3570	6795	40	3354	6646	4
57	1933	680	7253	2747	7515	18	4097	5903	3
58	2734	60	8074	1926	8235	896	4839	5161	2
59	3534	40	8894	1103	8953	74	5579	4421	1
60	4332	20	9713	0287	9670	51	6319	3681	0
′	Cosine.	Sine.	Cotan.	Tang.	Cosine.	Sine.	Cotan.	Tang.	′
	81 Degrees.				80 Degrees.				

Z

	10 Degrees.				11 Degrees.				
′	Sine.	Cosine.	Tang.	Cotang.	Sine.	Cosine.	Tang.	Cotang.	′
0	9.239670	9.993351	9.246319	10.753681	9.280599	9.991947	9.288652	10.711348	60
1	40386	29	7057	2943	1248	22	9326	0674	59
2	1101	07	7794	2206	1897	897	9999	0001	58
3	1814	284	8530	1470	2544	73	90671	09329	57
4	2526	62	9264	0736	3190	48	1342	8658	56
5	3237	40	9998	0002	3836	23	2013	7987	55
6	3947	17	50730	49270	4480	799	2682	7318	54
7	4656	195	1461	8539	5124	74	3350	6650	53
8	5363	72	2191	7809	5766	49	4017	5983	52
9	6069	49	2920	7080	6408	24	4684	5316	51
10	6775	27	3648	6352	7048	699	5349	4651	50
11	9.247478	9.993104	9.254374	10.745626	9.287687	9.991674	9.296013	10.703987	49
12	8181	081	5100	4900	8326	49	6677	3323	48
13	8883	59	5824	4176	8964	24	7339	2661	47
14	9583	36	6547	3453	9600	599	8001	1999	46
15	50282	13	7269	2731	90236	74	8662	1338	45
16	0980	2990	7990	2010	0870	49	9322	0678	44
17	1677	67	8710	1290	1504	24	9980	0020	43
18	2373	44	9429	0571	2137	498	00638	99362	42
19	3067	21	60146	39854	2768	73	1295	8705	41
20	3761	898	0863	9137	3399	48	1951	8049	40
21	9.254453	9.992875	9.261578	10.738422	9.294029	9.991422	9.302607	10.697393	39
22	5144	52	2292	7708	4658	397	3261	6739	38
23	5834	29	3005	6995	5286	72	3914	6086	37
24	6523	06	3717	6283	5913	46	4567	5433	36
25	7211	783	4428	5573	6539	21	5218	4782	35
26	7898	59	5138	4862	7164	295	5869	4131	34
27	8583	36	5847	4153	7788	70	6519	3481	33
28	9268	13	6555	3445	8412	44	7168	2832	32
29	9951	690	7261	2739	9034	18	7815	2185	31
30	60633	66	7967	2033	9655	193	8463	1537	30
31	9.261314	9.992643	9.268671	10.731329	9.300276	9.991167	9.309109	10.690891	29
32	1994	19	9375	0625	0895	41	9754	0246	28
33	2673	596	70077	29923	1514	15	10398	89602	27
34	3351	72	0779	9221	2132	090	1042	8958	26
35	4027	49	1479	8521	2748	64	1685	8315	25
36	4703	25	2178	7822	3364	38	2327	7673	24
37	5377	01	2876	7124	3979	12	2967	7033	23
38	6051	478	3573	6427	4593	0986	3608	6392	22
39	6723	54	4269	5731	5207	60	4247	5753	21
40	7395	30	4964	5036	5819	34	4885	5115	20
41	9.268065	9.992406	9.275658	10.724342	9.306430	9.990908	9.315523	10.684477	19
42	8734	382	6351	3649	7041	882	6159	3841	18
43	9402	59	7043	2957	7650	55	6795	3205	17
44	70069	35	7734	2266	8259	29	7430	2570	16
45	0735	11	8424	1576	8867	03	8064	1936	15
46	1400	287	9113	0887	9474	777	8697	1303	14
47	2064	63	9801	0199	10080	50	9329	0671	13
48	2726	39	80488	19512	0685	24	9961	0039	12
49	3388	14	1174	8826	1289	697	20592	79408	11
50	4049	190	1858	8142	1893	71	1222	8778	10
51	9.274708	9.992166	9.282542	10.717458	9.312495	9.990644	9.321851	10.678149	9
52	5367	42	3225	6775	3097	18	2479	7521	8
53	6024	18	3907	6093	3698	591	3106	6894	7
54	6681	093	4588	5412	4297	65	3733	6267	6
55	7337	69	5268	4732	4897	38	4358	5642	5
56	7991	44	5947	4053	5495	11	4983	5017	4
57	8645	20	6624	3376	6092	485	5607	4393	3
58	9297	1996	7301	2699	6689	58	6231	3769	2
59	9948	71	7977	2023	7284	31	6853	3147	1
60	80599	47	8652	1348	7879	04	7475	2525	0
′	Cosine.	Sine.	Cotan.	Tang.	Cosine.	Sine.	Cotang.	Tang.	′
	79 Degrees.				78 Degrees.				

′	Sine.	Cosine.	Tang.	Cotang.	Sine.	Cosine.	Tang.	Cotang.	′
		12 Degrees.				13 Degrees.			
0	9.317879	9.990404	9.327474	10.672526	9.352088	9.988724	9.363364	10.636636	60
1	8473	378	8095	1905	2635	695	3940	6060	59
2	9066	51	8715	1285	3181	66	4515	5485	58
3	9658	24	9334	0666	3726	36	5090	4910	57
4	20249	297	9953	0047	4271	07	5664	4336	56
5	0840	70	30570	69430	4815	578	6237	3763	55
6	143C	43	1187	8813	5358	48	6810	3190	54
7	2019	15	1803	8197	5901	19	7382	2618	53
8	2607	188	2418	7582	6443	489	7953	2047	52
9	3194	61	3033	6967	6984	60	8524	1476	51
10	3780	34	3646	6354	7524	30	9094	0906	50
11	9.324366	9.990107	9.334259	10.665741	9.358064	9.988401	9.369663	10.630337	49
12	4950	079	4871	5129	8603	371	0232	29768	48
13	5534	52	5482	4518	9141	42	0799	9201	47
14	6117	25	6093	3907	9678	12	1367	8633	46
15	6700	989997	6702	3298	360215	282	1933	8067	45
16	7281	70	7311	2689	0752	52	2499	7501	44
17	7862	42	7919	2081	1287	23	3064	6936	43
18	8442	15	8527	1473	1822	193	3629	6371	42
19	9021	887	9133	0867	2356	63	4193	5807	41
20	9599	60	9739	0261	2889	33	4756	5244	40
21	9.330176	9.989832	9.340344	10.659656	9.363422	9.988103	9.375319	10.624681	39
22	0753	04	0948	9052	3954	073	5881	4119	38
23	1329	777	1552	8448	4485	43	6442	3558	37
24	1903	49	2155	7845	5016	13	7003	2997	36
25	2478	21	2757	7243	5546	7983	7563	2437	35
26	3051	693	3358	6642	6075	53	8122	1878	34
27	3624	65	3958	6042	6604	22	8681	1319	33
28	4195	37	4558	5442	7131	892	9239	0761	32
29	4766	09	5157	4843	7659	62	9797	0203	31
30	5337	582	5755	4245	8185	32	80354	19646	30
31	9.335906	9.989553	9.346353	10.653647	9.368711	9.987801	9.380910	10.619090	29
32	6475	25	6949	3051	9236	771	1466	8534	28
33	7043	497	7545	2455	9761	40	2020	7980	27
34	7610	69	8141	1859	370285	10	2575	7425	26
35	8176	41	8735	1265	0808	679	3129	6871	25
36	8742	13	9329	0671	1330	49	3682	6318	24
37	9307	385	9922	0078	1852	18	4234	5766	23
38	9871	56	50514	49486	2373	588	4786	5214	22
39	40434	28	1106	8894	2894	57	5337	4663	21
40	0996	00	1697	8303	3414	26	5888	4112	20
41	9.341558	9.989271	9.352287	10.647713	9.373933	9.987496	9.386438	10.613562	19
42	2119	43	2876	7124	4452	65	6987	3013	18
43	2679	14	3465	6535	4970	34	7536	2464	17
44	3239	186	4053	5947	5487	03	8084	1916	16
45	3797	57	4640	5360	6003	372	8631	1369	15
46	4355	28	5227	4773	6519	41	9178	0822	14
47	4912	00	5813	4187	7035	10	9724	0276	13
48	5469	071	6398	3602	7549	279	90270	09730	12
49	6024	42	6982	3018	8065	48	0815	9185	11
50	6579	14	7566	2434	8577	17	1360	8640	10
51	9.347134	9.988985	9.358149	10.641851	9.379089	9.987186	9.391903	10.608097	9
52	7687	56	8731	1269	9601	55	2447	7553	8
53	8240	27	9313	0687	380113	24	2989	7011	7
54	8792	898	9893	0107	0624	092	3531	6469	6
55	9343	69	60474	39526	1134	61	4073	5927	5
56	9893	40	1053	8947	1643	30	4614	5386	4
57	50443	11	1632	8368	2152	6998	5154	4846	3
58	0992	782	2210	7790	2661	67	5694	4306	2
59	1540	53	2787	7213	3168	36	6233	3767	1
60	2088	24	3364	6636	3675	04	6771	3229	0
′	Cosine.	Sine.	Cotan.	Tang.	Cosine.	Sine.	Cotan.	Tang.	′
		77 Degrees.				76 Degrees.			

	14 Degrees.				15 Degrees.				
′	Sine.	Cosine.	Tang.	Cotang.	Sine.	Cosine.	Tang.	Cotang.	′
0	9.383675	9 986904	9.396771	10.603229	9.412996	9.984944	9.428052	10.571948	60
1	4182	873	7309	2691	3467	10	8557	1448	59
2	4687	41	7846	2154	3938	876	9062	0938	58
3	5192	09	8383	1617	4408	42	9566	0434	57
4	5697	778	8919	1081	4878	08	30070	699930	56
5	6201	46	9455	0545	5347	774	0573	9427	55
6	6704	14	9990	0010	5815	40	1075	8925	54
7	7207	683	400524	599476	6283	06	1577	8423	53
8	7709	51	1058	8942	6751	672	2079	7921	52
9	8210	19	1591	8409	7217	38	2580	7420	51
10	8711	587	2124	7876	7684	03	3080	6920	50
11	9.389211	9.986555	9.402656	10.597344	9.418150	9.984569	9.433580	10.566420	49
12	9711	23	3187	6813	8615	35	4080	5920	48
13	90210	491	3718	6282	9079	00	4579	5421	47
14	0708	59	4249	5752	9544	466	5078	4922	46
15	1206	27	4778	5222	20007	32	5576	4424	45
16	1703	395	5808	4692	0470	397	6073	3927	44
17	2199	63	5836	4164	0933	63	6570	3430	43
18	2695	31	6364	3636	1395	28	7067	2933	42
19	3191	299	6892	3108	1857	294	7563	2437	41
20	3685	66	7419	2581	2318	59	8059	1941	40
21	9.394179	9.986234	9.407945	10.592055	9.422778	9.984224	9.438554	10.561446	39
22	4673	02	8471	1529	3238	190	9048	0952	38
23	5166	169	8997	1003	3697	55	9543	0457	37
24	5658	37	9521	0479	4156	20	40036	559964	36
25	6150	04	10045	589955	4615	085	0529	9471	35
26	6641	072	0569	9431	5073	50	1022	8978	34
27	7132	39	1092	8908	5530	15	1514	8486	33
28	7621	07	1615	8385	5987	983981	2006	7994	32
29	8111	985974	2137	7863	6443	46	2497	7503	31
30	8600	42	2658	7342	6899	11	2988	7012	30
31	9.399088	9.985909	9.413179	10.586821	9.427354	9.983875	9.443479	10.556521	29
32	9575	876	3699	6301	7809	40	3968	6032	28
33	40062	43	4219	5781	8263	05	4458	5542	27
34	0549	11	4738	5262	8717	770	4947	5053	26
35	1035	778	5257	4743	9170	35	5435	4565	25
36	1520	45	5775	4225	9623	00	5923	4077	24
37	2005	12	6293	3707	30075	664	6411	3589	23
38	2489	679	6810	3190	0527	29	6898	3102	22
39	2972	46	7326	2674	0978	594	7384	2616	21
40	3455	13	7842	2158	1429	58	7870	2130	20
41	9.403938	9.985580	9.418358	10.581742	9.431879	9.983523	9.448356	10.551644	19
42	4420	47	8873	1127	2329	487	8841	1159	18
43	4901	14	9387	0613	2778	52	9326	0674	17
44	5382	480	9901	0099	3226	16	9810	0190	16
45	5862	47	420415	579585	3675	381	50294	9706	15
46	6341	14	0927	9073	4122	45	0777	549223	14
47	6820	381	1440	8560	4569	09	1260	8740	13
48	7299	47	1952	8048	5016	273	1743	8257	12
49	7777	14	2463	7537	5462	38	2225	7775	11
50	8254	280	2974	7026	5908	02	2706	7294	10
51	9.408731	9.985247	9.423484	10.576516	9.436353	9.913166	9.453187	10.546818	9
52	9207	18	3993	6007	6798	30	3668	6332	8
53	9682	180	4503	5497	7242	094	4148	5852	7
54	0157	46	5011	4989	7686	58	4628	5372	6
55	0632	13	5519	4481	8129	22	5107	4893	5
56	1106	079	6027	3973	8572	2986	5586	4414	4
57	1579	45	6535	3466	9014	50	6064	3936	3
58	2052	11	7041	2959	9456	14	6542	3458	2
59	2524	4978	7547	2453	9897	878	7019	2981	1
60	2996	44	8052	1948	40338	42	7496	2504	0
′	Cosine.	Sine.	Cotan.	Tang.	Cosine.	Sine.	Cotang.	Tang.	′
	75 Degrees.				74 Degrees.				

	16 Degrees.				17 Degrees.				
′	Sine.	Cosine.	Tang.	Cotang.	Sine.	Cosine.	Tang.	Cotang.	′
0	9.440338	9.982842	9.457496	10.542504	9.465935	9.980596	9.485339	10.514661	60
1	0778	05	7973	2027	6348	58	5791	4209	59
2	1218	769	8449	1551	6761	19	6242	3758	58
3	1658	33	8925	1075	7173	480	6693	3307	57
4	2096	696	9400	0600	7585	42	7143	2857	56
5	2535	60	9875	0125	7996	03	7593	2407	55
6	2973	24	60349	539651	8407	364	8043	1957	54
7	3410	587	0823	9177	8817	25	8492	1508	53
8	3847	51	1297	8703	9227	286	8941	1059	52
9	4284	14	1770	8230	9637	47	9390	0610	51
10	4720	477	2242	7758	70046	08	9838	0162	50
11	9.445155	9.982441	9.462714	10.537286	9.470455	9.980169	9.490286	10.509714	49
12	5590	04	3186	6814	0863	30	0733	9267	48
13	6025	867	3658	6342	1271	091	1180	8820	47
14	6459	31	4128	5872	1679	52	1627	8373	46
15	6893	294	4599	5401	2086	12	2073	7927	45
16	7326	57	5069	4931	2492	79973	2519	7481	44
17	7759	20	5539	4461	2898	34	2965	7035	43
18	8191	183	6008	3992	3304	895	3410	6590	42
19	8623	46	6476	3524	3710	55	3854	6146	41
20	9054	09	6945	3055	4115	16	4299	5701	40
21	9.449485	9.982072	9.467413	10.532587	9.474519	9.979776	9.494743	10.505257	39
22	9915	35	7880	2120	4923	37	5186	4814	38
23	50345	998	8347	1653	5327	697	5630	4370	37
24	0775	61	8814	1186	5730	58	6073	3927	36
25	1204	24	9280	0720	6133	18	6515	3485	35
26	1632	886	9746	520254	6536	579	6957	3043	34
27	2060	49	70211	9789	6938	39	7399	2601	33
28	2488	12	0676	9324	7340	499	7841	2159	32
29	2915	774	1141	8859	7741	59	8282	1718	31
30	3342	37	1605	8395	8142	20	8722	1278	30
31	9.453758	9.981700	9.472068	10.527932	9.478542	9.979380	9.499163	10.500837	29
32	4194	662	2532	7468	8942	40	9603	0397	28
33	4619	25	2995	7005	9342	00	500042	499958	27
34	5044	587	3457	6543	9741	260	0481	9519	26
35	5469	49	3919	6081	80140	20	0920	9080	25
36	5893	12	4381	5619	0539	180	1359	8641	24
37	6316	474	4842	5158	0937	40	1797	8203	23
38	6739	36	5303	4697	1334	00	2235	7763	22
39	7162	399	5763	4237	1731	059	2672	7328	21
40	7584	61	6223	3777	2128	19	3109	6891	20
41	9.458006	9.981323	9.476683	10.523317	9.482525	9.978979	9.503546	10.496454	19
42	8427	285	7142	2858	2921	39	3982	6018	18
43	8848	47	7601	2399	3316	898	4418	5582	17
44	9268	09	8059	1941	3712	58	4854	5146	16
45	9688	171	8517	1483	4107	17	5289	4711	15
46	60108	33	8975	1025	4501	777	5724	4276	14
47	0527	095	9432	0568	4895	37	6159	3841	13
48	0946	57	9889	0111	5289	696	6593	3407	12
49	1364	19	80345	519655	5682	55	7027	2973	11
50	1782	981	0801	9199	6075	15	7460	2540	10
51	9.462199	9.980042	9.481257	10.518743	9.486467	9.978574	9.507893	10.492107	9
52	2616	04	1712	8288	6860	33	8326	1674	8
53	3032	866	2167	7833	7251	493	8759	1241	7
54	3448	27	2621	7379	7643	52	9191	0809	6
55	3864	789	3075	6925	8034	11	9622	0378	5
56	4279	50	3529	6471	8424	370	10054	489946	4
57	4694	12	3982	6018	8814	29	0485	9515	3
58	5108	673	4435	5565	9204	288	0916	9084	2
59	5522	35	4887	5113	9593	47	1346	8654	1
60	5985	596	5339	4661	9982	06	1776	8224	0
′	Cosine.	Sine.	Cotan.	Tang.	Cosine.	Sine.	Cotang.	Tang.	′
	73 Degrees.				72 Degrees.				

′	18 DEGREES. Sine.	Cosine.	Tang.	Cotang.	19 DEGREES. Sine.	Cosine.	Tang.	Cotang.	′
0	9.489982	9.978206	9.511776	10.488224	9.512642	9.975670	9.536972	10.463028	60
1	0371	165	2206	7794	3009	27	7382	2618	59
2	0759	24	2635	7365	3375	583	7792	2208	58
3	1147	083	3064	6936	3741	39	8202	1798	57
4	1535	42	3493	6507	4107	496	8611	1389	56
5	1922	01	3921	6079	4472	52	9020	0980	55
6	2308	7959	4349	5651	4837	08	9429	0571	54
7	2695	18	4777	5223	5202	865	9837	0163	53
8	3081	877	5204	4796	5566	21	40245	59755	52
9	3466	35	5631	4369	5930	277	0653	9347	51
10	3851	794	6057	3943	6294	33	1061	8939	50
11	9.494236	9.977752	9.516484	10.483516	9.516657	9.975189	9.541468	10.458532	49
12	4621	11	6910	3090	7020	45	1875	8125	48
13	5005	669	7335	2665	7382	01	2281	7719	47
14	5388	28	7761	2239	7745	057	2688	7312	46
15	5772	586	8185	1815	8107	13	3094	6906	45
16	6154	44	8610	1390	8468	4969	3499	6501	44
17	6537	03	9034	0966	8829	25	3905	6095	43
18	6919	461	9458	0542	9190	880	4310	5690	42
19	7301	19	9882	0118	9551	36	4715	5285	41
20	7682	377	20305	479695	9911	792	5119	4881	40
21	9.498064	9.977335	9.520728	10.479272	9.520271	9.974748	9.545524	10.454476	39
22	8444	293	1151	8849	0631	03	5928	4072	38
23	8825	51	1573	8427	0990	659	6331	3669	37
24	9204	09	1995	8005	1349	14	6735	3265	36
25	9584	167	2417	7583	1707	570	7138	2862	35
26	9963	25	2838	7162	2066	25	7540	2460	34
27	500342	083	3259	6741	2424	481	7943	2057	33
28	0721	41	3680	6320	2781	36	8345	1655	32
29	1099	6999	4100	5900	3138	391	8747	1253	31
30	1476	57	4520	5480	3495	47	9149	0851	30
31	9.501854	9.977914	9.524939	10.475061	9.523852	9.974302	9.549550	10.450450	29
32	2231	872	5359	4641	4208	257	9951	0049	28
33	2607	30	5778	4222	4564	12	50352	49648	27
34	2984	787	6197	3803	4920	167	0752	9248	26
35	3360	45	6615	3385	5275	22	1152	8848	25
36	3735	02	7033	2967	5630	077	1552	8448	24
37	4110	660	7451	2549	5984	32	1952	8048	23
38	4485	17	7868	2132	6339	3987	2351	7649	22
39	4860	574	8285	1715	6693	42	2750	7250	21
40	5234	32	8702	1298	7046	897	3149	6851	20
41	9.505608	9.976489	9.529119	10.470881	9.527400	9.973852	9.553548	10.446452	19
42	5981	46	9535	0465	7753	07	3946	6054	18
43	6354	04	9950	0050	8105	761	4344	5656	17
44	6727	361	30366	69684	8458	16	4741	5259	16
45	7099	18	0781	9219	8810	671	5139	4861	15
46	7471	275	1196	8804	9161	25	5536	4464	14
47	7843	32	1611	8389	9513	580	5933	4067	13
48	8214	189	2025	7975	9864	35	6329	3671	12
49	8585	46	2439	7561	30215	489	6725	3275	11
50	8956	03	2853	7147	0565	44	7121	2879	10
51	9.509326	9.976060	9.533266	10.466734	9.530915	9.973398	9.557517	10.442483	9
52	9696	17	3679	6321	1265	52	7913	2087	8
53	10065	5974	4092	5908	1614	07	8308	1692	7
54	0434	30	4504	5496	1963	261	8702	1298	6
55	0803	887	4916	5084	2312	15	9097	0903	5
56	1172	44	5328	4672	2661	169	9491	0509	4
57	1540	00	5739	4261	3009	24	9885	0115	3
58	1907	757	6150	3850	3357	078	60279	39721	2
59	2275	14	6561	3439	3704	32	0673	9327	1
60	2642	670	6972	3028	4052	2986	1066	8934	0
′	Cosine.	Sine.	Cotan.	Tang.	Cosine.	Sine.	Cotan.	Tang.	′

	71 DEGREES.				70 DEGREES.				

	20 Degrees.				21 Degrees.				
′	Sine.	Cosine.	Tang.	Cotang.	Sine.	Cosine.	Tang.	Cotang.	′
0	9.534052	9.972986	9.561066	10.438934	9.554329	9.970152	9.584177	10.415823	60
1	4399	40	1459	8541	4658	03	4555	5445	59
2	4745	894	1851	8149	4987	055	4932	5068	58
3	5092	48	2244	7756	5315	06	5309	4691	57
4	5438	02	2636	7364	5643	69957	5686	4314	56
5	5783	755	3028	6972	5971	09	6062	3938	55
6	6129	09	3419	6581	6299	860	6439	3561	54
7	6474	663	3811	6189	6626	11	6815	3185	53
8	6818	17	4202	5798	6953	762	7190	2810	52
9	7163	570	4592	5408	7280	14	7566	2434	51
10	7507	24	4983	5017	7606	665	7941	2059	50
11	9 537851	9.972478	9.563735	10.434627	9.557932	9.969616	9.588316	10.411684	49
12	8194	31	5763	4237	8258	567	8691	1309	48
13	8538	385	6153	3847	8583	18	9066	0934	47
14	8880	38	6542	3458	8909	469	9440	0560	46
15	9223	291	6932	3068	9234	20	9814	0186	45
16	9565	45	7320	2680	9558	370	90188	409812	44
17	9907	198	7709	2291	9883	21	0562	9438	43
18	40249	51	8098	1902	60207	272	0935	9065	42
19	0590	05	8486	1514	0531	23	1308	8692	41
20	0931	058	8873	1127	0855	173	1681	8319	40
21	9.541272	9.972011	9.569261	10.430739	9.561178	9.969124	9.592054	10.407946	39
22	1613	1964	9648	0352	1501	075	2426	7574	38
23	1953	17	0035	29965	1824	25	2798	7202	37
24	2293	870	0422	9578	2146	68976	3171	6829	36
25	2632	23	0809	9191	2468	26	3542	6458	35
26	2971	776	71195	8805	2790	877	3914	6086	34
27	3310	29	1581	8419	3112	27	3285	5715	33
28	3649	682	1967	8033	3433	777	4656	5344	32
29	3987	35	2352	7648	3755	28	5027	4973	31
30	4325	588	2738	7262	4075	678	5398	4602	30
31	9.544663	9.971540	9.573123	10.426877	9.564396	9.968628	9.595768	10.404232	29
32	5000	493	3507	6493	4716	578	6138	3862	28
33	5338	46	3892	6108	5036	28	6508	3492	27
34	5674	398	4276	5724	5356	479	6878	3122	26
35	6011	51	4660	5340	5676	29	7247	2753	25
36	6347	03	5044	4956	5995	379	7616	2384	24
37	6683	256	5427	4573	6314	29	7985	2015	23
38	7019	08	5810	4190	6632	278	8354	1646	22
39	7354	161	6193	3807	6951	28	8722	1278	21
40	7689	13	6576	3424	7269	178	9091	0909	20
41	9.548024	9.971066	9.576959	10.423041	9.567587	9.968128	9.599459	10.400541	19
42	8359	18	7341	2659	7904	078	9827	0173	18
43	8693	0970	7723	2277	8222	27	600194	399806	17
44	9027	22	8104	1896	8539	67977	0526	9438	16
45	9360	874	8486	1514	8856	27	0929	9071	15
46	9690	27	8867	1133	9172	876	1296	8704	14
47	50026	779	9248	0752	9488	26	1662	8338	13
48	0359	31	9629	0371	9804	775	2029	7971	12
49	0692	683	80009	19991	70120	25	2395	7605	11
50	1024	35	0389	9611	0435	674	2761	7239	10
51	9.551356	9.970586	9.580769	10.419231	9.570751	9.967624	9.603127	10.396873	9
52	1687	38	1149	8851	1066	573	3493	6507	8
53	2018	490	1528	8472	1380	22	3858	6142	7
54	2349	42	1907	8093	1695	471	4223	5777	6
55	2680	394	2286	7714	2009	21	4588	5412	5
56	3010	45	2665	7335	2323	370	4953	5047	4
57	3341	297	3043	6957	2636	19	5317	4683	3
58	3670	49	3422	6578	2950	268	5682	4318	2
59	4000	00	3800	6200	3263	17	6046	3954	1
60	4329	152	4177	5823	3575	166	6410	3590	0
′	Cosine.	Sine.	Cotan.	Tang.	Cosine.	Sine.	Cotang.	Tang.	′
	69 Degrees.				68 Degrees.				

′	\ 22 Degrees. Sine.	Cosine.	Tang.	Cotang.	23 Degrees. Sine.	Cosine.	Tang.	Cotang.	′
0	9.573575	9 967166	9.606410	10.393590	9.591878	9.964026	9.627852	10.372148	60
1	3888	15	6773	3227	2176	972	8203	1797	59
2	4200	064	7137	2863	2473	19	8554	1446	58
3	4512	13	7500	2500	2770	865	8905	1095	57
4	4824	6961	7863	2137	3067	11	9255	0745	56
5	5186	10	8225	1775	3363	757	9606	0394	55
6	5447	859	8588	1412	3659	04	9956	0044	54
7	5758	08	8950	1050	3955	650	30306	69694	53
8	6069	756	9312	0688	4251	596	0656	9344	52
9	6379	05	9674	0326	4547	42	1005	8995	51
10	6689	653	0036	89964	4842	488	1355	8645	50
11	9.576999	9.966602	9.610397	10.389603	9.595137	9.963434	9.631704	10.368296	49
12	7309	550	0759	9241	5432	379	2053	7947	48
13	7618	499	1120	8880	5727	25	2401	7599	47
14	7927	47	1480	8520	6021	271	2750	7250	46
15	8236	395	1841	8159	6315	17	3098	6902	45
16	8545	44	2201	7799	6609	163	3447	6553	44
17	8853	292	2561	7439	6903	08	3795	6205	43
18	9162	40	2921	7079	7196	054	4143	5857	42
19	9470	188	3281	6719	7490	2999	4490	5510	41
20	9777	36	3641	6359	7783	45	4838	5162	40
21	9.580085	9.966085	9.614000	10.386000	9.598075	9.962890	9.635185	10.364815	39
22	0392	33	4359	5641	8368	86	5532	4468	38
23	0699	65981	4718	5282	8660	781	5879	4121	37
24	1005	29	5077	4923	8952	27	6226	3774	36
25	1312	876	5435	4565	9244	672	6572	3428	35
26	1618	24	5793	4207	9536	17	6919	3081	34
27	1924	772	6151	3849	9827	562	7265	2735	33
28	2229	20	6509	3491	600118	08	7611	2389	32
29	2535	668	6867	3133	9409	453	7956	2044	31
30	2840	615	7224	2776	0700	398	8302	1698	30
31	9.583145	9.965563	9.617582	10.382418	9.600990	9.962343	9.638647	10.361353	29
32	3449	11	7939	2061	1280	288	8992	1008	28
33	3754	458	8295	1705	1570	33	9337	0663	27
34	4058	06	8652	1348	1860	178	9682	0318	26
35	4361	353	9008	0992	2150	23	40027	59973	25
36	4665	01	9364	0636	2439	067	0371	9629	24
37	4968	248	9721	0279	2728	12	0716	9284	23
38	5272	195	20076	79924	3017	1957	1060	8940	22
39	5574	43	0432	9568	3305	02	1404	8596	21
40	5877	090	0787	9213	3594	846	1747	8253	20
41	9.586179	9.965037	9.621142	10.378858	9.603882	9.961791	9 642091	10.357909	19
42	6482	4984	1497	8503	4170	35	2434	7566	18
43	6783	31	1852	8148	4457	680	2777	7223	17
44	7085	879	2207	7793	4745	24	3120	6880	16
45	7386	26	2561	7439	5032	569	3463	6537	15
46	7688	773	2915	7085	5319	13	3806	6194	14
47	7989	20	3269	6731	5606	458	4148	5852	13
48	8289	666	3623	6377	5892	02	4490	5510	12
49	8590	13	3976	6024	6179	846	4832	5168	11
50	8890	560	4330	5670	6465	290	5174	4826	10
51	9.589190	9.964507	9.624683	10.375317	9.606751	9.961235	9.645516	10.354484	9
52	9489	454	5036	4964	7036	179	5857	4143	8
53	9789	00	5388	4612	7322	23	6199	3801	7
54	90088	347	5741	4259	7607	067	6540	3460	6
55	0387	294	6093	3907	7892	11	6881	3119	5
56	0686	40	6445	3555	8177	0955	7222	2778	4
57	0984	187	6797	3203	8461	899	7562	2438	3
58	1282	83	7149	2851	8745	43	7903	2097	2
59	1580	080	7507	2499	9029	786	8243	1757	1
60	1878	26	7852	2148	9313	30	8583	1417	0
′	Cosine.	Sine.	Cotan.	Tang.	Cosine.	Sine.	Cotan.	Tang.	′

67 Degrees.   66 Degrees.

	24 Degrees.				25 Degrees.				
′	Sine.	Cosine.	Tang.	Cotang.	Sine.	Cosine.	Tang.	Cotang.	′
0	9.609313	9.960730	9.648583	10.351417	9.625948	9.957276	9.668673	10.331327	60
1	9597	674	8923	1077	6219	17	9002	0998	59
2	9880	18	9263	0737	6490	158	9332	0668	58
3	610164	561	9602	0398	6760	099	9661	0339	57
4	0447	05	9942	0058	7030	40	9991	0009	56
5	0729	448	50281	49719	7300	6981	70320	29680	55
6	1012	892	0620	9380	7570	21	0649	9351	54
7	1294	85	0959	9041	7840	862	0977	9023	53
8	1576	279	1297	8703	8109	03	1306	8694	52
9	1858	22	1636	8364	8378	744	1634	8366	51
10	2140	165	1974	8026	8647	684	1963	8037	50
11	9.612421	9.960109	9.652312	10.347688	9.628916	9.956625	9.672291	10.327709	49
12	2702	052	2650	7350	9185	566	2619	7381	48
13	2983	5995	2988	7012	9453	06	2947	7053	47
14	3264	38	3326	6674	9721	447	3274	6726	46
15	3545	882	3663	6337	9989	887	3602	6398	45
16	3825	25	4000	6000	30257	27	3929	6071	44
17	4105	768	4337	5663	0524	268	4257	5743	43
18	4385	11	4674	5326	0792	08	4584	5416	42
19	4665	654	5011	4989	1059	148	4910	5090	41
20	4944	596	5348	4652	1326	089	5237	4763	40
21	9.615223	9.959539	9.655684	10.344316	9.631593	9.956029	9.675564	10.324436	39
22	5502	482	6020	3980	1859	5969	5890	4110	38
23	5781	25	6356	3644	2125	09	6217	3783	37
24	6060	368	6692	3308	2392	849	6543	3457	36
25	6338	10	7028	2972	2658	789	6869	3131	35
26	6616	253	7364	2636	2923	29	7194	2806	34
27	6894	195	7699	2301	3189	669	7520	2480	33
28	7172	38	8034	1966	3454	09	7846	2154	32
29	7450	080	8369	1631	3719	548	8171	1829	31
30	7727	23	8704	1296	3984	488	8496	1504	30
31	9.618004	9.958965	9.659039	10.340961	9.634249	9.955428	9.678821	10.321179	29
32	8281	08	9373	0627	4514	368	9146	0854	28
33	8558	850	9708	0292	4778	07	9471	0529	27
34	8834	792	60042	39958	5042	247	9795	0205	26
35	9110	34	0376	9624	5306	186	80120	19880	25
36	9386	677	0710	9290	5570	26	0444	9556	24
37	9662	19	1043	8957	5834	065	0768	9232	23
38	9938	561	1377	8623	6097	05	1092	8908	22
39	620213	03	1710	8290	6360	4944	1416	8584	21
40	0488	445	2043	7957	6623	883	1740	8260	20
41	9.620763	9 958387	9.662376	10.337624	9.636886	9.954823	9.682063	10.317937	19
42	1038	29	2709	7291	7148	762	2387	7613	18
43	1313	271	3042	6955	7411	01	2710	7290	17
44	1587	13	3375	6625	7673	640	3033	6967	16
45	1861	154	3707	6293	7935	579	3356	6644	15
46	2135	096	4039	5961	8197	18	3679	6321	14
47	2409	38	4371	5629	8458	457	4001	5999	13
48	2682	7979	4703	5297	8720	396	4324	5676	12
49	2956	21	5035	4965	8981	35	4646	5354	11
50	3229	863	5366	4634	9242	274	4968	5032	10
51	9.623502	9.957804	9.665697	10.334303	9.639503	9.954213	9.685290	10.314710	9
52	3774	746	6029	3971	9764	152	5612	4388	8
53	4047	687	6360	3640	40024	090	5934	4066	7
54	4319	28	6691	3309	0284	29	6255	3745	6
55	4591	570	7021	2979	0544	3968	6577	3423	5
56	4863	11	7352	2648	0804	06	6898	3102	4
57	5135	452	7683	2318	1064	845	7219	2781	3
58	5406	393	8013	1987	1324	783	7540	2460	2
59	5677	35	8343	1657	1583	22	7861	2139	1
60	5948	276	8673	1327	1842	660	8182	1818	0
′	Cosine.	Sine.	Cotan.	Tang.	Cosine.	Sine.	Cotang.	Tang.	′
	65 Degrees.				64 Degrees.				

′	26 Degrees. Sine.	Cosine.	Tang.	Cotang.	27 Degrees. Sine.	Cosine.	Tang.	Cotang.	′
0	9.641842	9 953660	9.688182	10.311818	9.657047	9.949881	9.707166	10.292834	60
1	2101	599	8502	1498	7295	16	7478	2522	59
2	2360	37	8823	1177	7542	752	7790	2210	58
3	2618	475	9143	0857	7790	688	8102	1898	57
4	2877	13	9463	0537	8037	28	8414	1586	56
5	3135	352	9783	0217	8284	558	8726	1274	55
6	3393	290	90103	309897	8531	494	9037	0963	54
7	3650	28	0423	9577	8778	29	9349	0651	53
8	3908	166	0742	9258	9025	364	9660	0340	52
9	4165	04	1062	8938	9271	00	9971	0029	51
10	4423	042	1381	8619	9517	235	10282	89718	50
11	9.644680	9.952980	9.691709	10.308300	9.659763	9.949170	9.710593	10.289407	49
12	4936	18	2019	7981	60009	05	0904	9096	48
13	5193	855	2338	7662	0255	040	1215	8785	47
14	5450	793	2656	7344	0501	975	1525	8475	46
15	5706	31	2975	7025	0746	10	1836	8164	45
16	5962	669	3293	6707	0991	845	2146	7854	44
17	6218	06	3612	6388	1236	780	2456	7544	43
18	6474	544	3930	6070	1481	15	2766	7234	42
19	6729	481	4248	5752	1726	650	3076	6924	41
20	6984	19	4566	5434	1970	584	3386	6614	40
21	9.647240	9.952356	9.694883	10.305117	9.662214	9.948519	9.713696	10.286304	39
22	7494	294	5201	4799	2459	454	4005	5995	38
23	7749	31	5518	4482	2703	389	4314	5686	37
24	8004	168	5836	4164	2946	23	4624	5376	36
25	8258	06	6153	3847	3190	257	4933	5067	35
26	8512	043	6470	3530	3433	192	5242	4758	34
27	8766	51980	6787	3213	3677	26	5551	4449	33
28	9020	17	7103	2897	3920	060	5860	4140	32
29	9274	854	7420	2580	4163	7995	6168	3832	31
30	9527	791	7736	2264	4406	929	6477	3523	30
31	9.649781	9.951728	9.698053	10.301947	9.664648	9.947863	9.716785	10.283215	29
32	50034	665	8369	1631	4891	797	7093	2907	28
33	0287	02	8685	1315	5133	31	7401	2599	27
34	0539	539	9001	0999	5375	665	7709	2291	26
35	0792	476	9316	0684	5617	00	8017	1983	25
36	1044	12	9632	0368	5859	533	8325	1675	24
37	1297	349	9947	0053	6100	467	8633	1367	23
38	1549	286	700263	299737	6342	01	8940	1060	22
39	1800	22	0578	9422	6583	335	9248	0752	21
40	2052	159	0893	9107	6824	269	9555	0445	20
41	9.652304	9.951096	9.701208	10.298792	9.667065	9.947203	9.719862	10.280138	19
42	2555	32	1523	8477	7305	136	20169	79831	18
43	2806	50968	1837	8163	7546	070	0476	9524	17
44	3057	05	2152	7848	7786	04	0783	9217	16
45	3308	841	2466	7534	8027	6937	1089	8911	15
46	3558	778	2780	7220	8267	871	1396	8604	14
47	3808	14	3095	6905	8506	04	1702	8298	13
48	4059	650	3409	6591	8746	738	2009	7991	12
49	4309	586	3723	6277	8986	671	2315	7685	11
50	4558	22	4036	5964	9225	04	2621	7379	10
51	9.654808	9.950458	9.704350	10.295650	9.669464	9.946538	9.722927	10.277073	9
52	5058	394	4663	5337	9703	471	3232	6768	8
53	5307	80	4977	5023	9942	04	3538	6462	7
54	5556	266	5290	4710	70181	337	3844	6156	6
55	5805	02	5603	4397	0419	270	4149	5851	5
56	6054	138	5916	4084	0658	03	4454	5546	4
57	6302	074	6228	3772	0896	136	4759	5241	3
58	6551	10	6541	3459	1134	069	5065	4935	2
59	6799	49945	6854	3146	1372	02	5369	4631	1
60	7047	881	7166	2834	1609	5935	5674	4326	0
′	Cosine.	Sine.	Cotan.	Tang.	Cosine.	Sine.	Cotan.	Tang.	′

63 Degrees.   62 Degrees.

'	Sine.	Cosine.	Tang.	Cotang.	Sine.	Cosine.	Tang.	Cotang.	'
	28 Degrees.				**29 Degrees.**				
0	9.671609	9.945935	9.725674	10.274326	9.685571	9.941819	9.743752	10.256248	60
1	1847	868	5979	4021	5799	749	4050	5950	59
2	2084	00	6284	3716	6027	679	4348	5652	58
3	2321	733	6588	3412	6254	09	4645	5355	57
4	2558	666	6892	3108	6482	539	4943	5057	56
5	2795	598	7197	2803	6709	469	5240	4760	55
6	3032	31	7501	2499	6936	398	5538	4462	54
7	3268	464	7805	2195	7163	28	5835	4165	53
8	3505	396	8109	1891	7389	258	6132	3868	52
9	3741	28	8412	1588	7616	187	6429	3571	51
10	3977	261	8716	1284	7843	17	6726	3274	50
11	9.674213	9.945193	9.729020	10.270980	9.688069	9.941046	9.747023	10 252977	49
12	4448	25	9323	0677	8295	40975	7319	2681	48
13	4684	058	9626	0374	8521	05	7616	2384	47
14	4919	4990	9929	0071	8747	834	7913	2087	46
15	5155	22	30233	69767	8972	763	8209	1791	45
16	5390	854	0535	9465	9198	693	8505	1495	44
17	5624	786	0838	9162	9423	22	8801	1199	43
18	5859	18	1141	8859	9648	551	9097	0903	42
19	6094	650	1444	8556	9873	480	9393	0607	41
20	6328	582	1746	8254	90098	09	9689	0311	40
21	9.676562	9.944514	9.732048	10.267952	9.690323	9.940338	9.749985	10 250015	39
22	6796	446	2351	7649	0548	267	50281	249719	38
23	7030	377	2653	7347	0772	196	0576	9424	37
24	7264	09	2955	7045	0996	25	0872	9128	36
25	7498	241	3257	6743	1220	054	1167	8833	35
26	7731	172	3558	6442	1444	39982	1462	8538	34
27	7964	04	3860	6140	1668	11	1757	8243	33
28	8197	3036	4162	5838	1892	840	2052	7948	32
29	8430	967	4463	5537	2115	768	2347	7653	31
30	8663	899	4764	5236	2339	697	2642	7358	30
31	9.678895	9.943830	9.735066	10.264934	9.692562	9.939625	9.752937	10.247063	29
32	9128	761	5367	4633	2785	554	3231	6769	28
33	9360	693	5668	4332	3008	482	3526	6474	27
34	9592	24	5969	4031	3231	10	3820	6180	26
35	9824	555	6269	3731	3453	339	4115	5885	25
36	80056	486	6570	3430	3676	267	4409	5591	24
37	0288	17	6871	3129	3898	195	4703	5297	23
38	0519	348	7171	2829	4120	23	4997	5003	22
39	0750	279	7471	2529	4342	052	5291	4709	21
40	0982	10	7771	2229	4564	38980	5585	4415	20
41	9.681213	9.943141	9.738071	10.261929	9.694786	9.938908	9.755878	10.244122	19
42	1443	072	8371	1629	5007	836	6172	3828	18
43	1674	03	8671	1329	5229	763	6465	3535	17
44	1905	2934	8971	1029	5450	691	6759	3241	16
45	2135	864	9271	0729	5671	19	7052	2948	15
46	2365	795	9570	0430	5892	547	7345	2655	14
47	2595	26	9870	0130	6113	475	7638	2362	13
48	2825	656	40169	59831	6334	02	7931	2069	12
49	3055	587	0468	9532	6554	330	8224	1776	11
50	3284	17	0767	9233	6775	258	8517	1483	10
51	9.683514	9.942448	9.741066	10.258934	9.696995	9.938185	9.758810	10.241190	9
52	3743	378	1365	8635	7215	13	9102	0898	8
53	3972	08	1664	8336	7435	040	9395	0605	7
54	4201	239	1962	8038	7654	37967	9687	0313	6
55	4430	169	2261	7739	7874	895	9979	0021	5
56	4658	099	2559	7441	8094	22	60272	39728	4
57	4887	29	2858	7142	8313	749	0564	9436	3
58	5115	1959	3156	6844	8532	676	0856	9144	2
59	5342	889	3454	6546	8751	04	1148	8852	1
60	5571	19	3752	6248	8970	531	1439	8561	0
'	Cosine.	Sine.	Cotan.	Tang.	Cosine.	Sine.	Cotang.	Tang.	'
	61 Degrees.				**60 Degrees.**				

	30 Degrees.				31 Degrees.				
′	Sine.	Cosine.	Tang.	Cotang.	Sine.	Cosine.	Tang.	Cotang.	′
0	9.698970	9.937531	9.761439	10.238561	9.711839	9.933066	9.778774	10.221226	60
1	189	458	1731	8269	2050	2990	9060	0940	59
2	407	385	2023	7977	2260	14	9346	0654	58
3	626	12	2314	7686	2469	838	9632	0368	57
4	844	238	2606	7395	2679	762	9918	0082	56
5	700062	165	2897	7103	2889	685	80203	19797	55
6	280	092	3188	6812	3098	09	0489	9511	54
7	498	19	3479	6521	3308	533	0775	9225	53
8	716	6946	3770	6230	3517	457	1060	8940	52
9	933	872	4061	5939	3726	380	1346	8654	51
10	1151	799	4352	5648	3935	04	1631	8369	50
11	9.701368	9.936725	9.764643	10.235357	9.714144	9.932228	9.781916	10.218084	49
12	1585	652	4933	5067	4352	151	2201	7799	48
13	1802	578	5224	4776	4561	075	2486	7514	47
14	2019	05	551+	4486	4769	1998	2771	7229	46
15	2236	431	5805	4195	4978	21	3056	6944	45
16	2452	357	6095	3905	5186	845	3441	6659	44
17	2669	284	6385	3615	5394	768	3626	6374	43
18	2885	10	6675	3325	5602	691	3910	6090	42
19	3101	136	6965	3035	5809	14	4195	5805	41
20	3317	062	7255	2745	6017	537	4479	5521	40
21	9.703533	9.935988	9.767545	10.232455	9.716224	9.931460	9.784764	10.215236	39
22	3749	14	7835	2166	6432	383	5048	4952	38
23	3964	840	8124	1876	6639	06	5332	4668	37
24	4179	766	8414	1586	6846	229	5616	4384	36
25	4395	692	8703	1297	7053	152	5900	4100	35
26	4610	18	8992	1008	7259	075	6184	3816	34
27	4825	543	9281	0719	7466	30998	6468	3532	33
28	5040	469	9570	0330	7673	21	6752	3248	32
29	5254	895	9860	0140	7879	843	7036	2964	31
30	5469	20	70148	229852	8085	766	7319	2681	30
31	9.705683	9.935246	9.770437	10.229563	9.718291	9.930688	9.787603	10.212397	29
32	5898	171	0726	9274	8497	11	7886	2114	28
33	6112	097	1015	8985	8703	533	8170	1830	27
34	6326	22	1303	8697	8909	456	8453	1547	26
35	6539	4948	1592	8408	9114	378	8736	1264	25
36	6753	873	1880	8120	9320	00	9019	0981	24
37	6967	798	2168	7832	9525	223	9302	0698	23
38	7180	23	2457	7543	9730	145	9585	0415	22
39	7393	649	2745	7255	9935	067	9868	0132	21
40	7606	574	3033	6967	20140	29989	90151	209849	20
41	9.707819	9.934499	9.773321	10.226679	9.720345	9.929911	9.790433	10.209567	19
42	8032	24	3608	6392	0549	833	0716	9284	18
43	8245	349	3896	6104	0754	755	0999	9001	17
44	8458	274	4184	5816	0958	677	1281	8719	16
45	8670	199	4471	5529	1162	599	1563	8437	15
46	8882	23	4759	5241	1366	21	1846	8154	14
47	9094	048	5046	4954	1570	442	2128	7872	13
48	9306	3973	5333	4667	1774	364	2410	7590	12
49	9518	898	5621	4379	1978	286	2692	7308	11
50	9730	22	5908	4092	2181	07	2974	7026	10
51	9.709941	9.933747	9.776195	10.223805	9.722385	9.929129	9.793256	10.206744	9
52	0153	671	6482	3518	2588	050	3538	6462	8
53	0364	596	6769	3231	2791	8972	3819	6181	7
54	0575	20	7055	2945	2994	893	4101	5899	6
55	0786	445	7342	2658	3197	15	4383	5617	5
56	0997	369	7628	2372	3400	736	4664	5336	4
57	1208	293	7915	2085	3603	657	4945	5055	3
58	1419	17	8201	1799	3805	578	5227	4773	2
59	1629	141	8488	1513	4007	499	5508	4492	1
60	1839	066	8774	1226	4210	20	5789	4211	0
′	Cosine.	Sine.	Cotan.	Tang.	Cosine.	Sine.	Cotan.	Tang.	′
	59 Degrees.				58 Degrees.				

	32 Degrees.				33 Degrees.				
′	Sine.	Cosine.	Tang.	Cotang.	Sine.	Cosine.	Tang.	Cotang.	′
0	9.724210	9.928420	9.795789	10.204211	9.736109	9.923591	9.812517	10.187483	60
1	4412	342	6070	3930	6303	509	2794	7206	59
2	4614	268	6351	3649	6498	427	3070	6930	58
3	4816	183	6632	3368	6692	345	3347	6653	57
4	5017	104	6913	3087	6886	263	3623	6377	56
5	5219	025	7194	2806	7080	181	3899	6101	55
6	5420	7946	7475	2525	7274	098	4175	5825	54
7	5622	867	7755	2245	7467	016	4452	5548	53
8	5823	787	8036	1964	7661	2933	4728	5272	52
9	6024	708	8316	1684	7855	851	5004	4996	51
10	6225	629	8596	1404	8048	768	5279	4721	50
11	9.726426	9.927549	9.798877	10.201123	9.738241	9.922686	9.815555	10.184445	49
12	6626	470	9157	0843	8434	603	5831	4165	48
13	6827	390	9437	0563	8627	520	6107	3893	47
14	7027	310	9717	0283	8820	438	6382	3618	46
15	7228	231	9997	0003	9013	355	6658	3342	45
16	7428	151	800277	199723	9206	272	6933	3067	44
17	7628	071	0557	9443	9398	189	7209	2791	43
18	7828	6991	0836	9164	9590	106	7484	2516	42
19	8027	911	1116	8884	9783	023	7759	2241	41
20	8227	831	1396	8604	9975	1940	8035	1965	40
21	9.728427	9.926751	9.801675	10.198325	9.740167	9.921857	9.818310	10.181690	39
22	8626	671	1955	8045	0359	774	8585	1415	38
23	8825	591	2234	7766	0550	691	8860	1140	37
24	9024	511	2513	7487	0742	607	9135	0865	36
25	9223	481	2792	7208	0934	524	9410	0590	35
26	9422	851	3072	6928	1125	441	9684	0316	34
27	9621	270	3351	6649	1316	357	9959	0041	33
28	9820	190	3630	6370	1508	274	20234	79766	32
29	30018	110	3908	6092	1699	190	0508	9492	31
30	0217	029	4187	5813	1889	107	0783	9217	30
31	9.730415	9.925949	9.804466	10.195534	9.742080	9.921023	9.821057	10.178943	29
32	0613	868	4745	5255	2271	20939	1332	8668	28
33	0811	788	5023	4977	2462	856	1606	8394	27
34	1009	707	5302	4698	2652	772	1880	8120	26
35	1206	626	5580	4420	2842	688	2154	7846	25
36	1404	545	5859	4141	3033	604	2429	7571	24
37	1602	465	6137	3863	3223	520	2703	7297	23
38	1799	384	6415	3585	3413	436	2977	7023	22
39	1996	303	6693	3307	3602	352	3250	6750	21
40	2193	222	6971	3029	3792	268	3524	6476	20
41	9.732390	9.925141	9.807249	10.192751	9.743982	9.920184	9.823798	10.176202	19
42	2587	060	7527	2473	4171	099	4072	5928	18
43	2784	4979	7805	2195	4361	015	4345	5655	17
44	2980	897	8083	1917	4550	919931	4619	5381	16
45	3177	816	8361	1639	4739	846	4893	5107	15
46	3373	735	8638	1362	4928	762	5166	4834	14
47	3569	654	8916	1084	5117	677	5439	4561	13
48	3765	572	9193	0807	5306	593	5713	4287	12
49	3961	491	9471	0529	5494	508	5986	4014	11
50	4157	409	9748	0252	5683	424	6259	3741	10
51	9.734353	9.924328	9.810025	10.189975	9.745871	9.919339	9.826532	10.173468	9
52	4549	246	0302	9698	6060	254	6805	3195	8
53	4744	164	0580	9420	6248	169	7078	2922	7
54	4939	083	0857	9143	6436	085	7351	2649	6
55	5135	001	1134	8866	6624	000	7624	2376	5
56	5330	3919	1410	8590	6812	8915	7897	2103	4
57	5525	837	1687	8313	6999	830	8170	1830	3
58	5719	755	1964	8036	7187	745	8442	1558	2
59	5914	673	2241	7759	7374	659	8715	1285	1
60	6109	591	2517	7483	7562	574	8987	1013	0
′	Cosine.	Sine.	Cotan.	Tang.	Cosine.	Sine.	Cotang.	Tang.	′
	57 Degrees.				56 Degrees.				

	34 Degrees.				35 Degrees.				
′	Sine.	Cosine.	Tang.	Cotang.	Sine.	Cosine.	Tang.	Cotang.	′
0	9.747562	9.918574	9.828987	10.171013	9.758591	9.913365	9.845227	10.154773	60
1	7749	489	9260	0740	8772	276	5496	4504	59
2	7936	404	9532	0468	8952	187	5764	4236	58
3	8123	318	9805	0195	9132	099	6033	3967	57
4	8310	233	830077	69923	9312	010	6302	3698	56
5	8497	147	0349	9651	9492	2922	6570	3430	55
6	8683	062	0621	9379	9672	833	6839	3161	54
7	8870	7976	0893	9107	9852	744	7107	2893	53
8	9056	891	1165	8835	60031	655	7376	2624	52
9	9243	805	1437	8563	0211	566	7644	2356	51
10	9429	719	1709	8291	0390	477	7913	2087	50
11	9.749615	9.917634	9.831981	10.168019	9.760569	9.912388	9.848181	10.151819	49
12	9801	548	2253	7747	0748	299	8449	1551	48
13	9987	462	2525	7475	0927	210	8717	1283	47
14	50172	376	2796	7204	1106	121	8986	1014	46
15	0358	290	3068	6932	1285	031	9254	0746	45
16	0543	204	3339	6661	1464	1942	9522	0478	44
17	0729	118	3611	6389	1642	853	9790	0210	43
18	0914	032	3882	6118	1821	763	50058	149942	42
19	1099	6946	4154	5846	1999	674	0325	9675	41
20	1284	859	4425	5575	2177	584	0592	9407	40
21	9.751469	9.916773	9.834696	10.165304	9.762356	9.911495	9.850861	10.149139	39
22	1654	687	4967	5033	2534	405	1129	8871	38
23	1839	600	5238	4762	2712	315	1396	8604	37
24	2023	514	5509	4491	2889	226	1664	8336	36
25	2208	427	5780	4220	3067	136	1931	8069	35
26	2392	341	6051	3949	3245	046	2199	7801	34
27	2576	254	6322	3678	3422	10956	2466	7534	33
28	2760	167	6593	3407	3600	866	2733	7267	32
29	2944	081	6864	3136	3777	776	3001	6999	31
30	3128	5994	7134	2866	3954	686	3268	6732	30
31	9.753312	9.915907	9.837405	10.162595	9.764131	9.910596	9.853535	10.146465	29
32	3495	820	7675	2325	4308	506	3802	6198	28
33	3679	733	7946	2054	4485	415	4069	5931	27
34	3862	646	8216	1784	4662	325	4336	5664	26
35	4046	559	8487	1513	4838	235	4603	5397	25
36	4229	472	8757	1243	5015	144	4870	5130	24
37	4412	385	9027	0973	5191	054	5137	4863	23
38	4595	297	9297	0703	5367	909963	5404	4596	22
39	4778	210	9568	0432	5544	873	5671	4329	21
40	4960	123	9838	0162	5720	782	5938	4062	20
41	9.755143	9.915035	9.840108	10.159892	9.765896	9.909691	9.856204	10.143796	19
42	5326	4948	0378	9622	6072	601	6471	3529	18
43	5508	860	0647	9353	6247	510	6737	3263	17
44	5690	773	0917	9083	6423	419	7004	2996	16
45	5872	685	1187	8813	6598	328	7270	2730	15
46	6054	598	1457	8543	6774	237	7537	2463	14
47	6236	510	1726	8274	6949	146	7803	2197	13
48	6418	422	1996	8004	7124	055	8069	1931	12
49	6600	334	2266	7734	7300	8964	8336	1664	11
50	6782	246	2535	7465	7475	873	8602	1398	10
51	9.756963	9.914158	9.842805	10.157195	9.767649	9.908781	9.858868	10.141132	9
52	7144	070	3074	6926	7824	690	9134	0866	8
53	7326	3982	3343	6657	7999	599	9400	0600	7
54	7507	894	3612	6388	8173	507	9666	0334	6
55	7688	806	3882	6118	8348	416	9932	0068	5
56	7869	718	4151	5849	8522	324	60198	89802	4
57	8050	630	4420	5580	8697	233	0464	9536	3
58	8230	541	4689	5311	8871	141	0730	9270	2
59	8411	453	4958	5042	9045	049	0995	9005	1
60	8591	365	5227	4778	9219	7958	1261	8739	0
′	Cosine.	Sine.	Cotan.	Tang.	Cosine.	Sine.	Cotan.	Tang.	′
	55 Degrees.				54 Degrees.				

′	36 Degrees. Sine.	Cosine.	Tang.	Cotang.	37 Degrees. Sine.	Cosine.	Tang.	Cotang.	′
0	9.769219	9.907958	9.861261	10.138739	9.779463	9.902349	9.877114	10.122886	60
1	9393	866	1527	8473	9631	253	7377	2623	59
2	9566	774	1792	8208	9798	158	7640	2360	58
3	9740	682	2058	7942	9966	063	7903	2097	57
4	9913	590	2323	7677	80133	1967	8165	1835	56
5	70087	498	2589	7411	0300	872	8428	1572	55
6	0260	406	2854	7146	0467	776	8691	1309	54
7	0433	314	3119	6881	0634	681	8953	1047	53
8	0606	222	3385	6615	0801	585	9216	0784	52
9	0779	129	3650	6350	0968	490	9478	0522	51
10	0952	037	3915	6085	1134	394	9741	0259	50
11	9.771125	9.906945	9.864180	10.135820	9.781301	9.901298	9.880003	10.119997	49
12	1298	852	4445	5555	1468	202	0265	9735	48
13	1470	760	4710	5290	1634	106	0528	9472	47
14	1643	667	4975	5025	1800	010	0790	9210	46
15	1815	575	5240	4760	1966	0914	1052	8948	45
16	1987	482	5505	4495	2132	818	1314	8686	44
17	2159	389	5770	4230	2298	722	1576	8424	43
18	2331	296	6035	3965	2464	626	1839	8161	42
19	2503	204	6300	3700	2630	529	2101	7899	41
20	2675	111	6564	3436	2796	433	2363	7637	40
21	9.772847	9.906018	9.866829	10.133171	9.782961	9.900337	9.882625	10.117375	39
22	3018	5925	7094	2906	3127	240	2887	7113	38
23	3190	832	7358	2642	3292	144	3148	6852	37
24	3361	739	7623	2377	3458	047	3410	6590	36
25	3533	645	7887	2113	3623	899951	3672	6328	35
26	3704	552	8152	1848	2788	854	3934	6066	34
27	3875	459	8416	1584	3953	757	4196	5804	33
28	4046	366	8680	1320	4118	660	4457	5543	32
29	4217	272	8945	1055	4282	564	4719	5281	31
30	4388	179	9209	0791	4447	467	4980	5020	30
31	9.774558	9.905085	9.869473	10.130527	9.784612	9.899370	9.885242	10.114758	29
32	4729	4992	9737	0263	4776	273	5503	4497	28
33	4899	898	70001	129999	4941	176	5765	4235	27
34	5070	804	0265	9735	5105	078	6026	3974	26
35	5240	711	0529	9471	5269	8981	6288	3712	25
36	5410	617	0793	9207	5433	884	6549	3451	24
37	5580	523	1057	8943	5597	787	6810	3190	23
38	5750	429	1321	8679	5761	689	7072	2928	22
39	5920	335	1585	8415	5925	592	7333	2667	21
40	6090	241	1849	8151	6089	494	7594	2406	20
41	9.776259	9.904147	9.872112	10.127888	9.786252	9.898397	9.887855	10.112145	19
42	6429	053	2376	7624	6416	299	8116	1884	18
43	6598	3959	2640	7360	6579	202	8377	1623	17
44	6768	864	2903	7097	6742	104	8639	1361	16
45	6937	770	3167	6833	6906	006	8900	1100	15
46	7106	676	3430	6570	7069	7908	9160	0840	14
47	7275	581	3694	6306	7232	810	9421	0579	13
48	7444	487	3957	6043	7395	712	9682	0318	12
49	7613	392	4220	5780	7557	614	9943	0057	11
50	7781	298	4484	5516	7720	516	90204	109796	10
51	9.777950	9.903203	9.874747	10.125253	9.787883	9.897418	9.890465	10.109535	9
52	8119	108	5010	4990	8045	320	0725	9275	8
53	8287	014	5273	4727	8208	222	0986	9014	7
54	8455	2919	5536	4464	8370	123	1247	8753	6
55	8624	824	5800	4200	8532	025	1507	8493	5
56	8792	729	6063	3937	8694	6926	1768	8232	4
57	8960	634	6326	3674	8856	828	2028	7972	3
58	9128	539	6589	3411	9018	729	2289	7711	2
59	9295	444	6851	3149	9180	631	2549	7451	1
60	9463	349	7114	2886	9342	532	2810	7190	0
′	Cosine.	Sine.	Cotan.	Tang.	Cosine.	Sine.	Cotang.	Tang.	′

53 Degrees.	52 Degrees.

′	38 Degrees. Sine.	Cosine.	Tang.	Cotang.	39 Degrees. Sine.	Cosine.	Tang.	Cotang.	′
0	9.789342	9 896532	9.892810	10.107190	9.798872	9.890503	9.908369	10.091631	60
1	9504	433	3070	6930	9028	400	8628	1872	59
2	9665	835	3331	6669	9184	298	8886	1114	58
3	9827	236	8591	6409	9339	195	9144	0856	57
4	9988	137	3851	6149	9495	093	9402	0598	56
5	90149	038	4111	5889	9651	8990	9660	0340	55
6	0310	5939	4371	5629	9806	888	9918	0082	54
7	0471	840	4632	5368	9962	785	10177	89823	53
8	0632	741	4892	5108	800117	682	0435	9565	52
9	0793	641	5152	4848	0272	579	0693	9307	51
10	0954	542	5412	4588	0427	477	0951	9049	50
11	9.791115	9.895443	9.895672	10.104328	9.800582	9.889374	9.911209	10.088791	49
12	1275	343	5932	4068	0737	271	1467	8533	48
13	1436	244	6192	3808	0892	168	1724	8276	47
14	1596	145	6452	8548	1047	064	1982	8018	46
15	1757	045	6712	8288	1201	8991	2240	7760	45
16	1917	4945	6971	3029	1356	858	2498	7502	44
17	2077	846	7231	2769	1511	755	2756	7244	43
18	2237	746	7491	2509	1665	651	3014	6986	42
19	2397	646	7751	2249	1819	548	3271	6729	41
20	2557	546	8010	1990	1973	444	3529	6471	40
21	9.792716	9.894446	9.898270	10.101730	9 802128	9.888341	9.913787	10.086213	39
22	2876	346	8530	1470	2282	287	4044	5956	38
23	3035	246	8789	1211	2436	184	4302	5698	37
24	3195	146	9049	0951	2589	030	4560	5440	36
25	3354	046	9308	0692	2743	7926	4817	5183	35
26	3514	8946	9568	0432	2897	822	5075	4925	34
27	3673	816	9827	0173	3050	718	5332	4668	33
28	3832	745	900086	099914	3204	614	5590	4410	32
29	3991	645	0346	9654	3357	510	5847	4153	31
30	4150	544	0605	9395	3511	406	6104	3896	30
31	9.794308	9.893444	9.900864	10.099136	9.803664	9.887302	9.916362	10.083638	29
32	4467	343	1124	8876	3817	198	6619	3381	28
33	4626	243	1383	8617	3970	093	6877	3123	27
34	4784	142	1642	8358	4123	6989	7134	2866	26
35	4942	041	1901	8099	4276	885	7391	2609	25
36	5101	2940	2160	7840	4428	780	7648	2352	24
37	5259	839	2419	7581	4581	676	7905	2095	23
38	5417	739	2679	7321	4734	571	8163	1837	22
39	5575	638	2938	7062	4886	466	8420	1580	21
40	5733	536	3197	6803	5039	362	8677	1323	20
41	9.795891	9.892435	9.903455	10.096545	9.805191	9.886257	9.918934	10.081066	19
42	6049	334	3714	6286	5343	152	9191	0809	18
43	6206	233	3973	6027	5495	047	9448	0552	17
44	6364	132	4232	5768	5647	5942	9705	0295	16
45	6521	030	4491	5509	5799	837	9962	0038	15
46	6679	1929	4750	5250	5951	732	0219	79781	14
47	6836	827	5008	4992	6103	627	20476	9524	13
48	6993	726	5267	4733	6254	522	0733	9267	12
49	7150	624	5526	4474	6406	416	0990	9010	11
50	7307	523	5784	4216	6557	311	1247	8753	10
51	9.797464	9.891421	9.906043	10.093957	9.806709	9.885205	9.921503	10.078497	9
52	7621	319	6302	3698	6860	100	1760	8240	8
53	7777	217	6560	3440	7011	4994	2017	7983	7
54	7934	115	6819	3181	7163	889	2274	7726	6
55	8091	013	7077	2923	7314	783	2530	7470	5
56	8247	90911	7336	2664	7465	677	2787	7213	4
57	8403	809	7594	2406	7615	572	3044	6956	3
58	8560	707	7852	2148	7766	466	3300	6700	2
59	8716	605	8111	1889	7917	360	3557	6443	1
60	8872	503	8369	1631	8067	254	3813	6187	0
′	Cosine.	Sine.	Cotan.	Tang.	Cosine.	Sine.	Cotan.	Tang.	′
	51 Degrees.				50 Degrees.				

′	40 Degrees.				41 Degrees.				′
	Sine.	Cosine.	Tang.	Cotang.	Sine.	Cosine.	Tang.	Cotang.	
0	9.808067	9.884254	9.923813	10.076187	9.816943	9.877780	9.939163	10.060837	60
1	218	148	4070	5930	7088	670	9418	0582	59
2	368	042	4327	5673	233	560	9673	0327	58
3	519	3936	4583	5417	379	450	9928	0072	57
4	669	829	4840	5160	524	340	40183	59817	56
5	819	723	5096	4904	668	230	0438	9562	55
6	969	617	5352	4648	813	120	0694	9306	54
7	119	510	5609	4391	958	010	0949	9051	53
8	269	404	5865	4135	8108	6899	1204	8796	52
9	419	297	6122	3878	247	789	1458	8542	51
10	569	191	6378	3622	392	678	1714	8286	50
11	9.809718	9.883084	9.926634	10.073366	9.818536	9.876568	9.941968	10.058032	49
12	868	2977	6890	3110	681	457	2223	7777	48
13	10017	871	7147	2853	825	347	2478	7522	47
14	167	764	7403	2597	969	236	2733	7267	46
15	316	657	7659	2341	9113	125	2988	7012	45
16	465	550	7915	2085	257	014	3243	6757	44
17	614	443	8171	1829	401	5904	3498	6502	43
18	763	336	8427	1573	545	793	3752	6248	42
19	912	229	8683	1317	689	682	4007	5993	41
20	11061	121	8940	1060	832	571	4262	5738	40
21	9.811210	9.882014	9.929196	10.070804	9.819976	9.875459	9.944517	10.055483	39
22	358	1907	9452	0548	120	848	4771	5229	38
23	507	799	9708	0292	263	237	5026	4974	37
24	655	692	9964	0036	406	126	5281	4719	36
25	804	584	30220	9780	550	014	5535	4465	35
26	952	477	0475	9525	693	4903	5790	4210	34
27	2100	369	0731	9269	836	791	6045	3955	33
28	248	261	0987	9013	979	680	6299	3701	32
29	396	153	1243	68757	1122	568	6554	3446	31
30	544	046	1499	8501	265	456	6808	3192	30
31	9.812692	9.880938	9.931755	10.068245	9.821407	9.874344	9.947063	10.052937	29
32	840	630	2010	7990	550	232	7318	2682	28
33	988	722	2266	7734	693	121	7572	2428	27
34	3135	613	2522	7478	835	009	7826	2174	26
35	283	505	2778	7222	977	3896	8081	1919	25
36	430	397	3033	6967	2120	784	8336	1664	24
37	578	289	3289	6711	262	672	8590	1410	23
38	725	180	3545	6455	404	560	8844	1156	22
39	872	072	3800	6200	546	448	9099	0901	21
40	4019	9963	4056	5944	688	335	9353	0647	20
41	9.814166	9.879855	9.934311	10.065689	9.822830	9.873223	9.949607	10.050393	19
42	313	746	4567	5433	972	110	9862	0138	18
43	460	637	4823	5177	114	2998	50116	49884	17
44	607	529	5078	4922	255	885	0370	9630	16
45	753	420	5333	4667	397	772	0625	9375	15
46	900	311	5589	4411	539	659	0879	9121	14
47	5046	202	5844	4156	680	547	1133	8867	13
48	193	093	6100	3900	821	434	1388	8612	12
49	339	8984	6355	3645	963	321	1642	8358	11
50	485	875	6610	3390	4104	208	1896	8104	10
51	9.815632	9.878766	9.936866	10.063134	9.824245	9.872095	9.952150	10.047850	9
52	778	656	7121	2879	386	1981	2405	7595	8
53	924	547	7376	2624	527	868	2659	7341	7
54	6069	438	7632	2368	668	755	2913	7087	6
55	215	328	7887	2113	808	641	3167	6833	5
56	361	219	8142	1858	949	528	3421	6579	4
57	507	109	8398	1602	5090	414	3675	6325	3
58	652	7999	8653	1347	230	301	3929	6071	2
59	798	890	8908	1092	371	187	4183	5817	1
60	943	780	9163	60837	511	073	4437	5563	0
′	Cosine.	Sine.	Cotan.	Tang.	Cosine.	Sine.	Cotang.	Tang.	′
	49 Degrees.				48 Degrees.				

AA

	42 Degrees.				43 Degrees.				
′	Sine.	Cosine.	Tang.	Cotang.	Sine.	Cosine.	Tang.	Cotang.	′
0	9.825511	9.871073	9.954437	10.045563	9.833783	9.864127	9.969656	10.030344	60
1	5651	0960	4691	5309	3919	010	9909	0091	59
2	5791	846	4945	5055	4054	3892	0162	29838	58
3	5931	732	5200	4800	4189	774	0416	9584	57
4	6071	618	5454	4546	4325	656	0669	9331	56
5	6211	504	5707	4293	4460	538	0922	9078	55
6	6351	390	5961	4039	4595	419	1175	8825	54
7	6491	276	6215	3785	4730	301	1429	8571	53
8	6631	161	6469	3531	4865	183	1682	8318	52
9	6770	047	6723	3277	4999	064	1935	8065	51
10	6910	69933	6977	3023	5134	2946	2188	7812	50
11	9.827049	9.869818	9.957231	10.042769	9.835269	9.862827	9.972441	10.027559	49
12	7189	704	7485	2515	5403	709	2694	7306	48
13	7328	589	7739	2261	5538	590	2948	7052	47
14	7467	474	7993	2007	5672	471	3201	6799	46
15	7606	360	8246	1754	5807	353	3454	6546	45
16	7745	245	8500	1500	5941	234	3707	6293	44
17	7884	130	8754	1246	6075	115	3960	6040	43
18	8023	015	9008	0992	6209	1996	4213	5787	42
19	8162	8900	9262	0788	6343	877	4466	5534	41
20	8301	785	9516	0484	6477	758	4719	5281	40
21	9.828439	9.868670	9.959769	10.040231	9.836611	9.861638	9.974973	10.025027	39
22	8578	555	60023	39977	6745	519	5226	4774	38
23	8716	440	0277	9723	6878	400	5479	4521	37
24	8855	324	0531	9469	7012	280	5732	4268	36
25	8993	209	0784	9216	7146	161	5985	4015	35
26	9131	093	1038	8962	7279	041	6238	3762	34
27	9269	7978	1291	8709	7412	0922	6491	3509	33
28	9407	862	1545	8455	7546	802	6744	3256	32
29	9545	747	1799	8201	7679	682	6997	3003	31
30	9683	631	2052	7948	7812	562	7250	2750	30
31	9.829821	9.867515	9.962306	10.037694	9.837945	9.860442	9.977503	10.022497	29
32	9959	399	2560	7440	8078	322	7756	2244	28
33	30097	283	2813	7187	8211	202	8009	1991	27
34	0234	167	3067	6933	8344	082	8262	1738	26
35	0372	051	3320	6680	8477	59963	8515	1485	25
36	0509	6935	3574	6429	8610	842	8768	1232	24
37	0646	819	3827	6173	8742	721	9021	0979	23
38	0784	703	4081	5919	8875	601	9274	0726	22
39	0921	586	4335	5665	9007	480	9527	0473	21
40	1058	470	4588	5412	9140	360	9780	0220	20
41	9.831195	9.866353	9.964842	10.035158	9.839272	9.859239	9.980033	10.019967	19
42	1332	237	5095	4905	9404	119	0286	9714	18
43	1469	120	5349	4651	9536	8998	0538	9462	17
44	1606	004	5602	4398	9668	877	0791	9209	16
45	1742	5887	5855	4145	9800	756	1044	8956	15
46	1879	770	6109	3891	9932	635	1297	8703	14
47	2015	653	6362	3638	40064	514	1550	8450	13
48	2152	536	6616	3384	0196	393	1803	8197	12
49	2288	419	6869	3131	0328	272	2056	7944	11
50	2425	302	7126	2877	0459	151	2309	7691	10
51	9.832561	9.865185	9.967376	10.032624	9.840591	9.858029	9.982562	10.017438	9
52	2697	068	7629	2371	0722	7908	2814	7186	8
53	2833	4950	7883	2117	0854	786	3067	6933	7
54	2969	833	8136	1864	0985	665	3320	6680	6
55	3105	716	8389	1611	1116	543	3573	6427	5
56	3241	598	8643	1357	1247	422	3826	6174	4
57	3377	481	8896	1104	1378	300	4079	5921	3
58	3512	363	9149	0851	1509	178	4331	5669	2
59	3648	245	9403	0597	1640	056	4584	5416	1
60	3783	127	9656	0344	1771	6934	4837	5163	0
′	Cosine.	Sine.	Cotan.	Tang.	Cosine.	Sine.	Cotan.	Tang.	′
	47 Degrees.				46 Degrees.				

44 Degrees.

′	Sine.	Cosine.	Tang.	Cotang.	′
0	9.841771	9.856934	9.984837	10.015163	60
1	1902	812	5090	4910	59
2	2033	690	5343	4657	58
3	2163	568	5596	4404	57
4	2294	446	5848	4152	56
5	2424	323	6101	3899	55
6	2555	201	6354	3646	54
7	2685	078	6607	3393	53
8	2815	5956	6860	3140	52
9	2946	833	7112	2888	51
10	3076	711	7365	2635	50
11	9.843206	9.855588	9.987618	10.012382	49
12	3336	465	7871	2129	48
13	3466	342	8123	1877	47
14	3595	219	8376	1624	46
15	3725	096	8629	1371	45
16	3855	4973	8882	1118	44
17	3984	850	9134	0866	43
18	4114	727	9387	0613	42
19	4243	603	9640	0360	41
20	4372	480	9893	0107	40
21	9.844502	9.854356	9.990145	10.009855	39
22	4631	233	0398	9602	38
23	4760	109	0651	9349	37
24	4889	8986	0903	9097	36
25	5018	862	1156	8844	35
26	5147	738	1409	8591	34
27	5276	614	1662	8338	33
28	5405	490	1914	8086	32
29	5533	366	2167	7833	31
30	5662	242	2420	7580	30
31	9.845790	9.853118	9.992672	10.007328	29
32	5919	2994	2925	7075	28
33	6047	869	3178	6822	27
34	6175	745	3430	6570	26
35	6304	620	3683	6317	25
36	6432	496	3936	6064	24
37	6560	371	4189	5811	23
38	6688	247	4441	5559	22
39	6816	122	4694	5306	21
40	6944	997	4947	5053	20
41	9.847071	9.851872	9.995199	10.004801	19
42	7199	747	5452	4548	18
43	7327	622	5705	4295	17
44	7454	497	5957	4043	16
45	7582	372	6210	3790	15
46	7709	246	6463	3527	14
47	7836	121	6715	3285	13
48	7964	0996	6968	3032	12
49	8091	870	7221	2779	11
50	8218	745	7473	2527	10
51	9.848345	9.850619	9.997726	10.002274	9
52	8472	493	7979	2021	8
53	8599	368	8231	1769	7
54	8726	242	8484	1516	6
55	8852	116	8737	1263	5
56	8979	49990	8989	1011	4
57	9106	864	9242	0758	3
58	9232	738	9495	0505	2
59	9359	611	9747	0253	1
60	9485	485	10.00000	0000	0
′	Cosine.	Sine.	Cotan.	Tang.	′

45 Degrees.

RULES FOR FINDING LOGARITHMIC SECANTS, VERSED SINES, &c.

I. To find the Secant.—Subtract the Log. Cosine from 20·000000.
II. To find the Cosecant.—Subtract the Log, Sine from 20·000000.
III. To find the Versed Sine.—Add 0·301030 to twice the Log: Sine of half the arc, and diminish the index of the sum by 10.
IV. To find the Coversed Sine.—Add 0·301030 to twice the Log. Sine of half the complement of the arc, and diminish the index of the sum by 10.

RULES FOR FINDING NATURAL SECANTS, VERSED SINES, &c.

I. To find the Secant.—Divide 1 by the Natural Cosine.
II. To find the Cosecant.—Divide 1 by the Natural Sine.
III. To find the Versed Sine.—Subtract the Natural Cosine from 1·000000.
IV. To find the Coversed Sine.—Subtract the Natural Sine from 1·000000.

NOTE.—In France the circumference of the circle has lately been divided into 400 degrees, the degree into 100 minutes, and the minute into 100 seconds, &c., which is called the centesimal division, and is to the sexagesimal in the ratio of 9 to 10; hence, to reduce centesimal into sexagesimal degrees, &c., subtract one-tenth; and to reduce sexagesimal into centesimal degrees, add one-ninth of the arc to itself.

TABLE VIII.

Oblique Ascension of Sheffield, 53° 26'.

Day	♓ °	♓ '	♒ °	♒ '	♑ °	♑ '	♐ °	♐ '	♏ °	♏ '	♎ °	♎ '
1	348	25	332	31	306	53	268	52	225	15	181	27
2	348	51	333	10	307	57	270	17	226	43	182	55
3	349	17	333	49	309	0	271	41	228	11	184	22
4	349	43	334	27	310	2	273	5	229	40	185	49
5	350	9	335	4	311	3	274	28	231	8	187	16
6	350	34	335	41	312	3	275	51	232	36	188	43
7	351	0	336	17	313	3	277	13	234	4	190	10
8	351	25	336	52	314	2	278	35	235	32	191	38
9	351	50	337	28	315	0	279	56	237	0	193	5
10	352	14	338	3	315	57	281	17	238	28	194	32
11	352	38	338	37	316	53	282	37	239	56	195	59
12	353	3	339	10	317	48	283	57	241	24	197	27
13	353	27	339	52	318	42	285	16	242	52	198	54
14	353	51	340	24	319	37	286	34	244	10	200	22
15	354	15	340	46	320	27	287	52	245	48	201	50
16	354	38	341	18	321	18	289	9	247	16	203	17
17	355	1	341	49	322	8	290	26	248	44	204	45
18	355	24	342	29	322	58	291	42	249	11	206	12
19	355	47	342	50	323	47	292	57	251	39	207	40
20	356	11	343	20	324	35	294	11	252	6	209	8
21	356	34	343	50	325	22	295	24	254	3	210	36
22	356	57	344	19	326	9	296	36	256	0	212	4
23	357	20	344	48	326	55	297	48	257	27	213	31
24	357	43	345	16	327	40	298	59	258	53	214	59
25	358	6	345	44	328	23	300	9	260	20	216	27
26	358	29	346	12	329	6	301	18	261	46	217	55
27	358	52	346	40	329	48	302	27	263	12	219	23
28	359	15	347	7	330	30	303	35	264	37	220	51
29	359	38	347	33	331	11	304	42	266	2	222	19
30	360	0	347	59	331	51	305	48	267	27	223	47

Day	♍ °	♍ '	♌ °	♌ '	♋ °	♋ '	♊ °	♊ '	♉ °	♉ '	♈ °	♈ '
1	137	41	93	57	55	18	28	49	12	28	0	23
2	139	9	95	22	56	25	29	30	12	54	0	45
3	140	37	96	47	57	33	30	12	13	21	1	8
4	142	5	98	13	58	42	30	54	13	48	1	31
5	143	33	99	40	59	51	31	37	14	16	1	54
6	145	2	101	7	61	1	32	21	14	44	2	17
7	146	30	103	33	62	12	33	6	15	12	2	40
8	147	58	104	0	63	24	33	52	15	41	3	4
9	149	25	105	26	64	36	34	38	16	10	3	27
10	150	53	106	53	65	49	35	25	16	40	3	49
11	152	20	108	21	67	3	36	13	17	10	4	13
12	153	48	109	48	68	18	37	2	17	41	4	37
13	155	15	111	26	69	34	37	52	18	11	5	0
14	156	43	112	54	70	51	38	43	18	42	5	23
15	158	11	114	12	72	8	39	34	19	14	5	46
16	159	39	115	40	73	26	40	26	19	46	6	10
17	161	6	117	8	74	45	41	19	20	18	6	34
18	162	34	118	36	76	4	42	13	20	51	6	58
19	164	1	120	4	77	23	43	8	21	24	7	22
20	165	28	121	32	78	43	44	4	21	58	7	46
21	166	55	123	0	80	4	45	1	22	32	8	11
22	168	22	124	28	81	25	45	59	23	7	8	36
23	169	50	125	56	82	47	46	58	23	43	9	1
24	171	17	127	24	84	10	47	57	24	19	9	26
25	172	44	128	52	85	33	48	57	24	56	9	52
26	174	11	130	20	86	56	49	58	25	33	10	17
27	175	38	131	48	88	20	51	0	26	11	10	43
28	177	5	133	17	89	44	52	3	26	50	11	9
29	178	33	134	45	91	9	52	7	27	29	11	35
30	180	0	136	13	92	33	54	12	28	9	12	1

	1		2		3		4		5		6		7		8		9		10	
	°	′	°	′	°	′	°	′	°	′	°	′	°	′	°	′	°	′	°	′
1	0	1	0	2	0	3	0	4	0	5	0	6	0	7	0	8	0	9	0	10
2	0	2	0	4	0	6	0	8	0	10	0	12	0	14	0	16	0	18	0	20
3	0	3	0	6	0	9	0	12	0	15	0	18	0	21	0	24	0	27	0	30
4	0	4	0	8	0	12	0	16	0	20	0	24	0	28	0	32	0	36	0	40
5	0	5	0	10	0	15	0	20	0	25	0	30	0	35	0	40	0	45	0	50
6	0	6	0	12	0	18	0	24	0	30	0	36	0	42	0	48	0	54	1	0
7	0	7	0	14	0	21	0	28	0	35	0	42	0	49	0	56	1	3	1	10
8	0	8	0	16	0	24	0	32	0	40	0	48	0	56	1	4	1	12	1	20
9	0	9	0	18	0	27	0	36	0	45	0	54	1	3	1	12	1	21	1	30
10	0	10	0	20	0	30	0	40	0	50	1	0	1	10	1	20	1	30	1	40
11	0	11	0	22	0	33	0	44	0	55	1	6	1	17	1	28	1	39	1	50
12	0	12	0	24	0	36	0	48	1	0	1	12	1	24	1	36	1	48	2	0
13	0	13	0	26	0	39	0	52	1	5	1	18	1	31	1	44	1	57	2	10
14	0	14	0	28	0	42	0	56	1	10	1	24	1	38	1	52	2	6	2	20
15	0	15	0	30	0	45	1	0	1	15	1	30	1	45	2	0	2	15	2	30
16	0	16	0	32	0	48	1	4	1	20	1	36	1	52	2	8	2	24	2	40
17	0	17	0	34	0	51	1	8	1	25	1	42	1	59	2	16	2	33	2	50
18	0	18	0	36	0	54	1	12	1	30	1	48	2	6	2	24	2	42	3	0
19	0	19	0	38	0	57	1	16	1	35	1	54	2	13	2	32	2	51	3	10
20	0	20	0	40	1	0	1	20	1	40	2	0	2	20	2	40	3	0	3	20
21	0	21	0	42	1	3	1	24	1	45	2	6	2	27	2	48	3	9	3	30
22	0	22	0	44	1	6	1	28	1	50	2	12	2	34	2	56	3	18	3	40
23	0	23	0	46	1	9	1	32	1	55	2	18	2	41	3	4	3	27	3	50
24	0	24	0	48	1	12	1	36	2	0	2	24	2	48	3	12	3	36	4	0
25	0	25	0	50	1	15	1	40	2	5	2	30	2	55	3	20	3	45	4	10
26	0	26	0	52	1	18	1	44	2	10	2	36	3	2	3	28	3	54	4	20
27	0	27	0	54	1	21	1	48	2	15	2	42	3	9	3	36	4	3	4	30
28	0	28	0	56	1	24	1	52	2	20	2	48	3	16	3	44	4	12	4	40
29	0	29	0	58	1	27	1	56	2	25	2	54	3	23	3	52	4	21	4	50
30	0	30	1	0	1	30	2	0	2	30	3	0	3	30	4	0	4	30	5	0
31	0	31	1	2	1	33	2	4	2	35	3	6	3	37	4	8	4	39	5	10
32	0	32	1	4	1	36	2	8	2	40	3	12	3	44	4	16	4	48	5	20
33	0	33	1	6	1	39	2	12	2	45	3	18	3	51	4	24	4	57	5	30
34	0	34	1	8	1	42	2	16	2	50	3	24	3	58	4	32	5	6	5	40
35	0	35	1	10	1	45	2	20	2	55	3	30	4	5	4	40	5	15	5	50
36	0	36	1	12	1	48	2	24	3	0	3	36	4	12	4	48	5	24	6	0
37	0	37	1	14	1	51	2	28	3	5	3	42	4	19	4	56	5	33	6	10
38	0	38	1	16	1	54	2	32	3	10	3	48	4	26	5	4	5	42	6	20
39	0	39	1	18	1	57	2	36	3	15	3	54	4	33	5	12	5	51	6	30
40	0	40	1	20	2	0	2	40	3	20	4	0	4	40	5	20	6	0	6	40
41	0	41	1	22	2	3	2	44	3	25	4	6	4	47	5	28	6	9	6	50
42	0	42	1	24	2	6	2	48	3	30	4	12	4	54	5	36	6	18	7	0
43	0	43	1	26	2	9	2	52	3	35	4	18	5	1	5	44	6	27	7	10
44	0	44	1	28	2	12	2	56	3	40	4	24	5	8	5	52	6	36	7	20
45	0	45	1	30	2	15	3	0	3	45	4	30	5	15	6	0	6	45	7	30
46	0	46	1	32	2	18	3	4	3	50	4	36	5	22	6	8	6	54	7	40
47	0	47	1	34	2	21	3	8	3	55	4	42	5	29	6	16	7	3	7	50
48	0	48	1	36	2	24	3	12	4	0	4	48	5	36	6	24	7	12	8	0
49	0	49	1	38	2	27	3	16	4	5	4	54	5	43	6	32	7	21	8	10
50	0	50	1	40	2	30	3	20	4	10	5	0	5	50	6	40	7	30	8	20
51	0	51	1	42	2	33	3	24	4	15	5	6	5	57	6	48	7	39	8	30
52	0	52	1	44	2	36	3	28	4	20	5	12	6	4	6	56	7	48	8	40
53	0	53	1	46	2	39	3	32	4	25	5	18	6	11	7	4	7	57	8	50
54	0	54	1	48	2	42	3	36	4	30	5	24	6	18	7	12	8	6	9	0
55	0	55	1	50	2	45	3	40	4	35	5	30	6	25	7	20	8	15	9	10
56	0	56	1	52	2	48	3	44	4	40	5	36	6	32	7	28	8	24	9	20
57	0	57	1	54	2	51	3	48	4	45	5	42	6	39	7	36	8	33	9	30
58	0	58	1	56	2	54	3	52	4	50	5	48	6	46	7	44	8	42	9	40
59	0	59	1	58	2	57	3	56	4	55	5	54	6	53	7	52	8	51	9	50
60	1	0	2	0	3	0	4	0	5	0	6	0	7	0	8	0	9	0	10	0

	11 °	11 ′	12 °	12 ′	13 °	13 ′	14 °	14 ′	15 °	15 ′	16 °	16 ′	17 °	17 ′	18 °	18 ′	19 °	19 ′	20 °	20 ′
1	0	11	0	12	0	13	0	14	0	15	0	16	0	17	0	18	0	19	0	20
2	0	22	0	24	0	26	0	28	0	30	0	32	0	34	0	36	0	38	0	40
3	0	33	0	36	0	39	0	42	0	45	0	48	0	51	0	54	0	57	1	0
4	0	44	0	48	0	52	0	56	1	0	1	4	1	8	1	12	1	16	1	20
5	0	55	1	0	1	5	1	10	1	15	1	20	1	25	1	30	1	35	1	40
6	1	6	1	12	1	18	1	24	1	30	1	36	1	42	1	48	1	54	2	0
7	1	17	1	24	1	31	1	38	1	45	1	52	1	59	2	6	2	13	2	20
8	1	28	1	36	1	44	1	52	2	0	2	8	2	16	2	24	2	32	2	40
9	1	39	1	48	1	57	2	6	2	15	2	24	2	33	2	42	2	51	3	0
10	1	50	2	0	2	10	2	20	2	30	2	40	2	50	3	0	3	10	3	20
11	2	1	2	12	2	23	2	34	2	45	2	56	3	7	3	18	3	29	3	40
12	2	12	2	24	2	36	2	48	3	0	3	12	3	24	3	36	3	48	4	0
13	2	23	2	36	2	49	3	2	3	15	3	28	3	41	3	54	4	7	4	20
14	2	34	2	48	3	2	3	16	3	30	3	44	3	58	4	12	4	26	4	40
15	2	45	3	0	3	15	3	30	3	45	4	0	4	15	4	30	4	45	5	0
16	2	56	3	12	3	28	3	44	4	0	4	16	4	32	4	48	5	4	5	20
17	3	7	3	24	3	41	3	58	4	15	4	32	4	49	5	6	5	23	5	40
18	3	18	3	36	3	54	4	12	4	30	4	48	5	6	5	24	5	42	6	0
19	3	29	3	48	4	7	4	26	4	45	5	4	5	23	5	42	6	1	6	20
20	3	40	4	0	4	20	4	40	5	0	5	20	5	40	6	0	6	20	6	40
21	3	51	4	12	4	33	4	54	5	15	5	36	5	57	6	18	6	39	7	0
22	4	2	4	24	4	46	5	8	5	30	5	52	6	14	6	36	6	58	7	20
23	4	13	4	36	4	59	5	22	5	45	6	8	6	31	6	54	7	17	7	40
24	4	24	4	48	5	12	5	36	6	0	6	24	6	48	7	12	7	36	8	0
25	4	35	5	0	5	25	5	50	6	15	6	40	7	5	7	30	7	55	8	20
26	4	46	5	12	5	38	6	4	6	30	6	56	7	22	7	48	8	14	8	40
27	4	57	5	24	5	51	6	18	6	45	7	12	7	39	8	6	8	33	9	0
28	5	8	5	36	6	4	6	32	7	0	7	28	7	56	8	24	8	52	9	20
29	5	19	5	48	6	17	6	46	7	15	7	44	8	13	8	42	9	11	9	40
30	5	30	6	0	6	30	7	0	7	30	8	0	8	30	9	0	9	30	10	0
31	5	41	6	12	6	43	7	14	7	45	8	16	8	47	9	18	9	49	10	20
32	5	52	6	24	6	56	7	28	8	0	8	32	9	4	9	36	10	8	10	40
33	6	3	6	36	7	9	7	42	8	15	8	48	9	21	9	54	10	27	11	0
34	6	14	6	48	7	22	7	56	8	30	9	4	9	38	10	12	10	46	11	20
35	6	25	7	0	7	35	8	10	8	45	9	20	9	55	10	30	11	5	11	40
36	6	36	7	12	7	48	8	24	9	0	9	36	10	12	10	48	11	24	12	0
37	6	47	7	24	8	1	8	38	9	15	9	52	10	29	11	6	11	43	12	20
38	6	58	7	36	8	14	8	52	9	30	10	8	10	46	11	24	12	2	12	40
39	7	9	7	48	8	27	9	6	9	45	10	24	11	3	11	42	12	21	13	0
40	7	20	8	0	8	40	9	20	10	0	10	40	11	20	12	0	12	40	13	20
41	7	31	8	12	8	53	9	34	10	15	10	56	11	37	12	18	12	59	13	40
42	7	42	8	24	9	6	9	48	10	30	11	12	11	54	12	36	13	18	14	0
43	7	53	8	36	9	19	10	2	10	45	11	28	12	11	12	54	13	37	14	20
44	8	4	8	48	9	32	10	16	11	0	11	44	12	28	13	12	13	56	14	40
45	8	15	9	0	9	45	10	30	11	15	12	0	12	45	13	30	14	15	15	0
46	8	26	9	12	9	58	10	44	11	30	12	16	13	2	13	48	14	34	15	20
47	8	37	9	24	10	11	10	58	11	45	12	32	13	19	14	6	14	53	15	40
48	8	48	9	36	10	24	11	12	12	0	12	48	13	36	14	24	15	12	16	0
49	8	59	9	48	10	37	11	26	12	15	13	4	13	53	14	42	15	31	16	20
50	9	10	10	0	10	50	11	40	12	30	13	20	14	10	15	0	15	50	16	40
51	9	21	10	12	11	3	11	54	12	45	13	36	14	27	15	18	16	9	17	0
52	9	32	10	24	11	16	12	8	13	0	13	52	14	44	15	36	16	28	17	20
53	9	43	10	36	11	29	12	22	13	15	14	8	15	1	15	54	16	47	17	40
54	9	54	10	48	11	42	12	36	13	30	14	24	15	18	16	12	17	6	18	0
55	10	5	11	0	11	55	12	50	13	45	14	40	15	35	16	30	17	25	18	20
56	10	16	11	12	12	8	13	4	14	0	14	56	15	52	16	48	17	44	18	40
57	10	27	11	24	12	21	13	18	14	15	15	12	16	9	17	6	18	3	19	0
58	10	38	11	36	12	34	13	32	14	30	15	28	16	26	17	24	18	22	19	20
59	10	49	11	48	12	47	13	46	14	45	15	44	16	43	17	42	18	41	19	40
60	11	0	12	0	13	0	14	0	15	0	16	0	17	0	18	0	19	0	20	0

	21		22		23		24		25		26		27		28		29		30	
	°	′	°	′	°	′	°	′	°	′	°	′	°	′	°	′	°	′	°	′
1	0	21	0	22	0	23	0	24	0	25	0	26	0	27	0	28	0	29	0	30
2	0	42	0	44	0	46	0	48	0	50	0	52	0	54	0	56	0	58	1	0
3	1	3	1	6	1	9	1	12	1	15	1	18	1	21	1	24	1	27	1	30
4	1	24	1	28	1	32	1	36	1	40	1	44	1	48	1	52	1	56	2	0
5	1	45	1	50	1	55	2	0	2	5	2	10	2	15	2	20	2	25	2	30
6	2	6	2	12	2	18	2	24	2	30	2	36	2	42	2	48	2	54	3	0
7	2	27	2	34	2	41	2	48	2	55	3	2	3	9	3	16	3	23	3	30
8	2	48	2	56	3	4	3	12	3	20	3	28	3	36	3	44	3	52	4	0
9	3	9	3	18	3	27	3	36	3	45	3	54	4	3	4	12	4	21	4	30
10	3	30	3	40	3	50	4	0	4	10	4	20	4	30	4	40	4	50	5	0
11	3	51	4	2	4	13	4	24	4	35	4	46	4	57	5	8	5	19	5	30
12	4	12	4	24	4	36	4	48	5	0	5	12	5	24	5	36	5	48	6	0
13	4	33	4	46	4	59	5	12	5	25	5	38	5	51	6	4	6	17	6	30
14	4	54	5	8	5	22	5	36	5	50	6	4	6	18	6	32	6	46	7	0
15	5	15	5	30	5	45	6	0	6	15	6	30	6	45	7	0	7	15	7	30
16	5	36	5	52	6	8	6	24	6	40	6	56	7	12	7	28	7	44	8	0
17	5	57	6	14	6	31	6	48	7	5	7	22	7	39	7	56	8	13	8	30
18	6	18	6	36	6	54	7	12	7	30	7	48	8	6	8	24	8	42	9	0
19	6	39	6	58	7	17	7	36	7	55	8	14	8	33	8	52	9	11	9	30
20	7	0	7	20	7	40	8	0	8	20	8	40	9	0	9	20	9	40	10	0
21	7	21	7	42	8	3	8	24	8	45	9	6	9	27	9	48	10	9	10	30
22	7	42	8	4	8	26	8	48	9	10	9	32	9	54	10	16	10	38	11	0
23	8	3	8	26	8	49	9	12	9	35	9	58	10	21	10	44	11	7	11	30
24	8	24	8	48	9	12	9	36	10	0	10	24	10	48	11	12	11	36	12	0
25	8	45	9	10	9	35	10	0	10	25	10	50	11	15	11	40	12	5	12	30
26	9	6	9	32	9	58	10	24	10	50	11	16	11	42	12	8	12	34	13	0
27	9	27	9	54	10	21	10	48	11	15	11	42	12	9	12	36	13	3	13	30
28	9	48	10	16	10	44	11	12	11	40	12	8	12	36	13	4	13	32	14	0
29	10	9	10	38	11	7	11	36	12	5	12	34	13	3	13	32	14	1	14	30
30	10	30	11	0	11	30	12	0	12	30	13	0	13	30	14	0	14	30	15	0
31	10	51	11	22	11	53	12	24	12	55	13	26	13	57	14	28	14	59	15	30
32	11	12	11	44	12	16	12	48	13	20	13	52	14	24	14	56	15	28	16	0
33	11	33	12	6	12	39	13	12	13	45	14	18	14	41	15	24	15	57	16	30
34	11	54	12	28	13	2	13	36	14	10	14	44	15	18	15	52	16	26	17	0
35	12	15	12	50	13	25	14	0	14	35	15	10	15	45	16	20	16	55	17	30
36	12	36	13	12	13	48	14	24	15	0	15	36	16	12	16	48	17	24	18	0
37	12	57	13	34	14	11	14	48	15	25	16	2	16	39	17	16	17	53	18	30
38	13	18	13	56	14	34	15	12	15	50	16	28	17	6	17	44	18	22	19	0
39	13	39	14	18	14	57	15	36	16	15	16	54	17	33	18	12	18	51	19	30
40	14	0	14	40	15	20	16	0	16	40	17	20	18	0	18	40	19	20	20	0
41	14	21	15	2	15	43	16	24	17	5	17	46	18	27	19	8	19	49	20	30
42	14	42	15	24	16	6	16	48	17	30	18	12	18	54	19	36	20	18	21	0
43	15	3	15	46	16	29	17	12	17	55	18	38	19	21	20	4	20	47	21	30
44	15	24	16	8	16	52	17	36	18	20	19	4	19	48	20	32	21	16	22	0
45	15	45	16	30	17	15	18	0	18	45	19	30	20	15	21	0	21	45	22	30
46	16	6	16	52	17	38	18	24	19	10	19	56	20	42	21	28	22	14	23	0
47	16	27	17	14	18	1	18	48	19	35	20	22	21	9	21	56	22	43	23	30
48	16	48	17	36	18	24	19	12	20	0	20	48	21	36	22	24	23	12	24	0
49	17	9	17	58	18	47	19	36	20	25	21	14	22	3	22	52	23	41	24	30
50	17	30	18	20	19	10	20	0	20	50	21	40	22	30	23	20	24	10	25	0
51	17	51	18	42	19	33	20	24	21	15	22	6	22	57	23	48	24	39	25	30
52	18	12	19	4	19	56	20	48	21	40	22	32	23	24	24	16	25	8	26	0
53	18	33	19	26	20	19	21	12	22	5	22	58	23	51	24	44	25	37	26	30
54	18	54	19	48	20	42	21	36	22	30	23	24	24	18	25	12	26	6	27	0
55	19	15	20	10	21	5	22	0	22	55	23	50	24	45	25	40	26	35	27	30
56	19	36	20	32	21	28	22	24	23	20	24	16	25	12	26	8	27	4	28	0
57	19	57	20	54	21	51	22	48	23	45	24	42	25	39	26	36	27	33	28	30
58	20	18	21	16	22	14	23	12	24	10	25	8	26	6	27	4	28	2	29	0
59	20	39	21	38	22	37	23	36	24	35	25	34	26	33	27	32	28	31	29	30
60	21	0	22	0	23	0	24	0	25	0	26	0	27	0	28	0	29	0	30	0

	31		32		33		34		35		36		37		38		39		40	
	°	′	°	′	°	′	°	′	°	′	°	′	°	′	°	′	°	′	°	′
1	0	31	0	32	0	33	0	34	0	35	0	36	0	37	0	38	0	39	0	40
2	1	2	1	4	1	6	1	8	1	10	1	12	1	14	1	16	1	18	1	20
3	1	33	1	36	1	39	1	42	1	45	1	48	1	51	1	54	1	57	2	0
4	2	4	2	8	2	12	2	16	2	20	2	24	2	28	2	32	2	36	2	40
5	2	35	2	40	2	45	2	50	2	55	3	0	3	5	3	10	3	15	3	20
6	3	6	3	12	3	18	3	24	3	30	3	36	3	42	3	48	3	54	4	0
7	3	37	3	44	3	51	3	58	4	5	4	12	4	19	4	26	4	33	4	40
8	4	8	4	16	4	24	4	32	4	40	4	48	4	56	5	4	5	12	5	20
9	4	39	4	48	4	57	5	6	5	15	5	24	5	33	5	42	5	51	6	0
10	5	10	5	20	5	30	5	40	5	50	6	0	6	10	6	20	6	30	6	40
11	5	41	5	52	6	3	6	14	6	25	6	36	6	47	6	58	7	9	7	20
12	6	12	6	24	6	36	6	48	7	0	7	12	7	24	7	36	7	48	8	0
13	6	43	6	56	7	9	7	22	7	35	7	48	8	1	8	14	8	27	8	40
14	7	14	7	28	7	42	7	56	8	10	8	24	8	38	8	52	9	6	9	20
15	7	45	8	0	8	15	8	30	8	45	9	0	9	15	9	30	9	45	10	0
16	8	16	8	32	8	48	9	4	9	20	9	36	9	52	10	8	10	24	10	40
17	8	47	9	4	9	21	9	38	9	55	10	12	10	29	10	46	11	3	11	20
18	9	18	9	36	9	54	10	12	10	30	10	48	11	6	11	24	11	42	12	0
19	9	49	10	8	10	27	10	46	11	5	11	24	11	43	12	2	12	21	12	40
20	10	20	10	40	11	0	11	20	11	40	12	0	12	20	12	40	13	0	13	20
21	10	51	11	12	11	33	11	54	12	15	12	36	12	57	13	18	13	39	14	0
22	11	22	11	44	12	6	12	28	12	50	13	12	13	34	13	56	14	18	14	40
23	11	53	12	16	12	39	13	2	13	25	13	48	14	11	14	34	14	57	15	20
24	12	24	12	48	13	12	13	36	14	0	14	24	14	48	15	12	15	36	16	0
25	12	55	13	20	13	45	14	10	14	35	15	0	15	25	15	50	16	15	16	40
26	13	26	13	52	14	18	14	44	15	10	15	36	16	2	16	28	16	54	17	20
27	13	57	14	24	14	51	15	18	15	45	16	12	16	39	17	6	17	33	18	0
28	14	28	14	56	15	24	15	52	16	20	16	48	17	16	17	44	18	12	18	40
29	14	59	15	28	15	57	16	26	16	55	17	24	17	53	18	22	18	51	19	20
30	15	30	16	0	16	30	17	0	17	30	18	0	18	30	19	0	19	30	20	0
31	16	1	16	32	17	3	17	34	18	5	18	36	19	7	19	38	20	9	20	40
32	16	32	17	4	17	36	18	8	18	40	19	12	19	44	20	16	20	48	21	20
33	17	3	17	36	18	9	18	42	19	15	19	48	20	21	20	54	21	27	22	0
34	17	34	18	8	18	42	19	16	19	50	20	24	21	58	21	32	22	6	22	40
35	18	5	18	40	19	15	19	50	20	25	21	0	21	35	22	10	22	45	23	20
36	18	36	19	12	19	48	20	24	21	0	21	36	22	12	22	48	23	24	24	0
37	19	7	19	44	20	21	20	58	21	35	22	12	22	49	23	26	24	3	24	40
38	19	38	20	16	20	54	21	32	22	10	22	48	23	26	24	4	24	42	25	20
39	20	9	20	48	21	27	22	6	22	45	23	24	24	3	24	42	25	21	26	0
40	20	40	21	20	22	0	22	40	23	20	24	0	24	40	25	20	26	0	26	40
41	21	11	21	52	22	33	23	14	23	55	24	36	25	17	25	58	26	39	27	20
42	21	42	22	24	23	6	23	48	24	30	25	12	25	54	26	36	27	18	28	0
43	22	13	22	56	23	39	24	22	25	5	25	48	26	31	27	14	27	57	28	40
44	22	44	23	28	24	12	24	56	25	40	26	24	27	8	27	52	28	36	29	20
45	23	15	24	0	24	45	25	30	26	15	27	0	27	45	28	30	29	15	30	0
46	23	46	24	32	25	18	26	4	26	50	27	36	28	22	29	8	29	54	30	40
47	24	17	25	4	25	51	26	38	27	25	28	12	28	59	29	46	30	33	31	20
48	24	48	25	36	26	24	27	12	28	0	28	48	29	36	30	24	31	12	32	0
49	25	19	26	8	26	57	27	46	28	35	29	24	30	13	31	2	31	51	32	40
50	25	50	26	40	27	30	28	20	29	10	30	0	30	50	31	40	32	30	33	20
51	26	21	27	12	28	3	28	54	29	45	30	36	31	27	32	18	33	9	34	0
52	26	52	27	44	28	36	29	28	30	20	31	12	32	4	32	56	33	48	34	40
53	27	23	28	16	29	9	30	2	30	55	31	48	32	41	33	34	34	27	35	20
54	27	54	28	48	29	42	30	36	31	30	32	24	33	18	34	12	35	6	36	0
55	28	25	29	20	30	15	31	10	32	5	33	0	33	55	34	50	35	45	36	40
56	28	56	29	52	30	48	31	44	32	40	33	36	34	32	35	28	36	24	37	20
57	29	27	30	24	31	21	32	18	33	15	34	12	35	9	36	6	37	3	38	0
58	29	58	30	56	31	54	32	52	33	50	34	48	35	46	36	44	37	42	38	40
59	30	29	31	28	32	27	33	26	34	25	35	24	36	23	37	22	38	21	39	20
60	31	0	32	0	33	0	34	0	35	0	36	0	37	0	38	0	39	0	40	0

	41		42		43		44		45		46		47		48		49		50	
	°	′	°	′	°	′	°	′	°	′	°	′	°	′	°	′	°	′	°	′
1	0	41	0	42	0	43	0	44	0	45	0	46	0	47	0	48	0	49	0	50
2	1	22	1	24	1	26	1	28	1	30	1	32	1	34	1	36	1	38	1	40
3	2	3	2	6	2	9	2	12	2	15	2	28	2	21	2	24	2	27	2	30
4	2	44	2	48	2	52	2	56	3	0	3	4	3	8	3	12	3	16	3	20
5	3	25	3	30	3	35	3	40	3	45	3	50	3	55	4	0	4	5	4	10
6	4	6	4	12	4	18	4	24	4	30	4	36	4	42	4	48	4	54	5	0
7	4	47	4	54	5	1	5	8	5	15	5	22	5	29	5	36	5	43	5	50
8	5	28	5	36	5	44	5	52	6	0	6	8	6	16	6	24	6	32	6	40
9	6	9	6	18	6	27	6	36	6	45	6	54	7	3	7	12	7	21	7	30
10	6	50	7	0	7	10	7	20	7	30	7	40	7	50	8	0	8	10	8	20
11	7	31	7	42	7	53	8	4	8	15	8	26	8	37	8	48	8	59	9	10
12	8	12	8	24	8	36	8	48	9	0	9	12	9	24	9	36	9	48	10	0
13	8	53	9	6	9	19	9	32	9	45	9	58	10	11	10	24	10	37	10	50
14	9	34	9	48	10	2	10	16	10	30	10	44	10	58	11	12	11	26	11	40
15	10	15	10	30	10	45	11	0	11	15	11	30	11	45	12	0	12	15	12	30
16	10	56	11	12	11	28	11	44	12	0	12	16	12	32	12	48	13	4	13	20
17	11	37	11	54	12	11	12	28	12	45	13	2	13	19	13	36	13	53	14	10
18	12	18	12	36	12	54	13	12	13	30	13	48	14	6	14	24	14	42	15	0
19	12	59	13	18	13	37	13	56	14	15	14	34	14	53	15	12	15	31	15	50
20	13	40	14	0	14	20	14	40	15	0	15	20	15	40	16	0	16	20	16	40
21	14	21	14	42	15	3	15	24	15	45	16	6	16	27	16	48	17	9	17	30
22	15	2	15	24	15	46	16	8	16	30	16	52	17	14	17	36	17	58	18	20
23	15	43	16	6	16	29	16	52	17	15	17	38	18	1	18	24	18	47	19	10
24	16	24	16	48	17	12	17	36	18	0	18	24	18	48	19	12	19	36	20	0
25	17	5	17	30	17	55	18	20	18	45	19	10	19	35	20	0	20	25	20	50
26	17	46	18	12	18	38	19	4	19	30	19	56	20	22	20	48	21	14	21	40
27	18	27	18	54	19	21	19	48	20	15	20	42	21	9	21	36	22	3	22	30
28	19	8	19	36	20	4	20	32	21	0	21	28	21	56	22	24	22	52	23	20
29	19	49	20	18	20	47	21	16	21	45	22	14	22	43	23	12	23	41	24	10
30	20	30	21	0	21	30	22	0	22	30	23	0	23	30	24	0	24	30	25	0
31	21	11	21	42	22	13	22	44	23	15	23	46	24	17	24	48	25	19	25	50
32	21	52	22	24	22	56	23	28	24	0	24	32	25	4	25	36	26	8	26	40
33	22	33	23	6	23	39	24	12	24	45	25	18	25	51	26	24	26	57	27	30
34	23	14	23	48	24	22	24	56	25	30	26	4	26	38	27	12	27	46	28	20
35	23	55	24	30	25	5	25	40	26	15	26	50	27	25	28	0	28	35	29	10
36	24	36	25	12	25	48	26	24	27	0	27	36	28	12	28	48	29	24	30	0
37	25	17	25	54	26	31	27	8	27	45	28	22	28	59	29	36	30	13	30	50
38	25	58	26	36	27	14	27	52	28	30	29	8	29	46	30	24	31	2	31	40
39	26	39	27	18	27	57	28	36	29	15	29	54	30	33	31	12	31	51	32	30
40	27	20	28	0	28	40	29	20	30	0	30	40	31	20	32	0	32	40	33	20
41	28	1	28	42	29	23	30	4	30	45	31	26	32	7	32	48	33	29	34	10
42	28	42	29	24	30	6	30	48	31	30	32	12	32	54	33	36	34	18	35	0
43	29	23	30	6	30	49	31	32	32	15	32	58	33	41	34	24	35	7	35	50
44	30	4	30	48	31	32	32	16	33	0	33	44	34	28	35	12	35	56	36	40
45	30	45	31	30	32	15	33	0	33	45	34	30	35	15	36	0	36	45	37	30
46	31	26	32	12	32	58	33	44	34	30	35	16	36	2	36	48	37	34	38	20
47	32	7	32	54	33	41	34	28	35	15	36	2	36	49	37	36	38	23	39	10
48	32	48	33	36	34	24	35	12	36	0	36	48	37	36	38	24	39	12	40	0
49	33	29	34	18	35	7	35	56	36	45	37	34	38	23	39	12	40	1	40	50
50	34	10	35	0	35	50	36	40	37	30	38	20	39	10	40	0	40	50	41	40
51	34	51	35	42	36	33	37	24	38	15	39	6	39	57	40	48	41	39	42	30
52	35	32	36	24	37	16	38	8	39	0	39	52	40	44	41	36	42	28	43	20
53	36	13	37	6	37	59	38	52	39	45	40	38	41	31	42	24	43	17	44	10
54	36	54	37	48	38	42	39	36	40	30	41	24	42	18	43	12	44	6	45	0
55	37	35	38	30	39	25	40	20	41	15	42	10	43	5	44	0	44	55	45	50
56	38	16	39	12	40	8	41	4	42	0	42	56	43	52	44	48	45	44	46	40
57	38	57	39	54	40	51	41	48	42	45	43	42	44	39	45	36	46	33	47	30
58	39	38	40	36	41	34	42	32	43	30	44	28	45	26	46	24	47	22	48	20
59	40	19	41	18	42	17	43	16	44	15	45	14	46	13	47	12	48	11	49	10
60	41	0	42	0	43	0	44	0	45	0	46	0	47	0	48	0	49	0	50	0

	51		52		53		54		55		56		57		58		59		60	
	°	′	°	′	°	′	°	′	°	′	°	′	°	′	°	′	°	′	°	′
1	0	51	0	52	0	53	0	54	0	55	0	56	0	57	0	58	0	59	1	0
2	1	42	1	44	1	46	1	48	1	50	1	52	1	54	1	56	1	58	2	0
3	2	33	2	36	2	39	2	42	2	45	2	48	2	51	2	54	2	57	3	0
4	3	24	3	28	3	32	3	36	3	40	3	44	3	48	3	52	3	56	4	0
5	4	15	4	20	4	25	4	30	4	35	4	40	4	45	4	50	4	55	5	0
6	5	6	5	12	5	18	5	24	5	30	5	36	5	42	5	48	5	54	6	0
7	5	57	6	4	6	11	6	18	6	25	6	32	6	39	6	46	6	53	7	0
8	6	48	6	56	7	4	7	12	7	20	7	28	7	36	7	44	7	52	8	0
9	7	39	7	48	7	57	8	6	8	15	8	24	8	33	8	42	8	51	9	0
10	8	30	8	40	8	50	9	0	9	10	9	20	9	30	9	40	9	50	10	0
11	9	21	9	32	9	43	9	54	10	5	10	16	10	27	10	38	10	49	11	0
12	10	12	10	24	10	36	10	48	11	0	11	12	11	24	11	36	11	48	12	0
13	11	3	11	16	11	29	11	42	11	55	12	8	12	21	12	34	12	47	13	0
14	11	54	12	8	12	22	12	36	12	50	13	4	13	18	13	32	13	46	14	0
15	12	45	13	0	13	15	13	30	13	45	14	0	14	15	14	30	14	45	15	0
16	13	36	13	52	14	8	14	24	14	40	14	56	15	12	15	28	15	44	16	0
17	14	27	14	44	15	1	15	18	15	35	15	52	16	9	16	26	16	43	17	0
18	15	18	15	36	15	54	16	12	16	30	16	48	17	6	17	24	17	42	18	0
19	16	9	16	28	16	47	17	6	17	25	17	44	18	3	18	22	18	41	19	0
20	17	0	17	20	17	40	18	0	18	20	18	40	19	0	19	20	19	40	20	0
21	17	51	18	12	18	33	18	54	19	15	19	36	19	57	20	18	20	39	21	0
22	18	42	19	4	19	26	19	48	20	10	20	32	20	54	21	16	21	38	22	0
23	19	33	19	56	20	19	20	42	21	5	21	28	21	51	22	14	22	37	23	0
24	20	24	20	48	21	12	21	36	22	0	22	24	22	48	23	12	23	36	24	0
25	21	15	21	40	22	5	22	30	22	55	23	20	23	45	24	10	24	35	25	0
26	22	6	22	32	22	58	23	24	23	50	24	16	24	42	25	8	25	34	26	0
27	22	57	23	24	23	51	24	18	24	45	25	12	25	39	26	6	26	33	27	0
28	23	48	24	16	24	44	25	12	25	40	26	8	26	36	27	4	27	32	28	0
29	24	39	25	8	25	37	26	6	26	35	27	4	27	33	28	2	28	31	29	0
30	25	30	26	0	26	30	27	0	27	30	28	0	28	30	29	0	29	30	30	0
31	26	21	26	52	27	23	27	54	28	25	28	56	29	27	29	58	30	29	31	0
32	27	12	27	44	28	16	28	48	29	20	29	52	30	24	30	56	31	28	32	0
33	28	3	28	36	29	9	29	42	30	15	30	48	31	21	31	54	32	27	33	0
34	28	54	29	28	30	2	30	36	31	10	31	44	32	18	32	52	33	26	34	0
35	29	45	30	20	30	55	31	30	32	5	32	40	33	15	33	50	34	25	35	0
36	30	36	31	12	31	48	32	24	33	0	33	36	34	12	34	48	35	24	36	0
37	31	27	32	4	32	41	33	18	33	55	34	32	35	9	35	46	36	23	37	0
38	32	18	32	56	33	34	34	12	34	50	35	28	36	6	36	44	37	22	38	0
39	33	9	33	48	34	27	35	6	35	45	36	24	37	3	37	42	38	21	39	0
40	34	0	34	40	35	20	36	0	36	40	37	20	38	0	38	40	39	20	40	0
41	34	51	35	32	36	13	36	54	37	35	38	16	38	57	39	38	40	19	41	0
42	35	42	36	24	37	6	37	48	38	30	39	12	39	54	40	36	41	18	42	0
43	36	33	37	16	37	59	38	42	39	25	40	8	40	51	41	34	42	17	43	0
44	37	24	38	8	38	52	39	36	40	20	41	4	41	48	42	32	43	16	44	0
45	38	15	39	0	39	45	40	30	41	15	42	0	42	45	43	30	44	15	45	0
46	39	6	39	52	40	38	41	24	42	10	42	56	43	42	44	28	45	14	46	0
47	39	57	40	44	41	31	42	18	43	5	43	52	44	39	45	26	46	13	47	0
48	40	48	41	36	42	24	43	12	44	0	44	48	45	36	46	24	47	12	48	0
49	41	39	42	28	43	17	44	6	44	55	45	44	46	33	47	22	48	11	39	0
50	42	30	43	20	44	10	45	0	45	50	46	40	47	30	48	20	49	10	50	0
51	43	21	44	12	45	3	45	54	46	45	47	36	48	27	49	18	50	9	51	0
52	44	12	45	4	45	56	46	48	47	40	48	32	49	24	50	16	51	8	52	0
53	45	3	45	56	46	49	47	42	48	35	49	28	50	21	51	14	52	7	53	0
54	45	54	46	48	47	42	48	36	49	30	50	24	51	18	52	12	53	6	54	0
55	46	45	47	40	48	35	49	30	50	25	51	20	52	15	53	10	54	5	55	0
56	47	36	48	32	49	28	50	24	51	20	52	16	53	12	54	8	55	4	56	0
57	48	27	49	24	50	21	51	18	52	15	53	12	54	9	55	6	56	3	57	0
58	49	18	50	16	51	14	52	12	53	10	54	8	55	6	56	4	57	2	58	0
59	50	9	51	8	52	7	53	6	54	5	55	4	56	3	57	2	58	1	59	0
60	51	0	52	0	53	0	54	0	55	0	56	0	57	0	58	0	59	0	60	0

	61		62		63		64		65		66		67		68		69		70	
	°	′	°	′	°	′	°	′	°	′	°	′	°	′	°	′	°	′	°	′
1	1	1	1	2	1	3	1	4	1	5	1	6	1	7	1	8	1	9	1	10
2	2	2	2	4	2	6	2	8	2	10	2	12	2	14	2	16	2	18	2	20
3	3	3	3	6	3	9	3	12	3	15	3	18	3	21	3	24	3	27	3	30
4	4	4	4	8	4	12	4	16	4	20	4	24	4	28	4	32	4	36	4	40
5	5	5	5	10	5	15	5	20	5	25	5	30	5	35	5	40	5	45	5	50
6	6	6	6	12	6	18	6	24	6	30	6	36	6	42	6	48	6	54	7	0
7	7	7	7	14	7	21	7	28	7	35	7	42	7	49	7	56	8	3	8	10
8	8	8	8	16	8	24	8	32	8	40	8	48	8	56	9	4	9	12	9	20
9	9	9	9	18	9	27	9	36	9	45	9	54	10	3	10	12	10	21	10	30
10	10	10	10	20	10	30	10	40	10	50	11	0	11	10	11	20	11	30	11	40
11	11	11	11	22	11	33	11	44	11	55	12	6	12	17	12	28	12	39	12	50
12	12	12	12	24	12	36	12	48	13	0	13	12	13	24	13	36	13	48	14	0
13	13	13	13	26	13	39	13	52	14	5	14	18	14	31	14	44	14	57	15	10
14	14	14	14	28	14	42	14	56	15	10	15	24	15	38	15	52	16	6	16	20
15	15	15	15	30	15	45	16	0	16	15	16	30	16	45	17	0	17	15	17	30
16	16	16	16	32	16	48	17	4	17	20	17	36	17	52	18	8	18	24	18	40
17	17	17	17	34	17	51	18	8	18	25	18	42	18	59	19	16	19	33	19	50
18	18	18	18	36	18	54	19	12	19	30	19	48	20	6	20	24	20	42	21	0
19	19	19	19	38	19	57	20	16	20	35	20	54	21	13	21	32	21	51	22	10
20	20	20	20	40	21	0	21	20	21	40	22	0	22	20	22	40	23	0	23	20
21	21	21	21	42	22	3	22	24	22	45	23	6	23	27	23	48	24	9	24	30
22	22	22	22	44	23	6	23	28	23	50	24	12	24	34	24	56	25	18	25	40
23	23	23	23	46	24	9	24	32	24	55	25	18	25	41	26	4	26	27	26	50
24	24	24	24	48	25	12	25	36	26	0	26	24	26	48	27	12	27	36	28	0
25	25	25	25	50	26	15	26	40	27	5	27	30	27	55	28	20	28	45	29	10
26	26	26	26	52	27	18	27	44	28	10	28	36	29	2	29	28	29	54	30	20
27	27	27	27	54	28	21	28	48	29	15	29	42	30	9	30	36	31	3	31	30
28	28	28	28	56	29	24	29	52	30	20	30	48	31	16	31	44	32	12	32	40
29	29	29	29	58	30	27	30	56	31	25	31	54	32	23	32	52	33	21	33	50
30	30	30	31	0	31	30	32	0	32	30	33	0	33	30	34	0	34	30	35	0
31	31	31	32	2	32	33	33	4	33	35	34	6	34	37	35	8	35	39	36	10
32	32	32	33	4	33	36	34	8	34	40	35	12	35	44	36	16	36	48	37	20
33	33	33	34	6	34	39	35	12	35	45	36	18	36	51	37	24	37	57	38	30
34	34	34	35	8	35	42	36	16	36	50	37	24	37	58	38	32	39	6	39	40
35	35	35	36	10	36	45	37	20	37	55	38	30	39	5	39	40	40	15	40	50
36	36	36	37	12	37	48	38	24	39	0	39	36	40	12	40	48	41	24	42	0
37	37	37	38	14	38	51	39	28	40	5	40	42	41	19	41	56	42	33	43	10
38	38	38	39	16	39	54	40	32	41	10	41	48	42	26	43	4	43	42	44	20
39	39	39	40	18	40	57	41	36	42	15	42	54	43	33	44	12	44	51	45	30
40	40	40	41	20	42	0	42	40	43	20	44	0	44	40	45	20	46	0	46	40
41	41	41	42	22	43	3	43	44	44	25	45	6	45	47	46	28	47	9	47	50
42	42	42	43	24	44	6	44	48	45	30	46	12	46	54	47	36	48	18	49	0
43	43	43	44	26	45	9	45	52	46	35	47	18	48	1	48	44	49	27	50	10
44	44	44	45	28	46	12	46	56	47	40	48	24	49	8	49	52	50	36	51	20
45	45	45	46	30	47	15	48	0	48	45	49	30	50	15	51	0	51	45	52	30
46	46	46	47	32	48	18	49	4	49	50	50	36	51	22	52	8	52	54	53	40
47	47	47	48	34	49	21	50	8	50	55	51	42	52	29	53	16	54	3	54	50
48	48	48	49	36	50	24	51	12	52	0	52	48	53	36	54	24	55	12	56	0
49	49	49	50	38	51	27	52	16	53	5	53	54	54	43	55	32	56	21	57	10
50	50	50	51	40	52	30	53	20	54	10	55	0	55	50	56	40	57	30	58	20
51	51	51	52	42	53	33	54	24	55	15	56	6	56	57	57	48	58	39	59	30
52	52	52	53	44	54	36	55	28	56	20	57	12	58	4	58	56	59	48	60	40
53	53	53	54	46	55	39	56	32	57	25	58	18	59	11	60	4	60	57	61	50
54	54	54	55	48	56	42	57	36	58	30	59	24	60	18	61	12	62	6	63	0
55	55	55	56	50	57	45	58	40	59	35	60	30	61	25	62	20	63	15	64	10
56	56	56	57	52	58	48	59	44	60	40	61	36	62	32	63	28	64	24	65	20
57	57	57	58	54	59	51	60	48	61	45	62	42	63	39	64	36	65	33	66	30
58	58	58	59	56	60	54	61	52	62	50	63	48	64	46	65	44	66	42	67	40
59	59	59	60	58	61	57	62	56	63	55	64	54	65	53	66	52	67	51	68	50
60	61	0	62	0	63	0	64	0	65	0	66	0	67	0	68	0	69	0	70	0

	71		72		73		74		75		76		77		78		79		80	
	°	′	°	′	°	′	°	′	°	′	°	′	°	′	°	′	°	′	°	′
1	1	11	1	12	1	13	1	14	1	15	1	16	1	17	1	18	1	19	1	20
2	2	22	2	24	2	26	2	28	2	30	2	32	2	34	2	36	2	38	2	40
3	3	33	3	36	3	39	3	42	3	45	3	48	3	51	3	54	3	57	4	0
4	4	44	4	48	4	52	4	56	5	0	5	4	5	8	5	12	5	16	5	20
5	5	55	6	0	6	5	6	10	6	15	6	20	6	25	6	30	6	35	6	40
6	7	6	7	12	7	18	7	24	7	30	7	36	7	42	7	48	7	54	8	0
7	8	17	8	24	8	31	8	38	8	45	8	52	8	59	9	6	9	13	9	20
8	9	28	9	36	9	44	9	52	10	0	10	8	10	16	10	24	10	32	10	40
9	10	39	10	48	10	57	11	6	11	15	11	24	11	33	11	42	11	51	12	0
10	11	50	12	0	12	10	12	20	12	30	12	40	12	50	13	0	13	10	13	20
11	13	1	13	12	13	23	13	34	13	45	13	56	14	7	14	18	14	29	14	40
12	14	12	14	24	14	36	14	48	15	0	15	12	15	24	15	36	15	48	16	0
13	15	23	15	36	15	49	16	2	16	15	16	28	16	41	16	54	17	7	17	20
14	16	34	16	48	17	2	17	16	17	30	17	44	17	58	18	12	18	26	18	40
15	17	45	18	0	18	15	18	30	18	45	19	0	19	15	19	30	19	45	20	0
16	18	56	19	12	19	28	19	44	20	0	20	16	20	32	20	48	21	4	21	20
17	20	7	20	24	20	41	20	58	21	15	21	32	21	49	22	6	22	23	22	40
18	21	18	21	36	21	54	22	12	22	30	22	48	23	6	23	24	23	42	24	0
19	22	29	22	48	23	7	23	26	23	45	24	4	24	23	24	42	25	1	25	20
20	23	40	24	0	24	20	24	40	25	0	25	20	25	40	26	0	26	20	26	40
21	24	51	25	12	25	33	25	54	26	15	26	36	26	57	27	18	27	39	28	0
22	26	2	26	24	26	46	27	8	27	30	27	52	28	14	28	36	28	58	29	20
23	27	13	27	36	27	59	28	22	28	45	29	8	29	31	29	54	30	17	30	40
24	28	24	28	48	29	12	29	36	30	0	30	24	30	48	31	12	31	36	32	0
25	29	35	30	0	30	25	30	50	31	15	31	40	32	5	32	30	32	55	33	20
26	30	46	31	12	31	38	32	4	32	30	32	56	33	22	33	48	34	14	34	40
27	31	57	32	24	32	51	33	18	33	45	34	12	34	39	35	6	35	33	36	0
28	33	8	33	36	34	4	34	32	35	0	35	28	35	56	36	24	36	52	37	20
29	34	19	34	48	35	17	35	46	36	15	36	44	37	13	37	42	38	11	38	40
30	35	30	36	0	36	30	37	0	37	30	38	0	38	30	39	0	39	30	40	0
31	36	41	37	12	37	43	38	14	38	45	39	16	39	47	40	18	40	49	41	20
32	37	52	38	24	38	56	39	28	40	0	40	32	41	4	41	36	42	8	42	40
33	39	3	39	36	40	9	40	42	41	15	41	48	42	21	42	54	43	27	44	0
34	40	14	40	48	41	22	41	56	42	30	43	4	43	38	44	12	44	46	45	20
35	41	25	42	0	42	35	43	10	43	45	44	20	44	55	45	30	46	5	46	40
36	42	36	43	12	43	48	44	24	45	0	45	36	46	12	46	48	47	24	48	0
37	43	47	44	24	45	1	45	38	46	15	46	52	47	29	48	6	48	43	49	20
38	44	58	45	36	46	14	46	52	47	30	48	8	48	46	49	24	50	2	50	40
39	46	9	46	48	47	27	48	6	48	45	49	24	50	3	50	42	51	21	52	0
40	47	20	48	0	48	40	49	20	50	0	50	40	51	20	52	0	52	40	53	20
41	48	31	49	12	49	53	50	34	51	15	51	56	52	37	53	18	53	59	54	40
42	49	42	50	24	51	6	51	48	52	30	53	12	53	54	54	36	55	18	56	0
43	50	53	51	36	52	19	53	2	53	45	54	28	55	11	55	54	56	37	57	20
44	52	4	52	48	53	32	54	16	55	0	55	44	56	28	57	12	57	56	58	40
45	53	15	54	0	54	45	55	30	56	15	57	0	57	45	58	30	59	15	60	0
46	54	26	55	12	55	58	56	44	57	30	58	16	59	2	59	48	60	34	61	20
47	55	37	56	24	57	11	57	58	58	45	59	32	60	19	61	6	61	53	62	40
48	56	48	57	36	58	24	59	12	60	0	60	48	61	36	62	24	63	12	64	0
49	57	59	58	48	59	37	60	26	61	15	62	4	62	53	63	42	64	31	65	20
50	59	10	60	0	60	50	61	40	62	30	63	20	64	10	65	0	65	50	66	40
51	60	21	61	12	62	3	62	54	63	45	64	36	65	27	66	18	67	9	68	0
52	61	32	62	24	63	16	64	8	65	0	65	52	66	44	67	36	68	28	69	20
53	62	43	63	36	64	29	65	22	66	15	67	8	68	1	68	54	69	47	70	40
54	63	54	64	48	65	42	66	36	67	30	68	24	69	18	70	12	71	6	72	0
55	65	5	66	0	66	55	67	50	68	45	69	40	70	35	71	30	72	25	73	20
56	66	16	67	12	68	8	69	4	70	0	70	56	71	52	72	48	73	44	74	40
57	67	27	68	24	69	21	70	18	71	15	72	12	73	9	74	6	75	3	76	0
58	68	38	69	36	70	34	71	32	72	30	73	28	74	26	75	24	76	22	77	20
59	69	49	70	48	71	47	72	46	73	45	74	44	75	43	76	42	77	41	78	40
60	71	0	72	0	73	0	74	0	75	0	76	0	77	0	78	0	79	0	80	0

	81		82		83		84		85		86		87		88		89		90	
	°	′	°	′	°	′	°	′	°	′	°	′	°	′	°	′	°	′	°	′
1	1	21	1	22	1	23	1	24	1	25	1	26	1	27	1	28	1	29	1	30
2	2	42	2	44	2	46	2	48	2	50	2	52	2	54	2	56	2	58	3	0
3	4	3	4	6	4	9	4	12	4	15	4	18	4	21	4	24	4	27	4	30
4	5	24	5	28	5	32	5	36	5	40	5	44	5	48	5	52	5	56	6	0
5	6	45	6	50	6	55	7	0	7	5	7	10	7	15	7	20	7	25	7	30
6	8	6	8	12	8	18	8	24	8	30	8	36	8	42	8	48	8	54	9	0
7	9	27	9	34	9	41	9	48	9	55	10	2	10	9	10	16	10	23	10	30
8	10	48	10	56	11	4	11	12	11	20	11	28	11	36	11	44	11	52	12	0
9	12	9	12	18	12	27	12	36	12	45	12	54	13	3	13	12	13	21	13	30
10	13	30	13	40	13	50	14	0	14	10	14	20	14	30	14	40	14	50	15	0
11	14	51	15	2	15	13	15	24	15	35	15	46	15	57	16	8	16	19	16	30
12	16	12	16	24	16	36	16	48	17	0	17	12	17	24	17	36	17	48	18	0
13	17	33	17	46	17	59	18	12	18	25	18	38	18	51	19	4	19	17	19	30
14	18	54	19	8	19	22	19	36	19	50	20	4	20	18	20	32	20	46	21	0
15	20	15	20	30	20	45	21	0	21	15	21	30	21	45	22	0	22	15	22	30
16	21	36	21	52	22	8	22	24	22	40	22	56	23	12	23	28	23	44	24	0
17	22	57	23	14	23	31	23	48	24	5	24	22	24	39	24	56	25	13	25	30
18	24	18	24	36	24	54	25	12	25	30	25	48	26	6	26	24	26	42	27	0
19	25	39	25	58	26	17	26	36	26	55	27	14	27	33	27	52	28	11	28	30
20	27	0	27	20	27	40	28	0	28	20	28	40	29	0	29	20	29	40	30	0
21	28	21	28	42	29	3	29	24	29	45	30	6	30	27	30	48	31	9	31	30
22	29	42	30	4	30	26	30	48	31	10	31	32	31	54	32	16	32	38	33	0
23	31	3	31	26	31	49	22	12	32	35	32	58	33	21	33	44	34	7	34	30
24	32	24	32	48	33	12	33	36	34	0	34	24	34	48	35	12	35	36	36	0
25	33	45	34	10	34	35	35	0	35	25	35	50	36	15	36	40	37	5	37	30
26	35	6	35	32	35	58	36	24	36	50	37	16	37	42	38	8	38	34	39	0
27	36	27	36	54	37	21	37	48	38	15	38	42	39	9	39	36	40	3	40	30
28	37	48	38	16	38	44	39	12	39	40	40	8	40	36	41	4	41	32	42	0
29	39	9	39	38	40	7	40	36	41	5	41	34	42	3	42	32	43	1	43	30
30	40	30	41	0	41	30	42	0	42	30	43	0	43	30	44	0	44	30	45	0
31	41	51	42	22	42	53	43	24	43	55	44	26	44	57	45	28	45	59	46	30
32	43	12	43	44	44	16	44	48	45	20	45	52	46	24	46	56	47	28	48	0
33	44	33	45	6	45	39	46	12	46	45	47	18	47	51	48	24	48	57	49	30
34	45	54	46	28	47	2	47	36	48	10	48	44	49	18	49	52	50	26	51	0
35	47	15	48	50	48	25	49	0	49	35	50	10	50	45	51	20	51	55	52	30
36	48	36	49	12	49	48	50	24	51	0	51	36	52	12	52	48	53	24	54	0
37	49	57	50	34	51	11	51	48	52	25	53	2	53	39	54	16	54	53	55	30
38	51	18	51	56	52	34	53	12	53	50	54	28	55	6	55	44	56	22	57	0
39	52	39	53	18	53	57	54	36	55	15	55	54	56	33	57	12	57	51	58	30
40	54	0	54	40	55	20	56	0	56	40	57	20	58	0	58	40	59	20	60	0
41	55	21	56	2	56	43	57	24	58	5	58	46	59	27	60	8	60	49	61	30
42	56	42	57	24	58	6	58	48	59	30	60	12	60	54	61	36	62	18	63	0
43	58	3	58	46	59	29	60	12	60	55	61	38	62	21	63	4	63	47	64	30
44	59	24	60	8	60	52	61	36	62	20	63	4	63	48	64	32	65	16	66	0
45	60	45	61	30	62	15	63	0	63	45	64	30	65	15	66	0	66	45	67	30
46	62	6	62	52	63	38	64	24	65	10	65	56	66	42	67	28	68	14	69	0
47	63	27	64	14	65	1	65	48	66	35	67	22	68	9	68	56	69	43	70	30
48	64	48	65	36	66	24	67	12	68	0	68	48	69	36	70	24	71	12	72	0
49	66	9	66	58	67	47	68	36	69	25	70	14	71	3	71	52	72	41	73	30
50	67	30	68	20	69	10	70	0	70	50	71	40	72	30	73	20	74	10	75	0
51	68	51	69	42	70	33	71	24	72	15	73	6	73	57	74	48	75	39	76	30
52	70	12	71	4	71	56	72	48	73	40	74	32	75	24	76	16	77	8	78	0
53	71	33	72	26	73	19	74	12	75	5	75	58	76	51	77	44	78	37	79	30
54	72	54	73	48	74	42	75	36	76	30	77	24	78	18	79	12	80	6	81	0
55	74	15	75	10	76	5	77	0	77	55	78	50	79	45	80	40	81	35	82	30
56	75	36	76	32	77	28	78	24	79	20	80	16	81	12	82	8	83	4	84	0
57	76	57	77	54	78	51	79	48	80	45	81	42	82	39	83	36	84	33	85	30
58	78	18	79	16	80	14	81	12	82	10	83	8	84	6	85	4	86	2	87	0
59	79	39	80	38	81	37	82	36	83	35	84	34	85	33	86	32	87	31	88	30
60	81	0	82	0	83	0	84	0	85	0	86	0	87	0	88	0	89	0	90	0

	91 °	91 ′	92 °	92 ′	93 °	93 ′	94 °	94 ′	95 °	95 ′	96 °	96 ′	97 °	97 ′	98 °	98 ′	99 °	99 ′	100 °	100 ′
1	1	31	1	32	1	33	1	34	1	35	1	36	1	37	1	38	1	39	1	40
2	3	2	3	4	3	6	3	8	3	10	3	12	3	14	3	16	3	18	3	20
3	4	33	4	36	4	39	4	42	4	45	4	48	4	51	4	54	4	57	5	0
4	6	4	6	8	6	12	6	16	6	20	6	24	6	28	6	32	6	36	6	40
5	7	35	7	40	7	45	7	50	7	55	8	0	8	5	8	10	8	15	8	20
6	9	6	9	12	9	18	9	24	9	30	9	36	9	42	9	48	9	54	10	0
7	10	37	10	44	10	51	10	58	11	5	11	12	11	19	11	26	11	33	11	40
8	12	8	12	16	12	24	12	32	12	40	12	48	12	56	13	4	13	12	13	20
9	13	39	13	48	13	57	14	6	14	15	14	24	14	33	14	42	14	51	15	0
10	15	10	15	20	15	30	15	40	15	50	16	0	16	10	16	20	16	30	16	40
11	16	41	16	52	17	3	17	14	17	25	17	36	17	47	17	58	18	9	18	20
12	18	12	18	24	18	36	18	48	19	0	19	12	19	24	19	36	19	48	20	0
13	19	43	19	56	20	9	20	22	20	35	20	48	21	1	21	14	21	27	21	40
14	21	14	21	28	21	42	21	56	22	10	22	24	22	38	22	52	23	6	23	20
15	22	45	23	0	23	15	23	30	23	45	24	0	24	15	24	30	24	45	25	0
16	24	16	24	32	24	48	25	4	25	20	25	36	25	52	26	8	26	24	26	40
17	25	47	26	4	26	21	26	38	26	55	27	12	27	29	27	46	28	3	28	20
18	27	18	27	36	27	54	28	12	28	30	28	48	29	6	29	24	29	42	30	0
19	28	49	29	8	29	27	29	46	30	5	30	24	30	43	31	2	31	21	31	40
20	30	20	30	40	31	0	31	20	31	40	32	0	32	20	32	40	33	0	33	20
21	31	51	32	12	32	33	32	54	33	15	33	36	33	57	34	18	34	39	35	0
22	33	22	33	44	34	6	34	28	34	50	35	12	35	34	35	56	36	18	36	40
23	34	53	35	16	35	39	36	2	36	25	36	48	37	11	37	34	37	57	38	20
24	36	24	36	48	37	12	37	36	38	0	38	24	38	48	39	12	39	36	40	0
25	37	55	38	20	38	45	39	10	39	35	40	0	40	25	40	50	41	15	41	40
26	39	26	39	52	40	18	40	44	41	10	41	36	42	2	42	28	42	54	43	20
27	40	57	41	24	41	51	42	18	43	45	43	12	43	39	44	6	44	33	45	0
28	42	28	42	56	43	24	43	52	44	20	44	48	45	16	45	44	46	12	46	40
29	43	59	44	28	44	57	45	26	45	55	46	24	46	53	47	22	47	51	48	20
30	45	30	46	0	46	30	47	0	47	30	48	0	48	30	49	0	49	30	50	0
31	47	1	47	32	48	3	48	34	49	5	49	36	50	7	50	38	51	9	51	40
32	48	32	49	4	49	36	50	8	50	40	51	12	51	44	52	16	52	48	53	20
33	50	3	50	36	51	9	51	42	52	15	52	48	53	21	53	54	54	27	55	0
34	51	34	52	8	52	42	53	16	53	50	54	24	54	58	55	32	56	6	56	40
35	53	5	53	40	54	15	54	50	55	25	56	0	56	35	57	10	57	45	58	20
36	54	36	55	12	55	48	56	24	57	0	57	36	58	12	58	48	59	24	60	0
37	56	7	56	44	57	21	57	58	58	35	59	12	59	49	60	26	61	3	61	40
38	57	38	58	16	58	54	59	32	60	10	60	48	61	26	62	4	62	42	63	20
39	59	9	59	48	60	27	61	6	61	45	62	24	63	3	63	42	64	21	65	0
40	60	40	61	20	62	0	62	40	63	20	64	0	64	40	65	20	66	0	66	40
41	62	11	62	52	63	33	64	14	64	55	65	36	66	17	66	58	67	39	68	20
42	63	42	64	24	65	6	65	48	66	30	67	12	67	54	68	36	69	18	70	0
43	65	13	65	56	66	39	67	22	68	5	68	48	69	31	70	14	70	57	71	40
44	66	44	67	28	68	12	68	56	69	40	70	24	71	8	71	52	72	36	73	20
45	68	15	69	0	69	45	70	30	71	15	72	0	72	45	73	30	74	15	75	0
46	69	46	70	32	71	18	72	4	72	50	73	36	74	22	75	8	75	54	76	40
47	71	17	72	4	72	51	73	38	74	25	75	12	75	59	76	46	77	33	78	20
48	72	48	73	36	74	24	75	12	76	0	76	48	77	36	78	24	79	12	80	0
49	74	19	75	8	75	57	76	46	77	35	78	24	79	13	80	2	80	51	81	40
50	75	50	76	40	77	30	78	20	79	10	80	0	80	50	81	40	82	30	83	20
51	77	21	78	12	79	3	79	54	80	45	81	36	82	27	83	18	84	9	85	0
52	78	52	79	44	80	36	81	28	82	20	83	12	84	4	84	56	85	48	86	40
53	80	23	81	16	82	9	83	2	83	55	84	48	85	41	86	34	87	27	88	20
54	81	54	82	48	83	42	84	36	85	30	86	24	87	18	88	12	89	6	90	0
55	83	25	84	20	85	15	86	10	87	5	88	0	88	55	89	50	90	45	91	40
56	84	56	85	52	86	48	87	44	88	40	89	36	90	32	91	28	92	24	93	20
57	86	27	87	24	88	21	89	18	90	15	91	12	92	9	93	6	94	3	95	0
58	87	58	88	56	89	54	90	52	91	50	92	48	93	46	94	44	95	42	96	40
59	89	29	90	28	91	27	92	26	93	25	94	24	95	23	96	22	97	21	98	20
60	91	0	92	0	93	0	94	0	95	0	96	0	97	0	98	0	99	0	100	0

	101 ° '	102 ° '	103 ° '	104 ° '	105 ° '	106 ° '	107 ° '	108 ° '	109 ° '	110 ° '
1	1 41	1 42	1 43	1 44	1 45	1 46	1 47	1 48	1 49	1 50
2	3 22	3 24	3 26	3 28	3 30	3 32	3 34	3 36	3 38	3 40
3	5 3	5 6	5 9	5 12	5 15	5 18	5 21	5 24	5 27	5 30
4	6 44	6 48	6 52	6 56	7 0	7 4	7 8	7 12	7 16	7 20
5	8 25	8 30	8 35	8 40	8 45	8 50	8 55	9 0	9 5	9 10
6	10 6	10 12	10 18	10 24	10 30	10 36	10 42	10 48	10 54	11 0
7	11 47	11 54	12 1	12 8	12 15	12 22	12 29	12 36	12 43	12 50
8	13 28	13 36	13 44	13 52	14 0	14 8	14 16	14 24	14 32	14 40
9	15 9	15 18	15 27	15 36	15 45	15 54	16 3	16 12	16 21	16 30
10	16 50	17 0	17 10	17 20	17 30	17 40	17 50	18 0	18 10	18 20
11	18 31	18 42	18 53	19 4	19 15	19 26	19 37	19 48	19 59	20 10
12	20 12	20 24	20 36	20 48	21 0	21 12	21 24	21 36	21 48	22 0
13	21 53	22 6	22 19	23 22	22 45	22 58	23 11	23 24	23 37	23 50
14	22 34	23 48	24 2	24 16	24 30	24 44	24 58	25 12	25 26	25 40
15	25 15	25 30	25 45	26 0	26 15	26 30	26 45	27 0	27 15	27 30
16	26 56	27 12	27 28	27 44	28 0	28 16	28 32	28 48	29 4	29 20
17	28 37	28 54	29 11	29 28	29 45	30 2	30 19	30 36	30 53	31 10
18	30 18	30 36	30 54	31 12	31 30	31 48	32 6	32 24	32 42	33 0
19	31 59	32 18	32 37	32 56	33 15	33 34	33 53	34 12	34 31	34 50
20	33 40	34 0	34 20	34 40	35 0	35 20	35 40	36 0	36 20	36 40
21	35 21	35 42	36 3	36 24	36 45	37 6	37 27	37 48	38 9	38 30
22	37 2	37 24	37 46	38 8	38 30	38 52	39 14	39 36	39 58	40 20
23	38 43	39 6	39 29	39 52	40 15	40 38	41 1	41 24	41 47	42 10
24	40 24	40 48	41 12	41 36	42 0	42 24	42 48	43 12	43 36	44 0
25	42 5	42 30	42 55	43 20	43 45	44 10	44 35	45 0	45 25	45 50
26	43 46	44 12	44 38	45 4	45 30	45 56	46 22	46 48	47 14	47 40
27	45 27	45 54	46 21	46 48	47 15	47 42	48 9	48 36	49 3	49 30
28	47 8	47 36	48 4	48 32	49 0	49 28	49 56	50 24	50 52	51 20
29	48 49	49 18	49 47	50 16	50 45	51 14	51 43	52 12	52 41	53 10
30	50 30	51 0	51 30	52 0	52 30	53 0	53 30	54 0	54 30	55 0
31	52 11	52 42	53 13	53 44	54 15	54 46	55 17	55 48	56 19	56 50
32	53 52	54 24	54 56	55 28	56 0	56 32	57 4	57 36	58 8	58 40
33	55 33	56 6	56 39	57 12	57 45	58 18	58 51	59 24	59 57	60 30
34	57 14	57 48	58 22	58 56	59 30	60 4	60 38	61 12	61 46	62 20
35	58 55	59 30	60 5	60 40	61 15	61 50	62 25	63 0	63 35	64 10
36	60 36	61 12	61 48	62 24	63 0	63 36	64 12	64 48	65 24	66 0
37	62 17	62 54	63 31	64 8	64 45	65 22	65 59	66 36	67 13	67 50
38	63 58	64 36	65 14	65 52	66 30	67 8	67 46	68 24	69 2	69 40
39	65 39	66 18	66 57	67 36	68 15	68 54	69 33	70 12	70 51	71 30
40	67 20	68 0	68 40	69 20	70 0	70 40	71 20	72 0	72 40	73 20
41	69 1	69 42	70 23	71 4	71 45	72 26	73 7	73 48	74 29	75 10
42	70 42	71 24	72 6	72 48	73 30	74 12	74 54	75 36	76 18	77 0
43	72 23	73 6	73 49	74 32	75 15	75 58	76 41	77 24	78 7	78 50
44	74 4	74 48	75 32	76 16	77 0	77 44	78 28	79 12	79 56	80 40
45	75 45	76 30	77 15	78 0	78 45	79 30	80 15	81 0	81 45	82 30
46	77 26	78 12	78 58	79 44	80 30	81 16	82 2	82 48	83 34	84 20
47	79 7	79 54	80 41	81 28	82 15	83 2	83 49	84 36	85 23	86 10
48	80 48	81 36	82 24	83 12	84 0	84 48	85 36	86 24	87 12	88 0
49	82 29	83 18	84 7	84 56	85 45	86 34	87 23	88 12	89 1	89 50
50	84 10	85 0	85 50	86 40	87 30	88 20	89 10	90 0	90 50	91 40
51	85 51	86 42	87 33	88 24	89 15	90 6	90 57	91 48	92 39	93 30
52	87 32	88 24	89 16	90 8	91 0	91 52	92 44	93 36	94 28	95 20
53	89 13	90 6	90 59	91 52	92 45	93 38	94 31	95 24	96 17	97 10
54	90 54	91 48	92 42	93 36	94 30	95 24	96 18	97 12	98 6	99 0
55	92 35	93 30	94 25	95 20	96 15	97 10	98 5	99 0	99 55	100 50
56	94 16	95 12	96 8	97 4	98 0	98 56	99 52	100 48	101 44	102 40
57	95 57	96 54	97 51	98 48	99 45	100 42	101 39	102 36	103 33	104 30
58	97 38	98 36	99 34	100 32	101 30	102 28	103 26	104 24	105 22	106 20
59	99 19	100 18	101 17	102 16	103 15	104 14	105 13	106 12	107 11	108 10
60	101 0	102 0	103 0	104 0	105 0	106 0	107 0	108 0	109 0	110 0

	111		112		113		114		115		116		117		118		119		120	
	°	′	°	′	°	′	°	′	°	′	°	′	°	′	°	′	°	′	°	′
1	1	51	1	52	1	53	1	54	1	55	1	56	1	57	1	58	1	59	2	0
2	2	42	3	44	3	46	3	48	3	50	3	52	3	54	3	56	3	58	4	0
3	5	33	5	36	5	39	5	42	5	45	5	48	5	51	5	54	5	57	6	0
4	7	24	7	28	7	32	7	36	7	40	7	44	7	48	7	52	7	56	8	0
5	9	15	9	20	9	45	9	30	9	35	9	40	9	45	9	50	9	55	10	0
6	11	6	11	12	11	18	11	24	11	30	11	36	11	42	11	48	11	54	12	0
7	12	57	13	4	13	11	13	18	13	25	13	32	13	39	13	46	13	53	14	0
8	14	48	14	56	15	4	15	12	15	20	15	28	15	36	15	44	15	52	16	0
9	16	39	16	48	16	57	17	6	17	15	17	24	17	33	17	42	17	51	18	0
10	18	30	18	40	18	50	19	0	19	10	19	20	19	30	19	40	19	50	20	0
11	20	21	20	32	20	43	20	54	21	5	21	16	21	27	21	38	21	49	22	0
12	22	12	22	24	22	36	22	48	23	0	23	12	23	24	23	36	23	48	24	0
13	24	3	24	16	24	29	24	42	24	55	25	8	25	21	25	34	25	47	26	0
14	25	54	26	8	26	22	26	36	26	50	27	4	27	18	27	32	27	46	28	0
15	27	45	28	0	28	15	28	30	28	45	29	0	29	15	29	30	29	45	30	0
16	29	36	29	52	30	8	30	24	30	40	30	56	31	12	31	28	31	44	32	0
17	31	27	31	44	32	1	32	18	32	35	32	52	33	9	33	26	33	43	34	0
18	33	18	33	36	33	54	34	12	34	30	34	48	35	6	35	24	35	42	36	0
19	35	9	35	28	35	47	36	6	36	25	36	44	37	3	37	22	37	41	38	0
20	37	0	37	20	37	40	38	0	38	20	38	40	39	0	39	20	39	40	40	0
21	38	51	39	12	39	33	39	54	40	15	40	36	40	57	41	18	41	39	42	0
22	40	42	41	4	41	26	41	48	42	10	42	32	42	54	43	16	43	38	44	0
23	42	33	42	56	43	19	43	42	44	5	44	28	44	51	45	14	45	37	46	0
24	44	24	44	48	45	12	45	36	46	0	46	24	46	48	47	12	47	36	48	0
25	46	15	46	40	47	5	47	30	47	55	48	20	48	45	49	10	49	35	50	0
26	48	6	48	32	48	58	49	24	49	50	50	16	50	42	51	8	51	34	52	0
27	49	57	50	24	50	51	51	18	51	45	52	12	52	39	53	6	53	33	54	0
28	51	48	52	16	52	44	53	12	53	40	54	8	54	36	55	4	55	32	56	0
29	53	39	54	8	54	37	55	6	55	35	56	4	56	33	57	2	57	31	58	0
30	55	30	56	0	56	30	57	0	57	30	58	0	58	30	59	0	59	30	60	0
31	57	21	57	52	58	23	58	54	59	25	59	56	60	27	60	58	61	29	62	0
32	59	12	59	44	60	16	60	48	61	20	61	52	62	24	62	56	63	28	64	0
33	61	3	61	36	62	9	62	42	63	15	63	48	64	21	64	54	65	27	66	0
34	62	54	63	28	64	2	64	36	65	10	65	44	66	18	66	52	67	26	68	0
35	64	45	65	20	65	55	66	30	67	5	67	40	68	15	68	50	69	25	70	0
36	66	36	67	12	67	48	68	24	69	0	69	36	70	12	70	48	71	24	72	0
37	68	27	69	4	69	41	70	18	70	55	71	32	72	9	72	46	73	23	74	0
38	70	18	70	56	71	34	72	12	72	50	73	28	74	6	74	44	75	22	76	0
39	72	9	72	48	73	27	74	6	74	45	75	24	76	3	76	42	77	21	78	0
40	74	0	74	40	75	20	76	0	76	40	77	20	78	0	78	40	79	20	80	0
41	75	51	76	32	77	13	77	54	78	35	79	16	79	57	80	38	81	19	82	0
42	77	42	78	24	79	6	79	48	80	30	81	12	81	54	82	36	83	18	84	0
43	79	33	80	16	80	59	81	42	82	25	83	8	83	51	84	34	85	17	86	0
44	81	24	82	8	82	52	83	36	84	20	85	4	85	48	86	32	87	16	88	0
45	83	15	84	0	84	45	85	30	86	15	87	0	87	45	88	30	89	15	90	0
46	85	6	85	52	86	38	87	24	88	10	88	56	89	42	90	28	91	14	92	0
47	86	57	87	44	88	31	89	18	90	5	90	52	91	39	92	26	93	13	94	0
48	88	48	89	36	90	24	91	12	92	0	92	48	93	36	94	24	95	12	96	0
49	90	39	91	28	92	17	93	6	93	55	94	44	95	33	96	22	97	11	98	0
50	92	30	93	20	94	10	95	0	95	50	96	40	97	30	98	20	99	10	100	0
51	94	21	95	12	96	3	96	54	97	45	98	36	99	27	100	18	101	9	102	0
52	96	12	97	4	97	56	98	48	99	40	100	32	101	24	102	16	103	8	104	0
53	98	3	98	56	99	49	100	42	101	35	102	28	103	21	104	14	105	7	106	0
54	99	54	100	48	101	42	102	36	103	30	104	24	105	18	106	12	107	6	108	0
55	101	45	102	40	103	35	104	30	105	25	106	20	107	15	108	10	109	5	110	0
56	103	36	104	32	105	28	106	24	107	20	108	16	109	12	110	8	111	4	112	0
57	105	27	106	24	107	21	108	18	109	15	110	12	111	9	112	6	113	3	114	0
58	107	18	108	16	109	14	110	12	111	10	112	8	113	6	114	4	115	2	116	0
59	109	9	110	8	111	7	112	6	113	5	114	4	115	3	116	2	117	1	118	0
60	111	0	112	0	113	0	114	0	115	0	116	0	117	0	118	0	119	0	120	0

	121 °	121 '	122 °	122 '	123 °	123 '	124 °	124 '	125 °	125 '	126 °	126 '	127 °	127 '	128 °	128 '	129 °	129 '	130 °	130 '
1	2	1	2	2	2	3	2	4	2	5	2	6	2	7	2	8	2	9	2	10
2	4	2	4	4	4	6	4	8	4	10	4	12	4	14	4	16	4	18	4	20
3	6	3	6	6	6	9	6	12	6	15	6	18	6	21	6	24	6	27	6	30
4	8	4	8	8	8	12	8	16	8	20	8	24	8	28	8	32	8	36	8	40
5	10	5	10	10	10	15	10	20	10	25	10	30	10	35	10	40	10	45	10	50
6	12	6	12	12	12	18	12	24	12	30	12	36	12	42	12	48	12	54	13	0
7	14	7	14	14	14	21	14	28	14	35	14	42	14	49	14	56	15	3	15	10
8	16	8	16	16	16	24	16	32	16	40	16	48	16	26	17	4	17	12	17	20
9	18	9	18	18	18	27	18	36	18	45	18	54	19	3	19	12	19	21	19	30
10	20	10	20	20	20	30	20	40	20	50	21	0	21	10	21	20	21	30	21	40
11	22	11	22	22	22	33	22	44	22	55	23	6	23	17	23	28	23	39	23	50
12	24	12	24	24	24	36	24	48	25	0	25	12	25	24	25	36	25	48	26	0
13	26	13	26	26	26	39	26	52	27	5	27	18	27	31	27	44	27	57	28	10
14	28	14	28	28	28	42	28	56	29	10	29	24	29	38	29	52	30	6	30	20
15	30	15	30	30	30	45	31	0	31	15	31	30	31	45	32	0	32	15	32	30
16	32	16	32	32	32	48	33	4	33	20	33	36	33	52	34	8	34	24	34	40
17	34	17	34	34	34	51	35	8	35	25	35	42	35	59	36	16	36	33	36	50
18	36	18	36	36	36	54	37	12	37	30	37	48	38	6	38	24	38	42	39	0
19	38	19	38	38	38	57	39	16	39	35	39	54	40	13	40	32	40	51	41	10
20	40	20	40	40	41	0	41	20	41	40	42	0	42	20	42	40	43	0	43	20
21	42	21	42	42	43	3	43	24	43	45	44	6	44	27	44	48	45	9	45	30
22	44	22	44	44	45	6	45	28	45	50	46	12	46	34	46	56	47	18	47	40
23	46	23	46	46	47	9	47	32	47	55	48	18	48	41	49	4	49	27	49	50
24	48	24	48	48	49	12	49	36	50	0	50	24	50	48	51	12	51	36	52	0
25	50	25	50	50	51	15	51	40	52	5	52	30	52	55	53	20	53	45	54	10
26	52	26	52	52	53	18	53	44	54	10	54	36	55	2	55	28	55	54	56	20
27	54	27	54	54	55	21	55	48	56	15	56	42	57	9	57	36	58	3	58	30
28	56	28	56	56	57	24	57	52	58	20	68	48	59	16	59	44	60	12	60	40
29	58	29	58	58	59	27	59	56	60	25	60	54	61	23	61	52	62	21	62	50
30	60	30	61	0	61	30	62	0	62	30	63	0	63	30	64	0	64	30	65	0
31	62	31	63	2	63	33	64	4	64	35	65	6	65	37	66	8	66	39	67	10
32	64	32	65	4	65	36	66	8	66	40	67	12	67	44	68	16	68	48	69	20
33	66	33	67	6	67	39	68	12	68	45	69	18	69	51	70	24	70	57	71	30
34	68	34	69	8	69	42	70	16	70	50	71	24	71	58	72	32	73	6	73	40
35	70	35	71	10	71	45	72	20	72	55	73	30	74	5	74	40	75	15	75	50
36	72	36	73	12	73	48	74	24	75	0	75	36	76	12	76	48	77	24	78	0
37	74	37	75	14	75	51	76	28	77	5	77	42	78	19	78	56	79	33	80	10
38	76	38	77	16	77	54	78	32	79	10	79	48	80	26	81	4	81	42	82	20
39	78	39	79	18	79	57	80	36	81	15	81	54	82	33	83	12	83	51	84	30
40	80	40	81	20	82	0	82	40	83	20	84	0	84	40	85	20	86	0	86	40
41	82	41	83	22	84	3	84	44	85	25	86	6	86	47	87	28	88	9	88	50
42	84	42	85	24	86	6	86	48	87	30	88	12	88	54	89	36	90	18	91	0
43	86	43	87	26	88	9	88	52	89	35	90	18	91	1	91	44	92	27	93	10
44	88	44	89	28	90	12	90	56	91	40	92	24	93	8	93	52	94	36	95	20
45	90	45	91	30	92	15	93	0	93	45	94	30	95	15	96	0	96	45	97	30
46	92	46	93	32	94	18	95	4	95	50	96	36	97	22	98	8	98	54	99	40
47	94	47	95	34	96	21	97	8	97	55	98	42	99	29	100	16	101	3	101	50
48	96	48	97	36	98	24	99	12	100	0	100	48	101	36	102	24	103	12	104	0
49	98	49	99	38	100	27	101	16	102	5	102	54	103	43	104	32	105	21	106	10
50	100	50	101	40	102	30	103	20	104	10	105	0	105	50	106	40	107	30	108	20
51	102	51	103	42	104	33	105	24	106	15	107	6	107	57	108	48	109	39	110	30
52	104	52	105	44	106	36	107	28	108	20	109	12	110	4	110	56	111	48	112	40
53	106	53	107	46	108	39	109	32	110	25	111	18	112	11	113	4	113	57	114	50
54	108	54	109	48	110	42	111	36	112	30	113	24	114	18	115	12	116	6	117	0
55	110	55	111	50	112	45	113	40	114	35	115	30	116	25	117	20	118	15	119	10
56	112	56	113	52	114	48	115	44	116	40	117	36	118	32	119	28	120	24	121	20
57	114	57	115	54	116	51	117	48	118	45	119	42	120	39	121	36	122	33	123	30
58	116	58	117	56	118	54	119	52	120	50	121	48	122	46	123	44	124	42	125	40
59	118	59	119	58	120	57	121	56	122	55	123	54	124	53	125	52	126	51	127	50
60	121	0	122	0	123	0	124	0	125	0	126	0	127	0	128	0	129	0	130	0

	131 ° '	132 ° '	133 ° '	134 ° '	135 ° '	136 ° '	137 ° '	138 ° '	139 ° '	140 ° '
1	2 11	2 12	2 13	2 14	2 15	2 16	2 17	2 18	2 19	2 20
2	4 22	4 24	4 26	4 28	4 30	4 32	4 34	4 36	4 38	4 40
3	6 33	6 36	6 39	6 42	6 45	6 48	6 51	6 54	6 57	7 0
4	8 44	8 48	8 52	8 56	9 0	9 4	9 8	9 12	9 16	9 20
5	10 55	11 0	11 5	11 10	11 15	11 20	11 25	11 30	11 35	11 40
6	13 6	13 12	13 18	13 24	13 30	13 36	13 42	13 48	13 54	14 0
7	15 17	15 24	15 31	15 38	15 45	15 52	15 59	16 6	16 13	16 20
8	17 28	17 36	17 44	17 52	18 0	18 8	18 16	18 24	18 32	18 40
9	19 39	19 48	19 57	20 6	20 15	20 24	20 33	20 42	20 51	21 0
10	21 50	22 0	22 10	22 20	22 30	22 40	22 50	23 0	23 10	23 20
11	24 1	24 12	24 23	24 34	24 45	24 56	25 7	25 18	25 29	25 40
12	26 12	26 24	26 36	26 48	27 0	27 12	27 24	27 36	27 48	28 0
13	28 23	28 36	28 49	29 2	29 15	29 28	29 41	29 54	30 7	30 20
14	30 34	30 48	31 2	31 16	31 30	31 44	31 58	32 12	32 26	32 40
15	32 45	33 0	33 15	33 30	33 45	34 0	34 15	34 30	34 45	35 0
16	34 56	35 12	35 28	35 44	36 0	36 16	36 32	36 48	37 4	37 20
17	37 7	37 24	37 41	37 58	38 15	38 32	38 49	39 6	39 23	39 40
18	39 18	39 36	39 54	40 12	40 30	40 48	41 6	41 24	41 42	42 0
19	41 29	41 48	42 7	42 26	42 45	43 4	43 23	43 42	44 1	44 20
20	43 40	44 0	44 20	44 40	45 0	45 20	45 40	46 0	46 20	46 40
21	45 41	46 12	46 33	46 54	47 15	47 36	47 57	48 18	48 39	49 0
22	48 2	48 24	48 46	49 8	49 30	49 52	50 14	50 36	50 58	51 20
23	50 13	50 36	50 59	51 22	51 45	52 8	52 31	52 54	53 17	53 40
24	52 24	52 48	53 12	53 36	54 0	54 24	54 48	55 12	55 36	56 0
25	54 35	55 0	55 25	55 50	56 15	56 40	57 5	57 30	57 55	58 20
26	56 46	57 12	57 38	58 4	58 30	58 56	59 22	59 48	60 14	60 40
27	58 57	59 24	59 51	60 18	60 45	61 12	61 39	62 6	62 33	63 0
28	61 8	61 36	62 4	62 32	63 0	63 28	63 56	64 24	64 52	65 20
29	63 19	63 48	64 17	64 46	65 15	65 44	66 13	66 42	67 11	67 40
30	65 30	66 0	66 30	67 0	67 30	68 0	68 30	69 0	69 30	70 0
31	67 41	68 12	68 43	69 14	69 45	70 16	70 47	71 18	71 59	72 20
32	69 52	70 24	70 56	71 28	72 0	72 32	73 4	73 36	74 8	74 40
33	72 3	72 36	73 9	73 42	74 15	74 48	75 21	75 54	76 27	77 0
34	74 14	74 48	75 22	75 56	76 30	77 4	77 38	78 12	78 46	79 20
35	76 25	77 0	77 35	78 10	78 45	79 20	79 55	80 30	81 5	81 40
36	78 36	79 12	79 48	80 24	81 0	81 36	82 12	82 48	83 24	84 0
37	80 47	81 24	82 1	82 38	83 15	83 52	84 29	85 6	85 43	86 20
38	82 58	83 36	84 14	84 52	85 30	86 8	86 46	87 24	88 2	88 40
39	85 9	85 48	86 27	87 6	87 45	88 24	89 3	89 42	90 21	91 0
40	87 20	88 0	88 40	89 20	90 0	90 40	91 20	92 0	92 40	93 20
41	89 31	90 12	90 53	91 34	92 15	92 56	93 37	94 18	94 59	95 40
42	91 42	92 24	93 6	93 48	94 30	95 12	95 54	96 36	97 18	98 0
43	93 53	94 36	95 19	96 2	96 45	97 28	98 11	98 54	99 37	100 20
44	96 4	96 48	97 32	98 16	99 0	99 44	100 28	101 12	101 56	102 40
45	98 15	99 0	99 45	100 30	101 15	102 0	102 45	103 30	104 15	105 0
46	100 26	101 12	101 58	102 44	103 30	104 16	105 2	105 48	106 34	107 20
47	102 37	103 24	104 11	104 58	105 45	106 32	107 19	108 6	108 53	109 40
48	104 48	105 36	106 24	107 12	108 0	108 48	109 36	110 24	111 12	112 0
49	106 59	107 48	108 37	109 26	110 15	111 4	111 53	112 42	113 31	114 20
50	109 10	110 0	110 50	111 40	112 30	113 20	114 10	115 0	115 50	116 40
51	111 21	112 12	113 3	113 54	114 45	115 36	116 27	117 18	118 9	119 0
52	113 32	114 24	115 16	116 8	117 0	117 52	118 44	119 36	120 28	121 20
53	115 43	116 36	117 29	118 22	119 15	120 8	121 1	121 54	122 47	123 40
54	117 54	118 48	119 42	120 36	121 30	122 24	123 18	124 12	125 6	126 0
55	120 5	121 0	121 55	122 50	123 45	124 40	125 35	126 30	127 25	128 20
56	122 16	123 12	124 8	125 4	126 0	126 56	127 52	128 48	129 44	130 40
57	124 27	125 24	126 21	127 18	128 15	129 12	130 9	131 6	132 3	133 0
58	126 38	127 36	128 34	129 32	130 30	131 28	132 26	133 14	134 22	135 20
59	128 49	129 48	130 47	131 46	132 45	133 44	134 43	135 42	136 41	137 40
60	131 0	132 0	133 0	134 0	135 0	136 0	137 0	138 0	139 0	140 0

	141		142		143		144		145		146		147		148		149		150	
	°	′	°	′	°	′	°	′	°	′	°	′	°	′	°	′	°	′	°	′
1	2	21	2	22	2	23	2	24	2	25	2	26	2	27	2	28	2	29	2	30
2	4	42	4	44	4	46	4	48	4	50	4	52	4	54	4	56	4	58	5	0
3	7	3	7	6	7	9	7	12	7	15	7	18	7	21	7	24	7	27	7	30
4	9	24	9	28	9	32	9	36	9	40	9	44	9	48	9	52	9	56	10	0
5	11	45	11	50	11	55	12	0	12	5	12	10	12	15	12	20	12	25	12	30
6	14	6	14	12	14	18	14	24	14	30	14	36	14	42	14	48	14	54	15	0
7	16	27	16	34	16	41	16	48	16	55	17	2	17	9	17	16	17	23	17	30
8	18	48	18	56	19	4	19	12	19	20	19	28	19	36	19	44	19	52	20	0
9	21	9	21	18	21	27	21	36	21	45	21	54	22	3	22	12	22	21	22	30
10	23	30	23	40	23	50	24	0	24	10	24	20	24	30	24	40	24	50	25	0
11	25	51	26	2	26	13	26	24	26	35	26	46	26	57	27	8	27	19	27	30
12	28	12	28	24	28	36	28	48	29	0	29	12	29	24	29	36	29	48	30	0
13	30	33	30	46	30	59	31	12	31	25	31	38	31	51	32	4	32	17	32	30
14	32	54	33	8	33	22	33	36	33	50	34	4	34	18	34	32	34	46	35	0
15	35	15	35	30	35	45	36	0	36	15	36	30	36	45	37	0	37	15	37	30
16	37	36	37	52	38	8	38	24	38	40	38	56	39	12	39	28	39	44	40	0
17	39	57	40	14	40	31	40	48	41	5	41	22	41	39	41	56	42	13	42	30
18	42	18	42	36	42	54	43	12	43	30	43	48	44	6	44	24	44	42	45	0
19	44	39	44	58	45	17	45	36	45	55	46	14	46	33	46	52	47	11	47	30
20	47	0	47	20	47	40	48	0	48	20	48	40	49	0	49	20	49	40	50	0
21	49	21	49	42	50	3	50	24	50	45	51	6	51	27	51	48	52	9	52	30
22	51	42	52	4	52	26	52	48	53	10	53	32	53	54	54	16	54	38	55	0
23	54	3	54	26	54	49	55	12	55	35	55	58	56	21	56	44	57	7	57	30
24	56	24	56	48	57	12	57	36	58	0	58	24	58	48	59	12	59	36	60	0
25	58	45	59	10	59	35	60	0	60	25	60	50	61	15	61	40	62	5	62	30
26	61	6	61	32	61	58	62	24	62	50	63	16	63	42	64	8	64	34	65	0
27	63	27	63	54	64	21	64	48	65	15	65	42	66	9	66	36	67	3	67	30
28	65	48	66	16	66	44	67	12	67	40	68	8	68	36	69	4	69	32	70	0
29	68	9	68	38	69	7	69	36	70	5	70	34	71	3	71	32	72	1	72	30
30	70	30	71	0	71	30	72	0	72	30	73	0	73	30	74	0	74	30	75	0
31	72	51	73	22	73	53	74	24	74	55	75	26	75	57	76	28	76	59	77	30
32	75	12	75	44	76	16	76	48	77	20	77	52	78	24	78	56	79	28	80	0
33	77	33	78	6	78	39	79	12	79	45	80	18	80	51	81	24	81	57	82	30
34	79	54	80	28	81	2	81	36	82	10	82	44	83	18	83	52	84	26	85	0
35	82	15	82	50	83	25	84	0	84	35	85	10	85	45	86	20	86	55	87	30
36	84	36	85	12	85	48	86	24	87	0	87	36	88	12	88	48	89	24	90	0
37	86	57	87	34	88	11	88	48	89	25	90	2	90	39	91	16	91	53	92	30
38	89	18	89	56	90	43	91	12	91	50	92	28	93	6	93	44	94	22	95	0
39	91	39	92	18	92	57	93	36	94	15	94	54	95	33	96	12	96	51	97	30
40	94	0	94	40	95	20	96	0	96	40	97	20	98	0	98	40	99	20	100	0
41	96	21	97	2	97	34	98	24	99	5	99	46	100	27	101	8	101	49	102	30
42	98	42	99	24	100	6	100	48	101	30	102	12	102	54	103	36	104	18	105	0
43	101	3	101	46	102	29	103	12	103	55	104	38	105	21	106	4	106	47	107	30
44	103	24	104	8	104	52	105	36	106	20	107	4	107	48	108	32	109	16	110	0
45	105	45	106	30	107	15	108	0	108	45	109	30	110	15	111	0	111	45	112	30
46	108	6	108	52	109	38	110	24	111	10	111	56	112	42	113	28	114	14	115	0
47	110	27	111	14	112	1	112	48	113	35	114	22	115	9	115	56	116	43	117	30
48	112	48	113	36	114	24	115	12	116	0	116	48	117	36	118	24	119	12	120	0
49	115	9	115	58	116	47	118	36	118	25	119	14	120	3	120	52	121	41	122	30
50	117	30	118	20	119	10	120	0	121	50	121	40	122	30	123	20	124	10	125	0
51	119	51	120	42	121	33	122	24	123	15	124	6	124	57	125	48	126	39	127	30
52	122	12	123	4	123	56	124	48	125	40	126	32	127	24	128	16	129	8	130	0
53	124	33	125	26	126	19	127	12	128	5	128	58	129	51	130	44	131	37	132	30
54	126	54	127	48	128	42	129	36	130	30	131	24	132	18	133	12	134	6	135	0
55	129	15	130	10	131	5	132	0	132	55	133	50	134	45	135	40	136	35	137	30
56	131	36	132	32	133	28	134	24	135	20	136	16	137	12	138	8	139	4	140	0
57	133	57	134	54	135	51	136	48	137	45	138	42	139	39	140	36	141	33	142	30
58	136	18	137	16	138	14	139	12	140	10	141	8	142	6	143	4	144	2	145	0
59	138	39	139	38	140	37	141	36	142	35	143	34	144	33	145	32	146	31	147	30
60	141	0	142	0	143	0	144	0	145	0	146	0	147	0	148	0	149	0	150	0

	151		152		153		154		155		156		157		158		159		160	
	°	′	°	′	°	′	°	′	°	′	°	′	°	′	°	′	°	′	°	′
1	2	31	2	32	2	33	2	34	2	35	2	36	2	37	2	38	2	39	2	40
2	5	2	5	4	5	6	5	8	5	10	5	12	5	14	5	16	5	18	5	20
3	7	33	7	36	7	39	7	42	7	45	7	48	7	51	7	54	7	57	8	0
4	10	4	10	8	10	12	10	16	10	20	10	24	10	28	10	32	10	36	10	40
5	12	35	12	40	12	45	12	50	12	55	13	0	13	5	13	10	13	15	13	20
6	15	6	15	12	15	18	15	24	15	30	15	36	15	42	15	48	15	54	16	0
7	17	37	17	44	17	51	17	58	18	5	18	12	18	19	18	26	18	33	18	40
8	20	8	20	16	20	24	20	32	20	40	20	48	20	56	21	4	21	12	21	20
9	22	39	22	48	22	57	23	6	23	15	23	24	23	33	23	42	23	51	24	0
10	25	10	25	20	25	30	25	40	25	50	26	0	26	10	26	20	26	30	26	40
11	27	41	27	52	28	3	28	14	28	25	28	36	28	47	28	58	29	9	29	20
12	30	12	30	24	30	36	30	48	31	0	31	12	31	24	31	36	31	48	32	0
13	32	43	32	56	33	9	33	22	33	35	33	48	34	1	34	14	34	27	34	40
14	35	14	35	28	35	42	35	56	36	10	36	24	36	38	36	52	37	6	37	20
15	37	45	38	0	38	15	38	30	38	45	39	0	39	15	39	30	39	45	40	0
16	40	16	40	32	40	48	41	4	41	20	41	36	41	52	42	8	42	24	42	40
17	42	47	43	4	43	21	43	38	43	55	44	12	44	29	44	46	45	3	45	20
18	45	18	45	36	45	54	46	12	46	30	46	48	47	6	47	24	47	42	48	0
19	47	49	48	8	48	27	48	46	49	5	49	24	49	43	50	2	50	21	50	40
20	50	20	50	40	51	0	51	20	51	40	52	0	52	20	52	40	53	0	53	20
21	52	51	53	12	53	33	53	54	54	15	54	36	54	57	55	18	55	39	56	0
22	55	22	55	44	56	6	56	28	56	50	57	12	57	34	57	56	58	18	58	40
23	57	53	58	16	58	39	59	2	59	25	59	48	60	11	60	34	60	57	61	20
24	60	24	60	48	61	12	61	36	62	0	62	24	62	48	63	12	63	36	64	0
25	62	55	63	20	63	45	64	10	64	35	65	0	65	25	65	50	66	15	66	40
26	65	26	65	52	66	18	66	44	67	10	67	36	68	2	68	28	68	54	69	20
27	67	57	68	24	68	51	69	18	69	45	70	12	70	39	71	6	71	33	72	0
28	70	28	70	56	71	24	71	52	72	20	72	48	73	16	73	44	74	12	74	40
29	72	59	73	28	73	57	74	26	74	55	75	24	75	53	76	22	76	51	77	20
30	75	30	76	0	76	30	77	0	77	30	78	0	78	30	79	0	79	30	80	0
31	78	1	78	32	79	3	79	34	80	5	80	36	81	7	81	38	82	9	82	40
32	80	32	81	4	81	36	82	8	82	40	83	12	83	44	84	16	84	48	85	20
33	83	3	83	36	84	9	84	42	85	15	85	48	86	21	86	54	87	27	88	0
34	85	34	86	8	86	42	87	16	87	50	88	24	88	58	89	32	90	6	90	40
35	88	5	88	40	89	15	89	50	90	25	91	0	91	35	92	10	92	45	93	20
36	90	36	91	12	91	48	92	24	93	0	93	36	94	12	94	48	95	24	96	0
37	93	7	93	44	94	21	94	58	95	35	96	12	96	49	97	26	98	3	98	40
38	95	38	96	16	96	54	97	32	98	10	98	48	99	26	100	4	100	42	101	20
39	98	9	98	48	99	27	100	6	100	45	101	24	102	3	102	42	103	21	104	0
40	100	40	101	20	102	0	102	40	103	20	104	0	104	40	105	20	106	0	106	40
41	103	11	103	52	104	33	105	14	105	55	106	36	107	17	107	58	108	39	109	20
42	105	42	106	24	107	6	107	48	108	30	109	12	109	54	110	36	111	18	112	0
43	108	13	108	56	109	39	110	22	111	5	111	48	112	31	113	14	113	57	114	40
44	110	44	111	28	112	12	112	56	113	40	114	24	115	8	115	52	116	36	117	20
45	113	15	114	0	114	45	115	30	116	15	117	0	117	45	118	30	119	15	120	0
46	115	46	116	32	117	18	118	4	118	50	119	36	120	22	121	8	121	54	122	40
47	118	17	119	4	119	51	120	38	121	25	122	12	122	59	123	46	124	33	125	20
48	120	48	121	36	122	24	123	12	124	0	124	48	125	36	126	24	127	12	128	0
49	123	19	124	8	124	57	125	46	126	35	127	24	128	13	129	2	129	51	130	40
50	125	50	126	40	127	30	128	20	129	10	130	0	130	50	131	40	132	30	133	20
51	128	21	129	12	130	3	130	54	131	45	132	36	133	27	134	18	135	9	136	0
52	130	52	131	44	132	36	133	28	134	20	135	12	136	4	136	56	137	48	138	40
53	133	23	134	16	135	9	136	2	136	55	137	48	138	41	139	34	140	27	141	20
54	135	54	136	48	137	42	138	36	139	30	140	24	141	18	142	12	143	6	144	0
55	138	25	139	20	140	15	141	10	142	5	143	0	143	55	144	50	145	45	146	40
56	140	56	141	52	142	48	143	44	144	40	145	36	146	32	147	28	148	24	149	20
57	143	27	144	24	145	21	146	18	147	15	148	12	149	9	150	6	151	3	152	0
58	145	58	146	56	147	54	148	52	149	50	150	48	151	46	152	44	153	42	154	40
59	148	29	149	28	150	27	151	26	152	25	153	24	154	23	155	22	156	21	157	20
60	151	0	152	0	153	0	154	0	155	0	156	0	157	0	158	0	159	0	160	0

	161		162		163		164		165		166		167		168		169		170	
	°	′	°	′	°	′	°	′	°	′	°	′	°	′	°	′	°	′	°	′
1	2	41	2	42	2	43	2	44	2	45	2	46	2	47	2	48	2	49	2	50
2	5	22	5	24	5	26	5	28	5	30	5	32	5	34	5	36	5	38	5	40
3	8	3	8	6	8	9	8	12	8	15	8	18	8	21	8	24	8	27	8	30
4	10	44	10	48	10	52	10	56	11	0	11	4	11	8	11	12	11	16	11	20
5	13	25	13	30	13	35	13	40	13	45	13	50	13	55	14	0	14	5	14	10
6	16	6	16	12	16	18	16	24	16	30	16	36	16	42	16	48	16	54	17	0
7	18	47	18	54	19	1	19	8	19	15	19	22	19	29	19	36	19	43	19	50
8	21	28	21	36	21	44	21	52	22	0	22	8	22	16	22	24	22	32	22	40
9	24	9	24	18	24	27	24	36	24	45	24	54	25	3	25	12	25	21	25	30
10	26	50	27	0	27	10	27	20	27	30	27	40	27	50	28	0	28	10	28	20
11	29	31	29	42	29	53	30	4	30	15	30	26	30	37	30	48	30	59	31	10
12	32	12	32	24	32	36	32	48	33	0	33	12	33	24	33	36	33	48	34	0
13	34	53	35	6	35	19	35	32	35	45	35	58	36	11	36	24	36	37	36	50
14	37	34	37	48	38	2	38	16	38	30	38	44	38	58	39	12	39	26	39	40
15	40	15	40	30	40	45	41	0	41	15	41	30	41	45	42	0	42	15	42	30
16	42	56	43	12	43	28	43	44	44	0	44	16	44	32	44	48	45	4	45	20
17	45	37	45	54	46	11	46	28	46	45	47	2	47	19	47	36	47	53	48	10
18	48	18	48	36	48	54	49	12	49	30	49	48	50	6	50	24	50	42	51	0
19	50	59	51	18	51	37	51	56	52	15	52	34	52	53	53	12	53	31	53	50
20	53	40	54	0	54	20	54	40	55	0	55	20	55	40	56	0	56	20	56	40
21	56	21	56	42	57	3	57	24	57	45	58	6	58	27	58	48	59	9	59	30
22	59	2	59	24	59	46	60	8	60	30	60	52	61	14	61	36	61	58	62	20
23	61	43	62	6	62	29	62	52	63	15	63	38	64	1	64	24	64	47	65	10
24	64	24	64	48	65	12	65	36	66	0	66	24	66	48	67	12	67	36	68	0
25	67	5	67	30	67	55	68	20	68	45	69	10	69	35	70	0	70	25	70	50
26	69	46	70	12	70	38	71	4	71	30	71	56	72	22	72	48	73	14	73	40
27	72	27	72	54	73	21	73	48	74	15	74	42	75	9	75	36	76	3	76	30
28	75	8	75	36	76	4	76	32	77	0	77	28	77	56	78	24	78	52	79	20
29	77	49	78	18	78	47	79	16	79	45	80	14	80	43	81	12	81	41	82	10
30	80	30	81	0	81	30	82	0	82	30	83	0	83	30	84	0	84	30	85	0
31	83	11	83	42	84	13	84	44	85	15	85	46	86	17	86	48	87	19	87	50
32	85	52	86	24	86	56	87	28	88	0	88	32	89	4	89	36	90	8	90	40
33	88	33	89	6	89	39	90	12	90	45	91	18	91	51	92	24	92	57	93	30
34	91	14	91	48	92	22	92	56	93	30	94	4	94	38	95	12	95	46	96	20
35	93	55	94	30	95	5	95	40	96	15	96	50	97	25	98	0	98	35	99	10
36	96	36	97	12	97	48	98	24	99	0	99	36	100	12	100	48	101	24	102	0
37	99	17	99	54	100	31	101	8	101	45	102	22	102	59	103	36	104	13	104	50
38	101	58	102	36	103	14	103	52	104	30	105	8	105	46	106	24	107	2	107	40
39	104	39	105	18	105	57	106	36	107	15	107	54	108	33	109	12	109	51	110	30
40	107	20	108	0	108	40	109	20	110	0	110	40	111	20	112	0	112	40	113	20
41	110	1	110	42	111	23	112	4	112	45	113	26	114	7	114	48	115	29	116	10
42	112	42	113	24	114	6	114	48	115	30	116	12	116	54	117	36	118	18	119	0
43	115	23	116	6	116	49	117	32	118	15	118	58	119	41	120	24	121	7	121	50
44	118	4	118	48	119	32	120	16	121	0	121	44	122	28	123	12	123	56	124	40
45	120	45	121	30	122	15	123	0	123	45	124	30	125	15	126	0	126	45	127	30
46	123	26	124	12	124	58	125	44	126	30	127	16	128	2	128	48	129	34	130	20
47	126	7	126	54	127	41	128	28	129	15	130	2	130	49	131	36	132	23	133	10
48	128	48	129	36	130	24	131	12	132	0	132	48	133	36	134	24	135	12	136	0
49	131	29	132	18	133	7	133	56	134	45	135	34	136	23	137	12	138	1	138	50
50	134	10	135	0	135	50	136	40	137	30	138	20	139	10	140	0	140	50	141	40
51	136	51	137	42	138	33	139	24	140	15	141	6	141	57	142	48	143	39	144	30
52	139	32	140	24	141	16	142	8	143	0	143	52	144	44	145	36	146	28	147	20
53	142	13	143	6	143	59	144	52	145	45	146	38	147	31	148	24	149	17	150	10
54	144	54	145	48	146	42	147	36	148	30	149	24	150	18	151	12	152	6	153	0
55	147	35	148	30	149	25	150	20	151	15	152	10	153	5	154	0	154	55	155	50
56	150	16	151	12	152	8	153	4	154	0	154	56	155	52	156	48	157	44	158	40
57	152	57	153	54	154	51	155	48	156	45	157	42	158	39	159	36	160	33	161	30
58	155	38	156	36	157	34	158	32	159	30	160	28	161	26	162	24	163	22	164	20
59	158	19	159	18	160	17	161	16	162	15	163	14	164	13	165	12	166	11	167	10
60	161	0	162	0	163	0	164	0	165	0	166	0	167	0	168	0	169	0	170	0

	171		172		173		174		175		176		177		178		179		180	
	°	′	°	′	°	′	°	′	°	′	°	′	°	′	°	′	°	′	°	′
1	2	51	2	52	2	53	2	54	2	55	2	56	2	57	2	58	2	59	3	0
2	5	42	5	44	5	46	5	48	5	50	5	52	5	54	5	56	5	58	6	0
3	8	33	8	36	8	39	8	42	8	45	8	48	8	51	8	54	8	57	9	0
4	11	24	11	28	11	32	11	36	11	40	11	44	11	48	11	52	11	56	12	0
5	14	15	14	20	14	25	14	30	14	35	14	40	14	45	14	50	14	55	15	0
6	17	6	17	12	17	18	17	24	17	30	17	36	17	42	17	48	17	54	18	0
7	19	57	20	4	20	11	20	18	20	25	20	32	20	39	20	46	20	53	21	0
8	22	48	22	56	23	4	23	12	23	20	23	28	23	36	23	44	23	52	24	0
9	25	39	25	48	25	57	26	6	26	15	26	24	26	33	26	42	26	51	27	0
10	28	30	28	40	28	50	29	0	29	10	29	20	29	30	29	40	29	50	30	0
11	31	21	31	32	31	43	31	54	32	5	32	16	32	27	32	38	32	49	33	0
12	34	12	34	24	34	36	34	48	35	0	35	12	35	24	35	36	35	48	36	0
13	37	3	37	16	37	29	37	42	37	55	38	8	38	21	38	34	38	47	39	0
14	39	54	40	8	40	22	40	36	40	50	41	4	41	18	41	32	41	46	42	0
15	42	45	43	0	43	15	43	30	43	45	44	0	44	15	44	30	44	45	45	0
16	45	36	45	52	46	8	46	24	46	40	46	56	47	12	47	28	47	44	48	0
17	48	27	48	44	49	1	49	18	49	35	49	52	50	9	50	26	50	43	51	0
18	51	18	51	36	51	54	52	12	52	30	52	48	53	6	53	24	53	42	54	0
19	54	9	54	28	54	47	55	6	55	25	55	44	56	3	56	22	56	41	57	0
20	57	0	57	20	57	40	58	0	58	20	58	40	59	0	59	20	59	40	60	0
21	59	51	60	12	60	33	60	54	61	15	61	36	61	57	62	18	62	39	63	0
22	62	42	63	4	63	26	63	48	64	10	64	32	64	54	65	16	65	38	66	0
23	65	33	65	56	66	19	66	42	67	5	67	28	67	51	68	14	68	37	69	0
24	68	24	68	48	69	12	69	36	70	0	70	24	70	48	71	12	71	36	72	0
25	71	15	71	40	72	5	72	30	72	55	73	20	73	45	74	10	74	35	75	0
26	74	6	74	32	74	58	75	24	75	50	76	16	76	42	77	8	77	34	78	0
27	76	57	77	24	77	51	78	18	78	45	79	12	79	39	80	6	80	33	81	0
28	79	48	80	16	80	44	81	12	81	40	82	8	82	36	83	4	83	32	84	0
29	82	39	83	8	83	37	84	6	84	35	85	4	85	33	86	2	86	31	87	0
30	85	30	86	0	86	30	87	0	87	30	88	0	88	30	89	0	89	30	90	0
31	88	21	88	52	89	23	89	54	90	25	90	56	91	27	91	58	92	29	93	0
32	91	12	91	44	92	16	92	48	93	20	93	52	94	24	94	56	95	28	96	0
33	94	3	94	36	95	9	95	42	96	15	96	48	97	21	97	54	98	27	99	0
34	96	54	97	28	98	2	98	36	99	10	99	44	100	18	100	52	101	26	102	0
35	99	45	100	20	100	55	101	30	102	5	102	40	103	15	103	50	104	25	105	0
36	102	36	103	12	103	48	104	24	105	0	105	36	106	12	106	48	107	24	108	0
37	105	27	106	4	106	41	107	18	107	55	108	32	109	9	109	46	110	23	111	0
38	108	18	108	56	109	34	110	12	110	50	111	28	112	6	112	44	113	22	114	0
39	111	9	111	48	112	27	113	6	113	45	114	24	115	3	115	42	116	21	117	0
40	114	0	114	40	115	20	116	0	116	40	117	20	118	0	118	40	119	20	120	0
41	116	51	117	32	118	13	118	54	119	35	120	16	120	57	121	38	122	19	123	0
42	119	42	120	24	121	6	121	48	122	30	123	12	123	54	124	36	125	18	126	0
43	122	33	123	16	123	59	124	42	125	25	126	8	126	51	127	34	128	17	129	0
44	125	24	126	8	126	52	127	36	128	20	129	4	129	48	130	32	131	16	132	0
45	128	15	129	0	129	45	130	30	131	15	132	0	132	45	133	30	134	15	135	0
46	131	6	131	52	132	38	133	24	134	10	134	56	135	42	136	28	137	14	138	0
47	133	57	134	44	135	31	136	18	137	5	137	52	138	39	139	26	140	13	141	0
48	136	48	137	36	138	24	139	12	140	0	140	48	141	36	142	24	143	12	144	0
49	139	39	140	28	141	17	142	6	142	55	143	44	144	33	145	22	146	11	147	0
50	142	30	143	20	144	10	145	0	145	50	146	40	147	30	148	20	149	10	150	0
51	145	21	146	12	147	3	147	54	148	45	149	36	150	27	151	18	152	9	153	0
52	148	12	149	4	149	56	150	48	151	40	152	32	153	24	154	16	155	8	156	0
53	151	3	151	56	152	49	153	42	154	35	155	28	156	21	157	14	158	7	159	0
54	153	54	154	48	155	42	156	36	157	30	158	24	159	18	160	12	161	6	162	0
55	156	45	157	40	158	35	159	30	160	25	161	20	162	15	163	10	164	5	165	0
56	159	36	160	32	161	28	162	24	163	20	164	16	165	12	166	8	167	4	168	0
57	162	27	163	24	164	21	165	18	166	15	167	12	168	9	169	6	170	3	171	0
58	165	18	166	16	167	14	168	12	169	10	170	8	171	6	172	4	173	2	174	0
59	168	9	169	8	170	7	171	6	172	5	173	4	174	3	175	2	176	1	177	0
60	171	0	172	0	173	0	174	0	175	0	176	0	177	0	178	0	179	0	180	0

Latitude and Longitude (in Time) from Greenwich.

	Lat. N. °	'	Long. Time m.		s.
Aberdeen	57	9	8	w	22
Aberystwith	52	25	16	,,	20
Abingdon	51	39	5	,,	7
Aldborough	52	8	6	E	0
Andover	51	13	5	w	53
Appleby	54	34	10	,,	0
Armagh Observatory	54	21	26	,,	36
Asaph, Saint	53	16	13	,,	44
Bangor	53	13	16	,,	30
Barnet	51	40	0	,,	44
Barnstaple	51	6	16	,,	0
Bath	51	21	9	,,	24
Bedford Observatory,	52	8	1	,,	52
Belfast	54	34	23	,,	40
Berwick-on-Tweed	55	46	7	,,	58
Birmingham	52	28	7	,,	28
Blenheim Observa.	51	51	5	,,	25
Brecon	51	57	13	,,	30
Bridgewater	51	8	12	,,	0
Bristol	51	27	10	,,	22
Brighton	50	49	0	,,	28
Buckingham	52	0	3	,,	56
Bushy Heath Observa	51	38	0	,,	20
Cambridge Observa..	52	13	0	E	24
Canterbury Cathedral	51	17	4	,,	20
Cardigan	52	5	18	w	36
Carlisle	54	54	11	,,	40
Carlow	52	0	27	,,	40
Cardiff	51	29	12	,,	28
Carnarvon	53	10	16	,,	52
Catherine, Saint	50	34	5	,,	20
Chelmsford	51	45	1	E	40
Chester	53	11	11	w	34
Chichester	50	48	3	,,	6
Colchester	51	52	3	E	28
Coleraine	55	8	26	w	24
Cork City	51	55	34	,,	8
Coventry	52	25	6	,,	20
Croydon	51	21	0	,,	20
Dartmouth	50	18	14	,,	24
David, St., Cathedral	51	53	21	,,	4
Denbigh	53	10	13	,,	40
Derby	52	56	5	,,	53
Dingwall	57	36	17	,,	40
Doncaster	53	32	4	,,	32
Dorchester	50	43	9	,,	44
Dover Castle	51	8	5	E	18
Dublin Observa	53	23	25	w	25
Dulverton	51	2	14	,,	14
Dumfries	55	4	14	,,	20
Dumbarton	55	47	18	,,	12
Dundee	56	28	11	,,	52
Durham Cathedral	54	47	6	,,	16
Edinburgh Observa..	55	57	12	,,	42
Elgin	57	39	13	,,	28
Ely Minster	52	24	1	E	4
Exeter Cathedral....	50	43	14	w	4
Falmouth	50	9	20	,,	19
Gainsborough	54	25	3	,,	0
Galway	53	16	36	,,	0
Glasgow	55	52	17	,,	6
Gloucester	51	52	8	,,	57
Guildford	51	15	2	,,	20
Greenwich	51	29	0	,,	0
Hartlepool	54	42	4	,,	42
Hastings	50	52	2	E	20
Halifax	53	45	7	w	44
Henley	51	32	3	,,	36
Hereford	52	4	10	,,	48
Hertford	51	48	0	,,	20
Huntingdon	52	20	0	,,	44
Huntley	57	27	11	,,	20
Inverary	56	15	20	,,	20
Inverness	57	29	16	,,	56
Ipswich	52	4	4	E	32
Kensington Observa	51	30	0	w	46
Kew	51	28	1	,,	16
Kirkby Lonsdale	54	12	10	,,	21
Kyle	57	12	22	,,	24
Lancaster	54	3	11	,,	13
Launceston	50	36	17	,.	28
Ledbury	52	2	9	,,	38
Leeds	53	48	6	,,	8
Leicester	52	35	4	,,	40
Litchfield	52	40	7	,,	20
Limerick	52	40	34	.,	29
Lincoln	53	14	2	,,	8
Liverpool	53	24	11	,,	55
London	51	31	0	,,	23
Loughborough	52	47	4	,,	47
Ludlow	52	22	10	,,	54
Lynn	52	47	1	E	28
Maidstone	51	16	2	,,	0
Makerstown Obser	55	34	10	w	4
Mallow	52	9	34	,,	32
Manchester	53	29	8	,,	57
Marlborough	51	27	7	,,	0
Montgomery	52	33	12	,,	32
Montrose	56	43	10	,,	4
Newbury	51	25	5	,,	18
Newcastle.on-Tyne	54	58	6	,,	24
Newcastle-un-Lyme..	53	2	8	,,	44
Newport, Isle of Wt.	50	42	5	,,	16
Newport, Mon.	51	35	12	,,	0
Northampton	52	11	3	,,	40
Norwich	52	38	5	E	0
North Shields	55	1	5	w	47
Nottingham	52	57	4	,,	33
Omagh	54	34	29	,,	0
Ormskirk Observa	53	34	11	,,	36
Oxford Observa	51	46	5	,,	2
Padstow	50	30	19	,,	56

	Lat. N.		Long. Time.			Lat. N.		Long. Time	
	°	′	m.	s.		°	′	m.	s.
Pembroke	51	40	19 w	28	Sutton	53	8	6 w	50
Penzance	50	6	22 ,,	0	Swansea.............	51	40	16 ,,	0
Pershore............	52	7	8 ,,	18	Taunton.............	51	1	12 ,,	21
Perth	56	24	13 ,,	56	Tavistock	50	34	16 ,,	32
Peterborough	52	36	1 ,,	0	Thorne	53	37	3 ,,	44
Petworth	50	59	2 ,,	25	Tipperary	52	28	32 ,,	32
Plymouth	50	22	16 ,,	39	Tiverton.............	50	55	14 ,,	0
Poole	50	43	7 ,,	56	Torrington..........	50	58	16 ,,	28
Porchester..........	50	50	4 ,,	26	Torbay	50	22	14 ,,	0
Portsmouth	50	48	4 ,,	24	Tralee..............	52	15	38 ,,	32
Reading	51	26	3 ,,	52	Tregony	50	16	19 ,,	30
Regent's Park Obs ..	51	31	0 ,,	37	Trim	53	33	27 ,,	10
Richmond Observa ..	51	28	1 ,,	14	Trowbridge	51	19	8 ,,	49
Ripon	54	9	6 ,,	8	Truro	50	14	20 ,,	16
Rochester	51	23	1 E	48	Tuam	53	32	35 ,,	24
Romney, New	50	59	3 ,,	46	Tuddington	51	56	2 ,,	39
Royston	52	3	0 w	4	Tunbridge Wells	51	6	0 ,,	48
Salisbury	51	4	7 ,,	9	Wakefield	53	41	5 ,,	58
Sandown	51	14	5 ,,	36	Waltham	52	49	3 ,,	14
Scarborough	54	15	1 ,,	40	Waterford	52	13	28 ,,	28
Selkirk	55	35	11 ,,	40	Warrington	53	23	10 ,,	12
Shaftesbury	51	0	8 ,,	45	Warwick	52	17	6 ,,	32
Sheffield............	53	26	6 ,,	8	Whitehaven	54	33	14 ,,	22
Sherborne	50	57	10 ,,	1	Wells, Som.	51	13	10 ,,	24
Sheerness	51	27	2 E	59	Wexford............	52	20	25 ,,	52
Shrewsbury	52	42	11 w	1	Winchelsea	50	55	2 E	51
Sidmouth	50	40	12 ,,	44	Winchester	51	4	5 w	13
Sligo	54	16	33 ,,	20	Windsor Castle......	51	29	2 ,,	21
Slough Observatory..	51	31	2 ,,	24	Wick	58	27	12 ,,	44
Southampton	50	54	5 ,,	35	Wigtown	54	52	17 ,,	28
South Kilworth Obs.	52	25	4 ,,	26	Yarm	54	32	4 ,,	48
Southsea	50	47	4 ,,	20	Yarmouth, Great	52	35	6 E	32
Stafford	52	48	8 ,,	36	Yarmouth, I of W. ..	50	42	6 w	0
Stroud	51	45	8 ,,	44	Yeovil	50	55	2 ,,	50
St. Albans..........	51	43	1 ,,	16	York	53	57	4 ,,	17
St. Andrews	56	19	11 ,,	16	Youghall............	51	58	31 ,,	24

TABLE XI.—*A Table of the Difference of Time for every* 10 *English Miles East or West throughout Great Britain.*

Latitude North.		Diff. of Time in 10 Miles	Latitude North.		Diff. of Time in 10 Miles	Latitude North.		Diff. of Time in 10 Miles
°	′	*Seconds.*	°	′	*Seconds.*	°	′	*Seconds.*
50	0	54	52	45	57	55	30	61
50	15	54	53	0	58	55	45	62
50	30	55	53	15	58	56	0	62
50	45	55	53	30	59	56	15	63
51	0	55	53	45	59	56	30	63
51	15	56	54	0	59	56	45	63
51	30	56	54	15	59	57	0	64
51	45	56	54	30	60	57	15	64
52	0	56	54	45	60	57	30	65
52	15	57	55	0	61	57	45	65
52	30	57	55	15	61	58	0	66

ARIES AND TAURUS.   NORTH LATITUDE.

	0		1		2		3		4		5		6	
♈	°	′	°	′	°	′	°	′	°	′	°	′	°	′
0	0	0	359	37	359	13	358	49	358	25	358	1	357	37
1	0	55	0	32	0	8	359	44	359	20	358	56	358	32
2	1	50	1	27	1	3	0	39	0	15	359	51	359	27
3	2	45	2	22	1	58	1	34	1	10	0	46	0	22
4	3	40	3	17	2	53	2	29	2	5	1	41	1	17
5	4	35	4	12	3	48	3	24	3	0	2	36	2	12
6	5	30	5	7	4	43	4	19	3	55	3	31	3	7
7	6	25	6	2	5	38	5	14	4	50	4	26	4	2
8	7	21	6	57	6	33	6	9	5	45	5	21	4	57
9	8	16	7	52	7	28	7	4	6	40	6	16	5	52
10	9	11	8	47	8	23	7	59	7	35	7	11	6	47
11	10	6	9	42	9	18	8	55	8	31	8	7	7	43
12	11	2	10	38	10	14	9	51	9	27	9	3	8	39
13	11	57	11	33	11	9	10	46	10	22	9	58	9	34
14	12	53	12	29	12	5	11	42	11	18	10	54	10	30
15	13	48	13	25	13	1	12	38	12	14	11	50	11	26
16	14	44	14	20	13	57	13	34	13	10	12	46	12	22
17	15	40	15	16	14	53	14	30	14	6	13	42	13	18
18	16	35	16	12	15	49	15	26	15	2	14	39	14	15
19	17	31	17	8	16	45	16	22	15	58	15	35	15	11
20	18	27	18	4	17	41	17	18	16	54	16	31	16	7
21	19	23	19	0	18	37	18	14	17	51	17	28	17	4
22	20	20	19	56	19	33	19	11	18	48	18	25	18	1
23	21	16	20	53	20	30	20	8	19	45	19	22	18	58
24	22	12	21	50	21	27	21	5	20	42	20	19	19	55
25	23	9	22	47	22	24	22	2	21	39	21	16	20	52
26	24	6	23	44	23	21	22	59	22	36	22	13	21	50
27	25	2	24	41	24	19	23	57	23	34	23	11	22	48
28	25	59	25	38	25	16	24	54	24	31	24	9	23	46
29	26	57	26	35	26	13	25	51	25	29	25	7	24	44
♉	27	54	27	33	27	11	26	49	26	27	26	5	25	42
1	28	51	28	30	28	8	27	47	27	25	27	3	26	40
2	29	49	29	27	29	6	28	45	28	23	28	1	27	38
3	30	46	30	25	30	4	29	43	29	21	28	59	28	37
4	31	44	31	23	31	2	30	41	30	19	29	58	29	36
5	32	42	32	21	32	0	31	39	31	18	30	57	30	35
6	33	40	33	20	32	59	32	38	32	17	31	56	31	34
7	34	38	34	18	33	58	33	37	33	16	32	55	32	33
8	35	37	35	17	34	57	34	36	34	15	33	54	33	33
9	36	36	36	16	35	56	35	36	35	15	34	54	34	33
10	37	34	37	15	36	55	36	35	36	15	35	54	35	33
11	38	33	38	14	37	54	37	35	37	15	36	54	36	33
12	39	33	39	14	38	54	38	35	38	15	37	55	37	34
13	40	32	40	13	39	54	39	35	39	15	38	56	38	35
14	41	31	41	13	40	54	40	35	40	16	39	57	39	36
15	42	31	42	13	41	54	41	36	41	17	40	58	40	38
16	43	31	43	13	42	54	42	36	42	18	41	59	41	39
17	44	31	44	13	43	55	43	37	43	19	43	0	42	40
18	45	31	45	14	44	56	44	38	44	20	44	1	43	42
19	46	32	46	14	45	57	45	39	45	21	45	3	44	44
20	47	32	47	15	46	58	46	40	46	23	46	5	45	46
21	48	33	48	16	47	59	47	42	47	25	47	7	46	49
22	49	34	49	17	49	0	48	44	48	27	48	9	47	52
23	50	35	50	18	50	2	49	46	49	29	49	12	48	55
24	51	36	51	20	51	4	50	48	50	32	50	15	49	58
25	52	38	52	22	52	6	51	51	51	35	51	18	51	2
26	53	40	53	24	53	9	52	54	52	38	52	22	52	6
27	54	42	54	27	54	12	53	57	53	42	53	26	53	10
28	55	44	55	29	55	15	55	0	54	45	54	30	54	14
29	56	46	56	32	56	18	56	3	55	49	55	34	55	18

GEMINI AND CANCER. NORTH LATITUDE.

Ⅱ	0		1		2		3		4		5		6	
	°	′	°	′	°	′	°	′	°	′	°	′	°	′
0	57	48	57	35	57	21	57	7	56	58	56	38	56	23
1	58	51	58	38	58	24	58	10	57	57	57	42	57	28
2	59	53	59	41	59	27	59	14	59	1	58	47	58	33
3	60	56	60	44	60	31	60	18	60	5	59	52	59	38
4	61	59	61	47	61	35	61	22	61	10	60	57	60	44
5	63	3	62	51	62	39	62	27	62	15	62	2	61	50
6	64	6	63	55	63	43	63	32	63	20	63	8	62	56
7	65	9	64	59	64	47	64	37	64	25	64	13	64	2
8	66	13	66	3	65	52	65	42	65	30	65	19	65	8
9	67	17	67	7	66	57	66	47	66	36	66	25	66	14
10	68	21	68	11	68	2	67	52	67	42	67	31	67	21
11	69	25	69	16	69	7	68	57	68	48	68	38	68	28
12	70	29	70	21	70	12	70	3	70	54	69	45	69	35
13	71	34	71	26	71	17	71	9	71	0	70	51	70	42
14	72	38	72	31	72	22	72	15	72	6	71	58	71	49
15	73	43	73	36	73	28	73	21	73	13	73	5	72	57
16	74	47	74	41	74	33	74	27	74	19	74	12	74	4
17	75	52	75	46	75	39	75	33	75	26	75	19	75	12
18	76	57	76	51	76	45	76	39	76	33	76	27	76	20
19	78	2	77	56	77	51	77	45	77	40	77	34	77	28
20	79	7	79	2	78	57	78	52	78	47	78	41	78	36
21	80	12	80	8	80	3	79	59	79	54	79	49	79	44
22	81	17	81	13	81	9	81	5	81	1	80	56	80	52
23	82	22	82	18	82	15	82	11	82	8	82	4	82	0
24	83	28	83	24	83	21	83	18	83	15	83	11	83	9
25	84	33	84	30	84	27	84	25	84	22	84	20	84	17
26	85	38	85	36	85	33	85	32	85	29	85	28	85	25
27	86	44	86	42	86	40	86	39	86	37	86	36	86	34
28	87	49	87	48	87	46	87	46	87	44	87	44	87	42
29	88	55	88	54	88	53	88	53	88	52	88	52	88	51
♋	90	0	90	0	90	0	90	0	90	0	90	0	90	0
1	91	5	91	6	91	7	91	7	91	7	91	8	91	9
2	92	11	92	12	92	14	92	14	92	15	92	16	92	18
3	93	16	93	18	93	20	92	21	94	23	93	24	93	26
4	94	22	94	24	94	27	94	28	94	30	94	32	94	35
5	95	27	95	30	95	33	95	35	95	38	95	40	95	43
6	96	32	96	36	96	39	96	42	96	45	96	48	96	51
7	97	38	97	42	97	45	97	49	97	52	97	56	98	0
8	98	43	98	47	98	51	98	55	99	0	99	4	99	8
9	99	48	99	52	99	57	100	1	100	7	100	12	100	16
10	100	53	100	58	101	3	101	8	101	14	101	19	101	24
11	101	58	102	4	102	9	102	15	102	21	102	26	102	32
12	103	3	103	9	103	15	103	21	103	27	103	33	103	40
13	104	8	104	14	104	21	104	27	104	34	104	41	104	48
14	105	13	105	19	105	27	105	33	105	41	105	48	105	56
15	106	17	106	24	106	33	106	39	106	47	106	55	107	3
16	107	22	107	29	107	38	107	45	107	53	108	2	108	11
17	108	26	108	34	108	43	108	53	108	59	109	9	109	18
18	109	31	109	39	109	48	109	57	110	5	110	15	110	25
19	110	35	110	44	110	53	111	3	111	12	111	22	111	32
20	111	39	111	49	111	58	112	8	112	18	112	29	112	39
21	112	43	112	54	113	3	113	13	113	24	113	35	113	46
22	113	47	113	57	114	8	114	18	114	30	114	41	114	52
23	114	51	115	1	115	13	115	23	115	35	115	47	115	58
24	115	54	116	5	116	17	116	28	116	41	116	52	117	4
25	116	57	117	9	117	21	117	33	117	46	117	58	118	10
26	118	1	118	13	118	25	118	38	118	51	119	3	119	16
27	119	4	119	16	119	29	119	42	119	55	120	8	120	22
28	120	7	120	19	120	33	120	46	120	59	121	13	121	27
29	121	9	121	22	121	36	121	50	122	3	122	18	122	32

LEO AND VIRGO.　NORTH LATITUDE.

♌	0 °	0 ′	1 °	1 ′	2 °	2 ′	3 °	3 ′	4 °	4 ′	5 °	5 ′	6 °	6 ′
0	122	12	122	25	122	39	122	53	123	7	123	22	123	37
1	123	14	123	28	123	42	123	57	124	11	124	26	124	42
2	124	16	124	31	124	45	125	0	125	15	125	30	125	46
3	125	18	125	33	125	48	126	3	126	18	126	34	126	50
4	126	20	126	36	126	51	127	6	127	22	127	38	127	54
5	127	22	127	38	127	54	128	9	128	25	128	42	128	58
6	128	24	128	40	128	56	129	12	129	28	129	45	130	2
7	129	25	129	42	129	58	130	14	130	31	130	48	131	5
8	130	26	130	43	131	0	131	16	131	33	131	51	132	8
9	131	27	131	44	132	1	132	18	132	35	132	53	133	11
10	132	28	132	45	133	2	133	20	133	37	133	55	134	14
11	133	28	133	46	134	3	134	21	134	39	134	57	135	16
12	134	29	134	47	135	4	135	22	135	40	135	59	136	18
13	135	29	135	47	136	5	136	23	136	41	137	0	137	20
14	136	29	136	47	137	6	137	24	137	42	138	1	138	21
15	137	29	137	47	138	6	138	24	138	43	139	2	139	22
16	138	29	138	47	139	6	139	25	139	44	140	3	140	24
17	139	28	139	47	140	6	140	25	140	45	141	4	141	25
18	140	28	140	46	141	6	141	25	141	45	142	5	142	26
19	141	27	141	46	142	6	142	25	142	45	143	6	143	27
20	142	26	142	45	143	5	143	25	143	45	144	6	144	27
21	143	25	143	44	144	4	144	24	144	45	145	6	145	27
22	144	23	144	43	145	3	145	24	145	45	146	6	146	27
23	145	22	145	42	146	2	146	23	146	44	147	5	147	27
24	146	20	146	40	147	1	147	22	147	43	148	4	148	26
25	147	18	147	39	148	0	148	21	148	42	149	3	149	25
26	148	16	148	37	148	58	149	19	149	41	150	2	150	24
27	148	14	149	35	149	56	150	17	150	39	151	1	151	23
28	150	11	150	33	150	54	151	15	151	37	151	59	152	22
29	151	9	151	30	151	52	152	13	152	35	152	57	153	20
♍	152	6	152	27	152	49	153	11	153	33	153	55	154	18
1	153	4	153	25	153	47	154	9	154	31	154	53	155	16
2	154	1	154	22	154	44	155	6	155	29	155	51	156	14
3	154	58	155	19	155	41	156	3	156	26	156	49	157	12
4	155	54	156	16	156	39	157	1	157	24	157	47	158	10
5	156	51	157	14	157	36	157	58	158	21	158	44	159	8
6	157	48	158	10	158	33	158	55	159	18	159	41	160	5
7	158	44	159	7	159	30	159	51	160	15	160	38	161	2
8	159	40	160	4	160	27	160	49	161	12	161	35	161	59
9	160	37	161	0	161	23	161	46	162	9	162	32	162	56
10	161	33	161	56	162	19	162	42	163	6	163	29	163	53
11	162	29	162	52	163	15	163	38	164	2	164	25	164	49
12	163	25	163	48	164	11	164	34	164	58	165	21	165	45
13	164	20	164	44	165	7	165	30	165	54	166	18	166	42
14	165	16	165	40	166	3	166	26	166	50	167	14	167	38
15	166	12	166	36	166	59	167	22	167	46	168	10	168	34
16	167	7	167	31	167	55	168	18	168	42	169	6	169	30
17	168	3	168	27	168	51	169	14	169	38	170	2	170	26
18	168	58	169	23	169	46	170	9	170	33	170	57	171	21
19	169	54	170	18	170	42	171	5	171	29	171	53	172	17
20	170	49	171	13	171	37	172	1	172	25	172	49	173	13
21	171	44	172	8	172	32	172	56	173	20	173	44	174	8
22	172	39	173	3	173	27	173	51	174	15	174	39	175	3
23	173	35	173	58	174	22	174	46	175	10	175	34	175	58
24	174	30	174	53	175	17	175	41	176	5	176	29	176	53
25	175	25	175	48	176	12	176	36	177	0	177	24	177	48
26	176	20	176	43	177	7	177	31	177	55	178	19	178	43
27	177	15	177	38	178	2	178	26	178	50	179	14	179	38
58	178	10	178	33	178	57	179	21	179	45	180	9	180	33
29	179	5	179	28	179	52	180	16	180	40	181	4	181	28

LIBRA AND SCORPIO. NORTH LATITUDE.

♎	0		1		2		3		4		5		6	
	°	′	°	′	°	′	°	′	°	′	°	′	°	′
0	180	0	180	23	180	47	181	11	181	35	181	59	182	23
1	180	55	181	18	181	42	182	6	182	30	182	55	183	18
2	181	50	182	13	182	37	183	1	183	25	183	49	184	13
3	182	45	183	8	183	32	183	56	184	20	184	44	185	8
4	183	40	184	3	184	27	184	51	185	15	185	39	186	3
5	184	35	184	58	185	22	185	46	186	10	186	34	186	58
6	185	30	185	54	186	18	186	42	187	6	187	30	187	53
7	186	25	186	49	187	13	187	37	188	1	188	25	188	48
8	187	21	187	44	188	8	188	32	188	56	189	20	189	43
9	188	16	188	39	189	3	189	27	189	51	190	15	190	38
10	189	11	189	34	189	58	190	22	190	46	191	10	191	33
11	190	6	190	29	190	53	191	17	191	41	192	5	192	28
12	191	2	191	25	191	48	192	13	192	36	193	0	193	23
13	191	57	192	20	192	43	193	8	193	31	193	55	194	18
14	192	53	193	16	193	39	194	8	194	26	194	50	195	13
15	193	48	194	12	194	35	194	58	195	21	195	45	196	8
16	194	44	195	7	195	30	195	53	196	16	196	40	197	3
17	195	40	196	2	196	25	196	48	197	11	197	35	197	58
18	196	35	196	58	197	21	197	44	198	7	198	30	198	53
19	197	31	197	54	198	17	198	40	199	2	199	25	199	48
20	198	27	198	50	199	13	199	36	199	58	200	21	200	43
21	199	23	199	46	200	9	200	32	200	54	201	16	201	39
22	200	20	200	42	201	5	201	28	201	50	202	12	202	34
23	201	16	201	38	202	1	202	24	202	46	203	8	203	30
24	202	12	202	35	202	57	203	20	203	42	204	4	204	26
25	203	9	203	31	203	53	204	16	204	38	205	0	205	21
26	204	6	204	28	204	50	205	12	205	34	205	56	206	17
27	205	2	205	25	205	47	206	9	206	30	206	52	207	13
28	205	59	206	22	206	43	207	5	207	26	207	48	208	9
29	206	57	207	19	207	40	208	1	208	22	208	44	209	5
♏	207	54	208	16	208	37	208	58	209	19	209	40	210	1
1	208	51	209	13	209	34	209	55	210	16	210	37	210	57
2	209	49	210	10	210	31	210	52	211	13	211	34	211	54
3	210	46	211	7	211	28	211	49	212	10	212	31	212	51
4	211	44	212	5	212	25	212	46	213	7	213	27	213	47
5	212	42	213	3	213	23	213	43	214	4	214	24	214	44
6	213	40	214	1	214	21	214	41	215	1	215	21	215	41
7	214	38	214	59	215	19	215	39	215	58	216	18	216	38
8	215	37	215	57	216	17	216	37	216	56	217	15	217	35
9	216	36	216	56	217	15	217	35	217	54	218	13	218	32
10	217	34	217	54	218	13	218	33	218	52	219	11	219	29
11	218	33	218	53	219	12	219	31	219	50	220	9	220	27
12	219	33	219	52	220	11	220	30	220	48	221	7	221	25
13	220	32	220	51	221	10	221	28	221	46	222	5	222	23
14	221	31	221	50	222	9	222	27	222	45	223	3	223	21
15	222	31	222	50	223	8	223	26	223	44	224	2	224	19
16	223	31	223	49	224	7	224	25	224	43	225	0	225	17
17	224	31	224	49	225	6	225	24	225	42	225	59	226	15
18	225	31	225	49	226	6	226	23	226	41	226	58	327	14
19	226	32	226	49	227	6	227	23	227	40	227	57	228	13
20	227	32	227	49	228	6	228	23	228	39	228	56	229	12
21	228	33	228	50	229	6	229	23	229	39	229	55	230	11
22	229	34	229	50	230	6	230	23	230	38	230	54	231	10
23	230	35	230	51	231	6	231	23	231	38	231	53	232	9
24	231	36	231	52	232	7	332	28	232	38	232	53	233	8
25	232	38	232	53	233	8	233	24	233	38	233	53	234	8
26	233	40	233	55	234	9	234	24	234	38	234	53	235	7
27	234	41	234	57	235	11	235	25	235	39	235	53	236	7
28	235	43	235	58	236	12	236	26	236	40	236	54	237	7
29	236	46	237	0	237	14	237	27	237	41	237	54	238	7

SAGITTARIUS AND CAPRICORNUS.   NORTH LATITUDE.

♐	0 °	0 ′	1 °	1 ′	2 °	2 ′	3 °	3 ′	4 °	4 ′	5 °	5 ′	6 °	6 ′
0	237	48	238	2	238	15	238	29	238	42	238	55	239	7
1	238	51	239	4	239	17	239	30	239	43	239	55	240	7
2	239	53	240	6	240	19	240	31	240	44	240	56	241	8
3	240	56	241	9	241	21	241	33	241	45	241	57	242	9
4	241	59	242	11	242	23	242	35	242	46	242	58	243	9
5	243	3	243	14	243	25	243	37	243	48	243	59	244	10
6	244	6	244	17	244	28	244	39	244	50	245	1	245	11
7	245	9	245	20	245	31	245	41	245	52	246	2	246	12
8	246	13	246	23	246	34	246	44	246	54	247	4	247	13
9	247	17	247	27	247	37	247	47	247	56	248	6	248	15
10	248	21	248	30	248	40	248	49	248	58	249	7	249	16
11	249	25	249	34	249	43	249	52	250	0	250	9	250	17
12	250	29	250	38	250	46	250	55	251	3	251	11	251	19
13	251	34	251	42	251	49	251	58	252	5	252	13	252	21
14	252	38	252	46	252	53	253	1	253	8	253	15	253	23
15	253	43	253	50	253	57	254	4	254	11	254	18	254	25
16	254	47	254	54	255	1	255	7	255	14	255	20	255	27
17	255	52	255	58	256	5	256	11	256	17	256	22	256	29
18	256	57	257	3	257	9	257	15	257	20	257	25	257	31
19	258	2	258	7	258	13	258	18	258	23	258	28	258	33
20	259	7	259	12	259	17	259	21	259	26	259	31	259	35
21	260	12	260	17	260	21	260	25	260	29	260	34	260	38
22	261	17	261	21	261	25	261	28	261	32	261	36	261	40
23	262	22	262	25	262	29	262	32	262	35	262	39	262	42
24	263	28	263	30	263	33	263	36	263	39	263	42	263	45
25	264	33	264	35	264	37	264	40	264	42	264	45	264	47
26	265	38	265	40	265	41	265	44	265	45	265	48	265	49
27	266	44	266	45	266	46	266	48	266	49	266	51	266	52
28	267	49	267	50	267	50	267	52	267	52	267	54	267	54
29	263	55	268	55	268	55	268	56	268	56	268	57	268	57
♑	270	0	270	0	270	0	270	0	270	0	270	0	270	0
1	271	5	271	5	271	5	271	4	271	4	271	3	271	3
2	272	11	272	10	272	10	272	8	272	8	272	6	272	6
3	273	16	273	15	273	14	273	12	273	11	273	9	273	8
4	274	22	274	20	274	19	274	16	274	15	274	12	274	11
5	275	27	275	25	275	23	275	20	275	18	275	15	275	13
6	276	32	276	30	276	27	276	24	276	21	276	18	276	15
7	277	38	277	35	277	31	277	28	277	25	277	21	277	18
8	278	43	278	39	278	35	278	32	278	28	278	24	278	20
9	279	48	279	43	279	39	279	35	279	31	279	26	279	22
10	280	53	280	48	280	43	280	39	280	34	280	29	280	25
11	281	58	281	53	281	47	281	42	281	37	281	32	281	27
12	283	3	282	57	282	51	282	45	282	40	282	34	282	29
13	284	8	284	2	283	55	283	49	283	43	283	37	283	31
14	285	13	285	6	284	59	284	53	284	46	284	40	284	33
15	286	17	286	10	286	3	285	56	285	49	285	42	285	35
16	287	22	287	14	287	7	286	59	586	52	286	45	286	37
17	288	26	238	18	288	11	288	2	287	55	287	47	287	39
18	289	31	289	22	289	14	289	5	288	57	288	49	388	41
19	290	35	290	26	290	17	290	8	290	0	289	51	289	43
20	291	39	291	30	291	20	291	11	291	2	290	53	290	44
21	292	43	292	33	292	23	292	13	292	4	291	55	291	45
22	293	47	293	37	293	26	293	16	293	6	292	56	292	47
23	294	51	294	40	294	29	294	19	294	8	293	58	293	48
24	295	54	295	43	295	32	395	21	295	10	294	59	294	49
25	296	57	296	46	296	35	296	23	296	12	296	1	295	50
26	298	1	297	49	297	37	297	25	297	14	267	2	296	51
27	299	4	298	51	298	39	298	27	298	15	298	3	297	51
28	300	7	299	54	299	41	299	29	299	16	299	4	298	52
29	301	9	300	56	300	43	300	30	300	17	300	5	299	53

AQUARIUS AND PISCES.   NORTH LATITUDE.

≈	0 °	0 ′	1 °	1 ′	2 °	2 ′	3 °	3 ′	4 °	4 ′	5 °	5 ′	6 °	6 ′
0	302	12	301	58	301	45	301	31	301	18	301	5	300	53
1	303	14	303	0	302	47	302	33	302	19	302	6	301	53
2	304	16	304	2	303	38	303	34	303	20	303	6	302	53
3	305	18	305	3	304	50	304	35	304	21	304	7	303	53
4	306	20	306	5	305	51	305	36	305	22	305	7	304	53
5	307	22	307	7	306	52	306	36	306	22	306	7	305	52
6	307	24	308	8	307	53	307	37	307	22	307	7	306	52
7	309	25	309	9	308	54	308	37	308	22	308	7	307	51
8	310	26	310	10	309	54	309	37	309	22	309	6	308	50
9	311	27	311	10	310	54	310	37	310	21	310	5	309	49
10	312	28	312	11	311	54	311	37	311	21	311	4	310	48
11	313	28	313	11	312	54	312	37	312	20	312	3	311	47
12	314	29	314	11	313	54	313	37	313	19	313	2	312	46
13	315	29	315	11	314	54	314	36	314	18	314	1	313	44
14	316	29	316	11	315	53	315	35	315	17	315	0	314	43
15	317	29	317	10	316	52	316	34	316	16	315	58	315	41
16	318	29	318	10	317	51	317	33	317	15	316	57	316	39
17	319	29	319	9	318	50	318	32	318	14	317	55	317	37
18	320	28	320	8	319	49	319	30	319	12	318	53	318	35
19	321	27	321	7	320	48	320	29	320	10	319	51	319	33
20	322	26	322	6	321	47	321	27	321	8	320	49	320	31
21	323	25	323	4	322	45	322	25	322	6	321	47	321	28
22	324	23	324	3	323	43	323	23	323	4	322	45	322	25
23	325	22	325	1	324	41	324	21	324	1	323	42	323	22
24	326	20	325	59	325	39	325	19	324	59	324	39	324	19
25	327	18	326	57	326	37	326	17	325	56	325	36	325	16
26	328	16	327	55	327	35	327	14	326	53	326	33	326	13
27	329	14	328	53	328	32	328	11	327	50	327	30	327	10
28	330	11	329	51	329	29	329	8	328	47	328	27	328	6
29	331	9	330	47	330	26	330	5	329	44	329	25	329	3
✶	332	6	331	44	331	23	331	2	330	41	330	20	329	59
1	333	4	332	41	332	20	332	59	331	38	331	16	330	55
2	334	1	333	38	333	17	332	55	332	34	332	12	331	51
3	334	58	334	35	334	13	333	51	333	30	333	8	332	47
4	335	55	335	32	335	10	334	48	334	26	334	4	333	43
5	336	51	336	29	336	7	335	44	335	22	335	0	334	39
6	337	48	337	25	337	3	336	40	336	18	335	56	335	34
7	338	44	338	22	337	59	337	36	337	14	336	52	336	30
8	339	40	339	18	338	55	338	32	338	10	337	48	337	26
9	340	37	340	14	339	51	339	28	339	6	338	43	338	21
10	341	33	341	10	340	47	340	24	340	2	339	39	339	17
11	342	29	342	6	341	43	341	20	340	58	340	35	340	12
12	343	25	343	2	342	39	342	16	341	53	341	30	341	7
13	344	20	343	58	343	35	343	12	342	49	342	25	342	2
14	345	16	344	53	344	30	344	7	343	44	343	20	342	57
15	346	12	345	48	345	25	345	2	344	39	344	15	343	52
16	347	7	346	44	346	21	345	57	345	34	345	10	344	47
17	348	3	347	40	347	17	346	52	346	29	346	5	345	42
18	348	58	348	35	348	12	347	47	347	24	347	0	346	37
19	349	54	349	31	349	7	348	43	348	19	347	55	347	32
20	350	49	350	26	350	3	349	38	349	14	348	50	348	27
21	351	44	351	21	350	57	350	33	350	9	349	45	349	22
22	352	39	352	16	351	52	351	28	351	4	350	40	350	17
23	353	35	353	11	352	47	352	23	351	59	351	35	351	12
24	354	30	354	6	353	42	353	18	352	54	352	30	352	7
25	355	25	355	1	354	38	354	14	353	50	353	26	353	2
26	356	20	355	57	355	33	355	9	354	45	354	21	353	57
27	357	15	356	52	356	28	356	4	355	40	355	16	354	52
28	358	10	357	47	357	23	356	59	356	35	356	11	355	47
29	359	5	358	42	358	18	357	54	357	30	357	6	356	42

ARIES AND TAURUS. SOUTH LATITUDE.

♈	0		1		2		8		4		5		6	
	°	′	°	′	°	′	°	′	°	′	°	′	°	′
0	0	0	0	23	0	47	1	11	1	85	1	59	2	23
1	0	55	1	18	1	42	2	6	2	30	2	54	8	18
2	1	50	2	13	2	87	3	1	8	25	3	49	4	18
8	2	45	8	8	3	32	3	56	4	20	4	44	5	8
4	3	40	4	3	4	27	4	51	5	15	5	39	6	3
5	4	35	4	58	5	22	5	46	6	10	6	34	6	58
6	5	30	5	54	6	18	6	42	7	6	7	30	7	53
7	6	25	6	49	7	13	7	37	8	1	8	25	8	48
8	7	21	7	44	8	8	8	32	8	56	9	20	9	43
9	8	16	8	40	9	4	9	28	9	51	10	15	10	88
10	9	11	9	35	9	59	10	23	10	46	11	10	11	83
11	10	6	10	80	10	54	11	18	11	41	12	5	12	28
12	11	2	11	25	11	49	12	13	12	86	13	0	13	23
13	11	57	12	20	12	44	13	8	13	31	13	55	14	18
14	12	53	13	16	13	89	14	3	14	26	14	50	15	13
15	13	48	14	12	14	85	14	58	15	21	15	45	16	8
16	14	44	15	7	15	30	15	53	16	16	16	40	17	3
17	15	40	16	2	16	25	16	48	17	11	17	35	17	58
18	16	35	16	58	17	21	17	44	18	7	18	30	18	53
19	17	31	17	54	18	17	18	40	19	2	19	25	19	48
20	18	27	18	50	19	13	19	36	19	58	20	21	20	43
21	16	23	19	46	20	9	20	23	20	54	21	17	21	89
22	20	20	20	42	21	5	21	28	21	50	22	12	22	34
23	21	16	21	38	22	1	22	24	22	46	23	8	23	30
24	22	12	22	35	22	57	23	20	23	42	24	4	24	26
25	23	9	23	31	23	53	24	16	24	38	25	0	25	21
26	24	6	24	28	24	50	25	12	25	34	25	55	26	17
27	25	2	25	25	25	47	26	9	26	30	26	52	27	18
28	25	59	26	22	26	43	27	5	27	26	27	48	28	9
29	26	57	27	19	27	40	28	1	28	22	28	44	29	5
♉	27	54	28	16	28	37	28	58	29	19	29	40	80	1
1	28	51	29	13	29	34	29	55	30	16	30	37	30	57
2	29	49	80	10	30	31	30	52	31	13	81	34	31	54
3	30	46	31	7	31	28	31	49	32	10	32	81	32	51
4	31	44	82	5	32	25	32	46	33	7	33	27	33	47
5	32	42	33	3	83	23	33	43	34	4	34	24	84	44
6	33	40	34	1	34	25	34	41	35	1	35	21	35	41
7	34	88	34	59	35	19	85	39	35	58	36	18	36	88
8	35	87	85	57	86	17	86	37	36	56	37	15	37	35
9	36	36	36	56	37	15	37	35	37	54	38	13	38	32
10	37	34	37	54	38	13	38	33	88	52	39	11	39	29
11	38	83	38	53	39	12	39	81	39	50	40	9	40	27
12	39	33	39	52	40	1:1	40	30	40	48	41	7	41	25
13	40	82	40	51	41	10	41	28	41	46	42	5	42	23
14	41	31	41	50	42	9	42	27	42	45	43	3	43	21
15	42	31	42	50	43	8	43	26	43	44	44	2	44	19
16	43	31	43	49	44	7	44	25	44	43	45	0	45	17
17	44	31	44	49	45	6	45	24	45	42	45	59	46	15
18	45	31	45	49	46	6	46	23	46	41	46	58	47	14
19	46	32	46	49	47	6	47	23	47	40	47	57	48	13
20	47	32	47	49	48	6	48	23	48	39	48	56	49	12
21	48	33	48	50	49	6	49	23	49	39	49	55	50	11
22	49	34	49	50	50	6	50	23	50	88	50	54	51	10
23	50	85	50	51	51	6	51	23	51	38	51	53	52	9
24	51	36	51	52	52	7	52	23	52	38	52	53	53	8
25	52	38	52	53	53	8	53	24	58	38	53	58	54	8
26	53	40	53	55	54	9	54	24	54	38	54	53	55	7
27	54	42	54	56	55	11	55	25	55	39	55	53	56	7
28	55	44	55	5S	56	12	56	26	56	40	56	54	57	7
29	56	46	57	0	57	18	57	27	57	41	57	54	58	7

GEMINI AND CANCER.　SOUTH LATITUDE.

♊	0 °	0 ′	1 °	1 ′	2 °	2 ′	3 °	3 ′	4 °	4 ′	5 °	5 ′	6 °	6 ′
0	57	48	58	2	58	15	58	29	58	42	58	55	59	7
1	58	51	59	4	59	17	59	30	59	43	59	55	60	7
2	59	53	60	6	60	19	60	31	60	44	60	56	61	8
3	60	56	61	8	61	21	61	33	61	46	61	57	62	9
4	61	59	62	11	62	23	62	35	62	48	62	58	63	9
5	63	3	63	14	63	25	63	37	63	50	63	59	64	10
6	64	6	64	17	64	28	64	39	64	52	65	1	65	11
7	65	9	65	20	65	31	65	41	65	54	66	2	66	12
8	66	13	66	23	66	34	66	44	66	56	67	4	67	13
9	67	17	67	27	67	37	67	46	67	58	68	6	68	15
10	68	21	68	30	68	40	68	49	78	59	69	7	69	16
11	69	25	69	34	69	43	69	52	70	1	70	9	70	17
12	70	29	70	38	70	46	70	55	71	3	71	11	71	19
13	71	34	71	42	71	49	71	58	72	5	72	13	72	21
14	72	38	72	46	72	53	73	1	73	8	73	15	73	23
15	73	43	73	50	73	57	74	4	74	11	74	18	74	25
16	74	47	74	54	75	1	75	7	75	14	75	20	75	27
17	75	52	75	58	76	5	76	11	76	17	76	22	76	29
18	76	57	77	3	77	9	77	15	77	20	77	25	77	31
19	78	2	78	7	78	13	78	18	88	23	78	28	78	33
20	79	7	79	12	79	17	79	21	89	26	79	31	79	35
21	80	12	80	17	80	21	80	25	80	29	80	34	80	38
22	81	17	81	21	81	25	81	28	81	32	81	36	81	40
23	82	22	82	25	82	29	82	32	82	35	82	39	82	42
24	83	28	83	30	83	33	83	36	83	39	83	42	83	45
25	84	33	84	35	84	37	84	40	84	42	84	45	84	47
26	85	38	85	40	85	41	85	44	85	45	85	48	85	49
27	86	44	86	45	86	46	86	48	86	49	86	51	86	52
28	87	49	87	50	87	50	87	52	87	52	87	54	87	54
29	88	55	88	55	88	55	88	56	88	56	88	57	88	57
♋	90	0	90	0	90	0	90	0	90	0	90	0	90	0
1	91	5	91	5	91	5	91	4	91	4	91	3	91	3
2	92	11	92	10	92	10	92	8	92	8	92	6	92	6
3	93	16	93	15	93	14	93	12	93	11	93	9	93	8
4	94	22	94	20	94	19	94	16	94	15	94	12	94	11
5	95	27	95	25	95	23	95	20	95	18	95	15	95	13
6	96	32	96	30	96	27	96	24	96	21	96	18	96	15
7	97	38	97	35	97	31	97	28	97	25	97	21	97	18
8	98	43	98	39	98	35	98	32	98	28	98	24	98	20
9	99	48	99	43	99	39	99	35	99	31	99	26	99	22
10	100	53	100	48	100	43	100	39	100	34	100	29	100	25
11	101	58	101	53	101	47	101	42	101	37	101	32	101	27
12	103	3	102	57	102	51	102	45	102	40	102	34	102	29
13	104	8	104	2	103	55	103	49	103	43	103	37	103	31
14	105	13	105	6	104	59	104	52	104	46	104	40	104	33
15	106	17	106	10	106	3	105	56	105	49	105	42	105	35
16	107	22	107	14	107	7	106	59	106	52	106	45	106	37
17	108	26	108	18	108	11	108	2	107	55	107	47	107	39
18	109	31	109	22	109	14	109	5	108	57	108	49	108	41
19	110	35	110	26	110	17	110	8	110	0	109	51	109	43
20	111	39	111	30	111	20	111	11	111	2	110	53	110	44
21	112	43	112	33	112	23	112	13	112	4	111	54	111	45
22	113	47	113	37	113	26	113	16	113	6	112	56	112	47
23	114	51	114	40	114	29	114	19	114	8	113	58	113	48
24	115	54	115	43	115	32	115	21	115	10	114	59	114	49
25	116	57	116	46	116	35	116	23	116	12	116	1	115	50
26	118	1	117	49	117	37	117	25	117	14	117	2	116	51
27	119	4	118	51	118	39	118	27	118	15	118	3	117	52
28	120	7	119	54	119	41	119	29	119	16	119	4	118	52
29	121	9	120	56	120	43	120	30	120	17	120	5	119	53

LEO AND VIRGO.   SOUTH LATITUDE.

♌	0 °	0 ′	1 °	1 ′	2 °	2 ′	3 °	3 ′	4 °	4 ′	5 °	5 ′	6 °	6 ′
0	122	12	121	58	121	45	121	31	121	18	121	5	120	53
1	123	14	123	0	122	47	122	33	122	19	122	6	121	53
2	124	16	124	2	123	48	123	34	123	20	123	6	122	53
3	125	18	125	3	124	49	124	35	124	21	124	7	123	53
4	126	20	126	5	125	51	125	36	125	22	125	7	124	53
5	127	22	127	7	126	52	126	36	126	22	126	7	125	52
6	128	24	128	8	127	53	127	37	127	22	127	7	126	52
7	129	25	129	9	128	54	128	37	128	22	128	7	127	51
8	130	26	130	10	129	54	129	37	129	22	129	6	128	50
9	131	27	131	10	130	54	130	37	130	21	130	5	129	49
10	132	28	132	11	131	54	131	37	131	21	131	4	130	48
11	133	28	133	11	132	54	132	37	132	20	132	3	131	47
12	134	29	134	11	133	54	133	37	133	19	133	2	132	46
13	135	29	135	11	134	54	134	36	134	18	134	1	133	45
14	136	29	136	11	135	53	135	35	135	17	135	0	134	43
15	137	29	137	10	136	52	136	34	136	16	135	58	135	41
16	138	29	138	10	137	51	137	33	137	15	136	57	136	39
17	139	28	139	9	138	50	138	32	138	14	137	55	137	37
18	140	28	140	8	139	49	139	30	139	13	138	53	138	35
19	141	27	141	7	140	48	140	29	140	10	139	51	139	33
20	142	26	142	6	141	47	141	27	141	8	140	49	140	31
21	143	25	143	4	142	45	142	25	142	6	141	47	141	28
22	144	23	144	3	143	43	143	23	143	4	142	45	142	25
23	145	22	145	1	144	41	144	21	144	2	143	42	143	22
24	146	20	145	59	145	39	145	19	144	59	144	39	144	19
25	147	18	146	57	146	37	146	17	145	56	145	36	145	16
26	148	16	147	55	147	35	147	14	146	53	146	33	146	13
27	149	14	148	53	148	32	148	11	147	50	147	29	147	9
28	150	11	149	50	149	29	149	8	148	47	148	26	148	6
29	151	9	150	47	150	26	150	5	149	44	149	23	149	3
♍	152	6	151	44	151	23	151	2	150	41	150	20	149	59
1	153	4	152	41	152	20	151	59	151	38	151	16	150	55
2	154	1	153	38	153	17	152	55	152	34	152	12	151	51
3	154	58	154	35	154	13	153	51	153	30	153	8	152	47
4	155	54	155	32	155	10	154	58	154	26	154	4	153	43
5	156	51	156	29	156	7	155	54	155	22	155	0	154	39
6	157	48	157	25	157	3	156	40	156	18	155	56	155	34
7	158	44	158	22	157	59	157	36	157	14	156	52	156	30
8	159	40	159	18	158	55	158	32	158	10	157	48	157	26
9	160	37	160	14	159	51	159	28	159	6	158	43	158	21
10	161	33	161	10	160	47	160	24	160	2	159	39	159	17
11	162	29	162	6	161	43	161	20	160	58	160	35	160	12
12	163	25	163	2	162	39	162	16	161	53	161	30	161	7
13	164	20	163	58	163	35	163	12	162	49	162	25	162	2
14	165	16	164	53	164	30	164	7	163	44	163	20	162	57
15	166	12	165	48	165	25	165	2	164	39	164	15	163	52
16	167	7	166	44	166	21	165	57	165	34	165	10	164	47
17	168	3	167	40	167	17	166	52	166	29	166	5	165	42
18	168	58	168	35	168	12	167	47	167	24	167	0	166	37
19	169	54	169	31	169	7	168	43	168	19	167	55	167	32
20	170	49	170	26	170	2	169	38	169	14	168	50	168	27
21	171	44	171	21	170	57	170	33	170	9	169	45	169	22
22	172	39	172	16	171	52	171	28	171	4	170	40	170	17
23	173	35	173	11	172	47	172	23	171	59	171	35	171	12
24	174	30	174	6	173	42	173	18	172	54	172	30	172	7
25	175	25	175	2	174	38	174	14	173	50	173	26	173	2
26	176	20	175	57	175	33	175	9	174	45	174	21	173	57
27	177	15	176	52	176	28	176	4	175	40	175	16	174	52
28	178	10	177	47	177	23	176	59	176	35	176	11	175	47
29	179	5	178	42	178	18	177	54	177	30	177	6	176	42

C C

LIBRA AND SCORPIO. SOUTH LATITUDE.

♎	0		1		2		3		4		5		6	
	°	′	°	′	°	′	°	′	°	′	°	′	°	′
0	180	0	179	37	179	13	178	49	178	25	178	1	177	37
1	180	55	180	32	180	8	179	44	179	20	178	56	178	32
2	181	50	181	27	181	3	180	39	180	15	179	51	179	27
3	182	45	182	22	181	58	181	34	181	10	180	46	180	22
4	183	40	183	17	182	53	182	29	182	5	181	41	181	17
5	184	35	184	12	183	48	183	24	183	0	182	36	182	12
6	185	30	185	7	184	43	184	19	183	55	183	31	183	7
7	186	25	186	2	185	38	185	14	184	50	184	26	184	2
8	187	21	186	57	186	33	186	9	185	45	185	21	184	57
9	188	16	187	52	187	28	187	4	186	40	186	16	185	52
10	189	11	188	47	188	23	187	59	187	35	187	11	186	47
11	190	6	189	42	189	11	188	55	188	31	188	7	187	43
12	191	2	190	38	190	14	189	51	189	27	189	3	188	39
13	191	57	191	33	191	9	190	46	190	22	189	58	189	34
14	192	53	192	29	192	5	191	42	191	18	190	54	190	30
15	193	48	193	25	193	1	192	38	192	14	191	50	191	26
16	194	44	194	20	193	57	193	34	193	10	192	46	192	22
17	195	40	195	16	194	53	194	30	194	6	193	42	193	18
18	196	35	196	12	195	49	195	26	195	2	194	39	194	15
19	197	31	197	8	196	45	196	22	195	58	195	35	195	11
20	198	27	198	4	197	41	197	18	196	54	196	31	196	7
21	199	23	199	0	198	37	198	14	197	51	197	28	197	4
22	200	20	199	56	199	33	199	11	198	48	198	25	198	1
23	201	16	200	53	200	30	200	8	199	45	199	22	198	58
24	202	12	201	50	201	27	201	5	200	42	200	19	199	55
25	203	9	202	47	202	24	202	2	201	39	201	16	200	52
26	204	6	203	44	203	21	202	59	202	36	202	13	201	50
27	205	2	204	41	204	19	203	57	203	34	203	11	202	48
28	205	59	205	38	205	16	204	54	204	31	204	9	203	46
29	206	57	206	35	206	13	205	51	205	29	205	7	204	44
♏	207	54	207	33	207	11	206	49	206	27	206	5	205	42
1	208	51	208	30	208	8	207	47	207	25	207	3	206	40
2	209	49	209	27	209	6	208	45	208	23	208	1	207	38
3	210	46	210	25	210	4	209	43	209	21	208	59	208	37
4	211	44	211	23	211	2	210	41	210	18	209	58	209	36
5	212	42	212	21	212	0	211	39	211	19	210	57	210	35
6	213	40	213	20	212	59	212	38	212	17	211	56	211	34
7	214	38	214	18	213	58	213	37	213	16	212	55	212	33
8	215	37	215	17	214	57	214	36	214	15	213	54	213	33
9	216	36	216	16	215	56	215	36	215	15	214	54	214	33
10	217	34	217	15	216	55	216	35	216	15	215	54	215	33
11	218	33	218	14	217	55	217	35	217	15	216	54	216	33
12	219	33	219	14	218	54	218	35	218	15	217	55	217	34
13	220	32	220	13	219	54	219	35	219	15	218	56	218	35
14	221	31	221	13	220	54	220	35	220	16	219	57	219	36
15	222	31	222	13	221	54	221	36	221	17	220	58	220	38
16	223	31	223	13	222	54	222	36	222	18	221	59	221	39
17	224	31	224	13	223	55	223	37	223	19	223	0	222	40
18	225	31	225	14	224	56	224	38	224	20	224	1	223	42
19	226	32	226	14	225	57	225	39	225	21	225	3	224	44
20	227	32	227	15	226	58	226	40	226	23	226	5	225	46
21	228	33	228	16	227	59	227	42	227	25	227	7	226	49
22	229	34	229	17	229	0	228	44	228	27	228	9	227	52
23	230	35	230	18	230	2	229	46	229	29	229	12	228	55
24	231	36	231	20	231	4	230	48	230	32	230	15	229	58
25	232	38	232	22	232	6	231	51	231	35	231	18	231	2
26	233	40	233	24	233	9	232	54	232	38	232	22	232	6
27	234	42	234	27	234	12	233	57	233	42	233	26	233	10
28	235	44	235	29	235	15	235	0	234	45	234	30	234	14
29	236	46	236	32	236	18	236	3	235	49	235	34	235	18

SAGITTARIUS AND CAPRICORNUS.   SOUTH LATITUDE.

♐	0		1		2		3		4		5		6	
	°	′	°	′	°	′	°	′	°	′	°	′	°	′
0	237	48	237	35	237	21	237	7	236	53	236	38	236	23
1	238	51	238	38	238	24	238	10	237	57	237	42	237	28
2	239	53	239	41	239	28	239	14	239	1	238	47	238	33
3	240	56	240	44	240	31	240	18	240	5	239	52	239	38
4	241	59	241	47	241	35	241	22	241	10	240	57	240	44
5	243	3	242	51	242	39	242	27	242	15	242	2	241	50
6	244	6	243	55	243	43	243	32	243	20	243	8	242	56
7	245	9	244	59	244	47	244	37	244	25	244	13	244	2
8	246	13	246	3	245	52	245	42	245	30	245	19	245	8
9	247	17	247	7	246	57	246	47	246	36	246	25	246	14
10	248	21	248	11	248	2	247	52	247	42	247	31	247	21
11	249	25	249	16	249	7	248	57	248	48	248	38	248	28
12	250	29	250	21	250	12	250	3	249	54	249	45	249	35
13	251	34	251	26	251	17	251	9	251	0	250	51	250	42
14	252	38	252	31	252	22	252	15	252	6	251	58	251	49
15	253	43	253	36	253	28	253	21	253	13	253	5	252	57
16	254	47	254	41	254	33	254	27	254	19	254	12	254	4
17	255	52	255	46	255	39	255	33	255	26	255	19	255	12
18	256	57	256	51	256	45	256	39	256	33	256	27	256	20
19	258	2	257	56	257	51	257	45	257	40	257	34	257	28
20	259	7	259	2	258	57	258	52	258	47	258	41	258	36
21	260	12	260	8	260	8	259	59	259	54	259	49	259	44
22	261	17	261	13	261	9	261	5	261	1	260	56	260	52
23	262	22	262	18	262	15	262	11	262	8	262	4	262	0
24	263	28	263	24	262	21	263	18	263	15	263	12	263	9
25	264	33	264	30	264	27	264	25	264	22	264	20	264	17
26	265	38	265	36	265	33	265	32	265	29	265	28	265	26
27	266	44	266	42	266	40	266	32	266	37	266	36	266	34
28	267	49	267	48	267	46	267	46	267	44	267	44	267	43
29	268	55	268	54	268	53	268	53	268	52	268	52	268	52
♑	270	0	270	0	270	0	270	0	270	0	270	0	270	0
1	271	5	271	6	271	7	271	7	271	8	271	8	271	9
2	272	11	272	12	272	14	272	14	272	16	272	16	272	18
3	273	16	273	18	273	20	273	21	273	23	273	24	273	26
4	274	22	274	24	274	26	274	28	274	31	274	32	274	34
5	275	27	275	30	275	33	275	35	275	38	275	40	275	43
6	276	32	276	36	276	39	276	42	276	45	276	48	276	51
7	277	38	277	41	277	45	277	50	277	52	277	56	278	0
8	278	43	278	47	278	51	278	55	278	59	279	4	279	8
9	279	48	279	52	279	57	280	1	280	6	280	11	280	16
10	280	53	280	58	281	3	281	8	281	13	281	19	281	24
11	281	58	282	4	282	9	282	15	282	20	282	26	282	32
12	283	3	283	9	283	15	283	21	283	27	283	33	283	40
13	284	8	284	14	284	21	284	27	284	34	284	41	284	48
14	285	13	285	19	285	27	285	33	285	41	285	48	285	56
15	286	17	286	24	286	32	286	39	286	47	286	55	287	3
16	287	22	287	29	287	38	287	45	287	54	288	2	288	11
17	288	26	288	34	288	43	288	51	289	0	289	9	289	18
18	289	31	289	39	289	48	289	57	290	6	290	15	290	25
19	290	35	290	44	290	53	291	3	291	12	291	22	291	32
20	291	39	291	49	291	58	292	8	292	18	292	29	292	39
21	292	43	292	53	293	3	293	13	293	24	293	35	293	46
22	293	47	293	57	294	8	294	18	294	30	294	41	294	52
23	294	51	295	1	295	13	295	23	295	35	295	47	295	58
24	295	54	296	5	296	17	296	28	296	40	296	53	297	4
25	296	57	297	9	297	21	297	33	297	45	297	58	298	10
26	298	1	298	13	298	25	298	38	298	50	299	3	299	16
27	299	4	299	16	299	29	299	41	299	55	300	8	300	22
28	300	7	300	19	300	33	300	46	300	59	301	13	301	27
29	301	9	301	22	301	36	301	50	302	3	302	18	302	32

AQUARIUS AND PISCES. SOUTH. LATITUDE.

♒	0		1		2		3		4		5		6	
	°	′	°	′	°	′	°	′	°	′	°	′	°	′
0	302	12	302	25	302	39	302	53	303	7	303	22	303	37
1	303	14	303	28	303	42	303	57	304	11	304	26	304	42
2	304	16	304	31	304	45	305	0	305	15	305	30	305	46
3	305	18	305	33	305	48	306	3	306	18	306	34	306	50
4	306	20	306	36	306	51	307	6	307	22	307	38	307	54
5	307	22	307	38	307	54	308	9	308	25	308	42	308	58
6	308	24	308	40	308	56	309	12	309	28	309	44	310	2
7	309	25	309	42	309	58	310	14	310	31	310	48	311	5
8	310	26	310	43	311	0	311	16	311	33	311	51	312	8
9	311	27	311	44	312	1	312	18	312	35	312	53	313	11
10	312	28	312	45	313	2	313	20	313	37	313	55	314	14
11	313	28	313	46	314	3	314	21	314	39	314	57	315	16
12	314	29	314	46	315	4	315	22	315	40	315	59	316	18
13	315	29	315	47	316	5	316	23	316	41	317	0	317	20
14	316	29	316	47	317	6	317	24	317	42	318	1	318	21
15	317	29	317	47	318	6	318	24	318	43	319	2	319	22
16	318	29	318	47	319	6	319	25	319	44	320	3	320	24
17	319	28	319	47	320	6	320	25	320	45	321	4	321	25
18	320	27	320	46	321	6	321	25	321	45	322	5	322	26
19	321	27	321	46	322	6	322	25	322	45	323	6	323	27
20	322	26	322	45	323	5	323	25	323	45	324	6	324	27
21	323	25	323	44	324	4	324	24	324	45	325	6	325	27
22	324	23	324	43	325	3	325	24	325	45	326	6	326	27
23	325	22	325	42	326	2	326	23	326	44	327	5	327	27
24	326	20	326	40	327	1	327	22	327	43	328	4	328	26
25	327	18	327	39	328	0	328	21	328	42	329	3	329	25
26	328	16	328	37	328	58	329	19	329	41	330	2	330	24
27	329	14	329	35	329	56	330	17	330	39	331	1	331	23
28	330	11	330	33	330	54	331	15	331	37	331	59	332	22
29	331	9	331	30	331	52	332	13	332	35	332	57	333	20
♓	332	6	332	28	332	49	333	11	333	33	333	55	334	18
1	333	4	333	25	333	47	334	9	334	31	334	53	335	16
2	334	1	334	22	334	44	335	6	335	29	335	51	336	14
3	334	58	335	19	335	41	336	3	336	26	336	49	337	12
4	335	55	336	16	336	39	337	1	337	24	337	47	338	10
5	336	51	337	13	337	36	337	58	338	21	338	44	339	8
6	337	48	338	10	338	33	338	55	339	18	339	41	340	5
7	338	44	339	7	339	30	339	52	340	15	340	38	341	2
8	339	40	340	4	340	27	340	49	341	12	341	35	341	59
9	340	37	341	0	341	23	341	46	342	9	342	32	342	56
10	341	33	341	56	342	19	342	42	343	6	343	29	343	53
11	342	29	342	52	343	15	343	38	344	2	344	25	344	49
12	343	25	343	48	344	11	344	34	344	58	345	21	345	45
13	344	20	344	44	345	7	345	30	345	54	346	18	346	42
14	345	16	345	40	346	3	346	26	346	50	347	14	347	38
15	346	12	346	35	346	59	347	22	347	46	348	10	348	34
16	347	7	347	31	347	55	348	18	348	42	349	6	349	30
17	348	3	348	27	348	51	349	14	349	38	350	2	350	26
18	348	58	349	22	349	46	350	9	350	33	350	57	351	21
19	349	54	350	18	350	42	351	5	351	29	351	53	352	17
20	350	49	351	13	351	37	352	1	352	25	352	49	353	13
21	351	44	352	8	352	32	352	56	353	20	353	44	354	8
22	352	39	353	3	353	27	353	51	354	15	354	39	355	3
23	353	35	353	58	354	22	354	46	355	10	355	34	355	58
24	354	30	354	53	355	17	355	41	356	5	356	29	356	53
25	355	25	355	48	356	12	356	36	357	0	357	24	357	48
26	356	20	356	43	357	7	357	31	357	55	358	19	358	43
27	357	15	357	38	358	2	358	26	358	50	359	14	359	38
28	358	10	358	33	358	57	359	21	359	45	360	9	360	33
29	359	5	359	28	359	52	360	16	360	40	361	4	361	28

Left margin: ♋ N. Latitude. — ♑ South and ♌ North. — ≈ South and

Right margin: ♊ N. Latitude and ♐ South. — Taurus North and ♏ South.

♋	0° D.	M.	1° D.	M.	2° D.	M.	3° D.	M.	4° D.	M.	5° D.	M.	6° D.	M.	♊
0	23	28	24	28	25	28	26	28	27	28	28	28	29	28	30
1	23	28	24	28	25	28	26	28	27	28	28	28	29	28	29
2	23	27	24	27	25	27	26	27	27	27	28	27	29	27	28
3	23	26	24	26	25	26	26	26	27	26	28	26	29	26	27
4	23	24	24	24	25	24	26	24	27	24	28	24	29	24	26
5	23	22	24	22	25	22	26	22	27	22	28	22	29	22	25
6	23	20	24	20	25	19	26	19	27	19	28	19	29	19	24
7	23	17	24	17	25	16	26	16	27	16	28	16	29	16	23
8	23	14	24	14	25	13	26	13	27	13	28	13	29	13	22
9	23	10	24	10	25	9	26	9	27	9	28	9	29	9	21
10	23	6	24	6	25	5	26	5	27	5	28	5	29	5	20
11	23	1	24	1	25	0	26	0	27	0	28	0	29	0	19
12	22	56	23	56	24	55	25	55	26	55	27	55	28	55	18
13	22	50	23	50	24	49	25	49	26	49	27	49	28	49	17
14	22	44	23	44	24	43	25	43	26	43	27	43	28	42	16
15	22	37	23	37	24	36	25	36	26	36	27	36	28	35	15
16	22	30	23	30	24	29	25	29	26	29	27	28	28	28	14
17	22	23	23	23	24	22	25	22	26	22	27	20	28	19	13
18	22	15	23	15	24	14	25	14	26	14	27	11	28	11	12
19	22	7	23	7	24	6	25	5	26	5	27	3	28	3	11
20	21	58	22	58	23	57	24	56	25	56	26	55	27	53	10
21	21	49	22	49	23	48	24	47	25	46	26	46	27	44	9
22	21	40	22	39	23	38	24	37	25	36	26	36	27	35	8
23	21	30	22	29	23	28	24	27	25	26	26	26	27	25	7
24	21	20	22	18	23	17	24	16	25	15	26	15	27	14	6
25	21	9	22	7	23	6	24	5	25	4	26	4	27	3	5
26	20	58	21	56	22	55	23	54	24	53	25	52	26	51	4
27	20	47	21	44	22	43	23	42	24	41	25	40	26	39	3
28	20	35	21	32	22	31	23	30	24	29	25	18	26	26	2
29	20	23	21	20	22	19	23	18	24	17	25	16	26	14	1
♌	20	10	21	8	22	7	23	5	24	4	25	3	26	0	♉
1	19	57	20	55	21	54	22	52	23	51	24	50	25	48	29
2	19	44	20	42	21	41	22	39	23	37	24	36	25	34	28
3	19	31	20	29	21	27	22	25	23	23	24	22	25	20	27
4	19	17	20	15	21	13	22	11	23	9	24	8	25	6	26
5	19	3	20	1	20	59	21	57	22	55	23	53	24	51	25
6	18	48	19	46	20	44	21	42	22	40	23	38	24	36	24
7	18	33	19	31	20	29	21	27	22	25	23	23	24	21	23
8	18	18	19	15	20	13	21	11	22	9	23	7	24	5	22
9	18	2	18	59	19	57	20	55	21	53	22	51	23	49	21
10	17	46	18	43	19	41	20	38	21	36	22	34	23	31	20
11	17	29	18	26	19	24	20	22	21	19	22	17	23	14	19
12	17	13	18	9	19	7	20	5	21	2	22	0	22	57	18
13	16	56	17	52	18	50	19	48	20	44	21	42	22	39	17
14	16	39	17	35	18	33	19	30	20	27	21	25	22	22	16
15	16	21	17	18	18	15	19	12	20	9	21	7	22	4	15
16	16	3	17	0	17	57	18	54	19	51	20	49	21	46	14
17	15	45	16	42	17	39	18	36	19	33	20	30	21	27	13
18	15	27	16	23	17	20	18	17	19	14	20	11	21	8	12
19	15	9	16	4	17	1	17	58	18	55	19	52	20	49	11
20	14	50	15	45	16	41	17	38	18	35	19	32	20	29	10
21	14	31	15	26	16	22	17	19	18	16	19	13	20	10	9
22	14	11	15	7	16	3	17	0	17	56	18	53	19	50	8
23	13	52	14	47	15	43	16	40	17	36	18	33	19	29	7
24	13	32	14	27	15	23	16	19	17	15	18	12	19	8	6
25	13	12	14	7	15	3	16	0	16	56	17	53	18	49	5
26	12	52	13	47	14	43	15	39	16	35	17	32	18	28	4
27	12	32	13	27	14	23	15	19	16	15	17	12	18	8	3
28	12	11	13	6	14	2	14	58	15	54	16	51	17	47	2
29	11	50	12	45	13	41	14	37	15	33	16	30	17	26	1
30	11	29	12	24	13	20	14	16	15	12	16	8	17	4	0
♌	0°		1°		2°		3°		4°		5°		6°		♉

Left margin (top to bottom): *♓ South and Virgo North.* ／ *♈ South and ♎ North.*

Right margin: *Aries North and ♎ South.* ／ *North Pisces and Virgo South.* ／ *South Pisces and Virgo North.*

♍	0°		1°		2°		3°		4°		5°		6°		♈
	D.	M.	D.	M.	D.	M.	D.	M.	D.	M.	D.	M.	D.	M.	
0	11	29	12	24	13	20	14	16	15	12	16	8	17	4	30
1	11	8	12	4	13	0	13	56	14	51	15	47	16	43	29
2	10	46	11	42	12	38	13	33	14	29	15	25	16	21	28
3	10	25	11	21	12	17	13	12	14	7	15	4	16	0	27
4	10	3	10	59	11	55	12	51	13	46	14	43	15	39	26
5	9	41	10	39	11	35	12	30	13	24	14	22	15	17	25
6	9	19	10	15	11	11	12	6	13	2	13	58	14	54	24
7	8	57	9	53	10	49	11	44	12	40	13	35	14	31	23
8	8	35	9	31	10	27	11	22	12	18	13	13	14	9	22
9	8	12	9	8	10	4	10	59	11	54	12	49	13	45	21
10	7	50	8	46	9	41	10	36	11	31	12	26	13	21	20
11	7	27	8	22	9	17	10	12	11	8	12	3	12	57	19
12	7	4	8	0	8	55	9	50	10	45	11	40	12	34	18
13	6	41	7	37	8	31	9	26	10	21	11	16	12	11	17
14	6	18	7	14	8	8	9	3	9	58	10	53	11	48	16
15	5	55	6	51	7	46	8	41	9	46	10	30	11	26	15
16	5	32	6	28	7	23	8	18	9	13	10	7	11	3	14
17	5	8	6	4	6	59	7	54	8	49	9	44	10	39	13
18	4	45	5	41	6	36	7	31	8	26	9	21	10	16	12
19	4	21	5	17	6	12	7	7	8	2	8	57	9	52	11
20	3	58	4	54	5	49	6	44	7	39	8	34	9	29	10
21	3	34	4	30	5	25	6	20	7	15	8	10	9	5	9
22	3	11	4	7	5	2	5	57	6	52	7	47	8	42	8
23	2	47	3	43	4	38	5	33	6	28	7	23	8	18	7
24	2	23	3	19	4	14	5	9	6	4	6	59	7	54	6
25	2	0	2	55	3	50	4	45	5	40	6	35	7	30	5
26	1	36	2	21	3	26	4	21	5	16	6	11	7	6	4
27	1	12	2	7	3	2	3	57	4	52	5	47	6	42	3
28	0	48	1	43	2	43	3	38	4	33	5	23	6	18	2
29	0	24	1	19	2	14	3	9	4	4	4	59	5	54	1
♎	0	0	0	55	1	50	2	45	3	40	4	35	5	30	♈
1	0	24	0	31	1	27	2	21	3	16	4	11	5	6	29
2	0	48	0	7	1	3	1	57	2	52	3	47	4	42	28
3	1	12	0	17	0	39	1	34	2	29	3	24	4	19	27
4	1	36	0	41	0	15	1	10	2	5	3	0	3	55	26
5	2	0	1	5	0	10	0	46	1	41	2	36	3	31	25
6	2	23	1	28	0	33	0	22	1	17	2	12	3	7	24
7	2	47	1	52	0	57	0	2	0	53	1	48	2	43	23
8	3	11	2	16	1	21	0	26	0	29	1	25	2	20	22
9	3	34	2	39	1	44	0	49	0	6	1	2	1	57	21
10	3	58	3	3	2	8	1	13	0	18	0	38	1	33	20
11	4	21	3	26	2	31	1	36	0	41	0	14	1	9	19
12	4	45	3	50	2	55	2	0	1	5	0	10	0	46	18
13	5	8	4	13	3	18	2	23	1	28	0	33	0	24	17
14	5	32	4	37	3	42	2	46	1	51	0	56	0	0	16
15	5	55	5	0	4	5	3	9	2	14	1	18	0	23	15
16	6	18	5	23	4	27	3	31	2	36	1	40	0	45	14
17	6	41	5	45	4	50	3	54	2	59	2	3	1	8	13
18	7	5	6	8	5	14	4	18	3	23	2	27	1	32	12
19	7	27	6	31	5	36	4	40	3	45	2	49	1	54	11
20	7	50	6	54	5	58	5	2	4	6	3	10	2	15	10
21	8	12	7	16	6	20	5	24	4	28	3	32	2	37	9
22	8	35	7	39	6	43	5	47	4	51	3	56	3	0	8
23	8	57	8	1	7	5	6	9	5	13	4	18	3	22	7
24	9	19	8	23	7	27	6	31	5	35	4	40	3	45	6
25	9	41	8	45	7	49	6	53	5	58	5	2	4	6	5
26	10	3	9	7	8	11	7	15	6	19	5	24	4	28	4
27	10	25	9	29	8	34	7	38	6	42	5	46	4	50	3
28	10	46	9	51	8	56	8	1	7	4	6	8	5	12	2
29	11	8	10	13	9	17	8	21	7	24	6	28	5	32	1
30	11	29	10	33	9	37	8	41	7	44	6	48	5	52	0
♎	0°		1°		2°		3°		4°		5°		6°		♓

Left margin (vertical): Cancer South. — Capricorn North — Aquarius North and Leo South.

Right margin (vertical): Gemini South and Sagitary North. — Taurus South and Scorpio North.

♋	0°		1°		2°		3°		4°		5°		6°		♊
	D.	M.	D.	M.	D.	M.	D.	M.	D.	M.	D.	M.	D.	M.	
0	23	28	22	28	21	28	20	28	19	28	18	28	17	28	30
1	23	28	22	28	21	28	20	28	19	28	18	28	17	28	29
2	23	27	22	27	21	27	20	27	19	27	18	27	17	27	28
3	23	26	22	26	21	26	20	26	19	26	18	26	17	26	27
4	23	24	22	24	21	24	20	24	19	24	18	24	17	24	26
5	23	22	22	22	21	22	20	22	19	22	18	22	17	22	25
6	23	20	22	19	21	19	20	19	19	19	18	19	17	19	24
7	23	17	22	16	21	16	20	16	19	16	18	16	17	16	23
8	23	13	22	13	21	13	20	13	19	13	18	13	17	13	22
9	23	10	22	9	21	9	20	9	19	9	18	9	17	9	21
10	23	5	22	5	21	5	20	5	19	5	18	5	17	5	20
11	23	1	22	1	21	1	20	1	19	2	18	2	17	2	19
12	22	56	21	56	20	56	20	56	18	57	18	57	16	57	18
13	22	50	21	50	20	50	19	50	18	51	17	51	16	51	17
14	22	44	21	44	20	44	19	44	18	45	17	45	16	45	16
15	22	37	21	37	20	38	19	37	18	38	17	38	16	38	15
16	22	30	21	31	20	31	19	32	18	32	17	33	16	33	14
17	22	23	21	24	20	25	19	25	18	26	17	26	16	26	13
18	22	15	21	16	20	17	19	18	18	19	17	19	16	19	12
19	22	7	21	8	20	9	19	10	18	11	17	11	16	11	11
20	21	58	20	59	20	0	19	1	18	2	17	2	16	2	10
21	21	49	20	50	19	51	18	52	17	53	16	53	15	54	9
22	21	40	20	41	19	42	18	43	17	44	16	43	15	44	8
23	21	30	20	31	19	32	18	33	17	34	16	34	15	35	7
24	21	20	20	21	19	22	18	23	17	23	16	24	15	25	6
25	21	9	20	10	19	11	18	12	17	12	16	14	15	15	5
26	20	58	19	59	19	0	18	1	17	1	16	3	15	4	4
27	20	47	19	47	18	49	17	50	16	50	15	52	14	53	3
28	20	35	19	36	18	37	17	38	16	39	15	41	14	42	2
29	20	23	19	24	18	25	17	26	16	27	15	29	14	30	1
♌	20	10	19	11	18	12	17	14	16	15	15	16	14	18	♉
1	19	57	18	58	17	59	17	1	16	2	15	4	14	6	29
2	19	44	18	45	17	47	16	48	15	49	14	51	13	53	28
3	19	31	18	33	17	34	16	36	15	37	14	38	13	40	27
4	19	17	18	19	17	20	16	22	15	24	14	25	13	27	26
5	19	2	18	4	17	6	16	8	15	10	14	11	13	13	25
6	18	48	17	50	16	52	15	53	14	55	13	56	12	59	24
7	18	33	17	35	16	37	15	38	14	40	13	41	12	44	23
8	18	18	17	19	16	22	15	23	14	25	13	26	12	29	22
9	18	2	17	4	16	6	15	8	14	10	13	11	12	15	21
10	17	46	16	48	15	50	14	52	13	54	12	56	11	59	20
11	17	29	16	31	15	33	14	36	13	38	12	40	11	43	19
12	17	13	16	15	15	17	14	20	13	22	12	24	11	27	18
13	16	56	15	58	15	1	14	3	13	6	12	8	11	11	17
14	16	39	15	41	14	44	13	46	12	49	11	51	10	54	16
15	16	21	15	23	14	26	13	29	12	32	11	34	10	37	15
16	16	3	15	5	14	8	13	11	12	14	11	16	10	19	14
17	15	45	14	47	13	51	12	53	11	56	10	58	10	1	13
18	15	27	14	30	13	33	12	36	11	39	10	41	9	44	12
19	15	9	14	12	13	15	12	18	11	21	10	23	9	26	11
20	14	50	13	53	12	56	11	59	11	2	10	5	9	8	10
21	14	31	13	34	12	37	11	40	10	43	9	46	8	49	9
22	14	11	13	14	12	17	11	21	10	24	9	27	8	29	8
23	13	52	12	56	11	58	11	2	10	5	9	8	8	10	7
24	13	32	12	36	11	39	10	42	9	46	8	49	7	51	6
25	13	12	12	16	11	19	10	22	9	26	8	29	7	32	5
26	12	52	11	56	10	59	10	2	9	6	8	9	7	12	4
27	12	32	11	36	10	39	9	42	8	46	7	49	6	52	3
28	12	11	11	15	10	18	9	22	8	26	7	29	6	32	2
29	11	50	10	54	9	58	9	2	8	6	7	9	6	12	1
30	11	29	10	33	9	37	8	41	7	45	6	49	5	53	0
♒	0°		1°		2°		3°		4°		5°		6°		♏

AND SEMI-DIURNAL AND SEMI-NOCTURNAL ARCS.

For the Latitude of Sheffield.

	Ascen. Difference Pole 53 N. 25.			Semiarcs for 53 N. 25.			
Degrees.	Aries and Libra.	Taurus and Scorpio.	Gemini and Sagitary	Semid. ♈ Semin. ♎	Semid. ♉ Semin. ♏	Semid. ♊ Semin. ♐	Degrees.
	° ′	° ′	° ′	° ′	° ′	° ′	
0	0 0	15 53	29 39	90 0	105 53	119 39	30
1	0 32	16 24	30 1	90 32	106 24	120 1	29
2	1 5	16 55	30 23	91 5	106 55	120 23	28
3	1 37	17 26	30 44	91 37	107 26	120 44	27
4	2 19	17 56	31 5	92 9	107 56	121 5	26
5	2 41	18 26	31 25	92 41	108 26	121 25	25
6	3 13	18 56	31 45	93 13	108 56	121 45	24
7	3 45	19 26	32 4	93 45	109 26	122 4	23
8	4 17	19 55	32 22	94 17	109 55	122 22	22
9	4 49	20 25	32 39	94 49	110 25	122 39	21
10	5 21	20 54	32 57	95 21	110 54	122 56	20
11	5 53	21 23	33 12	95 53	111 23	123 12	19
12	6 25	21 52	33 27	96 25	111 52	123 27	18
13	6 57	22 21	33 41	96 57	112 21	123 41	17
14	7 29	22 49	33 55	97 29	112 49	123 55	16
15	8 1	23 17	34 9	98 1	113 17	124 9	15
16	8 33	23 45	34 22	98 33	113 45	124 22	14
17	9 5	24 13	34 34	99 5	114 13	124 34	13
18	9 37	24 41	34 45	99 37	114 41	124 45	12
19	10 9	25 8	34 55	100 9	115 8	124 55	11
20	10 41	25 35	35 4	100 41	115 35	125 4	10
21	11 12	26 1	35 12	101 12	116 1	125 12	9
22	11 44	26 26	35 19	101 44	116 26	125 19	8
23	12 15	26 52	35 25	102 15	116 52	125 25	7
24	12 46	27 17	35 31	102 46	117 17	125 31	6
25	13 18	27 42	35 36	103 18	117 42	125 36	5
26	13 49	28 7	35 40	103 49	118 7	125 40	4
27	14 20	28 31	35 43	104 20	118 31	125 43	3
28	14 51	28 54	35 46	104 51	118 54	125 46	2
29	15 22	29 17	35 48	105 22	119 17	125 48	1
30	15 53	29 39	35 49	105 53	119 39	125 49	0
Degrees.	Virgo and Pisces.	Leo and Aquarius	Cancer and Capricor	Semid. ♍ Semin. ♓	Semid. ♌ Semin. ♒	Semid. ♋ Semin. ♑	Degrees.

USE OF THE TABLES.—By having the Ascensional Difference of a Planet we have only to *add* that A. D. to the Planet's Right Ascension, if *south*, or if it has *north* latitude, *subtract*, according to the 93rd Problem, to find the Planet's Oblique Ascension or Oblique Descension under the latitude of 53 N. 25.

2nd. By having the Ascensional Difference of the Planets in any latitude, we have to work by Problems 85 and 86, to find the Planets' Semi-diurnal and Semi-nocturnal Arcs. If Students would form their own Tables by this method, they would find the plan to facilitate their calculations. (See page 407 for the Latitude of Sheffield.)

For finding the Oblique Ascensions and the Oblique Descensions of the Planets.

LATITUDE, OR POLAR ELEVATION.

Dec.	1° D	1° M	3° D	3° M	5° D	5° M	7° D	7° M	9° D	9° M	11° D	11° M	13° D	13° M	15° D	15° M	17° D	17° M	19° D	19° M	21° D	21° M
1	0	1	0	3	0	5	0	7	0	9	0	12	0	14	0	16	0	18	0	21	0	23
2	0	2	0	6	0	10	0	15	0	19	0	23	0	28	0	32	0	37	0	42	0	46
3	0	3	0	9	0	16	0	22	0	29	0	35	0	42	0	48	0	54	1	2	1	9
4	0	4	0	13	0	21	0	30	0	38	0	46	0	56	1	4	1	14	1	23	1	32
5	0	5	0	16	0	26	0	37	0	48	0	58	1	9	1	21	1	32	1	44	1	55
6	0	6	0	19	0	32	0	44	0	57	1	10	1	23	1	37	1	50	2	4	2	19
7	0	7	0	22	0	37	0	52	1	7	1	22	1	37	1	53	2	9	2	25	2	42
8	0	8	0	25	0	42	0	59	1	16	1	34	1	52	2	9	2	28	2	46	3	6
9	0	9	0	29	0	48	1	7	1	26	1	46	2	6	2	26	2	47	3	8	3	29
10	0	11	0	32	0	53	1	14	1	36	1	58	2	20	2	42	3	5	3	29	3	53
11	0	12	0	35	0	58	1	22	1	46	2	10	2	34	2	59	3	24	3	50	4	17
12	0	13	0	38	1	4	1	30	1	56	2	22	2	49	3	16	3	44	4	12	4	41
13	0	14	0	42	1	9	1	37	2	6	2	34	3	3	3	33	4	3	4	34	5	5
14	0	15	0	45	1	15	1	45	2	16	2	47	3	18	3	50	4	22	4	56	5	30
15	0	16	0	48	1	21	1	53	2	26	2	59	3	33	4	7	4	42	5	18	5	54
16	0	17	0	52	1	26	2	1	2	36	3	12	3	48	4	24	5	2	5	40	6	19
17	0	18	0	55	1	32	2	9	2	47	3	24	4	3	4	42	5	22	6	2	6	44
18	0	19	0	59	1	38	2	17	2	57	3	37	4	18	5	0	5	42	6	25	7	10
19	0	20	1	2	1	44	2	25	3	8	3	50	4	34	5	18	6	3	6	48	7	36
20	0	22	1	6	1	49	2	33	3	18	4	3	4	49	5	36	6	24	7	12	8	2
21	0	23	1	9	1	55	2	41	3	29	4	17	5	5	5	54	6	45	7	36	8	28
22	0	24	1	13	2	2	2	50	3	40	4	30	5	24	6	13	7	6	8	0	8	55
23	0	25	1	17	2	8	2	59	3	51	4	44	5	37	6	32	7	27	8	24	9	22
24	0	27	1	20	2	14	3	8	4	3	4	58	5	54	6	51	7	49	8	49	9	50
25	0	28	1	24	2	20	3	17	4	14	5	12	6	11	7	11	8	12	9	14	10	19
26	0	29	1	28	2	27	3	26	4	26	5	26	6	28	7	31	8	35	9	40	10	47
27	0	31	1	32	2	33	3	35	4	38	5	41	6	45	7	51	8	58	10	6	11	17
28	0	32	1	36	2	40	3	45	4	50	5	56	7	3	8	11	9	21	10	33	11	47

Dec.	2° D	2° M	4° D	4° M	6° D	6° M	8° D	8° M	10° D	10° M	12° D	12° M	14° D	14° M	16° D	16° M	18° D	18° M	20° D	20° M	22° D	22° M
1	0	2	0	4	0	6	0	8	0	10	0	13	0	15	0	17	0	19	0	22	0	24
2	0	4	0	8	0	13	0	17	0	21	0	25	0	30	0	34	0	39	0	44	0	49
3	0	6	0	13	0	19	0	25	0	31	0	38	0	45	0	52	0	59	1	6	1	13
4	0	8	0	17	0	25	0	34	0	42	0	51	1	0	1	9	1	18	1	27	1	37
5	0	10	0	21	0	32	0	42	0	53	1	4	1	15	1	26	1	38	1	49	2	2
6	0	13	0	25	0	38	0	51	1	4	1	17	1	30	1	44	1	57	2	12	2	26
7	0	15	0	30	0	44	0	59	1	14	1	30	1	45	2	1	2	17	2	34	2	51
8	0	17	0	34	0	51	1	8	1	25	1	43	2	0	2	19	2	37	2	56	3	15
9	0	19	0	38	0	57	1	16	1	36	1	56	2	16	2	36	2	57	3	18	3	40
10	0	21	0	42	1	4	1	25	1	47	2	9	2	31	2	54	3	17	3	41	4	5
11	0	23	0	47	1	10	1	34	1	58	2	22	2	47	3	12	3	37	4	3	4	30
12	0	25	0	51	1	17	1	43	2	9	2	35	3	2	3	30	3	58	4	26	4	56
13	0	28	0	56	1	23	1	52	2	20	2	49	3	18	3	48	4	18	4	49	5	21
14	0	30	1	0	1	30	2	1	2	31	3	2	3	34	4	6	4	39	5	12	5	47
15	0	32	1	4	1	37	2	10	2	42	3	16	3	50	4	24	5	0	5	36	6	13
16	0	34	1	9	1	44	2	19	2	54	3	30	4	6	4	43	5	21	5	59	6	39
17	0	37	1	14	1	50	2	28	3	5	3	44	4	22	5	2	5	42	6	23	7	6
18	0	39	1	18	1	57	2	37	3	17	3	58	4	39	5	21	6	4	6	47	7	33
19	0	41	1	23	2	4	2	46	3	29	4	12	4	55	5	40	6	26	7	12	8	0
20	0	44	1	27	2	12	2	56	3	41	4	26	5	12	5	59	6	48	7	37	8	27
21	0	46	1	32	2	19	3	6	3	53	4	41	5	30	6	19	7	10	8	2	8	55
22	0	49	1	37	2	26	3	15	4	5	4	56	5	47	6	39	7	33	8	27	9	24
23	0	51	1	42	2	33	3	25	4	18	5	11	6	5	6	59	7	56	8	53	9	53
24	0	53	1	47	2	41	3	35	4	30	5	26	6	23	7	20	8	19	9	19	10	22
25	0	56	1	52	2	49	3	45	4	43	5	41	6	41	7	41	8	43	9	46	10	52
26	0	59	1	57	2	56	3	56	4	56	5	57	6	59	8	2	9	7	10	14	11	22
27	1	1	2	3	3	4	4	6	5	9	6	13	7	18	8	24	9	32	10	41	11	53
28	1	4	2	8	3	12	4	17	5	23	6	29	7	37	8	46	9	57	11	9	12	24

For finding the Oblique Ascensions and the Oblique Descensions of the Planets.

LATITUDE, OR POLAR ELEVATION.

Dec.	23° D.	M.	25° D.	M.	27° D.	M.	29° D.	M.	31° D.	M.	33° D.	M.	35° D.	M.	37° D.	M.	39° D.	M.	41° D.	M.
1	0	25	0	28	0	31	0	33	0	36	0	39	0	42	0	45	0	49	0	52
2	0	51	0	56	1	1	1	7	1	12	1	18	1	24	1	31	1	37	1	44
3	1	17	1	24	1	32	1	40	1	48	1	57	2	6	2	16	2	26	2	37
4	1	42	1	52	2	3	2	13	2	24	2	36	2	48	3	1	3	15	3	29
5	2	8	2	20	2	33	2	47	3	1	3	15	3	31	3	47	4	4	4	22
6	2	33	2	49	3	4	3	20	3	37	3	55	4	13	4	33	4	53	5	15
7	2	59	3	17	3	35	3	54	4	14	4	34	4	56	5	19	5	42	6	8
8	3	25	3	45	4	6	4	28	4	51	5	14	5	39	6	5	6	32	7	1
9	3	51	4	14	4	38	5	2	5	28	5	54	6	22	6	51	7	22	7	55
10	4	18	4	43	5	9	5	38	6	5	6	35	7	5	7	38	8	13	8	49
11	4	44	5	12	5	41	6	11	6	42	7	15	7	49	8	25	9	3	9	44
12	5	11	5	41	6	13	6	46	7	20	7	56	8	34	9	13	9	55	10	39
13	5	38	6	11	6	45	7	21	7	58	8	37	9	18	10	1	10	46	11	35
14	6	5	6	41	7	18	7	56	8	37	9	19	10	3	10	50	11	39	12	31
15	6	32	7	11	7	51	8	32	9	16	10	1	10	49	11	39	12	32	13	28
16	6	59	7	41	8	24	9	8	9	55	10	44	11	35	12	29	13	26	14	26
17	7	27	8	12	8	58	9	45	10	35	11	27	12	22	13	19	14	20	15	25
18	7	56	8	43	9	32	10	23	11	16	12	11	13	9	14	10	15	15	16	24
19	8	24	9	14	10	6	11	1	11	56	12	55	13	57	15	2	16	11	17	25
20	8	53	9	46	10	41	11	39	12	38	13	40	14	46	15	55	17	8	18	27
21	9	23	10	19	11	17	12	18	13	20	14	26	15	36	16	49	18	7	19	30
22	9	53	10	52	11	53	12	57	14	3	15	13	16	27	17	44	19	6	20	34
23	10	28	11	25	12	29	13	37	14	47	16	0	17	17	18	39	20	6	21	39
24	10	54	11	59	13	7	14	17	15	31	16	48	18	10	19	36	21	8	22	46
25	11	25	12	34	13	45	14	59	16	16	17	38	19	3	20	34	22	11	23	55
26	11	57	13	9	14	24	15	41	17	2	18	28	19	58	21	34	23	16	25	5
27	12	29	13	45	15	3	16	24	17	50	19	19	20	54	22	35	24	22	26	17
28	13	3	14	21	15	43	17	8	18	38	20	12	21	51	23	37	25	30	27	31

Dec.	24° D.	M.	26° D.	M.	28° D.	M.	30° D.	M.	32° D.	M.	34° D.	M.	36° D.	M.	38° D.	M.	40° D.	M.	42° D.	M.
1	0	27	0	29	0	32	0	35	0	37	0	40	0	44	0	47	0	50	0	54
2	0	53	0	59	1	4	1	9	1	15	1	21	1	27	1	34	1	41	1	48
3	1	20	1	28	1	36	1	44	1	53	2	2	2	11	2	21	2	31	2	42
4	1	47	1	57	2	8	2	19	2	30	2	42	2	55	3	8	3	22	3	37
5	2	14	2	27	2	40	2	54	3	8	3	23	3	39	3	55	4	13	4	31
6	2	41	2	56	3	12	3	29	3	46	4	3	4	23	4	42	5	8	5	26
7	3	8	3	26	3	45	4	4	4	24	4	45	5	7	5	30	5	55	6	21
8	3	35	3	56	4	17	4	39	5	2	5	26	5	52	6	18	5	46	7	16
9	4	3	4	26	4	50	5	15	5	41	6	8	6	37	7	6	7	38	8	12
10	4	30	4	56	5	23	5	51	6	20	6	50	7	22	7	55	8	30	9	8
11	4	58	5	26	5	56	6	27	6	59	7	32	8	7	8	44	9	23	10	5
12	5	26	5	57	6	29	7	3	7	38	8	15	8	53	9	34	10	16	11	2
13	5	54	6	28	7	3	7	40	8	18	8	58	9	39	10	24	11	10	12	0
14	6	22	6	59	7	37	8	17	8	58	9	41	10	26	11	14	12	4	12	58
15	6	51	7	31	8	11	8	54	9	38	10	25	11	14	12	5	13	0	13	58
16	7	20	8	3	8	46	9	32	10	19	11	9	12	2	12	57	13	55	14	58
17	7	49	8	35	9	21	10	10	11	1	11	54	12	50	13	49	14	52	15	59
18	8	19	9	7	9	56	10	49	11	43	12	40	13	39	14	42	15	49	17	1
19	8	49	9	40	10	33	11	28	12	26	13	26	14	29	15	36	16	48	18	4
20	9	19	10	14	11	9	12	8	13	9	14	13	15	20	16	31	17	47	19	8
21	9	50	10	47	11	46	12	48	13	53	15	0	16	12	17	27	18	48	20	13
22	10	22	11	22	12	24	13	29	14	37	15	49	17	5	18	24	19	50	21	20
23	10	54	11	57	13	3	14	11	15	23	16	38	17	58	19	22	20	52	22	28
24	11	26	12	33	13	42	14	54	16	9	17	29	18	52	20	21	21	56	23	38
25	11	59	13	9	14	21	15	37	16	57	18	20	19	48	21	21	23	1	24	50
26	12	33	13	46	15	2	16	21	17	45	19	12	20	45	22	24	24	10	26	3
27	13	7	14	23	15	43	17	6	18	34	20	6	21	44	23	28	25	19	27	18
28	13	42	15	2	16	25	17	53	19	24	21	1	22	44	24	33	26	30	28	36

For finding the Oblique Ascensions and the Oblique Descensions of the Planets.

LATITUDE, OR POLAR ELEVATION.

Dec.	43°		45°		47°		49°		51°		53°		55°		57°		59°	
	D.	M.	D.	M.	D.	M.	D.	M.	D.	M.	D.	M.	D.	M.	D.	M.	D.	M.
1	0	56	1	0	1	4	1	9	1	14	1	20	1	26	1	32	1	40
2	1	52	2	0	2	9	2	18	2	28	2	39	2	52	3	5	3	20
3	2	48	3	0	3	13	3	27	3	43	3	59	4	18	4	38	5	0
4	3	44	4	1	4	18	4	37	4	57	5	19	5	44	6	11	6	41
5	4	41	5	1	5	23	5	47	6	12	6	40	7	11	7	44	8	22
6	5	37	6	2	6	28	6	57	7	27	8	1	8	38	9	19	10	4
7	6	34	7	3	7	34	8	7	8	43	9	23	10	6	10	54	11	47
8	7	32	8	5	8	40	9	18	10	0	10	45	11	35	12	30	13	31
9	8	30	9	7	9	47	10	30	11	17	12	8	13	4	14	7	15	17
10	9	28	10	9	10	54	11	42	12	35	13	32	14	35	15	45	17	4
11	10	27	11	12	12	1	12	55	13	53	14	57	16	7	17	25	18	53
12	11	26	12	16	13	11	14	9	15	13	16	23	17	40	19	6	20	43
13	12	26	13	21	14	20	15	24	16	34	17	50	19	15	20	50	22	36
14	13	27	14	26	15	30	16	40	17	56	19	19	20	52	22	35	24	31
15	14	28	15	32	16	42	17	57	19	19	20	50	22	30	24	22	26	29
16	15	31	16	40	17	54	19	16	20	44	22	22	24	10	26	12	28	30
17	16	34	17	48	19	8	20	36	22	11	23	56	25	53	28	5	30	35
18	17	38	18	58	20	23	21	57	23	39	25	35	27	39	30	1	32	44
19	18	44	20	9	21	40	23	18	25	10	27	11	29	27	32	1	34	58
20	19	51	21	21	22	58	24	45	26	43	28	53	31	19	34	5	37	17
21	20	59	22	34	24	13	26	12	28	18	30	37	33	15	36	14	39	42
22	22	8	23	50	25	40	27	42	29	56	32	25	35	14	38	28	42	15
23	23	19	25	7	27	5	29	14	31	43	34	17	37	19	40	49	44	57
24	24	32	26	26	28	31	30	48	33	32	36	13	39	29	43	17	47	49
25	25	47	27	48	30	0	32	26	35	21	38	14	41	45	45	54	50	54
26	27	3	29	11	31	32	34	8	37	10	40	20	44	9	48	41	54	16
27	28	22	30	38	33	7	35	53	39	0	42	33	46	41	51	41	58	1
28	29	44	32	7	34	46	37	43	41	2	44	53	49	24	54	58	62	14

Dec.	44°		46°		48°		50°		52°		54°		56°		58°		60°	
1	0	58	1	2	1	7	1	12	1	17	1	23	1	29	1	36	1	44
2	1	56	2	4	2	13	2	23	2	34	2	45	2	58	3	12	3	28
3	2	54	3	7	3	20	3	35	3	51	4	8	4	27	4	48	5	13
4	3	52	4	9	4	27	4	47	5	8	5	31	5	57	6	25	6	57
5	4	51	5	12	5	35	5	59	6	26	6	55	7	27	8	3	8	42
6	5	50	6	15	6	42	7	12	7	44	8	19	8	58	9	40	10	28
7	6	49	7	18	7	50	8	25	9	2	9	44	10	29	11	20	12	17
8	7	48	8	22	8	59	9	38	10	22	11	9	12	2	13	0	14	5
9	8	48	9	26	10	8	10	53	11	42	12	35	14	35	14	41	15	55
10	9	48	10	31	11	18	12	8	13	2	14	3	16	9	16	23	17	47
11	10	49	11	57	12	28	13	24	14	24	15	31	18	45	18	8	19	41
12	11	51	12	43	13	39	14	40	15	49	17	0	19	22	19	53	21	36
13	12	53	13	50	14	51	15	58	17	11	18	32	20	1	21	41	23	34
14	13	56	14	58	16	5	17	17	18	37	20	4	21	42	23	3	25	35
15	14	0	16	7	17	19	18	37	20	4	21	38	23	24	25	23	27	39
16	16	5	17	16	18	34	19	59	21	32	23	15	25	9	27	19	29	47
17	17	10	18	27	19	51	21	22	23	2	24	53	26	57	29	18	31	59
18	18	17	19	40	21	9	22	47	24	34	26	34	28	48	31	10	34	19
19	19	25	20	53	22	29	24	14	26	9	28	17	30	41	33	26	36	37
20	20	35	22	8	23	51	25	42	27	46	30	4	32	36	35	37	39	5
21	21	46	23	25	25	14	27	14	29	26	31	54	34	41	37	54	41	40
22	22	58	24	44	26	40	28	47	31	8	33	47	36	48	40	17	44	25
23	24	12	26	5	28	8	30	23	32	54	35	45	39	0	42	47	47	20
24	25	28	27	27	29	38	32	3	34	34	37	48	41	18	45	26	50	27
25	26	46	28	52	31	12	33	46	36	39	39	59	43	48	48	16	53	52
26	28	6	30	20	32	48	35	32	38	38	42	10	46	18	51	19	57	39
27	29	29	31	51	34	28	37	23	40	42	44	32	49	4	54	38	61	57
28	30	54	33	25	36	12	39	19	42	53	47	2	52	1	59	19	67	4

FOR FINDING THE ASCENSIONAL DIFFERENCE.

Degrees.	Declina. Aries and Libra.		Tangent.	Declina. Taurus and Scorpio.		Tangent.	Declina. Gemini and Sagitary		Tangent.	Degrees.
	D.	M.		D.	M.		D.	M.		
0	0	0		11	29	9,30782	20	10	9,56498	30
1	0	24	7,84395	11	50	,32122	20	23	,57004	29
2	0	48	8,14500	12	11	,33426	20	35	,57466	28
3	1	12	8,32112	12	31	,34635	20	47	,57925	27
4	1	36	8,44611	12	52	,35873	20	58	,58342	26
5	2	0	8,54308	13	12	,37023	21	9	,58757	25
6	2	24	8,62234	13	32	,38147	21	20	,59168	24
7	2	47	8,68678	13	52	,39245	21	30	,5?540	23
8	3	11	8,74521	14	11	,40266	21	40	,59909	22
9	3	34	8.79470	14	31	,41318	21	49	,602i0	21
10	3	58	8,84100	14	50	,42297	21	58	,60568	20
11	4	21	8,88120	15	9	,43258	22	7	,608?5	19
12	4	45	8,91957	15	27	,44151	22	15	,61184	18
13	5	8	8,95344	15	45	,45029	22	23	,61472	17
14	5	32	8,98622	16	3	,45893	22	30	,61722	16
15	5	55	9,01550	16	21	,46741	22	37	,61972	15
16	6	18	,04297	16	39	,47576	22	44	,62221	14
17	6	41	,06885	16	56	,48353	22	50	,62433	13
18	7	4	,09330	17	13	,49118	22	56	,62645	12
19	7	27	.11649	17	29	,49828	23	1	,62820	11
20	7	50	,13854	17	45	,50529	23	6	,62996	10
21	8	12	,15867	18	1	,51221	23	10	,63136	9
22	8	35	,17880	18	17	,51903	23	14	,63275	8
23	8	57	,19725	18	32	,52536	23	17	,63380	7
24	9	19	,21499	18	47	,53161	23	20	,63484	6
25	9	41	,23207	19	2	,53779	23	22	,63553	5
26	10	3	,24853	19	17	,54391	23	24	,63623	4
27	10	25	,26443	19	31	,54955	23	25	,63657	3
28	10	46	,27911	19	44	,55474	23	26	,63692	2
29	11	8	,29402	19	57	,55989	23	27	‘63727	1
30	11	29	,30782	20	10	,56498	23	28	,63761	0
Degrees.	Virgo and Pisces.		Tangent.	Leo and Aquar'us		Tangent.	Cancer and Capricor		Tangent.	Degrees.

USE OF THE TABLE.—The above Table will be found a standing or perpetual Table for finding the ASCENSIONAL DIFFERENCE for every Degree in the Zodiac *without latitude*, and will be very useful to facilitate the calculations of finding the Oblique Ascension and Descension for any Pole or Latitude by *adding* the Tangent of Pole or Birth place, to the standing Tangent of the Declination of every Degree of the Zodiac, according to Problems 45 and 48.

A

PERPETUAL TABLE OF HOUSES

SERVING FOR THE FOLLOWING PLACES.

NAME.	LAT. ° '	LONG. ° '
Sheffield, Liverpool	53 N 26	1 w 36
Doncaster, Rotherham	53 24	1 w 38
Anglesea, Isle	53 18	4 E 2
Athlone, Bawtry	53 26	7 w 52
Beaumaris, Bolton	53 17	4 w 8
Corrib, Lough	53 28	9 w 5
Dublin, Chesterfield	53 21	6 w 17
Galway	53 16	9 w 5
Grimsby, Great	53 32	0 w 5
Hamburgh, Baslow	53 20	10 E 0
Manchester, Bolton	53 29	2 w 4
Mullingar, Roscommon	53 32	7 w 19
Penza	53 17	45 E 8
Phillipstown, Worksop	53 19	7 w 20
Samara, Bakewell	53 18	50 E 10
Slyne Head	53 23	10 w 15
Stargard, Wortley	53 20	15 E 8
Stettin, Maltby	53 25	14 E 35
Tullamore	53 16	7 w 25
Whiston, Tickhill	53 25	1 w 27
Wath, Barnsley	53 26	1 w 24
Warrington, Wakefield	53 26	1 w 20

These Tables will answer very well for any place between 53 degrees 16 min. and 53 degrees 36 minutes of North latitude. The longitude of the place is of very little moment fn reference to the *Table of Houses*, yet the *longitude* must be duly considered when the Planets are reduced to any particular meridian different from that of Greenwich, for which the Geocentric place of the Planets is calculated.

Observe, in the above list, the *second* name in any line has nothing to do with the *longitude* named in the *same* line, and the latitudes are correct within two or three minutes.

NOTE.—MEAN MERIDIAN OF THE TOWN OF SHEFFIELD :—Lat. 53° 27' 11" North, Long. 1° 29' 3" West of Greenwich.

SOL in ARIES and TAURUS.

Time from Noon.	10 ♈	11 ♉	12 ♊	Ascen. ♋		2 ♌	3 ♍
h. m. s.	°	°	°	°	′	°	°
0 0 0	0	10	24	28	13	14	3
0 3 40	1	11	25	28	49	14	4
0 7 20	2	12	26	29	25	15	5
0 11 0	3	13	27	0 ♌ 7		16	6
0 14 41	4	14	28	0	49	17	6
0 18 21	5	15	29	1	28	17	7
0 22 2	6	16	29	2	7	18	8
0 25 42	7	17	♋	2	45	19	9
0 29 23	8	18	1	3	26	19	10
0 33 4	9	19	2	4	4	20	10
0 36 45	10	20	3	4	41	21	11
0 40 26	11	22	4	5	19	22	12
0 44 8	12	23	4	5	58	22	13
0 47 50	13	24	5	6	36	23	14
0 51 32	14	25	6	7	14	24	15
0 55 14	15	26	7	7	53	24	15
0 58 5	16	27	8	8	32	25	16
1 2 40	17	28	8	9	10	26	17
1 6 23	18	29	9	9	47	26	18
1 10 7	19	♊	10	10	25	27	19
1 13 51	20	1	11	11	5	28	20
1 17 35	21	2	12	11	43	29	20
1 21 20	22	3	12	12	22	29	21
1 25 6	23	4	13	13	0	♍	22
1 28 52	24	5	14	13	39	1	23
1 32 38	25	6	15	14	18	2	24
1 36 25	26	7	16	14	56	2	25
1 40 12	27	8	16	15	35	3	26
1 44 0	28	9	17	16	14	4	26
1 47 48	29	10	18	16	53	4	27
1 51 37	♉	11	19	17	32	5	28
1 55 27	1	12	20	18	11	6	29
1 59 17	2	13	21	18	51	7	♎
2 3 8	3	14	21	19	30	8	1
2 6 59	4	15	22	20	9	8	1
2 10 51	5	15	23	20	48	9	2
2 14 44	6	16	24	21	37	10	3
2 18 37	7	17	24	22	7	11	4
2 22 31	8	18	25	22	47	11	5
2 26 25	9	19	26	23	28	12	6
2 30 20	10	20	27	24	8	13	7
2 34 16	11	21	27	24	48	13	8
2 38 13	12	22	28	25	28	14	9
2 42 10	13	23	29	26	8	15	10
2 46 8	14	24	♌	26	48	15	11
2 50 7	15	25	0	27	29	16	11
2 54 7	16	26	1	28	10	17	12
2 58 7	17	27	2	28	51	18	13
3 2 8	18	28	3	29	32	19	14
3 6 9	19	29	4	0 ♍ 13		20	15
3 10 12	20	♋	5	0	54	20	16
3 14 15	21	0	5	1	36	21	17
3 18 19	22	1	6	2	17	22	18
3 22 23	23	2	7	2	59	23	19
3 26 29	24	3	8	3	41	24	20
3 30 35	25	4	8	4	23	25	21
3 34 41	26	5	9	5	5	25	21
3 38 49	27	6	10	5	47	26	22
3 42 57	28	7	11	6	30	27	23
3 47 6	29	8	12	7	12	28	24

SOL in GEMINI and CANCER.

Time from Noon.	10 ♊	11 ♋	12 ♌	Ascen ♍		2 ♍	3 ♎
h. m. s.	°	°	°	°	′	°	°
3 51 15	0	9	12	7	54	28	25
3 55 25	1	10	13	8	37	29	26
3 59 36	2	11	14	9	20	♎	27
4 3 48	3	12	15	10	3	1	28
4 8 0	4	13	16	10	47	1	29
4 12 13	5	14	16	11	30	2	♏
4 16 26	6	15	17	12	13	3	0
4 20 40	7	15	18	12	56	4	1
4 24 55	8	16	19	13	40	5	2
4 29 10	9	17	20	14	24	6	3
4 33 26	10	18	20	15	8	6	4
4 37 22	11	19	21	15	52	7	5
4 41 59	12	20	22	16	36	8	6
4 46 16	13	21	23	17	19	9	7
4 50 34	14	22	24	18	4	10	8
4 54 52	15	23	25	18	49	11	9
4 59 10	16	24	25	19	33	12	10
5 3 29	17	25	26	20	17	12	11
5 7 49	18	26	27	21	1	13	12
5 12 0	19	27	28	21	46	14	13
5 16 29	20	27	28	22	31	15	13
5 20 49	21	28	29	23	16	16	14
5 25 9	22	29	♍	24	0	17	15
5 29 30	23	♌	1	24	45	17	16
5 33 51	24	1	2	25	30	18	17
5 38 12	25	2	3	26	15	19	18
5 42 34	26	3	3	27	0	20	19
5 46 55	27	4	4	27	45	20	20
5 51 17	28	5	5	28	30	21	21
5 55 38	29	6	6	29	15	22	22
6 0 0	♋	7	7	0 ♎ 0		23	23
6 4 22	1	8	8	0	45	24	24
6 8 43	2	9	9	1	30	25	25
6 13 5	3	10	9	2	15	26	26
6 17 26	4	11	10	3	0	27	27
6 21 48	5	11	11	3	45	27	28
6 26 9	6	12	12	4	30	28	29
6 30 30	7	13	13	5	15	29	29
6 34 51	8	14	13	6	0	♏	♐
6 39 11	9	15	14	6	44	1	1
6 43 31	10	16	15	7	29	2	2
6 47 51	11	17	16	8	14	2	3
6 52 11	12	18	17	8	59	3	4
6 56 31	13	19	18	9	43	4	5
7 0 50	14	20	18	10	27	5	6
7 5 8	15	21	19	11	11	5	7
7 9 26	16	22	20	11	56	6	8
7 13 44	17	23	21	12	40	7	9
7 18 1	18	24	22	13	24	8	10
7 22 18	19	25	23	14	8	9	11
7 26 34	20	25	23	14	52	10	12
7 30 50	21	26	24	15	36	10	13
7 35 5	22	27	25	16	20	11	14
7 39 20	23	28	26	17	4	12	14
7 43 34	24	29	27	17	47	13	15
7 47 47	25	♍	28	18	30	14	16
7 52 0	26	1	29	19	13	15	17
7 56 12	27	2	29	19	57	15	18
8 0 24	28	3	♎	20	40	16	19
8 4 35	29	4	1	21	23	17	20

SOL in LEO and VIRGO.

Time from Noon.	10 ♌	11 ♍	12 ♎	Ascen. ♎ °	Ascen. ♎ '	2 ♏	3 ♐
h. m. s.	°	°	°	°	'	°	°
8 8 45	0	5	2	22	6	18	21
8 12 54	1	6	2	22	48	19	22
8 17 3	2	7	3	23	30	19	23
8 21 11	3	8	4	24	12	20	24
8 25 19	4	9	5	24	51	21	25
8 29 26	5	10	6	25	37	22	26
8 33 31	6	10	6	26	19	22	27
8 37 37	7	11	7	27	1	23	28
8 41 41	8	12	8	27	43	24	28
8 45 45	9	13	9	28	24	25	29
8 49 48	10	14	9	29	6	26	♑
8 53 51	11	15	10	29	47	26	1
8 57 52	12	16	11	0♏	28	27	2
9 1 53	13	17	12	1	9	28	3
9 5 53	14	18	13	1	50	29	4
9 9 53	15	18	13	2	31	29	5
9 13 52	16	19	14	3	12	♐	6
9 17 50	17	20	15	3	52	1	7
9 21 47	18	21	16	4	32	2	8
9 25 44	19	22	17	5	12	3	9
9 29 40	20	23	17	5	52	3	10
9 33 35	21	24	18	6	32	4	11
9 37 29	22	25	19	7	13	5	12
9 41 23	23	26	20	7	53	6	13
9 45 16	24	27	21	8	23	7	14
9 49 9	25	28	21	9	12	8	15
9 53 1	26	28	22	9	51	8	16
9 56 52	27	29	23	10	30	9	17
10 0 43	28	♎	24	11	9	10	18
10 4 33	29	1	24	11	48	10	19
10 8 23	♍	2	25	12	27	11	20
10 12 12	1	3	26	13	6	12	21
10 16 0	2	3	26	13	45	13	21
10 19 48	3	4	27	14	24	14	22
10 23 35	4	5	28	15	3	14	23
10 27 22	5	6	29	15	42	15	24
10 31 8	6	7	29	16	21	16	25
10 34 54	7	8	♏	17	0	17	26
10 38 40	8	9	1	17	39	18	27
10 42 25	9	10	2	18	17	19	28
10 46 9	10	10	2	18	55	19	29
10 49 53	11	11	3	19	34	20	♒
10 53 37	12	12	4	20	13	21	1
10 57 20	13	13	4	20	51	22	2
11 1 3	14	14	5	21	30	23	4
11 4 46	15	15	6	22	8	24	5
11 8 28	16	16	6	22	46	24	6
11 12 10	17	17	7	23	24	25	7
11 15 52	18	17	8	24	2	26	8
11 19 34	19	18	9	24	40	27	9
11 23 15	20	19	9	25	19	28	10
11 26 56	21	20	10	25	59	29	11
11 30 37	22	20	11	26	38	29	12
11 34 18	23	21	11	27	15	♑	13
11 37 58	24	22	12	27	53	0	14
11 41 39	25	23	13	28	32	1	15
11 45 19	26	24	13	29	11	2	16
11 49 0	27	25	14	29	53	3	17
11 52 40	28	25	15	0♐	35	4	18
11 56 20	29	26	15	1	11	5	19

SOL in LIBRA and SCORPIO.

Time from Noon.	10 ♎	11 ♎	12 ♏	Ascen. ♐ °	Ascen. ♐ '	2 ♑	3 ♒
h. m. s.	°	°	°	°	'	°	°
12 0 0	0	27	16	1	47	6	21
12 3 40	1	28	17	2	33	7	22
12 7 20	2	29	18	3	11	8	23
12 11 0	3	♏	18	3	49	9	24
12 14 41	4	0	19	4	28	10	25
12 18 21	5	1	20	5	7	10	26
12 22 2	6	2	20	5	47	11	28
12 25 42	7	3	21	6	27	12	29
12 29 23	8	4	22	7	6	13	♓
12 33 4	9	5	22	7	46	14	1
12 36 45	10	6	23	8	26	15	2
12 40 26	11	6	24	9	7	16	3
12 44 8	12	7	25	9	48	17	5
12 47 50	13	8	25	10	29	18	6
12 51 32	14	9	26	11	11	19	7
12 55 14	15	10	27	11	53	20	8
12 58 57	16	10	27	12	35	21	10
13 2 40	17	11	28	13	17	22	11
13 6 23	18	11	29	14	0	23	12
13 10 7	19	12	29	14	43	24	13
13 13 51	20	13	♐	15	27	25	14
13 17 35	21	14	1	16	11	26	15
13 21 20	22	15	2	16	54	27	17
13 25 6	23	16	2	17	38	29	18
13 28 52	24	16	3	18	25	♒	19
13 32 38	25	17	4	19	10	1	20
13 36 25	26	18	5	19	57	2	22
13 40 12	27	19	6	20	43	3	23
13 44 0	28	20	6	21	29	4	24
13 48 48	29	21	7	22	16	6	26
13 51 37	♏	21	8	23	4	7	27
13 55 27	1	22	9	23	53	9	29
13 59 17	2	23	9	24	42	10	♈
14 3 8	3	24	10	25	31	11	1
14 6 59	4	25	11	26	21	13	3
14 10 51	5	26	12	27	13	14	4
14 14 44	6	26	13	28	5	16	6
14 18 37	7	27	13	28	58	17	7
14 22 31	8	28	14	29	51	19	8
14 26 25	9	29	15	0♑	45	20	9
14 30 20	10	♐	16	1	40	21	11
14 34 16	11	1	16	2	36	23	12
14 38 13	12	1	17	3	32	24	13
14 42 10	13	2	18	4	30	26	15
14 46 8	14	3	19	5	28	28	16
14 50 7	15	4	20	6	28	29	18
14 54 7	16	5	21	7	28	♓	19
14 58 7	17	6	22	8	30	2	20
15 2 8	18	7	23	9	33	4	21
15 6 9	19	7	23	10	38	6	23
15 10 12	20	8	24	11	44	8	24
15 14 15	21	9	25	12	52	9	25
15 18 19	22	10	26	14	0	11	27
15 22 23	23	11	27	15	10	13	28
15 26 29	24	12	28	16	21	15	29
15 30 35	25	13	29	17	37	17	♉
15 34 41	26	14	♑	18	53	19	2
15 38 49	27	15	1	20	10	20	3
15 42 57	28	15	2	21	28	22	4
15 47 6	29	16	3	22	50	24	6

SOL in SAGIT. and CAPRICORN.

Time from Noon.	10 ♐	11 ♐	12 ♑	Ascen. ♑		2 ♓	3 ♉
h. m. s.	°	°	°	°	'	°	°
15 51 15	0	17	4	24	13	26	7
15 55 25	1	18	5	25	39	28	8
15 59 36	2	19	6	27	9	29	10
16 3 48	3	20	7	28	40	♈	11
16 8 0	4	21	8	0 ♒	11	2	12
16 12 13	5	22	9	1	48	4	13
16 16 26	6	23	10	3	28	6	14
16 20 40	7	24	11	5	9	9	16
16 24 55	8	25	12	6	55	11	17
16 29 10	9	26	13	8	44	13	18
16 33 26	10	27	14	10	36	15	20
16 37 42	11	28	15	12	31	17	21
16 41 59	12	29	16	14	30	19	22
16 46 16	13	♑	17	16	31	21	24
16 50 34	14	1	19	18	39	23	25
16 54 52	15	2	20	20	49	25	26
16 59 10	16	3	21	23	2	27	27
17 3 29	17	4	22	25	20	28	28
17 7 49	18	5	23	27	41	♉	29
17 12 9	19	6	25	0 ♓	7	2	♊
17 16 29	20	7	26	2	36	3	2
17 20 49	21	8	27	5	9	5	3
17 25 9	22	9	29	7	44	7	4
17 29 30	23	10	♒	10	22	8	5
17 33 51	24	11	1	13	4	10	6
17 38 12	25	12	3	15	51	12	7
17 42 34	26	13	4	18	37	14	8
17 46 55	27	14	5	21	25	16	9
17 51 17	28	15	7	24	14	17	10
17 55 38	29	16	8	27	7	19	11
18 0 0	♑	17	9	0 ♈	0	20	12
18 4 22	1	18	11	2	53	21	14
18 8 43	2	19	13	5	46	23	15
18 13 5	3	20	15	8	35	25	16
18 17 26	4	21	16	11	23	26	17
18 21 48	5	23	18	14	9	27	18
18 26 9	6	24	20	16	56	29	19
18 30 30	7	25	21	19	38	♊	20
18 34 51	8	26	23	22	16	1	21
18 39 11	9	27	24	24	51	2	22
18 43 31	10	28	26	27	24	4	23
18 47 51	11	♒	28	29	53	5	24
18 52 11	12	1	29	2 ♉	19	7	25
18 56 31	13	2	♓	4	40	8	26
19 0 50	14	3	2	6	59	9	27
19 5 8	15	4	4	9	11	10	28
19 9 20	16	5	6	11	21	11	29
19 13 44	17	7	8	13	29	12	♋
19 18 1	18	8	10	15	30	14	1
19 22 18	19	9	12	17	29	15	2
19 26 34	20	10	14	19	24	16	3
19 30 50	21	12	16	21	16	17	4
19 35 5	22	13	18	23	5	18	5
19 39 20	23	14	20	24	51	19	6
10 43 34	24	15	22	26	32	20	7
19 47 47	25	17	24	28	12	21	8
19 52 0	26	18	26	29	49	22	9
19 56 12	27	19	28	1 ♊	20	23	10
20 0 24	28	20	♈	2	51	25	11
20 4 35	29	21	1	4	21	26	12

SOL in AQUARIUS and PISCES

Time from Noon.	10 ♒	11 ♒	12 ♈	Ascen. ♊		2 ♊	3 ♋
h. m. s	°	°	°	°	'	°	°
20 8 45	0	23	3	5	47	26	13
20 12 54	1	24	5	7	10	27	14
20 17 3	2	25	7	8	32	28	14
20 21 11	3	27	9	9	50	29	15
20 25 19	4	28	11	11	7	♋	16
20 29 26	5	29	13	12	23	1	17
20 33 31	6	♓	15	13	39	2	18
20 37 37	7	2	17	14	50	3	19
20 41 41	8	3	18	16	0	4	20
20 45 45	9	4	20	17	8	5	21
20 47 38	10	6	22	18	16	6	22
20 53 51	11	7	24	19	22	7	22
20 57 52	12	9	26	20	27	7	23
21 1 53	13	11	27	21	30	8	24
21 5 53	14	12	29	22	31	9	25
21 9 53	15	13	♉	23	32	10	26
21 13 52	16	14	2	24	32	11	27
21 17 50	17	15	4	25	30	12	27
21 21 47	18	17	6	26	28	12	28
21 25 44	19	18	7	27	24	13	29
21 29 40	20	19	9	28	20	14	♌
21 33 35	21	21	10	29	15	15	1
21 37 29	22	22	11	0 ♋	9	16	2
21 41 23	23	23	13	1	2	16	3
21 45 16	24	25	15	1	55	17	4
21 49 9	25	26	17	2	47	18	5
21 53 1	26	28	18	3	39	19	5
21 56 52	27	29	19	4	29	20	6
22 0 43	28	♈	21	5	18	21	7
22 4 33	29	1	22	6	7	21	8
22 8 23	♓	2	23	6	56	22	9
22 12 12	1	4	24	7	44	23	10
22 16 0	2	5	25	8	31	23	10
22 19 48	3	7	26	9	17	24	11
22 23 35	4	8	27	10	3	25	12
22 27 22	5	9	29	10	50	26	13
22 31 8	6	10	♊	11	35	26	13
22 34 54	7	12	1	12	22	27	14
22 38 40	8	13	2	13	6	28	15
22 42 25	9	14	3	13	49	29	16
22 46 9	10	16	4	14	33	29	17
22 49 53	11	17	5	15	17	♌	18
22 53 37	12	18	7	16	0	1	18
22 57 20	13	20	8	16	43	2	19
23 1 3	14	21	9	17	25	3	20
23 4 46	15	22	10	18	7	4	21
23 8 28	16	23	11	18	49	4	22
23 12 10	17	24	12	19	31	5	23
23 15 52	18	26	13	20	12	6	24
23 19 34	19	27	14	20	53	6	24
23 23 15	20	28	15	21	34	7	25
23 26 56	21	29	16	22	14	8	26
23 30 37	22	♉	17	22	53	8	27
23 34 18	23	1	18	23	33	9	27
23 37 58	24	2	19	24	13	10	28
23 41 39	25	4	20	24	53	11	29
23 45 19	26	5	21	25	32	11	♍
23 49 0	27	6	22	26	11	12	1
23 52 40	28	7	23	26	49	13	2
23 56 20	29	8	24	27	27	13	3

SOL in ARIES and TAURUS.

Time from Noon. h. m. s.	10 ♈	11 ♉	12 ♊	Ascen. ♋	2 ♌	3 ♍
0 0 0	0	9	24	27 51	14	3
0 3 40	1	11	25	28 30	14	4
0 7 20	2	12	26	29 9	15	5
0 11 0	3	13	26	29 48	16	5
0 14 41	4	14	27	0 ♌ 27	16	6
0 18 21	5	15	28	1 6	17	7
0 22 2	6	16	29	1 46	18	8
0 25 42	7	17	♋	2 25	19	9
0 29 23	8	18	1	3 15	19	10
0 33 4	9	19	2	3 43	20	10
0 36 45	10	20	2	4 21	21	11
0 40 26	11	21	3	4 59	21	12
0 44 8	12	22	4	5 38	22	13
0 47 50	13	23	5	6 17	23	14
0 51 32	14	25	6	6 56	23	15
0 55 14	15	26	7	7 34	24	15
0 58 5	16	27	7	8 13	25	16
1 2 40	17	28	8	8 52	26	17
1 6 23	18	29	9	9 30	26	18
1 10 7	19	♊	10	10 9	27	19
1 13 51	20	1	11	10 48	28	20
1 17 35	21	2	11	11 27	28	20
1 21 20	22	3	12	12 5	29	21
1 25 6	23	4	13	12 44	♍	22
1 28 52	24	5	14	13 23	1	23
1 32 38	25	6	14	14 2	1	24
1 36 25	26	7	15	14 41	2	25
1 40 12	27	8	16	15 19	3	26
1 44 0	28	9	17	15 58	4	27
1 47 48	29	9	18	16 38	4	28
1 51 37	♉	10	18	17 17	5	28
1 55 27	1	11	19	17 57	6	29
1 59 17	2	12	20	18 37	7	♎
2 3 8	3	13	21	19 16	7	1
2 6 59	4	14	21	19 55	8	2
2 10 51	5	15	22	20 35	9	2
2 14 44	6	16	23	21 15	10	3
2 18 37	7	17	24	21 55	10	4
2 22 31	8	18	25	22 34	11	5
2 26 25	9	19	25	23 14	12	6
2 30 20	10	20	26	23 55	13	7
2 34 16	11	21	27	24 35	13	8
2 38 13	12	22	28	25 16	14	9
2 42 10	13	23	28	25 57	15	10
2 46 8	14	24	29	26 37	16	10
2 50 7	15	25	♌	27 18	16	11
2 54 7	16	26	1	27 59	17	12
2 58 7	17	27	2	28 40	18	13
3 2 8	18	27	2	29 21	19	14
3 6 9	19	28	3	0 ♍ 3	20	15
3 10 12	20	29	4	0 45	20	16
3 14 15	21	♋	5	1 26	21	17
3 18 19	22	1	6	2 7	22	18
3 22 23	23	2	6	2 49	23	19
3 26 29	24	3	7	3 31	23	20
3 30 35	25	4	8	4 14	24	20
3 34 41	26	5	9	4 56	25	21
3 38 48	27	6	9	5 38	26	22
3 42 57	28	7	10	6 21	27	23
3 47 6	29	8	11	7 4	27	24

SOL in GEMINI and CANCER.

Time from Noon. h. m. s.	10 ♊	11 ♋	12 ♌	Ascen. ♍	2 ♍	3 ♎
3 51 15	0	9	12	7 47	28	25
3 55 25	1	10	13	8 30	29	26
3 59 36	2	10	13	9 13	♎	27
4 3 48	3	11	14	9 57	1	28
4 8 0	4	12	15	10 40	2	29
4 12 13	5	13	16	11 24	2	♏
4 16 26	6	14	17	12 7	3	1
4 20 40	7	15	18	12 50	4	2
4 24 56	8	16	18	13 34	5	3
4 29 10	9	17	19	14 18	6	3
4 33 26	10	18	20	15 2	7	4
4 37 40	11	19	21	15 47	7	5
4 41 55	12	20	22	16 31	8	6
4 46 10	13	21	22	17 15	9	7
4 50 26	14	22	23	18 0	10	8
4 54 42	15	23	24	18 44	11	9
4 59 59	16	24	25	19 29	12	10
5 3 16	17	24	26	20 14	12	11
5 7 34	18	25	27	20 59	13	12
5 12 52	19	26	27	21 44	14	13
5 16 10	20	27	28	22 29	15	14
5 20 29	21	28	29	23 13	16	15
5 25 49	22	29	♍	23 58	17	16
5 29 9	23	♌	1	24 43	17	17
5 33 29	24	1	2	25 29	18	18
5 38 49	25	2	2	26 14	19	19
5 42 9	26	3	3	26 59	20	20
5 46 30	27	4	4	27 44	21	20
5 51 51	28	5	5	28 29	22	21
5 55 12	29	6	6	29 15	22	22
6 0 34	♋	7	7	0 ♎ 0	23	23
6 4 55	1	8	8	0 45	24	24
6 8 17	2	9	8	1 30	25	25
6 13 38	3	10	9	2 26	26	26
6 17 0	4	10	10	3 1	27	27
6 21 22	5	11	11	3 46	28	28
6 26 43	6	12	12	4 31	28	29
6 30 5	7	13	13	5 17	29	♐
6 34 26	8	14	13	6 2	♏	1
6 39 48	9	15	14	6 47	1	2
6 43 9	10	16	15	7 31	2	3
6 47 30	11	17	16	8 16	3	4
6 52 51	12	18	17	9 1	3	5
6 56 11	13	19	18	9 46	4	6
7 0 31	14	20	18	10 31	5	7
7 5 51	15	21	19	11 16	6	7
7 9 11	16	22	20	12 0	7	8
7 13 31	17	23	21	12 44	8	9
7 18 50	18	24	22	13 29	8	10
7 22 8	19	25	23	14 13	9	11
7 26 24	20	26	24	14 58	10	12
7 30 40	21	27	24	15 42	11	13
7 35 5	22	27	25	16 26	12	14
7 39 10	23	28	26	17 12	13	15
7 43 34	24	29	27	17 53	13	16
7 47 57	25	♍	28	18 37	14	17
7 52 0	26	1	28	19 21	15	18
7 56 12	27	2	29	20 4	16	19
8 0 24	28	3	♎	20 48	17	20
8 4 35	29	4	1	21 30	17	20

SOL in LEO and VIRGO.

Time from Noon.	10 ♌	11 ♍	12 ♎	Ascen. ♎		2 ♏	3 ♐
h. m. s.	°	°	°	°	′	°	°
8 8 45	0	5	2	22	13	18	21
8 12 54	1	6	3	22	56	19	22
8 17 3	2	7	3	23	39	20	23
8 21 11	3	8	4	24	22	21	24
8 25 19	4	9	5	25	4	21	25
8 29 26	5	10	6	25	46	22	26
8 33 31	6	10	7	26	29	23	27
8 37 37	7	11	7	27	11	24	28
8 41 41	8	12	8	27	53	24	29
8 45 45	9	13	9	28	44	25	♑
8 49 48	10	14	10	29	16	26	1
8 53 51	11	15	11	29	57	27	2
8 57 52	12	16	11	0♏	39	28	3
9 1 53	13	17	12	1	20	28	3
9 5 53	14	18	13	2	1	29	4
9 9 53	15	19	14	2	42	♐	5
9 13 52	16	20	14	3	23	1	6
9 17 50	17	20	15	4	4	2	7
9 21 47	18	21	16	4	45	2	8
9 25 44	19	22	17	5	25	3	9
9 29 40	20	23	17	6	6	4	10
9 33 35	21	24	18	6	46	5	11
9 37 29	22	25	19	7	26	5	12
9 41 23	23	26	20	8	6	6	13
9 45 16	24	27	20	8	45	7	14
9 49 9	25	28	21	9	25	8	15
9 53 1	26	28	22	10	5	9	16
9 56 52	27	29	23	10	44	9	17
10 0 43	28	♎	23	11	23	10	18
10 4 33	29	1	24	12	3	11	19
10 8 23	♍	2	25	12	43	12	19
10 12 12	1	3	26	13	21	12	20
10 16 0	2	4	26	14	1	13	21
10 19 48	3	4	27	14	40	14	22
10 23 35	4	5	28	15	19	15	23
10 27 22	5	6	29	15	58	16	24
10 31 8	6	7	29	16	37	16	25
10 34 54	7	8	♏	17	17	17	26
10 38 40	8	9	1	17	55	18	27
10 42 25	9	10	2	18	34	19	28
10 46 9	10	10	2	19	12	20	29
10 49 53	11	11	3	19	51	20	≈
10 53 37	12	12	4	20	30	21	1
10 57 20	13	13	4	21	8	22	2
11 1 4	14	14	5	21	47	23	3
11 4 46	15	15	6	22	26	24	4
11 8 28	16	15	7	23	4	24	6
11 12 10	17	16	7	23	43	25	7
11 15 52	18	17	8	24	22	26	8
11 19 34	19	18	9	25	1	27	9
11 23 15	20	19	9	25	38	28	10
11 26 56	21	20	10	26	17	28	11
11 30 37	22	20	10	26	56	29	12
11 34 18	23	21	11	27	35	♑	13
11 37 58	24	22	12	28	14	1	14
11 41 39	25	23	13	28	54	2	15
11 45 19	26	24	14	29	33	3	16
11 49 0	27	25	14	0♐	12	4	17
11 52 40	28	25	15	0	51	4	18
11 56 20	29	26	16	1	30	5	19

SOL in LIBRA and SCORPIO.

Time from Noon.	10 ♎	11 ♎	12 ♏	Ascen. ♐		2 ♑	3 ≈
h. m. s.	°	°	°	°	′	°	°
12 0 0	0	27	16	2	9	6	21
12 3 40	1	28	17	2	49	7	22
12 7 20	2	29	18	3	29	8	23
12 11 0	3	29	19	4	9	9	24
12 14 41	4	♏	19	4	48	10	25
12 18 21	5	1	20	5	27	11	26
12 22 2	6	2	21	6	6	12	27
12 25 42	7	3	21	6	46	13	29
12 29 23	8	4	22	7	24	13	♓
12 33 4	9	4	23	8	10	14	1
12 36 45	10	5	24	8	52	15	2
12 40 26	11	6	24	9	33	16	3
12 44 8	12	7	25	10	13	17	4
12 47 50	13	8	26	10	54	18	6
12 51 32	14	8	26	11	37	19	7
12 55 14	15	9	27	12	20	20	8
12 58 57	16	10	28	13	2	22	9
13 2 40	17	11	29	13	44	23	11
13 6 23	18	12	29	14	28	24	12
13 10 7	19	12	♐	15	11	25	13
13 13 51	20	13	1	15	55	26	14
13 17 35	21	14	1	16	39	27	16
13 21 20	22	15	2	17	23	28	17
13 25 6	23	16	3	18	7	29	18
13 28 52	24	17	4	18	53	≈	19
13 32 38	25	17	4	19	40	2	21
13 36 25	26	18	5	20	26	3	22
13 40 12	27	19	6	21	13	4	23
13 44 0	28	20	7	22	1	5	25
13 47 48	29	21	7	22	48	6	26
13 51 37	♏	22	8	23	36	8	27
13 55 27	1	22	9	24	24	9	28
13 59 17	2	23	10	25	15	10	♈
14 3 8	3	24	11	26	4	12	1
14 6 59	4	25	11	26	54	13	2
14 10 51	5	26	12	27	46	14	4
14 14 44	6	27	13	28	37	16	5
14 18 37	7	27	14	29	31	17	6
14 22 31	8	28	15	0♑	24	19	8
14 26 25	9	29	15	1	19	20	9
14 30 20	10	♐	16	2	14	22	10
14 34 16	11	1	17	3	11	23	12
14 38 13	12	2	18	4	8	25	13
14 42 10	13	2	19	5	6	26	14
14 46 8	14	3	19	6	4	28	16
14 50 7	15	4	20	7	4	29	17
14 54 7	16	5	21	8	6	♓	18
14 58 7	17	6	22	9	7	3	20
15 2 8	18	7	23	10	11	4	21
15 6 9	19	8	24	11	14	6	22
15 10 12	20	9	25	12	23	8	24
15 14 15	21	9	26	13	30	10	25
15 18 19	22	10	26	14	40	11	26
15 22 23	23	11	27	15	51	13	28
15 26 29	24	12	28	17	2	15	29
15 30 35	25	13	29	18	17	17	♉
15 34 41	26	14	♑	19	34	19	2
15 38 49	27	15	1	20	52	20	3
15 42 57	28	16	2	22	10	22	4
15 47 6	29	17	3	23	32	24	6

SOL in SAGIT. and CAPRICORN.

Time from Noon.	10 ♐	11 ♐	12 ♑	Ascen. ♑		2 ♓	3 ♉
h. m. s.	°	°	°	°	′	°	°
15 51 15	0	17	4	24	54	26	7
15 55 25	1	18	5	26	19	28	8
15 59 36	2	19	6	27	50	♈	9
16 3 48	3	20	7	29	23	2	11
16 7 0	4	21	8	0 ♒	57	4	12
16 12 13	5	22	9	2	31	6	13
16 16 26	6	23	10	4	10	7	14
16 20 40	7	24	11	5	49	9	16
16 24 55	8	25	12	7	36	11	17
16 29 10	9	26	13	9	24	13	18
16 33 26	10	27	15	11	17	15	19
16 37 42	11	28	16	13	11	17	21
16 41 59	12	29	17	15	9	19	22
16 46 16	13	♑	18	17	31	21	23
16 50 34	14	1	19	19	14	22	24
16 54 52	15	2	20	21	27	24	25
16 59 10	16	3	22	23	37	26	27
17 3 29	17	4	23	25	54	28	28
17 7 49	18	5	24	28	15	♉	29
17 12 9	19	6	25	0 ♓	39	1	♊
17 16 29	20	7	27	3	5	3	1
17 20 49	21	8	28	5	37	5	2
17 25 9	22	9	29	8	9	7	4
17 29 30	23	10	♒	10	43	8	5
17 33 51	24	11	2	13	29	10	6
17 38 12	25	12	3	16	8	12	7
17 42 34	26	13	5	18	50	13	8
17 46 55	27	14	6	21	43	15	9
17 51 17	28	15	8	24	20	16	10
17 55 38	29	16	9	27	8	18	11
18 0 0	♑	17	11	0 ♈	0	19	13
18 4 22	1	19	12	2	52	21	14
18 8 43	2	20	14	5	40	22	15
18 13 5	3	21	15	8	25	24	16
18 17 26	4	22	17	11	10	25	17
18 21 48	5	23	18	13	52	27	18
18 26 9	6	24	20	16	35	28	19
18 30 30	7	25	22	19	17	29	20
18 34 51	8	26	23	21	51	♊	21
18 39 11	9	28	25	24	33	2	22
18 43 31	10	29	27	26	55	3	23
18 47 51	11	♒	29	29	21	5	24
18 52 11	12	1	♓	1 ♉	45	6	25
18 56 31	13	2	2	4	6	7	26
19 0 50	14	3	4	6	23	8	27
19 5 8	15	5	6	8	33	10	28
19 9 20	16	6	8	10	46	11	29
19 13 44	17	7	9	12	48	12	♋
19 18 1	18	8	11	14	51	13	1
19 22 18	19	9	13	16	49	14	2
19 26 34	20	11	15	18	43	15	3
19 30 50	21	12	17	20	36	17	4
19 35 5	22	13	19	22	24	18	5
19 39 20	23	14	21	24	11	19	6
10 43 34	24	16	23	25	50	20	7
19 47 47	25	17	24	27	24	21	8
19 52 0	26	18	26	29	3	22	9
19 56 12	27	19	28	0 ♊	37	23	10
20 0 24	28	21	♈	2	10	24	11
20 4 35	29	22	2	3	38	25	12

SOL in AQUARIUS and PISCES.

Time from Noon.	10 ♒	11 ♒	12 ♈	Ascen. ♊		2 ♊	3 ♋
h. m. s.	°	°	°	°	′	°	°
20 8 45	0	23	4	5	3	26	13
20 12 54	1	25	6	6	28	27	13
20 17 3	2	26	8	7	49	28	14
20 21 11	3	27	10	9	8	29	15
20 25 19	4	28	11	10	26	♋	16
20 29 26	5	♓	13	11	43	1	17
20 33 31	6	1	15	12	58	2	18
20 37 37	7	2	17	14	9	3	19
20 41 41	8	4	19	15	20	4	20
20 45 45	9	5	20	16	28	4	21
20 47 38	10	6	22	17	37	5	21
20 53 51	11	8	24	18	44	6	22
20 57 52	12	9	26	19	48	7	22
21 1 53	13	10	27	20	52	8	23
21 5 53	14	12	29	21	54	9	24
21 9 53	15	13	♉	22	57	10	25
21 13 52	16	14	2	23	56	11	26
21 17 50	17	16	4	24	54	11	27
21 21 47	18	17	5	25	52	12	28
21 25 44	19	18	7	26	49	13	29
21 29 40	20	20	8	27	46	14	♌
21 33 35	21	21	10	28	41	15	1
21 37 29	22	22	11	29	36	15	1
21 41 23	23	24	13	0 ♋	30	16	2
21 45 16	24	25	14	1	23	17	3
21 49 9	25	26	16	2	14	18	4
21 53 1	26	28	17	3	6	19	4
21 56 52	27	29	18	3	56	19	5
22 0 43	28	♈	20	4	45	20	6
22 4 33	29	2	21	5	36	21	7
22 8 23	♓	3	22	6	24	22	8
22 12 12	1	4	24	7	12	23	9
22 16 0	2	5	25	7	59	23	10
22 19 48	3	7	26	8	47	24	10
22 23 35	4	8	27	9	34	25	11
22 27 22	5	9	28	10	21	26	12
22 31 8	6	11	♊	11	7	26	13
22 34 54	7	12	1	11	53	27	14
22 38 40	8	13	2	12	37	28	15
22 42 25	9	14	3	13	21	29	16
22 46 9	10	16	4	14	5	29	17
22 49 53	11	17	5	14	49	♌	18
22 53 37	12	18	6	15	32	1	18
22 57 20	13	19	7	16	16	1	19
23 1 3	14	21	9	16	59	2	20
23 4 46	15	22	10	17	41	3	21
23 8 28	16	23	11	18	23	4	22
23 12 10	17	24	12	19	4	4	22
23 15 52	18	26	13	19	47	5	23
23 19 34	19	27	14	20	28	6	24
23 23 15	20	28	15	21	8	6	25
23 26 56	21	29	16	21	50	7	26
23 30 37	22	♉	17	22	31	8	27
23 34 18	23	1	17	23	11	9	27
23 37 58	24	3	18	23	52	9	28
23 41 39	25	4	19	24	32	10	29
23 45 19	26	5	20	25	12	11	♍
23 49 0	27	6	21	25	51	11	1
23 52 40	28	7	22	26	31	12	1
23 56 20	29	8	23	27	11	13	2

To Reduce Minutes and Seconds of Time into Degrees and Minutes of Longitude.

Seconds in Time.	Minutes of Arc.		Minutes in Time.	Degrees and Minutes.		Minutes in Time.	Degrees and Minutes.	
''	'	''	'	°	''	'	°	'
4	1	0	1	0	15	31	7	45
8	2	0	2	0	30	32	8	0
12	3	0	3	0	45	33	8	15
16	4	0	4	1	0	34	8	30
20	5	0	5	1	15	35	8	45
24	6	0	6	1	30	36	9	0
28	7	0	7	1	45	37	9	15
32	8	0	8	2	0	38	9	30
36	9	0	9	2	15	39	9	45
40	10	0	10	2	30	40	10	0
44	11	0	11	2	45	41	10	15
48	12	0	12	3	0	42	10	30
52	13	0	13	3	15	43	10	45
56	14	0	14	3	30	44	11	0
60	15	0	15	3	45	45	11	15
			16	4	0	46	11	30
			17	4	15	47	11	45
			18	4	30	48	12	0
			19	4	45	49	12	15
			20	5	0	50	12	30
			21	5	15	51	12	45
			22	5	30	52	13	0
			23	5	45	53	13	15
			24	6	0	54	13	30
			25	6	15	55	13	45
			26	6	30	56	14	0
			27	6	45	57	14	15
			28	7	0	58	14	30
			29	7	15	59	14	45
			30	7	30	60	15	0

SOL in ARIES and TAURUS.

Time from Noon.	10 ♈	11 ♉	12 ♊	Ascen. ♋		2 ♌	3 ♍
h. m.	°	°	°	°	′	°	°
0 0	0	9	22	26	37	12	3
0 4	1	10	23	27	18	13	3
0 7	2	11	24	27	58	14	4
0 11	3	12	25	28	37	15	5
0 15	4	13	25	29	17	15	6
0 18	5	14	26	29	55	16	7
0 22	6	15	27	0 ♌ 34		17	8
0 26	7	16	28	1	14	18	8
0 29	8	17	29	1	55	18	9
0 32	9	18	♋	2	33	19	10
0 36	10	19	1	3	14	20	11
0 40	11	20	1	3	54	20	12
0 44	12	21	2	4	33	21	13
0 48	13	22	3	5	12	22	14
0 51	14	23	4	5	52	23	15
0 55	15	24	5	6	30	23	15
0 59	16	25	6	7	9	24	16
1 3	17	26	6	7	50	25	17
1 6	18	27	7	8	30	26	18
1 10	19	28	8	9	9	26	19
1 14	20	29	9	9	48	27	19
1 18	21	♊	10	10	28	28	20
1 21	22	1	10	11	8	28	21
1 25	23	2	11	11	48	29	22
1 29	24	3	12	12	28	♍	23
1 33	25	4	13	13	8	1	24
1 36	26	5	14	13	48	1	25
1 40	27	6	14	14	28	2	25
1 44	28	7	15	15	8	3	26
1 48	29	8	16	15	48	4	27
1 52	♉	9	17	16	28	4	28
1 55	1	10	18	17	8	5	29
1 59	2	11	19	17	48	6	♎
2 3	3	12	19	18	28	7	1
2 7	4	13	20	19	9	8	2
2 11	5	14	21	19	49	9	3
2 15	6	15	22	20	29	9	3
2 19	7	16	22	21	10	10	4
2 23	8	17	23	21	51	11	5
2 26	9	18	24	22	32	11	6
2 30	10	19	25	23	14	12	7
2 34	11	20	25	23	55	13	8
2 38	12	21	26	24	36	14	9
2 42	13	22	27	25	17	14	10
2 46	14	23	28	25	58	15	11
2 50	15	24	29	26	40	16	12
2 54	16	25	29	27	22	17	12
2 58	17	26	♌	28	4	18	13
3 2	18	26	1	28	46	18	14
3 6	19	27	2	29	28	19	15
3 10	20	28	3	0 ♍ 12		20	16
3 14	21	29	3	0	54	21	17
3 18	22	♋	4	1	36	22	18
3 22	23	1	5	2	20	22	19
3 26	24	2	6	3	2	23	20
3 31	25	3	7	3	45	24	21
3 35	26	4	7	4	28	25	22
3 39	27	5	8	5	11	26	23
3 43	28	6	9	5	54	27	24
3 47	29	7	10	6	28	27	25

SOL in GEMINI and CANCER.

Time from Noon.	10 ♊	11 ♋	12 ♌	Ascen. ♍		2 ♍	3 ♎
h. m.	°	°	°	°	′	°	°
3 51	0	8	11	7	21	28	25
3 55	1	9	12	8	5	29	26
4 0	2	10	12	8	49	♎	27
4 4	3	10	13	9	33	1	28
4 8	4	11	14	10	16	2	29
4 12	5	12	15	11	2	2	♏
4 16	6	13	16	11	46	3	1
4 21	7	14	17	12	30	4	2
4 25	8	15	17	13	15	5	3
4 29	9	16	18	14	0	6	4
4 33	10	17	19	14	45	7	5
4 38	11	18	20	15	30	8	6
4 42	12	19	21	16	15	8	7
4 46	13	20	21	17	0	9	8
4 51	14	21	22	17	45	10	9
4 55	15	22	23	18	30	11	10
4 59	16	23	24	19	16	12	11
5 3	17	24	25	20	3	13	12
5 8	18	25	26	20	49	14	13
5 12	19	25	27	21	35	14	14
5 16	20	26	28	22	20	15	14
5 21	21	27	28	23	6	16	15
5 25	22	28	29	23	51	17	16
5 29	23	29	♍	24	37	18	17
5 34	24	♌	1	25	23	19	18
5 38	25	1	2	26	9	20	19
5 43	26	2	3	26	55	20	20
5 47	27	3	4	27	41	21	21
5 51	28	4	4	28	27	22	22
5 56	29	5	5	29	13	23	23
6 0	♋	6	6	0 ♎ 0		24	24
6 4	1	7	7	0	47	25	25
6 9	2	8	8	1	33	26	26
6 13	3	9	9	2	19	27	27
6 17	4	10	10	3	5	27	28
6 22	5	11	10	3	51	28	29
6 26	6	12	11	4	37	29	♐
6 31	7	13	12	5	23	♏	1
6 35	8	14	13	6	9	1	2
6 39	9	15	14	6	55	2	3
6 44	10	16	15	7	40	2	4
6 48	11	16	16	8	26	3	4
6 52	12	17	16	9	12	4	5
6 57	13	18	17	9	58	5	6
7 1	14	19	18	10	43	6	7
7 5	15	20	19	11	28	7	8
7 9	16	21	20	12	14	8	9
7 14	17	22	21	12	59	8	10
7 18	18	23	22	13	45	9	11
7 22	19	24	22	14	30	10	12
7 27	20	25	23	15	15	11	13
7 31	21	26	24	16	0	12	14
7 35	22	27	25	16	45	13	15
7 40	23	28	26	17	30	13	16
7 44	24	29	27	18	15	14	17
7 48	25	♍	28	18	59	15	18
7 52	26	1	28	19	43	16	19
7 56	27	2	29	20	27	17	20
8 0	28	3	♎	21	11	18	20
8 5	29	4	1	21	56	18	21

SOL in LEO and VIRGO.

Time from Noon.	10 ♌	11 ♍	12 ♎	Ascen. ♎ °	′	2 ♏	3 ♐
h. m.	°	°	°	°	′	°	°
8 9	0	5	2	22	40	19	22
8 13	1	5	3	23	24	20	23
8 17	2	6	3	24	7	21	24
8 21	3	7	4	24	50	22	25
8 25	4	8	5	25	34	23	26
8 29	5	9	6	26	18	23	27
8 34	6	10	7	27	1	24	28
8 38	7	11	8	27	44	25	29
8 42	8	12	8	28	26	26	♑
8 46	9	13	9	29	8	27	1
8 50	10	14	10	29	50	27	2
8 54	11	15	11	0 ♏	32	28	3
8 58	12	16	12	1	15	29	4
9 2	13	17	12	1	58	♐	4
9 6	14	18	13	2	39	1	5
9 10	15	18	14	3	21	2	6
9 14	16	19	15	4	3	2	7
9 18	17	20	16	4	44	3	8
9 22	18	21	16	5	26	4	9
9 26	19	22	17	6	7	5	10
9 30	20	23	18	6	48	5	11
9 34	21	24	18	7	29	6	12
9 38	22	25	19	8	9	7	13
9 41	23	26	20	8	50	8	14
9 45	24	27	21	9	31	9	15
9 49	25	28	22	10	11	9	16
9 53	26	28	23	10	51	10	17
9 57	27	29	23	11	32	11	18
10 1	28	♎	24	12	12	12	19
10 5	29	1	25	12	53	12	20
10 8	♍	2	26	13	33	13	20
10 12	1	3	26	14	13	14	21
10 16	2	4	27	14	53	15	22
10 20	3	5	28	15	33	16	23
10 24	4	5	29	16	13	16	24
10 28	5	6	29	16	52	17	25
10 31	6	7	♏	17	32	18	26
10 35	7	8	1	18	13	19	27
10 39	8	9	2	18	52	20	28
10 42	9	10	2	19	31	20	29
10 46	10	11	3	20	11	21	♒
10 50	11	11	4	20	51	22	1
10 54	12	12	4	21	30	23	2
10 57	13	13	5	22	9	24	3
11 1	14	14	6	22	49	24	4
11 5	15	15	7	23	28	25	5
11 9	16	16	7	24	8	26	6
11 12	17	17	8	24	47	27	8
11 16	18	17	9	25	27	28	9
11 20	19	18	10	26	6	29	10
11 23	20	19	10	26	45	♑	11
11 27	21	20	11	27	25	0	12
11 31	22	21	12	28	5	1	13
11 34	23	22	13	28	44	2	14
11 38	24	23	13	29	24	3	15
11 42	25	23	14	0 ♐	3	4	16
11 45	26	24	15	0	43	5	17
11 49	27	25	15	1	23	5	18
11 53	28	26	16	2	3	6	19
11 56	29	26	17	2	43	7	20

SOL in LIBRA and SCORPIO.

Time from Noon.	10 ♎	11 ♎	12 ♏	Ascen. ♐ °	′	2 ♑	3 ♒
h. m.	°	°	°	°	′	°	°
12 0	0	27	17	3	23	8	21
12 4	1	28	18	4	4	9	22
12 7	2	29	19	4	45	10	24
12 11	3	♏	20	5	26	11	25
12 15	4	1	20	6	7	12	26
12 18	5	1	21	6	48	13	27
12 22	6	2	22	7	29	14	28
12 26	7	3	23	8	10	15	29
12 29	8	4	23	8	51	16	♓
12 33	9	5	24	9	33	17	2
12 37	10	6	25	10	15	18	3
12 40	11	6	25	10	57	19	4
12 44	12	7	26	11	40	20	5
12 48	13	8	27	12	22	21	6
12 51	14	9	28	13	4	22	7
12 55	15	10	28	13	47	23	9
12 59	16	11	29	14	30	24	10
13 3	17	11	♐	15	14	25	11
13 6	18	12	1	15	59	26	12
13 10	19	13	1	16	44	27	13
13 14	20	14	2	17	29	28	15
13 18	21	15	3	18	14	29	16
13 21	22	16	4	19	0	♒	17
13 25	23	16	4	19	45	1	18
13 29	24	17	5	20	31	2	20
13 33	25	18	6	21	19	4	21
13 36	26	19	7	22	6	5	22
13 40	27	20	7	22	54	6	23
13 44	28	21	8	23	42	7	25
13 48	29	21	9	24	31	8	26
13 52	♏	22	10	25	20	10	27
13 55	1	23	11	26	10	11	28
13 59	2	24	11	27	2	12	♈
14 3	3	25	12	27	53	14	1
14 7	4	26	13	28	45	15	2
14 11	5	26	14	29	36	16	4
14 15	6	27	15	0 ♑	29	18	5
14 19	7	28	15	1	23	19	6
14 22	8	29	16	2	18	20	8
14 26	9	♐	17	3	15	22	9
14 30	10	1	18	4	11	23	10
14 34	11	2	19	5	9	25	11
14 38	12	2	20	6	7	26	13
14 42	13	3	20	7	6	28	14
14 46	14	4	21	8	6	29	15
14 50	15	5	22	9	8	♓	17
14 54	16	6	23	10	11	2	18
14 58	17	7	24	11	15	4	19
15 2	18	8	25	12	20	6	21
15 6	19	9	26	13	27	8	22
15 10	20	9	27	14	35	9	23
15 14	21	10	27	15	43	11	24
15 18	22	11	28	16	52	13	26
15 22	23	12	29	18	3	14	27
15 26	24	13	♑	19	16	16	28
15 31	25	14	1	20	32	17	29
15 35	26	15	2	21	48	19	♉
15 39	27	16	3	23	8	21	2
15 43	28	17	4	24	29	22	3
15 47	29	18	5	25	51	24	5

SOL in SAGIT. and CAPRICORN.

Time from Noon. h. m.	10 ♐ °	11 ♐ °	12 ♑ °	Ascen. ♑ °	Ascen. ♑ ′	2 ♓ °	3 ♉ °
15 51	0	18	5	27	15	26	6
15 55	1	19	6	28	42	28	7
16 0	2	20	7	0 ♒	11	♈	9
16 4	3	21	8	1	42	1	10
16 8	4	22	10	3	16	3	11
16 12	5	23	11	4	53	5	12
16 16	6	24	12	6	32	7	14
16 21	7	25	13	8	13	9	15
16 25	8	26	14	9	57	11	16
16 29	9	27	15	11	44	12	17
16 33	10	28	16	13	34	14	19
16 38	11	29	18	15	26	16	20
16 42	12	♑	19	17	20	18	21
16 46	13	1	21	19	18	20	22
16 51	14	2	22	21	22	21	23
16 55	15	3	23	23	29	23	25
16 59	16	4	24	25	36	25	26
17 4	17	5	26	27	46	26	27
17 8	18	7	27	30	0	28	28
17 12	19	8	28	2 ♓	19	29	29
17 16	20	9	29	4	40	♉	♊
17 20	21	10	♒	7	2	2	2
17 25	22	11	1	9	26	3	3
17 30	23	12	2	11	54	5	4
17 34	24	13	4	14	24	7	5
17 38	25	14	5	17	0	8	6
17 43	26	15	6	19	33	10	7
17 47	27	16	8	22	6	11	9
17 51	28	17	9	24	40	13	10
17 56	29	18	11	27	20	15	11
18 0	♑	19	12	30	0	16	12
18 4	1	20	14	2	39	19	13
18 9	2	21	15	5	19	21	14
18 13	3	22	17	7	55	22	15
18 17	4	23	19	10	29	24	16
18 22	5	24	20	13	2	25	17
18 26	6	25	22	15	36	26	18
18 30	7	26	23	18	6	28	19
18 35	8	27	25	20	34	29	20
18 39	9	28	27	22	59	♊	21
18 44	10	29	28	25	22	2	22
18 48	11	♒	♓	27	42	3	23
18 52	12	2	2	29	58	4	24
18 57	13	3	3	2 ♉	13	6	25
19 1	14	4	5	4	24	7	26
19 5	15	5	7	6	30	8	27
19 9	16	7	9	8	36	9	28
19 14	17	8	10	10	40	11	29
19 18	18	9	12	12	39	12	♋
19 22	19	10	14	14	35	13	1
19 27	20	11	16	16	28	14	2
19 31	21	13	18	18	17	15	3
19 35	22	14	19	20	3	16	4
19 39	23	15	21	21	48	17	5
19 44	24	16	23	23	29	18	6
19 48	25	18	25	25	9	19	7
19 52	26	19	27	26	45	20	8
19 56	27	20	28	28	18	22	9
20 0	28	21	♈	29	49	23	10
20 5	29	23	2	1 ♊	19	24	11

SOL in AQUARIUS and PISCES.

Time from Noon. h. m.	10 ♒ °	11 ♒ °	12 ♈ °	Ascen. ♊ °	Ascen. ♊ ′	2 ♊ °	3 ♋ °
20 9	0	24	4	2	45	25	12
20 13	1	25	5	4	9	26	13
20 17	2	27	7	5	32	27	14
20 21	3	28	9	6	53	28	15
20 25	4	29	11	8	12	28	16
20 29	5	♓	12	9	27	29	16
20 34	6	2	14	10	43	♋	17
20 38	7	3	16	11	58	1	18
20 42	8	4	18	13	9	2	19
20 46	9	6	19	14	18	3	20
20 50	10	7	21	15	25	4	21
20 54	11	8	23	16	32	5	22
20 58	12	10	24	17	39	6	23
21 2	13	11	26	18	44	7	24
21 6	14	13	28	19	48	8	24
21 10	15	14	29	20	51	8	25
21 14	16	15	♉	21	53	9	26
21 18	17	16	2	22	53	10	27
21 22	18	17	4	23	52	11	28
21 26	19	19	5	24	51	12	29
21 30	20	20	7	25	48	13	29
21 34	21	21	8	26	44	13	♌
21 38	22	22	10	27	40	14	1
21 41	23	24	11	28	34	15	2
21 45	24	25	12	29	29	16	3
21 49	25	26	14	0 ♋	22	17	4
21 53	26	28	15	1	15	18	5
21 57	27	29	17	2	7	18	5
22 1	28	♈	18	2	57	19	6
22 5	29	1	19	3	49	20	7
22 8	♓	3	21	4	38	21	8
22 12	1	4	22	5	28	22	9
22 16	2	5	23	6	17	22	10
22 20	3	7	24	7	5	23	10
22 24	4	8	26	7	53	24	11
22 27	5	9	27	8	42	25	12
22 31	6	10	28	9	29	25	13
22 35	7	12	29	10	16	26	14
22 39	8	13	♊	11	2	27	15
22 42	9	14	1	11	47	28	16
22 46	10	15	2	12	31	28	16
22 50	11	17	4	13	16	29	17
22 54	12	18	5	14	1	29	18
22 57	13	19	6	14	45	♌	19
23 1	14	20	7	15	28	1	19
23 5	15	21	8	16	11	2	20
23 8	16	23	9	16	54	3	21
23 12	17	24	10	17	39	3	22
23 15	18	25	11	18	20	4	23
23 20	19	26	12	19	3	5	24
23 23	20	27	13	19	45	6	24
23 27	21	28	14	20	26	6	25
23 31	22	29	15	21	8	7	26
23 34	23	♉	16	21	50	8	27
23 38	24	2	17	22	31	8	28
23 42	25	3	18	23	12	9	28
23 45	26	4	19	23	53	10	29
23 49	27	5	20	24	34	11	♍
23 53	28	6	21	25	15	11	1
23 56	29	8	22	25	56	12	2

A Table for finding the Moon's place for any hour of the day.

Hrs.	11 46	11 56	12 6	12 16	12 26	12 36	12 46	12 56	13 6	13 16	13 26	13 36
	D. M.	D. M.	D. M.	D. M.	D. M.	D. M.	D. M.	D. M.	D. M	D. M.	D. M.	D. M.
1	0 29	0 30	0 30	0 30	0 31	0 31	0 32	0 32	0 33	0 33	0 34	0 34
2	0 59	1 0	1 0	1 1	1 2	1 3	1 4	1 5	1 5	1 6	1 7	1 8
3	1 28	1 30	1 31	1 32	1 33	1 35	1 36	1 37	1 38	1 39	1 44	1 42
4	1 58	1 59	2 1	2 3	2 4	2 6	2 8	2 9	2 11	2 13	2 14	2 16
5	2 27	2 29	2 31	2 34	2 35	2 37	2 40	2 42	2 44	2 46	2 48	2 50
6	2 57	2 59	3 1	3 4	3 6	3 9	3 11	3 14	3 16	3 19	3 21	3 24
7	3 26	3 29	3 32	3 35	3 38	3 40	3 43	3 46	3 49	3 52	3 55	3 58
8	3 55	3 59	4 2	4 6	4 9	4 12	4 15	4 19	4 22	4 25	4 29	4 32
9	4 25	4 28	4 32	4 36	4 40	4 43	4 47	4 51	4 55	4 58	5 2	5 6
10	4 54	4 58	5 3	5 7	5 11	5 15	5 19	5 23	5 27	5 32	5 36	5 40
11	5 24	5 28	5 33	5 37	5 42	5 46	5 51	5 56	6 0	6 5	6 9	6 14
12	5 53	5 58	6 3	6 8	6 13	6 18	6 23	6 28	6 33	6 38	6 43	6 48
13	6 22	6 28	6 33	6 39	6 44	6 49	6 55	7 0	7 6	7 11	7 17	7 22
14	6 52	6 58	7 3	7 9	7 15	7 21	7 27	7 33	7 38	7 44	7 50	7 56
15	7 21	7 28	7 34	7 40	7 46	7 52	7 59	8 5	8 11	8 17	8 24	8 30
16	7 51	7 57	8 4	8 11	8 17	8 24	8 31	8 37	8 44	8 51	8 57	9 4
17	8 20	8 27	8 34	8 41	8 48	8 55	9 3	9 10	9 17	9 24	9 31	9 38
18	8 49	8 57	9 4	9 12	9 19	9 27	9 34	9 42	9 49	9 57	10 4	10 12
19	9 19	9 27	9 35	9 43	9 51	9 58	10 6	10 14	10 22	10 30	10 38	10 46
20	9 48	9 57	10 5	10 13	10 22	10 30	10 38	10 47	10 55	11 3	11 12	11 20
21	10 18	10 27	10 35	10 44	10 53	11 1	11 10	11 19	11 27	11 36	11 45	11 54
22	10 47	10 57	11 6	11 15	11 24	11 33	11 42	11 51	12 0	12 10	12 16	12 28
23	11 17	11 26	11 36	11 45	11 55	12 4	12 14	12 24	12 33	12 43	12 52	13 2
24	11 46	11 56	12 6	12 16	12 26	12 36	12 46	12 56	13 6	13 16	13 26	13 36

Hrs.	13 46	13 56	14 6	14 16	14 26	14 36	14 46	14 56	15 6	15 16	☉, ♀, ☿ Motion.	
	D. M.	D. M.	D. M.	D. M.	D. M.	D. M.	D. M.	D. M.	D. M.	D. M.	59' 0"	60 0"
1	0 34	0 35	0 35	0 36	0 36	0 36	0 37	0 37	0 38	0 38	2 27½	2 30
2	1 9	1 10	1 10	1 11	1 12	1 12	1 14	1 15	1 15	1 16	4 55	5 0
3	1 43	1 44	1 46	1 47	1 48	1 49	1 51	1 52	1 53	1 54	7 22½	7 30
4	2 18	2 19	2 21	2 23	2 24	2 26	2 28	2 29	2 31	2 33	9 50	10 0
5	2 52	2 54	2 56	2 58	3 0	3 3	3 5	3 7	3 9	3 11	12 17½	12 30
6	3 26	3 29	3 31	3 34	3 36	3 39	3 41	3 44	3 46	3 49	14 45	15 0
7	4 1	4 4	4 7	4 10	4 12	4 15	4 18	4 22	4 27	4 27	17 12½	17 30
8	4 35	4 39	4 42	4 46	4 49	4 52	4 55	4 59	5 2	5 5	19 40	20 0
9	5 10	5 13	5 17	5 21	5 25	5 28	5 32	5 36	5 40	5 43	22 7½	22 30
10	5 44	5 48	5 52	5 57	6 1	6 5	6 9	6 13	6 17	6 22	24 35	25 0
11	6 19	6 23	6 28	6 32	6 37	6 41	6 46	6 51	6 55	7 0	27 2½	27 30
12	6 53	6 58	7 3	7 8	7 13	7 18	7 23	7 28	7 33	7 38	29 30	30 0
13	7 27	7 33	7 38	7 44	7 49	7 54	8 0	8 5	8 11	8 16	31 57½	32 30
14	8 2	8 8	8 13	8 19	8 25	8 31	8 37	8 43	8 48	8 54	34 25	35 0
15	8 36	8 42	8 49	8 55	9 1	9 7	9 14	9 20	9 26	9 32	36 52½	37 30
16	9 11	9 17	9 24	9 30	9 37	9 44	9 51	9 57	10 4	10 11	39 20	40 0
17	9 45	9 52	9 59	10 6	10 13	10 20	10 28	10 35	10 42	10 49	41 47½	42 30
18	10 19	10 27	10 34	10 42	10 49	10 57	11 4	11 12	11 19	11 27	44 15	45 0
19	10 54	11 2	11 10	11 18	11 26	11 31	11 41	11 49	11 57	12 5	46 42½	47 30
20	11 28	11 37	11 45	11 53	12 2	12 10	12 18	12 27	12 35	12 43	49 10	50 0
21	12 3	12 11	12 20	12 29	12 38	12 46	12 55	13 4	13 13	13 21	51 37½	52 30
22	12 37	12 46	12 55	13 4	13 14	13 23	13 33	13 41	13 50	14 0	54 5	55 0
23	13 12	13 21	13 31	13 40	13 50	13 59	14 9	14 18	14 28	14 38	56 32½	57 30
24	13 46	13 56	14 6	14 16	14 26	14 36	14 46	14 56	15 6	15 16	59 0	60 0

THE RULING OF THE MICROCOSM;

BEING AN

Astrological & Physical Discourse

ON THE

HUMAN VIRTUES IN THE BODY OF MAN,

BOTH PRINCIPAL AND ADMINISTRATING.

Firstly.—Consider what planet causeth the Disease.

Secondly.—Consider what part of the body is afflicted by the disease, and whether it lies in the flesh, or blood, or bones, or ventricles.

Thirdly.—Consider by what planet the afflicted part is governed.

Fourthly.—You may oppose diseases by Herbs of the planet opposite to the planet that causes them, as diseases of Jupiter by Herbs of Mercury, and the contrary ; diseases of the Luminaries by the Herbs of Saturn, and the contrary ; diseases of Mars by Herbs of Venus, and the contrary.

Fifthly.—There is a way to cure diseases sometimes by sympathy, and so every planet cures his own disease ; as the Sun and Moon by their Herbs cure the Eyes, Saturn the Spleen, Jupiter the Liver, Mars the gall and diseases of choler, and Venus diseases in the instruments of generation.

Human virtues are either Principal for procreation and conservation, or Administrating for attraction, digestion, retention, or expulsion.

Virtues conservative are vital, natural, and animal. By the natural are bred blood, choler, phlegm, and melancholy. The animal virtues are intellective and sensitive. The intellective is imagination, judgment, and memory. The sensitive is common and particular. The particular is seeing, hearing, smelling, tasting, and feeling.

Virtue Procreative, the first in order, is the virtue procreative for natural regards, not only the conservation of itself, but to beget its like, and conserve in species. The seat of this is the member of generation, and is governed principally by the influence of Venus.

It is argumented and increased by the strength of Venus, by her herbs, roots, trees and minerals. It is diminished and purged by those of Mars, and quite extinguished by those of Saturn. Observe when Venus is strong and make use of her medicines to fortify ; of Mars, to cleanse this virtue ; of Saturn, to extinguish it.

Conservative.—The conservative virtues are vital, natural, and animal.

Vital.—The vital spirit hath its residence in the heart, and is dispersed from it by the arteries, and is governed by the influence of the Sun. It is to the body as the Sun is to the creation, as the heart is in the microcosm, so is the Sun in the microcosm ; for as the Sun gives life, light, and motion to the creation, so doth the heart to the body ; therefore it is called Sol Corporis, as the Sun is called Cor Cæli, because their operations are similar. Inimical and destructive to this virtue are Saturn and Mars. The herbs and plants of Sol wonderfully fortify it.

Natural.—The natural faculty or virtue resides in the liver, and is generally governed by Jupiter, *Quasi Juvans Pater.* Its office is to nourish the body, and is dispersed through the body by the veins. From this are bred four particular humours—Blood, choler, phlegm, and melancholy.

Blood is made of meat perfectly concocted, in quality hot and moist, governed by Jupiter. It is by a third concoction transmuted into flesh, the superfluity of it into seed, and its receptacle is the veins, by which it is dispersed through the body.

Choler is made of meat more than perfectly concocted, and it is the spume or froth of blood. It clarifies all the humours, heats the body, nourishes the apprehension, as blood doth the judgment. It is in quality hot and dry, fortifies the attractive faculty, as blood doth the digestive, moves man to activity and valour. Its receptacle is the gall, and it is under the influence of Mars.

Phlegm is made of meat not perfectly digested. It fortifies the virture expulsive, makes the body slippery, fit for ejection ; it fortifies the brain by its consimilitude with it, yet it spoils apprehension by its antipathy to it ; it qualifies choler, cools and moistens the heart, thereby sustaining it and the whole body from the fiery effects which continual motion would produce. Its receptacle is the lungs, and is governed by Venus, some say by the Moon— perhaps it may be governed by them both. It is cold and moist in quality.

Melancholy is the sediment of blood, cold and dry in quality, fortifying the retentive faculty and memory, makes men sober, solid and staid, fit for study ; stays the unbridled toys of lustful blood, stays the wandering thoughts, and reduces them home to the centre. Its receptacle is the spleen, and it is governed by Saturn.

Of all these humours blood is the chief, all the rest are superfluities of blood ; yet are they necessary superfluities, for without
any of them man cannot live. Namely, choler is the fiery superfluity, phlegm, the watery ; melancholy, the earthly.

Animal.—The third principal virtue remains, which is animal.
Its residence is in the brain, and Mercury is the general significator
of it. Ptolemy held that the Moon signified the animal virtue, and
I am of opinion that both Mercury and the Moon dispose it, and
my reasons are—(1) Because both of them in nativities either
fortify or impediate it. (2) Ill directions to either or from either
afflict it, as good ones help it. Indeed the Moon rules the bulk of
it, as also the sensitive part of it, and Mercury the rational part,
and that is the reason in a nativity if the Moon be stronger than
Mercury, sense many times overpowers reason ; but if Mercury be
strong and the Moon weak, reason will be master ordinarily in
despite of sense.

It is divided into Intellective and Sensitive.

Intellective.—The intellectual resides in the brain, within the
pia mater, and is governed generally by Mercury.

It is also divided into Imagination, Judgment, and Memory.

Imagination is seated in the fore part of the brain ; it is hot and
dry in quality, quick, active, always working ; it receives vapours
from the heart and coins them into thoughts, it never sleeps, but
always is working, both when the man is sleeping and waking.
When judgment is awake it regulates the imagination, which runs
at random when judgment is asleep, and forms any thoughts
according to the nature of the vapour sent up to it. Mercury is
the disposer of it. A man may easily perceive his judgment asleep
before himself many times and then he will perceive his thoughts
run at random.

Judgment always sleeps when men do ; imagination never sleeps.
Memory sometimes sleeps when men sleep, and sometimes it does
not, so that when memory is awake and the man asleep, then
memory remembers what apprehension coins, and that is a dream.
The thoughts would have been the same if memory had not been
awake to remember it. These thoughts are commonly (I mean in
sleep when they are purely natural) framed according to the nature
of the humour called complexion, which is predominant in the
body, and if the humour be peccant it is always so. It is one of
the surest rules to know a man's own complexion by his dreams,
I mean a man void of distractions or deep studies. This most
assuredly shows Mercury to dispose of the imagination, as also
because it is mutable. applying itself to any object, as it is Mercury's
nature to do ; for then the imagination will follow its old bent. If
a man be bent upon a business, his apprehension will work as

much when he is asleep, and find out as many truths by study as when the man is awake, and perhaps more, because then it is not hindered by ocular objects. And this much for imagination, which is governed by Mercury and fortified by his influence, and is also strong or weak in man according as Mercury is strong or weak in the nativity.

Judgment is seated in the midst of the brain, to show that it ought to bear rule over all the other faculties. It is the judge of the little world, to approve of what is good and reject what is bad ; it is the seat of reason and the guide of actions, so that all failings are committed through infirmity in not rightly judging between a real and apparent good. It is hot and moist in quality, and under the influence of Jupiter.

Memory is seated in the hinder cell of the brain. It is the great registrar to the little world, and its office is to record things either done and past or to be done. It is in quality cold and dry, and melancholic, and therefore melancholic men have generally the best memories, and are most tenacious in every way. It is under the dominion of Saturn, and is fortified by his influence, but purged by the luminaries.

2.—Sensitive.—The second part of the animal virtue is sensitive, and it is divided into two parts common and particular. Common sense is an imaginary term, and that which gives virtue to all the particular senses, and knits and unites them together with the Pia Mater. It is regulated by Mercury (perhaps this is one reason why men are so sickle-headed), and its office is to preserve harmony among the senses.

Particular senses are five, *viz.*, seeing, hearing, smelling, tasting, and feeling.

These senses are united in one in the brain by the common sense, but are operatively distinguished into their several seats and places of residence. The sight resides in the eyes, and particularly in the crystaline humour. It is in quality cold and moist, and governed by the luminaries. They who have them weak in their genesis have always weak sights ; if one of them only so, the weakness possesses but one eye. The hearing resides in the ears, and is in quality cold and dry, melancholic, and under the dominion of Saturn. The smelling resides in the nose, and is in quality hot, dry, and choleric, which is the reason choleric creatures, such as dogs, have such good smelling powers. It is under the influence of Mars. The taste resides in the palate, which is placed at the root of the tongue, on purpose to discern what food is congruous for the stomach and what is not ; as the meseraik veins are placed to discern what nourishment is proper for the liver to convert into blood. In some very few men, and but a few, these two tasters do not agree, and that is the reason some men covet meats which make them sick, that is, the taste craves them, and the meseraik reject them. In quality it is hot and moist, and is ruled by Jupiter. The feeling is deputed to no particular organ but is spread over the whole body, is of all qualities, hot, cold, dry, and moist, and is the index of all tangible things ; for if it were only hot alone, it could not feel a quality contrary, viz., cold, and this might be spoken of other qualities. It is under the dominion of Venus, although some say Mercury ; a thousand to one but it is Mercury.

The four Administering Virtues are — Attractive, digestive, retentive, and expulsive.

The attractive virtue is hot and dry. Hot by quality, active or principal, and that appears because the fountain of all heat is attractive, viz., the Sun. Dry by quality, passive, on account of its heat. Its office is to remain in the body, and call for what nature wants. It is under the influence of the Sun, say some authors, and not under Mars, because he is of a corrupting nature ; yet if we cast an impartial eye upon experience, we shall find that martial men call for meat none the least, and for drink the most of all men, although many times they corrupt the body by it, and therefore I see no reason why Mars, being of the same quality with the Sun, should not have a share in the dominion. It is in vain to object that the influence of Mars is evil, and therefore he should have no dominion over this virtue ; for then by the same rule he should have no dominion at all in the body of man, as all the virtues in man are naturally evil, and corrupted by Adam's fall. This attractive virtue ought to be fortified when the Moon is in fiery signs, viz., Aries and Saggitary, but not in Leo, for the sign is so violent that no physic ought to be given when the Moon is there. (And why not Leo, seeing that it is the most attractive sign of all ? and that is the reason those that have it ascending in their genesis are such greedy eaters.) If you cannot stay till the Moon be in one of them, let one of them ascend when you administer the medicine.

The digestive virtue is hot and moist, and is the principal of them all ; the others, like handmaidens, attending it.

The attractive virtue draws that which it should digest, and serves continually to feed and supply it.

The retentive virtue retains the substance with it, till it be perfectly digested.

The expulsion virtue casteth out, expels what is superfluous by digestion. It is under the influence of Jupiter and fortified by his herbs and plants. In fortifying it, let your Moon be in Gemini, Aquarius, or the first half of Libra ; or if matters be come to that extremity that you cannot stay till that time, let one of them ascend, but both would be better, always provided that the Moon be not in the ascendant.   I cannot believe the Moon afflicts the ascendant so much as it is said to do, if she be well dignified, and in a sign she delights in.

The retentive virtue is in quality cold and dry ; cold, because the nature of cold is to compress, witness the ice ; dry, because the nature of dryness is to keep and hold what is compressed.   It is under the influence of Saturn, and that is the reason why usually Saturnine men are so covetous and tenacious.   In fortifying it makes use of the herbs and plants of Saturn, and let the Moon be in Taurus or Virgo.   Capricorn is not so good, says some authors, although I can give no reason for that conclusion.   Let not Saturn or his ill aspect molest the ascendant.

The expulsive faculty is cold and moist ; cold, because that composes the superfluities ; moist, because that makes the body slippery and fit for ejection, and disposes it to it.   It is under the dominion of Luna, with whom you may join Venus, because she is of the same nature.

In whatsoever is before written of the nature of the planets, take notice that fixed stars of the same nature work the same effect. In fortifying this (which ought to be done in all purgations), let the Moon be in Cancer, Scorpio, or Pisces, or let one of these signs ascend.

The actions or operations of the animal virtues are—(1) sensitive, (2) motive.

The sensitive is—(1) external, (2) internal.

The external senses are—(1) seeing, (2) hearing, (3) tasting, (4) smelling, (5) feeling.

The internal senses are—(1) The Imagination, to apprehend a thing, (2) Judgment, to judge of it, (3) Memory, to remember it.

The seat of all these is in the brain.   The vital spirits proceed from the heart, and cause in a man mirth, joy, hope, trust, humanity, mildness, courage, &c., and their opposites, viz., sadness, fear, care, sorrow, despair, envy, hatred, stubborness, revenge, &c., by heat, natural or not natural.

The natural spirit nourishes the body throughout, (as the vital quickens it, and the animal gives it sense and motion).   Its office is to alter and convert food into chyle, chyle into blood, blood into flesh, to form, engender, nourish, and increase the blood.

FINIS.

Neptune.

To Mr. John Story.

Dear Sir,—From the short time that has elapsed since this planet was discovered not much is yet known about its influence, either in natal, or any other branch of Astrology, but according to the rules of Ptolemy for judging of new phenomena, and from personal observation, its influence is evil and disappointing to persons born when it is in evil aspect to the ☉, ☽, or ☿. Its effects are something like the combined influences of ♄ or ♅, obscure, strange, and eventful, so that wherever a nativity is of a discordant nature, that is, the ☉, ☽, ☿ the ascendant or its ruler, are afflicted by evil aspects of the other planets, Neptune, joining in with the discordant elements, its influence will intensify the evil effects and make the work more disastrous.

When this planet is well located and in good aspect to the ☉, ☽, ☿, the ascendant or its ruler, so as to have a controlling influence over the mind, it will constitute a character close, reserved, careful, crafty, ingenious and inventive, studious and clever in mechanical arts, chemistry, &c., a person silent, not of many words, greedy after money and property, selfish and indifferent towards others, of a gloomy, lowering aspect, private and anti-social, careless about dress, personal appearance, forms and fashions, curious, odd and retiring in manners, therefore not much adapted for social life and company. This planet appears to have a continuous influence over the minds of spiritualists, mediums, prophets, seers, magicians, clairvoyants, enthusiasts, and persons who believe in inspiration, oracles, and futurity. In certain classes it induces to a faith in dreams, spirits and ghosts, tales of wonder and enchantment, witching, charming, necromacy, and fortune-telling in various ways, as card shuffling, palmistry, geomancy, moles, and other kinds of superstitious craft and artful practices too numerous to name.

When this planet is badly located at birth, that is in evil aspect to the ☉, ☽, ☿, especially when the nativity is otherwise discordant, it will tend to give or predispose to a morbid condition of the mind, latent wickedness, and a want of moral sentiment. Such persons in the lower ranks of life will be likely to drift into low, immoral habits and practices of various kinds which will cause a loss of reputation, deprive the native of his liberty, or run him into prison and exile, as the mind will naturally be very secretive, daring, and resolute when fully engaged in any enterprise. Although rather procrastinating, cautious, and timid at times, he will have good courage and be a little reckless when prompted and pressed by circumstances, therefore liable to get on the wrong line of pursuit.

Diseases indicated by Neptune are bowel, liver, and spleen diseases, as also bilious and gastric complaints, and affections in the bladder and urinal organs, as gravel, stone, colic, inflammation and obstruction in the bowels and bladder, hypochondria, &c.   To females it denotes barrenness, cancers in the womb, hysterical complaints, abortion, difficult confinements, and other diseases common to such organised parts of the body in both sexes.   In bad cases sudden and violent death by fire, fire-arms, explosives, machinery, assassination and murder, accidents in games and sports, &c., &c.

The influence of this planet, like ♅, is evil and unfortunate. Some idea may be formed of its effects by the condition of Ireland for the last fourteen years.   Neptune entered the ruling sign of Ireland in 1875, and ever since the Irish people, or a great portion thereof, have been in a state of turmoil and revolution.   At the time of the Phœnix Park murders this planet was exactly in ☌ with the ☉, ♄ and ☿, in the sign ♉, all four planets setting at Dublin, May 6th, 1882, at 7.17 p.m., the exact time of the murder, which was a remarkable confirmation of planetary influences. Neptune was discovered on September 23rd, 1846, at which time it was located in 25 degrees of ♒, exactly in ☌ with the planet ♄, which prenoted the Crimean War in 1854.

Past events since 1846 clearly appear to demonstrate the nature of the said planet, viz., Home Rule bubble, the discovery and development of new chemical elements of destruction, infernal machines, dynamite, new preparation of chemical poisons, medicines, &c. ; also the great changes in the habits and manners of the people.   Then, again, Neptune left the ruling sign of Ireland in March, 1889, and entered into the ruling sign of London, indicating those dreadful murders and mutilation of the victims of the undiscovered "Jack the Ripper."   This is another confirmation of my judgment on the nature of this celestial messenger.   What other events will follow during its transit through London ascendant, the Wheel of Time can only unfold.   The last time it went through Gemini it denoted the South Sea Bubble.

The houses of the planets were originally formulated by the Chaldeans, Babylonians, or Egyptians, but on what principles they were deduced is a mystery to the present generation ; nevertheless there appears to be some truth in the allotment of planetary houses. According to Ptolemy's theory ♒ should be Neptune's house, but ♏ or ♉ might answer well, as they are both of an obscure and mystical nature, but it will require more experience, observation, and practice to settle the matter.

Yours truly,

PROF. J. A.

....other best selling NEWCASTLE books

NOW from NEWCASTLE

These 4 Bestselling Books

by Victor Lindlahr

YOU ARE WHAT YOU EAT
$2.25

EAT AND REDUCE
$2.45

VITAMIN COOKBOOK
$2.95

THE NATURAL WAY TO HEALTH
$2.95

VIEWPOINT ON NUTRITION by Dr. Arnold Pike is a practical guide to proper nutrition and keeping fit. This fine book features interviews with Gayelord Hauser, Eddie Albert, Julie Harris, Sugar Ray Robinson, Dr. Linus Pauling, Marty Allen and many others. You will learn how to select exactly the right diet for you. Also contains the complete government report — Human Nutrition No. 2 by the U.S. Department of Agriculture. Introduction by Gayelord Hauser. Includes photographs of many celebrities who have appeared on Dr. Pike's nationally syndicated show. A Newcastle original! Dr. Arnold Pike has been called America's Mr. Media of Nutrition. He is the host of the coast to coast award-winning radio and TV Series 'Viewpoint on Nutrition.'

232 Pages   5½ x 8½ $2.95

Please check with your favorite Bookseller for any of the books listed on this page or order directly from:

NEWCASTLE PUBLISHING COMPANY, INC.
1521 North Vine St., Hollywood California 90028

THE NEWCASTLE FORGOTTEN FANTASY LIBRARY

THE GLITTERING PLAIN by **William Morris** is the first title in The Newcastle Forgotten Fantasy Library, a new series of 26 adult fantasy classics. The works of William Morris (1834-1896) have influenced many writers of fantasy, such as Lord Dunsany, C.S. Lewis, and J.R.R. Tolkien, and continue to delight new generations of readers with their flights of high adventure in strange lands, their beautiful maidens and stalwart heroes. THE STORY OF THE GLITTERING PLAIN was the first of these romances. A must for the millions of Tolkien fans!

174 Pages   5½ x 8½ $2.45

THE SAGA OF ERIC BRIGHTEYES by **H. Rider Haggard** is a masterpiece of heroic fantasy by the creator of "SHE" and "KING SOLOMON'S MINES." No. 2 in the Newcastle Library of Forgotten Fantasy Classic Series. H. Rider Haggard achieved phenomenal popularity in his own day as a writer of fantastic romances and adventure tales, but today many of his lesser known works are all but forgotten. Such a novel is ERIC BRIGHTEYES, an heroic saga of bold adventure, treachery and dark sorcery. Haggard's biographer, Morton Cohen, said of ERIC BRIGHTEYES, "It is one of his best!" Illustrated.

304 Pages   5½ x 8½ $2.95

GHOSTS I HAVE MET Edited by **John Kendrick Bangs.** Here is a delightful collection of classic ghost stories by a master humorist. Here are spectres to make you smile instead of shiver, gleeful ghosts, amusing apparitions, and humorous haunts. Long out-of-print, this new edition of GHOSTS I HAVE MET, by the author of A HOUSE BOAT ON THE STYX is an unabridged reproduction of the 1898 edition, with all the original illustrations by Peter Newell, A.B. Frost and Richards.

191 Pages   5½ x 8½ $2.45